Contemporary

Inter-American Relations

Contemporary
Inter-American Relations

A Reader in
Theory and Issues

Edited by
YALE H. FERGUSON

Rutgers University

PRENTICE-HALL, INC., ENGLEWOOD CLIFFS, NEW JERSEY

13–169953–9

Library of Congress Catalog Card Number 78–143579

Printed in the United States of America

Current printing (last digit):

10   9   8   7   6   5   4   3   2   1

PRENTICE-HALL INTERNATIONAL, INC., London
PRENTICE-HALL OF AUSTRALIA, PTY. LTD., Sydney
PRENTICE-HALL OF CANADA, LTD., Toronto
PRENTICE-HALL OF INDIA PRIVATE LIMITED, New Delhi
PRENTICE-HALL OF JAPAN, INC., Tokyo

Contents

I

Analytical Perspectives
On Contemporary
Inter-American Relations

*Actors Systems, Linkages,
Integration, and Issue-Areas*

9

II

Patterns and Problems
Of Contemporary Inter-American Relations
In Key Issue-Areas

151

A. Security and Peaceful Settlement

B. Modernization: The Political Dimension

Preface

A decade or so ago compiling a reader on contemporary inter-American relations could only have served to expose the glaring deficiencies of the literature relevant to this subject, which with few exceptions was largely historical, highly polemical, and/or excessively legalistic in nature. Today a collection of this sort may still reveal that scholars and statesmen are far from fully understanding the multiplicity of factors inherent in inter-American relations—and are even farther from a consensus as to policies—but it can also offer evidence of a considerable intellectual advance in recent years.

There would seem to be at least two reasons for the progress that has been made. First, the late 1950s began a period of dramatic change (in retrospect, notwithstanding remarkable continuity) at the domestic level in Latin America and of bold international initiatives by the United States, the Soviet Union, and various Latin American states for a variety of ends in the hemisphere. In short, at least during the comparatively halcyon days of the Kennedy Administration, inter-American relations were of unprecedented concern to policy-makers and attentive publics. Second, the past few years have also seen a steady growth in sophistication of political science and the other social sciences, many of whose practitioners have turned their attention to the Latin American scene. Some have examined problems of public policy in the area. Still others, including those with special interests in international politics and foreign policy, linkages, international integration, international organization, and political development, have used area data to test old theories and build new ones.

So rapid is the continued march of events and the attendant crumbling of intellectual conventions and boundaries that it may well be premature for a scholar to attempt to synthesize the complex subject of inter-American relations in a single work of his own. Certainly, existing texts provide little grounds for optimism about his chances for success in such an ambitious project. On the other hand, it is definitely not too early to gather some of the recent literature from diverse quarters for the convenient use of students and scholars, policy-makers, and interested laymen alike. This is one purpose of the present collection.

Another twofold purpose is reflected in the basic organization of this reader: by a judicious choice of selections and editorial commentary, to offer both a modest theoretical introduction to inter-American relations and insights into key policy issues. These goals are by no means mutually exclusive, nor are selections with theoretical or issue content necessarily grouped under Part I or Part II of the book respectively. Part I merely highlights a few theoretical concepts which lend additional perspective to materials found in this section and elsewhere—even outside the confines of the anthology. Indeed, the editor would encourage those who read the selections to explore their multifunctional character by rearranging them to suit their own analytical pleasure. There is more than one organization possible and profitable here.

The scope of the reader is somewhat wider than its inter-American relations title might indicate. It includes selections dealing with significant intra- and extra-Western Hemisphere relationships as well as those between the United States and Latin America. Moreover, in recognition of the fact that much more than the bilateral and multilateral intercourse between governments is relevant to an understanding of international relations, it also encompasses items focusing on nongovernmental actors as well as political, economic, and social aspects of Latin American domestic environments. This volume testifies (if further testimony is needed) that along with the barriers between the social sciences, the traditional distinctions between international and domestic are fast breaking down.

Not surprisingly, the editor has experienced no little difficulty in deciding which specific selections to include and exclude. The quantity and quality of available literature varies sharply from topic to topic, and it has seemed advisable to treat some topics in greater depth than others. One might make a convincing case for giving preference to writings of "name" scholars or to neglected Latin American selections which have never before appeared in English translation. However, the editor's choices have generally turned on the usefulness of pieces to make particular points about theory and issues within his framework rather than the prominence or nationality of the authors involved.

For some of the reasons suggested above, this collection gives short shrift to historical (pre-1945) background, to OAS institutions and resolutions and inter-American legal controversies *per se,* to some ongoing hemisphere disputes (Ecuador-Peru over the Rio Marañon territory; Bolivia-Chile over the diversion of the Río Lauca waters and a Bolivian outlet to the sea; U.S.-Panama over the Canal, etc.), to the denuclearization movement in Latin America, and to anti-U.S. diatribes of the kind regularly produced by *some* Latin American intellectuals. Concerning the latter, fortunately, serious scholarship and thinking in many academic, policy-making—and even radical-activist—circles in the United States, Latin America, Europe, and elsewhere has now proceeded to a point where criticism of U.S. policies no longer need assume the insubstantial form of a polemic.

In closing, the editor should like to acknowledge the very helpful comments which he received on his table of contents at various stages in its evolution from Douglas A. Chalmers, Abraham F. Lowenthal, Richard L. Maullin, Per Olav Reinton, Jerome Slater, Miguel S. Wionczek, and Bryce Wood. Responsibility, of course, remains his alone. Prentice-Hall's political science editor, Roger G. Emblen, also merits a special vote of thanks for his interest and encouragement from the outset of this project. Thanks, too, to his former assistant, Ella Lennart, and to Amy Cicchetti in editorial-production. Finally, Kitty Ferguson eased the editor's task by her unfailing moral support, intelligent advice and criticism, and innumerable other wifely ministrations.

YALE H. FERGUSON

New York, N.Y.
November 17, 1970

Contemporary

Inter-American Relations

Introduction

As suggested in the Preface, the editor's label of inter-American relations for the subject of this collection is rather arbitrary. The truth of the matter is that we do not as yet have entirely adequate terms to describe the exceedingly complex web of actions and interactions that characterizes international relations in general—and the particular international relations of the Americas.

Even the notion of the Americas is vague. Does it, for instance, include Canada, certainly a part of North *America* but not a member of the Organization of *American* States? What of the islands of the Caribbean, some of which are independent states and OAS members (like Haiti, the Dominican Republic, and Trinidad and Tobago) and some of which remain colonial possessions of European powers (like Monserrat or Martinique)? What of Puerto Rico and its anomalous Commonwealth status within the purview of the United States? What of the Falkland Islands in the South Atlantic, disputed territory between the United Kingdom and Argentina; or of British Honduras (Belize), currently preparing for independence but claimed by Guatemala? What of Surinam (Netherlands Guiana) and French Guiana? What indeed of the 200 miles of ocean regarded as territorial waters by nine Latin American States?

As Latin America specialists never tire of pointing out, *any* strictly geographic conception of the Americas ignores vast political, economic, and social disparities between the American states. Equally or more significant from our standpoint, it also obscures sharp differences in the degree and character of intercourse across national boundaries within the area and stretching in some respects to the four corners of the globe.[1]

Given the definitional problem, it might be best to recognize that there are, in fact, *many* Americas, depending upon how we wish to conceive of them. *One* way of conceiving of them is in terms of their international relations; that is, emphasizing patterns in the cross-national intercourse mentioned above. This procedure allows us to leave the geographical boundaries of the area somewhat fuzzy and, in any case, forces us to consider pervasive links with the world outside.

We have disposed of one of the two difficulties raised at the outset, but the other remains: how to approach the analysis of international relations, including the special inter-American variety. Needless to say, this is not the

---

1 Similar objections might be raised to the more inclusive geographic concept of the Western Hemisphere.

place for a lengthy treatise on this subject.[2] All the editor proposes to do is to bring to the attention of inter-American relations students, a few analytically useful concepts developed by general international relations theorists.

Let us begin by identifying *actors,* those entities that engage in cross-national behavior originating and/or terminating within whatever geographical boundaries we desire to posit for the Americas. Note that each actor constitutes an actual or potential *symbol of identification* for the human individual, which may compete with other actors for a share of his normally divided loyalty.

The individual himself, of course, is the basic actor, whether he functions in the capacity of a private citizen, government official, or international civil servant. A Latin American student who tosses a stone at a visiting foreign dignitary participates *directly* in international relations. Likewise, the tourist from the United States who summers in Mexico, the Caribbean black whom the editor encountered working on an archeological site in Guatemala, the Otavaleño Indian of Ecuador who regularly travels abroad to market his textiles, and the Frenchman who mails a letter to a friend in Brazil.

Generally, however, individuals participate *indirectly* in international rela-tions through various human *collectivities.* The behavior of collectivities is something more (or less) than the sum of the behavior of their individual members, because they act on the basis of a decision-making process that maximizes consensus and/or allows some members more influence than others. From another perspective, although individual agents of collectivities participate directly in international relations, they do so under constraints from the wider membership. Thus collectivities may be considered international actors in their own right.

It is traditional to maintain that governments, as symbols and instruments of sovereign nation-states, are the leading actors in international relations. This interpretation seems to have a good deal of merit when the Soviet Union sends technicians to Cuba, United States marines land in the Dominican Republic, Castro lends material assistance to Che Guevara's guerrilla campaign in Bolivia, Ecuador or Peru seize fishing boats owned by U.S. companies, or El Salvador goes to war with Honduras.

However, the traditional view fails to do justice to the fact that, both above and below governments in what might be termed an international hierarchy of structures (not implying a chain of command),[3] there are other collectivi-

---

2 There are, of course, many available. The editor has leaned heavily upon the work of his former Rutgers colleague, James N. Rosenau. See esp.: Rosenau, ed., *International Politics and Foreign Policy: A Reader in Research and Theory* (2nd ed.; New York: The Free Press, 1969) ; Rosenau, ed., *Linkage Politics* (New York: The Free Press, 1969) ; Rosenau, "Foreign Policy as an Issue-Area" in Rosenau, ed., *Domestic Sources of Foreign Policy* (New York: *The Free Press,* 1967), pp. 11–50; and Rosenau, "Pre-theories and Theories of Foreign Policy"

in R. Barry Farrell, ed., *Approaches to Comparative and International Politics* (Evanston: Northwestern University Press, 1966), pp. 27–92.
3 This hierarchy presents what J. David Singer has labeled the "level-of-analysis" problem in international relations theory. See his "The Level-of-Analysis Problem in International Relations" in Klaus Knorr and Sidney Verba, eds., *The International System: Theoretical Essays* (Princeton: Princeton University Press, 1961), pp. 77–92

ties which engage in significant cross-national behavior. The recent Peruvian case serves as an illustration of, among other things,[4] the international relevance of entities *within* national societies: Precipitating the military coup of October 3, 1968, was a controversy over a new contract the incumbent Belaúnde government negotiated with the International Petroleum Corporation, a wholly–owned subsidiary of Standard Oil operating in Peru since 1924. Prior to the coup, various conservative business groups, newspapers, student organizations, labor unions, and political parties had conducted a long and vociferous campaign against foreign control of Peruvian oil. When the military intervened, it toppled a government closely associated with the United States and the Alliance for Progress, seized I.P.C. holdings (acting in this respect as a new government), and provided a "demonstration effect" which may be felt throughout Latin America for years to come. Indeed, following remarkably close upon the events in Peru, Anaconda Copper suddenly dropped its resistance to a plan for the nationalization of its industry in Chile and the Bolivian military came to power announcing the expropriation of Gulf Oil interests in that country.

Distinguishing sub-national actors is especially important in the light of the serious weakness of national governments in much of Latin America. Although most Latin Americans would regard themselves as Brazilians, Mexicans, Panamanians, etc., the *primary* symbol of identification for many of them is still not the nation and certainly not existing governments. Though the national government may fall, the military insists upon its prerogatives, rival political parties and party factions stalemate the President in Congress, businessmen express outrage at a modest new tax, unions stage violent demonstrations, students weekend with guerrilla bands, and so on.[5] Governments not only face the task of reconciling virtually irreconcilable domestic political factions but also the problem of maintaining their authority vis-à-vis foreign elements which are *physically* present on the nation's home ground. Foreign diplomats, economic aid and technical assistance personnel, military attachés and advisers, and foreign business enterprises exercise such substantial influence over the day-to-day conduct of national affairs that the concept of "penetrated" societies[6] appears eminently applicable to Latin America.

In spite of the weakness of many national governments, nationalism has

[reprinted in Rosenau, *International Politics,* pp. 20–29]; and "The Global System and Its Sub-Systems: A Developmental View" in Rosenau, *Linkage Politics,* pp. 21–43.
4 The theoretical implications of the case are extensive and obviously deserve a more detailed analysis than we can give them here. See also selection 29 in this reader.

5 Violence in the cities and on college campuses indicates that not even the United States is entirely immune to the problem of maintaining national identification and governmental legitimacy. Yet President Nixon's apparent success in mustering a "silent majority" in the face of an unpopular war, a declining economy, inflation, and high taxes, contrasts sharply with the Latin American norm.
6 Rosenau defines a "penetrated" system as "one in which nonmembers of a national society participate directly and authoritatively, through actions taken jointly with the society's members, in either the allocation of its values or the mobilization of support on behalf of its goals" (Rosenau, "Pretheories" in Farrell, *Approaches,* p. 65).

been a potent force in twentieth-century Latin America and may currently be on the rise. As Belaúnde could undoubtedly testify, nationalism can work either for or against governments, depending upon how effectively they manage to meet the dual demands of ever larger numbers of politically mobilized citizens for a better life and an end to extranational penetration and dependence. These goals are inconsistent insofar as economic and social development depend on external aid and trade; on the other hand, markedly "independent" domestic and international policies may to some extent compensate for a lack of rapid progress on the economic and social front.

We may identify and offer relevant examples of at least two additional types of actors engaged in cross-national behavior that overarch national governments in the international hierarchy of structures: international nongovernmental organizations (INGOs) and international governmental organizations (IGOs). The examples listed below demonstrate that each category includes entities which differ dramatically in their geographical scope, purposes, formal organization, supranational authority, autonomy with respect to other organizations, and internal cohesion. Therefore, although we shall not attempt the exercise, alternative classification schemes might be devised using one or more of the foregoing distinctions as a base.

(a) international nongovernmental organizations:

the Catholic Church

business and commercial enterprises which constitute an international network of parent organization and affiliates (in addition to their roles as subnational actors at home and abroad), such as Standard Oil of New Jersey and The Chase Manhattan Bank

congresses and conferences of Communist parties in Moscow and Havana

the World Union of Christian Democracy and its parent Latin American affiliate, the Christian Democratic Organization of America (ODCA)

the International Federation of Christian Trade Unions (CISC) and its Latin American affiliate, the Latin American Confederation of Christian Unions (CLASC)

the International Confederation of Free Trade Unions (ICFTU) and its Latin American affiliate, the Inter-American Regional Workers' Organization (ORIT)

ADELA, a private investment consortium pooling resources from corporations in the United States, Canada, Europe, and Japan

Association of American Chambers of Commerce in Latin America (AACCLA)

Lions International

(b) international governmental organizations:

> the United Nations, its regional Economic Commission for Latin America (ECLA), and UN specialized agencies like the World Bank (IBRD), the International Development Association (IDA), the International Finance Corporation (IFC), the International Monetary Fund (IMF), the International Atomic Energy Agency (IAEA), the General Agreement on Tariffs and Trade (GATT), and the UN Conference on Trade and Development (UNCTAD)
>
> the Organization of American States (OAS), the Inter-American Committee of the Alliance for Progress (CIAP), the Inter-American Commission on Human Rights (IACHR), and OAS specialized organizations like the Pan American Health Organization (PAHO)
>
> the Inter-American Development Bank (IDB)
>
> the Agency for the Prohibition of Nuclear Weapons in Latin America
>
> the Special Commission on Latin American Coordination (CECLA), an irregular meeting of Latin American government representatives designed to develop joint positions on questions of development assistance and trade
>
> the Organization of Central American States (ODECA)
>
> the Latin American Free Trade Association (LAFTA)
>
> the Andean Common Market (ANCOM)
>
> the Central American Common Market (CACM)
>
> the Caribbean Free Trade Association (CARIFTA)
>
> the European Economic Commission (EEC) and its Development Assistance Committee (DAC)

Having distinguished various types of international actors, we shall now shift our focus to the patterns of *interaction* arising from their cross-national behavior.

It is useful to conceive of the Americas as enmeshed in the global international *system* and many other less comprehensive and overlapping international *subsystems*. Considering the number of actors in all categories, the number of potential international subsystems is virtually limitless.[7] The internal decision-making processes of national

---

[7] The term *system* merely implies a relationship or interaction between the units therein; it does not specify the nature of that relationship or interaction. One might therefore want to make a distinction between "political" systems concerned with "the authoritative allocation of values" (following Easton) and other kinds of systems (economic, social, cultural, etc.); and also between "horizontal" and "vertical" systems, depending upon whether relationships exist on the same or different level(s) in the international hierarchy of structures. For slightly different, but not incompatible, definitions of horizontal and vertical systems, see Rosenau, "Pre-theories" in Farrell, *Approaches,* p. 74. As Rosenau suggests, an "issue-area" (discussed below) is a leading example of a vertical political system.

governments and of international governmental and nongovernmental organizations may themselves be regarded as subsystems, as may the relationships between individual international organizations and their members (OAS-U.S., IMF-Brazil, CLASC-an affiliated union); between international organizations and nonmembers (LAFTA-U.S., ANCOM-Venezuela, Communist Party congresses-"deviant" parties); and between international organizations and other international organizations (OAS-UN, EEC-CACM-LAFTA-CARIFTA, CLASC-ORIT). Likewise the relationships between an individual national government and another government (Soviet Union-Cuba, Cuba-Mexico, U.S.-Peru, Chile-Bolivia); among a group of nation-states that supposedly have a number of interests in common (Atlantic Triangle subsystem, inter-American subsystem, Latin American subsystem, North-South subsystem); between one nation-state and a group of nation-states (Canada-inter-American subsystem, Soviet Union-Latin American subsystem, Panama-Central American subsystem, United Kingdom-Commonwealth Caribbean subsystem); and between subnational actors in different nation-states (Brazilian military-Argentine military, Peruvian APRA Party-Venezuelan *Acción Democrática* Party). And these illustrations by no means exhaust the possibilities.

Some (sub)systems are obviously more significant than others in terms of their scope, their persistence through time, and their relevance to particular research projects. Each system has a *structure*—those actors whose international behavior sustains the system—and an *environment*. The latter includes all those human and nonhuman entities, behavior, and events which lie outside the relationships that constitute the system. Although it is external to the system, shifts in the environment may bring about changes in the system. For example, the emergence of a nationalist, development-oriented military in Peru has had an important impact on relations between the governments of the United States and Peru. Part of the environment of a system is, by definition, other systems; and, in the sense that changes in one system may affect another, we may add systems to our list of international actors.

International *integration* theory seeks to isolate the variables leading to more cooperative relationships between actors in international systems and to the establishment and expansion of international agreements and organizations. Conversely, it attempts to discover the reasons for continued or increased antagonisms and the failure of existing agreements or organizations (disintegration). This kind of theory is helpful not only to students of international organizations like the OAS and the CACM, but also to those who are concerned about systems which involve a pattern of relationships that is not yet highly institutionalized. The Latin American system, for instance, was a symbol of identification for many Latin American intellectuals and *técnicos* before it had any institutional underpinnings in ECLA, LAFTA, CACM, ANCOM, CECLA, and the projected Latin American Common Market. Its viability in the years ahead undoubtedly depends both upon the success of these cross-national ventures and further institution-building.

Linkage theory provides us with still another perspective on international relationships. As Rosenau defines the term, a linkage is "any recurrent sequence of behavior that originates in one system and is reacted to in another."[8] Central to the theory as it has developed is the interaction of national and international systems and such questions as: What kinds of linkages are there? What actors in national and international systems are the source or target of linkage behavior ("linkage groups")? What are consequences of linkage phenomena for national and international systems? Applying the theory to the Americas, one might ask: What impact has the Cuban Revolution had on other Latin American domestic systems? How did the series of Latin American military coups in the 1960s affect the activities of the OAS? and so on.

Finally, we may also organize international phenomena around the concept of *issue-areas*. Again quoting Rosenau: "[E]ach issue-area must be seen as comprised of certain kinds of actors whose values and interests are such that they can be expected to engage in certain kinds of behavior when issues are activated in the area."[9] Different kinds of issues cut across different national and international systems, engaging different sets of actors in different ways. For example, the constituencies, including international organizations, which participate in controversies over hemisphere security are not exactly the same as those involved in debates about economic aid or trade.

Even those actors who do participate in all three issue-areas do not bring the same attitudes to each of them. However, to the extent that the behavior of actors participating in more than one issue-area is conditioned by their experiences in each and that the policies in question have a generalized effect on the environment, issue-areas—like other systems—overlap and interact. Because of their experiences with the United States on the private investment question, many Latin American governments were inclined to believe Castro's initial argument that Washington opposed the Cuban Revolution solely because of his confiscation of enterprises belonging to U.S. nationals. The Kennedy Administration launched the Alliance for Progress in the belief that U.S. and OAS anti-Communist measures were of little use unless Latin American governments had the resources to provide an alternative to Castroism.

The foregoing survey of analytical approaches has been designed primarily to be suggestive and to make more comprehensible the content and organization of this book. Selections in Part I treat various actors in inter-American relations in greater depth, and some of them draw extensively upon the concepts of systems, linkages, and integration. The order of the selections in Part II derives largely from the editor's notion of the boundaries of key issue-areas, although the subheadings define rather broader boundaries.[10]

---

[8] "Toward the Study of National-International Linkages" in *Linkage Politics,* p. 45.
[9] "Foreign Policy in *Domestic Sources,* p. 16. See also "Pre-theories" in Farrell, *Approaches,* pp. 71–88.

[10] Partly because some selections overlapped issue-areas—as issue-areas themselves overlap! —the editor opted for more inclusive subheadings.

I

Analytical Perspectives

on Contemporary

Inter-American Relations

Actors, Systems, Linkages,
Integration, and Issue-Areas

Developing on the Periphery:
External Factors
in Latin American Politics

Douglas A. Chalmers

Douglas A. Chalmers is an Associate Professor of Government in the Institute of Latin American Studies at Columbia University.

Professor Chalmers's essay focuses on the principal actor in the international relations of Latin America, the Latin American nation-state and its domestic political system. However, his concern is less with the domestic political system as a source of outputs into its international environment than with the influence of the international environment upon the domestic system.[1] Although he warns of the dangers inherent in generalizing about Latin America, he maintains that the polities of the area do have features which distinguish them from other so-called developed and developing systems. Moreover, he argues that these distinctive features derive in large part from Latin America's unique linkage patterns. For over five hundred years Latin America has evolved in dependent fashion on the "periphery" of the developed world and, more specifically, within the sphere of influence of a succession of great powers.

Latin American nations are developing in a far different environment than did the nations of Europe, or even other areas presently classified as developing. Latin America's long-standing ties with an immensely more powerful Europe and United States, the rapidity of communications that send people, money, and resources swiftly back and forth, a century and a half of legal

---

[1] For another study which in many ways complements Professor Chalmers's, see Gino Germani, "Stages of Modernization," *International Journal*, XXIV, No. 3 (Summer 1969), pp. 463–85.

independence, but high economic and cultural dependence, these are elements of the distinctive relationship the area has with its environment. And this relationship profoundly affects politics in the area. Latin American political leadership must constantly deal with the advantages and dangers which such an environment presents. But even more, the political systems are linked to the environment not only as a whole, through the responsible elite, but also through the manifold linkages that exist between groups and institutions within and outside of the area. It is this pattern of linkages, its changes over time, and the consequences that it has for Latin American politics that is the subject of this chapter.[1]

The first task in analyzing the importance of linkages is to evolve a framework sufficiently flexible to describe the many variations involved in the relationships polities have with their environment. Based on this framework, some as yet highly speculative propositions will then be advanced concerning

the impact of linkage patterns on Latin American paths to development.

ASPECTS OF LATIN AMERICAN LINKAGE PATTERNS

Some of the dimensions that come to mind in trying to describe the relation of a polity to its environment are colonial dependency versus independence, cooperation versus exploitation and intervention versus nonintervention. However suggestive these terms might be, they are rigid, difficult to measure, and too gross to detect variations between countries and over a period of time. In addition, they are part of the language of polity-to-polity relationships whereas what is needed are categories that deal with the environment and the polity in more flexible terms, since many of the actors and events having an impact on Latin American politics are only loosely, if at all, identified with another polity.

To provide a framework for the description of the general Latin American type of linkage pattern, four aspects are explored:

1. The character of the international system.
2. The external linkage groups (polities, actors, or structures with whom the polity in question has most direct relations) and the relationship of the polity to those external linkage groups.
3. The internal linkage groups (groups, actors, or structures most directly responsive to external events) and the relationship of the internal linkage groups to the polity.[2]

---

[1] James N. Rosenau defines linkages as "any recurrent sequence of behavior that originates in one system and is reacted to in another." ("Toward the Study of National-International Linkages" in Rosenau, ed., *Linkage Politics* [New York: The Free Press, 1969], p. 45.) His challenge is to develop systematic analysis of linkages not only as international events affect domestic politics, but also vice versa. The present chapter, however, takes up only the first part of this challenge. It should be noted, too, that this chapter does not explore variations in linkage patterns and their consequences among Latin American polities, thereby perpetuating what for many experts is the lamentable tendency to generalize about a very diverse area. At this preliminary stage of analysis, however, I feel that the similarities are sufficient basis for a general treatment, although verification and refinement in the hypotheses offered here will surely require a more discriminating treatment of the area.

[2] The term linkage groups comes from the suggestive analysis of Karl Deutsch in his essay, "External Influences on the Internal Behavior of States" in R. Barry Farrell (ed.), *Approaches to Comparative and International Politics* (Evanston: Northwestern U.P., 1966), p. 5.

4. The character of the polity.

Within each of these categories, variables can be identified which, taken with the others, determine the sort of impact that the linkage pattern has on the polity. The following chart illustrates the categories by roughly indicating their content in several periods of Latin American history.

THE INTERNATIONAL SYSTEM

Rosenau has pointed out that the relevant environment of a polity is made up not of one system, but many —the contiguous, the regional, the global, and so on.[3] A lasting characteristic of the linkages Latin American polities have with the world, however, has been the overwhelming importance of the central arenas of international politics—Europe, the United States and the Soviet Union. It is true that ignoring the contiguous and regional environments has drawbacks, particularly in the period of boundary disputes and Latin American wars of the nineteenth century, and perhaps now with the growth of inter-American economic cooperation and communications. In general, however, it is the characteristics of the "central" system that are of primary concern and consequence for Latin America.

Another important characteristic has been the salience of the economic dimension. The world powers have, in the five centuries since the conquest, been competing with each other for economic advantage in Latin America —for precious metals, raw materials, markets and possibilities for investment. It is true, however, that the character of this economic dimension has

changed, most importantly by virtue of the fact that the increasing economic interdependence of the major powers and the effects of the world wars have created a situation that makes possible violent economic instability.

One of the most important characteristics of the international system relevant to Latin America emerged after World War I. The central international system expanded to include the United States and the Soviet Union. At the same time ideologically oriented political conflict was generated as both the Soviet Union and Nazi Germany defined their objectives and needs in world-wide terms. The fact that these conflicts led to world-wide war conditions—hot with respect to Nazi Germany and cold with respect to the Soviet Union—reinforced the ideological drive to build support among polities in such areas as Latin America. The competitive aspects of the international system ceased to be remote and Latin America has, on occasion, become the arena for great power confrontations.

EXTERNAL LINKAGE GROUPS

No matter what the state of international relations, the impact on a polity will vary according to the particular nations, structures and groups to which the polity is linked and the nature of that link. Nations do not react to the international system as a whole, but to the way it is reflected in particular actors with whom they have the most contact. One of the most enduring features of Latin American linkages has been the predominance of one other nation—a colonial power to begin with, and then a dominant commercial one, and finally, despite the growing importance of international markets and

3 Cf. Rosenau, *op. cit.*

TABLE 1. Summary of Latin America's Linkage Patterns in Selected Historical Periods

Aspect	Colonial	Late Nineteenth Century	Inter-War	1950 and After
			PERIOD	
International System	Colonization and mercantile competition	Aggressive commercial competition	Highly unstable international economic situation; emergence of ideological conflict	Somewhat stabilized international economy; intensified political conflict increasingly oriented towards winning "third world" allies
External Linkage Groups	Colonial powers who see Latin America as area for exploitation and religious conversion	The major commercial powers, especially Great Britain, who see area as source of raw materials, markets	The international trade pattern, in which LA is a subordinate participant; the major ideological powers begin to see LA polities as allies	The USA—economically sees LA as field of investment and markets; politically as area to be secured against Communism; International agencies, UN, ECLA, IMF, etc., with increasing attention to stimulating the area's development
Internal Linkage groups	Colonial administrators, church officials	Exporting and commercial elites often dominant. Intellectuals looking to Europe, U.S. Military establishments. Immigrants	Exporting and commercial elites, still often dominant. Intellectuals looking increasingly to all competing powers. Agents and agitators from all major powers	Government authorities and technicos receiving advice and aid. Intellectuals. Agents and agitators. Middle sectors, aware of external high standard of living. Church groups, especially lay
Nature of the Polities	Bureaucratic-authoritarian	Unstable oligarchy	Unstable oligarchy, with broadening to middle sectors and sporadic agitation from labor groups	Unstable, and broader oligarchy, much divided. Governments increasingly committed to broad development. Forceful nationalist reaction and efforts to control foreign influence

agencies, the United States. One might say that with marginal exceptions, for five hundred years each Latin American polity has been in someone's sphere of influence.

Further, after Independence, the linkages have generally been with countries considerably more developed economically than those in Latin America, creating a sharp inequality of capabilities. One may speak of the enduring peripherality of Latin America. Despite the presence of valuable resources that are needed by the major powers, Latin America's bargaining position has generally been weak. This has been modified with the evolution of a politically competitive international system in which major powers showed an increasing interest in winning Latin American allies. The countries with significant strategic value in World War II, for example—Brazil, Argentina, Panama, and Mexico—gained bargaining power with the United States. And in the post-war period, Latin American countries have sporadically been seen as important in the Cold War. This is a growing trend, although still a limited one, but it has led to a significant increase in the resources involved in the linkages.

The linkage pattern of Latin America is distinguished from other parts of the "third world," of course, by the fact that direct colonial ties were severed 150 years ago. This, in a way, has contributed to Latin America's peripherality, since a lack of authoritative bonds meant that the major powers had neither the opportunity nor the responsibility for a thoroughgoing and direct intervention in Latin American politics. Only in the areas near the United States like Cuba and Mexico did this country try, and some-

times succeed temporarily, in direct imposition.

A final point in this category of external linkage entities is the considerable growth and diversification of subsidiary, but still important, sources of influence, especially in the various sorts of international agencies—such as the Economic Commission for Latin America of the United Nations, which has been important in providing orientation and technical assistance, and the various international financial institutions, such as the International Monetary Fund, which is important in defining the economic issues, and, when there is a financial crisis, in applying direct pressure on political leaders. Although it would be too early to speak of a differentiated and specialized international set of linkage groups, the Latin American pattern is clearly moving in that direction.

INTERNAL LINKAGE GROUPS

With the possible exception of a full-scale invasion, the various elements of a political system do not respond equally to international events. Groups and structures within the polities have different levels of interest and awareness in the international environment. Another significant way of describing the linkage pattern, then, is to indicate the character and distribution of the most directly linked groups in the polity, and their position with respect to its decision-making processes.

The variables within this category which appear most significant in explaning the impact of the pattern on the polity are:

1. the dependence of the linkage groups on foreign sources of support and their

loyalties abroad, or, conversely, their commitments to the polity;

2. the extent to which important linkage groups are filling or controlling authoritative decision-making roles, or more vaguely, but flexibly, their influence;

3. the range of issues in which internal linkage groups are involved, and;

4. the coherence of the linkage groups—i.e., whether they are similarly oriented and coordinated, or whether they are diverse and competitive.

The Independence eliminated the viceroys and bureaucrats who were fully committed and dependent on foreign support and in positions of authority. Following the Wars of Independence in the nineteenth century, the influence of linkage groups was still very great, however, through the dominance of the exporting oligarchs—although the degree of their loyalty, and the permanence of their influence, varied according to the degree to which they were nationals or foreigners, and the degree to which they were able to establish hegemony. Since that time the linkage groups have certainly not decreased in size or importance, but they have become more diversified, less coherent, and more domestically oriented. Even foreign businessmen, wherever their loyalties lie, have become more dependent on internal factors, as indicated by the general shift in investment from exporting industries to manufacturing for the local market. Further, the competition of major powers for support has generated competing political groups (Communist parties, guerrilla groups, rightist parties, and more recently business and military groups) with fairly strong ties abroad. The technocrats and intellectuals who are in general sensitive to foreign ideas are less committed to particular foreign models, in general due to increasingly complex and differentiated sources, and their loyalties and perceptions appear to become somewhat more autonomous, as is shown in part by their growing espousal of nationalism.

Standing back, the relatively permanent characteristics of Latin American linkage patterns with respect to internal linkage groups in the last century and a half include the absence of direct colonial experience, but an expanding range of linkage groups having considerable influence. As was apparent from discussing external linkage groups, the constant theme has been linkages based on economic factors. While other groups have emerged, the foreign business community and the foreign-tied domestic banking, commercial, and manufacturing interests have been consistently important.

THE CHARACTER OF THE POLITY

The structure and behavior of the polity become the dependent variables in the next part of the chapter, but however much the linkage patterns influence the political system, it is clear that the relation is two-way, and that no matter what the international system and the pattern of linkage groups are, the impact will be different if, say, the polity in question is forcefully unified in an authoritarian fashion, or if it is a loose and conflict-ridden system.

The variables most useful in assessing the impact of linkage patterns are:

1. the unity and distinctiveness of national culture,

2. the demand-performance ratio with regard to socio-economic development,

3. the legitimacy and stability of existing decision-making procedures, and

4. the capability of the system to regulate the actors within the system—in particular the linkage groups.

Compared with other areas of the world each Latin American polity's national culture must be scored as unified but not sharply differing from each other or that of the major powers. It is relatively unified in that there are few "primordial" loyalties strong enough to threaten a fragmentation of the society. Latin America, despite the presence of the Indian, who is relatively quiescent politically, escapes the threat of national dissolution so prominent in Africa, Asia, and Central Europe. The last foreigner to use "divide and conquer" techniques (based on cultural cleavages) with any grand success was Cortez in the conquest of Mexico.

On the other hand, the culture of Latin American countries has always been heavily oriented toward Europe and the importance of Latin American culture as a source of political opposition to the foreigner has always been rather half-hearted, despite the existence of eloquent advocates. Even the relatively strong "latin" rejection of "anglo-saxon" attitudes seems to be of only peripheral importance.

With respect to the demand-performance ratio, Latin America has certainly experienced a "revolution of rising expectations" in ways to be discussed below, and also experiences relatively sharp crises engendered by the various strategies involved in satisfying those demands. There is no question but that inflationary spirals, political crises over demands to expand and make more effective the suffrage, or other crises associated with the process of development, provide an entry for direct political intervention

by outside groups—such as the power given to the International Monetary Fund and foreign bankers in the periodic monetary and payments crises that Latin American countries have recently been undergoing. If anything, this type of problem appears to be increasing.

The high turnover of regimes, and more particularly of presidents and groups in power, which has long provided the central topic for political scientists studying Latin America, also seems plausibly related to the significance of the pattern of linkages. This pattern has been variously termed a "lack of legitimacy," or "instability," although it is commonly noted that such instability rarely indicates major changes in policy orientation. More recently it has been suggested that there is, in addition, a relatively high degree of predictability about the *golpes* and sudden shifts in top personnel— at least in that they reflect a basic set of relationships among a series of elite groups, the "tentative" solution to which may change in detail, but not in general character.[4] In any case there is a weak sense of legitimacy about any fixed procedures of resolving political conflicts, and weak legitimacy for any particular set of top executive leaders. Once again, this would appear to provide opportunities for influence by exogenous groups that would be absent otherwise.

All of the factors so far discussed influence the regulative capability of the system, particularly as it is or can be applied to foreign-based groups. Fundamental and superficial crises im-

[4] For a discussion of the more or less enduring rules of the Latin American political game despite apparent instability, cf. Charles W. Anderson, *Politics and Economic Change in Latin America* (Princeton: Van Nostrand, 1967), ch. 4.

pair this ability, as does the lack of a cultural base on which to reject the foreigner. In Latin America, in general, though, there has clearly been a significant increase in this regulative capability, based in part on the strength of nationalistic movements, but probably more importantly, on the development of bureaucratic techniques to control the in- and outflow of money and resources, and the improving ability to provide for security, as in the increasingly sophisticated "insurgency" control tactics of the Latin American military (assisted by the United States military). It is obviously an uneven, and unevenly applied capability, but perhaps one of the strongest trends is in the direction of its improvement, most evident in Mexico, where the government appears to be able to absorb a very high degree of foreign involvement and foreign-tied linkage groups without losing control.

THE IMPACT OF LINKAGES ON LATIN AMERICAN POLITIES

Any effort to assess the over-all impact of this pattern of linkages on the structure and development of Latin American polities immediately runs up against the obvious complexity of the relationships involved. Linkages may affect the system, for example, in the following ways:

1. Groups with special ties abroad may emulate policies, organizations, standards of living, and so on, introducing exogenous patterns of behavior that may stimulate chains of disequilibria;
2. unequal access to foreign resources may alter the distribution of power;
3. unstable or exceptional demands may be injected into the system by groups acting "under orders" from abroad, or by local groups seeking to com-

pensate for deprivations experienced in their dealings abroad, and;
4. linkage groups, especially foreigners, may be under special constraints with regard to their participation in political life, which may be important enough to affect the style of politics and influence the range of viable political institutions.

Further, the impact of the linkage pattern may be felt in a very general and indirect way in changes brought about in the socioeconomic and cultural bases of the polity, or in a very specific way on the form and output of the day-to-day decision-making process. In order to provide some depth for the tentative conclusions about the over-all impact of linkages, the following pages will suggest some important "middle-range" hypotheses about the impact of linkages on the infrastructure of politics in Latin America, the issues facing decision makers and the policies they adopt, and the institutions through which the system operates.

IMPACT ON THE INFRASTRUCTURE

At the most general level, the history of socioeconomic change in Latin America has been strongly influenced by its linkage patterns. In the colonial period the impact was most direct, with decisions about land tenure, the treatment of the Indians and slaves, and the social status of foreigners and creoles being the subject of legislation in Spain and Portugal. Since the beginning of the nineteenth century, the impact has been more indirect, but strong enough so that histories of social and economic changes are taken up in large part with references to the impact of situations abroad with respect to markets, investments, immigration, and the like.

In a very general sense, the long-term trend, stimulated at least partly from abroad, has been in the direction of modernization—that is, the increasing secularization and differentiation of the population of Latin American polities and their social mobilization attendant on the processes of education, urbanization and industrialization. The question is, however, whether this process of modernization takes on any special characteristics by virtue of the linkage patterns. The answer is clearly in the affirmative, although it is difficult to be precise about distinguishing the importance of linkages from other factors—such as the particular patterns of resources and the influence of more or less indigenous cultural characteristics. A few of these special characteristics most plausibly related to linkages deal with the relationships to authority often denoted as paternalism, the sudden rise in political demands from the "revolution of rising expectations," and the existing pattern of political inequality.

Paternalism

One of the most often noted characteristics of Latin American politics is the tendency of many elements of the population to look to their leaders, political and otherwise, for the initiation, execution, and evaluation of policies, and to resist a mass, "class-conscious" mobilization to make demands. This has received various names, including the *authoritarian tradition,* the diffusion of *patron mentality,* the *subject culture,* and *paternalism.* It is manifested in the relation of the peasant to the landowner, the labor union members to their leaders, the businessmen to the government, and the followers of personalistic leaders in politics. As the terms used to describe

it indicate, this phenomenon is usually described or explained in terms of cultural attitudes. It can, however, at least in part be related to the pattern of linkages. This can best be demonstrated by looking at some particular groups.

With regard to the largest set of groups in Latin America, the peasantry, for example, the manner in which Latin American economies were tied into the world market contributed to the perpetuation of large-scale paternalistic social organization in the rural areas and has severely limited the rise of group-conscious small farmers or peasants. The purely Indian communities were destroyed or isolated, and the dominant early patterns of rural organization were large-scale land holdings based on slavery or debt peonage. Major changes in agriculture came with the development of more and more crops for export, rather than commercial production for domestic consumption. Such export production often entailed the perpetuation of the large paternalistic *hacienda* or *fazenda.* Even the most technologically advanced modern agricultural producers of the present time—a fair proportion of which, incidentally, are foreigners—employ a sort of modern paternalism designed to keep their workers tied to the land through provision of housing, schools, churches, and the like. As mechanization and the domestic demand grows, this paternalistic structure will probably change, but it seems clear that up to now, the typical pattern of a fragmented peasantry, tied closely with a local patron, has survived by virtue of the particular linkage pattern Latin America has experienced.

There are also factors related to the linkage pattern which affect the outlook of the urban working class, and may account for its low level of group or class solidarity, a generally low and probably declining level of radical political ideology, and the tendency to opt for rather diffuse "populistic" leadership rather than specific organizational leaders.

To begin with, Latin America's status as a late-comer has produced a particular pattern of industrial growth that emphasizes the demand for highly skilled labor in capital-intensive industries, creating incentives for paternalistic devices by management to hold these workers. At the same time the high level of immigration to the cities —much faster than the creation of industrial jobs (the industrial work force is declining as a percentage of the total in many countries) lead to a high level of internal stratification within the work force and has been suggested as a reason for the lack of solidarity.[5]

More directly, the pattern of linkages contributes to working-class dependency and involvement with agencies of the government. This dependency—with its resultant lack of labor militancy—can be seen most readily in countries like Mexico and Brazil, where the labor unions are more or less official, but it exists in more subtle ways throughout the continent.[6] Linkages play a role in creating this situation through the emu-

lation by elites in the 1930s and 1940s of world-wide trends toward adoption of "advanced" labor codes and welfare legislation, which in Latin America has created the legal and financial basis for tying the worker to the government. The fragile nature of Latin American industrialization in the face of international competition also makes public policy with regard to tariffs, exchange rates and regulation of credit exceptionally important for industry. If this makes the industrial and commercial interests of the country closely involved with the government, it also means that the workers, too, must depend more on government than on collective bargaining for significant economic gains. Although this orientation sometimes ends with the participation of labor leaders in government, for the rank and file the opportunity and incentive to form militant unions designed to win concessions from management is limited.

Some of the same factors have led to the prevalent posture of industrial and commercial groups, who are periodically chastised by North American writers for their preferences for personalistic dealings, family enterprises, and dependency on the favors of the government.[7] These groups have only recently approached the status of a coherent, politically organized group, and then only in the economically advanced Latin American countries. Developing on the periphery, however, has meant that such groups have always had more to gain—in terms of markets, credit, and technology—through direct dealings with the foreigner, or

[5] Cf. Frank Bonilla, "The Urban Worker," in John J. Johnson (ed.), *Continuity and Change in Latin America* (Stanford: Stanford U.P., 1964). Also Henry A. Landsberger, "The Labor Elite: Is it Revolutionary?" in S. M. Lipset and Aldo Solari (eds.), *Elites in Latin America* (New York: Oxford U. P., 1967).

[6] Cf. Robert Alexander, *Organized Labor In Latin America* (New York: Free Press, 1965), and for an analysis of the strategies used by labor in dealing with this situation in Peru, James L. Payne, *Labor and Politics in Peru* (New Haven: Yale U.P., 1965).

[7] Cf. Albert Lauterbach, *Enterprise in Latin America* (Ithaca: Cornell U.P., 1966) and Frank Brandenburg, *The Development of Latin American Private Enterprise* (Washington: National Planning Association, 1964).

through favors gained, often individually, from a government which increasingly controls access abroad.

Probes into the behavior and structure of other groups, I believe, would show similar patterns, providing a partial explanation, at least, for the failure on the part of many Latin American polities to evolve what in Gabriel Almond's terms would be a series of differentiated and autonomous interest groups.[8] Despite the general impulses from abroad towards socioeconomic development, which perhaps will produce this pattern in the long run, the combination of unequal levels of development, the pattern of emulation fostered by the cultural and political orientation towards Europe, and the necessarily crucial position of the government authorities in the highly linked economic system, all provide brakes to this process of modernization.

The Revolution of Rising Expectations

The concept of a *demonstration effect* producing a rising level of demands as the people of Latin America become aware of the high standards of living in the more developed countries is a familiar one. The basic conditions necessary—a sharp international inequality and a high level of communications—are clearly part of the Latin American linkage pattern. Some qualifications need to be made, however.

To begin with, the proposition must be applied separately to the various groups in the population. Access to information about the gap in living standards is unevenly distributed, for example, as are opportunities for use of nonpolitical means to satisfy the

demands created. Further, any reaction to awareness of the gap depends on the ability of the persons to empathize—imagine themselves on the other end of the scale of inequality—and to have the necessary instrumental attitudes which would lead them to believe that action on their part (i.e., expressing those demands) would be useful in bridging the gap.[9]

Taking these variables together, it seems a plausible and valid hypothesis that it is the middle sectors who would be most affected. The upper classes would either not find a gap between themselves and their reference group abroad, or, in many cases they would be able to rectify it not by pressure on the government, but by manipulating their contacts abroad—even moving there. The lower end of the socioeconomic scale, on the other hand, would be limited in its reaction by lack of access to detailed information, and because of attitudes which would limit their direct action.

These propositions seem in general to be valid in Latin America, since it is clearly this complex middle segment that provides much of the pressure for increasing output by governments. The image called forth by the notion of the *revolution of rising expectations,* that of the masses battering at the gates of the wealthy, is not, therefore, very appropriate. Latin American middle sectors are largely bureaucratic and white collar, and have a long-standing orientation towards assimilation into upper-class patterns. In many countries they are closely tied with the military. In Brazil in the early 1960s, for example, one segment of the much di-

8 Cf. Gabriel Almond and B. Powell, *Comparative Politics: A Developmental Approach* (Boston: Little, Brown, 1966).

9 Cf. Daniel Lerner, *The Passing of Traditional Society* (New York: Free Press, 1958).

vided middle class was to be found toying with appeals for a fundamental social change, only to be stopped short by another segment—equally insistent on development, but with different ideas about its achievement—supporting a military *coup d'état*.

The impact of the *demonstration effect* is very real in Latin America, and is providing some of the most important factors in its present dynamics, but as yet, in any case, it has not produced a clear confrontation, nor a general mobilization of energies, but conflicting and contradictory trends that have added a new stimulus to diffuse political instability.

*The Distribution of Power:
Linkages and Political Resources*

One of the most enduring consequences of linkages in Latin America has been the influence they have had on the distribution of economic resources, social status, and the means of violence among various groups, contributing thereby to the particular patterns of inequality of power in the system. For centuries, the special advantages that the top elite possessed in controlling the technology and finances from abroad, or the benefits of international trade, made possible a highly oligarchical system. The resources most crucial to maintaining the power of this oligarchy changed—the military technology of the conquerors, the access to markets and financing in the nineteenth century on the part of the exporting oligarchy, and the technical and bureaucratic skills available to governments throughout Latin American history. Until recently, however, the net impact has been to reinforce inequality.

The recent situation is changing, not

through creation of an egalitarian society, but by a trend towards so-called dispersed inequalities[10] in which there is more diffusion and, to some extent, competition among powerful groups. The way linkages have contributed to this latter phenomenon suggests some hypotheses concerning the conditions under which they affect the distribution of power.

1. The resulting power inequality will be greater the greater is the disparity between the resources available from abroad and those available domestically. Although technologically and in terms of wealth, the gap between Latin America and the rest of the world is increasing if it is changing at all, industrialization has generated competing resources within the country, and improved transportation has made the mobilization of political forces internally better able to counter the use of foreign resources.

2. Power inequality will be greater the greater is the capacity of relatively small groups to monopolize the access to foreign resources. The competitive nature of the international system and the proliferation of internal linkage groups has created a situation in which opposition groups as well as ruling elites, industrialists as well as exporters, and varying groups of technicians, intellectuals, academics, and civil servants have some opportunity to gain access to foreign resources of various types. The situation has become, therefore, considerably more diffuse.

3. Power inequality will be reduced, on the other hand, to the extent that either the outside source, or the government of the polity, is able to effectively limit the use of externally derived

[10] Cf. Robert A. Dahl, *Who Governs?* (New Haven: Yale U.P., 1961).

resources for general political purposes. There has been a continuing and probably, on the whole, not very successful effort on the part of United States authorities to prevent aid monies from being used for pay-offs and all sorts of political uses going under the name of corruption. The attitude of the United States has been much more equivocal and much more explosive with respect to the use of military assistance for domestic political objectives.[11] Given the apparently rather confused state of United States policies in this regard, the ability of foreigners to control the use of resources cannot yet be regarded as sufficient to or directed towards reducing political inequality.

More important, however, has been the growing capacity of domestic governments to control the use of resources. Better means of detecting arms shipments across the borders, better administration of export-import and exchange transactions and increasing capacity to regulate the use of foreign aid, sometimes through planning, have all limited the traditional concentration of power in the hands of the traditional oligarchies and their foreign allies within the system. This is an ambiguous trend, of course, since increasing the regulative capacity of government merely accentuates inequality if an oligarchy controls the government. It would seem fair to say, however, that political control of government has become increasingly diversified, although in widely differing degrees from one country to another.

11 There is a considerable literature on the uses and abuses of military assistance. With respect to Latin America, Edwin Lieuwen's *Arms and Politics in Latin America* (New York: Praeger, 1960) provided a basic critique which in many respects still stands.

THE IMPACT ON THE ISSUES OF LATIN AMERICAN POLITICS

One of the striking things about Latin American politics is the extent to which prominent issues are loaded with international overtones. Even, apparently, purely domestic issues, such as automobile and traffic control, have international dimensions, such as recently when the chief of a traffic department in Rio de Janeiro resigned with a statement blaming his failures on the fact that the United States government had not come through rapidly enough with a promised financial grant for equipment. This rather extreme example points to the fact that one of the ways linkages affect Latin American polities is through making certain types of issues prominent within the system and influencing the ways in which others are faced.

Two of the many aspects of the problem are first, the reflection of external ideological conflict within the polities, and second, the use of "imported" policies and programs in dealing with contemporary problems.

The Reflection of External Conflicts

Ideological conflict in Latin America has long reflected the conflicts of ideologies beyond its borders. The conflict over the role of the Church in civil society, for example, generated vehement controversy which borrowed a great deal from the ideological arguments in Europe. In the twentieth century, the conflicts between the Allies and the Axis and between the Communist and non-Communist world have provided much of the language used in internal political disputes in Latin America. Mere use of the language, however, is not enough, and the problem is to assess the degree to which international conflicts have real significance for Latin American politics. Such significance has had two forms in Latin America, first in the occasional situation in which the conflict among groups directly influenced by foreign powers is important, and second, when this is not the case but when some elites take over the means and definitions of political conflict used by international groups to identify and deal with their enemies.

The direct conflict of internationally responsive groups has been an occasional factor from earliest times—e.g., among commercial groups tied to England and to Spain in the later days of the colonial empire—but they have unquestionably become more important in the time since World War I as the major powers have sought directly to create allies among various groups in Latin America. A whole range of political groups in Latin America can be identified with foreign ones. Increasingly, on the left this identification is with foreign powers—the Russian groups, the Chinese groups, the Cuban groups—whereas on the right and center, since World War II, at least, the identification has been with such entities as the international Christian Democratic movement, the economic groups tied to international business, the military tied to the United States military, and so forth.

It is a mistake to believe, however, that because these groups exist and clearly do conflict, that the major political conflicts within Latin America always revolve around them. Despite the use of international ideological language, and the tendency of journalists to pick up and report such language, the importance of this domestic-international conflict appears to rise and

fall, correlated, it would appear, with the intensity of the international conflict, and the crises—from whatever origin—within the polity.

For example, the sharpening of international conflict leading to World War II saw numerous attempts at *coups* by fascist-sympathizing groups against those aligned with Great Britain and the United States, as in Argentina. The sharp rise in the temperature of the Cold War in the late forties saw a rise in the importance of conflicts with the Communists in Latin America. The conflict between Castro and the United States in the early 1960s also clearly accentuated the political conflict between sympathizing groups in Latin America, and this conflict was sharply diminished after the missile crisis of 1962 both on the domestic and international front.

Internally, crises within the polities also appear to provide opportunities for international involvement and an escalation of domestic-international conflict. By crisis is meant more than a *coup d'état,* of course, although specifying just what characteristics of an internal crisis lead to its internationalization is difficult. In any case, the Guatemalan upheaval that culminated in direct foreign intervention in 1954 is an obvious and extreme example. The Brazilian crisis following the resignation of Jânio Quadros that led ultimately to the military overthrow of Goulart in 1964 also saw heightened activity on the part of foreign powers and also by groups on the left and right who may be considered as directly responsive to them, even though the Brazilian crisis stemmed largely from internal factors, and was resolved largely by internal forces.

Although the consequences of these sorts of situations are complex, it might be suggested that since the United States so far has a much superior capacity of providing assistance to groups sympathetic to it, crises strengthen such groups; and that the apparent availability of external support in times of crisis may account to some extent for the sometimes puzzling fact that Latin American political leaders often seem strangely unwilling to build a political base within the country that they might call on in times of crisis. These must remain tentative suggestions, but they invite further investigation.

Even when direct conflict between internationally linked groups is not present, groups often adhere to strategies evolved internationally for "fighting communism" or "overthrowing the imperialists" in their domestic conflicts. There seem to be fashions on the left and the right. For example, left wing strategy has gone through accommodative and revolutionary phases, and a segment of it at present seems to have accepted the Mao - Castro emphasis on rural guerrilla war as the road to power. On the right, the influences of United States doctrine about fighting left-wing agitation have had their impact, too. Hemispheric defense to counter the Soviet military threat in the 1950s, support for the "non-Communist left" through diplomacy, private agencies and the CIA, and counter-insurgency tactics have all had their impact on thinking in Latin America, perhaps especially among the military. The conditions under which such transfer is likely are unclear, but it would appear to be a useful area of investigation, since the cues which are used to trigger political action by such groups as the military, or the tools that are likely to be used in internal conflict seem to be influenced by such factors.

Linkages and Latin American Problem Solving

Linkages affect the issues in Latin American political systems in another, more subtle way. Any decision-making process obviously responds to the demands of groups within the system, but the interpretation of those demands depends on the attitudes and perceptions of the decision makers as to the nature of the problem and the resources available. In Latin America these attitudes and perceptions are very often the product of linkages. The methods of collecting data, problem identification and diagnosis, and the programs and policies used often derive from experience in other countries. They are transmitted by a local intelligentsia that has worked and studied abroad, through international agencies such as the Economic Commission for Latin America, or through the technical advisers from foreign governments.

Faced with unrest, declining or stagnant economies, inflation, separatist tendencies, or whatever the problem, leaders in all countries at all times have, of course, cast about in international experience for guidelines for their responses. But because of the long-standing European orientation of Latin American elites and the importance of Latin America's colonial and then economic satellite status, the importance of these foreign definitions and policy models has always been very great. Perhaps the most often noted example of such borrowing was the imitation of European and North American constitutions in the establishment of the Republics after Independence. Despite increasing nationalism, this importation of ideas is more important than ever.

There are many reasons for its growth, primary among which is the vast increase in the rate of communication of ideas to and from Latin America. More Latin Americans are going abroad to study or to work, more international agencies are paying specific attention to Latin American problems, the number of North Americans alone who are involved in conveying advice, plans, and programs, aided by the leverage of financial and material assistance, is very great. Even the growth in the field of the social sciences in the United States dealing with Latin America—however deficient it may still appear in the eyes of specialists—constitutes a vast core of people and institutions giving advice, which is sometimes taken. Latin American decision makers at all levels of authority are increasingly bombarded with suggestions as to what their problems are and what they should do about them. Technical assistance is sometimes thought of in narrow terms of specific governmental programs. Looking at the overall linkage pattern, however, it is clear that generally construed as the transfer of ideas, technical assistance constitutes by now a very broad movement, and this cannot fail to have an effect on the approaches that decision makers take to the problems they face. And those effects come not only from the particular content of the advice that is given, but also in the channels through which it is given.

POLICY INSTABILITY. With regard to the content, one of the most obvious consequences for the system comes when policies or institutions evolved in foreign contexts are applied to quite different situations in Latin America—which happens quite often given Latin America's close ties with Europe and the United States. That such policies do not produce the expected results may contribute to (a) a disillusionment with the policy makers and the possibilities of reform, and (b) a highly volatile style of decision making, in which policies are adopted with fanfare and high hopes, only to be thoroughly condemned as useless when the expected results do not appear. This latter has been described as part of the Latin American decision-making style by Albert O. Hirschman.[12]

Again, the classic example of such a syndrome may be found in the adoption of liberal-democratic constitutions at a time when the social and economic structure of the Latin American republics could turn them into instruments of oligarchic rule. Although the continued prestige of the constitutions has been remarkable—in part no doubt because they could serve the interest of the oligarchies, there is a notable cynicism about them, and also a *de facto* shift back and forth in many countries between at least partial adherence to constitutional procedures and flagrant violation of them. Another example, admittedly covering many particular situations too generally, might be the Alliance for Progress concepts. This time, the projects are much more tailored to the Latin American reality, but they still reflect international strategies of stimulating economic growth, and the gap between expectations and reality has produced cynicism and waves of rejection and support. At least some of the instability in policies in Latin America, and the widespread cynicism about the effectiveness of official action must be credited to the continued and understandable efforts of Latin American

[12] Cf. Albert O. Hirschman, *Journeys Toward Progress* (New York: Twentieth Century Fund, 1963), esp. ch. 4.

decision makers to adopt the latest international program.

PRESERVING FOREIGN INFLUENCE. Although it is a highly explosive topic, it is also unquestionable that the content of much of the advice that comes from abroad has the effect of perpetuating certain kinds of arrangements and ties and particularly the power of some of the most important linkage groups. Given the dominance of the United States in the flow of ideas and resources, it is not surprising that much advice, along with sometimes subtle and sometimes blatant pressure to take such advice, tends to influence the system in the direction of approximating North American ideas about the organization of society and economy, and more particularly, to protect North American interests in Latin America. The policy of urging Latin American elites to define communism as a chief internal threat, or the austerity program for combating inflation urged by the International Monetary Fund, or the recommendations on the importance of encouraging foreign investment as a basic development strategy are all obvious cases in point. One should not make as much of this as some critics of North American foreign policy do, perhaps. Policies may be intended to protect North American interests but actually do the opposite—as when Latin Americans are brought to the United States for training and return as convinced anti-Yankees. Also there are competing groups within the United States and therefore competing interests to be protected. Finally, it is obviously not true that anything that serves United States interests is necessarily against the interests of Latin America. Nevertheless, as a general characteristic, it is still true that the predominance of

a single power in the Latin American environment has shaped the systems and, in a manner of speaking, allowed for a circular reinforcement of that tie.

Both policy instability and the reinforcement of foreign interests are probably diminishing, not because the borrowing of policies is any less, but because the sources of such borrowing are gradually becoming more numerous and competing, and because the growth of scientific interest in Latin America has meant that the facts of the Latin American case are becoming more important in the policies suggested by foreigners or suggested by foreign-oriented Latin Americans. There are other effects, however, which do not seem so likely to diminish, but rather to be reinforced by the swelling volume of ideas, advice, and resources in the linkage pattern.

ANTICIPATING DEMAND AND BUREAUCRATIC OVERLOAD. Despite the authoritarian and bureaucratic traditions presumably inherited from the colonial period, a fairly strong tradition approximating laissez-faire doctrines evolved in Latin America in the nineteenth century, represented by the Liberal parties in many countries. The prominence of such doctrines in Europe was at least partially responsible. Probably equally important, however, was the fact that much economic growth was stimulated by large scale foreign investment in primary commodity production, whose main political needs were to secure favorable concessions and then be left alone as much as possible, since the technology, personnel, transport, and physical construction was largely handled directly by the concerns themselves. The need for support from the local authorities had mostly to do with securing the necessary labor, and not with providing the elements of infrastructure, or a favorable internal market.

By mid-twentieth century, however, the situation changes completely. Not only are foreign investors more dependent on local conditions, but doctrines in the "developed" world have shifted strongly in the direction of an activist state, and much of the technical and financial resources available from abroad are being channeled through government bureaucracies. To this may be added the fact that international economic and political instability—another characteristic of the linkage pattern—makes it difficult to solve many problems without the active representation of Latin American interests in international negotiations on commodity prices, external financing, and so forth. The linkage pattern has come to reinforce an old tradition which assigns to the leaders the responsibility to identify problems, evolve strategies and apply them, which they do often by applying the latest model solution current in international circles.

Major innovations in governmental policy in Latin America over the last decades would include the introduction of labor codes and welfare policies, the various strategies designed to stimulate industrialization, the extension of the suffrage, and the beginnings of land reform. In each of these cases, the actions of leaders cannot be adequately explained as responses to the organized pressures of interested groups. With respect to the labor codes adopted in the 1930s and 1940s, for example, one can find sporadic strikes and unrest, but, at least on paper, the elites overreacted, creating extensive legislation to protect workers often before there were many workers, much less irresistible pressures. Part of the reason for

this can be found in the importance that even minor outbreaks of violence have for the delicately balanced arrangements among the governing elites in many Latin American countries. But at least in part, the availability of models from abroad—designed to deal with more serious threats in other countries—must be considered as a cause. Such influence is very easy to perceive with respect to labor codes, for which the Latin Americans could adopt all or part of the legislation being urged by such agencies as the International Labor Organization. In the case of extended suffrage, the models were more diffuse and varied. Land reform, perhaps the most recent general vogue in policy making, has also been imposed prior to organized peasant demands, either as part of a general revolutionary ideology, as in Cuba, or as part of a general developmental plan, as in Venezuela. However much these programs are adopted to the local circumstances, the fact remains that they are imposed rather than being demanded, at least in part because they are parts of the international models of what the problems of underdevelopment are, and what should be done about them.

The consequence of this anticipation of demands, although very complex, appears to entail a reinforcement of the role of the leadership in a paternalist fashion, a great emphasis on the administration of reform, and the opportunity for elites who initiate and execute these reforms to manipulate them in such a way as to avoid serious threats to their position. Thus, land reform can be turned in the direction of increasing productivity rather than destroying the power of the traditional landed oligarchs, as in many countries in Latin America today, or to becoming an instrument for cementing national political control of the country-side, as in Cuba and Mexico.

More fundamentally, this situation produces a particularly delicate problem for the "reform-mongers" who apparently are given a great advantage in the ability to make use of relatively sophisticated reform measures, but who must face the problem of maintaining these reforms in the absence of a firm political base which, having actively campaigned for the measure, might provide the necessary support for the leaders when opposition from entrenched interests develops.

Another consequence of the government-initiated problem solving stimulated by the pattern of linkages is the great load placed on the administrative apparatus. For example, land reform policies are adopted which require detailed knowledge of existing patterns of landholding, productivity and types of exploitation. Such information is often not available nor easily gathered by the existing agencies. It is often difficult to answer the criticism levelled at the advocates of planning that they assume a veritable miracle of administrative development.

In the long run, demands on the bureaucracy will no doubt produce investments in the training and organization of officialdom, but in the short run, the result is often inefficient operations, reinforcement of cynical attitudes toward the bureaucracy and a rise in personal favoritism and graft.

It would obviously be an exaggeration to consider the linkage pattern chiefly responsible for the attitudes and practices just discussed—corruption has long-standing roots in Latin American politics, for example—but the impact of developing on the periphery clearly plays some role. Of course the advantages of being able to exploit the latest

and most sophisticated analyses and policies are not to be overlooked, but as conditioning factors of the political system, they clearly have many unintended consequences.

LINKAGES AND THE PATTERN OF
INSTITUTIONALIZATION

Another aspect of the political systems of Latin America for which the pattern of linkages has been important is that of the manner and form of regular organized political action, or more simply, political institutions. In particular cases, external forces such as the United States have played a very important role in directly influencing the form of political institutions. Financial and military support for Batista in Cuba and Pérez Jiménez in Venezuela, for example, helped to perpetuate the dictatorial pattern established in those countries for a short period at least. Intervention in Guatemala in 1954 forestalled the imposition of radical leftist and perhaps Soviet style institutions in that country, and led to the return of oligarchical institutions of a particularly instable type.

I do not intend to discuss this further, however, since I am not sure there is any general effect, but rather contradictory and changing ones. The left in Latin America contends that United States policy promotes dictatorships, and the defenders of the United States contend that it promotes democracy. They both seem to be right at different times and different places.

At a somewhat more general level, however, it seems a plausible hypothesis that the type of linkage pattern characteristic of Latin America has some share of responsibility for the instability of political institutions in Latin America. The general argument would be as follows: Stable and effective institutions require among other things a high level of mutual expectations, shared norms, and an effective set of rewards and sanctions that will secure behavior in accordance with the norms. When there exists in a political system linkage groups with limited knowledge of, or allegiance to, the host system, the institutions are likely to be weakened. An obvious example is the threat that a large immigrant group might pose, although in Latin America the sanctions available to the government are quite large enough to prevent a fundamental threat to the system from that source.

The actors in contemporary systems in Latin America that are the most problematical, however, are foreign businessmen, foreign diplomats and military missions, and the foreign-linked revolutionary groups. Although I cannot cite particular examples of how faulty information, or lack of commitment of these groups directly stimulated the breakdown or change of political institutions in Latin American polities, it is hard to believe that the presence of these "foreign bodies" in the political system has no effect. It is at least interesting to speculate on the possibility that the ignorance of local patterns by powerful foreigners, or their unwillingness to play the game, might enter into some examples of institutional breakdown.

A more consistent influence, however, is that of the presence of foreigners and foreign-tied groups on the workings of liberal democratic institutions. The classic democratic institutions of Western Europe and the United States have been representative ones—parliaments linked with the electoral systems and political parties. The operation of these institutions has never completely re-

placed or pre-empted the networks of personal relationships among the elites even in the developed countries, and the pattern of interest groups interacting directly with administrative agencies in Europe and the United States has become increasingly important. The system of parties, elections, and parliaments, however, manages to establish basic legitimacy and carry out an overall regulation of the political game, chiefly by their control over the chief executive.

In Latin America, however, it is notorious that the system of representative institutions is weak. Elections have been manipulated and legislatures have been dominated by the executive or set aside by the military. Although this has many causes, it seems plausible to argue that the linkages have something to do with it in at least two senses. First, the powerful linkage groups, especially the foreigners, are usually not able, constitutionally or practically, to participate openly and fully in the kind of public competition which is demanded for party-political activity, participation in elections and representation in Congresses and parliaments. Although at an earlier stage it would be easy to identify the local representatives of foreign interests who might act quite openly as such, with the rise of nationalism this becomes more and more difficult. The natural habitat of the foreign businessman, the military attaché, the technician providing assistance, is not on the electoral hustings, but rather in the halls of bureaucracy, or in the personal interactions that take place with high government officials at cocktail parties and informal discussions.

In other words, linkages contribute to the tendency to develop means of resolving conflicts, aggregating and articulating interests, through traditional informal means, or through the more or less "private" representation through the bureaucracy. Although this does not necessarily lead to an authoritarian type of system, it would seem to increase its likelihood, especially in circumstances such as those often found in Latin America in which the evolution of pressure groups and regularized means of consultation—which might assure a more or less equal set of opportunities for all existing or potential participants —is, to say the least, not well developed. It is very often not a harsh form of authoritarianism, and may be highly paternalistic rather than ruthless. In part it is moderated, too, by the networks of personal relationships, in which friends can arrange that laws are not too harshly enforced in particular cases. Foreign businessmen, for example, who often have the advantage of rather substantial resources with which to buy such friends, apparently find this game not too difficult to play.

One might look at the same sort of factor from a somewhat different point of view, from that of the political leader with the problem of building the necessary type of long-term support for his policies. The strategies that he adopts are limited by the fact, that, as in all systems, he must find a "political base" which will not only return him or his friends to office and pass his legislation in Congress, but will secure the necessary cooperation for the policies that he adopts, or that will find ways to control potential opposition. The high incidence of linkage groups commanding important resources in Latin America means that in one fashion or another, he has to have their support. Also, many of his problems have to do with international questions. The ability of the political

leadership to adjust to, say, changes in international prices or the shifting fortunes of international political conflict is limited in any case, since many of the events are far beyond his control. But they are much more uncontrollable if he cannot count on the groups within his own system who are closest to, and have some influence over those external events. The problem of securing their support is more complicated than for domestic groups. First of all, if he brings pressure on them, they will either withdraw (to his detriment) or escalate the pressures they command in the international arena. To build them into his political base, however, requires concessions and communication which usually cannot be carried out as the president might attempt with his "domestic" support—that is, in organizing them through political parties and interest groups acting openly. The contacts must be more or less informal, or expressed—as they often are—in the innumerable "protocols" and "agreements" that are negotiated with foreign governments and international institutions.

The Latin American executives are, very often, caught in a rather difficult position in which their public (electoral and party) base sometimes differs radically from their informal base of support. There results what might be called the "Frondizi syndrome" after the Argentinian president who campaigned on a vigorously nationalistic program in 1958, and once elected, carried out a policy of courting various linkage groups, in particular the American Embassy and the international oil companies. His open political base, in other words, was quite at variance with his necessary base of support once in office. Although there are many factors which undermine the effectiveness of electoral and party systems in Latin America, this complex of national, linkage group and international interests, and the differentials in the ability or desire of these groups to express themselves in an acceptable manner in party and electoral competition is certainly an important factor.

Once again I have treated all linkage groups in the same fashion, and I believe that in general there is a consistency in the pattern, but it is true that there are great variations in the activities of foreign-based groups. In the late part of the nineteenth century, for example, the foreign business firms principally engaged in export trade were no doubt the most important groups in question. With the emergence of foreign business firms more tied to local markets, foreign business seems to play less of a role in promoting a personalistic-bureaucratic type of structure. This would not be true, however, of the huge firms that still remain as powerful entities, such as the United Fruit in Central America, the copper companies in Chile (at least until recently) and the oil companies, particularly in Venezuela.

The business community has been replaced by the embassies and international financial representatives, however, as the main actors of this type. But the basic problem remains the same, and until systematic relationships can be worked out and integrated into Latin American political institutions, the net effect will continue to be that of making the search for stable and secure political bases a complex and difficult task.

CONCLUSIONS

Given the highly speculative nature of the propositions offered here, any conclusions must be tentative. Assuming the validity of even some of these propositions, however, important implications follow for the study of comparative politics and for our understanding of Latin American political processes.

First of all, it is clear that any theories of comparative politics must pay more attention to external factors than has usually been the case. Economists have long done so, particularly with respect to Latin America, where economic history is largely a discussion of external factors and their influences. Political scientists have been much less assiduous about such analysis, however. The reasons for this are many, but one of them, perhaps, has been the dominance of an extremely simple model for analyzing external factors, namely that of polity-to-polity relationships. Overwhelming attention is given externally to the actions of the colonial power, of the intervention of the United States, and only very unsystematically to the impact of groups within other polities, international groups, or the characteristics of the international system as a whole. Further, the emphasis has been on the responses of the polity as a whole—the general "revolution of rising expectations" or the national response to external military threats— and again, only very unsystematically to the differentiated responses of particular groups or institutions. The four-term model offered at the beginning of this essay: (1) the international system; (2) the external linkage groups; (3) the internal linkage groups; and (4) the polity, may point the way to a rather more flexible type of analysis, and one which will allow for a more useful classification and analysis of linkage patterns.

The importance of this effort can be seen from a tentative conclusion about the impact of the linkage patterns on

Latin American political systems. Developing on the periphery of a set of powerful and technologically advanced polities, and linked to them in manifold and sometimes subtle ways, the character of Latin American polities cannot help but be different from that of a country at some hypothetically equivalent stage of development in Europe or North America. Not only does the pressure generated by the example of developed countries subject the decision makers to a greater sense of urgency, but the technological and material resources available to them are very much greater than for the leaders of polities developing earlier or in greater isolation. These resources and techniques are not an unmixed advantage—since they must be painfully adapted to the Latin American reality. Building support for the adoption of a foreign–inspired anti-inflationary policy or a set of civil service regulations, for example, requires tactical skills on the part of the leadership quite different from those required in implementing proposals that originate within the polity. A much higher emphasis on something akin to education is part of this, perhaps, as is the discovery of means to avoid or make use of the very wide swings in opinion which are likely to occur without a firmly fixed basis of political support.

The problem of building support for policies and political leadership is also profoundly affected by the presence of large numbers of foreigners and foreign-tied nationals in positions that are crucial to the economy, defense, and cultural affairs. Securing the support of such people is different from that of fully committed citizens by virtue of the special guarantees that must be given (or forceful but subtle means of control) to maintain their cooperation without making them choose the option of leaving the country. The pattern of institutionalization of such support-building practices, too, is different from a more isolated or less dependent polity, because the foreigners are far more difficult to integrate into the public framework of political parties and openly active organized interest groups.

Further, the ideological conflicts of the international system introduce special sorts of frictions into the open political system in Latin America, especially when they are linked with determined outside powers, or when they involve the question of the position of the foreigner within the system. Once again, the linkage pattern, therefore, presents obstacles to the institutionalization of the kind of representative institutions that we are familiar with in Western Europe and the United States.

For a long time, the speculation of political scientists about Latin America centered around the notion of the "pathology of Latin American democracy." Very often executive instability, weakness of parties, manipulation of elections, and *caudillo* type of leaders— taken as the indices of this pathology— were explained in terms of the Iberian Colonial heritage or from cultural factors. If the analysis presented here has any validity, however, the causes must be found also in the linkage pattern that has characterized the area.

But "pathology" is probably not the right word, or it may be applied wrongly to the over-all character of the political systems in Latin America. North Americans and Europeans are perhaps too ready to identify democracy with the health of the representative institutions with which they are familiar, despite the acknowledged signs of weakness into which many of their own have fallen— as is witnessed by the long-standing analysis of the "decline of parliaments."

Without judging whether Latin American democracy is "healthy" or not, the analysis here suggests that the forms in which representation and popular influence on the choice of executives and policy making are likely to be quite different in Latin America than in Europe and the United States. Along with other factors, the linkage pattern appears to encourage the evolution of bargaining and negotiation within the framework of the bureaucracy or the executive.

Concentrating the political process among the myriad agencies of the administration, stimulated by the linkage pattern and conforming to the traditional personalistic and paternalistic elements of Latin American political culture, unquestionably opens the way for elite manipulation and nondemocratic practices. But despite the conventional opinion which associates bureaucracies with nondemocratic and manipulative behavior, such is not necessarily the case. It may well be that in Latin America, as in Europe and the United States, the process most crucial to democratic values is the so far largely unobserved interactions that are going on behind the large solid doors of the ministries, autonomous agencies, and mixed enterprises of Latin American governments. The analysis of linkage patterns, in any case, appears to provide an explanation for the importance of these sorts of processes, and ought to stimulate political scientists to consider them as fundamental to the process of political development.

A final conclusion to be drawn relates to the changes in the Latin American linkage patterns. Although some features have remained constant—the basic peripherality, for example—the pattern has changed by virtue of the increasingly interdependent international system, the more competitive and more numerous external linkage groups, and finally, the increasingly integrated polities of Latin America. The sometimes expressed desire of Latin Americans to eliminate the influence of the foreigner seems quixotic in the face of such changes. But the very increase in the complexity of the linkages, coupled with increasing capacity of Latin American bureaucrats and decision makers, makes possible an increasingly rational control of the domestic situation within Latin American nations, in which the internal linkage groups are more systematically dealt with and their demands related to national objectives. The modern paradox of an increasingly interdependent world with increasingly "nationalist" assertion in such areas as Latin America is, perhaps, not a paradox at all, but rather a logical outcome of the particular ways in which polities are linked to international systems.

Whatever the validity of these analyses or projections, it is clear that techniques will have to be devised to systematically explore patterns of national-international linkages in order to obtain a satisfactory understanding of the factors involved in development. This essay has taken a small step in that direction.

2

Brazil's Experiment
with an
Independent Foreign Policy

Victor Wallis

From Victor Wallis, "La experiencia de Brazil con una política exterior inde-pendiente," *Estudios Internacionales* (Institute of International Studies, University of Chile, Santiago, Chile), I, No. 2 (July 1967), pp. 189–211. Reprinted by permission of the author and the publisher. The author has prepared the English translation and revised his article for this collection. (Footnotes in the original version have been omitted.)

Victor Wallis is an Assistant Professor of Political Science at Indiana University-Purdue University at Indianapolis.

This selection by Professor Wallis and the one by Richard L. Maullin that follows serve several purposes. Although neither is explicitly cast in a theoretical framework, both in fact offer case studies of linkages. Both also shed considerable light on domestic politics and the phenomenon of nationalism in Latin America.

One manifestation of Latin American nationalism has been the strategy of numerous governments in the area partially to counterbalance the overwhelming political, economic, and cultural influence of the United States through the maintenance or establishment of a broader pattern of international relations—without, at the same time, going as far as Arbenz's Guatemala or Castro's Cuba toward dependence on an international rival of the United States. Freedom from U.S. domination is, of course, a relative matter; and certainly the foreign policy of no Latin American state has consistently been just a mirror image of Washington's desires. However, examples of what might be termed militantly independent foreign policies have been rare: Argentina long remained aloof from the inter-American system, sheltered Axis operations in the Western Hemisphere during the Second World War, and under Perón claimed to represent a "Third Posi-

tion" in world affairs.[1] *Since the Revolution, Mexico has built something of an independent stance around the principles of nonintervention and self-determination, in the postwar era particularly evident in its skepticism about the viability of the OAS and tenacious opposition to anti-Communist measures directed against Guatemala and Cuba. Yet, in most other respects, Mexico's relations with its northern neighbor have been close and cordial.*[2]

The independent foreign policy pursued by Brazilian Presidents Jânio Quadros and João Goulart in the early 1960's stirred considerable interest not only because it came at a crucial time in the evolution of the Cuban question but also because Brazil was a major Latin American country with an almost unbroken tradition of strong support for the United States. Wallis discusses the nature and modest accomplishments of the Quadros-Goulart policy and analyzes its relationship both to major shifts in international politics and to changes in the Brazilian domestic environment.[3]

In Wallis's view, powerful currents of Brazilian economic nationalism provided much of the basis for the independent line and also indirectly contributed to its defeat. The trend toward independence really began under Kubitschek as a cautious response to opportunities presented by a gradual thaw in U.S.-U.S.S.R. relations and the emergence of the new African states. At this stage, the trend had widespread support from virtually all sectors of society in Brazil. In contrast, the later Quadros-Goulart posture towards Cuba represented a concession to reformist nationalists by governments that either would not or could not accede to demands to attack pro-U.S. economic elites on the domestic front. As polarization increased between the two groups, Goulart finally found himself in a position of being able to satisfy neither—undoubtedly part of the explanation for the lack of popular resistance when he fell. Wallis concludes that any future independent foreign policy in Brazil "will require far deeper structural changes."

I

As the language of the O.A.S. charter suggests, it is customary for Latin American countries to describe their foreign policies in terms of non-intervention and self-determination. These concepts, however, are subject to dras-

---

1 See esp. Thomas F. McGann, *Argentina, the United States, and the Inter-American System, 1880–1914* (Cambridge: Harvard University Press, 1957); Harold F. Peterson, *Argentina and the United States, 1810–1960* (New York: State University of New York, 1964), chaps. 18–20, 22–25; and Alberto A. Conil Paz and Gustavo E. Ferrari, *Argentina's Foreign Policy, 1930–1962,* trans. by Joseph J. Kennedy (Notre Dame: University of Notre Dame Press, 1966), chap. 6.
2 See esp. Carlos A. Astiz, ed., *Latin American International Politics* (Notre Dame: University of Notre Dame Press, 1969), section 2.
3 See also: Thomas E. Skidmore, *Politics in Brazil, 1930–1964* (New York: Oxford University Press, 1967), pp. 163–330; E. Bradford Burns, *Nationalism in Brazil: A Historical Survey* (New York: Frederick A. Praeger, 1968), chap. 6; and H. Jon Rosenbaum, "Brazil's Foreign Policy and Cuba," *Inter-American Economic Affairs,* XXIII, No. 3 (Winter 1969), pp. 25–45.

tic changes in their meaning depending on who uses them, and it is therefore hardly surprising that they should be invoked with equal passion by both the upholders and the challengers of traditional alignments. The same is true of the term "independence" as applied to the recent foreign policy of Brazil; for while it is undeniable that the real emphasis on independence was a product of the Quadros and Goulart administrations, the slogan itself proved to be too strong for outright repudiation, even in the context of so unqualified a pro-U.S. stance as that of the Castello Branco regime. Castello's spokesmen would take refuge in the concept of "interdependence"; but at the same time they would try to suggest that the innovations of the 1961–64 period constituted not an assertion of Brazil's identity, but rather the gradual subjection of Brazil to alien influences.

We may grant at the outset that the idea of independence is necessarily a relative one for an underdeveloped country: until the country succeeds in mobilizing its own resources, under its own initiative, whatever independence it has will lie simply in its ability to maneuver between alternative external influences. In the case of Brazil under Quadros and Goulart, what cannot be disputed is the fact that there was a major shift away from the deference which had previously been paid to the United States. Quadros gave a foretaste of this shift when he rejected an invitation to visit Washington during his travels as President-elect in the fall of 1960. The new style was repeatedly reaffirmed over the three following years in ways which we shall consider in some detail. What stamps the shift, however, as being essentially in the direction of independence, is the fact that from beginning to end of the

period in question, the United States never ceased to be the one foreign power which could exert real leverage on the Brazilian economy. This was due not only to its role as the biggest market for Brazilian exports but also to the magnitude of U.S. private investment and government loans which Brazil had obtained during the postwar period. Brazil was naturally driven into the position of contracting more and greater obligations; but at the same time the very weight of this relationship encouraged in some quarters a search for alternative courses of development.

Brazil's effort to pursue an independent foreign policy, vis-á-vis the United States, was not unprecedented among Latin American countries. Even apart from the recent Cuban example, there were the cases of Argentina, which declared itself neutral during World War II, and of Mexico, which remained aloof from the postwar military alliances. But prewar Argentina had experienced only limited U.S. influence, while Mexico, like Cuba, had gone through a social revolution. What was unique about the Brazilian thrust, then, was that it should have arisen as suddenly as it did, yet without the revolutionary impetus. In accounting for this peculiarity—which in turn explains the limitations in the degree of independence actually attained—it will be necessary to consider not only the nature of Brazil's economic development and its relations to the United States, but also the major changes which took place elsewhere in the world during the late 1950's and their particular significance to Brazil. Although the independent foreign policy derived its name with reference to a framework of U.S. domination, it was far from being grounded exclusively on anti-U.S. sentiment. This is shown most clearly in retrospect, by the fact that of the three main foreign-policy steps initiated by Quadros and Goulart—namely, (1) diplomatic relations with Soviet-bloc countries, (2) expanded contacts with underdeveloped countries outside the Western Hemisphere, and (3) resistance to U.S. pressure for sanctions against Cuba—only the step regarding Cuba was unequivocally repudiated by Castello Branco.

II

Two of the most important conditions favoring the independent foreign policy established themselves outside Brazil in the years immediately preceding Quadros's election. One of these was the partial relaxation of tensions between the United States and the Soviet Union; and the other was the emergence from colonialism of the new African nations, of which twenty-one came into existence between 1956 and 1960. Although each of these developments presented its own opportunities and problems, whether in the economic or the political sphere, they were alike in offering Brazil's leaders a more readily acceptable basis than had previously existed for departures from a strict Hemisphere-bloc orientation to world affairs. While they do not account for all aspects of the independent line, they at least set much of the framework in which it was debated.

The U.S.-Soviet détente, embodied in the Eisenhower–Khrushchev talks of August 1959, was significant to the Brazilian leadership as the climax to a long series of direct Soviet overtures to Brazil for closer ties. The Kubitschek administration had previously rejected such overtures and had made public reference to Soviet aid-offers primarily with the object of securing better finan-

cial arrangements with the United States. Whether Kubitschek would have gone further than this in the absence of the détente is of course an open question; and the importance of the U.S. example should not be allowed to obscure the pressure of strictly economic considerations, in particular, the severe drop in receipts from Brazil's coffee exports and the insufficient supply of Brazilian oil. Nevertheless, it was not until December 1959 that a major Soviet-Brazilian trade agreement was signed. Kubitschek himself continued to reject the possibility of diplomatic relations; but the desire for expanded commercial relations was becoming so widespread in political circles already before 1959 that the argument for a full diplomatic exchange began to gain influence, if only as a means of putting the trade benefits on a more stable basis.

As for the political implications of such a step, Professor Hélio Jaguaribe had indicated in 1958 the direct significance to Brazil of precisely those changes in the Communist world which were making the U.S.-Soviet détente possible. Pointing to the "break-up of the Communist monolith," the failure of the West European Communist parties, and the absence of Communist party influence in the African independence movements, he saw a general triumph of nationalism over communism as an ideology and considered it inconceivable that the Soviet Union would initiate a world war. His conclusion, under the circumstances, was that the prevailing concept of "national security" had become transformed into "a mechanism of the subordination of Brazilian national power to the strategic interests of the United States." Considering also the colonial aspects of Brazil's economy, he argued in general that "the most immediate threats to our capacity for self-determination come much more from the side of the United States than from that of the Soviet Union." Perhaps the most influential support for Soviet-Brazilian diplomatic relations, however, was that of Oswaldo Aranha, long-time political associate of Vargas and Foreign Minister under him during World War II. Aranha's arguments were based on (1) Brazil's claim to be one of the world's ten great powers, (2) the irrelevance of ideology to diplomatic recognition, (3) existing relations with Poland and Czechoslovakia, (4) commercial advantage, (5) the example of the United States, and (6) Brazil's need to participate in world decisions. Whatever the relative importance of these various points, it is notable that all of them except the argument from U.S. example and some aspects of the commercial argument could just as well have been used—by others as well as Aranha—to support recognition of the People's Republic of China. Jaguaribe indeed advocated the latter step, but the fact that it was less widely discussed in political circles suggests that whatever implications of the Soviet-Brazilian rapprochement the United States might find disturbing, it was still the U.S.-Soviet détente which at this stage made it possible.

The emergence of the African nations carried a potential threat to Brazil—as also to certain other Latin American countries—from a short-run economic point of view. This threat lay in the increasing competition which would face Latin American primary products on the world market. For Brazil, whose foreign exchange earnings in 1960 were still 56% dependent on coffee, it could hardly be comforting to note that while annual worldwide production of coffee had risen 90%

since the 1950–55 period, that of the African continent had risen 105%. This situation could only accelerate Brazil's already large loss of income, though the equally harmful effects it would have on African coffee producers in the long run might provide a good starting point for negotiations.

On the other hand, however, from the longer-term standpoint of working toward decreased reliance on coffee, full African independence could be beneficial to Brazil in the sense of (1) making possible for the first time a break in the extra low raw-material-costs enjoyed by the industries of the colonizing powers, thus removing at least one obstacle to the competitiveness of Brazilian manufactured goods on the world market, and (2) opening the African market itself to Brazilian manufactures. But discussion of these possibilities remained permeated with a note of skepticism; on the one hand, no doubt, because of the low purchasing power of the African population, and on the other, because of the evident success of the European Common Market countries in establishing special relationships in Africa. Both these conditions, of course, would have to be overcome eventually, but the process would at best be a slow one.

The immediate importance of African independence to Brazil lay not so much in any specific projects it opened up, as in the opportunity it gave for the formation of a positive national ideology. Up to this time, Brazil had failed to distinguish her international position from that of the Western Hemisphere, which meant in effect that of the United States. In arguing for relations with the Soviet Union, Brazilian leaders explicitly discounted all ideological considerations except an abstract desire for great-power status and perhaps a vague commitment to peace through understanding. With the emergence of Africa, however, Brazil could add to her international projection a general emphasis on her developmental interests, combined with specific reference to national characteristics of her own.

In the realm of geo-politics, Brazil could consider supplementing existing entities such as the "North Atlantic" or the "Western Hemisphere" with a new "South Atlantic" formation, which would include at least the East-coast nations of South America as well as West Africa. Behind this idea, as elaborated by Jaguaribe, was the experience of U.S. military bases in Brazil during World War II. In any future East-West conflict, such bases, far from contributing to Brazil's security, would lay Brazil open to attack: a prospect which technological advances had made much more immediate than before. With a separate South Atlantic alliance, no such imposition would have to be accepted, and Brazil would be able to work out any defense policy independently of the major conflicting powers.

While this idea was far-fetched, insofar as it was grounded on Brazilian-Argentinian military capabilities, the independence which it aimed at could be furthered in a general way (more economic and ideological than military) by some form of accommodation to existing ideologies of non-alignment or neutralism. The precise form which this accommodation would take remained a matter for debate, although the most widespread tendency in Brazil was to minimize as much as possible any break with the traditional ideology of the West. Insofar as new points of emphasis were suggested, the most popular seem to have been Brazil's ethnic bond with Africa, the relatively full integration of the African element into Brazil's national culture, and finally the possibility that with its size, population, and experience, Brazil would be able to provide some form of leadership for Africa—including the less expensive forms of aid, such as university training—that would not be tainted with imperialism, white supremacy, or Cold War considerations. All these points of emphasis, while compatible with even a radically changed pattern in Brazil's internal development, did not presuppose anything of the sort, and could in fact easily be used for propaganda purposes without any internal changes at all.

But if the existence of the new African states, along with the U.S.-Soviet détente, could encourage even a conservative-based government to reorient its foreign policy, other changes, more portentous in the long run, determined the specific problems which such a reorientation would have to confront. The opening in Africa was jeopardized from the outset by the role of Portugal, which held three of the territories still under colonial rule, maintained an intransigent position on the issue of their independence, and exercised a continuing pressure on Brazil through powerful commercial groups in Rio de Janeiro and São Paulo. Movements which the Brazilian government could welcome when they occurred in the rest of Africa, it had to greet with mixed feelings when they arose in the Portuguese colonies. The dilemma was squarely posed by the rise of the Angolan independence movement in the late 1950's; but Brazil's United Nations vote remained invariably aligned with that of the colonial powers, even on purely verbal resolutions regarding Africa, until late in 1960.

The most critical dilemma of all,

however, was that presented by the Cuban Revolution. Triumphing as it did two years before the inauguration of Quadros, it assured that there would be no premature flowering of visions founded exclusively on the U.S.-Soviet rapprochement or on ambiguously solicited African support. The urgent challenge which it embodied for the United States, together with its great psychological proximity to Brazil, as compared with any of the African developments, made a clear stand by the Brazilian government unavoidable. But at the same time, the Cuban problem meant that if an independent foreign policy were to exist at all, its sustained defense would be conditional not only on a possibly felicitous juridical formula, but also on developments over which the Brazilian government could have no control at all, namely, the course of U.S.-Cuban relations and the hardening of the U.S.-influenced conservative opposition in Brazil.

III

The problem in accounting for the full scope of the independent foreign policy is that it went beyond a mere response to the opportunities and challenges presented by the Soviet Union and Africa. By its very nature, the independent line pointed toward a change of direction domestically as well as an expansion of international horizons.

To understand this more fundamental aspect, we must begin by considering the problems of Brazilian economic development. We have already noted the phenomenon of declining terms of trade, which from around 1955 onward affected almost all exports of primary products. As an immediate response, this naturally sug-

gested a search for alternative markets offering better terms, which in turn pointed toward diplomatic relations with prospective buyers as well as closer understandings with possible rivals. But from a longer-run point of view, what was also needed was a change in the composition of the exports, away from primary products and toward manufactured goods. Brazil's interest in this latter course was clearly recognized in the deliberations on Africa; but in its actual ability to carry out such a program, the Brazilian economy was a victim, to some extent, of its previous development. By necessity during the depression years of the 1930's, but largely by choice during the 1950's, the industry which Brazil had built up was geared almost exclusively to the immediately felt demand of the domestic market. Apart from the restricted character of the market itself, this focus had at least two implications. (1) By giving more attention to effective demand than to Brazil's existing resources, it made possible the setting up of industries which for an indefinite time to come would remain dependent on imports for essential equipment or components. As a result, Brazil would be much less able than previously to resort to import-restriction as a corrective to foreign exchange difficulties. (2) At the same time that the reliance on particular imports was increasing, the declining prices of primary exports would continue to exercise the full weight of their influence over the balance of payments.

The looming crisis implicit in this mode of development underlay all the spectacular production-increases of the Kubitschek period (1956–61). The influx of foreign loans could soothe it in the short run only by aggravating it in the long run. As for foreign direct investment, the Kubitschek years indeed witnessed a reversal of the usual excess of annual profit-remittances over annual influx of new capital, but only at a high cost for the future; for in addition to signaling an eventual increase in remittances abroad, the new foreign investment brought with it a natural tendency to exaggerate even further the already excessive concentration on consumer-goods production for the local market. Despite the harmful effect of both these consequences on the balance of payments, Kubitschek encouraged the process by maintaining the exchange subsidies for foreign investors' imports which had been instituted in 1955. The result was a permanent inflationary tendency, which Kubitschek only exacerbated by his heavy deficit-financing of both productive and unproductive projects.

In response to this situation, there was a widespread rise of nationalist sentiment focusing on the problem of economic development, and advocating specifically a departure from the existing pattern of snow-balling foreign obligations as a necessary condition for Brazil's long-run growth. This nationalist sentiment did not embody a uniform conception of economic alternatives, although it generally favored at the very least a reduction of foreign privileges and foreign decision-making power; but it had an unmistakable implication for the international scene, namely, that Brazil should take orders from nobody and should defend the right of other nations to determine their own courses of development. While this position was just as readily available to nationalists of other countries, the particular force which it gained in Brazil around 1960 owed something to the speed, the sudden increase in foreign investment, and the financial instability which characterized the most recent period of Brazilian economic growth.

But however much such considerations pointed toward an independent foreign policy, they differed from both the Cold War thaw and the problem of Africa in the sense that, far from encouraging a reorientation on the part of conservatives, they implied an attack on the conservative position itself. Where expansion of markets and agreements with competitors could be viewed as supplementary to existing arrangements, the newer nationalist criticisms, with their emphasis on Brazil's export structure and on the related issue of foreign influence, tended to call these arrangements into question. In the sphere of foreign policy, moreover, they implied a clear defense of Cuba's right to plot its own course free of hostile interference: a position which, to say the least, would not be in the direct interest of the Brazilian ruling class.

From the standpoint of Brazil's established political leaders, however, this complex of nationalist criticisms and proposals did not necessarily have to be viewed as an undifferentiated whole. The option of trying to appropriate specific planks while rejecting any possible structural implications was a very real one, and the government in several respects had a well-suited instrument for such a strategy in the Cuban issue. First, by pointing at the Cuban development as a legitimate even if undesirable alternative, the government could pose an effective threat to foreign interests in its campaign for such external palliatives as new investments, increased loans, or delays in amortization. Secondly, by defending Cuba against international sanctions, the government could gain provisional support from some of its nationalist and left-wing critics without satisfying their economic demands, while at the same time—thirdly—adding to the effectiveness of its diplomatic initiatives elsewhere in the world.

It cannot be claimed, of course, that these exhaust the possible reasons for a government's defense of the Cuban Revolution. Nonetheless, the only type of regime for which they would automatically have to be seen as insufficient would be one that had clearly committed itself to a wide–ranging program of expropriation and structural change, i.e., one that was willing to identify itself directly with the Cuban model. In the absence of such a program, there can easily be room for speculation as to how far a government would be willing to carry its nationalism in terms of popular mobilization, with all its attendant risks. While such questions of intent are as unavoidable as they often are unanswerable, we may best focus our attention here upon factors which particular politicians would have to work with regardless of their personal convictions. In this sense, it will be useful to approach the perspective of the Brazilian government during the 1961–64 period by briefly reviewing (a) the tentative steps in an independent-line direction taken even by Kubitschek and (b) the sense in which the political alignments at work in 1960 pointed toward a campaign of the type actually conducted by Quadros.

Kubitschek's main ideological pronouncements in the realm of foreign policy were those connected with the *Operacão Panamericana*, the program for U.S. aid and closer ties which he proposed in the wake of the angry demonstrations that greeted Vice-President Nixon during his South American tour of 1958. In setting forth the OPA platform, Kubitschek paid full tribute both to the Monroe Doctrine and to anti-Communism. Nevertheless, he affirmed the authenticity of popular grievances in Latin America, and at the same time took explicit cognizance of the recent foreign aid initiatives of the Soviet Union. While not himself proposing any diminution of U.S. influence in Latin America, Kubitschek thus at least confronted the United States with an open, quasi-official threat that such a process might occur under other auspices in the foreseeable future. In the realm of economic policy, correspondingly, while Kubitschek encouraged an ever-increasing participation of foreign capital in Brazilian industry, he at the same time managed to do without the services of the International Monetary Fund when the fiscal demands it made were in conflict with his own plans. In other areas, his policies at one time or another included (1) adherence to the position of Marshall Lott and of those PSD elements which, along with the PTB, opposed foreign participation in petroleum production, (2) temporary resistance to U.S. demands for rights to radioactive minerals, (3) the sale of sugar to China, (4) a proposal to mediate the U.S.-Cuban dispute in 1960, and (5) quashing an attempt within the Foreign Ministry, also in 1960, to deny visas to visitors from Cuba.

These steps might seem limited in retrospect, but they were not without significance at the time. The mere fact that in his requests for U.S. aid Kubitschek resisted demands for financial orthodoxy when they did not suit him, would have made it difficult for anyone to oppose him primarily in the name of orthodoxy and debt-repayment without appearing totally subservient to U.S. interests. This, however, was precisely the position occupied by Quadros, as candidate of the conservative UDN, in the 1960 presidential campaign. Since Kubitschek's PSD, with Lott as its candidate, maintained its coalition with the officially nationalist PTB led by Vice-President Goulart (who was running for re-election), the logical way for Quadros to extend his area of support beyond those who backed his economic program and his attacks on corruption was by taking over the nationalist claims of his opponents. Quadros's campaign-image of personal integrity fit in perfectly with this logic, for there could be no better expression of such an image than the most complete disdain for established practices. In carrying over such disdain into the sphere of foreign policy, Quadros was undoubtedly helped by the fact that the Communist Party maintained its habitual support for the PTB and therefore also for Lott, and that Lott, wanting to disown this support, was driven to water down his nationalism by, for example, taking an unequivocal stand against diplomatic relations with the Soviet Union. Quadros, on the other hand, went beyond the minimal nationalist position of the government. He not only reversed an earlier stand in order to support government ownership of the oil industry; he also supported Soviet diplomatic ties, visited Cuba during his campaign (March, 1960), and spoke in favor of the Cuban agrarian reform.

The behavior of the two leading candidates in the 1960 election thus points toward a general practice of identifying oneself with the policy opposed to that of one's most conspicuous organized support. As for the alignment of forces leading up to the election, it suggests that a dual tendency to (a) look outside the Western Hemisphere for economic reasons and (b) make anti-U.S. statements for political reasons was proving increasingly useful even to groups which were largely identified with the growth of U.S. economic power in Brazil.

IV

The independent foreign policy extended with little change in its essential formulation over the seven months of Quadros's presidency and the two-and-a-half years of Goulart's. Quadros during his short tenure completed the difficult task of initiation, setting the main ideological lines for the entire period and carrying out all the decisive diplomatic steps except the actual exchange of ambassadors with the Soviet Union. Even with regard to Cuba, his consistent stand against U.S. intervention was certainly as strong as any proclamation of the Goulart period; and the final flourish with which he awarded the Cruzeiro do Sul decoration to Che Guevara just a week before resigning was perhaps even stronger, though its precise significance is still not altogether clear. Goulart's foreign policy was thus on the whole no more than a continuation of that of Quadros; but beyond this it should be noted that if the 1960 election campaign was at all indicative, Goulart would not have gone nearly so far as Quadros if he had been the one to set the initial pattern. Neither Quadros nor Goulart came to power with an immediate program of radical reform and neither was free to act politically without keeping in mind the possibility of forcible resistance from the right. For each of them, therefore, the independent line in foreign policy was simply one political option out of several. What the 1960 campaign showed was that, precisely because of the rightist threat, the option was most fully available to those who, like Quadros, remained unfettered by any programmatically nationalist organization.

The political merits of the independent line, from Quadros's stand-point, are suggested in part by the situation which confronted him in Congress on his taking office. He had just defeated the candidate of a coalition which, despite possible differences among its individual members, was on the whole committed to the pattern of inflationary "developmentalism" that prevailed during the Kubitschek years. However, Congressional elections did not coincide with the presidential election, and the Congress which Quadros would have to work with—elected in 1958 and not to be challenged until October 1962—was dominated by the very opposition which he had overcome in his campaign. Committed to an anti-inflationary program involving a reduction in government spending, Quadros faced a PSD-PTB coalition of generally opposed commitments which could outvote the UDN (most of whose members backed him in this respect) by as much as 182 (116 PSD + 66 PTB) to 66. Although the neatness of these figures overstates the actual degree of party discipline, it was clear that Quadros would have to effect some kind of reorientation if he was to have any hope of support for his program as a whole.

The area of foreign policy seemed to provide a unique opportunity in this respect. Background conditions, as we have seen, were such that much of what appeared necessary even to conservative interests, as a way out of the immediate dilemmas of international trade, was also desirable to the left, as a step toward restructuring the economy. With a special concession to the left on the issue of Cuba, which in any case would add to Brazil's stature in other parts of the world, Quadros might hope for a new coalition that would be united, if not in regard to every paticular question, at least in the sense of overall confidence in his leadership. To this end, Quadros worked in regular consultation with representatives of most of the major blocs in Congress, from the UDN's vice-president, Seixas Doria, to the leader of the PTB's left-wing "Grupo Compacto," Sergio Magalhães, both of whom supported his foreign policy. He also negotiated with PSD leaders, but his success in winning PTB support led PSD President Ernani do Amaral Peixoto to repudiate formally the PSD-PTB parliamentary accord, precisely on the grounds of foreign policy, just a day after Quadros's March 15 presentation of his independent line to Congress.

Already at this time, however, elements of the PTB including the party's secretary-general, Deputy Doutel de Andrade, were objecting to Quadros's position from the standpoint of its effects on their own organization. Doutel de Andrade charged that the independent foreign policy was a mere cover-up for Quadros's conservative domestic policy and that it was specifically devised to "neutralize" the organizing efforts of nationalist groups. This charge was given some confirmation a month later when the *Estado de São Paulo* reported open references on the part of "Janistas" to the desirability of co-opting potential PTB support in preparation for the 1962 elections.

But even if such charges and references give an accurate picture of Quadros's intent, it remains true that his tactic had a political logic of its own, which, regardless of prior calculations, tended to place him in a more extreme position than his original supporters could tolerate. Assuming that Quadros was indeed trying to undermine the PTB in the interest of a conservative economic policy, it nevertheless follows that if he was to capture the nationalists' thunder in the eyes of the electorate, his defense of Cuba against collective sanctions would have to involve more than behind-the-scenes clarifications to the United States. As time went on and his position became more and more clearly established, it might have occurred to Quadros's conservative supporters—or even to Quadros himself—that however little a foreign-policy stand might impinge on the immediate well–being of economically privileged groups, it could nonetheless have an educative or suggestive effect upon hitherto isolated sections of the population, particularly if it was being used as a substitute for attention to their material needs. It is most likely that Quadros's resignation reflected an awareness of this possibility, whether on his own part, on that of the right, or both.

In any case, the rapid sequence of the award to Guevara (August 19), the denunciation by Quadros's former ally Carlos Lacerda (on nationwide television, August 24), and the resignation itself (August 25) suggests something of the depth which the division over foreign policy was beginning to take on in Brazilian politics. The shift of the right away from Quadros seems to have come very suddenly, however. In April, for example, Lacerda, even while expressing solidarity with the Bay of Pigs invaders, still affirmed his support for Quadros, despite the latter's earlier rejection of U.S. demands that Brazil support collective sanctions against Cuba. And even as late as August 17,

the *Estado de São Paulo,* recording the appointment of PTB Deputy San Tiago Dantas as head of Brazil's U.N. delegation and noting the general disappointment with Quadros on the part of the UDN, nonetheless recommended editorially that the UDN continue to follow the president's policy without public criticism, so as not to let other parties usurp its "rightful" position.

With the decoration of Guevara, though, the battle lines were drawn. One can only wonder whether Quadros in fact considered the act—as his defenders in Congress claimed—a mere matter of protocol. But whatever his motives—and they remain as much in doubt as those of the resignation itself —it is highly probable that, even if he had remained in office, he would have lost any hope for the left-right coalition which had seemed possible at the outset. In this sense, the very act which set the stage for Quadros's resignation would most likely have placed him, had he not resigned, under political disabilities regarding foreign policy similar to those which his coalition opponents of 1960 had had to work with during the campaign. Where the latter had had to make apologies to the right for the support given them by the Communist Party, Quadros would have been increasingly pressed into making comparable apologies for his presumed sympathy with the Cuban Revolution.

Goulart likewise worked under the shadow of a constant rightist threat, though his position was strengthened at first by the success of armed resistance against the attempts of conservative military officers to prevent him from taking office. On the other hand, unlike Quadros, he was prevented by his reliance on organized labor from attempting any of the orthodox anti-inflationary steps advocated by the

UDN. Lacking from the outset any steady conservative support and unable to look to a strong left, he was driven to an inflationary immobilism based on concessions to all sides. He was further weakened until January 1963 by the parliamentary system which had been imposed on him; and by the time he recovered full presidential powers, the economic situation was so serious that his only immediate hope was for a new dose of loans from the United States. As a result of all these factors, not to mention whatever moderating personal predilections Goulart may have had, the only measure which linked his foreign policy in any direct way with one of economic nationalism was a law limiting the profit-remittances of foreign firms. The law does not seem to have been enforced, however; and even if it had been, it contained no provisions to require constructive allocation of the extra profits that would remain in Brazil. On the whole, then, although Goulart was in a better position to maintain an independent line than he would have been without Quadros's precedent, he was as powerless as Quadros to carry out those domestic changes which alone could have created a national consensus behind him.

V

Brazil's domestic conflicts were reflected not only in the support and the opposition which the independent policy aroused, but also in the content of the policy itself. If nationalist influence was strong enough to make Brazil criticize the United States, conservative influence remained strong enough throughout to assure that the criticism would be that of a "loyal opposition." This applied not only in relation to Cuba—where the Guevara decoration was in a sense the exception that proves the rule—but also, partly because of Portuguese influence, in relation to Africa and to the general question of non-alignment.

A few of the less controversial bi-products of the independent period can be briefly listed. Trade with the Soviet bloc rose slightly from less than 4% to roughly 6% of the total; but it remained "marginal and episodic" in the sense that little effort was made to work out complementarities different from those of Brazil's existing trade with the industrialized countries. Brazil established diplomatic relations with three of the new African states (Ghana, Nigeria, and Senegal), and also arranged to provide each of them with an annual number of university scholarships. In addition, Brazil signed an agreement in July 1961 with the Inter-African Coffee Organization, providing for mutual consultation with regard to production and prices. And as a further gesture toward Africa, Brazil in August 1963 pledged a contribution of US$20 million to the establishment of the African Development Bank. At a wider level, Brazil participated (along with Bolivia, Cuba, and Mexico) in the July 1962 Cairo Conference on economic development and subsequently issued a general critique of existing international trade organizations from the standpoint of the under-developed world: a position which it was to reiterate at the November 1963 conference of O.A.S. Ministers of Economy in São Paulo and again at the February 1964 preparatory meeting for the Geneva Trade Conference in Alta Gracia, Argentina. Finally, Brazil participated as one of the eight "non-aligned" states in the March 1962 Geneva Disarmament Conference, stressing among other things the desirability of establishing denuclearized zones in underdeveloped areas and of planning not only for disarmament and inspection, but also for economic reconversion.

The bedrock of the independent foreign policy, however, was the stand taken with regard to Cuba. The first major challenge which Goulart faced on this issue was at the Punta del Este meeting of O.A.S. Foreign Ministers in January 1962, called specifically to consider collective sanctions. It is worth noting that in the actual vote on whether or not to hold the conference, Brazil, along with four other countries, was content to abstain, leaving Mexico as the only country besides Cuba to vote No. At the conference itself, Brazil, represented by Goulart's Foreign Minister San Tiago Dantas, joined with Mexico, Argentina, Bolivia, Chile, and Ecuador in (a) voting in favor of the clauses condemning Marxism-Leninism and the current Cuban regime as being incompatible with the Inter-American system, but (b) abstaining on juridical grounds over the clauses expelling revolutionary Cuba from the O.A.S. In addition, along with three countries, Brazil abstained from voting economic sanctions. San Tiago Dantas's main speech was in part a plea for moderation based on the conviction that democracy could triumph over communism under peaceful conditions; but at the same time it included a restatement of the view that the democratic concept was not fundamentally violated by traditionalist social structures, in which, as he put it, democracy suffered only a "momentary loss". Brazil did not alter this official position on subsequent occasions. The other major challenge regarding Cuba was that posed by the October 1962 missile crisis. In this case, Brazil supported the U.S. arms blockade, but abstained from

a motion to permit forceful measures in connection with Cuba's existing stock of arms. It is clear, then, that Brazil's independent line remained very moderate even at its sorest point. Whatever Goulart's ultimate plans might have been, the most he could tell the United States was, as San Tiago Dantas had put it at Punta del Este, that "we differ not over ends but over means."

The hesitancy associated with the dilemma over Cuba was also apparent in Brazil's dealings with the non-aligned countries. In regard to Africa, Quadros largely compromised his initiatives in the new states by pressing for expanded trade with the Republic of South Africa and by avoiding any major statements on the Angolan question. The strongest position taken was that of the San Tiago Dantas Ministry in January 1962, when Brazil voted in favor of a U.N. study of the Portuguese territories. But even then, Brazil's U.N. representative, Afonso Arinos de Mello Franco, excluded any possible support for sanctions against Portuguese rule by exhorting Portugal herself "to assume direction of the movement for the liberty of Angola." In December 1963, Brazil took a step back toward her practices of the 1950's when she abstained—along with the United States, Great Britain and France, and in contrast to Venezuela—from a Security Council vote in favor of a clause deploring Portuguese non-compliance with earlier U.N. Resolutions. Far from acting as Latin America's leading anti-colonial power, Brazil frequently lagged behind other countries, a further example being Argentina on the issue of Algeria.

In relation to the non-aligned countries as a group, Brazil repeatedly emphasized the distinction between her

3

The Colombia-IMF Disagreement
of November-December 1966:
An Interpretation of its Place
in Colombian Politics

Richard L. Maullin

From Richard L. Maullin, *The Colombia-IMF Disagreement of November-December 1966: An Interpretation of Its Place in Colombian Politics*, Rand Memorandum RM-5314-RC (June 1967). Reprinted by permission of the author and The Rand Corporation. The author has revised his essay for this collection.

Richard L. Maullin is on the staff of The Rand Corporation.

Among the conclusions to be drawn from the preceding selection is that nationalistic policies may well prove insufficient to bind a deeply divided nation and may even divide it further when polarizing issues like Cuba are involved. On the other hand, Maullin's study of a 1966 dispute between Colombia and the International Monetary Fund illustrates that a skillful president may seize upon the right issue and trigger nationalist sentiments to his short-run political advantage.

From a theoretical standpoint, this study examines a single series of interactions between an international governmental organization and the key decision-maker of a national government, himself constrained by a domestic political system. It also holds relevance for issue-areas considered under headings II-B and II-C. For all its unique features (the National Front included), the Colombian political system resembles others in Latin America in its clash between traditional and modern elements and the centrality of the presidential role. President Lleras's handling of the dispute with the IMF demonstrates that the achievement of reform in such a system has an international as well as a domestic dimension. Finally, the IMF's conduct in the case highlights a familiar Latin American complaint that international development institutions impose orthodox policies ill-suited to the political and economic conditions prevailing in the area. There has been some indication that the IMF has become at least a little more flexible in its policies after its recent experiences in Colombia and elsewhere. To the extent that it has done so, we may suggest that the Fund's international outputs occasioned domestic outputs which, in turn, altered its subsequent behavior.

The Colombian domestic political system sets up a number of constraints on the types of economic development policy Colombian presidents may follow.

This study, focusing on a dispute between the International Monetary Fund and the administration of recent Colombian President Carlos Lleras Restrepo (1966–1970), illustrates some ways in which domestic politics can influence presidential policy options in regard to desired international economic aid. It also discusses presidential use of Colombia's recurrent foreign exchange crises for the enhancement of the president's domestic political positions.

Colombian presidents and would-be presidents have to manage the power that accrues to them as the chief of two different systems of influence and obligation. The style of power in the first system may be called classic or traditional, and its symbolic components are the time-honored rhetoric of Colombia's two massed based traditional political parties, the Liberals and the Conservatives, the hierarchical social prestige attached to family name, occupation, and regional origin, and the premium placed upon formal courtesies and religiosity. The style of power in the second system may be termed pragmatic or industrial, and its symbolic components, while not necessarily excluding traditional elements, reflect efforts to increase productivity in scientifically–based enterprises. The chief executives of Colombia find that the promotion of a transitional or developing economy resolves itself into the difficult political job of providing leadership for two worlds that are often poorly connected and from time to time in direct conflict.

The government which the President administers must contend with the demands placed upon it by political interests representative of both styles. The constraints to which President Carlos Lleras Restrepo found himself subject were imposed in part by Colombia's National front system of government and in part by the nature of the election which placed him in the Presidency.

As embodied in the Colombian Constitution, the National Front system provides for alternation in the Presidency between candidates of the Liberal and Conservative Parties exclusively through 1974, and for equal representation in The National Congress at least until 1972. Since its inception (1957) serious divisions within both parties have produced permanent factions. At the time of Colombia's dispute with the IMF—December 1966—there were five factions operating in three groupings. The first grouping was composed of traditional party factions opposing the National Front system. The second was composed of the followers of a former President, General Gustavo Rojas Pinilla, who are for the most part urban lower-middle and working class voters at the base, and conservative, neo-fascist and populist enthusiasts at the activist level. The third group is made up of the traditional party factions supporting the National Front. All three groupings were strongly oriented to the Congress as a vehicle for political expression; they supported its prerogatives vis-à-vis the Presidency. Initiating his administration in this political climate, President Lleras encountered both overt and covert opposition in the Congress to his economic development and political reform programs.

Initially, Lleras's 1966 election campaign showed a certain aloofness toward the traditional parties. It used mass media and personal tours to project his image and economic development message directly to the voters. His strongest opponent, the Rojas Pinilla electoral movement, the National Popular Alliance (ANAPO), elicited impressive demonstrations of public support by harping on the theme that the National Front had caused public suffering by promoting currency devaluations. Faced with the possibility that Rojas would win a large vote in Congressional elections held six weeks prior to the presidential contest, Lleras switched his tactics and began to rely more heavily on the vote-getting networks of the Liberal Party and its National-Front-supporting Conservative allies. The coalition supporting the National Front won a Congressional majority, thus assuring Lleras of a victory in the subsequent presidential election.

The inescapable conclusion was that Carlos Lleras owed as much to the National Front politicians of classical style as to his own personal election campaign for producing his winning majority. After his inauguration in August 1966, Lleras found himself confronted by a vehement Congressional opposition, a predominantly unsympathetic public, and a lack of cooperation on the part of his own National Front copartisans in the Congress.

Problems with the International Monetary Fund arose just as Lleras was beginning to consolidate his executive position.

In the short period, November 29 through December 10, 1966, President Carlos Lleras Restrepo and his Ministers carried out an extraordinary executive maneuver in response to a breakdown in negotiations between his government and the International Monetary Fund. Lleras's government was negotiating with the IMF for a standby loan of sixty million dollars with which Colombia would be able to meet a good part of the public and private foreign debt about to fall due.

The IMF position was an orthodox call for diversification of Colombia's foreign exchange earning products and for an immediate devaluation of the peso from its officially pegged rate of 13.50 to 16 to 20 per U.S. dollar.[1] The intent of this devaluation was to lower domestic demand for imported products to a level Colombia's foreign exchange earning capability indicated it could more realistically support. The IMF also hoped to stimulate exports by the resultant lower prices for Colombian goods. Implicit in the IMF's orthodox position was a skeptical attitude toward the various exchange rate schemes advocated by the Lleras administration.

Lleras and his government planners had been pressing upon the IMF a program for lifting Colombia out of her continuing balance of payments and foreign exchange problems by improving a "disequilibrium" foreign exchange

[1] *El Espectador*, November 30, 1966, pp. 1-A and 10-A. Lleras outlined the situation in his lengthy national TV-radio speech on November 29. He implied he was surprised that Colombia-IMF differences over the standby loan were also affecting Colombia's negotiations with AID over its Program Loan to Colombia.

system. Lleras's program rested upon rationalized governmental direction of economic development plans and effective import controls rather than faith in the automatic market mechanisms favored by the IMF.

The balance-of-payments problem, it should be noted, had been aggravated in the months prior to the impasse with the IMF by generally adverse international market conditions for Colombia's largest export products. Coffee, which earns over two-thirds of Colombia's foreign exchange, and on which all Colombian governments since the late forties have relied to create an industrial sector, was earning six to eight cents a pound less in late 1966 than it had been earning earlier in that year. Even at the previous price of roughly fifty cents a pound, coffee earnings were incapable of supplying the capital necessary to spur large-scale industrial expansion and just barely able to supply foreign exchange requirements for existing domestic industries. World prices for cotton, another large export, were also depressed, and sugar was adversely affected by a weak world market and a modest U.S. market quota. While these export market conditions prevailed, the Lleras government continued an import policy initiated by the previous regime's Finance Minister that allowed much uncontrolled importation using foreign exchange obtained on the legal free dollar market.[2] To illustrate Colombia's serious financial straits, Lleras revealed that at the

time when the IMF negotiations turned sour, the *Banco de la República,* Colombia's central bank, owed 126 million dollars in debts for which it had no funds. This deficit did not include the foreign debt of governmental and semi-governmental entities or private persons.

Lleras held, as he had for several years, that the solution to the long-term crisis of Colombia as an agrarian coffee-producing but nascent industrial economy lay in what he termed an "economy of abundance." This view, an ideology of economic growth, favors government controls for limiting price instability and handling foreign exchange crises. It encourages increases in domestic production, while paradoxically permitting increased consumption, both domestic and foreign, of that production. Thus, as he stated publicly in innumerable election campaign speeches and presidential addresses, Lleras was in principle not inclined to restrict demand, except when necessary to meet special crises and to regulate development.

In Lleras's view, a vital element of his approach was the continued sympathetic assistance of public international lending and credit institutions such as the IMF. In reference to the broad outline of his policies, he said, "We thought we might work in perfect harmony with the IMF. Our program contemplated a constant search for equilibrium in the balance of payments with the understanding that we could count on a certain amount of foreign financing."[3]

Prior to the breakdown of conversations with the IMF Lleras said very little in public about the foreign ex-

---

[2] Employing a policy favored by AID, Colombia allowed many imports to pass to the uncontrolled list, but it never completely removed controls on imports. Controlled imports enjoyed a dollar exchange rate of 13.50 pesos; uncontrolled imports were valued at the free market price of the peso.

[3] El Espectador, *op. cit.*

change problem, especially in its more acute short-run manifestations, other than to state quite clearly that he expected creditors and credit institutions to carry him until he could work some changes for the better in the exports' and coffee markets' picture. From the Colombian Government's point of view the IMF, and by implication, AID, countered Lleras's optimistic evaluation of his own crisis management skills with a stock-in-trade set of loan conditions that strongly implied little confidence in Colombia's future without devaluation. Indeed, one could sense in the IMF response a certain amount of weariness with rhetorical dynamism and less-than-spectacular economic management on the part of the Colombian Government. At the time, this weariness seemed curiously similar to the notable distrust or perhaps lack of confidence in government, politicians, and their promises found in many Colombians. Such attitudes were reflected by the flight of Colombian domestic capital and in the continuation of downward trends in electoral participation in the 1966 election.

The IMF's firmness did not dim Lleras's drive to manage Colombia out of its balance of payment troubles on his own terms. Faced with the IMF refusal to provide psychological support as well as monetary credit, Lleras attempted both to carry out his general policies and to demonstrate to his foreign creditors and loan sources that the Colombian economy, under his constant leadership, was worthy of their support on the terms he proposed for it.

The IMF's position seems to have piqued the Colombians on more than economic grounds. The program proposed by IMF, assuming as it did the devaluation of the peso, would have put Lleras in an exposed political position at a moment when he was just beginning to build up political strength with the voting public as well as with various politically powerful special-interest communities. While Lleras had been propounding his tightly managed economic expansion approach throughout the protracted presidential campaign, he and his National Front backers were accused of supporting the other devaluations (1962 and 1965) which had caused a great deal of inflation and unemployment distress.[4] His opposition, especially the Rojas Pinilla forces, endlessly accused him of preparing another devaluation. These charges, together with Lleras's less-than-spectacular showing at the polls, seem to have made it an article of political faith for his regime that overt devaluations were to be avoided like the plague. As one Colombian close to Lleras put it: "Politically, devaluation goes hand in hand with extreme unction."

Lleras and a few close friends, veterans of what may be termed a circuitous thirty-year struggle for the presidency and with it the power to direct the national economy, showed open irritation with the IMF's seeming indifference to the delicate political situation and the fragile state of popular support, a support necessary for combating political opponents in the Colombian Congress and departmental administrations on a wide range of issues. Such a direct challenge to Lleras's skills and point of view could

[4] John Sheahan, *Imports, Investment, and Growth: Colombian Experience Since 1950,* Economic Development Series Report No. 38, Center for International Affairs, Harvard University, Cambridge, June 1966, pp. 21–24.

not be tolerated, for political as well as economic reasons. In effect Lleras was forced by the IMF to insist forcefully and publicly that he, not the Fund, really understood the nature of the crisis and the true range of ameliorative measures. Lleras was determined, if he could, not to accept from foreign sources what he called limits on the management of policy.[5]

When negotiations with IMF came to a standstill on November 26, 1966, Lleras and his ministers moved quickly to tighten the already existing partial controls over the movement of foreign exchange and the flow of imports. Lleras's task was aided by the fact that the state of siege declared in May 1965 by his predecessor, Guillermo León Valencia, was still in effect. Drawing upon the authority of Article 121 of the Colombian Constitution, which permits the President to issue decree-laws during states of siege, on November 29 Lleras issued Decree 2867 of 1966. This decree froze all dollar accounts in Colombian banks and in the local branches of foreign banks. It also suspended the sale of dollars on the free market and required all holders of dollars to declare their holdings. Subsequent decrees, it stated, would establish the priorities by which foreign exchange would be allocated to Colombian purchasers, and at what price and under what conditions dollars formerly available on the free market would again be offered for sale.

Bogotá hummed with speculation over the President's move.

Forty-eight hours after the publication of Decree 2867 of 1966, Lleras published the details of his foreign exchange and import control proce-

dures in two somewhat overlapping resolutions of the *Junta Monetaria*,[6] Resolution 48 in the morning, and Resolution 49 in the afternoon of December 1, 1966.[7] Resolution 48 specified the powers and procedures of the *Junta Monetaria* and other government agencies for allocating foreign exchange in general. Resolution 49 detailed the priorities and procedures for determining the use of formerly free dollars. Taken together, these resolutions represented the Lleras administration's solution for the foreign exchange issue: controls on all imports, no official devaluation, and no free dollar market.

The question of the efficacy of these measures for encouraging IMF and AID support seems partially answered by the agreements negotiated at the end of January 1967 for a standby loan from the IMF.[8] At that time Colombia agreed to institute a certificate-auction system for the sale of foreign exchange. Under this arrangement—formalized in Decree-Law 444, March 22, 1967—licenses to import were maintained and the sale of foreign exchange certificates was controlled, thus giving the government a means to regulate the level of imports. Importers,

---

[5] *El Espectador,* November 30, 1966, p. 10-A.

[6] The *Junta Monetaria,* created in late 1963, is a body composed of the Ministers of Development, Treasury, and Agriculture, the Chief of the Administrative Department of Planning and Technical Services, and the Director of the Bank of the Republic. It is given broad powers in the field of monetary policy, credit, and banking. For the laws covering its functions, see *Código Administrativo, 1965,* Oscar Peña Alzate, ed., Editorial Bedout, Bogotá, 1965, pp. 648–651.

[7] *La República,* Bogotá, December 2, 1966, pp. 1, 14–15. Additional resolutions soon amplified Resolutions 48 and 49, but Lleras's policy was indicated clearly enough in the December 1st resolutions.

[8] *El Espectador,* February 1, 1967, p. 1-A.

however, would have to buy foreign exchange certificates on auction with the price determined essentially by demand. This system, in effect through the remainder of Lleras's term, allowed the effective exchange rate to drift upwards gradually so that in fact the peso was devalued to the IMF advocated rate by early 1968, but in a manner that the devaluation-sensitive political system could tolerate.

One interpretation of the Lleras regime's success in resisting the IMF's 1966 devaluation plan is that the Fund, while not approving of controls as a long-term solution for Colombia's foreign exchange problem, found the certificate-control system acceptable as a short-term device. Another interpretation might see this as an indication that the IMF became more attuned to the social and political delicacy of devaluation in Colombia, as Lleras had insisted in his speech of November 29, 1966, that they should be.[9]

These measures of *de facto* devaluation showed an element of consistency and coherence in Colombia's policy for dealing with the long-term exchange crisis. By moving ahead with a program of strict government management, Lleras was able to maintain the policy line he advocated before his immediate problem with the IMF. Given the impasse, he demonstrated an ability to adjust quickly to the new situation and thus minimize the possible loss of IMF support. In addition, he showed his skill in the use of a particular economic crisis to deliver blows on other more political fronts where his authority and influence were being tested.

Troublesome as the November 1966 breakdown in negotiations was for

Colombia, President Lleras was able to use it to make political gains for himself. The impasse with the IMF gave the young administration its first major opportunity to regain for the office of the President some of the public support, prestige, and power lost—in the public view—because of the failure of his National Front predecessors to handle the long-term economic development situation with much success.

The capture of mass public support by any Colombian president seems largely contingent on his ability to create a reputation for himself as an economic savior among the salaried and shabby who predominate in the urban centers.

In his public address announcing the emergency measures taken in the wake of the impasse with the IMF, Lleras expressed himself in explicit nationalistic terms. The crisis of the moment was portrayed as an attempt by the IMF to force Colombia to follow a policy that its President deemed, in essence, contrary to national sovereignty and independence, productive of as much harm as good, and insulting to the national administration's governing ability. The President's plan, one of resistance, was announced, and Colombians were marshalled to support the national alternative to the IMF devaluation program. With its nationalistic language and programs, the Colombian Government faced the IMF, not as weak-kneed or devoid of policy alternatives as might have been assumed, but with a consistent policy, firmly stated.

The hard note of nationalism, as much psychological as economic, presented Lleras's political opposition with a dilemma. Unless they agreed, not only with Lleras's immediate specific proposals, but also with his general

9 *El Espectador,* November 30, 1966, p. 10-A.

economic orientations, they risked being characterized as non-patriotic. Having a concrete situation replete with foreign badmen gave Lleras an important opportunity to capture public fancy and to deal some heavy blows at groups which might have proven, under less crisis-ridden circumstances, more effective in their opposition to his initiatives in land reform,[10] tax policy reforms, and administrative and constitutional reorganization.

The tone of Lleras's rebuttal to the IMF, his clever use of the themes of national self-respect and staunch rhetorical opposition to devaluation—the devil incarnate for a low-income, but acquisitive urban people—created an environment of popular approval previously absent in spite of a year's constant campaigning.

Lleras played on the popular desire for a strong man and, for the first time since winning the Presidency, the murmur heard in Bogotá cafes and streets was that the President *"tenía pantolones"*; he had his pants on, the mark of a man. Nor was the man in the street the only endorser of Lleras's move. Important organizations and interest groups such as the Coffee Federation, the labor unions, and the bankers' association voiced their support in numerous statements to the national press in the week following the first exchange and import controls decree. Furthermore, since the situation was concrete and his talk about national prestige and control of national policy referred to a real situation, Lleras placed Colombia

in the peculiar but emotionally-satisfying position of snarling at the hand that has helped to feed it. For a people accustomed to being a nation of heavy debtors, this rebellious stance must have been a welcome release from the hat-in-hand pose.

Consider, too, that a policy crisis vis-à-vis an international credit institution is nearly exclusively an area for executive action (even if in private all sorts of forces can potentially exert influence over policy). Lleras had in this case a free shot at the goal of public sympathy and support. In contrast, his parliamentary opposition was left very much in the background simply by the nature of the issue. At best they could only agree with or dispute this major initiative on his part, a policy issue that strongly animated public opinion in his favor.

Although only one among many politicians, the President alone has the legal power to set Colombia's political course. The initiative taken by Lleras and the nationalistic coloration he gave it assumed great political significance because he used the power unique to his office. Under the state of siege then in force this power was enhanced, even though the state of siege itself was indicative of malaise in the political process. With a few words the President committed the nation to a major policy and defined Colombia's attitude toward business, international bodies, and other countries. When he firmly articulated a nationalist posture and translated it into action by decree, contrary opinion had to contend with the President's legal power to determine policy as well as to contest him in the various political arenas.

In the current political environment in Colombia, a president can probably follow a policy that is less than

---

[10] Lleras, as a senator, was the principal force behind Colombia's 1961 agrarian reform law. For a vitally important analysis of the politico-economic manuevers to adopt this law, see Albert O. Hirschmann, *Journeys Towards Progress* (New York: Twentieth Century Fund, 1963).

optimal for a specific technical problem, but he will not survive too long without at least the *credible appearance* of making strong policy. If his action proves disadvantageous in a technical sense, so long as it is not an absolute, total blunder, no other political personality or group can prove him wrong by promulgating an alternative policy formula. The potency of this presidential role is not lost on the various publics, nor is the expectation that it will be exercised absent. As so many Colombians are anxious for the holder of the presidential office to act as well as talk, political benefit in the form of public approval can be, and was in this case, the dominant initial domestic result.

It is a political asset for a Colombian president that the opposition, both overt and covert, think he is running strong with the masses.

Simply stated, both the classical and pragmatic-technocratic styles of politics depend ultimately on popular support, especially in crisis situations. In any case they seek their legitimacy in popular consent. Recall that Colombia has a political system in which the interests served by either the more classical or the more pragmatically modern styles of handling mass public demands will at times come into conflict. Nevertheless, common to both styles and to the men who have roles in their related political processes is the constant necessity of dealing with the *pueblo,* or the people of less than middle-class station, as well as the more educated and economically comfortable classes. Common to both political styles, it may be argued, is the fear of violent reactions on the part of this *pueblo* when its socio-economic and psychological needs are not satisfied by the distributive capacities of existing social, political,

and economic institutions. In Colombia, where institutional modes are in a state of flux, an element of societal crisis and a potential for violence always seems to be present.

For many practitioners of the classical style of politics as well as for many who bridge both the classical and the pragmatic, the experience of the populist Rojas Pinilla regime (1953–1957) is a vivid memory of an attempt to win away from both the Liberals and the Conservatives their popular following, especially in the fast growing cities. Classically-oriented political people are faced with the necessity of continually convincing the laboring and lower-middle-class elements flirting with the Rojas-led ANAPO that such institutions as the traditional parties and the Congress, and such issues as local and partisan loyalties, are legitimate and relevant in the context of Colombia's economic development.

For the more convinced pragmatists, men like Carlos Lleras, most of whom began as traditional politicians and who have evolved—not revolted—from that style and are still influenced by it, the problems of legitimacy for their programs and approach are similar. The peculiar mixture of Catholic tradition and state intervention for economic development currently expressed by Rojas and the ANAPO truly contends with more secular and rationalized bureaucratic approaches for the prize of significant popular support.

Lleras's major political task during the IMF dispute and afterwards was distinguishing his actions from alternatives presented both by his old comrades in the traditional parties and by the populist Rojas.

A review of the obstacles facing Colombia as it seeks further economic development does not indicate any easy road to success. Transforming the economy in a fairly open and democratically intentioned society is time-consuming and guaranteed to involve high political risk. One way to minimize the adverse political effects of moving ahead toward long-range goals is to build vitally needed public support whenever the opportunity presents itself. As Lleras's handling of the 1966 IMF dispute illustrates, a skillful President may find a means of manipulating nationalist resentment against foreign interference to gain a short period in which to breathe, regroup his forces, and then move again.

4

Linkages to World Society:
International Labor Organizations
in the Western Hemisphere

Henry A. Landsberger

From Henry A. Landsberger, "International Labor Organization" in Samuel Shapiro, ed., *Integration of Man and Society in Latin America* (Notre Dame: University of Notre Dame Press, 1967), pp. 101–28. Reprinted by permission of the author, the editor, and the publisher. (Footnotes in the original version have been omitted.)

Henry A. Landsberger is a Professor of Sociology at the University of North Carolina at Chapel Hill.

As his title indicates, Professor Landsberger offers us yet another study of linkages, in this instance: between Latin American labor movements and labor movements in Western Europe and the United States (subnational-subnational); between international labor organizations and their counterparts in the Western Hemisphere (INGO-INGO); between rival Western Hemisphere international labor organizations (INGO-INGO); and between Western Hemisphere international labor organizations and domestic unions (INGO-subnational). His principal thesis is that international labor organizations are relatively insignificant in Latin America because they are primarily engaged in "organizational conquest" at the behest of non-Latin American "contestants" and lack the capacity to shape the course of "day-to-day unionism" on the national level. Although Landsberger's example is labor, his essay in fact suggests some of the reasons for the weakness of many international nongovernmental organizations—for instance, party organizations purporting to support a particular ideological position in the "international Communist movement."

I
DESCRIPTION

INTRODUCTION

In some not-quite-clear manner, the United States labor movement (or important parts thereof), and perhaps the United States Government, are in head-on collision with a Latin American labor group which, in some equally unclear fashion, seems to be Catholic. Some much publicized feuding has been going on for some time between, on the one hand, the Latin American Confederation of Christian Unions (CLASC—the Latin American regional affiliate of CISC, the International Federation of Christian Trade Unions) and, on the other hand, the Inter-American Regional Workers' Organization, ORIT, which bears the same formal relationship to the International Confederation of Free Trade Unions (ICFTU) as CLASC does to CISC. Of late, the AFL-CIO and the training institute sponsored by it and by certain United States companies, and financed largely by United States Government funds, have also been involved in the dispute.

In the second half of this paper we will analyze the causes of this dispute. But, before doing so, let me take some heat out of the dispute by that old and well-tried technique of providing facts about the history and structure of the chief *dramatis personae*. . . .

.   .   .

Profound differences as to ideologies, goals, tactics, organizational structure, and all other conceivable aspects of trade union life have been characteristic of the trade union movement from its inception in practically all parts of the world and at all levels of the movement. The quarrel is no fiercer in Latin America today than it is elsewhere, and it is no fiercer today than it has been in Latin America at other times or in other places at other times. It comes as a surprise only because most of us have not previously been aware of what went on in the house of labor. . . .

By the early fifties the lines had been drawn at the international level: a Communist international, the WFTU; a Christain (mainly, but not exclusively,

Catholic) international, CISC; and finally, the ICFTU—the largest of all —in part with a now even-more softened European socialist ideology, in part with less even than that, due to the membership and power of the AFL-CIO, no proponent of socialism or even laborism. . . .

WESTERN HEMISPHERE REGIONAL MOVEMENTS

Culturally, much of what has occurred in Latin America has been influenced by Western Europe, particularly by the Latin countries of Western Europe. Of few fields is this truer than that of labor. When French labor was riven by struggles between anarchosyndicalists and socialists in the late nineteenth and early twentieth centuries, so was Argentinian labor. Not long after Christian unions were established in Belgium and France, they were established in Chile, where Father Guillermo Viviani was instrumental in the establishment of unions of chauffeurs, railroad men, retail workers, and needle trade workers.

And so, too, it was at the level of regional organizations. Already the First International (the International Workingmen's Association) had affiliated groups in Latin America. In 1907 the anarchosyndicalist trade union movement of Argentina—the *Federacion Obrera Regional Argentina* (FORA)—called a hemispheric meeting in Buenos Aires, to which were invited the United States IWW, the famous "Wobblies," the Industrial Workers of the World. They did not attend, nor did the projected hemispheric organization materialize. These events are nevertheless of prognostic importance. As in Europe, and influenced by Europe, attempts at regional unity would be made on the basis of ideological compatibility.

In 1918, however, the first serious and relatively effective inter-American organization was established: the Pan-American Federation of Labor (PAFL). It was the fruit of the joint efforts of Samuel Gompers, president of the AFL; Santiago Iglesias, a Puerto Rican socialist labor leader; and the leaders of the Mexican labor movement. The story of the founding of this organization is fascinating because it contains many different strands of much relevance today. In part it represented the sympathy of Samuel Gompers, dominant figure on the American labor scene for over thirty years, for the struggle of Mexican labor and of the Mexican people in general, and his desire to prevent the United States Government from helping counterrevolutionary attempts. In part it represented a reaction to, an opposition to, the meeting of the Pan-American Financial and Trade Conference of 1915, which was regarded as a business threat to hemispheric labor. Yet in part the planning of the Federation from 1916 onwards also represented an attempt of a patriotic Gompers to help the United States war effort against Germany. Money seems to have flowed from the United States Government to the organizers of the conference who were trying to create an appropriate climate for it, while information on German activities in Mexico flowed from Gompers to the United States Government.

When the founding convention actually took place in Laredo, Texas, in mid-November, 1918, themes could be heard which are today major issues in the regional labor situation.

1. There was, on the part of some Latin Americans, e.g., Luis N. Morones, the Mexican labor leader, a pronounced fear that the United States labor movement would dominate the organization and expect others to obey it— *monroismo obrero,* as it came to be called.

2. There were implicit suggestions by some United States spokesmen (Secretary of Labor William B. Wilson, who made the keynote address in President Wilson's name) that the United States labor movement might well serve as a model and example to the labor movements of Latin America insofar as structure, policies, and methods were concerned.

3. Gompers, against bitter resistance from the Mexicans in particular, who did not want to get involved in larger political problems, convinced the convention to go along with a resolution supporting the United States Government on an issue of international politics outside the labor sphere as such; in this case, President Wilson's peace terms.

4. Also as a harbinger of things to come, Gompers and his Latin American colleagues spent much time and effort in attempts to have representatives of PAFL incorporated in the growing number of organizations and committees dealing with inter-American affairs which were springing up under the auspices of the Pan American Union. This is, of course, reminiscent of the vigorous activity of ORIT from the 1961 Punta del Este Conference onwards, to increase labor representation on all inter-American (that is, Alliance and OAS) bodies as well as on the national planning bodies stimulated by the Alliance.

5. PAFL is of interest because the United States labor movement—in effect, Gompers—was several times in the role of middleman and conveyed to the United States Government protests from labor groups in Latin American countries—for example, from those of Nicaragua and (shades of 1965!) the Dominican Republic—about their

own dictatorial governments and/or the action of the United States Government and its military forces. The impression one has is that Gompers, despite his closeness to the United States Government and to President Wilson in particular, was decidedly more ready than his counterparts in the 1960's to speak up on behalf of his Latin American counterparts, and that he was less ready than his counterparts today to defend the actions of the United States Government. Indeed, resolutions severely condemning United States policies were passed at the Fifth Congress of PAFL in 1927.

6. And finally, it was notable that some of the Latin groups (again, the Mexicans, but also the Argentinians) were restive over having their international contacts confined to the Western Hemisphere. They wanted more direct contact with Europe. The attempt to organize a Latin American federation excluding the United States and affiliating itself with the IFTU failed. But the effort is significant.

We have dwelt at some length on this early venture in inter-American labor organization because it is fascinating that forty and more years ago some of the issues argued with vehemence today were already visible. Almost all these issues involve the role of the North American colossus: its government and its labor movement, their relationship to each other and their relationship to their weaker southern colleagues. In part these issues were resolved differently then than now; in part they were resolved in very much the same way.

When the AFL began to interest itself in Latin America in 1948 after a pause of almost twenty years (the PAFL expired in the late twenties), it was a very different group of men who

did so. But the traditions of organizations and certain immanent policies live on beyond the men who made them. So do the problems, issues, and dilemmas external to these men and their organizations with which they are faced and which they have to try to resolve. These dilemmas are relived anew, therefore, and often resolved in the same way. The AFL gave early signs of strong leanings toward a robust, perhaps rather limited, patriotism on the basis of which it maintains the sympathy of a public easily aroused to suspicions of left radicalism. The AFL's posture also preserved, and still preserves, government goodwill and occasional support of a more tangible kind (for example, jobs in government) which are as important to its institutional well-being as is approval by the general public. This patriotic theme was adopted early in the life of the AFL. It is in crescendo today, but even when more muted during certain periods, it has never disappeared, and it is unlikely that it ever will.

We may review other efforts at regional labor movements more briefly, not because they were less important, but because their significance was so clear that little of our precious time and space needs to be spent elaborating on them. First, toward the end of the twenties there was founded not only an inter-American anarchosyndicalist organization (ACAT) but also a hard-line, purely Communist Latin American Labor Confederation (CSLA). It affiliated, of course, as did its national members, with the Red International of Labor Unions. This, too, we may regard as a permanent tendency in Latin America: the temporary congregation of sharply radical groups, soon to disintegrate as "openings to the right" are deemed expedient, and as isolation and loss of support lead to ineffectiveness.

Later, in the course of the thirties, when Communists everywhere rejoined other groups in a spirit of popular frontism, several of the newly enlarged major Latin American movements founded the *Confederación de Trabajadores de America Latina* (CTAL). This occurred largely under the inspiration of the newly established Mexican Confederation of Labor (CTM) and its general-secretary, Vicente Lombardo Toledano, with the encouragement of President Cárdenas. But it was vigorously supported by Argentina's CGT and Chile's CTCH. This effort, too, symbolizes much that is typical for Latin America: first, its restriction to Latin American to the exclusion of North American unions, and second, a confederation which, while radical, is broader by far than the extreme left. But this kind of regional confederation also is unstable. Before long it shrinks in effect into being little more than another extremist group. This occurs both because nonextremists tend to leave it and because extremists tend to win out in the internal struggle for power. That is exactly what happened to the WFTU in the late forties at the international level. That is exactly what happened in the late forties to CTAL at the Latin American level, though CTAL continued in formal existence until the early sixties.

Finally, in 1948, under stimulus from the AFL and its Latin American representative Serafino Romualdi, greatly concerned over the existence of CTAL as a radical regional organization excluding the United States, there was founded the *Confederación Interamericana de Trabajadores* (CIT) in close cooperation with several Latin American movements which had eliminated Communist influence. In 1951 this organization converted itself into ORIT, the Inter-American Regional Organization of the newly established ICFTU.

And is it to be wondered that at about the same there should be founded the first Latin American Christian Regional Association (CLASC), affiliated, of course, with CISC?

I believe I have adequately illustrated that ideological rivalry is a permanent characteristic of the inter-American labor scene, as it is of the international labor scene. We can now pass on to take stock of the present situation.

THE PRESENT SITUATION

1. Nonaffiliated.

Let it be recognized at the outset that as of May, 1964, over one-third of all workers south of the Rio Grande *who were in unions* were yet not affiliated with any of the three international organizations. The members of several more unions might have belonged to the international trade secretariats of one or other of the world federations, particularly those of the ICFTU. However, Argentina, the country with perhaps the Southern Hemisphere's most powerful and well-developed labor movement, had in that year none of its two and a half million members affiliated to an international or regional trade union federation. In Bolivia practically none of the unions or their members were affiliated; in Mexico almost 50 percent were not; in Uruguay 85 percent were not, and in Chile over 60 percent were not. As of the same date—1964—the only countries with important labor movements where the percentage of nonaffiliated was low were Brazil (5 percent), Colombia (27 percent), and Peru (12 percent). We note, therefore, that very important national labor movements may exist without affiliation to either regional or one of the three international trade union movements.

2. The "radical" camp.[1]

There exists at present no regional confederation of radical orientation. A planning meeting was held in Santiago, Chile, in 1962, to plan for a further planning meeting in Brazil in 1964. The latter—during which CTAL was officially dissolved—met under difficult circumstances just prior to the fall of President Goulart. It decided to set up, in Santiago, Chile, a permanent commission to plan for a new Latin American confederation! It is doubtful that much will come of it.

Nor does the WFTU have many direct affiliates. Only in Ecuador, Venezuela, and in the tiny French Caribbean departments is a substantial sector of the unionized working population in unions affiliated with the WFTU. Altogether the WFTU, which claims a worldwide membership of 138 million, actually has little strength outside the Communist-bloc countries, including Cuba, with the exception of France, Italy, and India.

Yet neither the failure to have a viable Latin American regional confederation nor the meager direct affiliation with the WFTU can be regarded as an accurate measure of the strength of radical ideologies and of radically oriented leaders in Latin American labor. Important sections of the Uru-

guayan and Chilean labor movements have strong radical leadership, and it is not far below the surface in the metal manufacturing industry in Brazil, as well as in Colombia and in the Dominican Republic. The failure to form an overt regional movement or to affiliate with the WFTU is, therefore, to be understood as a very sober and accurate assessment of the fact that at this particular juncture, with hostile governments almost everywhere, a Latin American confederation of openly radical orientation, or in the hands of radical elements, could achieve nothing except draw fire.

A temporizing policy may well be eminently sensible not only for these radical groups but also for others. This point takes on added force when we recall, once again, how many of Latin America's organized workers—as well as, by definition, all its unorganized workers—are unaffiliated with any international labor organization.

3. CISC and its Latin American affiliate, CLASC.

At the Eleventh Congress of CISC, in 1951, Latin American groups from five countries were admitted for the first time. But for lack of money they were unable to attend. At the Fifteenth Congress in Liège, in 1964, of the sixty-two nations represented, twenty-three—the largest single bloc—came from Latin America. Twenty African, thirteen European, and six Asian nations were also represented.

Nevertheless, CISC is not strong worldwide. It is generally estimated to have three or three and a half million affiliated members. And the numerical strength of CLASC, the Latin American affiliate, is not great, and it is certainly indeterminate. Only in the Dominican Republic is a major move-

[1] The descriptive material in this and the following sections is for the period 1965–1967.

ment (the *Confederación Auténtico Sindical Cristiano* [CASC] with perhaps forty or fifty thousand members) affiliated to it. To this can be added certain nuclei in Venezuela and an important segment of Chile's newly flourishing rural movement, as well as rural movements of indeterminate size in Peru, Ecuador, and Guatemala.

Painful for CLASC has always been the fact that the two most substantial Latin labor movements of Christian inspiration—the Colombian UTC and *Rerum Novarum* of Costa Rica—have been steadfast affiliates of ORIT, not of CLASC. More recently CLASC has felt compelled to expel the 200,000-member Brazilian Confederation of Christian Workers (CBTC) for its early support of the 1964 military coup (a support since rescinded). And finally it should be noted that Chile's Christian Democratic Party, while on record against ORIT, has not by virtue of that fact endorsed CLASC with any notable degree of enthusiasm.

However sound the policy positions taken by CLASC may or may not be, it cannot, in fact, speak for a large number of organized workers, nor even for a substantial sector of the Christian inspired unions of Latin America. On the matter of financing it is equally necessary to be frank and realistic about CLASC. While the sums at the disposal of CLASC may be far smaller than those of which "the ORIT complex" disposes, these funds are probably no more indigenous to Latin America than are those of its rival. They come from CISC in Brussels and from other Western European, particularly German, sources.

4. The ORIT complex.

The ORIT complex, therefore, is by all odds the largest numerically, the best financed, and institutionally the most powerfully supported grouping. It consists of (1) ORIT itself, the Western Hemisphere regional organization of the ICFTU, in which the voice of the AFL-CIO is undoubtedly the dominant voice, and (2) various international trade secretariats active in the Western Hemisphere, such as the International Transport Workers Federation; the Metal Workers; the Postal, Telephone, and Telegraph Workers; and others. ORIT has by far and away the largest number of affiliates, among them some of Latin America's most firmly established national federations, such as Mexico's CTM; Venezuela's CTV; Peru's CTB; the two main Colombian federations, UTC and CTC; massive sectors of the Brazilian labor movement; and important sectors from many of the smaller countries where unions are, however, generally weak: El Salvador, Guatemala, and many of the Caribbean islands (where unions are strong). In 1964 ORIT may have had approximately 50 percent of all organized workers, and it may have had over 95 percent of all workers who were affiliated with an international labor organization.

The most controversial member of the "ORIT complex" is, however, (3) the American Institute for Free Labor Development. This controversy is ironic because AIFLD was set up in part to permit the United States labor movement to deal more directly with Latin American labor movements without passing through a regional organization which, it was realized in the early sixties, was controversial and unattractive to many Latin American trade unionists. The Institute is sponsored directly by the AFL-CIO and in effect run by it. But its board also contains representatives of large United

States companies operating in Latin America, such as Grace and Anaconda, and Latin Americans of the democratic moderate left, such as Rómulo Betancourt and José Figueres. It has perhaps fourteen field offices in Latin America; over forty thousand students have passed through educational short courses sponsored by it in Latin America itself, over four thousand through longer resident courses, and over four hundred through longer training in Washington. Apart from its educational program it has a social projects program under which housing, credit, and consumer cooperatives and the building of medical clinics are sponsored. The social projects department has a resident United States staff in Latin America which has been estimated at over sixty, and this number may be over two hundred if United States citizens servicing Latin America, but stationed at Washington headquarters, are included. Through obtaining United States Government guarantees of loans extended by AFL-CIO unions to Latin American (trade union) borrowers, and through its contacts with the Agency for International Development (AID) in general, the Institute is involved in the channeling of tens, if not hundreds, of millions of dollars. Of its direct budget, probably 80 percent comes from United States Government sources, the remainder being approximately evenly distributed between business and unions.

ORIT in general and the AFL-CIO more particularly are closely linked to various inter-American and Alliance for Progress bodies, and they have easy access to United States Government agencies. Human nature being what it is, it is only to be expected that this influence and power as well as the immense resources for education,

housing, etc., of which the ORIT complex disposes would be cause enough for feelings of envy and suspicion. These feelings are enormously reinforced by the ambiguous political role which the ORIT complex is seen as having played in recent critical events in Latin America. Despite its claim, sincerely meant and not really illogical, that its long-run aim is to foster "independent" trade unionism and an apolitical labor movement, some of its actions are highly political and interventionist. Key figures have stated proudly that they or their trainees played important roles in the toppling of the Bosch Government in the Dominican Republic and of President Goulart in Brazil. These acts, the support of strikes against Cheddi Jagan in Guyana, ORIT support of the Castillo Armas regime after it had ousted Arbenz, and the belated condemnation of Batista all seem to many to form a pattern of political support for right-wing regimes. In addition, accusations have been made of intimate connections between AIFLD personnel and United States intelligence services, accusations voiced, for example, by Victor Reuther, brother of Walter Reuther, a long-time critic of the AFL-CIO's president, George Meany, particularly on foreign policy as well as other matters.

The issues, then, are rather unpleasant ones. The "ORIT complex" is accused, first, of teaching to others a nonpolitical pure trade union approach to the solution of labor's problems in a setting where no such solutions are likely to be effective unless a substantial change in political power has first occurred. In short, it is accused of misunderstanding the nature of Latin American society. The participation of United States company representatives in an educational venture for Latin

American trade unionists is regarded as symbolic of this lack of comprehension of Latin America's problems, or at least of its psychology. Second, the "ORIT complex" is accused of preaching a doctrine of nonpolitical unionism while actually engaging in political activity and even supporting or condoning right-wing violence. In particular, its fierce anti-Communism is regarded as sterile, a highly political act undermining its claim to be nonpolitical. Third, it is regarded as an instrumental part of United States Government policy, which may be good or bad, but means that it is not engaged in *bona fide* union activity. Fourth, there is a generalized fear that the immense wealth and power of the United States labor movement will have the practical effect of preventing the growth of strong local, autonomous labor movements. Fifth, there is a feeling that ORIT, in practice, utilizes as its standard bearers unionists in ill-repute with their fellows.

In the quarrel with CLASC, ORIT counterattacks by questioning for whom CLASC really speaks when voicing these fears, in view of its unknown representativeness, its numerical thinness, and its practical inexperience even at the top leadership level. CLASC's emphasis on the need for a genuine social revolution and changes in institutional structure are seen either as pure demagogy, empty phrases lacking any specific programmatic content, or as dangerously similar to Communist preachings of class warfare. In the latter connection, CLASC's strident anti-Yankeeism and its failure to condemn the USSR and China with equal frequency are also noted (CLASC has condemned aspects of Castro-Cuban policy). Finally, its foreign financing and its attempts to split and reaffiliate existing union movements are criticized.

Concerning the left tone of CLASC pronouncements coming from Santiago and, more recently, from its new headquarters in Caracas, as well as its lack of emphasis on religious matters, it is important to note that this is in line with CISC trends at the international level and is not confined to Latin America. The reformulated 1962 program of CISC has removed all references to God and Christianity and stated its goal to be a democratic rather than a Christian society. One of CISC's most important affiliates—the French CFTC—recently removed the final "C" (*chrétiens*) from its title and substituted for it a "D" for *democratique* (CFDT). CISC and its affiliates may be adopting a more flexible policy toward the WFTU and Communism generally than does the ICFTU. Rumored strains between CLASC and its parent body, CISC, may, therefore, be only partially true. On the whole, CLASC's policies with exception of its stress on political action may represent CISC policies quite well regardless of how many Latin Americans it represents.

II

INTERPRETATION

How can we best understand what is going on today in Latin America at the level of regional and hemispheric labor organizations? What functions are they really performing? Who controls them and for what ends? At what points are they succeeding and why? Where do they fail and why?

The interpretations which follow are unusual because their basic theme is that we are not dealing with ordinary trade union phenomena but with struggles for power, influence, and control between quite unusual contestants applying pressure at points not normally considered when thinking about the ways and means of trade unions. These interpretations may even appear cynical. But the aim is not that of seeking notoriety by the crude device of shocking.

REGIONAL ORGANIZATIONS CANNOT, ON THE WHOLE, HELP MUCH IN DAY-TO-DAY UNIONISM

A long-time student of international labor organizations has divided the goals and functions of these organizations into three: (1) representational, or "placing a generalized trade union point of view on current issues before intergovernmental agencies, such as the United Nations, the ILO, or regional bodies" (note the reference to regional bodies); (2) missionary goals: "the propagation of trade unionism, or rather of a particular brand of trade unionism, to areas where it does not yet exist or where its weakness requires external support"; and (3) servicing: "support of their affiliates, as through international strike support, research and welfare work, exchange of trade information, and assistance to migrating union members." It is this latter which we have called "help in day-to-day unionism."

Both Windmuller and another long-time observer, George E. Lichtblau, agree that of the three functions, the missionary activity and not service in day-to-day union affairs has become the most important. "The 'cold war' remains the principal preoccupation of the international labor movements. . . . (and) consumes most of the energy and resources of the labor internationals." Concentration on the cold war gives the missionary activity a peculiar twist. It means that as much or more energy may be spent in attempting to get already established unions to change their affiliation from one international organization to another, or to oust one group of leaders and replace them with ideologically more acceptable ones, as in organizing previously unorganized workers.

The day-to-day activities of a union at the local plant level, or at the company or industry level, may be divided into (1) its organization and establishment in the first place; (2) gaining recognition from the employer and the government; (3) negotiating agreements (this may include fewer or more steps, such as appearing before mediation and arbitration boards, and organizing and executing strikes); (4) administering the agreement; (5) directing the internal life of the union, holding meetings, and the like; (6) educating members and especially those elected to be officials in the activities just outlined. These are the activities which most directly and immediately affect the individual worker.

When international organizations were first established, they were of some help in these activities. They could occasionally provide strike funds, stop employers from importing strikebreakers across European boundaries, refuse to handle his goods when exported, and so forth. The ICFTU international trade secretariats continue to be of some help in this general area of service in the day-to-day activities of unions, mostly in connection with initial organization and recognition or during critical negotiations. In particular, a visit by some senior (generally European) officer of the ITS's to a government official may be important in a critical labor dispute or if the very existence of a local union is threatened.

But clearly it is not logical that regional organizations should address themselves to thousands of local situations. They do not have the financial or human resources to do so. Immersion in a local situation by an outsider is immensely difficult, and international organizations do not dispose of large quantities of such wise men, if, indeed, they exist at all. Nor does the problem usually lend itself to solution from the outside. The reaction of both the Chilean workers whom it is intended to help, and of the Chilean minister before whom representations are made, may be imagined if the spokesman for a regional labor organization happened to be, for example, a Bolivian or Argentinian. Regional organizations do not generally have sufficient time or resources to see a problem through to its solution. In the organization of new unions, for example, though the outsider is often gratified by his initial success in establishing one, he generally does not and cannot stay long enough to see it collapse a month, a year, or two years after the initiation ceremony.

By comparison with most national organizations, international organizations are as a rule poorly provided with those instruments that are essential to effective action, in particular, a well-functioning apparatus under authoritative leadership, adequate human and material resources, and certain devices for inducing or compelling adherence to their policies. In general their secretariats are weak, their resources scanty, and their coercive and persuasive powers exceedingly small.

THE REAL GOAL OF INTERNATIONAL AND REGIONAL LABOR ORGANIZATIONS IN LATIN AMERICA IS THAT OF ORGANIZATIONAL CONQUEST

We are doing little more than restating what has been said by the two experts we have cited above. The chief objective of international organizations is a missionary, not service, one. We would wish only to add one important clarifying footnote to that idea and to the term "missionary." It is our impression that the aim of these organizations is not really, in the first and most important instance, that of spreading their ideologies and thereby leading to different trade union practices and activities. Certainly this is not their aim in the short run or even the medium run. It is for this reason that not much space has been devoted to analyzing in what way the CISC-CLASC ideology concerning trade union aims differs from that of the ICFTU-ORIT or from that of the WFTU. As organizations, these entities are too weak, and local situational pressures too strong, for them to impose any philosophy of trade unionism on their affiliates even if they have any distinctive ones, which is not at all certain in the case of the CISC-CLASC and ICFTU-ORIT. In this sense they are not really missionaries.

International labor organizations in Latin America seem to be missionaries only in that less desirable sense of seeking formal converts, of increasing the numbers of those formally registered and affiliated, and, in particular, in ousting the representatives of rival groups. The anti-Communism of ORIT is, therefore, not so much or not only ideological. It is organizational. And the anti-Yankeeism and anti-ORITism of CLASC likewise represents in part a desire to remove persons whom it can never control and whose organizations it can never hope to capture while these persons are in charge.

This game of organizational raiding, of affiliating and reaffiliating, of plotting the ouster of one group of officers to install another because of their greater organizational loyalty, does not arouse this author to great heights of enthusiasm in favor of any of the contestants. It is an unending game which absorbs a great deal of energy and is of dubious advantage to the ordinary worker. Unfortunately, since the game is being played, it is impossible to ignore it.

THE CONTESTANTS AT THE REGIONAL AND INTERNATIONAL LEVEL ARE, TO AN IMPORTANT DEGREE, NOT LATIN AMERICAN

It is reasonably clear that without the administrative know-how and drive, and especially without the immense financial resources, of the United States labor movement (and, in part, that of the United States Government) ORIT would be but a shadow of itself. AIFLD and its manifold activities would, obviously, cease to exist. This is not to deny, let this be equally clear, that their help may not be welcomed in many cases by those who receive it. But it is not help by Latin Americans to Latin Americans. It is doubtful that the Mexican CTM, Venezuela's CTV, or Peru's CTP—the Latin American affiliates of ORIT which are strongest organizationally and financially—would band together without United States help in anything but the most perfunctory regional grouping. The reason is that there would not be—and there is not at present—very much "in it for them." It is not likely that they would get together to send teams of well-financed experts to the northeast of Brazil or that they would contribute to the financing of a well-appointed union hall in Ecuador.

The reason behind the intense interest of those leaders of the AFL-CIO who are interested in this organizational race is not fully clear. We might note that their number is small and that the goals they pursue are of little interest to their North American members, though these clearly also do not oppose them. The easiest answers are ones which can be traced back historically. First, the AFL leadership has a long tradition of being fiercely anti-Communist. Second, like all organizations which have had to fight for their place in the sun, it is conscious of its power now that it has some and likes to exercise it in a variety of settings. These two motives, in combination, imply that the AFL-CIO's vigorous hunt of Communists in Latin America must not be seen as a simple, passive execution of United States Government policy. On the contrary, there is perhaps as much unhappiness as satisfaction with the massive and forceful activities of the "ORIT complex" among those U.S. government officials and policy makers who are aware of them but who cannot speak out for a variety of reasons. United States labor is leading, as much as following, the United States Government. In addition to anti-Communism and the desire to exercise power, the AFL leadership is genuinely patriotic, and this is certainly one motive for its action, however much one or another person may differ with it on what is appropriately patriotic at any given moment of time. The AFL-CIO leadership is also desirous of helping the Government because certain *quid pro quos* are involved, for example support for legislation which the AFL-CIO needs at home. And, finally, humanitarianism, of course, plays an important motivating role: the desire to organize the unorganized and to help them toward a better life. But it must be remembered that there is much similar work to be done along these lines in the United States, and those leaders of the AFL-CIO who have been most concerned with overseas affairs have often given least indication of being motivated by this kind of drive at home.

The case of CLASC is basically not dissimilar. Its outside sponsors are, of course, also moved by humanitarian reasons, organizing the unorganized. But the classical religious motivation behind trade union activities, that of not abandoning the ground to capitalist or socialist-communist materialism, surely also plays a role. In this instance ideological motives are, we suspect, strongly reinforced by discomfort at the thought of organizationally abandoning Latin American workers to the North American colossus no matter what his ideology. And this discomfort exists not only in Latin America but in Western Europe.

THE METHODS IN THIS STRUGGLE FOR
ORGANIZATIONAL POWER ARE:
(1) EDUCATION, (2) DISBURSEMENT
OF RESOURCES, (3) REPRESENTATION
IN DECISION-MAKING BODIES

1. Education.

At all levels trade unions sponsor educational activities. But the further away, and the further up, that one moves from the grass-roots level, the more likely it is that the intent—and certainly the main effect—of this education is that of morale-lifting and, particularly, the building of loyalty rather than the building of specific organizational skills. Speaking as an educator and as someone who has participated in and observed the educational efforts of CLASC, ORIT, and of some more radical groups, I am dubious that much new skill or much information was learned, that it ever could be learned

in the kind of setting in which it was offered, or that it was the chief purpose of the organizers that it be learned.

Administrative skills, skills in organizing and negotiating, and skills in conducting meetings and in otherwise communicating with union members, can be well learned, not in this kind of setting, but only over long periods of actual experience, perhaps in an apprentice relationship to an experienced man. Invariably courses run by regional organizations contain a good deal of general political, doctrinal, and so-called historical material, and this alone is sufficient to indicate its real intention.

Its efficacy in any direction is difficult to assess. That many trainees are "lost" in one way or another is quite apparent. But one or two trainees in the right spot at the right time may compensate for them. More information on the efficacy of educational programs is clearly needed, though each organization will undoubtedly wish to conduct its own study. Lacking more concrete information, we can only go by impressions, and these are strong that the purpose and the effect of training programs conducted by international labor organizations is primarily that of instilling organizational loyalty and giving a general boost to morale rather than equipping the student with specific skills.

2. Disbursement of Resources.

The giving and withholding of resources in order to get the right man elected or to achieve affiliation or reaffiliation of a particular union is probably a more powerful weapon than education. In fact, the disbursing of educational fellowships—a weekend or a week or four weeks at a training center, perhaps in another country or even another continent—is itself a resource which is used to make friends and win allegiance. More massive efforts are loans to housing or consumer cooperatives or the donation of a union hall. Less massive efforts are the supply of office equipment and jeeps. The price is the promise of affiliation or at least a good deal of publicity for the organization granting the benefit.

3. *Representation in Decision-making Bodies.*

The third and final technique used by regional organizations to increase their power is that of seeking representation on inter-American organizations. There is here a parallel with European integration which in part is deceptive and misleading. Western Europe is, of course, in a relatively advanced stage of integration, and its union movement is relatively affluent and firmly established. Consequently, the union movements of the countries involved (West Germany, France, Belgium, and others) have been in a position to set up effective advisory committees to provide expert representation of worker interests. Thus, there is a European Trade Union Secretariat (established by ICFTU affiliates) which acts as an interest group vis-à-vis the European Economic Community. The European Free Trade Association and the Organization of Economic Cooperation and Development also have such trade union bodies attached to them.

The parallel is, of course, COSATE, the Trade Union Technical Advisory Committee to the Department of Social Affairs of the Organization of American States. Moreover, this group—from which CLASC has withdrawn as we have already mentioned—is pressing that trade unionists be involved in social and economic policy-making bodies at the national level in all countries participating in the Alliance for Progress. But the real question is whether the OAS, or the newly projected national planning entities, are in the foreseeable future likely to influence important policy-making bodies to the degree to which they are in Europe. Even if we assume that they are, there is a further question whether Latin American trade unions have the kind of personnel available, or trainable, who could effectively influence such important policies as are made. What seems much more certain is that positions on inter-American bodies and on national bodies can be important in the organizational fight to which we have drawn attention, even if they are not important in affecting major economic and social policies. It should be noted that in Europe, ICFTU and CISC unions have a reasonable *modus vivendi* at the continental level and at many national levels which CLASC and ORIT clearly do not have. The likelihood of using representation in inter-American or national bodies for organizational rather than policy purposes is, therefore, great. Thus, the parallel with Europe is partial, though it will become more real with the passage of time as Latin America becomes more integrated and as its labor movement has the resources to maintain staff experts who can participate in deliberations on problems such as continental social security systems, tariffs, prices, and other such issues. In the meantime, these European-looking forms have a different significance in Latin America.

5

The Decline of the OAS

Jerome Slater

From Jerome Slater, "The Decline of the OAS," *International Journal*, XXIV, No. 3 (Summer 1969), pp. 497–506. Reprinted by permission of the author and the publisher.

Jerome Slater is an Associate Professor of Political Science at the State University of New York at Buffalo.

In this selection, the leading student of the OAS maintains that the principal international governmental organization actor in inter-American relations "has entered a period of disarray and political decline." Slater discusses the limited convergence of U.S. and Latin American interests that gave the inter-American system considerable vitality in the 1940s and 1950s and the debilitating effects of U.S. anti-Communism, ideological conflict, and Latin American nationalism in the 1960s, which he finds reflected in recent action (and inaction) on proposed changes in the OAS.[1] Neverthe-

---

[1] For historical surveys of U.S. hemisphere security policies and the evolution of the inter–American system, see esp.: Arthur P. Whitaker, *The Western Hemisphere Idea* (Ithaca: Cornell University Press, 1954); Dexter Perkins, *A History of the Monroe Doctrine* (2nd ed.; Boston: Little, Brown and Company, 1955); Donald M. Dozer, ed., *The Monroe Doctrine: Its Modern Significance* (New York: Alfred A. Knopf, 1965); John A. Logan, Jr., *No Transfer: An American Security Principle* (New Haven: Yale University Press, 1961); Dana G. Munro, *Intervention and Dollar Diplomacy in the Caribbean, 1900–1921* (Princeton: Princeton University Press, 1964); Thomas L. Karnes, *The Failure of Union: Central America 1824–1960* (Chapel Hill: University of North Carolina Press, 1961); Bryce Wood, *The Making of the Good Neighbor Policy* (New York: Columbia University Press, 1961); Bryce Wood, *The United States and Latin American Wars, 1932–1942* (New York: Columbia University Press, 1966); J. Lloyd Mecham, *The United States and Inter-American Security, 1889–1960* (Austin: University of Texas Press, 1961); and Gordon Connell-Smith, *The Inter-American System* (London: Oxford University Press, 1966).

General works on the OAS: By far the best is Jerome Slater, *The OAS and United States Foreign Policy* (Columbus: Ohio State University Press, 1967). The volumes by Mecham and Connell-Smith above deal partly with the OAS experience. Useful as reference works but legalistic are M. Margaret Ball, *The OAS in Transition* (Durham: Duke University Press, 1969); Ann Van Wynen Thomas and A. J. Thomas, Jr., *The Organization of American States* (Dallas: Southern Methodist University Press, 1963); and Charles G. Fenwick, *The Organization of American States* (Washington: n.p., 1963).

On OAS structural reforms, see also: John C. Dreier, "New Wine and Old Bottles: The Changing Inter-American System," *International Organization*, XXII, No. 2 (Spring 1968), pp. 477–93; and William Manger, "Reform of the OAS: The 1967 *less, he cautions against a conclusion that the organization is or is likely soon to be "moribund," none-the-least because it is a useful mechanism for Latin Americans' exercise of collective influence over United States policies.*

Several other factors which Slater cites as evidence of the continued viability of the OAS were conspicuously present in the organization's role in ending the El Salvador-Honduras "Soccer War" during the summer of 1969.[2] The threat of inter-American sanctions raised at an emergency OAS Meeting of Foreign Ministers and the personal diplomacy of Secretary General Galo Plaza Lasso were apparently instrumental in obtaining a cease-fire and El Salvador's military withdrawal from Honduras. OAS observers patrolled the international boundary, while the Inter-American Commission on Human Rights investigated charges of gross mistreatment of foreign nationals by both parties to the conflict.[3]

It seems clear that the Organization of American States (OAS) has entered a period of disarray and political decline. The signs are everywhere present: the bitterness in Latin America over the unilateral United States intervention in the Dominican Republic and the failure of the OAS to constrain effectively Washington's actions there, the refusal of the organization to adopt internal structural reforms long considered desirable, and the unwillingness of the majority of the member states to allow an inter-American role in problems of political change in Latin America.

In retrospect, curiously enough, the period of the greatest political vitality for the inter-American system seems to have been the 1940s and 1950s. Curiously, because during this period the organization was rent with most of the same conflicts that exist in heightened form today, and OAS participants and observers alike hardly thought they were living through a golden era of inter-American co-operation. Yet, despite the decline of the goodwill that had characterized the days of the Good Neighbor policy, despite the bitter disappointment at the failure of the United States to provide substantial economic assistance to Latin America, and despite the heavy-handed diplomacy of John Foster Dulles, the organization somehow succeeded in playing a significant role in the management and control of interstate political conflict

---

Buenos Aires Protocol of Amendment to the 1948 Charter of Bogotá: An Appraisal," *Journal of Inter-American Studies,* X, No. 1 (January 1968), pp. 1–14.

[2] For an analysis of the origins of the war and its impact on the CACM, see selection 32.

[3] The IACHR is a fascinating example of organizational task expansion under what would appear to be exceedingly unfavorable conditions. See Anna P. Schreiber and Philippe S. E. Schreiber, "The Inter-American Commission on Human Rights in the Dominican Crisis," *International Organization,* XXII, No. 2 (Spring 1968), pp. 508–28; and Anna P. Schreiber, *The Inter-American Commission on Human Rights* (Leyden: A. W. Sijthoff, 1970).

in the hemisphere.[1] It succeeded in settling or at least damping down a number of small-scale, but potentially explosive conflicts in the Central American and Caribbean area. Backed by the strong support of the United States, with all that such support implied in the way of heavy political, economic, and even military pressures, the organization typically was able to interpose itself in conflicts in a variety of ways—gathering facts by on-the-spot investigations, separating belligerents through the establishment of OAS patrols, facilitating consultation between contestants or directly mediating disputes, and sometimes even spelling out and imposing settlements.

Despite all the political differences within the hemisphere, then, a number of factors had converged to make it possible for the OAS to act. For one thing, the "western hemisphere idea" —the notion that the hemispheric states shared a common history, philosophy, and destiny that distinguished them from the rest of the world—had not yet lost all its force as an integrative mechanism. In operation, the idea provided the rationale for the attempted insulation of the hemisphere from European political influences. During the 1930s and early 1940s, with the development of the Nazi threat to Western civilization, this traditional hemispheric goal had taken on added meaning. As a result, during World War II there was a considerable degree

of ad hoc inter–American political and military collaboration, and in the immediate postwar years there was nearly unanimous agreement on the need to create much more effective and institutionalized mechanisms.

The postwar consensus was also a reflection of two new factors: changes in United States policy and the development of the cold war. In the past, Latin American distrust of the United States had precluded the creation of an effective hemispheric organization with strong political functions, for it was feared that such an organization would serve only to institutionalize and legitimate United States domination of the hemisphere. Roosevelt's Good Neighbor policy, however, resting as it did on strict non-intervention in Latin American internal affairs, had so quieted these fears that they were now outweighed, particularly among the many conservative and oligarchical Latin American governments, by the spectre of a worldwide communist challenge. Besides, it was hoped that the formal adherence of the United States to a permanent inter-American system might increase the constraints on Washington and make more unlikely a return to the interventionist policies of the early twentieth century. The outbreak of the postwar crisis in Europe settled all remaining doubts and provided the final impetus to the drive for greater inter-American cooperation that culminated in the signing of the Rio Treaty in 1947 and the OAS Charter in 1948.

Later, even after Latin American fears of the USSR began to fade and disenchantment with the United States again set in, common interests remained. With the revolutionary and populist currents that were to erupt in

[1] For a detailed discussion of these activities, see especially my monograph *A Revaluation of Collective Security,* Mershon Center for Education in National Security Pamphlet No. 1 (Cleveland, 1965) and my book, *The OAS and United States Foreign Policy* (Cleveland, 1967).

Latin America in the 1960s still mostly below the surface or successfully repressed, most of the hemispheric governments—certainly including that of the United States—wanted little more from the inter-American system than the preservation of peace and the maintenance of the political status quo. And that the organization was able to do fairly well. Most of the conflicts that broke out among the Caribbean states in the late 1940s and again in the late 1950s stemmed from attempts of exile groups, based in and supported by friendly countries, to overturn existing governments in their homelands. Thus, the effect of organizational action was not only to dampen and contain interstate conflict but also to insulate the Caribbean dictatorships from pressures for change.

By the 1960s, however, this limited convergence of interests had largely broken down. With fear of a dangerous common enemy no longer providing external pressure for co-operation, the impact of the western hemisphere idea on operational policy had markedly diminished. Moreover, as the United States increasingly sought to use the OAS as an anticommunist alliance to mobilize the hemispheric states on behalf of its cold war policies, the value of the organization to the Latin Americans sharply declined—one of the primary functions of the system in Latin American eyes was to insulate the hemisphere from rather than involve it in world conflict. Similarly, the emergence of anti–communism as the overriding concern of American hemispheric policy undermined the ability of the inter-American system to constrain American unilateralism. Beginning with the Guatemalan crisis in 1954, continuing through the Bay of Pigs affair, and culminating in the Dominican intervention, the United States made it clear that it considered the exigencies of the cold war, as defined exclusively by itself, to override its multilateral commitments, no matter how explicit and solemnly formalized. Thus, Latin American concern with American domination of the hemisphere once again became paramount.

Finally, rising Latin American ideological conflict and nationalism have further weakened the bonds of the inter-American system. Ideological conflict has undercut the peacekeeping system, for Cuban dedication to the spread of revolution and, conversely, the determination of the status quo or counter-revolutionary states to prevent radical change have overridden commitments to the norms of non-intervention and the maintenance of international peace. Nationalism, at least in its current emotional and exaggerated state, has dealt yet another blow to international co-operation, which of necessity involves a certain subordination of sovereignty to the collective will. Moreover, in the inter-American setting nationalism is particularly devastating to multilateralism, for it usually takes the form of anti-Americanism, and the instrument for collaboration is frequently seen as a mere extension of Washington's will.

Let us turn now to more specific evidence of fragmentation and debilitation in the inter-American system.

There has apparently been a sharp increase in the disenchantment of Latin America with the OAS as a result of the failure of the organization to prevent, or even to condemn verbally, the United States intervention in the Dominican Republic. The reputation of the organization throughout the hemisphere seems to be at an all-time low.[2] Another recent manifestation of the OAS decline was the refusal of the organization, in three hemispheric conferences in 1965–67, to implement a number of structural reforms widely considered to be both necessary and politically realistic. The political capabilities and defined scope of action of the OAS have always been quite limited, reflecting the unwillingness of the Latin American states to dilute their "sovereignty" any more than is absolutely essential, the general distrust of the United States, and the fear of dictatorial and/or conservative régimes of a strong organization that might be capable of applying pressures for domestic change. None the less, before the Dominican crisis there seemed to be considerable agreement throughout the hemisphere on the desirability of revising and strengthening the organization in several important ways.

First, there was strong support for giving the OAS Council a greater role in the peaceful settlement of hemispheric disputes that had not yet broken out into armed hostilities but which had that potential if not defused by international action. Under its existing statutes, the council could deal with political questions only through the mechanism of the Rio Treaty. Invoking that treaty was considered to be a very serious matter, however, for it implied that an act of "aggression" had taken place and suggested the possibility that sanctions would be imposed on the disturber of the peace. Given this interpretation, Rio Treaty action over minor territo-

rial or jurisdictional disputes was usually politically impossible. To fill this gap in organizational political authority and to provide a more flexible mechanism for quiet mediation, the proposed changes authorized the council to suggest methods for the solution of any hemispheric political problem at the request of any member state.

Secondly, there was an apparent convergence of views on the desirability of authorizing the secretary-general to play a role in peaceful settlement procedures. Unlike the United Nations secretary-general, the OAS office had not developed an important political capacity, and there was general agreement that the organization should at least partially remedy this situation. The new roles envisaged were quite modest: the secretary would be authorized to bring to the attention of the council any matter that in his view might threaten the peace of the hemisphere, and he could help mediate such disputes when specifically authorized to do so by the council.

Other more controversial reforms were in the air, although no consensus for them had been attained. Proposals by Ecuador and Bolivia (which had unsatisfied territorial claims against, respectively, Peru and Chile) would in effect have made the council into a compulsory arbitration board, authorizing it not merely to mediate conflicts but to dictate the terms of settlement by threatening to apply sanctions against recalcitrant states. Proposals by Costa Rica and Venezuela would require mandatory diplomatic and economic sanctions (including exclusion from the inter-American system, collective non-recognition, and the denial of economic assistance) against régimes coming into power as a result of coups d'état against democratically elected

2 This theme is developed in my article "The Limits of Legitimization in International Organizations: The OAS and the Dominican Crisis," *International Organization*, XXXIII (winter 1969), 48–72. [See selection 13 (Ed.).]

governments. Finally, some states, led by the United States, were calling for the creation of a permanent inter-American peace force, to serve as the military arm of the organization in future collective actions.

Whatever consensus had existed for even the most modest of these proposals abruptly disappeared in the wake of the American intervention in the Dominican revolution. Suddenly, the overriding concern of most Latin American states became the traditional one of *minimizing* the political role of the OAS, not expanding it. In the ensuing three charter-reform conferences—at Rio de Janeiro in the autumn of 1965, Panama in the spring of 1966, and Buenos Aires in early 1967—the position of the majority progressively hardened. It is an open question whether the council was actually strengthened more than it was weakened. On the one hand, its peaceful settlement role was modestly expanded, for it was given the authority to play a conciliatory role in non-violent hemispheric disputes so long as *all* the contending parties agreed.[3] While this meant, of course, that a state standing to lose by international action could veto a council role, the expansion of the council's formal jurisdiction represented a step forward from the existing situation. (Although the rejection of more far-reaching proposals was in part a reflection of the hostility of states satisfied with their existing borders to the possible reopening of old disputes, it was also clearly a function of the larger reaction

against adding major new powers to an organization that rarely seemed to differ with Washington.)

On the other hand, in some ways the role of the council was diminished. The most important of these is a new provision that the foreign ministers must meet annually instead of in emergency situations only. Thus, in the future many even fairly routine matters that until now have been handled by the council will probably be dealt with at higher levels. The change in procedures reflected the growing suspicion that council delegates, many of whom double as ambassadors to the United States, are more likely to defer to Washington's views than are the foreign ministers.

The strong opposition to any expanded political role for the organization was also reflected in the fate of the other proposed revisions. Hostility to the United States plan for a permanent inter-American military force was so great that it was dropped before the conferences even began. The much more modest suggestions for an increase in the authority of the secretary-general also had to be dropped; indeed the only action taken in this area was a *reduction* in the secretary's term from ten to five years. In an even more significant cutback, the Panama conference terminated the temporary authority granted to the Peace Committee in 1959[4] that later had helped lay the basis for the OAS's post-Trujillo role in the Dominican Republic;[5] just for good measure it was also specified

---

[3] The Ecuadoran proposal authorizing a council role at the request of *any* of the parties was defeated by a vote of six in favor, nine opposed, and five abstaining. (Document 113, Minutes of the 15th Plenary Session, Panama Conference on Amendments to the Charter, 1966).

[4] To "study the relationship between violations of human rights or the nonexercise of representative democracy, on the one hand, and the political tensions that affect the peace of the hemisphere, on the other."
[5] See chapter 5 of Slater, *The OAS and United States Foreign Policy*.

that no future amendment to the statutes of the Peace Committee could restore that authority. Finally, the Costa Rican proposal for sanctions against *golpistas* was whittled down to a meaningless provision for hemispheric "consultation" after the overthrow of elected governments. (Since then, hemispheric consultations after the Brazilian and Peruvian military power seizures have led to no action whatever.)

The decline of the OAS as an important mechanism for the resolution of hemispheric conflicts has been confirmed by the organization's inability to affect, or even deal with, the several South American border disputes (Argentina-Chile, Ecuador-Peru, Bolivia-Chile) that have recently heated up, occasionally even to the point of small-scale military skirmishes. More significantly, the organization has been unable to develop a meaningful role in the process of political change in Latin America. To be sure, this is nothing new, for since its inception the OAS has been deliberately excluded from the internal politics of the hemispheric states (except for its role in the Dominican Republic, a product of some very special circumstances); thus, although the organization in the 1950s periodically reaffirmed its commitment to democracy and social change, it did practically nothing about it. None the less, in the 1960s this gap in organizational action is more serious, for the increased political instability that will almost certainly accompany the process of urbanization and industrialization in Latin America may simply make the OAS irrelevant to the major problems of the hemisphere.

Some qualifications are in order. There are some indications that the organization is not yet moribund. For one thing, the election of Galo Plaza Lasso to succeed José Mora as secretary-general was an encouraging sign, for it was hardly likely that a man of Plaza's experience and stature would have accepted the position without strong private assurances that the office would not be relegated to an administrative clerkship. For another, the Human Rights Commission has been able to continue and even to expand a little its modest work. Despite its clear "interference" in the internal affairs of some hemisphere states, the commission's prestige is now apparently great enough to preclude attacks on it by even the repressive states. In the last few years, the commission has reported on human rights violations in the Dominican Republic, Haiti, Cuba, Paraguay, Ecuador, Guatemala, Nicaragua, and Honduras, and, according to commission members, has often succeeded in obtaining remedial action.

A third indicator of the system's continued viability has been the unwillingness of the Latin American majority to turn in wholesale fashion to the United Nations or other extrahemispheric actors to offset the power of the United States.[6] To be sure, there no longer is automatic Latin American support for the old United States tactic of using the OAS as a shield to fend off any United Nations role in hemispheric

6 See the essay by Michael O'Leary in Robert Gregg, ed., *International Organization in the Western Hemisphere* (Syracuse, 1968). For other discussions of the recent relation of the OAS to the United Nations see Ronald Yalem, *Regionalism and World Order* (Washington, 1965) and Bryce Wood and Minerva Morales, "Latin America and the United Nations," in Norman J. Padelford and Leland M. Goodrich, eds., *The United Nations in the Balance* (New York, 1965).

affairs (e.g., Guatemala, 1954), and as a result the United States was forced to acquiesce in a nominal United Nations role in the Dominican crisis. None the less, even in the Dominican affair there was no Latin American disposition to work *primarily* through the world body rather than the OAS, and after the first wave of anger at the unilateral American intervention, the traditional inclination to close ranks and solve hemispheric problems within the family reasserted itself to a surprising degree.

Finally, despite the recent Latin American refusal to institutionalize important new political capabilities in the OAS, the door to an ad hoc political role is far from closed. Whatever the reluctance to resort to the Rio Treaty, its vague authorization of collective action in the event of any "fact or situation that might endanger the peace of America" continues to provide the juridical vehicle for multilateral action when the majority is so disposed. It is safe to predict that in the foreseeable future organizational political capabilities will not be significantly increased or decreased, with the action of the system reflecting, as in the past, the balance of political forces in each case.

Pursuing this train of thought, one can imagine several kinds of situations in which the OAS might play a major political role, even in the face of the general trend toward minimal organizational action. Paradoxically enough, some of the very forces that have thus far contributed to the decline of the organization could, in certain circumstances, lead to strong collective action. For example, as Latin American political instability, ideological conflict, and even civil warfare intensify, there are likely to be occasions in which domestic political conflict will become so violent or will spill over into interstate conflict at such a level that the organization will be forced to intervene. The tragic Haitian situation already contains all the seeds for that kind of crisis. It is widely feared in both State Department and OAS circles that upon the passing of the Duvalier régime, whether through the death of the Haitian dictator or an internal uprising, the thin fabric of Haitian society will dissolve into bloody chaos. Under such circumstances a major OAS intervention would be far from out of the question, particularly if humanitarian considerations should be reinforced by a Dominican threat to intervene unilaterally or a Cuban attempt to foster a Castroite revolution. Indeed, current contingency planning in Washington envisages the possibility of a long period of OAS trusteeship over Haiti, for the abysmal poverty of the country and the absence of established and reliable political institutions and leadership may leave no other responsible choice.

Similarly, a continuation of United States anticommunist or counter-revolutionary activism in the Caribbean could precipitate reluctant OAS action, much as unilateral American intervention quickly forced the OAS to involve itself in the Dominican crisis. Like the Cuban missile crisis before it, the Dominican affair suggests an interesting hypothesis that is only superficially ironic: the more likely the United States is to act unilaterally if necessary, the more likely it is that in fact the OAS will act. The logic is persuasive enough—in crisis situations defined by the United States as vital to its national interests, the only way the Latin Americans can exercise leverage over Washington's policies is through at least partial co-operation with it.

There are several general directions in which the Organization of American States could now go. One possibility that has considerable support in Latin America as well as some in the United States (e.g., Senator Fulbright) would be a gradual loosening of inter-American ties in favour of all-Latin American groupings. There are some signs that this is already happening, as the Latins increasingly are caucusing together to develop common policies—especially in economic matters—vis-à-vis the United States. Still, as with other such movements in the past, it is doubtful that in the last analysis this trend will go very far, for even the most anti-American governments recognize that it is hardly sensible for

them to jettison gratuitously their major forum for collective influence over United States economic and political policies. It is far more likely that, for the present, the organization will simply continue its recent emphasis on economic and other widely accepted non-political tasks. Later, if the United States should abandon its efforts to use the OAS as an anticommunist alliance and the current wave of nationalistic militarism in Latin America should subside, it is not impossible that the organization could once again emerge as a central institution for common political tasks.

6

Reflections on the Inter-American Principle of Nonintervention: A Search for Meaning in Ambiguity

Yale H. Ferguson

From Yale H. Ferguson, "Reflections on the Inter-American Principle of Non-intervention: A Search for Meaning in Ambiguity," *Journal of Politics*, XXXII, No. 3 (August 1970), pp. 628–54. Reprinted by permission of the publisher.

The editor's aim in this essay is to place the inter-American system's "cornerstone" principle of nonintervention in the perspective of contemporary international legal theory. He rejects as fruitless the search for a "timeless" definition of "intervention" couched in terms of behavior. Nevertheless, he insists that the principle is meaningful when understood as the "flow of decisions" by hemisphere decision-makers regarding the legitimacy of particular kinds of behavior by given actors in the pursuit of specific purposes. Lastly, he suggests how and why norms like the principle of nonintervention change, and he explores some of the implications of this analysis for the Americas.

As any student of diplomatic intercourse in the Western Hemisphere—and undoubtedly many a layman—knows, nonintervention is reputed to be one of the main principles governing inter-American relations.

In its present formulation in the Charter of the Organization of American States, the principle stands as a monument to generations of Latin American statesmen and jurists who labored for its adoption. This nonintervention norm goes far beyond the rule often attributed to general international law, as well as the Article 2(4) prohibition in the United Nations Charter of "the threat or use of force against the territorial integrity or political independence of any state, or in any other manner inconsistent with the Purposes of the United Nations," and perhaps also beyond Article 2(7) of the UN Charter which (with the sole exception of enforcement measures under Chapter VII) requires the world organization to abstain from intervening in matters that are "essentially within the domestic jurisdiction of any state."

Article 15 of the OAS Charter provides:

No State or group of States has the right to intervene, directly or indirectly, for any reason whatever, in the internal or external affairs of any other State. The foregoing principle prohibits not only armed force but also any other form of interference or attempted threat against the personality of the State or against its political, economic and cultural elements.

Article 16 elaborates on the principle to include "the use of coercive measures of an economic or political character in order to force the sovereign will of another State and obtain from it advantages of any kind." Article 17 adds: "The territory of a State is inviolable; it may not be the object, even temporarily, of military occupation or of other measures of force taken by another State, directly or indirectly, on any grounds whatever." Moreover, Article 8 declares that "the fundamental rights of States may not be impaired in any manner whatever"; and Article 13, that "each State has the right to develop its cultural, political and economic life freely and naturally." Taking all of these provisions together, one can hardly imagine the norm of nonintervention stated in more sweeping terms.

Thus speaks the OAS Charter, and it is a pronouncement of considerable significance. As John C. Dreier comments perceptively, the OAS is "first of all a repository or an institutionalization of those principles and ideals which form the mystique so dear to the Hispanic mind." "Mystique" is the key word. To Latin Americans, legal doctrine has always been linked in Plato-like fashion to an "ideal world of absolutes and perfect forms," those matters of supreme importance by which the real world is to be judged.[1]

In this sense, the nonintervention rule has been the object of "ritualistic veneration."

On the other hand, it is impossible to appreciate fully the special sanctity and emotional aura—let alone the repeated controversies—surrounding the nonintervention principle[2] without an awareness of the long and bitter struggle from which it emerged and a grasp of many aspects of the complex hemispheric environment of today. Obviously, there is more to understanding the nonintervention norm than pouring over treaty phraseology or noting the frequency of its invocation on official occasions. However, what else is necessary to understanding is far from clear.

What indeed is the nature of the "intervention" that the principle forbids and the practical effect of the norm's existence upon inter-American relations?

Regrettably, despite the prominent place which the principle of nonintervention has occupied in the affairs of this hemisphere, scholars have yet to subject it to the kind of rigorous examination and systematic analysis that it deserves. Many writers content themselves with the hardly profound (and even somewhat misleading) remarks that the principle is the cornerstone of the inter-American system and that it

---

[1] "The Special Nature of Western Hemisphere Experience with International Organization," in Robert W. Gregg, ed., *Inter-*

national Organization in the Western Hemisphere, (Syracuse: Syracuse University Press, 1968), pp. 20, 13.
[2] Robert N. Burr suggests the "almost sacred role" of nonintervention in the foreign policies of Latin American governments and the "minds and emotions" of Latin American leaders is analogous to that of the Monroe Doctrine in the United States. (*Our Troubled Hemisphere: Perspectives on United States-Latin American Relations* [Washington: The Brookings Institution, 1967], p. 82.)

constitutes the formal expression of Latin American governments' concern for the protection of their sovereign rights vis-à-vis the "Colossus of the North." Some proceed with an explicit or implicit assumption that the meaning of the rule is obvious; others, noting seemingly contradictory behavior on the part of the American states, dismiss it as a shibboleth; still others feel obliged to define it for themselves, apparently hoping to settle questions of meaning once-and-for-all or (more defensibly) attempting to make research more manageable. A number of authors neglect the wider implications of the patterns they casually observe.

At the root of the problem of comprehension is the fact that serious discussion of intervention has been nearly monopolized by scholars who maintain a traditional legalistic view of international law or by students of international relations who regard law as at most tangential to their concerns. Both groups have failed to place the nonintervention principle in the perspective of an increasingly substantial body of contemporary international legal theory, which might help to reveal the deficiencies in current scholarship and point the way to better.

DEFICIENCIES OF TIMELESS DEFINITIONS

A perennial approach to giving meaning and content to the principle of nonintervention which must be rejected at the outset is the search for a firm, timeless definition of intervention couched in terms of behavior. One might be inclined to pass over this approach with little comment, except that several distinguished scholars and even the OAS itself have suc-

cumbed to its surface promise of being a relatively easy way to bring intellectual order out of empirical chaos.

Among those who emphasize definitions are both those who place their confidence in existing treaty phraseology and those who offer or grope for an "improved" definition of their own.

One of the most prominent writers who stressed the "plain and natural meaning" of the written rule was the late Mexican jurist and scholar, Isidro Fabela. In his ambitious study *Intervención,* he strongly asserted that the language of the OAS (and UN) Charter(s) was clear enough for anyone to understand who had a sincere desire to do so. To Fabela, the OAS Charter meant what it said and said what it meant: absolute nonintervention except for the inter-American peace and security measures specifically exempted by Article 19. And, incidentally, in his opinion, Article 15 undoubtedly prohibited the sort of collective meddling that the United States was promoting in the hemisphere as essential to defense against Communism.[3]

For an example of a legalistic attempt to write a new definition, one may turn to the major works of Ann Van Wynen Thomas and A. J. Thomas, Jr.[4] They note that "there is no satisfactory agreement among jurists as to the meaning and content of intervention in international law" and that "not only the authorities but also the

---

[3] Fabela (México: Escuela Nacional de Ciencias Políticas y Sociales, 1959), pp. 266–291, 300–307.
[4] *Non-intervention: The Law and Its Import in the Americas* (Dallas: SMU Press, 1956) and *The Organization of American States* (Dallas: SMU Press, 1963).

practices of states are in confusion."[5] Nevertheless, they seem intrepid enough in developing their own definition, "reasoning from principles and sources of the law of nations and evaluating acts and declarations of states." According to the Thomases, "intervention occurs when a state or group of states interferes, in order to impose its will, in the internal or external affairs of another state, sovereign and independent, with which peaceful relations exist and without its consent, for the purpose of maintaining or altering the condition of things."[6] In their view:

It is then the constraining nature of the act of interference which undoubtedly constitutes intervention whether the act is one involving the use of force or one involving a lesser type of compulsion, i.e., political or economic. A mere friendly interference such as a tender of advice or an official communication requesting a state to take or refrain from taking certain measures, or the offer of good offices or mediation wherein there is no element of compulsion present, is not intervention. . . . The essence of intervention is the attempt to compel, . . .[7]

The Thomases emphasize the fact that their definition concerns itself with "intent" in the legal sense rather than with the more general concept of "motive." "In law, it is properly inferred that one who does an act wilfully intends the natural and proximate consequences of the act. A state is thus presumed to have willed the results of its action."[8] The principal determinant

is still the nature of the act in question.

The OAS itself has condoned and even encouraged attempts to express the principle of nonintervention in a more definitive manner. Most notably, in 1959 the Fifth Meeting of Consultation of Ministers of Foreign Affairs in Santiago, Chile, called for the preparation of "a draft instrument listing the greatest possible number of cases that constitute violations of the principle of nonintervention."[9] This initiative did not envisage changes in the language of the Charter; rather, it aimed at authoritative interpretation through an enumeration of the types of situations to which the hemisphere norm applied.

Fulfilling the Santiago meeting's mandate, the Inter–American Juridical Committee (IAJC) formulated a Draft Instrument on Violations of the Principle of Nonintervention for the eventual attention of the projected Eleventh Inter–American Conference. Drawing in scissors-and-paste fashion from the OAS Charter, the 1928 Habana Convention on the Rights and Duties of States in the Event of Civil Strife, and various inter-American resolutions and declarations, the IAJC

---

5 Thomas and Thomas, *Non-intervention,* p. 69.
6 *Ibid.,* p. 71.
7 *Ibid.,* p. 72. For the same definition and concomitant explanation in *The Organization of American States,* see pp. 160–162.
8 Thomas and Thomas, *Non-intervention,* pp. 72–73.

9 Text of Santiago conference Resolution VII is reprinted in OAS, PAU, IAJC, *Instrument Relating to Violations of the Principle of Nonintervention,* Doc. No. CIJ-51 (English) (Washington, 1959).
  The decision to prepare such an instrument was largely a response to the Caribbean turbulence that had occasioned the Santiago meeting. In the spring of 1959, Panama and Nicaragua were the targets of abortive invasions, apparently encouraged by Castro's success in overthrowing the Batista dictatorship. Moreover, the Trujillo regime charged that the Cuban and Venezuelan governments had supported two unsuccessful landings on Dominican shores and that more invasions were in preparation.

enumerated only twelve forms of intervention. Among these were the following:

1. Any form of interference or attempted threat against the personality of a state or against its political, economic, social, and cultural elements;
2. The permitting of traffic in arms and war material that it is suspected are intended for the purpose of starting, promoting, and aiding civil strife in an American state;
3. Acts of duress that constitute a direct effort to impose upon another country a particular organization or government and also any subsequent acts designed to maintain the imposed situation;
4. Acts by which it is attempted to impose or there is imposed upon a state the recognition of a privileged status for aliens beyond the rights, remedies, and guarantees granted to its nationals under local law;
5. The abusive use of recognition of governments in contravention of the norms established by international law as a means of obtaining unjustified advantages.[10]

James N. Rosenau, a leading international relations theorist, also attempts to formulate a definition of intervention, but with quite a different objective in mind from those seen by Fabela, the Thomases, and the OAS. He is not directly concerned with illuminating the content of the nonintervention rule, but with finding an "operational" concept of intervention that will give the scholar a workable framework for further theoretical inquiry. Rosenau draws a careful distinction between intervention as "empirical phenomenon" (tied to the "common sense" usage of citizens and statesmen) and "analytic concept" (his

operational definition).[11] He questions the utility of the common sense usage that he reads as allowing "any action directed against another nation"—or "even the absence of action"—to be regarded as intervention. In his view, interventions can be distinguished from other phenomena in international politics by their "convention-breaking character" *and* their "authority–oriented nature." He thus suggests that we "describe the behavior of one international actor towards another as interventionary whenever the form of the behavior constitutes a sharp break with then-existing forms *and* whenever it is directed at changing or preserving the structure of political authority in the target society."[12] In addition to avoiding a vague, common sense usage, Rosenau argues, a decided advantage of such an operational definition is that it "obviates the enormously difficult task of tracing motivation."[13]

Attempts such as all of the foregoing to offer a timeless definition of intervention are well-intentioned, but they do not accomplish their purpose. They confuse more than they clarify.

10 *Ibid.,* pp. 16–17. The listing here does not follow the same order as the original.

11 "The Concept of Intervention," *Journal of International Affairs,* 22, No. 2 (1968), pp. 174–75.
12 *Ibid.,* pp. 166–67. Rosenau does not specifically relate his definition to norms, although one may perhaps assume that norms, written or unwritten, formal or informal, are analogous to the "convention" that he sees intervention as "breaking." The second half of his definition is considerably less flexible and less time-conscious than the first. It should also be noted that Rosenau does remark: "No claim is made, . . . that my formulation can or should be the last word on the subject" (p. 172). For Rosenau's later attempt to construct an initial theory of intervention based on his definition, see "Intervention as a Scientific Concept," *Journal of Conflict Resolution,* 13 (June 1969), pp. 49–71.
13 "The Concept of Intervention," pp. 170–71.

Those scholars and statesmen like Fabela who place their faith in the plain and natural meaning of Article 15 and other provisions suffer in their reasoning from what Myres S. McDougal has called the "fallacy of the unambiguous meaning" or the "fallacy of univocalism," the assumption "that words have an absolute meaning, independent of their users and interpreters, and independent of objectives and contexts." As McDougal asserts: "It is no longer revolutionary, . . . to point out that the effort to impose upon any language of a complicated multilateral treaty . . . —an 'absolute,' 'literal,' 'plain,' or 'natural' meaning puts an impossible burden on words,"[14] What is unfortunate is that "the language of the rule encourages an exaggerated assumption of clairvoyance on the part of the reader of a text, and de-emphasizes an open–eyed quest for relevant information."[15] Those who lean heavily on Vattel's dictum that "it is not permissible to interpret what has no need of interpretation" undoubtedly deserve the tongue-lashing that McDougal and his associates deliver, to wit: "Among the reiteraters of Vattel's maxim, we can observe the unmistakable spore of unacknowledged failure which would appear inevitably to accompany bringing an analytic sequence to a premature end."[16]

The absurdity of the plain and natural meaning approach is even more apparent when one recalls not only the continuing controversy over Article 15 but also a few other examples of the past indeterminacy of the concept of intervention both in and out of the hemispheric context. For instance one might refer to the confusion in classical international law over the distinction between "self-serving interference" and actions undertaken by states supposedly to enforce general community standards of behavior.[17] Or to the question of what forms of coercion constitute illegal intervention in the light of UN Charter Articles 2(4)[18] and 2(7),[19]

---

obvious fact is that the phrase-focused interpreter cannot entirely blind himself to the larger features of the dispute, although his cadaver-like obedience to the textualist command may result, when his glance strays toward *travaux préparatoires,* in sensations akin to those said to be enjoyed by a peeping Tom. At the margin of full waking attention the decision–maker may allow himself to learn enough about the relative strength of the contending parties at the time of negotiation, and other realistic detail, to accept— or to question—his first reading of the provisions of the treaty. Whether the interpreter fully admits the necessity to himself or not, the judgment of the supposed 'plainness' or 'simplicity' of meaning of the words depends on these elicit glimpses of the context. When relevance is a grudging concession to that which cannot be avoided, realism of interpretation is not done away with entirely; rather it is either mutilated or shriveled to a caricature of its potentiality" (pp. 363–64).

[14] "International Law, Power and Policy," in Academie de Droit International, *Recueil des Cours,* 82 (1953), p. 151.

[15] McDougal, Harold D. Lasswell, and James C. Miller, *The Interpretation of Agreements and World Public Order: Principles of Content and Procedure* (New Haven: Yale University Press, 1967), p. 97.

[16] *Ibid.,* p. 361. For further discussion of the necessity for active interpretation of *any* written rule, see especially pp. 6–12, 35–39, and 361–78. A single quotation reflects the tenor of the argument on this point: "The

[17] See Richard A. Falk, "The Legitimacy of Legislative Invervention by the United Nations," in Ronald J. Stranger, ed., *Essays on Intervention* (Columbus: Ohio State University Press, 1964), pp. 37–38.

[18] See William T. Burke, "The Legal Regulation of Minor International Coercion: A Framework of Inquiry" in Stanger, *Essays,* pp. 92–93.

[19] See Leland M. Goodrich, *The United*

especially as these provisions are qualified by Article 51's guarantee of the "inherent right of individual or collective self-defense" in the event of an "armed attack" and the grant of a measure of autonomy to regional organizations under Articles 52–53.[20] Or to the evolution of the United States government's interpretation of the pre-OAS nonintervention principle initially accepted at the Montevideo Conference in 1933.[21]

If one thing in the record is clear, it is that the concept of intervention has defied unambiguous formulation in general international law and the particular international law of the United Nations and the Americas. No formal legal provision relating to it has ever had a plain and natural meaning in the sense that Fabela and others imply. This background might also give fair warning to those who seek to develop their own timeless definitions. Upon closer examination, such definitions appear to be open to the preliminary objection that they are either too general or too specific. Definitions on the order of the Thomases' and Rosenau's are unlikely to gain widespread acceptance because they are hardly improvements over the existing rules. Each of them has within it its own incipient controversies. Were the Thomases' general definition somehow

miraculously substituted for Article 15, one could easily imagine the debates that would rage as to whether a given unilateral or collective action was an "attempt to compel" or merely "friendly interference" or whether a state had or had not given its "consent" to intervention. For his part, Rosenau himself constructively offers his readers a sample of the criticisms directed at his relatively specific definition when he presented it before a Princeton conference on intervention:

In the words of one critic, "The definition sacrifices relevance for precision." A number of conferees reiterated this idea by citing examples of significant historical episodes that endured for years—thus losing their convention-breaking character —and that they had always classified as interventions, but that fell outside the scope of the definition. Others criticized the narrowness of the formulation by noting that it omitted foreign aid programs, which they had always regarded as interventionary because the aid-givers can profoundly alter economic and social structures even though alteration may not also occur in the authority structures of the recipient societies.[22]

Any effort to list various cases of interventions like that undertaken by the OAS is also too specific in intent. It is virtually impossible to draw up a list of violations that will satisfy all those who have a say in its adoption. One practical political virtue of a general definition is its very generality, its convenient susceptibility to a wide range of interpretations and thus acceptability to a number of different points of view. The outlook for the draft instrument prepared by the IAJC

Nations (New York: Crowell, 1959), pp. 74–79.

[20] See Inis L. Claude, Jr., "The OAS, the UN, and the United States," *International Conciliation*, No. 547 (March 1964).

[21] See the following by Bryce Wood: *The Making of the Good Neighbor Policy* (New York: Columbia University Press, 1961) and *The United States and Latin American Wars, 1932–1942* (New York: Columbia University Press, 1966), esp. Introduction and Part Four.

[22] Rosenau, "The Concept of Intervention," pp. 171–72.

has never been auspicious principally because it includes such questionable cases as the following: "Acts by which it is attempted to impose or there is imposed upon a state the recognition of a privileged status for aliens beyond the rights, remedies, and guarantees granted to its nationals under local law." In an era when the American states maintain divergent positions on the rights of aliens, consideration of this provision would be sure to reopen a great many old wounds. Moreover, many governments undoubtedly share the opinion of James Oliver Murdock, the dissenting U.S. jurist on the IAJC, that the adoption of any list of cases might well "create a false sense of security." He warned:

The appropriate organs of the Organization of American States would have a tendency to consider of less importance the acts not mentioned in such a list. The omissions would encourage the intervenor to distort the definition or might delay action by the Organization of American States. Furthermore, in the other cases listed, automatic action by the appropriate organ of the Organization of American States might bring premature application of corrective measures.[23]

At the center of many of the difficulties encountered by all the above and similar definitional attempts is the fact that they inevitably reflect the subjectivities of their author. The danger is that this subjectivity may be unrepresentative of a broader spectrum of much more relevant opinions. In this vein, and even more basic than our criticism that definitions do not offer an improvement over Article 15, is the

point that they are certainly less "official." The Charter version enjoys an exalted position today precisely because (at least in 1948) it was a compromise formula acceptable to all the American governments—a mutual statement of *their shared* subjectivities. To date there is no formal substitute or supplement, and the non-progress of the IAJC draft declaration indicates that there are unlikely to be drastic developments in this regard for the foreseeable future.

There remain difficult decisions to make, and it matters very much who makes them. Each decision-maker unavoidably brings various predispositions to bear on his (its) conclusions as to the legitimacy or illegitimacy of certain forms of behavior. Fabela and John Foster Dulles, for example, held quite different views on the legality of the anti-Communist declarations that the United States presented for approval at the 1954 Caracas Conference. Not the least important consideration is which decision-maker(s) is (are) most authoritative in each individual case. The opinions of Fabela and Dulles aside, the decision of the Caracas Conference itself was perhaps the one that counted the most at the time. Or were the most significant decision–makers those many Latin American governments who voted with fingers crossed at Caracas and whose subsequent decisions gave little support to the "Dulles Doctrine"?

Another closely-related shortcoming of timeless definitions is that they do not—cannot—make allowances for the various contexts that are going to prove relevant in their application. For instance, a diplomat decision-maker normally brings not only his country's policy objectives to bear in arriving at

23 IAJC, *Instrument Relating to Violations of the Principle of Nonintervention*, p. 23.

his conclusions but often his own personal values as well. Other possible relevant contexts include the precedents from which he reads selectively to determine the content of the nonintervention norm itself and other aspects of the prevailing national and international environments that influence him to defer to what he regards as the community rule to a greater or lesser extent. In this connection, any decision-maker is necessarily influenced by the immediate facts surrounding the behavior alleged to constitute "intervention." As Murdock put it, with reference to the IAJC's draft instrument: *"A priori* definition without regard to the facts of a specific case is unwise. What may be intervention in one instance may by no means be intervention in another instance. Each case must be decided on its merits."[24]

And this brings us to a final criticism: It is futile to rely on timeless definitions precisely because of their timeless quality, or at least their ostensible timelessness. At their potential best, they might derive their inspiration from, and therefore constitute a more-or-less accurate statement of, *current* reality. Any pretense to being something more would be rapidly shattered when the events that mold decisions march on, leaving them as abstract formulations disengaged from the real world.

Thus, to quote Murdock once again, the principle of nonintervention belongs in the category of "primary notions, which by their nature are not susceptible of definition."[25] Likewise, Gordon Connell-Smith is correct in his judgment that nonintervention is "impossible... to define,"[26] and Jerome Slater, in his comment that the Article 15 rule is "quite vague."[27]

On the other hand, we must be careful to avoid the defeatist attitude of writers who are apparently more bewildered than enlightened by past and present practice and who therefore conclude that the inter-American doctrine of nonintervention is a mere platitude. There is no justification for hasty statements such as the following by Norman A. Bailey: "Since [the signing of the Charter in 1948], and, especially since the United States has once again felt its hemispheric paramountcy threatened..., nonintervention, which never, in any case, even in its mildest form, had any validity beyond the willingness of the United States to abide by it, and, in its more extreme forms, never had any validity at all, has in reality become nonexistent as a rule of Inter-American public international law."[28]

To assert that the text of Article 15 is basically ambiguous and to insist that seeking another timeless definition is an exercise in futility is *not* the same as saying that the principle of nonintervention is or has ever been altogether *meaningless*. Quite apart from its specific formulation in various hemisphere agreements, the norm has had a tremendous practical impact on inter-American relations ever since it began to emerge, primarily as a challenge to U.S. policy, in pre-Good Neighbor days. And, as far as the contemporary

---

24 *Ibid.,* p. 25.
25 *Ibid.,* p. 22. The words "definition" and "define" presumably are used here and in the next sentence respectively in the timeless, couched-in-terms-of-behavior sense we have been employing.

26 *The Inter-American System* (London: Oxford University Press, 1966), p. 311.
27 *The OAS and United States Foreign Policy* (Columbus: Ohio State University Press, 1967), p. 24.
28 *Latin America in World Politics* (New York: Walker, 1967), p. 134.

period is concerned, two decades of post-OAS Charter experience in the hemisphere have, so to speak, picked up where Article 15 left off. This experience has demonstrated that the nonintervention rule is in fact anything but nonexistent[29] and indeed has gone a long way towards giving real content to the phraseology of the Charter.

THEORETICAL PERSPECTIVES

How, then, may we view the principle of nonintervention and comprehend the hemispheric experience that gives it meaning?

One may begin by conceding due importance to the status of the principle as a norm in a formal international agreement, the OAS Charter. The very fact that a norm comes to rest in a treaty both gives it an added degree of legitimacy *and* limits the number of possible interpretations of it which bear even the semblance of reasonableness. As Kaplan and Katzenbach remark: "The explicit language of treaties, even if quite general, tends to limit the discretion of national officials rather more than do several formulations over a period of time by several decision makers."[30] To the extent that interpretation rests in the hands of decision-makers trained in the traditional plain and natural meaning

school of legal theory,[31] language becomes even more significant.[32]

Yet Article 15 is hardly a model of verbal clarity; and, in any event, treaty phraseology is invariably ambiguous if only because words do not have absolute meanings. Moreover, the inter-American principle of nonintervention cannot be regarded as existing in isolation from the rest of international law. Even in the OAS Charter, there are inherent conflicts between norms that can never be completely reconciled. Central among these conflicts is that between the nonintervention principle and other norms which either give, or can be interpreted as giving, the organization interventionary authority. As Richard A. Falk remarks about the international legal order in general: "The possibilities of adversary process and the presence of complementary structures of legal norms suggest that challenged action can simultaneously be described as legal and illegal depending upon the doctrinal line of argument adopted."[33]

It is helpful to get away from treaty phraseology and to conceive instead of the principle of nonintervention as

---

[29] Even Bailey concedes: "Latin American statesmen still deal, verbally, in the shibboleths of the 1930's, so that 'nonintervention' as a propaganda device is still a force to be dealt with" (*ibid.*).

[30] Morton A. Kaplan and Nicholas deB. Katzenbach, *The Political Foundations of International Law* (New York: Wiley, 1961), p. 23.

[31] This description would fit most Latin American diplomats. See, for example, H. Jon Rosenbaum, "A Critique of the Brazilian Foreign Service," *The Journal of the Developing Areas,* 2 (April 1968), pp. 384–385.

[32] One of the principal criticisms leveled at the so-called Yale (or New Haven) school of legal theory, which we draw heavily upon below, is that it fails to take into account the fact that decision-makers so often do earnestly strive to discern the meaning of treaty texts—and then turn to the broader purposes of the agreement for guidance in interpretation when provisions are hopelessly unclear. See Gidon Gottlieb, "The Conceptual World of the Yale School of International Law," *World Politics,* 21 (October 1968), pp. 108–132.

[33] *Law, Morality, and War in the Contemporary World* (New York: Praeger, 1963), p. 33.

part of a network of what Falk has called "horizontal norms," arising from the common or converging behavior of the international community. According to Falk: "A horizontal norm is a descriptive proposition about what nations will probably do in the light of the interplay of event, interest, conscience, and rule; it is a predictive generalization that acts as a comprehensive ground rule for behavior."[34] We may take Falk one step further and classify such norms on the basis of their existence on various levels of international society; for instance, there are regional and subregional as well as universal norms. Furthermore, at any given time some norms are more formal than others, depending upon whether they have been stated in an international agreement. Finally, reflecting the degree of generality or specificity of regular behavior, norms range from the very general to the very specific.

Falk's concept of horizontal norms is a liberating one, but it still leaves the scholar with a minimum of guidance as to exactly where to look to determine "what the law is." At this juncture, we may welcome McDougal's advice to focus on decisions. McDougal describes decision-making as "a dynamic process in which decision-makers, located in many institutional positions and contexts, are continually creating, interpreting and reinterpreting rules and continually formulating and reformulating, applying and terminating, policies."[35] When we wish to know "what the law is," we must also ask

the question "who are the relevant decision-makers." And, as McDougal explains, the answer involves considerations of both "formal authority" and "effective control." Traditional legal theory views states as the sole subjects of international law and their governments as the only authoritative decision-makers. More progressive theorists would include international organizations as authoritative also, especially as concerns their own powers. But we must in addition look behind or beyond authority to other decision-makers whose decisions are at most controlling and at least influential in the final outcome—to actors, such as national and transnational political parties and non-party groups and their leaders, whose decisions either presently or potentially register at the authoritative level.

It is the task of the scholarly observer to view the decision-making process as a whole, to weigh the relative importance of decisions emanating from numerous sources, and thereby as far as possible to identify current international horizontal norms. From this standpoint, international law *is*—in McDougal's phrase—the "flow of decisions."

McDougal-Lasswell-Miller in their recent study, *The Interpretation of Agreements and World Public Order*,[36] recommend a somewhat less comprehensive outlook than the foregoing to any *community* decision-maker who

---

[34] *Ibid.*, 78. Falk's concept of horizontal norms bears some resemblance to the familiar notion of "custom" in international law but avoids the stringent standard-practice-over-long-periods-of-time requirements of the latter.

[35] McDougal, "International Law, Power and Policy," pp. 182–83.

[36] For an analysis and assessment of the significance of this work, see Richard A. Falk, "On Treaty Interpretation and the New Haven Approach: Achievements and Prospects," *Virginia Journal of International Law,* 8 (April 1968), pp. 323–55. For Falk's further comments, taking into account the reactions of other reviewers, see "Charybdis Responds: A Note on Treaty Interpretation," *The American Journal of International Law,* 63 (July 1969), pp. 510–14.

must render an *authoritative* interpretation of a disputed *agreement*. They suggest that he adopt as his "primary goal" ascertaining the "genuine shared expectations" of parties to the agreement,[37] and they offer him an exhaustive checklist of principles of interpretation ("principles of content and procedure") as a guide in his quest for relevant information.[38] This framework is of interest to the scholarly observer as well, since the decisions of parties to agreements are obviously basic in the flow of decisions which he monitors for indications of current norms (though the scholar may be equally or more concerned with, among other things, the results of the community decision-making process).[39] The factors that McDougal-Lasswell-Miller admit as evidence of "shared expectations" include, but go far beyond, those allowed by even the least restrictive traditional legal theory: *travaux préparatoires,* explicit interpretations of previous agreements by the parties, and so forth.[40] Perhaps most significantly, McDougal-Lasswell-Miller place as much or more stress on the "post-outcome phases" (subsequent conduct and performance) as they do upon "pre-outcome phases" (preliminary negotiations) and the "outcome phase" itself ("the moment of moments, after

---

[37] *The Interpretation of Agreements,* p. 40. Where the community decision-maker cannot ascertain the parties' intentions "because of gaps, contraditions, or ambiguities" in their communications, the authors recommend a "second or ancillary goal" of "supplementing" the expressions of the parties "by making reference to the basic constitutive policies of the larger community which embraces both parties and decision-maker." Finally, McDougal-Lasswell-Miller's third goal for the community decision-maker is "policing and integration," in accordance with which he must refuse to give effect to parties' expectations that stand in "grave contradiction" to "the requirements of fundamental community policy" (p. 41).
[38] See *ibid.,* esp. pp. 44–77.
[39] The information about expectations highlighted by the application of McDougal-Lasswell-Miller principles is of concern to both the scholarly observer and community decision–maker. On the other hand, the nonauthoritative scholar is naturally in no position to undertake "policing and integration," and insofar as he makes recommendations in this respect, he engages in special pleading.
Furthermore, we must be continually aware that few *national* decision-makers are following the McDougal-Lasswell-Miller approach or—if they are—are using it in an "objective" fashion. Drawing on a review by Burns Weston, Falk complains of the "failure of McDougal, Lasswell, and Miller to make explicit the differential considerations that apply in national (as opposed to international) arenas of interpretation. According to Falk: "A decision-maker in [an authoritarian or totalitarian political system] is *capable* of making an enlightened interpretation of a contested provision of an international agreement, but he is virtually incapable, regardless of the merits, of making an interpretation adverse to the policy preferences of the government he serves. I would contend that this element of biased interpretation is present to some extent whenever an agreement is interpreted by a domestic court or foreign office, whatever the national political system, ... The New Haven Approach, if followed, provides a self-aware interpreter acting in good faith with a procedure for attaining greater objectivity than do alternative approaches, but it also provides a way of masking partisanship in an elaborate explication of a decision. In my judgment, McDougal and his direct associates have never adequately acknowledged or dealt with this double potentiality of their method, the one its fulfillment and the other its perversion" ("Charybdis Responds," pp. 512–13).
[40] However, the authors do effectively demonstrate in *The Interpretation of Agreements* (chaps. 3–5) that their principles are generally in accord with many current trends in interpretation. See pp. 361–78 for a summary discussion of "past inadequacies."

past differences have been reconciled and before future differences arise, when the parties integrate and express their shared expectations of common commitment to a future policy"). They hold that the "distinctive significance" of post-outcome phases is their "reflection of the parties' continuing consensus, or want thereof, about the content of their commitment."[41]

Let us recapitulate at this point: The author is suggesting that if we would know what the inter-American principle of nonintervention forbids (or, alternatively, what the regional concept of "intervention" includes), we must turn to the hemisphere actors who are continually engaged in assessing this matter for themselves. We may stress the shared expectations of the parties to the written rule, their consensus or lack of consensus about the nature of their commitment as evidenced by their present conduct and performance. However, our focus must eventually encompass the normally broader spectrum of all relevant decisions stemming from a variety of sources with varying degrees of authority and influence. In a sense, then, we *are* offering a definition of "intervention," but it is one framed in highly relative terms—relative to decisions through time.

As we proceed with our analysis of decisions, we may find it most realistic to posit the existence at any given time of several, perhaps many, nonintervention norms[42]—distinguishable at least by their reference to either uni-lateral or multilateral (organization) behavior and to the purpose(s) that this behavior furthers. Action or even inaction on the part of an individual government may be regarded as "intervention," while the same action or inaction by an international organization may not. Action or inaction in pursuit of one purpose may be regarded as "intervention," while the same action or inaction in pursuit of another purpose may not. Hence a complete statement of a single norm should include no less than a description of what behavior is forbidden or allowed to either an individual government or an international organization in pursuit of what purpose.

It is possible to break down the actor categories of individual government and international organization somewhat further. For example, what is forbidden or allowed by hemisphere decision-makers to the United States (the Colossus of the North) *may* not be the same as that forbidden or allowed to Cuba (a self-styled Marxist-Leninist regime), to Venezuela (a democratic-left government), to Peru (a neo-Nasserite military government), to Paraguay (a rightist dictatorship) —or to particular *ad hoc* coalitions of governments.[43] Moreover, decision-

---

[41] For an analysis of the process of agreement, from which McDougal-Lasswell-Miller derive many of their principles, see *ibid.,* pp. 14–20.

[42] Or a single norm with several or many different facets.

[43] It is obvious that Latin Americans have customarily been more concerned about Yankee incursions than those of Latin American governments in general. C. Neale Ronning writes of Latin Americans' "obsession with 'the one great threat' ": "There is a definite tendency among Latin American writers to avoid the unpleasant facts of conflict among the Latin American states, . . . Thus the problem of intervention in the Western Hemisphere has been viewed almost exclusively as a struggle in which Latin American states were defending themselves against intervention by the United States (and a few Great Powers in Europe)...."

makers naturally also make important distinctions between the OAS,[44] LAFTA, CACM, ODECA, and other subregional organizations or alliances.

Likewise, one can imagine various classifications of action-inaction, ranging from the use/non-use of force (landing marines, assassination, guer-

---

(*Law and Politics in Inter-American Diplomacy* [New York: Wiley, 1963], pp. 64–65. See also Ronning, ed., *Intervention in Latin America* [New York: Knopf, 1970].)

However, the political leaders of Latin America have not been able to avoid passing formal and informal judgment on various confrontations between Latin American governments (especially in the Caribbean) over the past two decades, and this gives the scholar an interesting set of decisions to analyze. The record at least reveals a tendency to condemn actual physical assaults on other governments and the extension of direct material aid to guerrilla or exileinvasion groups, whatever the character of the regimes involved or the ideological implications of the change that has been sought by these actions. Regardless of their diverse attitudes towards the Castro regime, Latin American governments were virtually unanimous in expressing strong disapproval of Cuba's assistance to guerrilla campaigns in Venezuela and Bolivia. They also denounced the pro-democracy machinations of the "Caribbean Legion" in the late 40's, resolved to aid Costa Rica in fending off Somoza-supported exile attacks in 1948 and 1955, levied sanctions against Trujillo for his role in a plot to assassinate President Betancourt of Venezuela in 1960, and on several occasions reminded both the Dominican Republic and Haiti to respect one another's sovereignty.

[44] Whether the OAS is itself bound by the nonintervention rule has been a question of some importance to scholars and within the organization. The language of Article 15, forbidding intervention by a "group of States," offers little guidance; indeed, there is every evidence that at the time of the framing of the Charter, the American governments were of different minds as to the desirability of hamstringing the OAS and purposely seized upon the "group of States" phrase as a means of leaving the issue open. (See the Pan American Union Governing Board's *Draft Declaration of the Rights and Duties of American States* and governmental comments thereon [esp. pp. 22–24, 29] and

the debates at Bogotá, in Colombia, Ministerio de Relaciones Exteriores, *Novena Conferencia Internacional Americana, . . .: Actas y documentos,* 3 [Bogotá, 1953–1954], esp. pp. 8, 162, 221–223.) In 1959, the Fifth Meeting of Foreign Ministers requested an opinion from the IAJC on a Mexican proposal for a declaration specifically prohibiting the OAS from intervening "in matters that are essentially within the domestic jurisdiction of its members." (The texts of the Mexican proposal and Santiago conference Resolution V are reprinted in OAS, PAU, IAJC, *Opinion on the Legal Aspects of the Draft Declaration on Nonintervention Presented by the Mexican Delegation,* OEA/Ser.I/VI.2/CIJ-58 [English] [Washington, 1961], pp. 1–2.) The IAJC concluded that "there is no vacuum in the inter-American system that makes necessary a special rule to protect the reserved jurisdiction of the states, a circumstance that was surely taken into account by the draftsmen of the Charter who, with knowledge of the provisions of Article 2(7) [of the UN Charter] did not adopt them" (*Ibid.,* p. 18).

As a matter of fact, those governments anxious to see the OAS take a more active role in hemispheric affairs have *not* generally seized upon the potential loophole in Article 15 in support of their proposals. They have not done so, in the first place, because they have been well aware of the strength of the opposition. But the major reason is that they have found better arguments, principally that pursuit of the principles and purposes embodied in the Charter (equally vague as Article 15) is *not* "intervention." Only "measures adopted for the maintenance of peace and security in accordance with existing treaties" are explicitly exempted from the constraints of the nonintervention norm by the Charter (Article 19); however, it has been quite possible to maintain that Article 19 says nothing about such measures being the *sole* exception and/or to insist that the collective action proposed has a direct or indirect bearing on peace and security.

rilla infiltration, show of force, etc.) to the mere expression/non-expression of opinion (official condemnation, unofficial "leaks" to the press, etc.). And purposes: protection against threats to security emanating from outside the hemisphere, meeting subversion stemming from a hemisphere source like Cuba, squashing internal radical revolution, promoting democracy, protecting human rights, fostering economic development, engineering social change, protecting the lives of nationals, safeguarding the foreign investments of nationals, and so on.

We should note, too, that these categories are inherently interrelated. It might be hypothesized that decision-makers make distinctions between actors at least in part on the basis of the prevailing "images" of these actors, which images themselves are an amalgam of actors' presumed actions and purposes. For instance, many Latin Americans have long viewed the OAS with blanket suspicion because of its identification with U.S. security interests, and Latins were also more inclined to give the United States the benefit of the doubt during the Kennedy than the Johnson years. Actions are also taken as evidence of purposes: Witness the fact that, quite apart from what Washington thought or said it intended to do in the 1965 Dominican crisis, critics gauged from press reports that U.S. forces on the spot were interpreting "neutrality" in ways prejudicial to the Constitutionalists.

It is worthy of re-emphasis that what we are seeking in the end are merely "predictive generalizations" or "ground rules of behavior." We surely cannot expect to discover norms applying to actor behavior in all situations. Neither can we expect actors to abide by norms, nor decision-makers to reaffirm (let alone enforce) them, under all circumstances.[45] We have not entirely eliminated the problem of deviant cases arising from the immediate context in which behavior occurs, one of the bases for criticizing the timeless-definition approach above. But by keying our observations to decisions through time we have a better notion of where explanation for deviant cases lies (in decisions and their sources), and we can recognize the need—beyond simple scholarly open-mindedness —continuously to reassess the viability of the norms we identify.

There is no denying that the suggested approach involves formidable tasks of observation and judgment. Rosenau warns: "What officials and citizens call 'intervention' may be the complex result of multiple processes for the analyst, and he will never comprehend these processes if he allows the subject of his investigation to define his terms for him."[46] Nevertheless, there would seem to be little choice except to do generally what Rosenau deplores, though we may avoid a strictly common-sense conception by weeding out the opinions of the proverbial man on the street. "Convention-breaking, authority-oriented" behavior certainly merits the attention of the scholar; but it is not necessarily the

[45] Norms in the sense of standards of behavior may exist even though "violations" call forth no greater penalty than widespread expressions of disapproval. Of course, decision-makers' attempts (especially successful attempts) to force compliance with standards by means of sanctions or reprisals give norms additional substance.

[46] Rosenau, "The Concept of Intervention," p. 175.

same notion of "intervention" that holds practical meaning in diplomacy. Why confuse matters by so labeling it? One can learn a great deal by recalling that few hemisphere decision-makers cried "intervention" when President Kennedy dispatched U.S. warships to Dominican waters to forestall a coup by the remnants of the Trujillo family in 1961. Convention-breaking, authority-oriented behavior? Undoubtedly. Lesson? At least in 1961, a U.S. attempt to prevent the reestablishment of a widely despised dictatorship by a modest unilateral show of force was *not* "intervention." Similarly, there was strikingly little overt hostility in Latin America to the Kennedy government's policy of nonrecognition of governments arising from coups.

Not all experience resolves in such a clear-cut fashion. The scholar following the flow of decisions may often find actors in serious disagreement. Since the late 19th century, there have been no less than two contending positions regarding the legitimacy of diplomatic pressures exercised on behalf of private claims. Latin Americans have increasingly subscribed to the Calvo Doctrine, holding that aliens have no right of appeal beyond that established by law for nationals in the country involved; on the other hand, the United States has doggedly defended the traditional rule that diplomatic protection is legitimate when citizens abroad are "denied international minimum standards of justice." In the period after the Second World War, Latin Americans have also differed markedly with the United States—and among themselves—regarding the seriousness of the Communist threat to the hemisphere and the nature of appropriate unilateral and multilateral responses to it. Many Latins initially viewed radical-left regimes in Guatemala and Cuba as largely domestic products, and they suspected that Washington's concern derived primarily from these regimes' attacks on U.S. private investment and general anti-Yankee postures. At the same time, conservative civilian and military governments have exceeded even the United States in anti-Communist zeal. To the extent that investigation reveals a divergence of views comparable to the foregoing examples, norms can be said to be presently in a state of greater or lesser flux.

Thus far we have concentrated on the task of assigning current meaning to the principle of nonintervention. We can gain additional perspective with the realization that many norms are changing even as we attempt to identify them. The word "flow" in the "flow of decisions" is a happy choice, implying as it does that the process of norm-building and norm-destruction is a dynamic and continuing one. What, in fact, are the salient features of this process? How and why do norms change?

Norms develop in an immediate sense through a pattern of claim and concession or assertion and response. For instance: In 1965 the United States sent troops into the Dominican civil war; shortly thereafter, on the grounds that "another Cuba" was in the making, sought and obtained OAS formal underwriting of the operation; and subsequently insisted that the handling of the crisis had not violated the inter-American nonintervention rule. Such an assertion occasions a series of decisions that, taken together, constitute a response that has an unavoidable impact on the norm(s) in question.[47]

In the last analysis, norms change because the behavior of men and their governments changes as they both shape, and find their choices circumscribed by, the world in which they live (their "total environment," to borrow from David Easton). Norms change no more rapidly than they usually do because the environment is relatively stable, significant changes customarily occurring so gradually that they are almost imperceptible for a period of years. The Calvo Doctrine controversy serves as an illustration: It has been as lengthy and indecisive as it has largely because nationalism in Latin America has never increased to a point where governments were prepared to launch a final assault against foreign control of key economic sectors and against the rule of international minimum standards developed in an age of imperialism.

Although the environment is relatively stable, it is often a sudden tide of events that precipitates a flurry of assertions and responses. The Peruvian military government's recent seizure of IPC oil holdings and its other reforms affecting foreign investments have now reawakened interest in the hoary rights-of-aliens problem. One may find evidence of a "demonstration effect" operating out of Peru in the Ovando regime's subsequent expropriation of

---

[47] From an overview standpoint, the crisis represents yet another example of incomplete resolution in the "security against alleged Communist penetration" issue-area, identified above as one in which norms are currently in a state of considerable flux.

The Dominican case was particularly complicated because of decision-makers' lack of information about the character of the revolution taking place in the Dominican Republic and about the Johnson Administration's real motives and actions (whether the U.S. actually feared a Communist take-over or was simply determined to prevent *any* shift to the left in the Dominican government). Regardless of these considerations, most Latin American governments—including a surprising number of conservative regimes—where openly critical of the United States failure to consult with the OAS before acting unilaterally. Hence, although the U.S. disclaimer weighed heavily in the balance, it might be fair to conclude that the scales tipped in the direction of branding the unilateral landing of the marines as "intervention."

On the other hand, reactions to the proposal for a temporary Inter-American Peace Force were mixed and leave the observer with a much more ambiguous impression. Decidedly conservative governments were strongly in favor of OAS action; several more progressive and democratic governments, including Costa Rica and Venezuela, offered reluctant support or abstained; and Chile, Ecuador, Mexico, Peru, and Uruguay were adamantly opposed. Query: In the view of member governments, was the purpose of the OAS action to meet the threat of another Cuba? To facilitate the eventual establishment of another "experiment in democracy" like the eight months of the Bosch regime in 1963? Or to gain influence in an ongoing situation after the Johnson Administration had engineered a *fait accompli?* One or more (and possibly additional) purposes were undoubtedly motivating supporting decision-makers; but the outcomes of earlier OAS debates on the democracy issue and later discussion concerning the establishment of a permanent inter-American peace force indicate that a desire to recapture the initiative from Washington was paramount.

See Jerome Slater, "The Limits of Legitimization in International Organizations: The Organization of American States and the Dominican Crisis," *International Organization,* 23 (Winter 1969), pp. 48–72. Slater argues that the effect of the creation of the OAS peace force was not so much to lend an aura of "collective legitimacy" to previous U.S. measures as it was to "delegitimize" the organization. [See selection 13(Ed.).]

Gulf Oil interests in Bolivia. Earlier, caught up in the vicissitudes of the Cold War, the new radicalism of the Guatemalan and Cuban governments challenged the relevance of security norms built upon World War II precedents (when only Perón provided a hint of things to come). A wave of Latin American democratic-left successes at the domestic level beginning in 1957–58 led to a crisis over the democracy issue in U.S. unilateral policy and the OAS, which eventually subsided after military coups decimated pro-democracy ranks. The Nixon incident and the Castro Revolution dramatized what was hardly a "revolution" in rising expectations and paved the way for the Alliance for Progress— a program not widely regarded as "intervention" in spite of its strong original emphasis on social reform.

As our framework suggests, in an intermediate position between the larger environment and the flow of decisions about norms stand decision-makers. Within the limits of their perceptions, the occupants of interrelated decision-making roles on all levels of national and international society adjust their decisions to environmental change.[48] Over time, new occupants come to fill old roles, new roles develop, and different vertical relationships between roles emerge. The locus of formal authority and effective control over the allocation of values is constantly shifting.

Our capacity to predict future norms therefore hinges primarily upon our ability to predict future patterns of decision-making. Which elites carrying which values will be occupying deci-sion-making roles tomorrow, and at what level(s) will the most important decisions be made? Will future governments in Latin America, by choice or necessity, be more or less responsive to what domestic social sectors (classes, groups, etc.)? What will be the demands and supports emanating from these sectors? Likewise, for inputs from the international environment? Will civilian-oligarchical or conservative military governments continue to predominate in Latin America, or will we see the rise of more democratic–reformist, neo-Nasserite-military, or radical-left regimes? Whatever their character, will hemisphere governments see fit to cede more authority to international organizations? What degree of authority over which values? To which existing or yet-to-be-created organizations? These are some of the questions that remain to be answered.

We are describing the cumulative effect of many shifts in the environment and decision-making structures when we speak of the progressive interdependence that has characterized inter-American relations for the last century-and-a-half. John Bartlow Martin writes: "Sumner Welles' hope for non-intervention in the Hemisphere seems now to belong with Booth Tarkington and heliotrope and the swish of the garden hose at summer dusk."[49] In actuality, the hope antedated Mr. Welles and was always illusory, although it still lingers on in some Latin American circles and among those holding extreme "disengagement" sentiments in Washington today. Absolute nonintervention, like the traditional concept of sovereignty, implies the

[48] No determinism is implied: Decisions themselves may impede, halt, or hasten various kinds of changes in the environment.

[49] *Overtaken by Events: The Dominican Crisis—from the Fall of Trujillo to the Civil War* (New York: Doubleday, 1966), p. 733.

complete separation of domestic and international, of internal and external, affairs. However, as Falk convincingly argues:

In fact, the domestic order has never enjoyed autonomy in any strict sense. It is now commonplace to accept the interdependence of economic, cultural, and military affairs. In fact, nations have always had vital concern with what goes on elsewhere, even if elsewhere is a foreign state. Sovereignty only confers a primary competence upon a nation; it is not, and never was, an exclusive competence. Intervention in some form is an unavoidable concomitant of national existence.[50]

And again:

The power to intervene, whether used or not, is what influences domestic outcomes in another state in an "interventionary" manner. The choice, then, concerns the *form* of intervention. Paradoxically enough, "nonintervention" is one form of intervention.[51]

To recognize the interdependence of states, then, is to recognize the impossibility of nonintervention in any absolute sense. The exercise of influence across national boundaries is inevitable.[52] Indeed the growing literature on "linkages" is only now beginning to reveal just how extensive and deeply embedded in domestic societies cross-national ties are.[53]

International organization in the Western Hemisphere has, of course, built upon interdependence. Advancing by fits and starts and not without periods of reversal or virtual standstill, the *trend* in inter-American relations has been towards curbing the unilateral and extending the multilateral exercise of influence. This trend has naturally been reflected in the flow of decisions regarding the nonintervention rule: While unilateral behavior has been regarded as subject to greater constraints, decisions have, in effect, increasingly narrowed the concept of "intervention" as far as organizations are concerned.

Part of the explanation for the multilateral aspect of the trend is that governments have perceived ends held in common and realized that shared goals can most effectively be pursued through joint effort. For example: Both Washington and Latin American governments have been sufficiently interested in stability to support an active OAS role in the peaceful settlement of disputes, evident most recently in the El Salvador-Honduras "Soccer War." The Alliance was possible because both the United States and Latin Americans were anxious to speed development and believed that a vast hemispheric program was necessary to that end. Visions of a broader base for development and a measure of Latin American

---

[50] Falk, "The Legitimacy of Legislative Intervention," p. 36.

[51] *Ibid.,* p. 39.

[52] Ronning expresses it in terms of the United States role in the Western Hemisphere: "Thus *absolute* non-intervention becomes an impossible and utopian objective as far as the United States is concerned. The political and economic power of the United States is so great that anything it *does* or *does not do* in relation to another American republic influences the political affairs of that republic. Responsible persons in the United States and Latin America will have to face the fact that it will be a matter of deciding *how* and *with what objective* to intervene rather than taking an utterly impossible and unrealistic 'non-intervention' position" (p. 84).

[53] See especially James N. Rosenau, "Pre-Theories and Theories of Foreign Policy," in R. Barry Farrell, ed., *Approaches to Comparative and International Politics* (Evanston: Northwestern University Press, 1966), pp. 27–92; and Rosenau, ed., *Linkage Politics* (New York: The Free Press, 1969).

solidarity vis-à-vis the United States have kept the regional common market idea alive in the face of many obstacles.

On the other hand, especially in the OAS and with respect to security against alleged Communist penetration, task expansion has often derived less from what might be termed creative consensus than from Latin Americans' grudging acceptance of collective responsibility as the only apparent alternative to unilateralism run riot. Presidents Kennedy and Johnson both made it extremely clear that the United States would not hesitate to act alone if the OAS failed to meet its obligations as defined by Washington. A barely sufficient number of Latin American governments responded to Johnson's call in the latest Dominican crisis, not because all of them were enthusiastic about the unprecedented Dominican operation, but because most were loath to forego whatever leverage multilateralizing it could provide them.

In closing, we should stress that the inter-American trend towards de-legitimizing the unilateral and legitimizing the multilateral exercise of influence is only part of the story. Most hemispheric intercourse remains bilateral. Under the Kennedy Administration, a dramatic upsurge in the exercise of unilateral influence for democracy and economic and social development found a generally warm reception in Latin America. Alliance multilateral and Latin American common market institutions still have at best only modest grants of authority. Moreover, the record of OAS task expansion includes the defeat of many bold proposals, an occasional step backward (such as the

successive downgrading of the Inter-American Peace Committee in 1956 and 1966), and numerous initiatives approved by such narrow decisions that they proved inconsequential or even counterproductive. Majority rule has allowed task expansion to proceed along the lines desired by a majority coalition but often, as in the 1965 Dominican case, at the price of alienating an important minority that never came around. Dissenters against the trend of increasing authority for the OAS have judged that sufficient common interests do not exist to provide the basis for common action and/or that, given the fact that one of the members of the organization is a superpower, genuine collective action is impossible. Some of the greatest crises of confidence the OAS has faced have stemmed from the unwillingness of key Latin American states to lend a multilateral figleaf to essentially unilateral policies.[54] Whatever the reasons behind their recalcitrance, however, dissenters virtually one and all have buttressed their positions by invoking the principle of nonintervention.

To the extent that they have done so, and insofar as unilateral and other multilateral behavior is regularly put to the test of its conformity to the nonintervention rule, the inter-American principle of nonintervention remains a formidable barrier between nation and nation and between national and international jurisdiction.

[54] The figleaf metaphor is Slater's. For his insightful overview of the OAS today, which is not quite as pessimistic as his title, see "The Decline of the OAS," *International Journal*, 24 (Summer 1969), pp. 497–506. [See selection 5 (Ed.).]

7

The Relevance of Latin America
to the Foreign Policy of
Commonwealth Caribbean States

Roy Preiswerk

From Roy Preiswerk, "The Relevance of Latin America to the Foreign Policy of Commonwealth Caribbean States," *Journal of Inter-American Studies*, XI, No. 2 (April 1969), pp. 245–71. Reprinted by permission of the author and the publisher.

Roy Preiswerk is a Professor at the Graduate Institute of International Studies in Geneva, Switzerland.

As Professor Preiswerk observes, the emergence of new states faces their leaders and citizens with a question of the "conceptualization of their position in world affairs." The same might be said for the task of students of international relations. In the case of the Caribbean, we are seeing the substitution of much looser Commonwealth ties for the former colonial relationship with the United Kingdom; the development of a new Caribbean subsystem of independent and semi-independent states, which is partially undergirded by CARIFTA; and the convergence of the Caribbean subsystem with the United States and Canada, the Afro-Asian subsystem, and the inter-American and Latin American subsystems. Preiswerk notes that Caribbean leaders have recently been attributing increasing importance to relationships with Latin America, and he examines some of the interests— primarily but not entirely economic—which the two areas appear to have in common. Although he also discerns numerous political and some economic obstacles to a closer association between the Caribbean and Latin America, he believes that there is reason for "moderate optimism" about the future in this regard.[1]

[1] See the following volumes edited by Professor Preiswerk: *Regionalism and the Commonwealth Caribbean* (Trinidad: Institute of International Relations, University of the West Indies, Trinidad, 1970) and *Documents on International Relations in the Caribbean* (Rio Piedras, P.R.: Institute of Caribbean Studies, University of Puerto Rico, 1970). See also Havelock Brewster and Clive Y. Thomas, *The Dynamics of West Indian Economic Integration* (Jamaica: Institute of Social and Economic Research, University of the West Indies, 1967); and Aaron Segal, *The Politics of Caribbean Economic Integration* (Rio Piedras, P. R.: Institute of Caribbean Studies, University of Puerto Rico, 1968).

For the leaders and people of every new state of Asia, Africa and the Caribbean, independence has brought about a dramatic awakening with respect to the conceptualization of their position in world affairs. The loosening of ties with the metropolis, which had been the primary aim of the struggle for independence, suddenly appears in a double perspective. On the one hand, it contains the threat of disintegration of the established social and economic order and, on the other hand, it opens prospects for new bonds and opportunities. After decades or centuries of predominantly bilateral relationships between colony and metropolis, historical links are confronted with the pressures resulting from geographic proximity. The diversification of foreign contacts is a phenomenon of the very recent past. The leaders and inhabitants of Ghana and the Ivory Coast, Nigeria and Niger, Trinidad and Venezuela, or Guyana and Brazil are only now realizing the full impact of their relationship as neighbours. To understand the shock which this process of regional familiarization creates in some situations, the analyst may still study the source of the difficulty of adjustment in a "live" situation. Indeed, the totality of colonial bilateralism, encompassing commercial, political, human, and spiritual relations, can be witnessed in such countries as Martinique or Angola where the outlook of the elites continues to be exclusively oriented towards the metropolis in total ignorance of the Caribbean or African environment.

In the case of the new English-speaking Caribbean States,[1] the development of regional and extra-regional links to compensate for the disintegration of the colonial relationship plays a particularly important role in the formulation of foreign policy. The peculiarity of the situation stems from the fact that the clash of historical and geographical determinants of foreign policy is exceptionally violent: here is a group of Commonwealth countries, appearing on the world scene as small, separate units, with constitutional systems framed according to the Westminster model and with a majority of the populations of African and Asian descent, participating in the same historical push towards self-determination as Asia and Africa, but squeezed geographically between the highly developed and expansive North American continent and the economically underdeveloped Latin American mainland. This sketch of some of the objective determinants of foreign policy reveals four options for the new Caribbean States other than the traditional links with the metropolis.

Firstly, the common bonds established during the eighteenth and nineteenth centuries through forced migration and the joint effort to attain independence call for a political rapprochement with the Afro-Asian group of countries. This is substantiated by the voting behavior of Jamaica and Trinidad and Tobago in the United Nations General Assembly, particularly on such issues as colonialism and racialism. It is also reflected in the visits of the Prime Minister of Trinidad and Tobago, Dr. Eric Williams, to India in 1961 and to Africa in 1964, in the

---

[1] At the recent Heads of Government Conference the term "Commonwealth Caribbean" was officially accepted to designate the English-speaking territories regardless of constitutional status. "Commonwealth Caribbean States" consequently applies to Jamaica, Trinidad and Tobago, Barbados, and Guyana. The term "West Indies" shall be applied as consistently as possible to cover English-speaking Caribbean islands only, exclusive of Guyana and British Honduras.

establishment of a Trinidad Embassy in Addis Ababa, and in the visits to the West Indies of President Leopold Senghor of Senegal, Emperor Haile Selassie of Ethiopia, President Kenneth Kaunda of Zambia, and Prime Minister Indira Gandhi of India.

Secondly, increased relations with the North American continent partly substitute for the declining involvement of the United Kingdom in the Caribbean. The United States and Canada provide new markets for West Indian products, while their private investments and public aid are on the increase. Potential conflicts, such as the liquidation of American military establishments, have been avoided by peaceful settlement, and two West Indian countries, Trinidad and Barbados, have joined the hemispheric collective security system.[2]

The third element in the diversification of the foreign relations of West Indian States and Guyana is reflected in the serious attempts made since 1967 to bring about increased intra-regional cooperation and integration. The establishment of the Caribbean Free Trade Association (CARIFTA) and of the Regional Secretariat on the one hand, and the proposals for the creation of a Caribbean Development Bank and new regional Common Services on the other hand, contain a certain degree of hope that the region can achieve progress in unity despite the failure of the colonial administration to introduce effective and lasting federal structures of government.

Finally, the latest development is to be seen in the increased interest which the West Indies and Guyana begin to attribute to Latin America. In many

ways, some Latin American countries respond favourably to Caribbean overtures and a consciousness of common problems and common goals evolves on both sides. Concrete evidence for this is now sufficiently abundant to justify some detached reflection on the subject. The foremost task of the analyst consists in detecting the motives justifying a rapprochement. These might be rather impressive and could actually lead to rash assertions and false hopes. Thus, an inventory of the obstacles to be overcome may help in measuring the scope of the action required by governments, the business community, the universities and voluntary organizations, as well as the period of time which will evolve, before any tangible changes can be discerned.

EVIDENCE OF COMMONWEALTH CARIBBEAN INTEREST IN LATIN AMERICA

The first significant move towards Latin America originated from Trinidad and Tobago after the advent of the People's National Movement (PNM) in 1956. The aim of the PNM was to liquidate a number of disputes which had affected the relations between Great Britain and Venezuela and to initiate a series of cooperative ventures with the latter country. The disputes concerned such matters as the delimitation of territorial waters, illegal immigration, contraband, fishing, and discriminatory trade practices.[3] When Trinidad and Tobago attained inde-

---

[2] Jamaica also joined the OAS in mid-1969 (Ed.).

[3] See Eric Williams, *History of the People of Trinidad and Tobago* (Port-of-Spain: PNM Publishing Company, 1962), pp. 257–259. See also a summary of the efforts undertaken by the Trinidad Government in a speech by the then Premier, Dr. Eric Williams, to the Legislative Council, 28 August, 1959.

pendence under the PNM's leadership in 1962, most differences with Venezuela had either been eliminated or their resolution had been agreed upon in principle. Some are still unsolved but have lost their inflammatory attributes. The abolition in 1965 of the thirty per cent surtax previously imposed by Venezuela on the products originating from independent Commonwealth Caribbean countries constituted the major reciprocation of the goodwill policy of the Trinidad Government. It cemented the relations existing between the two countries to an extent which made possible, in June 1967, the formal constitution of a Mixed Commission whose terms of reference include the preparation of Trinidad's participation in Latin American integrative schemes, expansion of trade, technical cooperation, education, tourism, migration, joint planning in industrialization, and the harmonization of policies with regard to mineral and petroleum resources.[4]

The second major indication of West Indian interest in Latin America again originated from Trinidad and Tobago, when, in 1967, the Government for the first time propagated the idea of a possible entry into a wider Latin American economic institution. The occasion was the Punta del Este Conference of American Presidents where the Prime Minister of Trinidad and Tobago represented his country as the first West Indian member of the Organization of American States. Together with the other Latin American countries, a firm

pledge to join in setting up a Latin American Common Market by 1980 was made by the Trinidad Government. This means, as an immediate step, that Trinidad must seek association with a particular Latin American integration bloc which would subsequently be merged with others into the Common Market. The choice is, of course, very limited: apart from the rather remote Central American Common Market, the projected Andean Common Market is the only imaginative and promising integrative scheme in Latin America at the present time.[5] Trinidad has indicated her strong interest in this project, although very little publicity has been given to a possible Andean dimension of her foreign policy.[6] In the meantime, the Andean project itself is not progressing sufficiently due, among other factors, to the articulate opposition professed by the Venezuelan business community.

4 A.N.R. Robinson, *The Foreign Policy of Trinidad and Tobago,* paper presented at the Institute of International Relations, University of the West Indies, St. Augustine, 29 May, 1968. The Mixed Commission met in Port-of-Spain in November, 1967, and in Caracas in September, 1968.

5 For an introduction to Andean integration, see Rodrigo Botero, *La Comunidad Económica Caribe-Andina* (Bogotá: Ediciones Tercer Mundo, 1967).
6 In February, 1968, when answering a question from an independent member, the Leader of the Senate only indicated briefly that diplomatic approaches had been made to members of LAFTA and that an invitation to join the Central American Common Market had been received. See *Debates of the Senate* (Hansard) vol. 7, No. 10 (6 February 1968), pp. 612–614. Soon after, the Washington correspondent of a major Caracas newspaper reported that Trinidad was actively preparing to join the Andean Common Market. See "Trinidad Ingresaría en el Grupo Andino de Acelerada Integración", *El Universal,* 17 Febrero, 1968, p. 6. An announcement to this effect by an official of the Trinidad Government was made in Caracas on the occasion of the visit of a trade mission in September, 1968. See "Trinidad Bids to Join Andean Pact", *Trinidad Guardian,* 13 September, 1968, p. 2.

Participation in the Andean group is, according to the draft Pact, restricted to members of the Latin American Free Trade Association. Consequently, it appears that Trinidad and Tobago will, after all, have to join this wider Latin American group, despite the serious deficiencies in the operation of the scheme admitted by the Latin Americans themselves. Based on a concept of simple trade liberalization which has failed to bring about an expansion of trade and the protection of the interests of less developed members,[7] LAFTA is presently undergoing an "agonizing reappraisal" by the protagonists of Latin American integration. The most recent trade figures reveal that, after a period of stagnation, LAFTA has now entered a phase of regression. Indeed, in 1967, intra-regional trade in Latin America has declined for the first time since the Association was founded.[8] Thus, the joining of LAFTA could in no case constitute an achievement in itself; it becomes merely a formal step designed to open access to the Andean group with the ultimate aim of becoming a part of the proposed Latin American Common Market.

The third significant indication of West Indian interest in Latin America comes from Barbados where, a few months after independence in 1966, a senior minister was appointed to the post of Minister for Caribbean and Latin American Affairs. Having joined the Organization of American States too late to participate in the Punta del Este meeting, the country subsequently professed its intention to seek a transformation of its foreign policy which may be considered to be as far-reaching as the one sought by Trinidad and Tobago.[9] The Prime Minister, Mr. Errol Barrow, in a declaration made at the headquarters of the Organization of American States in September, 1968, went even to the point of asserting that

Our community of interests now resides with the members of the O.A.S.

Speaking of future links with Great Britain, he said:

I do not think that anyone in the Western Hemisphere will shed a tear if these connections in the way of trade are severed, because it appears that they will be severed in a unilateral fashion and it is better that we are forewarned and forearmed so that we can make our new alliance with those people who have a community of interests with us.[10]

Jamaica, whose major post-independence shift in foreign policy was in the direction of the United States and

---

[7] See Sidney Dell, *A Latin American Common Market?* (London: Oxford University Press, 1966), particularly at pp. 70–94; 206–217.

[8] Global trade decreased by 45.2 million dollars (U.S.) or 3.1% in 1967. See "A Monthly Report on Latin American Integration," *Comercio Exterior* (Mexico), XIV, No. 11 (November, 1968), 7.

[9] "LBJ looks forward to Barbados Visit," *Trinidad Guardian,* 13 September, 1968, p. 1. Within hours of the adoption of the Punta del Este Resolution, the Prime Minister had announced that Barbados would subscribe to the idea of a Latin American Common Market. See *Sunday Advocate,* 16 April, 1967.

[10] If this severance of trade relations actually occurred, Barbados would be plunged into a serious economic crisis. The other Commonwealth Caribbean countries have always presented their desire to establish new hemispheric links as an additional, not alternative, dimension of foreign policy. See, Government of Barbados, *Address by the Rt. Hon. Errol W. Barrow at the Protocolary Session of the OAS Council Held in His Honour,* 1968, p. 4.

Canada, stretched out a first feeler towards Latin America with the establishment of an embassy in Mexico in 1966. The Prime Minister's report on foreign affairs of that year for the first time mentioned closer links with Latin America as a priority. Plans were made to set up another embassy in Costa Rica, which would also serve Panama, two countries that have traditionally received a strong flow of Jamaican immigrants.[11] In 1968, the Jamaican High Commissioner in Port-of-Spain was also accredited to Venezuela. These moves are only of a preliminary nature and will be followed, if a dynamic Latin American policy is the true aim of the Jamaican Government, by efforts of official and private bodies at increasing trade, cultural relations and, functional cooperation.

In her post-independence attempts to follow the continental vocation which geographical considerations dictate to her, Guayana, the only English-speaking territory on the South American continent, has been severely hampered by Venezuela's claim on a large portion of her territory.[12] However, in September, 1968, she succeeded in establishing closer relations with her other powerful neighbour, Brazil. Apart from the exchange of diplomatic envoys, the two countries agreed on increased commercial and cultural relations and on an improvement of communications.[13] This, incidentally, occurred at about the same time as

Trinidad opened a permanent diplomatic mission in Rio de Janeiro. Brazil thus suddenly emerged as a new partner in economic and cultural cooperation for the Eastern Caribbean countries.

While all the above-mentioned efforts are based primarily on economic considerations or on particular political objectives, the independent Commonwealth countries of the Caribbean have also given evidence of a rapprochement with Latin America in their voting behavior on wider political issues at the United Nations. This observation applies primarily to Trinidad and Jamaica. Both countries identified themselves quite strongly with the Afro-Asian group after their independence in 1962, but later began to operate as effective members of the Latin American group.[14] This was largely the result of the evolution which occurred after the adoption of the Act of Washington in December, 1964, in the attitude of the Latin Americans towards the Commonwealth Caribbean.[15] The change in attitude is striking, when one considers, for instance, that Mr. Robert Lightbourne, Jamaica's representative at UNCTAD in Geneva (1964), together with the representative of Trinidad and Tobago, were rebuffed by the Latin American group when the question of representation on the Trade

<hr>

[11] See Hugh Shearer's report to the House of Representatives, *Activities of the Ministry of External Affairs during the year 1966 and Forecast for 1967/68* (Ministry Paper No. 45, 28 July, 1967).
[12] See below, pp. 107–108.
[13] See *Guyana Journal* (Georgetown: Ministry of External Affairs, 1968) No. 2, pp. 73–76.

[14] In 1963, when outlining the possible alignments of Trinidad and Tobago with particular blocs within the United Nations, the Prime Minister merely mentioned the Latin American group and elaborated in great detail on the importance of the African group. Cf. *The Foreign Relations of Trinidad and Tobago,* Speech to the House of Representatives, 6 December, 1963 (Port-of-Spain: Government Printing Office, 1963), pp. 5–10.
[15] On the Act of Washington, see below pp. 107–108.

and Development Board arose, whereas in 1967, Dr. Patrick Solomon, Trinidad's Permanent Delegate to the United Nations, was the President of the Latin American group in the United Nations and introduced, on its behalf, the compromise resolution on the Middle East Crisis. Today, it is a generally accepted practice to include the Commonwealth Caribbean States in the quota granted to Latin America for representation on international bodies. However, on certain specific issues such as colonialism and racialism, particularly in the southern part of Africa, the Commonwealth Caribbean States feel strongly that their first allegiance continues to lie with the Afro-Asian group.

REASONS FOR COMMONWEALTH CARIBBEAN INTEREST IN LATIN AMERICA

1. ECONOMIC MOTIVES. First and foremost among the reasons explaining the new orientation of some Commonwealth Caribbean States is the desire to devise a foreign policy that will promote the general economic well-being of the population by opening markets capable of absorbing indigenous products, by finding supplies at the most advantageous terms, and by obtaining financial and technical support for economic development. It was the threat of Britain's entry into the European Economic Community under terms unfavorable to the Commonwealth which sparked off the search for new economic partners in 1962 and, again, in 1966. Britain, of course, remains the major market for West Indian agricultural products and is a source of aid, but in view of the uncertainty of the E.E.C.'s position on

the Commonwealth preferential system, the West Indies had to begin, not only to seek a diversification of trade links, but to plan the restructuralization of their economies in order to make their production compatible with the needs of potential customers and suppliers. The pledge made by the Prime Minister of Trinidad and Tobago at Punta del Este came only months after Britain's second move towards the E.E.C.

An alternative course of action was to follow Britain's initiative and to seek association with the E.E.C. Apart from Jamaica, no Commonwealth Caribbean State considered this possibility in 1966. A realistic assessment of the chances of association leads to the conclusion that the E.E.C. has no interest in accepting the Caribbean States and that the continental European markets are already crowded with most of the products of which the Commonwealth Caribbean is a potential supplier.[16] The only reasonable objective of association would, in fact, be to preserve the privileged position which the Commonwealth Caribbean enjoys on the British market, in the event of British membership in the E.E.C.[17] This, however, is no realistic long-term objective, as preferential systems linking an individual E.E.C. member to an outside group are bound to be either rejected at the time of

16 On this point, see the study by the West India Committee, *The Commonwealth Caribbean and the European Economic Community* (London, 1967).

17 Jamaica's position is explained by a stronger dependence on the British market than that of the other Caribbean States. See the statement of the Jamaican Prime Minister, Mr. Hugh Shearer, to the House of Representatives after a visit to Britain, France, Holland and Germany, 2 November, 1967.

admission or phased out rapidly. The bargaining position of Britain in the E.E.C. is rather weak and, despite present assertions to the contrary, will not be exhausted by Britain for a cause which ranks merely among her secondary objectives on the agenda of negotiation with the E.E.C. It would be advisable to remember that twice within five years, Britain was ready to relinquish her position in the European Free Trade Association for membership in the E.E.C. after repeatedly asserting her solidarity with the "Outer Seven."

The foregoing is not intended to mean that efforts at increasing exports to Britain and to the European continent or at obtaining European aid should not be pursued by the governments, business companies or Chambers of Commerce in the Commonwealth Caribbean. On the contrary, there are concrete possibilities of increased economic relations which could be explored much in the same way as in the case of the United States and Canada. The difference with the attempts at closer relations with Latin America is, however, that the economic partners in the developed world, although they may for a long time to come be the most important customers and suppliers, are not prepared to enter into any new, strong, institutional arrangements. The trend in present-day economic policies is towards the liquidation of preferential systems which are an outcome of colonial or other special relationships,[18] and the establishment of regional groupings among

developing countries to balance some of the losses suffered from the gradual closure of traditional markets.

The negative effect of Britain's disengagement from the Caribbean is not the sole motive for a reorientation of West Indian and Guyanese foreign policy. Latin America has enough potential to become an attractive economic partner in its own right. Its population will expand to approximately 600 million by the end of the century and its purchasing power is expected to grow at the rate of 5% per annum.[19]

With regard to economic aid, it must be noted that the participation of Commonwealth Caribbean States in regional integrative schemes promises to lead to additional assistance from the United States. It is a well-known fact that President Johnson encouraged the willingness of Latin American leaders to cooperate among themselves with promises of additional development funds from the United States.[20] Similarly, Caribbean integration has received the support of Britain, the United States, and Canada in the form of contributions to the regional Development Bank. Furthermore, should the United States eventually agree to establish a preferential hemispheric trade system as a new form of aid, despite present trends against the concept, it would be of the utmost importance for the Commonwealth Caribbean to be part of such an arrangement.

As for private foreign investments,

18 For an analysis of the reasons for which even the beneficiaries of preferences should work towards the liquidation of such a system, see Alister McIntyre, "Decolonization and Trade Policy," *The Caribbean in Transition* (Puerto Rico: Institute of Caribbean Studies, 1965), pp. 196–200.

19 See the reports of the Economic Commission for Latin America, for instance, the annual *Economic Survey of Latin America,* published by the United Nations, New York. 20 Meeting of American Chiefs of State, *Declaration of the Presidents of America,* Punta del Este, April, 1967 (Washington: Organization of American States, 1967).

membership in a Latin American Common Market may permit Caribbean countries to end the under-utilization of their production lines for manufactures, which results from the smallness of their markets.[21] Foreign investors are already attracted to the English-speaking countries by virtue of easier communication, exceptionally high literacy rates and political stability. The prospect of being able to cater from such a base for Latin American markets may constitute an important additional incentive to invest.[22]

On still a very small scale, Trinidad's efforts at improving its trade balance with Venezuela are beginning to produce results. The meetings of the Mixed Commission, other negotiations for trade concessions and several exploratory missions of business representatives are bound, in not too distant a future, to increase these gains to a tangible size. Other countries may discover that bilateral arrangements of the same kind are effective in bringing about short-term gains. Thus, there is scope for making a partnership with Latin America a proposition of immediate interest, despite the fact that structural problems will probably account for the postponement of substantial benefits to the long-run perspective.

Since any association between sovereign states must be solidly grounded on mutual interests, it is necessary to briefly point out that Latin America may also expect substantial benefits from increased relations with the Commonwealth Caribbean. Foremost among the elements which West Indian negotiators may throw into the balance are the relatively high purchasing power of the Commonwealth Caribbean equivalent to that of the much larger Central American region, and the low degree to which the import substitution process has been completed in the Caribbean. Furthermore, Latin America, as evidenced by the Table on page 120 has a very large export surplus towards the Caribbean. The beneficiary countries, Venezuela and Colombia, may find it desirable to consolidate their privileged position as oil suppliers by influencing the behaviour of international oil companies through inter-governmental arrangements with the oil-importing countries. Finally, the Caribbean is an important source of bauxite and laterites and constitutes the natural partner in the development of Latin America's metallurgic industry.

2. POLITICAL MOTIVES. In the balkanized third world, the search for a united front defending the interests of the new states and, in some cases, of the other developing countries, is an essential objective of foreign policy. It explains the solidarity, which all West Indian leaders have proclaimed at one stage or another, with the Afro-Asian countries. It also explains, to some extent, the efforts for regional integration in the Caribbean and the new orientation towards Latin America. However, politically, and even more so, economically, the trends towards Afro-Asian solidarity appear to offer little concrete advantage to the newly in-

---

[21] This may be difficult in the short run since most Latin American countries have completed their import substitution programme. See Alister McIntyre, *op. cit.* pp. 208–209. McIntyre argues that the low degree of import substitution in the Commonwealth Caribbean makes regional integration among Caribbean countries more attractive than an association with Latin America.

[22] See Frank Dowdy, "OAS vs ECM: Can We Manage Both?" *Enterprise* (Trinidad and Tobago Federation of Chambers of Industry and Commerce Inc., December, 1967), p. 19.

dependent West Indian States and Guyana. Trade relations are seriously hampered by the cost of transportation. On the political scene, the African and Asian states have only limited opportunities to reciprocate the support received in the United Nations from Caribbean states. On the other hand, the Caribbean itself has no weight as a separate part of the third world under the pressure of Western or Eastern power politics. This is true, not only because of the fragmentation of the Caribbean into English-, French-, Spanish-, and Dutch-speaking parts, but also in view of the more real than apparent rift between Jamaica and the rest of the Commonwealth Caribbean.

The desire to manifest strength through unity naturally points towards an increased alignment with Latin America for the joint defense of common interests on the international scene. The most important such interest is in the field of security. It entails for each Latin American state protection from extra-hemispheric aggression, from unilateral intervention by the United States and from aggression by another Latin American state. The present solution for collective security is the system adopted by the Organization of American States. The Rio Treaty of 1947 protects signatories from extra-regional or mutual aggression. It does not, however, eliminate the danger of unilateral U.S. action, and it is particularly in this respect that the unity of the other states in the hemisphere may be of vital importance.

One of the more recent threats to the security of the established regimes in the hemisphere comes through subversive activities encouraged by the Castro Government in Cuba. Venezuela is a declared target of guerrilla warfare supported by Cuba and there-fore has an active interest in obtaining the cooperation of Trinidad, which has traditionally served as a springboard for infiltrators.[23] But West Indian leaders themselves are fearful of Communist subversion and make no secret of their desire to resist such activities, if necessary in cooperation with other states in the hemisphere.

It is interesting to note that the rapprochement of the Commonwealth Caribbean with Latin America has been paralleled by increased relations with the United States. Membership in the Organization of American States has been widely interpreted in the West Indies as a move towards Latin America, although its major objective was the participation in hemispheric collective security and aid programmes, which are founded primarily upon the military potential and the financial resources of the United States. In fact, the increasing influence of the United States in the Commonwealth Caribbean cannot be separated from the rapprochement between the latter and Latin America. The entry into the Organization of American States serves a variety of purposes, some of which can be attained in partnership with the United States, some in cooperation with Latin America and some by the Organization as a whole.[24] The power vacuum and the economic difficulties

[23] This is true even in the most recent past according to a report in the Venezuelan press. See "Agentes subversives entraron por Trinidad," *El Universal* (Caracas), 10 November, 1968. On 24 September, 1967, the Minister of External Affairs of Trinidad and Tobago told the 12th Meeting of Consultation of Foreign Ministers of the OAS, that Trinidad stood firmly with Venezuela in the conflict with Cuba.

[24] The motives of OAS membership are in themselves worthy of a separate study and will not be further explored here.

which are a result of Britain's disengagement from the Caribbean cannot be compensated for by the Latin American countries, which lack the military capability and the economic resources to provide an immediate alternative. Interestingly enough, strategic and financial considerations are forcing the United States to liquidate her military bases in the West Indies at the very moment of the disengagement from the same area by a friendly extra-hemispheric power. The removal of American troops from the Chaguaramas base, a major element in the control of the Southern Caribbean, may be partly responsible for Trinidad's entry into the OAS, which now extends collective security to an area previously controlled by the United States and Britain. One may speculate about whether this actually means that the United States will, in the future, pursue its interests in the Caribbean with a multilateral blessing. One might think that the United States would hesitate to expose itself again to the hostility of Latin America, which resulted from the originally unilateral intervention in the Dominican Republic in 1965. On the other hand, the action of the Soviet Union in Czechoslovakia, endorsed from the outset by a regional collective security system, gives new strength to the concept of the "immediate spheres of interest," in which either the Soviet Union or the United States are unrestricted in the choice of means for the attainment of vital goals.

The establishment of closer links with the United States is not necessarily a popular idea in the Commonwealth Caribbean. The feeling of substituting one form of foreign domination for another and the unpleasant experiences suffered by many black West Indians in the United States account for the limited enthusiasm which large segments of the West Indian public are able to generate for this development. However, Commonwealth Caribbean Governments have little choice in the matter. They welcome the opportunity which the new relations with Latin America offer to them to balance the increased presence of the United States exercised directly or through the Organization of American States.

OBSTACLES TO A RAPPROCHEMENT OF THE COMMONWEALTH CARIBBEAN AND LATIN AMERICA

1. POLITICAL OBSTACLES The history of the last 150 years has divided the West Indies and Latin America into two entirely separate worlds. Up to 1797 Trinidad was an integral part of the same Spanish Empire as Venezuela. Today, it is a country with a different language, a different population and a different political system.

The struggle between monarchism and republicanism, which was won by the latter ideology through the conversion of the Western Hemisphere in the late eighteenth and early nineteenth centuries, has left a barrier between the West Indies and Latin America until the very recent past. Most Latin Americans were somewhat reluctant to accept the membership in the Organization of American States of Commonwealth countries with a governmental system based on the concept of constitutional monarchy. They had a vague feeling that no state could claim to be truly independent as long as the Queen of England remained its Head. When the Charter of the Organization of American States was drawn up in 1948, the possibility of membership for countries other than the United States and the Latin American Republics was not present in the minds of the draftsmen. Article 3 of the Charter merely referred to the possibility of a "new political entity that arises from the union of several Members" becoming a new member in the place of its composite parts. Awareness of Canada's special position emerged much later and the need to adopt a proper procedure for the admission of new members was only fully realized after the independence of Jamaica and Trinidad. The idea that Latin American countries were generally favorable to the Commonwealth Caribbean during the negotiations leading to the adoption of the Act of Washington in 1964 can hardly be accepted.[25] In fact, the opposition was so substantial that an Associated Press report from Washington in October, 1964, quoted "diplomatic sources" as saying that Trinidad would probably complain to the United Nations if the Organization of American States was unable to fulfill its role as a regional organization by failing to provide rules for the admission of new members.[26]

Monarchism, membership in the Commonwealth, the Queen, and other historical and temperamental differences between the countries and peoples are only partial motives for Latin American suspicions about the new Caribbean states. The major sources of antagonism are disputes over former or present British territories in the hemisphere. Guatemala's claim over the entire territory of British Honduras (Belize), Venezuela's claim over two-thirds of the territory of Guyana[27] and Argentina's claim over the Falkland Islands have resulted in a provision included in the Act of Washington (§ 3) according to which no political entity can be admitted to the Organization of American States "whose territory, in whole or in part, is subject, prior to the date of this resolution, to litigation or claim between an extra-continental country and one or more member States of the Organization of American States, until the dispute has been ended by some peaceful procedure."[28] Guatemala, in particular, has persisted in reserving its position on Belize. In 1955,

---

25 Charles Fenwick argues that "From the discussions attending the possible membership of Canada in the Organization, it would appear that membership in the British Commonwealth of Nations would not be an obstacle. On the occasion of Jamaica's independence, August 6, 1962, the Secretary-General of the OAS sent his congratulations and expressed the hope that emergence as a new State may be a first step which could ultimately lead to its incorporation in the American community of nations." See *The Organization of American States* (Washington, 1963), p. 83. The cable of congratulations was actually a compromise after a heated debate in the Council had persuaded the Secretary-General not to accept the invitation of the British Government to attend the independence celebrations personally.
26 *Trinidad Guardian,* 7 October, 1964. The Act of Washington was adopted in Decem-

ber, 1964. Already on 6 December, 1963, the Prime Minister of Trinidad and Tobago had said that "...there has been...a certain resentment that our rights were being tampered with, that our rights as a member of the American family are not recognized, and that we have to depend upon what ultimately appears to be something as of grace, instead of, as we insist, on something as of right." *The Foreign Relations of Trinidad and Tobago,* Speech to the House of Representatives (Port–of-Spain: Government Printing Office, 1963), p. 15.
27 In June, 1970, Venezuela and Guyana signed an agreement suspending their border dispute for a period of at least twelve years (Ed.).
28 See Gordon Connell-Smith, *The Inter-American System* (London: Oxford University Press, 1966), p. 298. The three major claims were restated in an appendix to the Final Act.

it ratified the Inter-American Treaty of Reciprocal Assistance with the following reservation:

The present Treaty poses no impediment whatever to Guatemala's assertion of its rights over the Guatemalan territory of Belize by whatever means it considers most appropriate; . . .[29]

It is quite obvious from the behaviour of a number of Latin American states that the admission of the new Caribbean States constituted a potential threat to the validity of their arguments about the illegality of some British territorial conquests in the hemisphere. It is partly because of Jamaica's and Trinidad's independence that Venezuela, Argentina, and Guatemala have raised their territorial claims in the United Nations since 1962.

While the Act of Washington has opened the way for the admission of Trinidad and Barbados and the establishment of good relations between these countries and Latin America, it has also created much uncertainty with regard to the security of Belize and Guyana. It is not appropriate at this point to speculate on the future of Belize, which is in a most delicate position after the rejection, by all sides, of the U.S. mediation attempt. The case of Guyana, already an independent country, is as good an illustration for the difficulties which must still be overcome. The security of Guyana is not guaranteed effectively at the present moment. The 1966 Geneva Agreement with Britain and Venezuela, which calls for a peaceful settlement of the dispute, has already been broken by Venezuela with the occupation of the Ankoko Island in 1967 and the extension of Venezuela's territorial waters in

[29] See *ibid*, p. 192.

1968.[30] The other Commonwealth Caribbean countries are themselves interested in developing good relations with Venezuela. Britain and the United States have given no unilateral assurances to protect the territorial integrity of Guyana. The support which Guyana may obtain from an Afro-Asian majority in the United Nations is of little practical significance in the face of possible military aggression committed by Venezuela.

The question may be raised whether Guyana could become a party to the Inter-American Treaty of Reciprocal Assistance without being a member of the OAS and receive OAS support in case of a crisis. Although there is no legal provision in the Rio Treaty debarring a nonmember of the OAS from undertaking the obligations set forth in the Treaty, it is most unlikely that a majority of OAS members would support Guyana's stand. An indication of this can be seen in the fact that Guyana and Belize are excluded from the efforts to guarantee the de-nuclearization of Latin America. The Treaty for the Prohibition of Nuclear Weapons in Latin America, which was negotiated under the auspices of the United Nations, contains, in identical terms, the provision embodied in paragraph 3 of the Act of Washington for the exclusion of countries whose territory is under dispute.[31]

[30] The Venezuelan Decree of 9 July, 1968, annexes a belt of sea lying along the coast of Guyana between the Essequibo River and Waini Point. See *Guyana/Venezuela Relations* (Georgetown: Ministry of External Affairs, 1968), p. 20.
[31] Article 25, section 2. See *Guyana Journal* (Georgetown: Ministry of External Affairs, 1968), No. 1, pp. 29–31, on the protest made by the Guyana Government in the General Assembly of the United Nations.

Thus, despite the position of the United States and several Latin American countries, the claims of Venezuela, Guatemala, and Argentina are a living reality and will increasingly affect the relations between the newly independent Caribbean States and Latin America. A recent incident in the United Nations shows how Caribbean countries whose territory is undisputed can also be drawn into the quarrels of the others. Barbados was a candidate for membership of the Committee of 24[32] in which her presence would have been particularly useful, since it discusses annually the situation in the Eastern Caribbean. However, the President of the General Assembly, who happened to be the Foreign Minister of Guatemala, somewhat arbitrarily appointed Ecuador to serve on the Committee. He may have felt that an English-speaking Caribbean country would lend its support to the point of view of Belize in forthcoming debates. The Government of Barbados did not hide its disapproval and protested strongly, together with the other Commonwealth Caribbean States. Guyana felt particularly perturbed, since its Permanent Representative to the United Nations, although at the time the President of the Latin American group, was not consulted on the matter.[33]

It must be clearly underlined that membership in any of the Latin American regional groups does not presuppose membership in the Organization of American States. Article 59 of the Montevideo Treaty, for instance, provides simply for the admission to LAFTA of "Latin American States," a term which is now generally interpreted to include Commonwealth Caribbean States. Quite apart from the legal provisions, it is, however, possible to imagine that members of LAFTA and the CACM might oppose the admission to the LACM of Guyana and Belize on the same political grounds as they oppose admission to the OAS. However, there is at present no indication that they will do so or that their point of view would find the support of other Latin American states.

A new element in present-day international relations which may also affect the relations between the Commonwealth Caribbean and Latin America is

32 Special Committee on the Situation with regard to the Implementation of the Declaration on the Granting of Independence to Colonial Countries and Peoples, established by General Assembly resolutions 1514 (XV), 1654 (XVI), 1810 (XVII), and 1956 (XVIII).
33 According to the *Trinidad Guardian* of 29 October, 1968 ("W.I. States Take Offence in UN"), the Deputy Prime Minister of Barbados, Mr. Cameron Tudor, said: "...it would be most unfortunate if countries like mine, eager to cooperate with our neighbours on the mainland and in the Spanish-speaking Caribbean, were to gain the impression that there are signs of systematic discrimination against those countries which do not belong to the Iberian tradition." The Barbados *Advocate–News* of 28 October ("Barbados in UN Issue"), not representing an official view, went much further: "Informed Caribbean sources, pointing out that this was not the first occasion that the 22-nation group had been divided between its old white Spanish-speaking countries and the newly independent English-speaking black countries, said it was quite possible that four Caribbean countries might soon leave the regional group and join the Afro-Asian group." To support its argument that there is discrimination within the Latin American group along linguistic and racial lines, the commentator points out that Haiti and Brazil were not consulted when the appointment was made. In the case of Brazil, this may be due to the fact that "...it was sympathetic towards Guyana in its dispute with Venezuela."

the mini-state issue. With the admission of Barbados to the OAS, the Latin American countries have acknowledged the concept of the mini-state within the Organization.[34] A few of the Organization's members actually began to realize the implications of this step only after the debate on admission had started. At that stage, they preferred not to make their real feelings known for reasons of international courtesy. The fact remains, however, that a number of Latin American countries are now concerned about the proliferation of statehood in the eastern Caribbean if the present trend results in the application for membership of approximately a dozen islands with a population of less than a hundred thousand inhabitants each. This would bring about a dramatic change in the balance of the English and Spanish/Portuguese-speaking members. A situation of this kind is bound to stir up usually dormant suspicions in the minds of the Latin Americans. Their major fear, which may not be altogether unjustified, is that a small Caribbean island emerging from British colonial rule may align itself too easily to the U.S. point of view in controversial issues arising between North and South America.

If the admission of new mini-states to the Organization of American States is brought up again, the Latin Americans may have themselves partly to blame. The reason for this is that, much as the United Nations in the Committee of 24, the OAS has actively promoted the idea of complete and separate independence of all territories regardless of size and population. While the United Nations is motivated by the principle of self-determination and by the strong anti-colonialist feelings of a majority of members, the OAS acted primarily on the basis of the principle of noninterference in hemispheric affairs enshrined in the Monroe Doctrine. Neither the UN nor the OAS has ever given priority to the creation of regional groupings of dependent territories over the attainment of independence as separate island-states. As far back as 1948, the Ninth International Conference of American States in Bogotá called for the creation of an American Committee on Dependent Territories, which carried out substantial research on the various territories involved.[35] In the Final Act, signed at Havana in 1949, the Committee resolved:

> To address to the non-American countries having possessions in America a request for their cooperation with a view to definitive solution of the colonial problem on the basis of the principles of democracy and liberty, to the end that their colonies and possessions may be established as independent and democratic states.[36]

The recommendations and resolutions of the Committee were subsequently endorsed and expanded at the Fourth Meeting of Consultation of Ministers of Foreign Affairs of the OAS (Washington, 1951) and at the Tenth Inter-American Conference of the OAS (Caracas, 1954). There is no

---

[34] See Patricia Wohlegemuth-Blair, *The Ministate Dilemma* (New York: Carnegie Endowment for International Peace, 1967), who suggests a population of less than 300,000 people as a criterion to define the mini-state.

[35] See Comisión Americana de Territorios Dependientes, *Memoria/Informe*, 2 vols., (La Habana, 1949).

[36] *Final Act of the American Committee on Dependent Territories*, signed at Habana on 21 July, 1949 (Washington: Pan American Union, 1949), Congress and Conference Series No. 60, p. 10.

doubt that the OAS must be commended for thus lending strong support to the process of decolonization as a whole and in the hemisphere in particular. However, the point must be stressed that the Organization, by failing to call initially for the creation of larger units, has encouraged a movement towards the proliferation of mini-states which may ultimately have an adverse effect on its own operations and lead to serious quarrels among members on the question of admission and voting rights.

2. ECONOMIC OBSTACLES Three major economic obstacles are in the way of the integration of the Commonwealth Caribbean with Latin America: the traditional links of the West Indies and Guyana with the Commonwealth, the incompatibility of the economies from a static point of view, and the lack of cohesion of CARIFTA with regard to foreign economic policies of members.[37]

From the point of view of the Latin Americans, the Commonwealth preferential system is a serious obstacle to regional integration. Manufactured goods purchased in Latin America are already quite uncompetitive in view of the high tariff protection which most producers have traditionally enjoyed. To come up with a product which is not only internationally competitive but which can outdo, in quality and price, the Commonwealth goods admitted to the West Indies and Guyana

at preferential customs tariff is a matter of impossibility for practically every Latin American manufacturer.

The West Indian business community maintains close links with British and North American suppliers and customers. The expansion of trade with Latin America requires better travel facilities and telecommunications. Bankers must gain faith in new partners. Clerks must learn to calculate in meters and kilos. Everyone encounters the language barrier. It may take ten to twenty years to make the adjustments necessary to overcome these difficulties.

Importers in the Commonwealth Caribbean can take advantage of the export credit facilities offered by the developed countries. No Latin American country has, at present, the financial resources and the promotional attitude to set up equivalent facilities with a view to outdoing the traditional suppliers. The same can be said of the West Indian producers who are interested in getting a foothold in the Latin American market.

The impact of traditional links, acquired habits and metropolitan advantages is clearly reflected in the foreign trade statistics of Commonwealth Caribbean States. For those observers who adopt a static point of view, the discussion on Caribbean-Latin American integration reaches a final deadlock when the figures of interregional trade are revealed. The Table shows that, in 1965, the Commonwealth Caribbean States sent between 0.02 per cent (Barbados) and 2.9 per cent (Trinidad) of their total exports to Latin America, which is indeed quite negligible. The only substantial Latin American trade connection of any Caribbean country is reflected by the heavy imports by Trinidad of crude oil from Venezuela and Colombia. (This element reap-

---

[37] One might add to this the present protectionist policies adopted by Latin American countries as well as a host of other factors which are impediments to the integration of Latin America itself. These elements cannot be adequately dealt with here. See Sidney Dell, *A Latin American Common Market?* (London: Oxford University Press, 1966); Miguel Wionczek (Ed.), *Latin American Economic Integration* (New York: Praeger, 1966).

Trade with Latin America[38]

		Imports			*Exports*	
TRINIDAD ($ mill. TT.)	1956	1961	1965	1956	1961	1965
Trade with Latin America ...	81.6	144.1	204.4	19.4	19.1	20.2
Total Trade	301.5	584.5	817.0	330.2	593.9	690.6
Percentage of Latin America in Total Trade ...	27.1%	24.7%	25.0%	5.9%	3.2%	2.9%
JAMAICA (£ mill.)						
Trade with Latin America ...	1.1	1.5	9.5	.12	.06	1.0
Total Trade	58.3	75.4	105.0	39.3	61.5	76.7
Percentage of Latin America in Total Trade ...	1.8%	2.0%	9.1%	.31%	.10%	1.3%
BARBADOS ($ mill. E.C.)						
Trade with Latin America ...	n.a.	3.1	13.0	n.a.	.02	.01
Total Trade	n.a.	80.3	116.2	n.a.	43.3	64.2
Percentage of Latin America in Total Trade ...	n.a.	3.9%	11.2%	n.a.	.05%	.02%
GUYANA ($ mill. G.)						
Trade with Latin America ...	.37	3.1	0.7	.21	1.0	1.6
Total Trade	99.9	146.5	178.8	94.7	148.3	166.7
Percentage of Latin America in Total Trade ...	.37%	2.1%	.40%	.22%	.69%	.94%

pears in Trinidad's balance of trade through exports of refined oil to North America). All four countries, incidentally, have an unfavorable balance of

[38] Trinidad: *The Balance of Payments of Trinidad and Tobago 1956–65* (Port-of-Spain: Central Statistical Office, 1968) and *Overseas Trade 1956, 1961, 1965* (Port-of-Spain: Central Statistical Office, 1957, 1962, 1966).
Jamaica: *External Trade of Jamaica 1956, 1961, 1965* (Kingston: Department of Statistics, 1958, 1962, 1966).
Barbados: *Overseas Trade—1961 and 1965* (Bridgetown: Statistical Service, 1962 and 1966).
Guyana: *Annual Account Relating to External Trade, 1956, 1961* (Georgetown: Department of Customs and Excise, 1957, 1962).
For more details on Caribbean-Latin American Trade, see Alister McIntyre "Aspects of Development and Trade in the Commonwealth Caribbean", *Economic Bulletin for Latin America*, X, No. 2 (October, 1965), 149–150; 161–162.

trade towards Latin America. Trinidad, Barbados, and Jamaica have substantially increased their imports, while exports have remained insignificant.

The static interpretation of trade statistics is, of course, not satisfactory. The fact that a country has a high export rate to another country does not mean that the two must become part of an institutional arrangement for integration. The traditional markets for the exports of Commonwealth Caribbean States must be safeguarded through the maintenance of quality standards at competitive prices, commodity agreements, and economic policies which permit export-oriented firms to function adequately. On the other hand, a low export rate is not an impediment to integration. The entire concept of trade expansion through regional integration is obviously based on a dynamic view of production and export promotion.[39] The attempt to reduce the reliance on exports of primary products to developed countries by an increase in exports of manufactured goods to developing countries is the only feasible avenue for developing countries in the light of high protection and competition in the markets for manufactured goods of the developed countries. But this solution requires an enormous effort on behalf of the participating countries, such as regional coordination of development plans, improvement of communications, complementarity agreements, allocation of investments, and, above all, a promotional export policy on behalf of both governments and private circles.

From a static point of view, it is correct to assert that export crops, such as sugar, citrus, and bananas, which because of the labour-intensive production process are of the greatest significance to the economic well-being and political stability of the West Indies, have no future in Latin American markets. In fact, all Latin American countries are either self-sufficient in the production of these crops or cover their needs through imports from neighbouring countries. If the West Indies, rather than enjoying quantitative protection and preferential prices on the British market, had to compete with Latin America on free world markets, they would encounter the most serious economic difficulties. To this extent, the incompatibility of West Indian and Latin American economies is real and cannot be resolved in the short-run. Integration must therefore be directed

primarily at the increased exchange of manufactured goods, raw materials, oil, chemicals and processed foodstuff.

Current trade statistics do not reflect indirect interregional trade resulting from the corporate integration of sources of raw materials in one region, processing plants in a developed economy, and markets in the other region. Thus, for example, Latin America covers its imports of aluminium mainly through purchases from American and Canadian companies, which extract bauxite and alumina in the Caribbean and process it in North America.[40] The economic integration of the two regions may create an incentive for foreign companies to establish local processing plants and thus bring about a substantial increase in direct interregional trade.

The problem of integration with Latin America is further complicated by the attempt of some Commonwealth Caribbean countries to obtain simultaneous affiliation with various integrative schemes, which is due to differences in the structure of their foreign economic relations. At present, only Trinidad and Barbados are committed to participation in the future Latin American attempts at integration. Jamaica is still looking towards the E.E.C. and is a very lukewarm supporter of Caribbean integration. Guyana is excluded from the Latin club and sees Commonwealth and Caribbean ties as the only immediate solution. Trinidad and Barbados will

---

39 United Nations Conference on Trade and Development, *Trade Expansion and Economic Integration among Developing Countries,* TD/B/85, 2 August, 1966.

40 See Norman Girvan and Owen Jefferson, "Institutional Arrangements and the Economic Integration of the Caribbean and Latin America." Paper presented at a Conference on International Relations at Mona (Jamaica), April, 1967, mimeographed, p. 13.

face a very serious dilemma when called upon to participate in the establishment of the Latin American Common Market: either they will succeed in both persuading Jamaica to go along and eliminating Latin resistance against Guyana and Belize, thus allowing for CARIFTA to be associated with Latin America as a regional formation, or the future of CARIFTA will become highly precarious. The simultaneous affiliation of Trinidad and Barbados with the Commonwealth, CARIFTA, and the LACM will, in itself, create some, although not insurmountable, difficulties with the Latin Americans. However, if Jamaica, as a member of CARIFTA were to gain associate status with the E.E.C. rather than following the other Commonwealth Caribbean countries, some intricate technical problems would arise. For instance, to the extent that the control of origin would not be effectively enforced, goods produced in the E.E.C. could be imported into Latin America through CARIFTA at preferential tariffs without reciprocity for Latin America on the E.E.C. market. But even if Jamaica's plea for association with the E.E.C. is unsuccessful, as it will probably be, the unity of CARIFTA is threatened by Jamaica's lack of interest in Latin America. If Trinidad and Barbados were to be the only members to join the LACM, the evolution of CARIFTA from a free trade association to an economic union, which is an avowed aim of the group, comes to an end. Indeed, the formulation of a common foreign economic policy of CARIFTA would then be incompatible with the obligation of Trinidad and Barbados to adopt the foreign economic policy of the LACM.

On a similar line of thought, the continued formal dependence of the smaller CARIFTA countries on Britain may complicate the Association's relationship with Latin America. Members of the East Caribbean Common Market (Antigua, Dominica, Grenada, St. Lucia, St. Kitts-Nevis-Anguilla, St. Vincent) which forms a sub-regional group within CARIFTA, and Montserrat have certain special relationships with Britain. Their currency, the East Caribbean dollar, is linked to sterling in such a way that devaluation of the latter extends automatically to the former.[41] In a general way, their right to decide on foreign economic policy is restricted by their status as colonies (Bahamas, Montserrat, St. Vincent) or by the new arrangements for associated statehood with Britain (Antigua, Dominica, Grenada, St. Lucia, St. Kitts-Nevis-Anguilla). This, then, is a major handicap for participation in the elaboration of a common foreign economic policy within a larger Caribbean or Latin American unit.[42]

CONCLUSION

When choosing an order of presentation of the motives for, and obstacles to, increased relations between the Commonwealth Caribbean and Latin America, we have been guided by the conviction that *economic motives* are the prime force behind any new developments and that the *political obstacles*

[41] For the functioning of the East Caribbean Currency Board, see Clive Thomas, *Monetary and Financial Arrangements in a Dependent Monetary Economy* (Mona: Institute of Social and Economic Research, 1965), pp. 15–36.

[42] For details on division of power between Britain and the Associated States in the field of foreign affairs, see Margaret Broderick, "Associated Statehood—A New Form of Decolonisation," *The International and Comparative Law Quarterly*, 17, Part 2 (April, 1968), 375–383.

appear to be particularly strong at the present time. This observation is a source of moderate optimism about the feasibility of increased relations. Indeed, as long as economic reasons motivate the need for cooperation, the chances of tangible results are reasonable. This is illustrated by the success of regional economic groupings whose members had just emerged from a mutual war (European Economic Community) or where a break in diplomatic relations among some members had little effect on the functioning of common institutions (Central American Common Market). Where economic needs dictate a certain course of action, political obstacles can be overcome....

The Commonwealth Caribbean and Latin America find themselves at the threshold of a vast undertaking which will preoccupy an entire generation. Achievements made so far are embryonic and the difficulties which have already been identified contain promises of hard labour under tough conditions. There is no room for illusions and excessive enthusiasm. But there are sufficient elements to justify the expectation of reasonable, mutual benefits in the long run....

8

International Structure
and International Integration:
The Case of Latin America

Per Olav Reinton

From Per Olav Reinton, "International Structure and International Integration: The Case of Latin America," *Journal of Peace Research*, IV (1967), pp. 334–65. Reprinted by permission of the author and the publisher.

Per Olav Reinton is associated with the International Peace Research Institute in Oslo, Norway.

The emergence and convergence of international subsystems discussed in the preceding selection invite investigation in terms of international integration theory. Building integration theory—using Latin American subsystems as the major source of data—is the purpose of this study by Reinton.[1] Since Reinton's is a difficult essay, a brief survey of some of his key concepts and conclusions may be in order by way of introduction.

Reinton starts with the question "Who [in Latin America] cooperates with

[1] For recent general theoretical studies of international regions and regional integration—with relevance to Latin America—and additional bibliographical information, see esp.: Leon N. Lindberg and Stuart A. Scheingold, eds., *Regional Integration: Theory and Research*, entire issue of *International Organization*, XXIV, No. 4 (Autumn 1970); Joseph S. Nye, Jr., ed., *International Regionalism: Readings* (Boston: Little, Brown, 1968); Bruce M. Russett, *International Regions and the International System: A Study in Political Ecology* (Chicago: Rand McNally, 1967); Roger W. Cobb and Charles Elder, *International Community: A Regional and Global Study* (New York: Holt, Rinehart and Winston, 1970); Karl Kaiser, "The Interaction of Regional Subsystems: Some Preliminary Notes on Recurrent Patterns and the Role of Superpowers," *World Politics*, XXI, No. 1 (October 1968), pp. 84–107; Roger D. Hansen, "Regional Integration: Reflections on a Decade of Theoretical Efforts," *World Politics*, XXI, No. 2 (January 1969), pp. 242–71; Joseph S. Nye, Jr., "Comparative Regional Integration: Concept and Measurement," *International Organization*, XXII, No. 2 (Autumn 1968), pp. 855–80; Philippe C. Schmitter, "Three Neo-Functional Hypotheses About International Integration," *International Organization*, XXIII, No. 1 (Winter 1969), pp. 161–66; Mario Barrera and Ernst B. Haas, "The Operationalization of Some Variables Related to Regional Integration: A Research Note," *International Organization*, XXIII, No. 1 (Winter 1969), pp. 150–60; Philippe C. Schmitter, "Further Notes on Operationalizing Some Variables Related to Regional Integration," *International Organization*, XXIII, No. 2 (Spring 1969), pp. 327–36; Mario Barrera, "Reply to Philippe C. Schmitter's 'Further Notes on Operationalizing Some Variables Related to Regional Integration,'" *International Organization*, XXIII, No. 4 (Autumn 1969), pp. 969–70; and Kenneth A. Dahlberg, "Regional Integration: The Neo-Functional Versus a Configurative Approach," *International Organization*, XXIV, No. 1 (Winter 1970), pp. 122–28. See also selections 30–33.

whom, and why?" and the hypothesis that a nation's status in an international system "determines" various aspects of its behavior in the system and the character of other nations' responses. Comparing four indices of international stratification, he demonstrates that it is possible to rank Latin American nations in high-medium-low status categories with some degree of certitude. He then proceeds to measure the interaction between different pairs of nations (units), with interaction defined largely as trade transactions. (He later employs interaction data other than trade to further substantiate conclusions and explain deviant cases.)

From the foregoing exercise emerge some interesting findings and a wealth of valuable information about Latin America. Reinton finds that the intensity of interaction increases with the average status of nations within a pair. A nation of higher rank may interact with one of lower rank with any degree of intensity, but the former "dominates" the relationship in proportion to the discrepancy in status between the two—there is a "disequilibrated pair" with respect to transaction flows. According to Reinton, Latin America is an area with "a fairly low level of interaction where most of the transactions take place between nations with similar position in the system": in pairs of nations with high-medium, medium-medium, and medium-low ranks.

At this point Reinton introduces the concept of "influence," which in his usage is synonymous with behavior that elicits a genuinely imitative, emulative, and/or cooperative response. He maintains that influence prevails whenever one nation is not dominating another in terms of transaction flows, that is, when there is an "equilibrated pair." Since interaction between nations of different rank has previously been found to involve domination and disequilibrium, influence can prevail only among nations of equal rank. Thus, in Reinton's view, what passes for cooperation (etc.) in the relationship between the United States and the nations of Latin America is really domination. Moreover, middle-level nations are especially important in Latin American integration precisely "because they have more equals."

1. INTRODUCTION

Asking 'Who cooperates with whom, and why?', we shall in this paper[1] investigate the implications of the structure of the international society, to see if the positions of nation-pairs in the

[1] This article is part of a general study of Latin American integration, and is PRIO publication no. 22–5. I am particularly grateful to Johan Galtung for suggestive criticism and comments, without which this paper would have been even more unclear and wearisome than it is, and to my wife Ragnhild Reinton, who participated in the work with imaginative logic.

Data were collected during a year-long trip in Latin America, made financially possible by the Norwegian Council for Science and the Humanities (NAVF) and the University of Oslo. The field work was performed in cooperation with Centro Latino-Americano de Investigaciones en Ciencias Sociales, Mexico D.F., Instituto para la Integración en America Latina, Buenos Aires, Facultad Latinoamericana de Ciencias Sociales, Santiago de Chile, and Centro Latino-Americano de Pesquisas em Ciencias Sociais, Rio de Janeiro. All institutions contributed with helpful support during the investigation.

structure determine their behavior towards each other. Our starting point is the hypothesis that a nation's status in a particular system determines its intensity of participation, the character of its behaviour, and its capability of influence in the system. If that is true, the structure of the system will necessarily modify the development of integration within the system. . . .

We have chosen Latin America as the system of nations to be studied.[2] During the last twenty years a movement towards international integration has developed on that continent. The ideology of this movement is to push Latin American nations from a situation where they only tolerate each other, to a state where they are mutually dependent and act in common, both internally and externally. These ideas developed during the 1950's around CEPAL, the United Nations' Economic Commission for Latin America in Santiago de Chile, and became institutionalised by the creation in 1961 of ALALC, the Latin American Free Trade Area, with its secaretariat in Montevideo, Uruguay, and the creation in 1962 of MCC, the Central American Common Market, with its headquarters in Guatemala. Because of the organizational development of the movement we must qualify our statement that this study concerns 'Latin America': We exclude all data concerning the Antilles, because they do not take part in the movement at present. We shall also exclude Panama, which is not considered part of Central America nor does it behave as if it were. Guyana became independent too late to be included, and French Guyana and Surinam are not considered parts of the continent as long as they are European colonies. This is valid also for Belize, or British Honduras.

Bolivia, however, is included in the study. Representatives from this country took part in the deliberations leading to the creation of ALALC; today Bolivia has observers at meetings in Montevideo, and expects to enter the organization as a member.[3]

We are then left with two different systems of nations: South America plus Mexico (11 nations), on one hand; and Central America (5 nations) on the other. Both are systems with a co-operative climate, a fairly stable pattern of interaction, and constantly interacting units. The two most important parts of their environment consist of Europe and the United States, which can be treated as constants during the study, and their impact can be controlled throughout the analysis.

When we speak of interaction, this is generally in terms of commerce. But as far as other data are available, notably on weekly air-flights between pairs of nations, or participation in international conferences and international activities in general, they will also be presented and compared with conclusions drawn from trade statistics.

The advantages Latin America presents us with are relevant for the data-gathering, but do not make the two systems different in character from any other system which might be selected among the units of the global system of nations. Though the data concern

[2] A study on international stratification in Latin America, using nations as units, has been done by Johan Galtung, Manuel Moya y Araujo and Simon Schwartzman: 'El Sistema Latino–americano de Naciones: un Analisis Estructural', *América Latina*. Ano 9, no. 1. Janeiro–Março de 1966, pp. 59–95. A more general study is Gustavo Lagos: *International Stratification and Underdeveloped Countries* (Chapel Hill 1963).

[3] Bolivia is now a member (Ed.).

Latin America alone, we believe that the conclusions are valid for any system of nations, not just for systems of nations with a cooperative climate, with constantly interacting units, with stable patterns of interaction, and so on.

Inevitably, however, some characteristics of the Latin American setting will determine the formulations of the conclusions, give them a particular colour, so that they are not always directly applicable to other systems. Only similar studies investigating other systems of nations than Latin America can eliminate such blurring particularities.

2. STRUCTURE

In speaking of a system of nations, we imply that the system has a particular structure which explains the direction and intensity of interaction between units. In which manner does international stratification determine international interaction?

To make the analysis valid, we must describe the structure accurately and in detail. . . . 1) the units should be presented in a rank order, each unit measured relative to the other units in relation to a list of criteria that appear relevant in conveying power and development, factors influencing the environment's image of the unit, or the unit's capability to influence or dominate its environment; 2) the units should be ranked in relation to how they are perceived as high, medium, or low ranking units by people living in these units; 3) if the units in interaction disclose an unambiguous rank order, or if they have ranked themselves as big, medium, or small, this should be put on an index; and 4) if there is high correlation among the different rank indices, an accurate description is achieved.

2.1. THE LATIN AMERICAN STRUCTURE

The Galtung-Mora-Schwartzman objective index[4] fulfills the first prerequisite. It is called 'objective' because the criteria determining ranking order are chosen by the researchers themselves. This is in contrast to the 'subjective' index that they use, where Latin American students rank the nations in their own way and order. The subjective index, then, fulfills the second prerequisite.

The ALALC Conference has ranked their members as big, medium, and small according to each member's economic capacity.[5] In that way prerequisite number three is fulfilled.

We have chosen to present a fourth index, or rather a diagram. Power is measured along one axis, communication along the other, and the distribution of units in accordance with the two variables are presented in Figure 1. . . .

The four indices are presented in Table 1 and compared in Table 2.

The correlation between the four indices are high; consequently, we find the stratification inside the system quite accurately described.

Which index shall we choose in our analysis? There is no way of deciding which is 'best', but we have preferred the ALALC index. It is developed by the countries themselves. Though the ALALC index measures economic

---

[4] The objective criteria in the Galtung-Mora-Schwartzman study were these: a) area, b) population, c) GNP, d) production per capita, e) illiteracy, f) newspapers/population, g) per cent of population in middle and high class, h) urbanization, i) population, j) per cent of white people.

[5] See the amendments to the Montevideo Treaty.

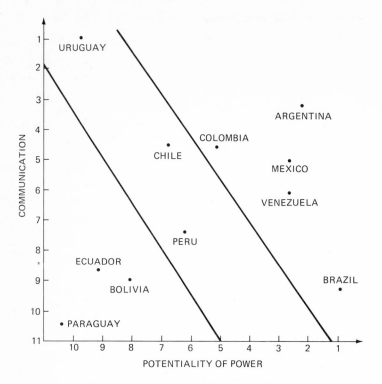

FIGURE 1. Power-communication index

Communication: Average rank of 1) daily newspaper circulation +2) Radio distribution +3) Annual increase of radios. *Power:* Average rank of 1) Total population +2) Area +3) GNP. Data from: Russett et al.: *World Handbook of Political and Social Indicators.* For a discussion of using communication as a measure of political development, see: Phillip Cutright: 'National Political Development: Measurement and Analysis,' *American Sociological Review,* Vol. 28, no. 2 April 1963, p. 260.

TABLE 1. Four Indices Measuring the Rank of Nations Within the ALALC System

	The Galtung, Mora, Schwartzman index	The subjective index	Communication Power index	The ALALC index
High	Argentina	Argentina	Argentina	Argentina
	Chile	Brazil	Brazil	Brazil
	Venezuela	Chile	Mexico	Mexico
	Brazil	Mexico	Venezuela	
	Uruguay		Colombia	
	Colombia			
Medium	Mexico	Venezuela	Chile	Chile
	Peru	Uruguay	Uruguay	Peru
	Ecuador	Colombia	Peru	Colombia
		Peru		Uruguay
				Venezuela
Low	Bolivia	Ecuador	Ecuador	Ecuador
	Paraguay	Bolivia	Bolivia	Bolivia
		Paraguay	Paraguay	Paraguay

TABLE 2. Correlation Matrix of Indices (γ). γ is Based on a 3 × 3 Table, with N = 11

	GMS	*subj.*	*power-comm.*	*ALALC*
GMS	(1.00)	0.71	0.87	0.72
subj.	0.71	(1.00)	0.88	1.00
power-comm.	0.87	0.88	(1.00)	1.00
ALALC	0.72	1.00	1.00	(1.00)

capacity and we shall test each unit's interaction capacity, we avoid any tautological reasoning by the fact that there is high correlation between the different indices.

3.1 COMMUNICATION IN LATIN AMERICA

Since this paper focuses on communications and transactions among units, we shall briefly describe the setting, the milieu, from which our data are selected. Before we look at the interaction in pairs of nations, an idea of the total picture is needed. The communication network in Latin America remains characteristic of a colonial economy, with a large part of the transport relying on mules, and the best facilities promoting the exporting sector. In an absolute sense—not thinking of per capita distributions—Africa is better off than Latin America in terms of transportation of goods. A comparison between all continents in the world places South and Central America at the bottom of the list as to the extension of the communications network.[6]

We may single out four periods of traffic development in Latin America: 1) the colonial times, dominated by mules and horses; 2) the railways era from 1870 to 1914. The railways were, almost without exception, built by

foreigners—the United States in Central America and the northern part of South America, and England and France in the southern part of the continent. There was no central planning, and competition among different companies prohibited cooperation. Only in some parts have railways later been integrated. 3) the development of air traffic from 1914 to 1939; 4) modern times, dominated by road-building and further development of airborne transport.

Despite the development since 1914, the railways are still responsible for the geo-economic structure of the Latin American countries and the continent as a whole. Eighty per cent of all railways are found in Argentina, Chile, and Mexico alone, which means that vast areas like Brazil, Venezuela, and Colombia, together with the 14 other countries, are left with one fifth of the low total. Since 1945 the railways in Latin America have increased only 5%, and have in some countries decreased. From 1960 to 1963, 93% of all railways were decreasing 4%. This development does not indicate a decisive trend towards less communication, however. The importance of the Latin American railways is limited by the fact that there exist ten different rail gauges in the area, and few connections between the countries. . . .

Lessons from the economic history of the United States show that the railroad situation in Latin America

6 Franz Henning: *Intra-kontinentaler Verkehr in Lateinamerika. Situation und Entwicklungsmöglichkeiten* (Hamburg 1965), p. 25.

may have little influence on international transactions of the continent,[7] as long as the modern times are characterised by the development of air traffic and road building. While the railroads are diminishing and very often kept in bad condition, roads are built and improved. This is true only for industrial centers, however. Road-building in the countryside is still embryonic.

Shipping is today most important in transportation: 90% of all goods are shipped—but only 6% on Latin American ships. In 1962 there were 821 Latin American cargo ships, and they were 20.7 years in average—while the world average is 10 years. While the increase in tonnage of commercial ships was 60.5% in the world during the years 1952–1963, the Latin American increase was only 44.2%.

The fourth sector of modern transportation, air traffic, is more important in personal than in goods transport, but there are planes used in mining industries far away from traditional centers. From 1955 to 1962 air traffic almost doubled, from 4 billion person-kilometres to 7 billion person-kilometres. Data on air communication are presented in Table 3.

3.2 THE PATTERN OF TRADE TRANSACTIONS

Trade among Latin American nations is small relative to total trade. Like Scandinavia in the first part of this century, intra-Latin American trade constitutes approximately ten per cent of the total.[8]

Focusing on the ALALC system of

nations, it is our intention to chart the relative interdependence among units in the system. How is the correlation between total rank and volume of interaction among pairs of units?

With 11 nations we get 55 pairs of nations. The data are presented in Table 4. We shall, however, partly operate with 110 pairs. We get 110 pairs when we calculate the trade between A and B as *a percentage of A's total exports in the ALALC system* and its *total imports in the ALALC system,* because the percentage of A's exports to B is not equal to the percentage of B's imports from A.

When we calculate A's imports from B and exports to B as a percentage of A's total imports and exports in the ALALC system, we get an AB pair. When we calculate B's imports and exports from A, the score of this pair is different from the AB pair, and is consequently named the BA pair.

This simple method can give us much information on interaction among nations. Here are two examples:

1) Argentina's exports to Brazil in 1963 were 39% of Argentina's total exports to the system, while Argentina's imports from Brazil were 46% of Argentina's total imports from the system. Adding the percentages we get the number 85, the score of the AB pair, or Argentina's score in interaction with Brazil.

   Brazil's imports from Argentina in 1963 constituted 34% of Brazil's total imports from the system. Brazil's exports to Argentina represented 59% of Brazil's total exports to the system. The score of the BA pair is then 93, or the score of Brazil in interaction with Argentina.

2) Argentina's exports to Paraguay were in 1963 only 5% of Argentina's total exports to the system, and Argentina's imports from Paraguay were 8% of Argentina's total imports from

[7] Holland Hunter: 'Transport in Soviet and Chinese Development', *Economic Development and Cultural Change.* Vol. XIV, no. 1. Oct. 1965, p. 71.

[8] Amitai Etzioni: *Political Unification* (N.Y. 1965), pp. 196–197.

TABLE 3. Weekly International Passenger Flights 1965

	Argentina	Brazil	Chile	Colombia	Ecuador	Mexico	Paraguay	Peru	Uruguay	Venezuela	Bolivia	Costa Rica	El Salvador	Guatemala	Honduras	Nicaragua	Panama	Tot. to ALALC-count. + Bolivia	Tot. to Central America	Tot. to Latin America*	To United States	Tot. to the whole world flights	countries
Argentina		21	40	2	5	4	18	18	158	1	3						11	270	11	281	26	366	28
Brazil			7	4	0	3	3	8	13	5	4						10	68	10	78	26	183	33
Chile				2	5	4	1	17	10	2	1						10	82	10	92	12	154	28
Colombia					9	4	1	18	1	8	1				2		19	46	21	67	32	133	26
Ecuador						3	2	17	0	2	2						13	45	13	58	13	81	18
Mexico							0	9	0	0	0	16	17	21	8	13	21	16	96	112	154	317	30
Paraguay								4	7	2	2						2	36	2	38	3	44	11
Peru									2	1	10						29	99	29	128	38	209	27
Uruguay										4	2						0	180	0	180	6	226	20
Venezuela											0			2			10	20	12	32	26	144	29
Bolivia												0					3	21	3	24	4	32	10
Costa Rica													14	14	7	11	19	17	65	82	13	97	9
El Salvador														27	14	20	12	21	87	108	17	125	8
Guatemala															14	18	17	25	90	115	27	145	10
Honduras																10	9	24	54	78	8	86	9
Nicaragua																	11	15	70	85	12	100	9
Panama																		119	68	187	48	209	27

* Latin America = ALALC + Mercomun + Bolivia + Panama.

TABLE 4. Total of Exports of Each Country to Each Country and to ALALC as a Percentage of Grand Total to ALALC plus Bolivia and Venezuela. Total of Imports of Each Country from Each Country and from ALALC as a Whole Taken as a Percentage of Grand Total from ALALC plus Bolivia and Venezuela.

Exports to & Imports from Country	Year	Argentina		Brazil		Chile		Colombia		Ecuador		Mexico		Paraguay		Peru		Uruguay		ALALC		Bolivia		Venezuela		Total	
		Ex-port	Im-port	Ex-port	Im-port	Ex-port	Im-port	Ex-port	Im-port	Ex-port	Im-port	Ex-port	Im-port	Ex-port	Im-port	Ex-port	Im-port	Ex-port	Im-port	Ex-port	Im-port	Ex-port	Im-port	Ex-port	Im-port	Ex-port	Im-port
Argentina	1959	—	—	59.8	26.2	16.9	12.9	0.2	0	0	0	0.6	0.5	5.6	4.2	5.6	4.4	4.1	0.2	92.7	48.7	3.5	2.5	3.8	48.8	100	100
	1963	—	—	39.2	46.2	21.2	13.7	4.1	0	0.2	0	1.0	1.3	4.8	7.5	18.0	7.3	4.9	1.8	93.5	80.6	2.3	2.4	4.2	17.0	100	100
Brazil	1959	56.2	45.9	—	—	12.9	3.8	0.3	0.1	0	0	0.1	0.3	1.1	0	0.2	0.7	27.2	0.6	98.1	51.3	0.3	0.2	1.6	48.5	100	100
	1963	59.0	33.6	—	—	11.8	12.0	0.7	0	0	1.7	1.7	6.8	2.5	0.3	1.3	5.9	17.2	3.9	94.2	62.7	1.4	0	4.3	37.3	100	100
Chile	1959	57.0	48.4	19.4	13.1	—	—	2.0	0.2	5.6	2.4	3.1	2.4	0	0	7.1	29.5	2.9	0.5	93.8	99.3	4.0	0.5	2.1	0.2	100	100
	1963	28.3	41.1	52.7	14.7	—	—	1.7	1.1	5.7	1.4	2.3	8.6	0.1	0	7.2	20.8	2.7	1.6	94.6	94.0	1.0	0.2	2.7	5.8	100	100
Colombia	1959	1.4	1.9	0.7	1.0	20.0	4.8	—	—	7.7	41.9	0.8	17.1	0	0	33.4	15.2	0.4	3.8	64.4	85.7	0.1	0	35.5	14.3	100	100
	1963	7.8	38.8	1.9	2.2	3.9	4.5	—	—	38.7	19.6	3.2	13.8	0.1	0	26.3	8.5	4.2	7.6	86.6	95.1	0.2	0	13.3	4.9	100	100
Ecuador	1959	0.5	0	0	0	21.9	16.3	55.8	6.1	—	—	0	0	0	0	1.9	28.6	0.1	0	80.3	51.0	0.2	0	19.0	49.0	100	100
	1963	3.3	1.2	1.2	0	25.8	4.7	52.5	13.4	—	—	0.1	5.2	0.8	4.8	17.0	5.2	0.3	1.2	99.0	30.8	0.3	0	0.5	69.2	100	100
Mexico	1959	5.0	28.5	3.3	0	15.0	35.7	13.6	2.4	3.8	0	—	—	0	0	8.8	16.7	1.0	4.8	51.3	92.8	0.3	2.4	48.4	4.8	100	100
	1963	7.7	26.3	31.5	8.8	15.5	13.2	12.9	1.8	2.9	0	—	—	0.2	0	9.3	32.5	1.5	12.3	81.5	94.7	0.6	0	17.9	5.3	100	100
Paraguay	1959	82.2	97.4	0.4	0	2.2	0	0	0	0	0	0	0	—	—	0	0.5	10.9	2.6	95.7	100.0	4.3	0	0	0	100	100
	1963	80.7	96.2	3.7	0	1.5	0	0	0	0	0	0.1	0	—	—	0	0.2	14.0	3.8	100.0	100.0	0	0	0	0	100	100
Peru	1959	17.8	64.3	2.7	0.9	61.3	15.0	2.4	11.7	5.4	1.4	1.2	3.8	0	0.5	—	—	1.5	0	92.3	97.7	6.5	1.9	1.2	0.5	100	100
	1963	11.8	74.6	18.7	1.5	45.9	6.7	3.3	3.5	2.7	3.5	4.6	3.5	0	0.2	—	—	4.6	0.9	91.6	94.4	2.8	0.2	5.7	5.5	100	100
Uruguay	1959	12.0	6.0	46.1	52.1	0	3.0	8.0	0	3.4	0	0.7	0.2	2.6	2.3	18.3	1.8	—	—	93.0	65.5	2.0	0	6.9	34.5	100	100
	1963	6.1	23.5	64.5	34.0	9.8	3.4	11.0	1.5	1.6	0	0.6	3.2	2.5	5.9	3.7	7.3	—	—	99.5	78.7	0.5	0	0.1	21.3	100	100
Bolivia	1959	62.7	53.3	20.6	2.6	2.0	16.4	0	0	0	0	5.8	0	0	0	7.4	27.6	1.1	0	99.9	100.0	—	—	0	0	100	100
	1963	70.0	43.6	23.3	17.0	3.3	17.0	0	0	0	0	0	3.2	0.4	0	3.3	18.1	0	1.1	100.0	100.0	—	—	0	0	100	100
Venezuela	1959	42.6	29.9	42.1	12.6	4.1	3.3	1.6	8.9	2.0	9.8	0.2	31.3	0	0	0.2	2.8	7.2	1.4	99.9	100.0	0	0	—	—	100	100
	1963	12.3	29.0	67.7	3.7	5.0	4.5	0.9	3.3	2.2	3.3	0.3	45.7	0.1	0	3.3	10.2	8.1	0.4	99.9	100.0	0	0	—	—	100	100

Data from: Donald W. Baerresen, Martin Carnoy & Joseph Grunwald: *Latin American Trade Patterns*. The Brookings Institution, Washington DC, 1965. The export figures are taken from Table XI-1 and XI-5. The import figures are based on Tables VI-1 to VI-11.

the system. This gives the AP pair a score of 13.

Paraguay's exports to Argentina, however, were in 1963 81% of Paraguay's total exports to the system, and Paraguay's imports from Argentina were 96% of Paraguay's total imports from the system. The PA pair scores 177.

This treatment of data gives us information on two relevant points: 1) We shall know if a pair scores relatively high or relatively low in relation to other pairs in the system. 2) We shall know if there is *interactive equilibrium* inside a pair, i.e. whether the AB pair is similar to the BA pair, or the scores of AB are high in relation to be scores of BA.

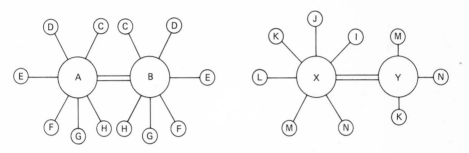

FIGURE 2. An equilibrated and a disequilibrated pair

3.3 INTERACTIVE DISEQUILIBRIUM

When pairs are equilibrated, the score of one unit is similar to the score of the other unit, within a chosen limit. When pairs are disequilibrated, one unit dominates the other in interaction. The dominating unit will get a low score in the pair, while the dominated unit will get a high score. The dominated unit is directed towards the dominating unit, so to speak; the dominated unit means less to the dominating unit than vice versa. This is illustrated in Figure 2. Characteristic of an equilibrated pair is that units *either* score relatively high in interaction with other units in the system, *or* both units score low in interaction with other units. If a pair has one of these two characteristics, it is certainly not disequilibrated.

A pair, *xy,* where unit *x* has a relatively high score with other units, but not *y,* may be either an equilibrated or a disequilibrated pair. Such a pair is disequilibrated only if *x* scores high in interaction with other units, but relatively low in interaction with unit *y,* while unit *y* scores high in interaction with unit *x,* and relatively low in interaction with other units.

4.1 RANK AND INTENSITY OF INTERACTION

Having constructed methods of measuring rank and interaction, we shall investigate the intensity of interaction within pairs. As shown by Figure 3 there will be two types of interaction-scores: 1) those where each unit has a similar score within the pair, 2) those where one unit scores considerably more than the other.

When both unit A and unit B score

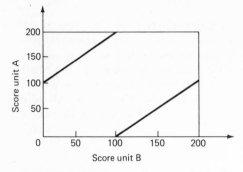

FIGURE 3. The range of scores within the ALALC system

200, they are the only interacting units in the system; and if they both score zero, there is no interaction between them. Most pairs will fall within the dotted lines, and towards the left and bottom corner of the diagram. Such pairs may be easy to categorize as having high or low interaction intensity.

Pairs where unit x scores 20 and unit y 120 cannot be characterised as a pair with either low or high interaction intensity. They fall outside the dotted lines in Figure 3. We have chosen two categories for such pairs: 1) strong one-unit domination, and 2) weak one-unit domination, for pairs that fall within the dotted lines, but nevertheless demonstrate a clear disequilibrium. Table 5 shows which scores fall in which category.

To see the correlation between the rank of units within a pair and the character of interaction, we compare rank and interaction-intensity in Table 6. A nation of high status is given the value 2, a medium status nation the value 1, and a low status nation the value 0. In a pair of one unit of top status and another of medium status, for instance, the average rank of units within the pair is 1.5. Table 6 shows that *the lower the average status of units within a pair, the lower the inten-*

TABLE 5. The Character of Interaction and Scores Within Pairs

Character of interaction	*Scores*
High intensity	Over 80 for both units
Medium intensity	Between 80 and 30 for both units
Low intensity	Between 30 and 5 for both units
Minimal intensity	Less than five, but above zero, for both units
No interaction	Zero for both units
Strong one-unit domination	The dominating unit below 20
	The dominated unit above 100
Weak one-unit domination	The dominating unit below 5
	The dominated unit above 40

TABLE 6. Character of Interaction Related to the Rank Units Within Pairs

Average rank of units within the pair		*Character of interaction*
2		High
1.5		Medium
1		Low
0.7		Minimal
0.5		No interaction
The dominating unit:	2	Strong one-unit domination
The dominated unit:	0.3	
The dominating unit:	1.6	Weak one-unit domination
The dominated unit:	0.8	

TABLE 7. Interaction Scores

Country		High	Medium	Low	N	Interaction score: High — (med. + low)	
Argentina		6	3	1	10	+2	
Brazil		5	2	3	10	0	
Chile		5	4	1	10	0	High
Venezuela		5	3	2	10	0	
Peru		4	4	2	10	−2	
Mexico		3	4	3	10	−4	Medium
Colombia		3	4	3	10	−4	
Ecuador		2	2	6	10	−6	
Uruguay		2	6	2	10	−6	
Bolivia		2	2	6	10	−6	Low
Paraguay		1	2	7	10	−8	
	N	38	36	36	110		

sity of interaction; and the greater the discrepancy in status between units within a pair, the stronger is the domination of one unit in interaction.[9]

4.2 INTERACTION SCORES

We may go deeper into the question of interaction within pairs, in order to investigate if there are units that do not behave in accordance with the finding presented above. If a unit scores less in interaction than expected in relation to its status in the system, we expect that it will gain in interaction-intensity when transactions become more intensified and the communication-network is more developed, granted that the unit is a topdog.

Table 7 and 8 show that Mexico and Uruguay are such units. Both have a

[9] This is only a confirmation of a proposition tested earlier, by Johan Galtung, Simon Schwartzman, and Manuel Mora y Araujo in the article mentioned above; and by Johan Galtung: 'East–West Interaction Patterns', *Journal of Peace Research,* no. 2, 1966, pp. 146–178. See also William A. Hachten: *The Flow of News and Under-development.* A Pilot Study of the African Press (University of Wisconsin, unpublished). The author is highly indebted to authors who pointed at the structural implications of interaction, but is in this article trying to investigate the case further.

lower score on interaction than could be expected from their rank position in the system, which means that they are found too seldom in pairs with high interaction scores and too often in pairs with low and medium scores. Mexico is safely situated among typical medium-nations as Peru and Colombia, while Uruguay has dropped down into the company of Ecuador and Bolivia.

We will discuss this further in sections dealing with the correlation between position in the system and behaviour in integration processes. Here we may only mention that we expect Mexico to profit more from Latin American integration than any

TABLE 8. Rank and Interaction Scores

Country	Rank	Interaction score
Argentina	2	+2
Brazil	2	0
Mexico	2	−4
Chile	1	0
Venezuela	1	0
Peru	1	−2
Colombia	1	−4
Uruguay	1	−6
Ecuador	0	−6
Bolivia	0	−6
Paraguay	0	−8

other nation, at least as long as there is no supra-nationality built into the system allocating values on new criteria non-existent in the system today. It is not self-evident that the same argument concerns Uruguay, since this unit is no topdog in the system. Uruguay ranks very low on power-variables and very high on development-variables. I find it natural to hypothesize that the *integration-process in Latin America today rewards development-values very little and power-values considerably more.*

This will mean a relatively low position for Uruguay at the time being.

TABLE 9a. Total of Exports of Each Country to Each Country as a Percentage of Total to Mercomun

		Guatemala	El Salvador	Honduras	Nicaragua	Costa Rica	Total
Guatemala	1962		71	21	7	1	100
	1963		65	20	13	2	100
	1964		58	18	15	9	100
El Salvador	1962	41		32	18	9	100
	1963	54		28	10	9	100
	1964	52		28	11	9	100
Honduras	1962	24	73		1	2	100
	1963	24	71		2	1	100
	1964	24	67		5	4	100
Nicaragua	1962	12	54	5		29	100
	1963	13	42	13		33	100
	1964	10	31	18		41	100
Costa Rica	1962	6	69	9	16		100
	1963	11	50	7	32		100
	1964	21	47	10	22		100

TABLE 9b. Total Imports of Each Country from Each Country as a Percentage of Total from Mercomun

		Guatemala	El Salvador	Honduras	Nicaragua	Costa Rica	Total
Guatemala	1962		72	24	2	2	100
	1963		61	22	14	3	100
	1964		73	14	3	11	100
El Salvador	1962	38		47	9	6	100
	1963	48		33	10	9	100
	1964	42		33	7	18	100
Honduras	1962	33	64		1	2	100
	1963	15	81		3	1	100
	1964	32	50		9	9	100
Nicaragua	1962	30	57	3		10	100
	1963	5	63	12		20	100
	1964	35	30	7		28	100
Costa Rica	1962	10	61	5	24		100
	1963	9	46	8	37		100
	1964	33	35	9	23		100

Sources: *Quarto Compendio Estadistico Centroamericano.* SIECA, marzo 1965. Cuadro 1–22. *Anuario Estadistico Centroamericano de Comercio Exterior.* SEICA, 12 de octubre 1965. pp. 2–6.

TABLE 9c. Total of Imports from the World to Each Country in Mercomun

Imports from		Mercado Comun 10³ $CA	%	Total Latin America 10³ $CA	%	United States 10³ $CA	%	Western Europe 10³ $CA	%	Others 10³ $CA	%	Total Imports 10³ $CA
Guatemala	62	6,526	5	20,490	15	65,266	48	38,630	29	11,580	8	135,966
	63	20,773	13	26,417	15	79,609	48	45,261	27	12,046	7	165,550
	64	26,357	13	36,693	18	89,885	44	52,788	26	22,744	11	202,109
El Salvador	62	22,058	18	26,556	20	45,471	36	40,810	33	11,958	10	124,795
	63	24,151	16	40,736	27	51,336	34	46,060	31	12,353	8	151,746
	64	39,234	20	53,790	28	66,419	35	49,512	26	21,412	11	191,123
Honduras	62	8,911	11	16,596	21	41,251	52	15,377	19	6,569	8	79,793
	63	13,318	14	20,819	21	45,440	48	17,876	19	8,784	9	95,081
	64	18,004	18	20,310	20	49,604	49	17,083	17	14,636	14	101,634
Nicaragua	62	5,343	5	17,045	17	49,477	50	22,084	23	9,620	10	98,226
	63	3,876	4	21,001	19	53,652	48	25,680	23	10,513	10	110,787
	64	14,419	11	25,996	19	64,966	48	32,047	23	13,968	10	136,978
Costa Rica	62	3,308	3	13,335	12	52,588	46	34,309	30	13,114	12	113,346
	63	4,455	4	14,537	12	59,127	48	36,154	29	12,820	10	123,847
	64	8,285	6	15,585	11	64,144	46	37,863	27	21,008	15	138,601

TABLE 9d. Total of Exports to the World from Each Country in Mercomun

Exports to		Mercado Comun 10³ $CA	%	Total Latin America 10³ $CA	%	United States 10³ $CA	%	Western Europe 10³ $CA	%	Others 10³ $CA	%	Total Exports 10³ $CA
Guatemala	62	8,732	8	9,626	8	55,734	49	37,584	33	11,569	10	114,513
	63	17,294	11	18,294	11	66,274	44	49,739	33	17,205	11	151,512
	64	29,558	18	29,735	18	52,954	32	56,839	35	24,940	15	164,347
El Salvador	62	18,695	14	18,880	14	46,052	34	44,205	32	27,165	20	136,300
	63	30,228	20	30,658	20	37,780	25	45,374	29	40,032	26	153,844
	64	36,795	21	36,877	21	45,428	25	57,729	32	38,060	21	178,095
Honduras	62	12,630	16	17,914	23	45,717	58	12,564	16	2,683	3	78,905
	63	12,807	15	17,219	21	48,953	58	14,121	17	3,208	4	83,501
	64	16,442	18	17,125	18	48,954	53	16,390	18	10,290	11	92,760
Nicaragua	62	3,531	4	8,544	10	34,486	38	26,515	29	20,625	23	90,170
	63	4,741	4	9,543	9	39,103	37	29,258	28	28,836	27	106,767
	64	7,926	6	8,470	7	32,824	26	45,703	37	38,064	30	125,061
Costa Rica	62	1,720	2	5,475	6	54,266	58	32,039	35	1,190	1	92,970
	63	3,945	4	6,333	7	52,527	57	32,466	35	1,174	1	92,500
	64	15,389	13	17,434	15	59,564	52	32,945	29	4,108	4	113,899

The numbers are in thousands of centeramerican pesos. Imports—cif, exports—fob. Columns Total Latin America, United States, Western Europe and Others add up to 100%.

The same hypothesis will lead us to the conclusion that Brazil is rated very high in the integration-process, because of its power-potentialities, though it scores very low on development.[10]

[10] That is: in our power-communication index, as shown in Figure 1, Brazil is in fact

Uruguay and Brazil are the countries most 'unbalanced' in power-develop- the most un-categorizable nation in Latin America because of its enormous and surprising diversity and contrasts. In some ways it may be categorized as rich and developed, in other ways as poor and underdeveloped; it depends on procedure.

TABLE 10. The Distribution of Units in the Central American System of Three Levels of Interaction-Intensity

Country	High	Medium	Low	N
El Salvador	2	2	0	4
Guatemala	1	1	2	4
Honduras	1	1	2	4
Costa Rica	0	2	2	4
Nigaragua	0	2	2	4
N	4	8	8	20

ment values (as shown in Figure 1).

By such treatment of data, we show which units are central and which are peripheral in interaction within the system. If we use the data on Central America presented in Table 9, we get the results presented in Table 10.

Table 10 shows that we can name El Salvador, Guatemala, and Honduras 'central' in Central American interaction, while Nicaragua and Costa Rica constitute the 'periphery'.

The varieties and combinations in Central American interaction are so few,[11] however, that it is not fruitful to elaborate more on these data. Central America and its 'Mercomun' will, for this reason, be treated scantily here.

4.3 THE PLACE OF EACH UNIT IN THE STRUCTURE

In Table 11 we show some of the implications for the system of nations that we are particularly interested in at the moment. Two characteristics are immediately visible: more than 60% of all units fall within pairs with low or minimal interaction, and more than 70% of the units fall within pairs of the three categories high-medium, medium-medium, and medium-low. Interaction among units is scanty, not only in absolute but also in relative terms. The extreme categories high-high, low-low, and low-high are under-represented in the Latin American system. In other words, we have a fairly low level of interaction where most of the transactions take place between nations with similar position in the system. The implications of this finding will be discussed later; first we shall analyse the distribution of countries in the Table more in detail.

Group 1. Pairs with units of high rank have either high or medium interaction. There exist only three pairs of this sort. The Mexico-Argentina case, which appar-

TABLE 11. Distribution of Units According to Degree of Interaction and Rank within Pairs

Rank of units Degree of Interaction	Group 1 high-high	Group 2 high-med.	Group 3 med.-med.	Group 4 med.-low	Group 5 low-high	Group 6 low-low	N
High	1	0	0	0	0	0	1
Medium	1	6	1	1	0	0	9
Low	0	5	8	5	0	0	18
Minimal	0	1	1	7	5	2	16
No interaction	0	0	0	1	1	1	3
Strong dom.	0	1	0	0	2	0	3
Little dom.	1	2	0	1	1	0	5
N	3	15	10	15	9	3	55

[11] It may appear almost ridiculous to rank Central American nations in relation to each other. We may note, however, that Costa Rica is rather peripheral in Central American interaction though it is often considered the most important country in the isthmus. It does not turn enough of its interaction potential inward.

ently disturbs the whole picture, is found in the category 'little domination'. Whether a pair is put into category 'low' or 'little domination' may be unimportant. But the particular character of the Argentina-Mexico pair still holds, and we have seen that Mexico plays a role rather different from its rank in interaction in the present system of nations. The direction of Mexican trade has not traditionally gone south, at least not as far south as to South America proper. Thus, its position, which may have a connection with the country's peripheral geographical position in the system, is more like that of a unit of medium status than top status. We shall later see that this discrepancy between status and action gives Mexico some peculiar characteristics in the program-creation of the integration movement.

If Venezuela and Chile are given top rank, there will be five more pairs with high rank and medium interdependence. The proposition that high status implies high degree of interaction is not shaken by the strange behaviour of the Argentina–Mexico pair.

Group 2. The mixed pairs of high and medium rank units are found inside the categories denoted medium interaction or low interaction. Two pairs are found in 'little domination'; what has been said above on this category may also be applied here. Coincidence, more than actual difference, may have guided those pairs into category 'little domination'.

One deviant case is interesting, however: this is the Brazil-Uruguay pair. If we look at pairs in the category with low interaction, we will to our surprise discover Argentina-Uruguay. For an observer visiting Latin America, Uruguay and Argentina have apparently more mutual contact than any other pair of countries in the continent. Do the data on trade blur any important information in this case? Is trade after all a bad indicator when describing that type of behaviour called interaction? It sounds strange indeed that Uruguay's relations with Brazil are equivalent with Bolivia's and Paraguay's relations with Argentina.

Thus, if we take a look at other data,

for instance weekly direct flights between units that are presented in Table 3, we see that there are ten times as many flights between Uruguay and Argentina than between Uruguay and Brazil (158 and 13 respectively). Uruguay's dependence on Brazil, as the data on trade show, does not tell the whole story, probably also because the Argentina-Uruguay economy is competitive. The Brazilian dominance in trade is compensated by a highly developed communication network with its other great neighbour, Argentina. Argentinian newspapers may be bought in Montevideo the same day they are printed in Buenos Aires and sold in the streets, but it is far more difficult to get Journal do Brasil fresh from press.

The two giants in trade on the continent, Argentina and Brazil, exchange only 21 flights a week, in comparison with the 158 that the Argentina-Uruguay pair scores. If we take a closer look at Uruguay, we find that the country is less dependent on the United States than any other unit in the system, and less dependent on Europe than Argentina, measured in terms of commerce.

This elegant balance between four great powers—the neighbour giants Argentina and Brazil and the far-off giants the United States and Europe—is striking. No one dominates Uruguay, though it is a small country. We have seen that Uruguay and Mexico—which behave as dissonances in our data—have some particular traits when they appear in the integration processes, different from units that behave more typically.

The lone pair in category 'minimal', is Brazil-Peru. If we look at the table of weekly flights, Brazil has most flights with Uruguay, Chile *and* Peru, so the slight deviance the pair demonstrates may even be narrowed if we introduce other data for adjustment.

Group 3. The pairs consisting of medium rank units are easily located in group 3, that of low interaction. One pair has more interaction than expected: the Peru-Chile axis. There are two 'axes of interaction' whose degree of intensity makes them penetrate into a level usually reserved for topdogs. The one axis is the Colombia-Ecuador pair (medium-small unit) and the other is the Peru-Chile pair. This may be explained as a consequence of the transportation problem. 90% of all goods are transported by ships in Latin America, and Peru and Chile have easy access to each other through the Pacific. The Chile-Colombia pair scores less than expected, and the reasons may here be the obstacles to transportation within the pair.

Group 4. The mixed pairs with medium rank and low rank units have mostly low or minimal interaction. That one pair has no interaction is not surprising, nor that one pair may be found in category "little domination." The Ecuador-Venezuela pair, which scores most, is a marginal case, difficult to define. Both Ecuador and Venezuela may be put in other status-groups and as well constitute a medium-medium, medium-high, or high-low pair.

Group 5. The pairs with high-rank and low-rank units are distributed perfectly. There is either minimal or no interaction, or the low-rank unit is dominated by the high-rank unit. I have put this category after the medium-low on the Table, to elucidate the symmetry of the Table. The Table would have been perfect if the values were distributed on a diagonal starting at box 'high-high' and ending in the box where 'low interaction' and 'low-low' columns meet. The groups six and seven are adding to the picture new information: all values (except the a-typical Mexico-Argentina case) are found in columns with disequilibrated pairs—high-med., med.-low, low-high. In 75% of the cases of disequilibrated pairs that also show disequilibrium in interaction, a high-status unit is involved.

Group 6. The pairs with low-rank units are also distributed perfectly in the Table. There is either minimal or no interaction.

5. *RESPONSIVENESS AND INFLUENCE*

Invariably there are connections between transactions and responsiveness.

Our task will be to find the associations between responsiveness and the structure of the system where units interact. We are now in a field that may be described as the role of systemic referents[12] in the creation of national foreign policy, and we are almost touching the problems of how a program for integration is developing in Latin America.

By responsiveness we mean the ability to respond to stimuli from other units, referring to the capability of emulation, reaction, imitation—and cooperation. . . .

5.1. DEFINITION OF INFLUENCE

Our concept 'responsiveness' is almost similar to the concept 'influence'. When a unit is responsive towards another, it is capable of influencing the other unit. With the word 'influence' we imply a causal effect between the behaviour of two units, while the word 'responsiveness' denotes that there are correlations between the behaviour of two units. 'Influence' means that a unit modifies the behaviour of another unit.

It may be unsatisfactory to infer that there is influence whenever there is

[12] For a discussion on systemic referents, see Wolfram Hanrieder: 'Actor objectives and international systems', *Journal of Politics*. Vol. 27, no. 1, 1965, pp. 109–133. His systemic referents are considered ideal types, but are attempts at solving the problem posed by J. David Singer: 'The Level-of-Analysis Problem in International Relations", in Klaus Knorr and Sidney Verba ed.: *The International System*, (Princeton 1961).

It is our contention that the structural approach may eliminate the problem whether or not internal and external contingencies are impossible to unite in one model. A low status unit has simply another frame of reference than the high status unit, and the effects of position in the structure may determine the behaviour of a unit, as described and analysed in this paper.

responsiveness, or just to infer that there is influence in some cases. If we rely on our general insight and information of the units we are treating, we may, however, say that there is systematic influence when the internal situation of the unit is such that we should have expected another development if the impulse from outside had not been received. The crucial point in the influence concept is of course the measurement of 'might-have-beens', as long as we have no controlled experimental situation.[13] Our methodological basis may look weak, but we are forced to accept the method as it is until the tools are sharpened. To use a psychological concept, we may in general say that *there is influence among two units, when the impulses from one unit are received and internalized in the other unit.* It may be difficult to grasp and point at the impulses, but we may anticipate their existence when there are similarities where we expected dissimilarities.

5.2 CONDITIONS FOR INFLUENCE

Our proposition says that *unit x is not inflencing unit y, if unit x is dominating unit y.* This is equal to saying that there is no flow of influence within a disequilibrated pair. An impulse from *x* may be regarded as an order or a guide for *y*, but the impulse is not internalised and developed inside its new context.

When there is dominance in interac-

[13] This is a central point in James N. Rosenau: *Public Opinion and Foreign Policy* (Random House, N.Y. 1961). He decides to abandon the concept of influence altogether, and starts out constructing a conceptual edifice around the transmission of opinion. (p. 16). Our conclusion on this problem is rather different. We believe that it is more difficult to catch and measure the

tion among units within a pair, one unit is able to control the other unit's behaviour to a certain extent, by limiting the other unit's interaction with others in the system. 'Influence' and 'dominance' are two facets of the power-aspect that work contrarily: *the more dominance, the less influence.* This proposition is in sharp opposition to conventional ideas of power politics. . . .

Interaction among equals in the international society is not usual, because the system is highly stratified and almost feudal in structure. Equal and low-ranking pairs will tend to have little interaction, if any at all. Equal and high-ranking pairs, on the contrary, have a higher degree of interaction; and we may expect that they will imitate each other, emulate each other, and cooperate with each other. We may expect the demonstration effect to work on this level between equals, and also the spill-over effect; this may mean—for instance—that treaties on this level among equals are likely to trigger off more treaties than among equals on lower levels. There is one important policy implication in this: *If a unit wants to influence another, it should do as much as possible to help the other unit reach its own position in the world system of nations.*

5.3 DATA ON INFLUENCE

In the class-like, or feudal-like, world society of today, we are observing a widening of gaps between rich and poor countries. We may count institutional links between topdogs in the world, between topdogs and underdogs, and between underdogs, to find out at which level the institutional network

concrete impulses, the transmissions, than the consequences of the impulses.

is best developed. We will expect the links between Western Europe and the United States to be broad and strong, while links between North and South of the globe are considerably less developed, and the institutional connections among underdogs almost non-important.

According to our theory, influence will work between Europe and the United States, while dominance will characterize the North-South interaction. Typical pairs of interaction characterised by domination are those with the United States as one unit and any Latin American nation as the other.

Data on commerce show that the Latin American nations behave with characteristics of small nations towards the United States:[14] the closer to the United States' border, the more dependent on the United States. The dependence on Europe is constant, not influenced by geographical positions of units. The data are given in Table 12, and indices on dependence of Europe and the United States in Table 13.

The United States and the Latin American nations give us examples of how rank influences interaction, not only its intensity, but also its consequences in terms of influence and dominance. The transaction flow from the United States to Mexico is striking, both in terms of trade and in terms of information through newspapers. The two dailies *Excélsior* and *Novedades* carry more material from the United States than seven Latin American dailies give to all foreign material. *Novedades* carries almost as much on the United States in thirty days as the *New York Times* carries about all foreign

nations in about the same number of days; and *Excélsior* carries considerably more United States material than the big New York daily carries foreign material.[15]

This example may indicate several things: 1) despite the immense flow of goods from the United States to Mexico, the United States does not influence the behaviour of Mexico, neither in internal affairs, nor in foreign affairs. The United States domination of Mexico leads to the negative effect of no-influence, but not to the positive effect of control, because Mexico's rank in the system is relatively high. 2) The United States and Mexico might have influenced each other to a greater extent if the flow of goods and information had been reciprocal and equal. 3) It is wrong to assume that the amount of transactions alone indicates degree of integration, simply because the perception of transactions is very important in cooperation and integration.

Similar to the United States-Mexico pair is the Argentina-Paraguay pair. In our data Paraguay looks like an Argentine satellite, and there is no indication that Argentina and Paraguay are imitative, emulative, or cooperative towards each other. It is probably difficult to find two neighbours as different as these two.

On the other hand, we have the Brazil-Argentina pair, which also shows many dissimilarities in social structure and historical development. But it has been remarkable for an observer to see all the similarities in politics that characterise this pair of units. Inside this pair we find the political behaviour

---

14 On small nations and their dependence on geographical position, see Galtung, Mora, Schwartzman, op.cit.

15 John C. Merrill: 'The United States as seen from Mexico', *Journal of Inter-American Studies*. Vol. V, no. 1, 1963, pp. 53–66.

TABLE 12. Trade of Latin American Nations

Exports

Exports to & imports from Country	Year	To ALALC 10⁶ $	%	To ALALC & Boliv. & Venez. 10⁶ $	%	To all Latin America 10⁶ $	%	To United States 10⁶ $	%	To Western Europe 10⁶ $	%	To others 10⁶ $	%	Total exports 10⁶ $
Argentina	1959	137.6	13.6	148.4	14.7	149.3	14.8	107.8	10.7	655.0	64.9	86.9	9.6	1,009.0
	1963	197.7	14.3	185.0	13.6	200.0	14.6	153.6	11.2	884.1	64.8	90.6	9.3	1,364.6
Brazil	1959	75.1	5.9	76.3	6.0	76.9	6.0	592.2	46.2	540.4	42.2	72.4	5.6	1,281.9
	1963	76.0	5.4	78.3	5.6	83.8	6.0	530.9	37.7	584.4	45.1	207.9	14.8	1,407.0
Chile	1959	38.7	7.8	42.0	8.5	45.6	9.2	193.5	39.0	245.7	49.5	11.8	2.3	496.6
	1963	49.4	9.1	51.2	9.5	54.0	10.0	185.0	34.2	257.6	47.6	45.0	8.3	541.6
Colombia	1959	2.8	0.6	4.3	0.9	7.3	1.6	321.4	69.0	117.1	25.1	19.9	4.3	466.0
	1963	6.0	1.3	6.9	1.5	12.4	2.8	233.7	52.3	150.0	33.6	50.5	11.3	446.6
Ecuador	1959	7.8	8.1	9.4	9.7	10.4	10.8	58.1	60.1	24.7	25.5	3.5	3.6	96.7
	1963	7.8	5.9	8.1	6.2	8.3	6.3	74.0	56.4	31.6	24.1	17.3	13.2	131.2
Mexico	1959	4.9	0.7	9.6	1.3	25.4	3.4	439.6	58.6	66.0	8.8	218.8	29.2	749.8
	1963	25.9	2.7	32.2	3.3	52.8	5.4	597.5	61.5	80.4	8.3	240.5	24.8	971.2
Paraguay	1959	7.5	24.0	7.8	25.0	7.8	25.0	10.3	33.0	9.0	28.8	4.1	13.2	31.2
	1963	10.1	25.1	10.1	25.1	10.1	25.1	9.1	22.6	13.1	32.5	8.0	19.8	40.3
Peru	1959	46.6	14.9	50.4	16.1	51.8	16.5	98.4	31.4	123.6	39.4	39.9	12.7	313.7
	1963	49.1	9.1	53.8	9.9	54.2	10.0	190.9	35.3	230.8	42.6	65.2	12.1	541.1
Uruguay	1959	2.7	2.7	3.0	3.0	3.4	3.4	11.6	11.7	53.2	53.8	30.6	31.0	98.8
	1963	15.1	9.1	15.1	9.1	15.8	9.6	19.2	11.6	108.7	65.8	21.6	13.1	165.3
Bolivia	1959	7.4	9.6	7.4	9.6	7.4	9.6	27.0	34.9	40.2	52.0	2.7	3.5	77.3
	1963	3.0	3.5	3.0	3.5	3.0	3.5	27.9	32.3	53.9	62.5	1.5	1.7	86.3
Venezuela	1959	202.1	8.5	202.1	8.5	268.0	11.3	988.2	41.8	369.5	15.6	740.9	31.3	2,366.6
	1963	125.6	4.8	125.6	4.8	166.9	6.3	882.5	33.5	573.0	21.8	1,006.6	38.3	2,629.0

Data from: Donald W. Baerresen, Martin Carnoy & Joseph Grunwald: *Latin American Trade Patterns*. The Brookings Institution Washington DC, 1965.

TABLE 12 (cont'd)

Imports

Exports to & Imports from Country	Year	From Boliv. & Venez. ALALC 10⁶ $	%	From ALALC & America Boliv. & Venez. 10⁶ $	%	From all Latin America 10⁶ $	%	From United States 10⁶ $	%	From Western Europe 10⁶ $	%	From others 10⁶ $	%	Total Imports 10⁶ $
Argentina	1959	107.3	10.8	220.3	22.2	222.0	22.4	191.1	19.3	409.8	41.3	169.3	17.1	992.2
	1963	101.0	10.3	125.3	12.6	129.0	13.2	241.7	24.6	457.7	46.7	152.5	15.5	980.9
Brazil	1959	116.9	8.5	227.9	16.7	233.8	17.0	461.3	33.6	451.2	32.8	228.1	16.6	1,374.4
	1963	164.0	11.3	261.6	17.6	262.4	17.6	456.5	30.7	475.8	32.0	292.7	19.7	1,487.4
Chile	1959	54.6	13.2	55.0	13.3	56.9	13.8	218.9	53.1	119.4	29.0	16.7	4.1	411.9
	1963	120.0	18.8	127.7	20.0	140.1	22.0	223.9	35.1	221.3	34.7	52.2	8.2	637.5
Colombia	1959	9.0	2.2	10.5	2.6	20.3	4.9	245.4	59.2	112.6	27.2	35.9	8.7	414.2
	1963	21.3	4.2	22.4	4.4	36.5	7.3	259.9	51.9	161.8	32.3	42.5	8.5	500.7
Ecuador	1959	2.5	2.8	4.9	5.6	5.4	5.9	47.2	51.8	32.0	35.1	6.6	7.2	91.2
	1963	5.3	17.2	13.3	17.5	17.5	13.5	49.9	38.6	45.1	34.8	16.9	13.1	129.4
Mexico	1959	3.9	0.4	4.2	0.4	12.4	1.2	733.9	73.0	202.0	20.1	57.0	5.7	1,005.3
	1963	10.8	0.9	11.4	0.9	19.2	1.5	850.2	68.6	269.0	21.7	101.1	8.2	1,239.5
Paraguay	1959	7.6	28.9	7.6	28.9	7.6	28.9	5.3	20.2	7.9	30.0	5.5	20.9	26.3
	1963	7.9	24.2	7.9	24.2	7.9	24.2	9.6	29.4	8.4	25.8	6.7	20.6	326.6
Peru	1959	20.8	7.1	21.3	7.2	23.7	8.1	132.6	45.1	106.8	36.3	31.0	10.5	294.1
	1963	62.0	11.1	65.7	11.8	66.8	12.0	207.6	37.3	210.3	37.7	72.5	13.0	557.1
Uruguay	1959	28.7	17.9	43.8	27.3	44.3	27.7	32.0	20.0	62.6	39.1	21.0	13.1	159.9
	1963	32.2	18.2	40.9	23.1	45.5	25.7	27.3	15.4	77.0	43.4	27.4	15.5	177.2
Bolivia	1959	15.2	26.0	15.2	26.0	16.7	28.6	28.8	49.3	10.0	17.1	2.9	5.0	58.4
	1963	9.4	9.1	9.4	9.1	10.0	9.6	49.5	47.7	33.7	32.5	10.6	10.2	103.8
Venezuela	1959	21.4	1.5	21.4	1.5	39.8	2.8	750.2	53.2	511.1	36.2	109.5	7.8	1,410.6
	1963	24.5	2.8	24.5	2.8	26.2	3.0	470.3	54.0	274.1	31.5	100.0	11.5	870.6

The figures for ALALC, All Latin America, United States, Western Europe and Total are taken from Tables V-1 to V-11. The figures in 'Others' are figured out from the numbers in the present table. The figures in 'ALALC + Bolivia and Venezuela' are figured out from the numbers in the present table and Tables VI-1 to VI-11.

TABLE 13. Indices on Each Country's Trade with the United States and Europe

Country	Trade US/LA	Trade Eu/LA
1. Mexico	18.6	4.3
2. Venezuela	9.8	5.9
3. Colombia	9.4	6.6
4. Bolivia	6.2	7.3
5. Ecuador	4.8	2.9
6. Peru	4.1	4.4
7. Brazil	2.8	3.2
8. Chile	2.2	2.6
9. Argentina	1.3	4.0
10. Paraguay	1.1	1.2
11. Uruguay	0.8	3.7

Spearman's Rho is -0.2.

called populism more deeply based than in any other unit in the system, exemplified by the two foremost populists on the continent, Getulio Vargas in Brazil and Juan Perón in Argentina. The revolution in Brazil in April 1964 and the revolution in Argentina in June 1966 showed many striking similarities in origin and performance—and not least in character and purpose.[16]

5.4 The Importance of The Middle Level Unit

What we have said so far points at the importance of the medium status unit: it is less likely to dominate than a top status unit, and less likely to be dominated than a low status unit. Hence it should be capable of influence, more so than other types of units.

In relation to Table 9, we observed that 70% of the units in the ALALC-system fall within the three categories high-medium, medium-medium, and

medium-low. This indicates that the medium status nation may have an important role to play in Latin America. There is, however, one caution: all units *defined* in this paper as medium status may not necessarily play *the role* of the medium status unit. There may be some medium status units that dominate their opposition party in the pair, or are dominated by topdogs in the interaction.

The diplomatic history of Latin America demonstrates how medium nations have tried to cooperate, and had to do so alone because top status and low status nations were not interested. We shall also show how the Latin American nations behaved when a 'super-dog' entered the scene.

We must first protest against the commonly-held belief that the Latin American continent was 'united' during the colonial occupation. First of all, occupation by military forces over an area very seldom means that the area is integrated.[17] Secondly, we know that the local 'caudillos' and the traditional provincial forces claiming autonomy were stronger than the we-feeling at the time of independence: the conflicts between unitarians, who wanted a strong and unified state, versus the federalists, who agitated for local autonomy, show the local interests to be deeply located in Latin America during and after the fall of the Spanish empire, and difficult to reconcile. Above this fractioned continent, almost like a super-structure, lingered the dreams of continental unification, as expressed in poetic language by the great liberators of the struggle for in-

16 Egil Fossum: 'Factors influencing the occurrence of military coups d'etat in Latin America', *Journal of Peace Research,* no. 3, 1967, pp. 228–251, shows how military coups d'etat occur simultaneously in neighbour nations, provided these are topdogs in the system.

17 Karl W. Deutsch et. al: *Political Community and the North Atlantic Area* (Princeton 1957), p. 29, demonstrates the inefficiency of military occupation in integration processes.

TABLE 14. Participation in Latin American Conferences 1847–1864

Country	1 meeting	2 meeting	3 meeting	4 meeting	Meeting-frequency
Peru	X	X	X	X	4
Chile	X	X	—	X	3
Ecuador	X	X	—	X	3
Colombia	X	—	X	X	3
Bolivia	X	—	—	X	2
Guatemala	—	—	X	X	2
Venezuela	—	—	X	X	2
El Salvador	—	—	X	X	2
Mexico	—	—	X	—	1
Costa Rica	—	—	X	—	1

dependence. They hoped to create a united America 'from Canada to Patagonia', which should 'present America to the world in an aspect of majesty and grandeur unexampled among the nations of antiquity'.

The liberators initiated international politics in Latin America. The first international congress was organised by Simon Bolivar in Panama in 1826, when he was president of Colombia. His attempt to unify the continent was unsuccessful, as only Colombia, Mexico and Peru took part in the congress. Important countries as Argentina, Brazil, Chile, the United States, and England did not participate.

In continental meetings from 1847 to 1864, we can see the sense of cohesion among units of medium rank, as demonstrated by Table 14.

Peru was the most frequent participator in the congresses, probably not so much because of overwhelming military and political strength, as because of tradition. Lima had been the center of the Spanish empire, and after the shocks of the independence movement, Spanish America was relaxing with some remnants of the old picture still intact. Not participating were some of the biggest nations, like the United States, Argentina, and Brazil, and

smallest, like Uruguay and Paraguay.

It is, however, difficult to deduce any conclusions about the international structure's influence on interaction. The values determining stratification might have been completely different at that time. We may, nevertheless, be able to put items of information on nineteenth century Latin American interaction into the general picture.

Significantly, the countries not participating were the biggest and the smallest ones, another example of how equals appear more responsive towards each other. If the big nations had taken part, the small nations would also have followed. That is what happened in 1889 and later at the Pan American Conferences. *When a great power takes the initiative, the small ones follow; and the smaller they are, the more eagerly they participate.*[18]

[18] As predicted by Johan Galtung: 'International Relations and International Conflicts: A Sociological Approach'. Transactions of the Sixth World Congress of Sociology. (Evian, 4–11 September 1966) p. 160.

This was also discovered by Amitai Etzioni: *Political Unification* (Holt, Rinehart and Winston 1965), p. 292, where he states that units tend to be more oriented to the external elite, the weaker the units are.

We shall see how this proposition holds in three different contexts: 1) when international conferences take place, 2) in determining participation in the two world wars, 3) when international agreements are negotiated. The first time all Latin American nations were represented at a conference was in 1889, when the United States took the initiative, having refused to participate in all former conferences.

The president of Uruguay, José Batlle y Ordoñez, tried in 1907 to convince the United States that the conferences should be reorganized into a tighter political institution. Bolivia tried the same at the third conference and the Dominican Republic at the fourth.

When the United States became involved in World War I and asked its Latin American allies for assistance, both Uruguay and Paraguay asked for inter-American conferences (with no response). This showed the smaller nations' eagerness to come into cooperation and commit themselves to the big nation. In another spirit Argentina sent out invitations to a strictly Latin American conference in 1917, trying to keep the United States outside the deliberations that they wanted to take place on the continent. The United States' State Department declared that the congress should not be held, referring to a Peruvian statement: 'The government of Peru considers that the policy of this continent should be one with the policies of the United States'. That was the last word in the case, and the conference was never held.

When the United States declared war on Germany in 1917, together went seven underdogs (Cuba, Costa Rica, Guatemala, Haiti, Honduras, Nicaragua, Panama)—but only one topdog: Brazil. The only non-collaborators were Argentina and Mexico.

Five more countries were neutral, of which three had a relatively high position (Chile, Venezuela and Colombia) while El Salvador and Paraguay were the only neutral underdogs. Five underdogs broke diplomatic relations with Germany. The thirteen countries that thus either declared war or severed diplomatic relations with the Central Powers, had bilateral defense agreements with the United States. No Pan-American meeting was held.[19]

This had changed in 1938, when the threats from Europe were discussed at meetings of foreign ministers from all America, and fear of German acquisition of European territories in South and Central America was mentioned. In that situation Argentina was the only non-collaborator, and Brazil behaved just as it did in 1917.

Rank influences behaviour in international negotiations also, as shown when the United States took an initiative to secure its private capital in Latin American nations in 1951 by the Mutual Security Act—after the negotiations of the Treaty of Friendship, Commerce, and Economic Development had proved a failure and only was signed by Nicaragua. The Act was signed by the low-status nations Ecuador, Bolivia, and Paraguay, and the Central American countries Costa Rica, Guatemala, Honduras, Nicaragua, and Cuba and Haiti in the Antilles, while Peru and Colombia—the most typical medium rank units—were the only na-

[19] Because of the absence of the 'super-dog' at the League of Nations, Latin American participation was weak. The absence of the United States was characterized as a betrayal, and Brazil and Costa Rica were the first countries to leave the League forever. The weak participation and the absence of the United States make data on participation in the League of Nations rather uninteresting in this context, and they are left out of this report.

tions of relatively high rank that participated in the Act. Brazil and Mexico did not want to have anything to do with the Act, and Argentina was not even asked.

The units with a higher position in the system—Argentina, Brazil, and Mexico—behave more individually, i.e. more independently. Argentina was the top-ranking nation in Latin America during the whole period, second only to the United States in inter-American affairs, and denied any close cooperation with the 'super-dog'. Brazil took the opposite stand in both wars, even directly participating in Italy. Mexico was a non-collaborator in 1917, but a collaborator in 1941.

Even units dominated by a 'super-dog' behave more freely when their position in the system is high. They do not identify with the United States at all, nor imitate, nor cooperate—though the United States ranks on the top level to which they may aspire. This finding is apparently contrary to what is accepted as good stratification theory.[20] The theory says that mobile persons identify in norms and behaviour with the upper level to which they may aspire. Our finding does not refute the old one, but simply stresses the importance of *mobility*. The inter-American system is definitely not mobile, and this fact accounts for the lack of responsiveness between the 'super-class' and the 'top-class' in the inter-American system.

6. STRUCTURAL IMPLICATIONS ON INTEGRATION

Starting with a 'catastrophe theory', stating that units with a high position

20 Bernhard Berelson & Gary A. Steiner, *Human Behavior* (Harcourt, Brace & World, Inc., 1964), p. 487.

would probably monopolize capabilities of mutual influence because of high intensity of interaction, we modified the proposition by pointing at the important position of the medium rank unit. The 'catastrophe theory' has furthermore been modified by three propositions. The first one says that perception of transactions is important for the outcome; it is not only the amount of transactions that count (for instance in the Mexico-United States pair of nations). The second proposition states that even dominated states behave independently when ascribed relatively high position in the system (for instance Argentina's, Mexico's, and Brazil's attitudes towards the World Wars). We may add a *third*, saying that the values of internal elites in units may heavily influence the behaviour of states (for instance in behaviour towards Cuba). We shall now look at the integration experiment in Latin America in the light of these propositions.

According to the 'catastrophe theory', Argentina and Brazil in interaction with Mexico should determine the direction and speed of the process. As we shall see, this is only partly true.

Argentina, Uruguay, Brazil, and Chile—the Cono Sur—took the initiative and the lead in negotiations before ALALC was created. They are the countries least dependent on the United States and with the highest degree of interaction in the system—80% of the system's trade is exchanged between these units. They did not *start* the negotiations, however. Many years of analysis background work had been done by a professional administrative elite partly outside any of the units, acting through the United Nations Economic Commission for Latin America at least since 1950. In negotiations before 1960, Mexico sided with this group of experts, in opposition to the Cono Sur countries, in the debates concerning the creation of the first institution through which planned integration was to take place.

Mexico wanted ALALC to go much further than the Cono Sur countries would admit, and demonstrated the most aggressive attitude towards future institutionalised cooperation. In the opinion of the Mexican representatives, the integration institution should have a character more similar to a common market from the beginning; while the Cono Sur countries were more occupied with holding a position closer to the status quo, in order to pursue the profits they already had gained by earlier efforts between themselves. They already enjoyed a privileged position in interaction in the system. The discrepancy between Mexico's rank and its role in system interaction inspired the more aggressive attitude of the Mexican representatives. Mexico was optimistically regarding its role in an integrated Latin America.

This optimism has been proved right; Mexico is today satisfied with her new role. The free trade area has made the ratio between status and interaction more balanced, and Mexico, and Mexico's behaviour is more similar to that of Argentina and Brazil than it was before ALALC was created.

Chile is at present least satisfied with the state of affairs, taking Mexico's earlier place as the 'de-nationalised' professional administrative elite's most faithful ally. It is a country just on the border-line between topdogs and 'mediumdogs', with certain aspirations to level Argentina and Brazil. We expect Venezuela to be in the same situation as Chile; but as this unit entered ALALC in 1966, there is too little information on Venezuela's attitudes after it entered the free trade area.[21]

The markets of Argentina and Brazil are defined as 'sufficient' for national development by the ALALC treaty, and they thus behave more as sedate participants in the processes. The same can today be said of Mexico probably to a lesser extent, but it is difficult to measure adequately differences of content and discontent between the three countries. Mexico finds the development inside ALALC satisfactory and does not favour the more aggressive attitude articulated in the early sixties.

One of the most important later events in the slow integration process trying to catch root in Latin America was the Bogota meeting in 1966 with Peru, Chile, Colombia, Bolivia, and Ecuador participating. The fact that the meeting was held made the Brazilian government send a note to Chile expressing its concern about the future division of the continent in different blocs. As nothing else in the year 1966 this meeting seems to have frightened and inspired talk about integration on high levels, and perhaps the problem of integration gained in saliency in the continent. . . .

From what we have said above, it is necessary to keep an eye on nations like Chile, Venezuela, and probably Colombia and Peru, because the most aggressive behaviour must be expected from those units in the integration processes. The nations have the crucial characteristics of the middle-group level that Karl Deutsch mentions:[22] 1) Without them, taken all together, little can be

21 [See selection 33 (Ed.).]
22 Karl Deutsch: *The Nerves of Government* (N.Y. 1963), pp. 154–157.

done, and particularly, little can be done, and particularly, little can be changed. The top status nations may stop the integration process if they ally with certain elites in other countries, otherwise they will be isolated. 2) Each of the middle-level nations must count with the group of topdogs, with whose support much can be done, but against whom they are more helpless.

The topdogs are the *generals* in the integration process, content with the state of affairs. The 'mediumdogs' are the *colonels,* more open for changes in the system.

The 'mediumdog' nations have also a stronger capability of influence up and down in the hierarchy of nations, because they have more equals. . . .

II

Patterns and Problems of Contemporary Inter-American Relations in Key Issue-Areas

A

SECURITY AND PEACEFUL SETTLEMENT

9

Soviet Policy in Latin America

Herbert S. Dinerstein

From Herbert S. Dinerstein, "Soviet Policy in Latin America," *The American Political Science Review*, LXI, No. 1 (March 1967), pp. 80–90. Reprinted by permission of the author and the publisher. (Footnotes in the original version have been omitted.)

Herbert S. Dinerstein is a Professor in The Washington Center of Foreign Policy Research at The School of Advanced International Studies of The Johns Hopkins University.

Since independence, the three principal extracontinental *threats to the security of Latin America have emanated from the Holy Alliance and successor imperialist governments in Europe in the nineteenth and early twentieth centuries; the Axis during the Second World War; and the Soviet Union, primarily in the post-World War II era. Professor Dinerstein focuses on the latter.*

Drawing largely upon Soviet literature[1], Dinerstein traces the evolution of Soviet doctrine on the likelihood of Communist revolutions in Latin America, from an early "geographic fatalism" through an abrupt rise and decline in optimism with the changing fortunes of the Cuban Revolution and the Cuban Missile Crisis. He asserts that, although another guerrilla victory in Latin America could force the Soviets to clarify their calculatedly ambivalent position on violent revolutions and risk a confrontation with the United States, they now appear content with the modest goal of lessening U.S. influence in the hemisphere by giving cautious support to radical (and even not so radical) nationalist governments and groups.

[1] See also: Robert G. Carlton, ed., *Soviet Image of Contemporary Latin America: A Documentary History, 1960–1968* (Austin: University of Texas Press, 1970); Stephen Clissold, ed., *Soviet Relations with Latin America 1918–68: A Documentary Survey* (London: Oxford University Press, 1970); and J. Gregory Oswald and Anthony J. Strover eds., *The Soviet Union and Latin America* (New York: Praeger, 1970).

The Chinese Communists have largely limited their involvement to factional struggles within traditional Latin American Communist parties and strictly verbal backing of indigenous guerrilla movements.[2] *Castro's rapprochement with the Soviets in 1964 precipitated a clash with Peking which has had a lasting impact on Cuban-Chinese relations.*

When Dinerstein wrote in 1966, he detected some strains in Castro's accord with Moscow and concluded: "Only time will tell whether the uneasy Cuban-Soviet agreement on policy toward insurrection can be maintained. . . ." Since then, in fact, the Cuban line has again come almost full circle. The years 1966–67 saw what Jackson, an analyst of the ideological juggling between Havana and Moscow, has termed a dramatic "reassertion of theoretical Castroism."[3] *Early in 1967 the Cuban government published Regis Debray's* Revolution Within the Revolution?, *which strongly condemned Latin American Communist parties for a lack of revolutionary fervor and advanced a strategy of revolution centering on the mobile guerrilla striking force (see selection 11). Castroite pronouncements on violent insurrection reached a peak of sorts at the Latin American Solidarity Conference the following July. Jackson attributes this shift mainly to Castro's determination to keep the Soviets from taking his regime for granted and to refurbish his image as a revolutionary leader in the face of criticism from the Latin American "New Left."*[4]

However, Castro delivered a remarkably mild speech on the tenth anniversary of the Cuban Revolution in January, 1969; and subsequently there was a decided lowering of the tone and level of Cuban publicity (and seeming support) for guerrilla activity in Latin America. Castro appeared to draw closer to both the USSR and Latin America as he supported the Soviet invasion of Czechoslovakia and joined the Soviets in approbation of the Peruvian and Bolivian militaries' expropriations and reforms and of Allende's electoral victory in Chile. The latest Cuban stance is undoubtedly related to Guevara's failure in Bolivia in the fall of 1967, to flagging guerrilla campaigns elsewhere in Latin America, and to Castro's renewed concern with domestic political and economic problems.[5] *The stance itself may yet prove to be either just another development in the tortuous foreign policy*

---

2 See esp.: Cecil Johnson, *Communist China and Latin America, 1959–1967* (New York: Columbia University Press, 1970); Ernst Halperin, "Peking and the Latin American Communists," *The China Quarterly,* No. 25 (January-March 1967), pp. 111–54; George Ginsburg and Arthur Stahnke, "Communist China's Trade Relations with Latin America," *Asian Survey,* X, No. 9 (September 1970), 803–19.

3 D. Bruce Jackson, *Castro, the Kremlin, and Communism in Latin America* (Washington: The Johns Hopkins Press, 1969), p. 121. This volume is a study of the period 1964–1967. See also Andrés Suárez, *Cuba Castroism and Communism* (Cambridge: M.I.T. Press, 1967).

4 *Castro, the Kremlin,* chap. 8 *passim.*

5 See Edward Gonzales, "Castro: The Limits of Charisma," *Problems of Communism,* XIX, No. 4 (July-August 1970), pp. 12–24.

*course of the Cuban Revolution or—more likely—the beginning of the end
of Cuba's partially self-imposed isolation in the hemisphere.*

I. INTRODUCTION

The general conclusions of the study will be stated at the outset in the broadest terms to aid the reader in his evaluation of the argument as it is unfolded in more detail.

The Soviet leaders expected to make great advances in the underdeveloped world as it decolonized. They hoped that the Communists would lead the nationalist rebellions and convert them into Communist states. Only in the North of Indochina has the Communist party been able to do so; the South is still in contest. High hopes in Indonesia, Algeria, and the Congo have come to naught. The successful seizure of power in Cuba has taken place in an unanticipated manner.

In this case, a non-Communist revolution converted itself into a Communist one. Before Castro's assumption of power in Cuba, the Soviet Union viewed Latin America in general, and the Caribbean in particular, as an area where American power severely limited Communist opportunities. The overthrow of the Arbenz regime in Guatemala in 1954 seemed to prove the point. But for a time after the Bay of Pigs episode, the Cubans believed, and seemed to have convinced the Soviets, that the Cuban revolution could be exported. But the failure of several attempts to do so, and the outcome of the missile crisis in the fall of 1962, caused first the Soviets and somewhat later the Cubans to revise their hopes for new Communist states in Latin America in the near or foreseeable future. Now several years after the windfall of Castro's conversion, Soviet attention is increasingly centered on the costs to be borne. First, although Castro will probably remain a Communist, he will continue to be as defiant as he can afford to be. Second, Castro has cost the Soviet Union a great deal of money and, although these contributions have been reduced, the end is not yet in sight. Third, the appearance in Latin America of regimes seemingly on the road to communism has been shown to provoke United States intervention. Such intervention is less costly to the Soviet Union when the loss of a Communist state is not at issue than after the Soviets have made large commitments, or after a Communist regime has been established. For this reason, and because the Soviets do not foresee the victory of traditional Communist parties in Latin America and have all sorts of reservations about parties headed by "Johnny-come lately" Communists like Castro, they prefer a long transition from coalition governments to communism, and indeed favor an extended period of national democracy in which many social elements participate. As long as the situation is one which might be called "creeping revolution," the Soviet Union's commitment, economic and military, can be kept within the bounds of what the Soviets are willing to invest. But once a country labels itself Communist, the Soviet options are greatly restricted. Hence the Soviet Union's preference for a gradual transition in Latin American countries to such rapid communization as in the case of Cuba. But the Soviets are not free to follow their preferences if they want to maintain influence, let alone control, over revolutionary parties. In

Central America, particularly in Guatemala, Venezuela, and Peru, there are partisan movements, most of which are run by indigenous, non-Communist revolutionaries who are willing to take greater risks and resort more readily to violence than do the traditional Communist parties. The Cubans and the Chinese are potential sponsors of these movements and thus a threat to Soviet influence. To preserve its influence, the Soviet Union has to grant these movements greater autonomy, and this in turn creates conflicts with the traditional Communist parties in Latin America, which stand to suffer as a result of communist support of violence in any one country.

It is unlikely that the Soviets will be able to have revolutions in Latin America when and how they want them. Much more likely, in any future case, the Soviet Union will be confronted with a revolutionary situation where it will have to either support or reject the incipient Communist revolution. Soviet doctrine, which is to be examined in the next pages, does not enable us to predict which choice Soviet leaders will make, but it can furnish a better notion of the intellectual atmosphere in which Soviet policymakers move.

II. SOVIET DOCTRINE ON POLITICAL DEVELOPMENT IN UNDERDEVELOPED COUNTRIES

Soviet scholars writing on the underdeveloped world recognize that its political problems represent a special category and that Communist revolutions in these areas will differ from earlier Communist revolutions elsewhere. Few go as far as did a young French Communist [Debray] writing in a Cuban weekly, who said, in effect, that the history of the Communist revolutions of the past was a poor guide to the future. "The true value of the Cuban revolution is perhaps more forcefully perceived within the revolution itself: it dispenses with the revolutionary models of the Soviet Union, China, and *even Cuba....*" If one reviews American and even Soviet accounts of the revolution in Russia itself, and of the creation of Communist states in Eastern Europe and China, it becomes obvious that all the peering into the entrails of a political situation to see if the pattern of Moscow 1917, Peking 1947, Prague 1948, or Havana 1959 is being repeated has been wasted effort. Some such realization seems to inform Soviet analyses of the underdeveloped world, as we shall presently see.

Not only is any future seizure of power likely to follow different rules, but the model of the development of the Soviet Union has little relevance for underdeveloped countries. For years before and after the Second World War, the experience of the modernization of a backward part of the Soviet Union, Soviet Central Asia, was compared to the situation in colonial countries. By almost any definition, Soviet Central Asia was an underdeveloped country. In almost fifty years of Soviet rule the situation has changed radically. But how was this achieved? Enormous amounts of Soviet capital and trained personnel (a special form of capital) have been invested in this area over a period of fifty years. The equalization of living standards between the backward and the more advanced areas of the Soviet Union was one consequence of planning on an all-Union scale. But who is going to provide the capital for the four hundred millions of India? For the six or seven hundred millions of China?

Such questions throw into sharp relief the dilemma that foreign economic development poses for the Soviet Union (and indeed for the United States). It is becoming increasingly evident that the present situation in almost all the underdeveloped countries makes both the Soviet and the American model only marginally relevant.

Marxian analysts can neither expect the underdeveloped countries to undertake industrialization on the model of capitalist development, nor can they expect them to follow the example of the Soviet Union. The latter, paradoxically, has followed Marx's model of capitalist industrialization more closely than any other country. Capital was accumulated almost exclusively on the basis of forced savings, for the Soviet leaders made an early decision to go it alone and refused to permit foreign capital to be invested in their state. Although some leaders of the underdeveloped world believed that their only course was to follow the Soviet example, political realities in their own countries have ruled this out. It is possible to force present generations to sacrifice themselves for the future, but only if the state is run by ruthless leaders who are convinced that immutable laws of economics exist and that they alone understand them. Thus far, only Communist regimes have met these criteria.

If regimes of this kind should continue to appear, they would present a peculiar problem to the Soviet Union because of the political and economic demands they would make on it. Even had it desired to do so, the Soviet Union obviously would have been incapable of helping China on the same scale that it did its own Central Asian republics. Therefore, successful Communist revolutions in poor and overpopulated countries hereafter will not be able to emulate the Soviet experience without aid from the Soviet Union of a magnitude far beyond that nation's resources. Thus a new problem has emerged, the problem of "premature communism."

The Soviet Union has contributed to the Cuban economy, but reluctantly and without any genuine choice in the matter. Yet Cuba is smaller and has a much better articulated infrastructure than many other underdeveloped countries. There is a limit to the potential number of new Communist states which could expect economic support from the established Communist powers, and "premature" Communist regimes that could not count on Soviet economic support might well founder. In a sense, the Soviet Union has been forced into the very position for which it criticized the Mensheviks in 1917. It prefers that capital be accumulated before the socialist revolution so that the new Communist states will have a better chance of success and not make embarrassing demands upon the Soviet Union. Naturally, the Soviet formulation is not so blunt but the meaning is clear. As we go on to examine Soviet doctrine on the economic and political development of underdeveloped countries, the basis for so radical a shift in Soviet preferences will emerge.

Soviet economists argue that improving labor productivity is a better way to accumulate capital than concentrating on large capital installations with scant reference to productivity. Therefore, some underdeveloped countries are advised against following the Soviet example of developing large steel mills and all the paraphernalia of heavy industry, but are urged instead to develop whatever pays best and use the profits from that to capitalize. Thus, Che

Guevara, who created a mystique of sacrifice and was willing to industrialize Cuba without regard to whether it was economically expedient, was overruled by the Soviets, who would have had to foot much of the bill. The Cubans were advised to industrialize by starting with what they could do most profitably, which was to grow sugar.

The Soviets have also stressed the need for agricultural reforms, particularly for Latin America, as a way to increase the size of the internal market. Their argument, familiar enough in Western economic writings, is that large segments of the peasant populations of the world produce so inefficiently that they can do little more than feed themselves and are unable to buy any of products of industry, thereby putting a ceiling on the expansion of domestic manufactures. To expand the internal market, therefore, agricultural reforms (not argicultural revolutions, it should be noted) are advocated. Given such reforms, the peasants will have some surplus; they will enter the market; the bourgeoisie and the proletariat will expand; and economic progress will have begun.

Soviet economists advise underdeveloped countries to get their capital from both the Soviet Union and the United States. They say, in so many words, that the Soviet Union has neither the capital nor the skills to help the entire underdevleoped world, and that these countries therefore must have recourse to Western capital.

Soviet writers profess to see an important political difference between countries that are on the path to socialism and those that are not. Since many of the leaders of the underdeveloped world reject the capitalist system and tend to take out much of their frustration on the capitalist world, Soviet writers expect that in the transition period many of these countries will be adjuncts to the Soviet diplomatic system rather than the capitalist. If countries espouse the doctrine of socialism, say the Soviet writers, even if it is not socialism in the Soviet sense, this represents an important predisposition for socialism and against capitalism. If medium-term gains from a policy can be anticipated, it is not necessary to make a strong case for the long-term gains.

A crucial factor in this new type of socialist revolution is the concept of what the Soviet writers call intermediate, or interstitial, strata and what Western scholars would call the technocratic elite: a service class composed of people with skills rather than property. Its members may belong to the military, the bureaucracy, or the professional classes. According to Soviet theory, in a country developed on a state-capitalist rather than a private-capitalist basis this new class grouping will have a vested interest in pushing toward a state-managed system rather than a traditional, capitalist state. As the political power of private capital will be small, the "new class" will meet little opposition as it moves toward socialism. When the prince becomes a Christian, the people follow; when the managers become Communists, so does the state. These intermediate groups, then, are unwittingly preparing a socialist revolution.

In practice, the foregoing is used to justify the Soviet support of transitional regimes by a modest program of loans and grants, as the Soviet Union can argue that history will help bring the new countries into the socialist camp. As might be expected, the Chinese have mocked the theory that nonsocialists will make socialist revolutions despite themselves. Soviet concentration on intermediate rather than ultimate goals (a counterrevolutionary tendency, in Chinese terms) is not the result of ideological reassessment alone but the consequence of successive defeats. Except in Cuba, Soviet intervention in the underdeveloped world has brought very little but headaches. Recent events in Algeria and Indonesia demonstrated how precarious even the most touted "national democracies" can be.

III. SOVIET DOCTRINE ON LATIN AMERICAN POLITICAL DEVELOPMENT

Before World War II, Moscow had little success in Latin America and great difficulty in controlling Communist parties. In the immediate postwar period, this pattern continued; Soviet leaders believed the influence of the United States to be controlling, and the ease with which the Guatemala of Arbenz, a government friendly to the Soviet Union, was overthrown in 1954 confirmed their conviction. The Communist phrase that described this state of affairs was "geographic fatalism." For this reason the breakneck speed of the radicalization of Cuba after January 1, 1959, startled Soviet observers. Theodore Draper's *Castroism: Theory and Practice* demonstrates conclusively that neither the Soviet Union nor the Cuban Communists viewed Castro as an ally until very late in the game, when the Communist Party of Cuba established liaison with him and assisted him in his victory, very much as a last-minute junior partner. Even after Castro entered Havana, the Soviets and the Cuban Communists regarded him as another petit-bourgeois leader, more promising than most, but still a man who might make his peace with the United States and continue the social structure essentially unchanged. However, as 1959 wore on and Castro became more radical in his internal policies, and as his relations with the United States worsened, the Soviets began to believe that here indeed was a new political phenomenon: a genuine social revolution in Latin America, seemingly tolerated by the United States. Moscow now supported him, first verbally and then economically, and even gave very carefully qualified assurances of military aid. When Castro seized upon these vague Soviet formulas and tried to make them more specific, Khrushchev replied that his promise of missile support had been only figurative. But Castro was inexorable in his pursuit of the reluctant Soviets and insisted that he had always been a Marxist-Leninist—one of many untruths. Castro's becoming a Communist meant two things. First, it would now be harder for the Soviet Union to evade helping him both politically and economically; and second, it put the Communist Party of Cuba under his discipline. Castro did not hesitate to alter the Communist Party of Cuba to his own needs and to establish his dominance by eliminating many of the old Communist Party members from positions of power.

Here, then, was yet another kind of Communist revolution. It began as an essentially middle-class revolution (with only a rudimentary, but much-advertised, rural base) against a tottering dictatorship. The middle-class revolutionary, who had studied the lessons of Guatemala and Cuba very carefully, came to power with the conviction that the United States would not let him go very far. Castro wanted to be the Bolivar of the Caribbean. If he were to be only a more liberal Batista, he could not realize such a dream. In the assessment of the Latin American Left, the Guatemalan revolution had failed because it had left the army intact and had not really enlisted the peasants' support. It was the exigencies of holding power, not doctrinal conviction, that drove Castro leftward. By expropriating the large landowners, by moving rapidly to appropriate foreign property, and by forming a new army, Castro systematically did all the things that Arbenz had not done. In addition, he forced a reluctant Soviet Union to become his ally.

Once Castro had made these important changes in the political structure of his country, it needed more than a trumpet to blow down the walls of that Jericho. A small action from outside could not have the catalytic effects in Cuba that it had in Guatemala. This was the lesson of the abortive Bay of Pigs invasion of 1961.

The Soviets were confronted with an unexpected victory and an unusual new Communist. Castro at first tried to export his revolution, but had little success. As the prospects for further Castroite revolutions in the Caribbean went glimmering, the Soviets had to take on the costs of fortifying the existing enterprise and to see if they could get more than political advantage from it. The cost in money was high, and money was hardly in abundant supply in the Soviet Union. Another and far from negligible cost was the complication of relations with Latin American Communist parties, which will be considered later.

Some time in the spring or early summer of 1962, the Soviets began planning to put medium- and intermediate-range missiles into Cuba. The frustration of that scheme was a great defeat for the Soviet Union and Castro. After the missile crisis, both the Soviet Union and Cuba had to lower their sights. To be sure, communism in Cuba was a considerable accomplishment, even if the most optimistic hopes had not been realized. But Cuba had cost, and continued to cost, a great deal of money, and the very existence of a Communist Cuba had provoked an American response which reduced the likelihood of new Cubas. It was clear even before the Dominican crisis that a new Castroite revolution would not be tolerated by the United States. However, even if this judgment had been mistaken and such a revolution might have succeeded, could the Soviet Union have afforded it? Brazil in 1964 offers a good hypothetical case. The Soviets, unlike most American political analysts, believed that the chief purpose of Goulart's approaches to the Communist Party and to the Soviet Union was to enable him to extract better terms from the United States. But even if they hoped that Goulart might follow the Castroite path and change his political color once he had consolidated power in Brazil, they could not have viewed such an eventuality with any enthusiasm. Cuba is a country of about seven million people; Brazil has a population of over seventy-seven million. Obviously, the Soviet Union could not support Brazil economically on anything like the scale on which it was supporting Cuba. A Communist regime under Goulart would pose very serious problems for the Soviet Union while it existed, and its viability was uncertain. Perhaps in this case, as in many others, the wish was father to the analysis, leading the Soviets to believe that Goulart could not come to power.

Whether their diffidence is cause or effect, Soviet writers on Latin America are hardly sanguine about the prospects for revolution on that continent. The starting point of their analysis is that, by comparison with other underdeveloped areas, Latin America has a better-developed middle class, which opposes the assumption of power by the proletariat or by modernizing revolutionaries like Castro. Given the connection of this middle class with American imperialism and the immediate benefits that it derives from the relationship, so the Soviet theory goes, members of this group can be relied on to suppress Communist revolutions in Latin America. But some sections of the middle class suffer more from America's dominance than they gain from being its agent. From the Soviet point of view, the growth of this sector of the middle class is to be encouraged, and a precondition for doing so is the expansion of the internal market. In time, then, the *comprador* (middleman between foreign imperialism and native business) is expected to yield political power to the national, and nationalistic, bourgeoisie. For the latter to flourish, the internal market must grow, and to this end there must be land reforms (*not* an agrarian revolution). As the nationalistic, patriotic components of the bourgeoisie in Latin American countries become preponderant, Soviet writers expect that they will break with the United States, the first step being the confiscation of American property. This process will take much longer in Latin America than in Africa, say the Soviet analysts, precisely because the *comprador* class is so strong in Latin America. Although in Africa the economy as a whole is less developed, the prospects for the transition to socialism are better because a concomitant of backwardness is a weak middle class.

At best, the Soviet prediction for Latin American communism is not wildly optimistic. Also, there remains the question of why Latin American radical nationalists, once having shaken loose from the United States, should turn to socialism rather than to new types of govenment which do not fit present categories tidily. Of course, if the Soviets insist on calling whatever system emerges a variety of communism, they are assured of victories; conversely, if we do the same, we are assured of defeats. But on the basis of any reasonably objective definition of communism, one must agree with the Soviets' pessimism about their opportunities in Latin America, especially when one recognizes that the Soviet Union is not prepared to grant large-scale economic assistance to the development of these new, presumably anti-American, governments. The dominant and unvarying theme of all Soviet analysts is that Castroism will not be the model. Why, they never say. One could imagine another situation in which a non-Communist leader, once having taken power, finds it opportune to turn Communist. It appears, however, that this alternative is never discussed in Soviet literature, as much, one suspects, because the Soviets find it unpalatable as because the United States is not expected to permit such a development.

IV. THE SOVIET POLICIES IN LATIN AMERICA

Actual Soviet policy toward Latin American states and their Communist parties conform generally to the theoretical analysis just summarized, but, naturally, with many modifications to meet local situations. The variations are most obvious in the differentiated policies toward Latin American Communist parties. One of the consequences of the Sino-Soviet competition has been that the Soviet Union is holding Communist parties on increasingly loose strings in order to be able to hold them at all. But it has not been possible to satisfy one party, or group of parties, without dissatisfying another. Thus far, Cuba has presented the most awkward case. The Cuban revolution cannot be popular with such long–established Communist parties as those in Uruguay, Chile, Argentina, and Brazil, whose leaders have held their offices for years, in some cases more than a quarter of a century, and do not relish the prospect of being displaced, humiliated, and expelled from the Party by a Communist of such recent vintage as Castro. For them, Castroist infiltration in their respective countries is not only subversive of their authority within the Communist party, but it furnishes a pretext for hostile state authorities to declare the party illegal. Since they share the Soviet view that the best course is to rely on growing nationalism to further the movement toward communism, they want to retain the legality of their position so as to be able to exert maximum influence on the radical nationalists. The old Communist leadership does not want to frighten the nationalists into making their peace with the United States and spurning the cooperation so eagerly offered by the Communists. Thus far, although the Soviet Union has had problems in balancing the interests of Castro against those of the traditional Latin American Communist parties, it has succeeded on the whole.

A major adjustment in this complex relationship seems to have taken place in a secret meeting in Havana in the latter part of 1964. Following Togliatti's recommendation to convene regional meetings of Communist parties,

the Soviets had called the meeting in Havana, which presumably was to be attended by all the Communist parties of Latin America but which excluded the pro-Chinese splinters. In agreeing to such a meeting, Castro went a long way toward estranging the Chinese. The communiqué of the conference, published in Moscow in January, 1965, gave some indication of what the compromise between the Soviet Union, Castro, and the other parties must have involved. The critical issue was the employment of violence at that time in Latin America. On this issue Moscow's position had been changing. Two articles in consecutive issues of *Kommunist* in the summer of 1964 signaled the change.

In their dispute with the Chinese the Soviets had never taken the position that peaceful parliamentary transition was the only path to Communist revolution. They always insisted that both the violent and the nonviolent paths were possible and that the choice in any given case depended on the circumstances, but Communist parties that did not consider the armed struggle suitable for their countries were cited as examples.

The first *Kommunist* article follows the pattern just described. The second article repeats the generalization that the choice of means must depend on the local situation, but then specifically approves armed struggle and guerrilla activity in some Latin American countries and peaceful means in others. The two articles are, of course, logically consistent, but an important policy shift has been signaled.

At an undisclosed date at the end of 1964, the Communist party of the Soviet Union and the Communist parties of Latin America met in Havana and adopted a resolution which reflected the policy change which the CPSU had initiated in the summer or, more likely, had accepted at Castro's urging. The resolution called for "support in an active form to those who at present are subjected to severe repression, such as the Venezuelan, Colombian, Guatemalan, Honduran, Paraguayan, and Haitian fighters." It took the Soviet side in the Sino-Soviet conflict and called for the unity of each Communist party. Since none of the Chinese splinters among the Latin American Communist parties had been invited to the meeting, it was obvious that unity within each of the Latin American parties was to be interpreted as applying to parties which followed the Soviet lead. In addition, Castro, after his initial reluctance, agreed to come to the Moscow Party meeting scheduled for March, 1965, which was directed against the Chinese.

What seems to have happened at Havana is that the Soviet Union on the one hand secured the support of Cuba and other Latin American parties against the Chinese, but on the other hand made support of its position on China easier for those parties by making explicit that there were several Soviet lines in Latin America. The Havana communiqué called for a further meeting, or meetings, of groups of Latin American Communist parties, implying that they should either concert their activities or agree to pursue different policies in different areas. Unity of the Latin American parties was restored by the explicit endorsement of diversity of policy.

At first sight, the Soviet Union's encouragement and support of guerrilla movements in Latin America, whether grudging or spontaneous, seems to contradict its estimate of the prospects for revolution in Latin America. But if the

Soviet Union is to maintain its influence over Latin American parties (control being no longer in question), it must be responsive to their needs. When guerrillas are active in Latin American countries, the Communist parties find themselves in a quandary. (Castro's guerrilla movement from 1957 to 1959 is a good example of this.) The guerrilla leaders often are not Communists. Sometimes only a minority of them are Communists; in no case in the past have they all been Communists. Typically, the guerrillas operate in the countryside and are thus relatively elusive; only in exceptional cases will they be active in the cities, as they were for a while in Venezuela. The established Communist parties often are opposed to guerrilla activity because they are convinced that it will fail and that their support of any movements which they do not control may uselessly jeopardize legal rights they have. However, in weighing their own opposition, they have to take into account the danger of losing the support of young militants who admire those who are fighting. Most typically, the relations between the Communist parties and the guerrillas are very strained. In one unusual case, Castro denounced the Sosa movement in Guatemala as a political mistake. But more commonly, Communist parties will furnish limited support to the guerrillas and some personnel, in an effort to ensure some control over them and to avoid the onus of being against those who are "fighting with weapons in their hands." The police often arrest and harry the Communists, a circumstance which impels them to try to get the guerrillas to desist. As one can imagine, such alliances are fearsomely complicated, constantly shifting, and almost always embittered. Generalizations are of course perilous, but apparently the Cubans have remained more optimistic about the prospects of guerrilla movements than the Russians, and the relations between the Russians and the Cubans seem to include agreement on particular cases, concessions by one to the other, as well as agreements which one or both seek to subvert—the marks of a normal alliance, in other words. The Cubans are showing signs of greater discrimination in their support of guerrilla movements, and the Soviets still seem to be chasing the guerrilla movements leftward without being able to overcome the contempt of the guerrilla leaders for the old-line Communists.

Such a situation, while hardly ideal for the Soviets' point of view, is tolerable as long as their thesis that the guerrillas really have no chance of seizing power proves correct. If, however, in some small country where relatively few people participate in political life, a modest guerrilla force were to seize power, the Soviet Union would have to make the hard choice between supporting and scuttling a guerrilla group in power which it had previously been helping. Either choice would entail unpleasant consequences for the Soviet Union. If it supported the guerrillas' seizure of power with more than vague statements of support, it would lose heavily in prestige if the United States intervened successfully; a policy of inaction, on the other hand, would furnish ammunition to those guerrilla elements who have contended that the Soviet Union does not want them to succeed. Perhaps the Soviets are willing to risk having to make such a choice because they are convinced that the likelihood of the event is very small and that the objective of preserving their influence over the Communist movement in the face of the Chinese challenge is worth such a risk.

Although Soviet attention to guerrillas has increased, in most of the populous countries of Latin America the Soviet Union has adopted a vigorous united front policy, and it is doing so also in other parts of the world. In Europe, alliances with left and moderate parties have been projected. Even *rapprochement* with the Catholics has been advocated in the pages of the *World Marxist Review*. The policy of the united front is essentially a policy of broad alliances for limited ends. Given the Soviet Union's low estimate of the likelihood, or perhaps desirability, of Communist revolution at the present stage, its emphasis throughout the world is on alliances with other parties.

In Latin America the goal is clear: the isolation of the United States and an end to its influence in Latin America. In pursuit of this goal, the large Communist parties all over Latin America have been instructed to give conditional support to nationalist reformist movements. For instance, the Communist party of Chile in coalition with the Socialists, after losing the last election to the Christian Democrat Frei, has now moved to a position in support of Frei. At the last congress of the Communist Party of Chile it seemed as if the party would have supported Frei even more vigorously if its socialist allies had permitted it. In the Soviet analysis, Frei is pursuing a triangular policy in trying to balance off the United States by making arrangements with Europe, and in this endeavor the Communists wish him well. The Soviets are aware that Latin American politicians will try to use Europeans, including the East Europeans, as a way of getting better terms in their bargaining with the United States. The Soviet Union, for one, is quite willing to be used in this way, and the political color of the regime with which it is so dealing makes little difference. Thus, the Soviets were prepared to go along with Goulart, and are now willing to arrange trade agreements with his successor, Castello Branco. This policy has the virtue of being extremely cheap, and almost automatically assured of success because its objectives are so modest. The Soviets understand as well as others that the most powerful political force in Latin America today is radical nationalism, which is naturally antiforeign. As a foreigner who is far away, with very little "presence" in Latin America, the Soviet Union is not the target of Latin American radical nationalism. The favorite target is the United States. Therefore, the Soviet Union, simply by continuing to talk generally about national liberation movements, and by encouraging native Communist parties, wherever it has influence over them, to cooperate with nationalist movements, is swimming with the tide. This is not a policy that promises the transition of the Latin American states to communism in the near or approximate future, but it has the virtue of avoiding embarrassing complications for the Soviet Union.

The same issues were reexamined at the Tricontinental Conference in Havana in January, 1966, where the main actors—the Chinese, the Russians, the pro-Soviet Communist parties, and representatives of the guerrilla groups that are in uneasy alliance with Communist parties—were able to confront each other in the flesh. Information on the proceedings of the conference is still incomplete, and the statement of its results that follows may have to be revised in its details, and perhaps even in its essentials, when the full data are available.

The Chinese in attacking Castro pushed him closer to the Soviet Union, although he is still not in agreement with the latter on all issues. Apparently, the central issue between Cuba and China has been the treatment of the guerrilla movement. The Cubans have rethought the problems of the guerrilla movements in Latin America, and the aforementioned article by Regis Debray, published in Havana on the eve of the conference, is primary evidence of their rethinking. Debray makes the general point that no models for revolution really exist, but that each revolution in the past has found its own strategy and tactics in action. Many attempts at an exact imitation of the Cuban revolution in Latin America have failed, says Debray, because they were unsuited to local conditions, but also, more generally, because the very precedent of the Cuban revolution has made its repetition difficult if not unlikely. The opponents of Communist revolution in Latin America are now alert to the possibility that a non-Communist guerrilla movement may become Communist after taking power. As one Colombian guerrilla leader told Debray, "Herbert Matthews will not interview me nor will a Betancourt send me arms." Debray does not present a formula for successful revolutions growing out of guerrilla movements in Latin America; the main burden of his argument is that the formula will emerge from the struggle. "Engage the enemy and then play it by ear" is his prescription. But he foresees that battles may be lost, and he does not specify how many enemies should be engaged.

One may conclude from Debray's article that the Cubans are less sanguine than they once were about the possibility of revolution but that they still favor assistance in selected cases.

The drama of the conference itself and the pressure on Castro determined the form in which Castro conveyed this new line. Sino–Cuban relations reached their lowest point when China refused to continue to barter rice for sugar. This refusal would appear to have been a mistake, because Castro's estrangement from China has sharply reduced his bargaining power with the Russians, now that he can no longer play the Russians off against the Chinese. Castro is properly very sensitive about the charge that he is a Soviet puppet, and frequently talks and acts in a way calculated to demonstrate his independence. A journalist who had talked with Castro for several hours after the Havana conference then quoted an unnamed high Cuban official as saying: "It is the USSR which has attached itself to the Cuban line."

On the guerrilla movement the Cubans demonstrated their difference with the Soviets in two cases, and their agreement in another. Their varying positions most probably reflect the Cubans' appraisal of the situation, but they also serve to demonstrate Cuban independence. Let us first examine the instances of disagreement with other Communist parties (including, presumably, the Soviets). Cuba was in charge of the invitations to the Tricontinental Conference. She invited, as members of the Peruvian and Venezuelan delegations, persons who were critical both of the Communists in their respective countries and of the Soviet Union. In a recent article, the Peruvian delegate, who came under the assumed name Roberto García Urrutia, is quoted as

frankly admitting that the Peruvian guerrillas do not enjoy wide support and have suffered reverses. But if the guerrilla movement continues, he maintains, conditions for wider support will be created because, as the movement grows, American intervention will follow, and the guerrilla struggle will then become identified with the patriotic struggle of the whole Peruvian people. The Americans, because they fear that the Peruvian middle class will aid the guerrillas, support the conciliatory reformism of the ruling party. And the writer adds: "Certain leftist parties [read, the Communists]...have the illusion that in making agreement with the bourgeoisie which permits them to publish four or five periodicals—which only the militants read anyhow—they have discharged their revolutionary duty. In reality this is an attitude of collaboration with imperialism...."

By inviting García to the Tricontinental Conference, Castro was clearly intervening in the affairs of the Communist party of Peru and departing from the practices of fraternal and friendly conferences among the Latin American Communist parties. The Soviets were forced either to swallow this defiance or try to change Castro's mind.

In Guatemala, on the other hand, Castro took the opposite course. For a long time he favored the MR-13 wing of the Guatemalan guerrilla movement led by Sosa, a non-Communist who typically is more strongly committed to extensive guerrilla warfare than is the Guatemalan Communist party. In a speech right after the Havana conference, Castro switched the Cuban position and attacked Sosa possibly because he disapproved of this policy but more likely because he was resentful of his connection with the Trotskyites.

Latin American Trotskyites have criticized Castro very sharply, and apparently effectively, for the change of policy which they connect with the disappearance of Che Guevara.

The Trotskyites interpret Che Guevara's eclipse as meaning that Castro has ceased to be a genuine revolutionary. He failed to offer vigorous opposition to the American landing in Santo Domingo, they say; perhaps he murdered Guevara; he is really opposed to guerrilla movements in Latin America; he has withdrawn arms from the militia because he is afraid that the "Guevara group" might use them to overthrow him. Nothing could be better calculated to infuriate Castro than to be accused of having the same relationship to the guerrilla movements of Latin America that the Cuban Communist party had to his movement. Only time will tell whether the uneasy Cuban–Soviet agreement on policy toward insurrection can be maintained at the present level or whether it will deteriorate.

In the above pages, Soviet foreign policy objectives in Latin America have been described as more limited and realistic today than in the period before the missile crisis. Soviet Latin American policy is of a piece with the changes in Soviet policy the world over. The Soviet Union has lowered its sights and now aims for more modest but more realistic goals. The question in Latin America as in the rest of the world is whether this is a temporary, a medium-range, or a long-range trend. Given a Soviet military inferiority that is now recognized as likely to continue, and given the Soviet Union's preoccupation with an unsatisfactory domestic political situation and with the Chinese problem, one would expect this tendency to be of longer rather than shorter duration. But these projections are always uncertain because, in the Soviet-American confrontation, events unexpected by either side, sometimes undesired by either side, often push matters into new directions.

It is on this note of caution and ambivalence that this paper ends. Although the Russians may prefer and expect to pursue limited objectives in Latin America, unexpected events could force them to take sides in an unanticipated crisis.

10

On the Cuban Revolution
and Armed Struggle

Ernesto ("Che") Guevara

From George Lavan, ed., *Che Guevara Speaks* (New York: Grove Press, Inc., 1967), pp. 26–33, 85–90, 157–59. *Che Guevara Speaks,* © 1967 by Merit Publishers, New York. Reprinted by permission of the publisher.

From the outset of the Cuban Revolution until his apparently abrupt and voluntary departure in 1965, Ernesto ("Che") Guevara was the Revolution's chief theoretician. Guevara pledged to make the Andes "the Sierra Maestra of Latin America" and was the principal source of the doctrine that only through the "subjective" willingness of guerrillas to initiate "armed struggle" in the countryside could Latin America's "objective" potential for radical revolution be realized. This doctrine frequently bedeviled relations between Havana and Moscow in the early years of the Revolution and later re-emerged in a more extreme and intellectualized form in the work of Debray.

Guevara was a superb polemicist, and he captures in his often-eloquent prose not only the high idealism of the Cuban Revolution but also its appeal to many throughout Latin America and the underdeveloped world (and on college campuses everywhere) as a symbol of the "struggle against imperialism." Moreover, in spite of his near-romantic view of the heroic guerrilla and the noble peasant, undergirding his writings is a strong thread of realism. He was aware that the Cuban precedent was not entirely applicable to the rest of Latin America, especially in that the Revolution itself had placed anti-revolutionary forces on their guard. Unlike Debray, he gave some attention to the political, as distinct from the military, task involved in the making of a revolution.

Guevara was confident that revolutions were virtually inevitable in Latin America because of "the people's hunger, their reaction to that hunger, the terror unleashed to crush the people's reaction, and the wave of hatred that the repression creates." In the latter respect, one may argue that he was entirely wrong, overly optimistic, or simply premature.

What follows are excerpts (separated by ellipses) from Guevara's articles on "Cuba: Exceptional Case or Vanguard in the Struggle Against Colonialism?" (1961) and "Guerrilla Warfare: A Method" (1963); and his message "from somewhere in the world" to the Organization of Solidarity of the Peoples of Africa, Asia and Latin America, published by the Cuban press on April 16, 1967, less than six months before his death.

...Some sectors, in good faith or with axes to grind, claim to see in the Cuban Revolution a series of exceptional origins and features whose importance for this great historical event they inflate to that of the decisive factor. They speak of the exceptionalism of the Cuban Revolution as compared with the course of other progressive parties in America and conclude therefrom that the form and road of the Cuban Revolution are unique and that in the other countries of America the historic transition of the peoples will be different.

We accept that there are exceptions which give the Cuban Revolution its peculiar characteristics. It is a clearly established fact that every revolution has this type of specific factor, but it is no less an established fact that all of them follow laws which society cannot violate. Let us analyze, then, the factors of this purported execeptionalism.

The first, perhaps the most important, the most original, is that cosmic force called Fidel Castro Ruz, a name that in a few years has attained historic proportions. The future will accord our Prime Minister's merits their exact place, but to us they appear comparable to those of the greatest historic figures of all Latin America....

However, no one could assert that there were political and social conditions in Cuba totally different from those in the other countries of America, and that precisely because of that difference the revolution took place. Nor could anyone assert, on the other hand, that Fidel Castro made the revolution despite that difference. Fidel, a great and able leader, led the revolution in Cuba, at the time and in the way he did, by interpreting the profound political disturbances that were preparing the people for the great leap onto the revolutionary road. Also certain conditions existed which were not confined to Cuba, but which it will be hard for other peoples to take advantage of again because imperialism—in contrast to some progressive groups—does learn from its errors.

The condition that we would describe as exceptional was that North American imperialism was disoriented and was never able to measure accurately the true scope of the Cuban Revolution. Here is something that explains many of the apparent contradictions in North American policy. The monopolies, as is habitual in such cases, began to think about a successor for Batista precisely because they knew that the people were not compliant and were also looking for a successor to Batista—but along revolutionary paths. What more intelligent expert stroke then than to get rid of the now unserviceable little dictator and to replace him with the new "boys" who could in their turn serve the interests of imperialism very well? The empire gambled on this card from its continental deck for a while, and lost miserably. Prior to our military victory they were suspicious, but not afraid of us; rather, with all their experience at this game, which they were accustomed to winning, they played with two decks. On various occasions, emissaries of the State Department, disguised as newspapermen, came to investigate our rustic revolution, but they never found any trace of imminent danger in it. When imperialism wanted to react, when the imperialists discovered that the group of inexperienced young men, who were marching in triumph through the streets of Havana, had a clear awareness of their political duty and an iron determination to carry out that duty, it was already too late. And thus in January, 1959, dawned the first social revolution of the Caribbean zone and the most profound of the revolutions in America.

We don't believe that it could be considered exceptional that the bourgeoisie, or at least a good part of it, showed itself favorable to the revolutionary war against the tyranny at the same time it was supporting and promoting movements seeking for negotiated solutions which would permit them to substitute for the Batista regime elements disposed to curb the revolution.

Considering the conditions in which the revolutionary war took place and the complexity of the political tendencies which opposed the tyranny, it was not at all exceptional that some latifundist elements adopted a neutral, or at least non-belligerent, attitude toward the insurrectionary forces. It is understandable that the national bourgeoisie, struck down by imperialism and the tyranny, whose troops sacked small properties and made extortion a daily way of life, felt a certain sympathy when they saw those young rebels from the mountains punish the military arm of imperialism, which is what the mercenary army was.

So non-revolutionary forces indeed helped smooth the road for the advent of revolutionary power.

Going further, we can add as a new factor of exceptionalism the fact that in most places in Cuba the peasants had been proletarianized by the needs of big semi-mechanized capitalist agriculture, and had reached a stage of organization which gave them greater class-consciousness. We can admit this. But we should point out, in the interest of truth, that the first area where the Rebel Army—made up of the survivors of the defeated band that had made the voyage on the *Granma*—operated was an area inhabited by peasants whose social and cultural roots were different from those of the peasants found in the areas of large-scale semi-mechanized agriculture. In fact, the Sierra Maestra, locale of the first revolutionary beehive, is a place where peasants struggling barehanded against latifundism took refuge. They went there seeking a new piece of land—somehow overlooked by the state or the voracious latifundists—on which to create a modest fortune. They constantly had to struggle against the exactions of the soldiers, who were always allied to the latifundists; and their ambition extended no farther than a property deed. Concretely, the soldiers who belonged to our first peasant-type guerrilla armies came from the section of this social class which shows most strongly love for the land and the possession of it; that is to say, which shows most perfectly what we can define as the petty-bourgeois spirit. The peasant fought because he wanted land for himself, for his children, to manage it, sell it, and get rich by his work.

Despite his petty-bourgois spirit, the peasant soon learned that he could not satisfy his land hunger without breaking up the system of latifundist property. Radical agrarian reform, the only kind that could give land to the peasants, clashed directly with the interests of the imperialists, latifundists and sugar and cattle magnates. The bourgeoisie was afraid to clash with those interests. But the proletariat wasn't. In this way the revolution's course itself brought together the workers and peasants. The workers supported the demands against the latifundists. The poor peasant, rewarded with ownership of the land, loyally supported the revolutionary power and defended it against its imperialist and counter-revolutionary enemies.

In our opinion no further factors of exceptionalism can be claimed. We have been generous in stating those listed in their strongest form. Now we shall examine the permanent roots of all social phenomena in America, the contradictions which, ripening in the womb of present societies, produce changes that can attain the scope of a revolution like Cuba's.

First in chronological order, though not in the order of importance at present, is latifundism. Latifundism was the economic power base of the ruling class throughout the entire period which followed the great liberating anticolonialist revolution of the last century. . . .

In most countries the latifundist realized he couldn't survive alone and promptly entered into alliances with the monopolies, that is, with the strongest and cruelest oppressor of the American peoples. North American capital arrived on the scene to make the virgin lands fruitful, so that later it could carry off unnoticed all the funds so "generously" given, plus several times the amounts originally invested in the "beneficiary" country.

America was a field of inter-imperialist struggle, and the "wars" between Costa Rica and Nicaragua, the separa-

tion of Panama from Colombia, the infamy committed against Ecuador in its dispute with Peru, the fight between Paraguay and Bolivia, are nothing but manifestations of the gigantic battle between the world's great monopolistic combines, a battle decided almost completely in favor of the North American monopolies following World War II. From that point on, the empire dedicated itself to strengthening its grip on its colonial possessions and perfecting the whole structure to prevent the intrusion of old or new competitors from other imperialist countries. All this resulted in a monstrously distorted economy which has been described by the shamefaced economists of the imperialist regime in an innocuous term which reveals the deep compassion they feel for us inferior beings (they call our miserably exploited Indians, persecuted and reduced to utter wretchedness, "little Indians"; all Negroes and mulattos, disinherited and discriminated against, are called "colored"; individually they are used as instruments, collectively, as a means of dividing the working masses in their struggle for a better economic future). For us, the peoples of America, they have another polite and refined term: "underdeveloped."

What is "underdevelopment"?

A dwarf with an enormous head and a swollen chest is "underdeveloped," inasmuch as his weak legs or short arms do not match the rest of his anatomy. He is the product of an abnormal formation that distorted his development. That is really what we are—we, who are politely referred to as "underdeveloped," but in truth are colonial, semicolonial or dependent countries. We are countries whose economies have been twisted by imperialism, which has abnormally developed in us those branches of industry or agriculture needed to complement its complex economy. "Underdevelopment," or distorted development, brings dangerous specialization in raw materials, inherent in which is the threat of hunger for all our peoples. We, the underdeveloped, are also those with monoculture, with the single product, with the single market. A single product whose uncertain sale depends on a single market that imposes and fixes conditions—that is the great formula for imperialist economic domination. It should be added to the old, but eternally young, Roman slogan *Divide and Conquer!*

Latifundism, then, through its connections with imperialism, completely shapes the so-called underdevelopment, whose results are low wages and unemployment. This phenomenon of low wages and unemployment is a vicious circle which produces ever lower and ever more unemployment, as the great contradictions of the system sharpen and—constantly at the mercy of the cyclical fluctuations of its own economy—provides the common denominator of all the peoples of America, from the Rio Bravo[1] to the South Pole. This common denominator, which we shall print in capital letters and which serves as the starting point for analysis by all who think about these social phenomena, is called THE PEOPLE'S HUNGER; weary of being oppressed, persecuted, exploited to the limit; weary of the wretched selling of their labor-power day after day (faced with the fear of swelling the enormous mass of unemployed) so that the greatest profit can be wrung from each human body, profits that are later squandered

[1] The Latin American name for the river called the Rio Grande in the United States.

in the orgies of the masters of capital. . . .

The objective conditions for struggle are provided by the people's hunger, their reaction to that hunger, the terror unleashed to crush the people's reaction, and the wave of hatred that the repression creates. America lacked the subjective conditions, the most important of which is awareness of the possibility of victory through violent struggle against the imperialist powers and their internal allies. These conditions were created through the armed struggle which made clearer the need for change (and permitted it to be foreseen) and the defeat and subsequent annihilation of the army by the people's forces (an absolutely necessary condition for every true revolution).

Having already shown that these conditions are created through the armed struggle, we have to explain once more that the scene of the struggle should be the countryside. A peasant army, pursuing the great objectives for which the peasantry should fight (the first of which is the just distribution of the land), will capture the cities from the countryside. The peasant class of America, basing itself on the ideology of the working class, whose great thinkers discovered the social laws governing us, will provide the great liberating army of the future, as it has already done in Cuba. This army, created in the countryside, where the subjective conditions keep ripening for the taking of power, proceeds to take the cities, uniting with the workers and enriching itself ideologically from contributions of the working class. It can and must defeat the oppressor army, at first in skirmishes, engagements, surprises; and in big battles at the end, when the army will have grown from its small-scale guerrilla footing to the proportions of a great popular army of liberation. One stage in the consolidation of the revolutionary power, as we indicated above, will be the liquidation of the old army. . . .

.   .   .

The Yankees will intervene because of solidarity of interests and because the struggle in America is decisive. In fact, they are already intervening in the preparation of repressive forces and the organization of a continental apparatus of struggle. But from now on they will do so with all their energy; they will strike the people's forces with all the destructive weapons at their disposal. They will try to prevent the consolidation of revolutionary power; and if it should be successful anywhere, they will renew their attack. They will not recognize it. They will try to divide the revolutionary forces. They will introduce all types of saboteurs, create frontier problems, engage other reactionary states to oppose it, and will try to strangle the new state economically —in a word, to annihilate it.

This being the picture in America, it is difficult to achieve and consolidate victory in a country that is isolated. The unity of the repressive forces must encounter the unity of the people's forces. In all the countries in which oppression becomes unbearable, the banner of rebellion must be raised, and this banner of historical necessity will have a continental character. As Fidel said, the Andes will be the Sierra Maestra of America, and all the immense territories that make up this continent will become the scene of a life-and-death struggle against the power of imperialism.

We cannot tell when this struggle

will acquire a continental character nor how long it will last; but we can predict its advent and its triumph, because it is the inevitable result of historical, economic and political conditions and its direction cannot be changed. It is the task of the revolutionary force in each country to initiate it when the conditions are present, regardless of the situation in other countries. The general strategy will emerge as the struggle develops. The prediction of the continental character of the struggle is borne out by analysis of the strength of each contender, but this does not in the least exclude independent outbreaks. Just as the beginning of the struggle in one part of a country is bound to develop it throughout its area, the beginning of a revolutionary war contributes to the development of new conditions in the neighboring countries.

The development of revolution has normally produced high and low tides in inverse proportion: to the revolutionary high tide corresponds the counter-revolutionary low tide; and conversely at moments of revolutionary decline, there is a counter-revolutionary ascendency. At such moments the situation of the people's forces becomes difficult, and they should resort to the best defense measures in order to suffer the least loss. The enemy is extremely powerful, continental in stature. Therefore the relative weaknesses of the local bourgeoisie cannot be analyzed with a view to making decisions within restricted limits. Still less can one think of an eventual alliance of these oligarchies with an armed people. The Cuban Revolution has sounded the alarm. The polarization of forces is becoming complete: exploiters on one side and exploited on the other. The mass of the petty bourgeoisie will lean to one side or the other according to their interests and the political skill with which it is handled; neutrality will be an exception. This is how revolutionary war will be.

Let us consider the way a guerrilla center can start.

Nuclei of relatively few persons choose places favorable for guerrilla warfare, sometimes with the intention of launching a counter-attack or to weather a storm, and there they begin to take action. But the following must be made clear: At the beginning, the relative weakness of the guerrilla fighters is such that they should only endeavor to pay attention to the terrain in order to become acquainted with the surroundings, establish connections with the population and fortify the places which eventually will be converted into bases.

A guerrilla unit can survive only if it starts by basing its development on the three following conditions: constant mobility, constant vigilance, constant wariness. Without the adequate use of these elements of military tactics, the unit will find it hard to survive. It must be remembered that the heroism of the guerrilla fighter at such times consists in the scope of the planned objective and the long series of sacrifices that must be made in order to attain it.

These sacrifices will not mean daily combat or face-to-face struggle with the enemy; they will assume forms more subtle and difficult for the individual guerrilla fighter to endure physically and mentally.

The guerrillas will perhaps suffer heavily from the attacks of enemy armies, at times be split up while those taken prisoner will be martyred. They will be pursued like hunted animals in the areas they have chosen to operate in, with the constant anxiety of having the enemy on their track, and on top of all this with the constant doubt that in some cases the terrorized peasants will give them away to the repressive troops in order to save their own skins. They have no alternative but death or victory at times when death is a concept a thousand times present, and victory a myth only a revolutionary can dream of.

That is the heroism of the guerrilla. That is why it is said that to be on the march is also a form of fighting, and to avoid combat at a given moment is another form. Faced with the general superiority of the enemy, the way to act is to find a form of tactics with which to gain a relative superiority at a chosen point, either by being able to concentrate more troops than the enemy or by making the best use of the terrain to secure advantages that upset the correlation of forces. In these conditions tactical victory is assured; if relative superiority is not clear, it is preferable not to take action. As long as one is in a position to choose the "how" and the "when," no battle should be fought which will not end in victory.

Guerrilla forces will grow and be consolidated within the framework of the great politico-military action of which they are a part. And within this framework they will go on forming the bases, which are essential for their success. These bases are points which the enemy can penetrate only at the cost of heavy losses; they are bastions of the revolution, both shelters and starting points for bolder and more distant raids.

Such a time will come if the difficulties of both tactical and political discipline have been overcome. The guerrillas must never forget their function as vanguard of the people, the mandate entrusted to their care, and therefore they should create the necessary political conditions for the establishment of a revolutionary power based on the full support of the masses. The main demands of the peasantry should be met to the degree and in the form which circumstances permit, so as to bring about the unity and solidarity of the whole population.

If the military situation is difficult from the first moments, the political situation will be no less delicate; and if a single military error can wipe out the guerrillas, a political error can check their development for a long period.

The struggle is politico-military; so it must develop, and so it must be understood.

In the course of its growth guerrilla fighting reaches a point at which its capacity for action covers a given region, for which there are too many men and too great a concentration. Then begins the beehive action, in which one of the commanding officers, a distinguished guerrilla, hops to another region and repeats the chain development of guerrilla warfare, but still subject to a central command.

Now, it is necessary to point out that one cannot hope for victory without the formation of a people's army. The guerrilla forces can be expanded to a certain size; the people's forces, in the cities and in other enemy-occupied zones, can inflict losses, but the military potential of the reactionaries would remain intact. It must always be remembered that the final outcome should be the annihilation of the enemy. Therefore all these new zones that have been created, as well as the penetrated zones behind the enemy lines and the forces operating in the principal cities, should be under a unified command. It cannot be claimed that there exists among guerrilla forces the closely linked chain of command that characterizes an army, but there is a strategic command. Within certain conditions of freedom of action, the guerrillas should carry out all the strategic orders of the central command, which is set up in one of the safest and strongest areas, preparing conditions for the union of the forces at a given moment.

The guerrilla war or war of liberation will generally have three stages: First, the strategic defensive when a small force nibbles at the enemy and makes off, not to shelter in passive defense within a small circumference, but rather to defend itself by limited attacks which it can carry out successfully. After this, comes a state of equilibrium, during which the possibilities of action on the part of both the enemy and the guerrillas are established; then comes the final stage of overrunning the repressive army, ending in the capture of the big cities, large-scale decisive encounters and the total annihilation of the enemy.

After reaching a state of equilibrium, when both sides are on guard against each other, in the ensuing development guerrilla war acquires new characteristics. The concept of maneuver is introduced: big columns attack strong points; and mobile warfare with the shifting of forces and of considerable means of attack. But owing to the capacity of resistance and counter-attack that the enemy still retains, this war of maneuver does not entirely replace guerrilla fighting; it is only one form of action taken by the larger guerrilla forces until finally they crystallize into a people's army with army corps. Even at this time, the guerrillas will play their "original" guerrilla role, moving ahead of the actions of the main forces, destroying communications and sabotaging the whole defensive apparatus of the enemy.

We have predicted that the war will be continental. This means it will have many fronts, and will cost much blood and countless lives over a long period. But besides this, the phenomena of polarization of forces that are occurring in America, the clear division between exploiters and exploited that will exist in future revolutionary war, mean that when the armed vanguard of the people seizes power, the country or countries that attain it will, at one and the same time, liquidate both their imperialist and national exploiting class oppressor. The first stage of the socialist revolution will have crystallized; the people will be ready to staunch their wounds and begin to build socialism. . . .

.   .   .

And let us develop genuine proletarian internationalism, with international proletarian armies; let the flag under which we fight be the sacred cause of benefiting all humanity, so that to die under the colors of Vietnam, Venezuela, Guatemala, Laos, Guinea, Colombia, Bolivia, Brazil—to mention only the current scenes of armed struggle—is equally glorious and desirable for an American, an Asian, an African and even a European.

Every drop of blood spilled in a land under whose flag one was not born is an experience that is treasured by anyone who survives and who can then apply the lessons learned in the struggle for freedom in his own place of origin. And every people that frees itself is a step won in the battle for freedom of one's own people. . . .

We would sum up, as follows, our aspirations for victory, destruction of imperialism by means of eliminating its strongest bulwark—the imperialist domain of the United States of North America. . . .

How close and bright would the future appear if two, three, many Vietnams, flowered on the face of the globe, with their quota of death and immense tragedies, with their daily heroism, with their repeated blows against imperialism, obliging it to disperse its forces under the lash of the growing hate of the people of the world!

And if we were capable of uniting so as to give our blows greater solidity and certainty, so that the effectiveness of aid of all kinds to the people locked in combat was increased—how great the future would be, and how near!

If we, on a small point on the map of the world, fulfill our duty and place at the disposition of the struggle whatever little we are able to give, our lives, our sacrifice, it can happen that one of these days we will draw our last breath on a bit of earth not our own, yet already ours, watered with our blood. Let it be known that we have measured the scope of our acts and that we consider ourselves no more than elements in the great army of the proletariat; but we feel proud at having learned from the Cuban Revolution and its great leader the great lesson to be drawn from Cuba's attitude in this part of the world: "What difference the dangers to a man or a people, or the sacrifices they make, when what is at stake is the destiny of humanity?"

Our every action is a call for war against imperialism and a cry for the unity of the peoples against the great enemy of the human species: the United States of North America.

Wherever death may surprise us, let it be welcome if our battle cry has reached even one receptive ear, and another hand reaches out to take up our arms, and other men come forward to join in our funeral dirge with the chattering of machine guns and new calls for battle and for victory.

II

Revolutionary Theory:
Guevara and Debray

Peter Worsley

From Peter Worsley, "Revolutionary Theory: Guevara and Debray" in *Violence and Politics (The Fourth Dimension of Warfare)* (Manchester: Manchester University Press, 1970). Reprinted by permission of the author and the publisher.

Peter Worsley is a Professor of Sociology at the University of Manchester, Manchester, England.

In this essay, Professor Worsley places the Cuban Revolution and its principal theoretical spokesmen, Guevara and Debray, in the perspective of other leading Marxist revolutions and theorists of the nineteenth and twentieth centuries. Every major revolution, Worsley maintains, has been essentially a unique experience, but each has given rise to theorists claiming to have distilled from that experience the only "correct" road to power. The Cuban Revolution, "the least dogmatic revolution of all," is no exception: "The pragmatism of Castro himself, the absorption in the revolutionary act of fighting in Guevara, are reduced to an intellectual schema in Debray"—to a "unitary formula" largely irrelevant to the tremendous variety of domestic situations empirically discernable in Latin America and elsewhere.[1] Worsley finds it ironic that dogma has tended to obscure the real significance of the Cuban Revolution, "its 'demonstration effect' at a much more diffuse level." Cuba has shown that "revolution is possible" and, in any event, that "action by dedicated minorities in the context of mass dissatisfaction, and repudiating orthodox polities, can produce striking results."[2]

[1] See also esp.: Robert F. Lamberg, "Che in Bolivia: The 'Revolution' That Failed," *Problems of Communism*, XIX, No. 4 (July-August 1970), pp. 25–37; José Moreno, "Che Guevara on Guerrilla Warfare: Doctrine, Practice and Evaluation," *Comparative Studies in Society and History*, XII, No. 2 (April 1970), pp. 114–33; Luis E. Aguilar, "Fragmentation of the Marxist Left," *Problems of Communism*, XIX, No. 4 (July-August 1970), pp. 1–12; John D. Martz, "Doctrine and Dilemmas of the Latin American 'New Left'," *World Politics*, XXII, No. 2 (January 1970), pp. 171–96; Luis Mercier Vega, *Guerrillas in Latin America* (New York: Praeger, 1969); and Malcolm Deas, "Guerrillas in Latin America: A Perspective," *The World Today* (February 1968), pp. 72–78.

[2] See also esp.: James P. O'Connor, *The Origins of Socialism in Cuba* (Ithaca, N.Y.: Cornell University Press, 1970); Richard R. Fagen, *The Transformation of Political Culture in Cuba* (Stanford: Stanford University Press, 1969); and Maurice Zeitlin, *Revolutionary Politics and the Cuban Working Class* (New York: Harper & Row, 1970).

It is appropriate, in a lecture in Manchester devoted to revolution and war, to take as our starting point the work of a revolutionary whose importance is both world-historic and local: world-historic, because his ideas influenced millions of subsequent revolutionaries, and local, because his pioneer sociological fieldwork study of the working class of this city is commemorated by the place of honor accorded his photograph in our faculty building in Dover Street, where he once lived. I refer, of course, to Friedrich Engels.

Engels, indeed, was more than simply a *theorist* of revolution: he was a practitioner, who served with the artillery in the German Revolution of 1848, and who was intensely interested in the specifically military aspects of insurrection (his nickname was "the general"). His knowledge of military affairs in general was so profound that it enabled him to write articles, under Marx's name, for the *New York Tribune,* the income from which, however, cannot have been very substantial compared to the money he made in the family cotton business in Manchester, which helped keep the Marx family afloat while Marx got on with writing *Capital.*[1]

In 1871, however, the experience of the Paris Commune shocked Engels into a new and ominous realization that things were not what they had been in 1848, and that the prospects for armed insurrection in urban areas —never favorable—had become even more unfavorable due to the rationalization of armies, the improvement of communications systems, and new technological innovations in weaponry, notably vastly improved rifles and artillery. The unsuitability of the city for street

fighting was greater in 1871 than in 1848, particularly in Paris, where Baron Haussmann had built a system of wide and straight boulevards which provide a magnificent field of fire for gunners. The day of the street barricade, of urban insurrection, it seemed, was over. After recent events in Paris, and the Tet offensive, after Watts, Detroit and Newark, we know better. But in 1871, it seemed that urban revolution, henceforth, was going to be very difficult, if not impossible: paving-stones, spontaneous amateur militia, and periodic upsurges of revolutionary fervor were no longer enough.

And, indeed, revolution in the advanced, urbanized industrial countries has not occurred. An explanation of why this has been so, however, would have to go far beyond the largely technological and infrastructural factors mentioned by Engels. Yet elsewhere in his writings, he did foreshadow some of these other analytical elements which we would need to build into any more satisfactory explanatory model for the failure of socialist revolution in "the West": the "self-defeating" effect of organized labor in societies whose ruling classes were not simply flexible and skillful in giving economic and political concessions, but who could *afford* to be, since they had the lion's share of the wealth of the richest countries in the world at their disposal. The very success of organized labor, under such conditions, meant that they themselves gradually became institutionalized parts of the political culture. They now had *some* interest, at least, in its economic continuity and expansion; similarly, they were involved in the running of the capitalist polity, via the party system, participation in Parliament, and the operation of labor, cooperative, and other organizations and pressure groups under conditions of constitutional legal-

---

[1] See W. H. Chaloner and W. O. Henderson, *Engels as Military Critic,* Manchester, 1959.

ity. Allowing for national variations, the pattern in countries such as France and Italy has been similar, though the mass working-class parties there have been Communist. One of the significant results of this process of institutionalization was the emergence of a new kind of "vertical" identification with the dominant cultural emphasis of the nation-state rather than a "horizontal" class identification with the "international proletariat": an imperial legacy now maturing in the form of Powellism. As Che Guevara has remarked,[2] the workers of the imperialist countries have "a certain complicity" in the exploitation of dependent countries, the effect of which, he notes, "wears away the militant spirit of the masses" in the imperialist country itself.

These views depend upon acceptance of the classical Leninist analysis of imperialism, with its emphasis upon the "super-profits" of the imperialist countries, and the division of the world into haves and have-nots. Yet they depart from Leninism in that they consider the corrupting effects of imperialism upon the workers in the industrial countries to be so deep that revolution in these countries is to be discontinued. Lenin believed firmly in the prospects of revolution in Europe (though he had pointed to the growth of revolutionary ideas and movements in India, China, and the colonial world as the ultimate assurance of the eventual triumph of world revolution). Moreover, he believed that West European Communism, unlike social democracy (indeed corrupted by imperialism), would be unaffected by its location in

the heartlands of developed capitalism.

This view is sharply challenged in the Third World today, even by those who are quite faithful disciples of Lenin in many other key respects. The two crucial Leninist postulates they do adhere to are (a) the model of a capitalist world economy composed of imperialist countries, on the one hand, and the countries they exploit on the other; (b) the Leninist model of a small, dedicated, trained, and highly organized body of revolutionary fighters at the head of a mass movement as the midwife of the revolution. Both the macro-conceptualization of the world situation, then, and the conception of the revolutionary agency are thoroughly Leninist.

Of course, severe revolutionary challenges did occur in Europe after 1917. Even in Britain we had 1919 and 1926. But whatever the revolutionary *potential* of that period, in the event, empirically, it did not eventuate, even in Germany. One classical Marxist explanation—in terms of human agency—is that there was defective leadership: the Soviet turn towards an inward-looking "socialism in one country"; the reduction of other Communist Parties to the status of instruments of the Soviet state; the Stalinist cessation of revolutionism from the Popular Front era onwards, etc. Others find this too demonological an explanation and emphasize, more deterministically, the "situation logic" by virtue of which revolutionism in wealthy countries necessarily became absorbed.

Whatever the relative explanatory power of these two models (and surely *both* are required in any sophisticated explanatory model, for they are not mutually exclusive), the fact remains that the looked-for revolutions in the West did not materialize. More than

---

2 Ernesto Che Guevara, *Man and Socialism in Cuba,* Guairas, Book Institute, Havana, 1967, p. 19.

that, many revolutionaries found themselves abandoned by the USSR, which failed to assist, consciously abandoned, or discouraged Communist revolution in Greece, Egypt, and other countries.

The single most important Communist revolutionary movement, in the largest country in the world, was that in China. Stalin's advice, in 1946, was to enter a coalition with Chiang Kai Shek. The Chinese listened respectfully, and proceeded to do the opposite. It was to be many years before they allowed any crack to appear in the verbal façade of Sino-Russian solidarity, for these differences in policy, involving the blatant flouting and defiance of Soviet advice, were papered over even as late as a decade after the achievement of power, as if no differences had ever arisen, and as if Soviet and Chinese policies were inherently in harmony. The facts were quite other, and had been for a long time.

Soviet assistance to the Chinese Communists had begun long before World War II, with the dispatch of key political and military advisers to China in the 1920's. It would be far too demonological to attribute the subsequent disastrous setbacks experienced by the Chinese Communists (particularly the hideous slaughter of tens of thousands in the Canton "commune" of 1927) entirely to Soviet advice, however, for the theoretical deficiencies which underlay these disasters were deeply ingrained in the Marxism of the day in general, rather than simply in Soviet Marxism. For the Marxist emphasis on the "leading role" of the proletariat necessarily carried with it an implicit military strategy: the revolution would be waged in the cities, and waged by the industrial workers.

As we know, the disasters encountered when this policy was followed led Mao Tse Tung to move the revolution just about as far as he could possibly get from the urban centers: to Yenan. It is true that, as an independent factor, his theoretical analyses of Chinese society, conducted in the light of Marxist methodological principles, begun in Hunan in the mid-1920's, had led him to a new realization that what was possibly true for the advanced industrial countries was not necessarily true for the vastly different agrarian society of China. And so we had the elaboration of a new strategy in which the revolution was spearheaded, not by the city proletariat, but by the peasantry of a remote and backward liberated territory, led by a nucleus of those who survived the Long March.

In time, the cadres of the revolution —whether Party, Army, or other—were increasingly men and women of peasant origin. The mass support for the revolution was peasant, and the cities, classically developed on the coast under the influence and control of the imperialist powers, were the last strongholds to be liberated.

The lesson was not lost on other rising revolutionaries. Even European experience showed that successful revolutionary war had to be fought in the countryside. Whatever the social composition of the armies themselves, that meant having the support of the rural population. Thus one of the few effective Communist-led partisan movements in Europe, that of Yugoslavia, was able to succeed, not because it was able to turn the peasantry red (it has not done that yet), but because, under the conditions of a national war against Nazi Germany, the peasantry was nevertheless prepared to accept predominantly Communist leadership.

It should be clearly noted, though, that what the Chinese Communists did, while involving *guerrilla* warfare proper on a great scale, was something rather different from what happened in Cuba. The Chinese strategy involved the establishment of a very large liberated area as a base from which the rest of the country could ultimately be won. Moreover, very large forces were involved, including whole military units up to the level of divisions, some of which had defected from the Kuomintang, others of which had been trained by the Communists before and after the Long March. They administered an enormous and populated territory, no matter how marginal it was. All this, then, is a far cry from the tiny, constantly moving groups of five to fifteen men which Guevara posits as the module for the Latin American guerrilla band.

The possession of a liberated territory has profound implications. Isolation itself gives security. This security can be exploited to proselytize among the peasants, to commence land and other social reforms, to train armies. Continuity is possible—as it is not in the city, where guerrillas can only work effectively at night—and centralized control is easier. Moreover, the process the Cubans call "proletarianization" takes place. The leadership is decisively cut off from all their former external attachments and comforts. In the liberated area, they have to live the lives of the peasantry—though not nearly to the extent that the small guerrilla band has to do, of necessity, even to the growing of its food. (Nothing is more fatal than to *take* food, to use force against the peasantry, as the Greek Communist guerrillas found to their cost.) For the guerrillas depend for recruits, intelligence, guides, supplies, transportation, for virtually everything, upon the peasants. This they cannot win by pointing

guns at them. The revolutionary, in Mao's famous phrase, is like the fish in the peasant sea: he is supported by the medium in which he lives.

The guerrilla army not only establishes its *own* security by securing a liberated zone: it also provides it for the peasantry of that zone, who are no longer subject to landlord police, counter-insurgency forces, warlord armies, and all the varieties of repressive agents who intervene and make their land a battleground. Military security in turn produces that psychological assurance which political propaganda reinforces; then the peasant feels confident enough, in Mao's graphic phrase, to "stand up." Ideologically secure, and socially supported by army, party and society, he is prepared to place the revolution before everything. "Revolutionary leaders," Guevara has said, "are not often present to hear their children's first hesitant words; their wives must also share in their sacrifice."[3] Commitment, indeed, to that most elemental of human interests—life itself—is equally renounced. An ideological, social "super-ego" becomes more powerful than any primitive desire to survive. Rather, survival for him has meaning and possibility only via taking up arms.

This theory—principally Maoist—of the relationship between guerrillas and peasantry is familiar enough. It is not the product of one man's mind, however; it is the distillation of the social experience of one hundred years of revolution and war from the Taiping Revolution, the largest mass revolution of the nineteenth century, to the Communist era. During this century, every ideology was tried successively: Bud-

---

[3] Quotation prefacing his *Reminiscences of the Cuban Revolutionary War,* New York and London, 1968.

dhist millenarism; syncretic messianic doctrines with a Christian flavor during the Taiping; a people-and-empire nationalism, belonging to the same family as European Bonapartism, Boulangism, or Hobsbawm's "Church and King" movements, during the "Boxer" Rising; modern nationalism under Sun Yat Sen; an authoritarian degenerated version under Chiang Kai Shek; and the ultimate victory of Marxism. But *people* as well as *ideologies* are tried out during such a period of extended trial: very few poltroons, vacillators, idiots, or rash or weak men survived the stormy times from 1911 onwards, particularly among those in the forefront of events. Many heroic and competent men died, too.

No such experience has occurred in Latin America. True, as Debray shows in his careful, highly informed and quite brilliant survey of the Latin American scene in 1965, "Latin America: The Long March,"[4] the condition of the entire continent is much more promising, objectively, to the revolutionary's eye than the African continent Chou En Lai designated ripe for revolution in 1965. The objective features are: the "culture of poverty" described by Oscar Lewis; the pressure on the land; the growth of population; urban explosion; massive unemployment; politico-military repression; degenerating terms of trade; and United States economic and political intervention, whether direct or of the kind the French describe as "tele-guidance."

The mortality rate, or the market-value of the *cruzeiro* are not abstract things to those who die or have to find money to live. They are not "objective" facts, to be placed in separate concep-

4 *New Left Review*, No. 33, September-October, 1965, pp. 17–58.

tual categories from so-called "subjective" ones. For though the banker and the guerrilla have to operate with the same data, these are different kinds of people, who bring different kinds of interpretation to the facts. They mean different things to each, have different life-consequences, and each draws different conclusions for action. The so-called objective facts thus only exist within a framework of meaning. And even the same cognitive interpretation can give rise to differential conclusions for action. Thus both the military and the guerrillas recognize what Daniel Bell called the "exhaustion" of orthodox politics. The military move the army in; the guerrillas take to the backlands. Even such a purely physical fact as the jungle only becomes a social resource in a context of meaning and action: the guerrillas *create* it as a resource, while, for a parliamentarian, it is no kind political resource. Of course, we can crudely and usefully distinguish such physical elements as the nature of the terrain, the equipment available to each side, and the density of the population from social factors, such as their class composition. However, I emphasize the subjective variability of response to the same physical and social facts, because it is human *response* to these quite plastic facts that is crucial. The way people think is equally a condition of action, and the physical facts are always subjectively interpreted, according to the mental set, cultural assumptions, predispositions, degree of politicization, social experience, and ideological exposure of the actors.

Normally omitted from these simplistic objective/subjective models is the structure and culture of the enemy. Yet we ought not to forget that there are negative relationships as well as positive, that hostility and warfare are social relationships quite as much as love, mutual aid, or any positive relationships. The Other, to use George Herbert Mead's term (or Parsons' Alter), affects powerfully your own capacity to act, your range of choice. In older and simpler military parlance, it is necessary to know the enemy. But this entails a great deal more than simply being informed about the disposition of his troops, his plans, his equipment, or his movements. It is not only ordinary military intelligence that is needed, but a total socio-military appraisal of his relationship to you, and of the differential relationship of each of you to the *tertium quid* in this equation: the people among whom you are fighting, and for whose souls both are competing. For in warfare, of this kind above all, guns are not enough. They never have been enough, in good military theory. Clausewitz, after all, spoke of war as "the *continuation* of politics," and politicians are rarely stupid enough to rely on force alone. They attempt to win men's minds, to gain "legitimacy," to sell "noble lies," to make it unnecessary to have continually to occupy their own country with troops. In revolutionary warfare, the winning-over of the population—here one's own people—is vital. Even in non-revolutionary war, these factors are central, whether they concern the commitment of one's own troops or of the civilian population. The fall of France in 1940 is a notorious instance; Soviet resistance to the Nazis a converse case.

Thus, in the era of mass warfare, which the Taiping and the American Civil War introduced, the masses are crucial—their loyalty, will to fight, commitment, everything. Now mass consciousness is a highly various thing, to be empirically studied. It encom-

passes, to take Latin America alone, the "traditional" non-revolutionary communism and socialism of the established city proletariat; the temporal perspective of the peasant oriented to the eternal agricultural year and the eternal landlord; the persistent Peronism of the workers of Buenos Aires "for whom everything that isn't Peronist is as far away as Mars"; that "feverish and urgent passion not to sit still" in the wretched northeast of Brazil; that "mystique of starving" that has constantly generated millenarian movements infused with "a vague feeling of imminent salvation," and today infused with "Fidelista impatience"; the ghastly bloodletting anarchy of the Colombian countryside where two to three hundred thousand died in *la violencia* of the fifties for quite un-ideological causes; the resigned despair and submission to authority of the drugged Indians of the Andes.

These varying consciousnesses are what the revolutionary has to take into account, and has to change. This is the whole rationale underlying land reform programs, the provision of medical aid, education, agricultural work by the army, and so on, which are all normal features of guerrilla activity in liberated areas.

Thus the enemy, oneself, and the people are three structural elements in the revolutionary social equation. All of these, naturally, can be broken down further. Each possesses different social and cultural characteristics, and disposes of different kinds and quantities of social and physical resources. Each has a characteristic cultural equipment, too, which has to be assessed before any meaningful estimation of the situation or appropriate strategy can be arrived at.

Let us apply a little of this to Latin

America, and in particular to the revolutionary theory of Guevara and Debray. First, the social equation. It is quite clear that the enemy in 1968 is not the enemy that the twelve survivors of the *Granma* faced in Batista's Cuba in 1958, two days after they landed in the Sierra Maestra. Debray himself is quite clear about this. "The revolution," he writes, "has revolutionized the counter-revolution."[5] More than this, "Cuba has raised the material and ideological level of imperialist reaction *in less time than that of the revolutionary vanguard.*" "Imperialism," he writes, "is in a better position to put the lessons which it has learned from the Cuban Revolution into practice rapidly, because it has at its command all the material means of organized violence." He then goes on to document the vast input of money, men, and military equipment, into specifically *military* counterinsurgency programs in Latin America, plus the supportive political and economic programs and institutions such as the Alliance for Progress (which Debray contemptuously describes as a plan for transforming Latin America into a "paradise of golden latrines"), the Organization of American States, the Inter-American Defense Council, the Inter-American Development Bank, etc. Noting that the ratio of capital exported to aid and investment received was of the order of 3:1 for the whole continent in 1961[6] (this exodus of capital going via repatriated foreign profits, the worsening of terms of trade, and

amortization of debts, to finance what C. Wright Mills once delightfully described as the "over-development" of the United States), Cuban political leaders measure this input against, not simply the number of those who have died in revolutionary warfare (for these are a mere handful), but against what Debray calls the "peaceful genocide" that goes on every day in the suburbs of Recife, Brazil, where 500 out of every 1,000 born die before they are two years old, or among the Bolivian miners and the workers on the *latifundia* of Brazil who can expect to be dead soon after their thirtieth birthday. In the Second Declaration of Havana (February 4, 1962), the flow of capital to the United States was thus not only calculated at $4,000 a minute, but computed, against some unspecified death-rate, as "$1,000 per corpse and four corpses a minute."

The activity of the United States has thus been enormously stepped up since the Cuban Revolution. Between Batista's flight and the Bay of Pigs invasion there was an initial phase during which eyeball-to-eyeball confrontation was not intense. But nationalization of foreign enterprises frightened the United States into countermeasures which were to lead to the Bay of Pigs, the turn to the Communist countries, the missile crisis, the blockade, and the subsequent massive program of counterinsurgency. All this, known well enough by revolutionary theorists, constitutes a major change in one of the elements in the social equation of revolution. The Cuban rebels even enjoyed at times a limited degree of support from some other Latin American governments, initially. But today, the President of Costa Rica no longer sends arms to guerrillas as he did to the 26th of July Movement, nor do finances and military equipment

5 "Problems of Revolutionary Strategy in Latin America," *New Left Review*, No. 45, September-October, 1967, pp. 13–41.
6 See Andre Gunder Frank, *Capitalism and Underdevelopment in Latin America*, New York, 1967.

come from Venezuela with official or quasi-official approval. (Initially, too, British, French and some American journalists gave Cuba a good press.) Two years later, Cuba was fighting for its life against an invasion launched from Nicaragua, and mild reforms in the Dominican Republic evoked instant invasion from American Marines.

A further element in the equation is the existence of other political movements competing for mass support. With the establishment of the Cuban Revolution, *focismo* has become a rival to existing parties and movements, revolutionary or otherwise, and it now has a social base, reference point, and source of inspiration and support. Of course, the 26th of July Movement itself had to cope with the existence of an established Communist Party, of trade unions, with the division between the "Llano" and the "Sierra." But the contemporary guerrilla movements face the problem of resistance and criticism from rival institutionalized revolutionary movements, more severely in countries like Brazil and Venezuela.

The implications of these changes in the equation are clear. They are not that revolution is impossible: an infinitely greater American effort in Vietnam has been a signal failure. But it is going to be infinitely more difficult than it ever was in Cuba. It is surely symbolic that Guevara is dead, and that Debray has thirty years in which to reflect upon the accuracy of his theoretical model.

The Cuban Revolution never went in for prophetic models of "what it will be like": what Marx sardonically called "Comtist cookshop recipes for the future." Theory, for them, emerged in the *act* of revolution. It is noteworthy that Fidel Castro never held a political meeting in seventeen months

in the Sierra Maestra. Guerrillas theorize about armed revolution, not post-revolution. Castro's program during the Sierra Maestra campaign, it has been said (by a Brazilian "traditional-Communist" critic),[7] amounted to little more than "the overthrow of the dictatorship and the formation of a democratic government free from corruption." It owed more to José Martí than Marx.

Whatever his personal exposure to Marxism, either via books, at the University of Havana, or in the shape of involvement with "acted-out" Marxism in revolutionary circles, Castro's own evaluation seems accurate enough. His political ideas at that time, he says, were embodied in "History Will Absolve Me," his famous speech to the court after the failure of the assault on the Moncada barracks. "Even then I analyzed the class composition of our society, the need to mobilize the workers, the farmers, the unemployed, the teachers, the intellectual workers and the small proprietors against the Batista regime. Even then I proposed a program of planned development for our economy, utilizing all the resources of the country to promote its economic development. . . . It could be called Marxist if you wish, but probably a true Marxist would have said that it was not. Unquestionably though, it was an advanced revolutionary program."[8]

Today, however, the Cuban Revolution *has* produced a very distinct body of Marxist theory, and present-day guerrillas are definitely Marxist. Read-

7 G. Luiz Araujo, "A Revolução Cubano e a Teoria dos Focos Insurrecionais," *Revista Civilização Brasileira*, 14, Year III, July, 1967, pp. 85–108.
8 In the famous interview "Fidel Castro—Candid Conversation," in *Playboy*, January, 1967, pp. 64, 68.

ing Castro's own voluminous writings and speeches, and examining his turns of policy since the revolution, one sees that his own personal thinking is much more pragmatic than that of others around him. One finds in it the same kind of extraordinary flexibility, and acuteness—opponents call it "opportunism" —that stamped Lenin, who could return from exile to the Finland Station, only to repudiate the whole party line arrived at by the Bolshevik leadership in his absence. Neither Lenin nor Castro (nor Mao), then, waited for "objective conditions" to "mature" to some point of inevitability. They *created* the revolution in what they judged to be a chronically revolutionary situation. They made the inevitable.

Nevertheless, Castro no doubt completely endorses the recommendations for guerrilla warfare embodied in the various calls to arms sent out from Havana and was a principal source of theoretical guidance to Debray, who articulated the main ideas: the strategy of detonating a popular mass response by small guerrilla bands embarking on armed struggle. But the general conceptualization of *focismo* has been the work of Debray. Guevara's book, *Guerrilla Warfare,* is very much a practical do-it-yourself field manual focused on the techniques of guerrilla struggle; his *Reminiscences of the Cuban Revolutionary War* is a straightforward blow-by-blow personal account, rather than a severely political document.

The real schematization comes with Debray, though not in his earliest essay, "The Long March," which is a carefully-documented, detailed distillation of the experience of political encounter over the postwar period, particularly the successive attempts to create guerrilla armies. All of this is located within the framework of an analysis of the social structure and cultures of Latin America. His essay, "Problems of Revolutionary Strategy in Latin America" written two years later in 1967, is stamped by an enhanced sensitivity to the increased counterattack of the United States; a critical rejection of parliamentarism (even for the relatively "developed" countries of the "southern cone"—Chile, Uruguay, Argentina); and an examination of the process through which, he considers, parties of bourgeois revolution (Partido Revolucionaria in Bolivia; Acción Democrática in Venezuela) have either been strangled by the military or become "demo-bourgeois fascist" regimes. To play the game of revolution within the rules of constitutional legality, i.e., without a popular armed organization, has one of two possible endings, he declares. Either the player is sent to prison, exile, or the grave (military coup), or he is put in power and is *himself* charged with sending revolutionaries to prison, exile, or the grave.

Some see in Debray's work a consistent theoretical whole, the two earlier essays forming "an indispensable complement, the theoretical-political premises of the call to arms in *Revolution in the Revolution?*" This is unhistoric, for *Revolution in the Revolution?*, the latest of these three works, is also markedly the most schematic. Gone is the detailed empirical documentation of the earliest essay, the concrete analysis of the *variety* of Latin American situations. In its place, we find a paradigm of guerrilla warfare, largely abstracted from its social context, an absorption with the techniques of guerrilla warfare, and an inward-turning preoccupation with the guerrillas themselves. Now, too, the *foco*, the act, become primary. This is not new: we have seen that the absence of theoretical programatics is authentically Cuban, the emphasis upon *creating* the revolution authentically Castroist. Yet Debray's critics have always accused him of a tendency towards a kind of modernized Blanquism. I think this criticism *was* misplaced. It has, perhaps, become increasingly true. Let me illustrate by a quotation from Mao Tse Tung:

We must go to the masses; arouse them to activity; concern ourselves with their weal and woe; . . . work earnestly and sincerely in their interests and solve their problems of salt, rice, shelter, clothing, and childbirth. . . . The . . . women want to learn ploughing and hoeing. . . . The children want to go to school. . . . The wooden bridge over there is too narrow. . . . All such problems concerning the living standards of the masses should be placed on our agenda. . . . We should make the broad masses realize that we represent their interests, that our life and theirs are intimately interwoven. (*Selected Works,* London, 1954, Vol. I, pp. 135, 136, 149, 150, 151.)

Contrast this, from Debray:

During the first [of guerrilla operations] the initial group experiences at the outset a period of absolute nomadism . . . the guerrilla force is *independent* of the civilian population, . . . the guerrilla *foco* . . . independent of the families residing within the zone of operations . . . the guerrilleros avoid going to the villages . . . "constant vigilance, constant mistrust, constant mobility" the three golden rules. . . . A given group of armed propagandists [should abandon] all hope of remaining unnoticed, "like fish in water."

The contrast could not be sharper. Of course, one may simply say that this is an adaptation to the new conditions facing guerrillas in Latin America. That may be so. It does, however, sug-

gest that it is going to be extremely difficult to organize peasants whom you never stop to speak to and constantly mistrust, and who are constantly policed by counterinsurgency forces. One knows that Debray is talking about the *initial* phase, and schematically envisages a subsequent phase of rootedness among the peasantry of a guerrilla-controlled zone. But are the rural guerrillas whom he describes as "a handful of hunted men [living] 24 hours out of 24, neither in the day or the night but in the half-light of the enervating, humid, protecting sunless forest" really any less constricted than the urban revolutionary whose world, he says, is one of "solitude, fleeting human relationships, oppressive silence, confinement, symbolized by the night"? In becoming "invisible to the enemy" do they not become also invisible to the peasants?

Guatemalan guerrillas have, in fact, adopted strategies that appear to reject the "self-defense zone" concept and Debray's model of the *foco*. Their strategy and tactics of armed revolution are the product of a different experience—the Arbenz debacle in particular. In contrast to the Cuban model of the primacy of the guerrilla *foco,* the Guatemalans see "the function of the guerrillas. . . as that of organizing the peasants and *becoming their revolutionary instrument.* The corresponding strategy puts more emphasis on the political—on breaking up the existing state power—than on the military. The climax of the revolution is seen, not as a series of pitched battles, but rather as an armed insurrection, with the action of the guerrillas in the countryside being closely coordinated with that of the workers and students in the cities and towns. Out of this would emerge *from the outset* a workers' and peasants' state based directly on the workers' and peasants' committees organized and developed during the preceding stages."[9] Thus Adolfo Gilly's account of the Guatemalan movement emphasizes that military action is subordinated to the organization of the peasants, whom the guerrillas constantly talk to, educating them politically but also receiving *their* ideas, discovering their wants; the guerrillas act as a coordinating mechanism for the emergent struggles of a "people in arms," not as a "directorate" and in no way self-isolated from, or suspicious of, the peasantry.

One appreciates that, after the elimination of the "self-defense zones" established in Marquetalia, in Southern Colombia, eliminated by the army in May, 1964, and in the mines of Bolivia —similarly invaded in May and September, 1965—Debray fears the premature establishment of guerrilla base zones. Of course, seven months before Batista's fall, the Cuban Rebel Army itself numbered only 300 rifles, and it probably never contained more than 1,500–2,000 men.[10] Yet it becomes increasingly difficult to see how the move from "absolute nomadism" to cleared autonomous zones is to be made today, and Debray has no theoretical answers. He is, in the event, against such "self-defense zones."

Debray might well answer that Latin America is not China, and that tactics and strategy must differ. But neither is Latin America Cuba. It is Bolivia, Uruguay, Brazil, Colombia, and so on, each country having regions with vastly differing social characteristics which do not disappear at the wave of a schematic wand from however gifted a French intellectual. Take urbanization: Brazil has two cities with more than five million people in them, and three more of over a million each; in Argentina, 70 percent of the population is urban; 600,000 people live in the *barriadas* around Lima, a city of one and a half million inhabitants; a so-called "primate city," like Guatemala City, embraces a fifth of the entire population of the country. Nor do these people necessarily have work. In Venezuela, 48 percent of the *bidonville* dwellers are completely unemployed, 38 percent work three days a week, and only 18 percent a full week.[11] Potentially, these people are, of course, highly volatile politically, as Fanon has reminded us. Moreover, for those countries unfortunately endowed by nature with *pampas* instead of jungles and mountains, Debray has little to recommend, except to tell them that their liberation depends upon guerrilla warfare in more favored regions: a strangely passive message for the bulk of the population of a continent, many of whom are already politicized and organized.

All the factors in the revolutionary equation, in fact, differ greatly from country to country: armies are more or less reliable; the rural population includes landless laborers, independent smallholders, workers on *latifundia,* and so on. Only one thing is common, as Debray points out: the United States' presence.

[9] "The Breakthrough in Guatemala," editorial, MONTHLY REVIEW, Vol. 17, No. 1, May, 1965, pp. 6–7. See also Adolfo Gilly's "The Guerrilla Movement in Guatemala," pp. 9–39.
[10] Robin Blackburn, "Prologue to the Cuban Revolution," *New Left Review,* No. 21, October, 1963, p. 76.

[11] Jeanne Habel, "L'Amérique Latine et la Lutte des Classes," *Partisans,* April-June, 1967, No. 37, p. 76. See also the following issue, No. 38, which, like No. 37, is entirely devoted to Latin American guerrilla problems.

Preoccupied increasingly with the internal organization and political culture of the guerrilla army, Debray said very little in *Revolution in the Revolution?* about what used to be the central theme of Marxist analysis of guerrilla warfare: the relationship between the guerrillas and peasants. Now the peasants are treated principally as a danger. Questions of military technique preoccupy Guevara: how to make Molotov cocktails, or how to demolish strongpoints. In Debray, it is the demolition of all other political strategies and tactics: urban revolutionism, alliances, "excessive deliberation," self-defense zones, the peasantry, Trotskyism, Maoists, traditional communism, all are witheringly rejected as contaminated. There remains the band of hunted men, acting and creating the revolution, increasingly focused upon themselves and preoccupied with the military act. It may be that the Sorel whose name appears in his book (true, to be rejected) is not too far below the surface of Debray's mind. The pragmatism of Castro himself, the absorption in the revolutionary act of fighting in Guevara, are reduced to an intellectual schema in Debray in the shape of a unitary formula, and a continent of two hundred millions of diversified people is reduced to a monotonal revolutionary design.

All revolutions export their ideas; they always protest that this is the last thing they want to do. The Russian Revolution forced its conceptions on other Communist Parties directly via the Comintern; China has split the world Communist movement because she knows her strategy is correct; Cuba, the least dogmatic revolution of all, a veritable "revolution without doctrines" ends up by projecting *focismo*. Debray's

schematism, then, is not simply an individual intellectual proclivity. His thinking is indeed that of the Cuban revolutionaries he admires. But he brings to it a Gallic systematization appropriate to an *Agregé de Philosophie* and a product of the Ecole Normale Supérieure. A revolution proud of its achievements naturally finds an articulating voice. Perhaps a revolution headed by actors and men of flexibility, given the social division of labor, had to import an outsider when its requirement became systematization.

What is crucial, however, in the Cuban Revolution is its "demonstration effect" at a much more diffuse level. It has shown that revolution is possible; it has shown it to be possible in a micro-country without the immense resources of Russia or China, in a country dominated by the United States, and not too far from its colonial past. It has also taught others that action, including action by dedicated minorities in the context of mass dissatisfaction, and repudiating orthodox politics, can produce striking results—and not only in underdeveloped countries. These lessons are of wider significance, especially when backed up by the experience of Vietnam, culminating in the urban Tet offensive, for they threaten, as France shows, to stimulate revolutionary action once more in countries long politically becalmed, where huge electoral Communist parties have been reduced to impotence for decades, and where the largest one in non-Communist Asia—that of Indonesia—allowed itself to be wiped out. I doubt that these tendencies will be characteristic of the communism and the non-Communist revolutionism of the next decade. Even Guevara's death, in the longer run, has a symbolic positive value. Of course he failed, but so did Christ. Yet Christianity subsequently became quite important. Moreover, an hypothesis is not falsified by a single negative instance (though, to be exact, there have been many other such failures). However, enough people feel that what 82 crazy men did in landing in Cuba (after an initial rebuff at Moncada)—both of these events "theoretical and historical scandals"—they can do. What those men went through in deaths, desertions, betrayals, disappointments, would have led any determinist to give up. The Cubans did not have it easy either. But they were not determinists; they were revolutionists and voluntarists.

We are back to the problem that faces all political actors, but notably those out to create radical change. When is the moment ripe? "European Marxism," Debray has written, "is flawed by positivism (with an empiricist basis)." It waited for conditions to mature. Cuban Marxism has been called "idealist" Marxism; it seems better, however, simply to call it revolutionary Marxism, which is neither an "objective" nor a "subjective" variant, but a dialectical approach to the interplay of the actor and his environment, in which the agency of the actor, his human assertions, are crucial.

Raúl Castro recently gave a piece of free advice to counterrevolutionary governments. He explained how *they* had coped with 179 CIA bands dropped into Cuba by July 1967: very simply, they had armed 50,000 workers and 50,000 peasants. "All you have to do to destroy guerrilla bands," he remarked, "is the same." But that, of course, is just what cannot be done. Moreover, the contingency tables needed for revolutionary prediction contain different numbers from those used in counterrevolutionary calculations. I am reminded of the paradox of nuclear deterrence theory. It *has* been the case, many times, that major crises, even the Cuban missile crisis, have not led to nuclear world war. Yet this theory has one distinctive property, which distinguishes it from most other social theories. It only has to be proved wrong once, and none of us will have much need for theory thereafter. Similarly, *focos* may be wiped out time and again, but the guerrillas need only succeed once. From that point onwards, the revolution has won.

12

United States-Cuban Relations

Richard R. Fagen

Published for the first time in this collection, in a slightly revised form from the original working paper, by permission of the author.

Richard R. Fagen is a Professor of Political Science at Stanford University.

When the Castro Revolution was ten years old, the Center for Inter-American Relations of New York convened a study group to examine continuing problems of United States-Cuban relations. Following is the working paper which resulted from the group's discussions, drafted by study director Professor Richard R. Fagen, a prominent student of the Cuban Revolution.

The paper sets forth what at this writing still remain current United States goals and policies regarding Cuba, and it asserts that some of the same and other goals might be better served by a shift in policies. Specifically, the paper recommends a gradual accommodation with the Castro regime— we should emphasize, solely on the pragmatic basis that such a course is in the best interests of the United States.[1]

Although the policy recommendations in the study group's document are clearly modest ones, its circulation in the spring of 1969 stirred considerable controversy. Senator Strom Thurmond (Democrat-South Carolina) decried a "rising tide of pro-Castro propaganda" and incorporated into the Congressional Record an article by conservative journalist Paul Bethel which denounced the Center study group as having been "packed with members from the Left."[2] The reader may also be interested in Fagen's own retrospective observations, excerpted with permission from his personal correspondence with the editor:

[I]t seems to me that if one wants to understand why working papers of the sort that I wrote about U.S.-Cuban relations have literally no chance of being taken seriously by policy makers, one must also understand the kind of climate or ambiente which pollutes even discussions of sweet reasonableness concerning such

---

[1] See also John Plank, "We Should Start Talking with Castro," *The New York Times Magazine* (March 30, 1969), pp. 29–31 ff; and Irving Louis Horowitz, "United States-Cuba Relations: Beyond the Quarantine," *TRANS-action*, VI, No. 6 (April 1969), pp. 43–47.

[2] *Congressional Record—Senate* (April 3, 1969), pp. S3557–S3558.

matters. In other words, I am saying that for understanding the parameters of the policy-making and policy-changing process in the United States, one must also understand how excruciatingly difficult it is to get a discussion going on certain topics without being attacked by people like Thurmond and Bethel. . . . I should also add (as more or less of an aside) that my paper received only negative comments in print and in personal correspondence. Almost all of this negative comment was political: "Communist, sell-out, Pinko," etc., etc. No one really discussed the merits of the situation as a situation. . . . What I say [in the paper] about "quasi-professional anticommunists, sugar importers, Cuban refugees, and a business community stung by confiscations" certainly came home to roost.

The goals and purposes of the United States posture toward Cuba have changed through time.[1] In the early 1960's, and particularly at the time of the Bay of Pigs invasion, it was clear that the overthrow of the Castro government was the primary objective of the government of the United States. At the present, although "getting rid of Castro" may still be the highest priority goal for some politicians and administrators, the mainstream of official thinking seems to focus on the following three goals:

1) To isolate the "revolutionary virus," thus protecting other people and nations from the spread of Castroite activities, influence, and violent revolution.
2) To make the Cuban developmental effort as costly and sluggish as possible, thus both discrediting the Cuban developmental model and weakening the legitimacy of the current regime (in official thinking, progress toward this goal should contribute to progress toward goal number one).

3) To embarrass, instruct, and increase costs to the Soviet Union by forcing the Russians to "relate to" and support a Communist government that they cannot easily control and which might, in fact, prove to be a developmental failure.

Again, progress toward goal number two should contribute (in the official view) to progress toward goal number three.[2]

The *actual practices* which comprise the official posture toward Cuba must be kept distinct from these three goals. A summary of official, public practices

[1] Those who attended the several meetings of the Study Group on United States-Cuban relations of the Center for Inter-American Relations have contributed to this paper in innumerable and important ways. No attempt has been made, however, to represent all points of view in this written report. The author wishes to thank the participants while at the same time absolving them of responsibility for what is herein expressed and advocated.

The word *posture* is used instead of the more conventional *policy* to convey the notion that the manner in which the United States relates to the Castro regime does not constitute a group of practices that are as consistent and fully articulated as a strict usage of the word *policy* would suggest.

[2] Publicly, United States officials do not usually articulate and defend the United States posture toward Cuba in terms of any except the first of these three goals. Thus, Assistant Secretary of State Covey Oliver, testifying before the Senate Foreign Relations Committee on March 6, 1968, said the following: "I would like to explain my personal view about the interdiction of Cuba. The interdiction is not designed to topple a government. . . . The purpose in Cuba of the denial program is to bring about a situation in which Castro's Cuba will be less prone and less able to engage in hemispheric hooliganism. . . ." Senate Foreign Relations Committee, *Hearings on the Alliance for Progress*, 1968, pp. 257–258.

currently in force would include, at the minimum, the following:[3]

1) No diplomatic or consular relations with Cuba (United States representation is handled through the Swiss).
2) No monetary, trade, or commercial relations with Cuba except as specifically authorized by the president or his representative.
3) No travel by United States citizens to Cuba except as specifically authorized by the Department of State.
4) Various administrative and political pressures brought to bear on governments that sell, ship, or otherwise furnish goods to the Castro government.
5) Exclusion of the Castro government from participation in the inter-American system (through a series of OAS resolutions directly attributable to actions taken by the United States).

This basic distinction between a set of goals and a set of practices (not necessarily related to those goals) raises four questions:

TO WHAT EXTENT DO CURRENT PRACTICES ACTUALLY CONTRIBUTE TO THE IMPLEMENTATION OF THE GOALS SET OUT?

The practices listed above are in large part an accumulation of retaliatory decisions, accidents, antagonisms, inattentions and not a fully rational linking of means to ends. Of course, in this they do not differ dramatically

from the practices relating the United States to many other small (and sometimes large) countries. Nor do their accidental and retaliatory characteristics necessarily imply that they do not contribute to the articulated goals. However, the extent to which certain United States policy goals in regard to Cuba have actually been achieved is only weakly related to the practices which in fact have been employed. For example, the failure of Castroite activities and armed rebellion in Latin America is probably best explained by the technological and tactical sophistication of United States-Latin American military teams, the opposition of the Soviet Union to armed struggle in the hemisphere, the nationalism of large numbers of politically articulate Latin Americans, and the difficulty of politicizing peasant populations and turning the lower and middle sectors against moderate and centrist regimes. In short, apparently, the "objective" conditions for the spread of Castroism do not exist on any substantial scale, and thus the success achieved in containing Castroism should not be attributed to the diplomatic, economic, or cultural isolation of the regime. Similarly, Cuban mismanagement, economic romanticism, and precipitous centralization as well as problems with East European trading partners and assorted natural disasters have been more responsible for the sluggishness and costliness of the development effort than has been the policy of economic denial.

---

[3] The list is limited to officially acknowledged, openly promulgated practices intended to "hurt" or "contain" the Castro government directly. Thus, practices such as air and sea surveillance and the various activities of the CIA are excluded because of their non-public character; the arrangements which regulate the flow of Cuban exiles into the United States are excluded because they are not necessarily intended to "hurt" or "contain" the Castro government; and United States military, political, and economic policies in other Latin American countries (although deeply influenced by the fear of Castroism) are not included because they are not directly part of the U.S. posture toward the Castro government.

WHAT ARE SOME OF THE LESS DESIRABLE CONSEQUENCES AND UNANTICIPATED COSTS OF THE PRACTICES NOW ENGAGED IN?

The opposition and hostility of the United States directly benefits the Cuban regime in at least two ways. First, the sense of emergency created on the island stimulates and reinforces a sense of solidarity, of will, of "being in it together." This is a variant of the wartime, belt-tightening ethic frequently noted by visitors to besieged lands. Second, the leadership is in part spared from having to face the consequences of its own mistakes, because the opposition and hostility of the United States are readily available to explain whatever shortages, shortcomings, and problems exist. It is probably fair to say, however, that the benefits to the Cuban regime of United States hostility are considerably fewer now than they were in the early 1960's when Sartre (paraphrasing others) said that if the United States did not exist, the Cuban revolutionaries would be forced to invent it.

A certain amount of prestige is lost by the United States and a considerable amount of ill-will is generated both in Western Europe and in Latin America among the democratic center and the left as a result of the almost unilateral attempts to "interdict" the Castro government. Although the costs of trying to get Europeans to cooperate fully in the policy of economic denial have usually been perceived by U.S. decision-makers to be unacceptably high, the United States nevertheless applies pressure to otherwise friendly governments in the hope that they will climb on the anti-Cuban bandwagon in some fashion.[4] Despite United States success

in guiding sanctions and punitive measures against Cuba through the OAS, many Latin Americans unquestionably feel ill-used by the manner in which they came to have—and now must operate with—a Cuban policy not of their making. Furthermore, it is entirely possible that substantial sympathy for the Cuban cause has been generated as a natural reaction to the David and Goliath aspects of the Cuban-United States confrontation.

The lack of almost all types of contacts with Cuba at all levels increases the potential for something "going wrong" in the governance of the hemisphere. Thus, although it is difficult to predict just what form a new Cuban crisis might take were one to occur in the next few years, the isolation of Cuba in the hemisphere increases the number of potential scenarios leading to such a crisis. In general, the predictability and stability of regional systems are not enhanced when attempts are made to isolate and exclude one geo-political space. As a corollary, it is somewhat bizarre and probably dangerous (even after the "agreements" following the missile crisis of 1962) to have to deal with the Soviet Union in this hemisphere in large part through the "black box" of Cuba.

WHAT MIGHT OTHER AND ALTERNATIVE PERSPECTIVES OR GOALS FOR A UNITED STATES CUBAN POLICY BE?

The following four points cannot be developed in detail here; however, none is outlandish given the most generally expressed goals of United States

[4] Even generally friendly Europeans react with bewilderment and scorn in the face of United States practices toward Cuba. See, for example, Raymond Aron and Alfred Grosser, "A European Perspective," in John Plank, ed., *Cuba and the United States* (Washington, D.C.: The Brookings Institution, 1967).

policy around the world. Also, these four points should not be viewed as independent policy perspectives and goals, but rather as partially inter-related segments of an adjusted posture toward Cuba.

1. To End or Contain Cuban Mischief-Making in the Hemisphere.

This is currently claimed to be the prime objective of U.S. policy toward Cuba, and—at the same time—the end of such mischief-making is usually characterized by U.S. officials as a "requisite" to the normalization of United States-Cuban relations. Thus, Assistant Secretary Covey Oliver, in his testimony before the Senate Foreign Relations Committee, said,

. . . a logic is seen in the public expressions by leaders of our government that the United States would consider some degree of normalization of relations with Cuba, with Castro's Cuba, if the government should do two things: One, cut off military associations with an extracontinental power or powers; and two, cease and desist from the said hemispheric hooliganism.

We know, however (or at least we should know by now), that this is a sterile and unproductive way of conceptualizing the problem. If Cuban "hemispheric hooliganism" is really as bad as Oliver and others say, then its termination or containment should become a goal of policy not a prior condition to a bargain that the other party might not want. At the very least, we should admit that the punitive measures against Cuba were in part imposed for reasons other than the regime's "hemispheric hooliganism," and lifting some of those measures can just as well be seen as a requisite for a reciprocal termination of the "hooliganism" as the other way around.

2. To Break Cuba Away From Substantial Military and Economic Dependence on the Soviet Union.

There is a certain ambivalence in official attitudes toward Cuban-Soviet relations. On the one hand, there are those who seem satisfied to see the Soviet Union burdened and at times embarrassed by the Cubans. On the other hand, Oliver and others emphasize the "unacceptability" of the current Soviet presence in Cuba. Both juridically (under the OAS resolutions) and politically (in terms of costs, dangers, and benefits) the latter perspective would seem preferable to the former. That is, it would seem to be a sounder policy to concentrate on lessening the Soviet presence in Cuba than to try to use that presence to discredit or burden the U.S.S.R. Again, however, it must be emphasized that nothing is gained by demanding that the Cubans renounce Soviet military (and/or economic) support as a precondition to some degree of normalization of relations with the United States. It is not clear how fully they desire the latter, and they certainly cannot afford —under current conditions—to do the former. Cuban economic dependence on the Soviet Union is not best understood in zero-sum terms. That is, lessening this dependence does not imply that the United States will have to start picking up all of Cuba's unpaid bills and developmental costs. Above all, it is not necessary to think of the United States as having to "buy" Cuba away from the Soviet Union through especially attractive offers of trade and aid. Simply allowing Cuba to trade on ordinary terms in the hemisphere would in itself lessen its dependence on the Soviet Union. Furthermore, a non-socialist basis for developmental aid is already established in the technological assistance that the Cubans now receive from Canada, Japan, Israel, and many Western European countries, and this base could easily expand if restrictions on the movement of men, goods, and money were eased. It is unlikely, however, that much can be done about Cuba's military dependence on the Soviet Union until the antagonism toward the United States is somewhat reduced or reversed.

3. To Democratize or Liberalize the Domestic Policies of the Castro Regime. It has been suggested that to the extent that the United States is truly interested in bettering the conditions under which citizens other than its own live, elements of a new Cuban policy could be directed toward goals such as releasing political prisoners, strengthening legal due process, securing greater scope for criticism in the mass media, and securing various other institutional and procedural reforms that would increase individual freedom and enhance individual dignity in Cuba. It is not easy, however, to imagine any direct and immediate mechanisms for affecting the process and substance of Cuban political life. Nevertheless, there is evidence from Eastern Europe that autocratic and centrist political regimes are relatively vulnerable (through time) to the "liberal virus." Increased exposure to the diversity and ferment of both socialist and non-socialist cultures has led to changes in Eastern Europe that were almost unimaginable only a decade ago. At the very least, a partial loosening of the diplomatic and cultural noose around Cuba would probably make the continuance of certain antidemocratic practices more difficult (on the assumption that it is harder and more costly to oppress one's population in public than in private).

4. To Win Some Substantial Measure of Hemispheric and Even Extra-hemispheric Respect, Credibility, and Leadership. It need hardly be emphasized that the United States is not exactly viewed around the world as the champion of "liberty and justice for all." Outside of the hemisphere, there are probably few national elites or articulate publics that respect, defend, or even fully understand the current United States posture toward Cuba. In Latin America, however, the situation is more complex. Without question, sectors of official and public opinion in many countries (for example, Brazil, Argentina, Venezuela, and some Central American countries) support our posture. Some Latin American elites would certainly go even further, advocating increased harassment and military pressure directed against the Castro regime. Despite the verbal battering that the political center and much of the Latin American left has taken from the Cuban leadership, however, some moderates and almost all of the noncommunist left in many countries would probably applaud a shift toward increased trade and/or diplomatic exchange with Cuba. It is difficult to think of hemispheric initiatives by the United States since the first years of the Alliance for Progress that could—by any stretch of the imagination—be called progressive, and thus be likely to appeal to those Latin Americans on the left of the current political center of gravity. On the other hand, the record is heavy with political, military, and commercial initiatives that—although clothed in modern rhetoric—smack of the 1920's. Yet the United States can ill-afford in the long run to continue to ignore and alienate the progressive elements active in Latin American politics. As many have ar-

gued, these sectors can only increase their influence in the next decade, and our current standing with them is marginal.[5] A more rational Cuban posture might ease access into and improve credibility with those groups now waiting in the wings for their chance to wrestle with problems of governance and development.

WHAT PRACTICES OR ARRANGEMENTS MIGHT BE MOST CONDUCIVE TO THE ACCOMPLISHMENT OF A NEW OR REVISED SET OF GOALS?

It was argued above that whatever success has been achieved to date in containing the hemispheric mischief-making of the Cuban regime is attributable more to exogenous factors than to the specific content of the United States posture toward Cuba. If this is, in fact, an accurate assessment, then it follows that the United States does not run the risk of encouraging higher levels of mischief-making by removing or readjusting sanctions that are not operating to deter or inhibit the regime's activity. In fact, the opposite argument can be made: Cuba's capacity to engage in the kind of hemispheric activities that are viewed as "subversive" is directly proportional to the island's degree of political, economic, and cultural isolation. Once the

Castro regime is at least partially tied to the hemisphere through trade, travel, and diplomacy, outright subversive activities become more difficult rather than easier for the regime to support. Certain costs of fomenting trouble accrue and are perceived where none previously existed. For example, the revolutionary leadership would have to think twice before sending arms and men to the guerrillas in Venezuela if it were at the same time buying oil from the Venezuelan Petroleum Corporation (if one can imagine such a state of affairs coming to pass!).[6] Similarly, opening Cuba and the revolutionary experience to the rest of the hemisphere would probably exercise a moderating influence over both the friends and enemies of the regime. The Cuban revolution has its fair share of both strengths and weaknesses, successes and failures, and no sensible or enduring purpose is served by limiting the number of persons who can experience and interpret it first-hand. Returning to the metaphor dear to those who oppose the regime, if the Cuban revolution is a virus, then exposure to its carriers should result in increased immunity on the part of target populations.

5 This argument is well made by John J. Johnson in "The United States and the Latin American Left Wings," *The Yale Review*, Vol. LVI (March 1967), pp. 322–335. Johnson's argument is almost pure pragmatism: "...it is easy but dangerous to stick with a loser, but that is just what we are doing at this moment in each of the Latin American countries. The proof is that Washington is supporting the most socially conservative elements that could possibly win an honest election, and doing that grudgingly" (p. 335).

6 In this respect, Cuban-Mexican relations are instructive. As the one member of the OAS maintaining diplomatic, trade, and cultural relations with the Castro government, Mexico has received relatively "correct" treatment from the Cubans. Although it is doubtful that the revolutionaries approve of the Mexican political system, they explicitly exclude it from most of their attacks on the systems and rulers of the rest of Latin America. At the moment, in fact, the Cubans and Mexicans are negotiating an agreement designed to control hijackings involving the aircraft of either nation through the extradition and return of the hijackers. [This pact has since been signed. (Ed.)]

The argument just sketched suggests two specific policy innovations.[7] First, the travel ban should be lifted, and all United States citizens who wish to do so and are able to secure a visa from the Cuban authorities should be allowed to visit Cuba. Current travel regulations are undemocratic and unenforceable (owing to bureaucratic overload in Washington and recent Federal Court decisions relating to passports and travel); and telling U.S. citizens that they must ask special permission from their own government before visiting certain foreign areas is demeaning. It would be difficult to find anyone—inside of government—who would publicly defend the rationality of current travel policy and enforcement procedures. At the very least, even those who believe in the necessity and morality of telling U.S. citizens that they cannot go to countries X, Y, and Z would probably agree that the proper administrative agency for enforcing such policy is the Department of Justice (rather than the State Department) and that the proper statutory base is congressional legislation rather than presidential and/or administrative whim.[8] More generally,

and somewhat more cynically, the lifting of the travel ban shifts the onus of being exclusionist onto the Cuban authorities. The spectacle of the most powerful nation in the world admitting, at least implicitly, that it cannot trust its own citizens to visit a small Communist island for fear that they might be seduced by the revolution is ludicrous. If, on the other hand, the Cubans fear —for whatever reasons—an increased flow of North Americans, let them guard their own gates; but certainly the United States should not be protecting them from the necessity of facing the issue.[9]

Second, the economic denial policy should be lifted and limited trade

---

7 It is not suggested that these two moves should be undertaken immediately. Rather, they are proposed as logical *low cost* initiatives that are available at executive discretion for use when a climate conducive to further negotiations exists. For instance, concern with Peruvian-United States relations probably pre-empts the energies and attention of official United States policy circles at the present moment. To bring up Cuban-United States at such a moment would weaken our already marginal capacity (in terms of men, good will, new ideas) to cope with the problems at hand.

8 The case against travel restrictions in general and the use of the passport as an instrument of control in particular is powerfully made in Thomas Ehrlich, "Passports,"

Stanford Law Review, Vol. 19, No. 1 (November 1966), pp. 129–149.

9 Two immediate, preliminary initiatives to a lifting of the travel ban are suggested: first, the United States government should stop opposing a commercial air-link between either Nassau and Cuba or Canada and Cuba. Under existing arrangements, the Mexicans are being pressured to act as watchdogs over our travel policy because the Mexico City-Havana flights are the only ones into Cuba from airports in the Western Hemisphere (or at least they are the only non-restricted commercial flights). Needless delays, antagonisms, and expenses for legitimate travelers result from this bottleneck. There is also the possibility that additional British and/or Canadian flights would end or substantially reduce the hijacking of airplanes. Little is known of the personal motivations and states of mind of the hijackers, however, so that prediction in this area is risky.

In the second place, restrictions on the exchange of printed and filmed materials with Cuba should be lifted. Again, if the Cubans wish to protect themselves from American books, magazines, and newspapers, let them assume the burden of imposing or maintaining such restrictions. But when imposed by the United States, such restrictions fly squarely in the face of the most elementary concepts of freedom of access to information.

should be re-established between the United States and Cuba. The most difficult issue that would eventually have to be faced involves the sugar quota, but a first round of commercial arrangements could be established without having to reach an agreement on sugar. In fact, it is possible that the sale of Cuban tobacco alone—or simply accumulated currency reserves—could float an initial round of purchases of the sort that the Cubans might like to make under a commercial agreement. Certainly, it would be a mistake to think of such a first round in anything except commercial terms: they have goods to sell or dollars that the United States wants; the United States has goods to sell that they want. With some simplification, this is the basis of Cuban trade with Spain. Above all, the lifting of the denial policy should not be confounded with either threats or promises of aid. Lifting the denial policy does not necessarily involve extending credits or aid in any form to the Castro government. It means allowing North American firms to do cash and carry business with the Cuban government. The immediate economic consequences and costs of such a first step in the re-establishment of commercial relations with Cuba would be minimal. From the Cuban point of view, the arrangements would facilitate securing spare parts for existing American machinery, while at the same time lessening transportation costs (and some basic costs) on other goods purchased. But the initial volume of trade of the cash-and-carry variety proposed would not be great. The Cuban economy simply does not generate sufficient convertible foreign exchange to enable the planners to make large dollar purchases in the United States. From the American point of

view, these commercial arrangements would constitute a relatively low cost, low risk opportunity for the exploration of other kinds of arrangements while at the same time appearing relatively cautious by virtue of falling far short of the web of agreements that the United States has with many other Communist nations.[10]

It is not easy to suggest in detail, or to predict, what actions might follow the two moves just outlined; however, since both are relatively free of risk, they should be tried despite the lack of clear vision of the next stake in U.S.-Cuban relations. Subsequent moves would necessarily be deeply conditioned by Cuban responses and other ongoing determinants of the policy process.[11] Eventually, however, the larger issue of Cuba's relationship with the rest of the hemisphere will have to be faced, and it is useful to understand from the outset that the revolution has irrevocably changed the nature of intra-hemispheric relations. This means that phrases such as "the return of Cuba to the OAS" and the "normalization of hemispheric relations" mask rather than illuminate the nature of the problem. Any substantial diplomatic and economic re-incorporation of revolutionary Cuba into the hemisphere will

[10] Implied in this second move is the expectation that the pressures brought to bear on other governments that sell, ship, or otherwise furnish goods to the Castro government would be terminated. In fact, these costly and ineffectual pressures should be ended immediately.

[11] For example, the Guantanamo naval base has little if any military importance now although its symbolic significance to both the Cuban and U.S. elites is great. There might come a moment when returning it to the Cubans would make good sense as part of a negotiated package of settlements of outstanding differences.

constitute a redefinition of allowable intra-hemispheric relations and will probably not involve a return to the OAS.[12] The vocabulary of "normalization" with all of its unfortunate connotations of a *status quo ante* is inadequate to an understanding of—or prescriptions for—possible relationships between Cuba and the rest of the hemisphere. Maintaining certain aspects of the status quo is imaginable and perhaps desirable, but the *status quo ante* is unimaginable given all that has happened in the past decade.

To this point we have paid less attention to the viability than to the desirability and rationality of certain kinds of changes. Although nothing discussed above is *prima facie* fanciful, a realistic view of the policy-changing process forces us to consider the various publics and groups relevant to Cuban-United States relations and what their reactions or postures might be when confronted with the possibility of changes in these relations. Although this topic cannot here be given anything like the attention that it deserves,

a few words about United States, Cuban, Soviet, and other Latin American publics will help to set the stage for further discussions.

UNITED STATES. There is substantial policy inertia in the United States system; moreover, from certain perspectives the United States "is not doing badly" vis-à-vis Cuba. Proponents of this point of view imply that only fools and idealists would counsel change, that experience suggests the fewer waves made, the better. With all the problems that the United States confronts at home and abroad, why open up the Cuban issue until forced to do so by events? The briefest answer to this argument is that it was exactly such a "reactive" style of decision-making that led to the anomalies, contradictions, and costs which now characterize the United States posture toward Cuba. A second and more political consideration is that much of the official United States posture toward Cuba is for domestic (United States) consumption, and even (or especially) a well thought-out revision of our Cuban policy would have to be sold in some fashion to Congress, quasi-professional anti-communists, sugar importers, Cuban refugees, and a business community stung by confiscations. It should also be pointed out, however, that the specific moves suggested above entail the mobilization of a minimum of political and bureaucratic machinery. Travel restrictions can be lifted by an agreement between the White House and State Department, and limited trade with Cuba could be established by presidential order under the "national interest" clauses of existing legislation. Politically, it might not be that easy, but statutory changes are not needed in either case.

12 For example, even relatively conservative Mexican news media continue to talk about the possibility of Cuba rejoining the OAS. See, for instance, the editorial in *Excelsior,* December 4, 1968, pp. 6, 8. However, Castro's view of the OAS and Cuba's relationship to it is very clear:

> To believe that one can even speak of Cuba's ever returning to that disreputable indecency known as the OAS! If some day we join a regional organization, it will be a regional organization of revolutionary countries of Latin America. There is no other historical possibility and no other route (*Granma, Weekly Review,* April 28, 1968, p. 6).

The point is that if "normalization" and "a return to the OAS" are thought of as the only possible paths to a re-incorporation of revolutionary Cuba into the hemisphere, then no progress at all is likely.

CUBA. As a starting point we can accept Philip Bonsal's estimate that a key organizing principle of the Cuban revolution is that the island had to win and must maintain its independence from the United States whatever the costs.[13] Said more formally, from the standpoint of the revolutionary leadership, Cuba's sovereignty is not negotiable (at least in dealing with the United States). This does not preclude negotiated settlements of differences, however, and in assessing the possibility of such settlements, three other characteristics of the Castro regime deserve emphasis. First, the Cubans have a tangled and conflicting relationship with the Soviet Union, and there are no signs that the conflict is easing. Second, there is a strain of pragmatism in the regime's foreign policy (for example, trade with Spain, technical aid from Israel, diplomatic relations with the Vatican) that is overlooked by those who concentrate too much on subversive activities in the hemisphere or the fanaticism with which independence from the United States is asserted. Third—and unlike the first two points this works against negotiated settlements with the United States— Castro is probably concerned that were the hostility eased and were various kinds of transactions with the United States increased, the materialism and "spirit" of American culture could easily penetrate Cuba once again, sapping the revolutionary movement of much of its vigor and sense of direction. This is not the same as saying that the Cuban revolution "needs" the hostility of the United States, but rather that it is not yet ready (in the view of its leaders) to handle the kinds of threats posed by a liberal, expansionist, and materialistic culture. As Castro's analysis of events in Czechoslovakia makes clear, the Cuban perspective on what constitutes the good society is very different from that held by certain socialist and liberal reformers, either of East or West.

SOVIET UNION. There is widespread agreement that the Soviet Union got more than it bargained for in a number of ways when it hooked itself into the Cuban economy and—at least in the early 1960's—into the defense of the island. In fact, Cuba probably represents more of a problem for the Soviet Union than for the United States. Russian attempts to establish commercial and diplomatic relations in the rest of Latin America are certainly not helped by their Cuban albatross, and certainly no great power enjoys being verbally and politically abused by a smaller nation that is, at the same time, taking its money. Most importantly, the uncertainty which the Cubans introduce into Soviet hemispheric and even global calculations is probably not viewed lightly by Kremlin policy makers. Thus, without going into specifics, the ingredients seem to be present for some significant types of Soviet-United States cooperation on various aspects of Cuban relationships as long as such cooperation does not turn on United States demands that the Soviets abandon the Castro regime.

LATIN AMERICA. The diversity in Latin America of regimes and of their perspectives on Cuba makes generalizations both difficult and dangerous. Cer-

---

13 Philip W. Bonsal, "Cuba, Castro and the United States," *Foreign Affairs*, Vol. 45, no. 2 (January 1967), pp. 260–276. In Bonsal's rather harsh language, "Through all Castro's gyrations, the only constant has been his determination to free Cuba from American influence (which he equates with domination) even at the eventual cost of submitting his country to the Soviet Union" (p. 267).

tainly the armed forces and important publics in a number of countries would react negatively to almost any policy initiative that did not involve stronger sanctions or punitive measures against the Castro regime. However, there are other important groups and sectors of hemispheric opinion that might welcome the kinds of initiatives suggested here. At the least, involving the several governments and posing Cuban-United States relations as only one aspect of a web of relations of vital concern to all nations in the hemisphere is an improvement over the unilateral action (usually presented as "the will of the majority") that has been the pattern to date. In involving the several governments, however, great care must be exercised so as not to precipitate the Cuban question into the public arena prematurely. Bilateral and perhaps multilateral consultations are needed before any United States action is taken, but these should be as private as possible. To urge Latin American governments to take a stand, either at home or in the OAS, on the entire complex package of relations with Cuba is to invite posturing, ringing speeches in defense of freedom, general statements intended for domes-

tic consumption, and considerable embarrassment to those who would ease the hard line but hesitate to say so for the record. Although eventually the OAS will have to consider the Cuban question, if only to legitimate in some fashion national decisions either contemplated or already in force, it is not the proper forum in which to begin. Consultation in the hemisphere does not necessarily imply public hearings, and the incremental revision of Cuban policy suggested here would be undercut by public, hemispheric debate of the "great issues" posed by the Cuban revolution. Moreover, this kind of modest and cautious policy revision process offers even greater scope for leadership on the part of the United States—and substantial scope for the participation of other interested parties in Latin America—than does a "great debate." There is sufficient work for all to do under the circumstances, and few guidelines for how to go about doing it. Just as there was no historical precedent for isolating Cuba in the hemisphere, so there are no clear paths to follow if a decision is made to attempt a reintegration of the Castro regime under conditions that do not conform to the *status quo ante.*

13

The Limits of Legitimization in International Organizations: The Organization of American States and the Dominican Crisis

Jerome Slater

From Jerome Slater, "The Limits of Legitimization in International Organizations: The Organization of American States and the Dominican Crisis," *International Organization*, XXIII, No. 1 (Winter 1969), pp. 48–72. Reprinted by permission of the author and the publisher.

Jerome Slater is an Associate Professor of Political Science at the State University of New York at Buffalo.

Essentially distinct from the matter of relations with the now-entrenched Castro regime in Cuba is the problem of the United States, OAS, and UN responses to future revolutions and other changes at the domestic level in Latin America perceived as raising the threat of additional Communist penetration. The increasing radicalism of the Arbenz government in Guatemala in the early fifties and the Cuban Revolution led U.S. policy-makers to act unilaterally under the obviously not-entirely-multilateralized Monroe Doctrine—supporting the Castillo Armas and Bay of Pigs exile invasions respectively—and also to launch a diplomatic offensive against the two regimes in the inter-American organization. Moreover, the U.S. attempted to deter the UN from acting on Guatemalan and Cuban complaints. The 1965 Dominican Crisis differed from previous cases mainly in that it arose precipitously, and ultimately saw the United States, the OAS, and the UN more directly and deeply involved in channeling the course of domestic events.

As the next seven selections indicate,[1] the crisis was clearly one of the most

---

[1] In addition, see esp.: Jerome Slater, *The United States and the Dominican Revolution* (New York: Harper & Row, 1970); Theodore Draper, *The Dominican Revolt: A Case Study in American Policy* (New York: Commentary, 1968); Tad Szulc, *Dominican Diary* (New York: Delacorte Press, 1965; and Dell, 1966); Dan Kurzman, *Santo Domingo: Revolt of the Damned* (New York: G. P. Putnam's Sons, 1965); José A. Moreno, *Barrios in Arms: Revolution in Santo Domingo* (Pittsburgh: University of Pittsburgh Press, 1970); Richard R. Fagen and Wayne A. Cornelius, Jr.,

significant episodes in the long history of inter-American relations, and, in many respects, it is still controversial. One might well ponder such questions as these: Was there a real threat of a Communist revolution in the Dominican Republic? Was the U.S. unilateral landing of marines justified? Are there parallels between the U.S. action in the Dominican case and its involvement in Vietnam—or the Soviet intervention in Czechoslovakia in 1968? Was the operation a success in terms of U.S. goals in the Dominican Republic? What has been the impact of the crisis on the OAS and extra-OAS United States-Latin American relations? Are other similar crises likely to arise in the future? If so, will they elicit similar responses?

In this essay, Slater observes that in the more than twenty years of its existence the OAS has performed "certain widely approved tasks" and has thereby given considerable substance to the "Western Hemisphere Idea." Chief among these tasks has been the organization's role in the peaceful settlement of disputes in the hemisphere, reflecting a high degree of compatibility between the United States' interest in stability and the Latin American objective of the protection of sovereignty.[2] In these cases and in other respects, the OAS has often provided a multilateral stamp of legitimacy for essentially unilateral U.S. actions in support of mutual goals.

On the other hand, efforts to convert the OAS system of collective security and peaceful settlement into an anti-Communist alliance have severely strained the organization's "legitimizing capacity." These strains were most evident in the 1965 Dominican episode. As Slater's careful analysis reveals, even in the Dominican case—when the United States was in an unusually dominant position—there remained substantial (if sometimes reluctant) Latin American support for "collective legitimization" and the OAS was not without some leverage over U.S. policies. Nevertheless, Slater argues, OAS underwriting of the Dominican operation may have been counterproductive both for the organization and the United States. It failed to provide much legitimacy for U.S. actions, antagonized key member governments, and seemed to confirm the Latin American radical-left's stereotype of the OAS as a tool of Washington.

---

eds., *Political Power in Latin America: Seven Confrontations* (Englewood Cliffs, N.J.: Prentice-Hall, Inc., 1970), pp. 231–96; Abraham F. Lowenthal, "Purpose or Process? A Study of the 1965 Dominican Intervention" (Doctoral dissertation, Department of Government, Harvard University, 1970).

2 For background on a few still-unsettled disputes, see: David H. Zook, Jr., *Zarumilla-Marañon: The Ecuador-Peru Dispute* (New York: Bookman Associates, 1964); Mary Jeanne Reid Martz, "Ecuador and the Eleventh Inter-American Conference," *Journal of Inter-American Studies*, X, No. 2 (April 1968), pp. 306–27; Robert D. Tomasek, "The Chilean-Bolivian Lauca River Dispute and the OAS," *Journal of Inter-American Studies*, IX, No. 3 (July 1967), pp. 351–66; and Lawrence O. Ealy, *Yanqui Politics and the Isthmian Canal* (University Park, Pa.: Pennsylvania State University Press, 1971).

INTRODUCTION

In recent years political scientists have given increasing attention to the phenomenon of legitimacy, defined, following Richard Merelman,[1] as the quality of "oughtness" perceived by members of a political system to inhere in the system's authorities and/or regime.[2] The more the regime is regarded as morally proper and elicits generalized favorable attitudes from its constituency—i.e., is perceived to be legitimate—the more the members are predisposed to comply with directives of the authorities even when they are under no serious compulsion to do so or their own immediate self-interest does not so dictate.

Political scientists utilizing systems models tend to postulate the existence of an international political system in which international organizations function as rudimentary regimes performing at least some allocative functions.[3] It has been further hypothesized that international organizations have developed a certain amount of legitimacy

(to some degree with governments but more definitely with important sectors of elite public opinion) lending greater weight to their decisions or outputs. Still, with but few exceptions, not much systematic attention has been given to this phenomenon. Ernst Haas was probably the first to deal rigorously with legitimacy in the context of international organizations; more recently Inis Claude has examined the "collective legitimization" function of the United Nations.[4] In Claude's view collective legitimization—the capacity of the United Nations to elicit worldwide approval for national policies successfully channeled through that body—has emerged as one of the UN's major political functions. Moreover, while distinguishing between the UN and other international organizations, Claude nonetheless implies that the capacity to legitimize national policies inheres in at least some of them as well: "The function of legitimization in the international realm has tended in recent years to be increasingly conferred upon international political institutions."[5]

To go further, it is not unfair to say that at least some of the literature implicitly assumes that international organizations *in general* are normally bearers of legitimacy and, further, that there is a secular trend toward their

This article was originally prepared for delivery at the 1968 meeting of the American Political Science Association, Washington, September 2–7. The author would like to thank Professors Glenn Snyder, Lester Milbrath, Terry Nardin, and Richard Johnson of State University of New York at Buffalo, Joseph Nye of Harvard, Robert Keohane of Swarthmore, Yale Ferguson of Rutgers, and Abraham Lowenthal of the Brookings Institution for their suggestions and criticisms.
[1] Richard M. Merelman, "Learning and Legitimacy," *American Political Science Review,* September 1966 (Vol. 60, No. 3), pp. 548–561.
[2] See David Easton, *A Systems Analysis of Political Life* (New York: John Wiley and Sons, 1965) for a general discussion of legitimacy and for the distinction between authorities and regimes.
[3] Especially Easton, pp. 484–488.

[4] Ernst B. Haas, *The Uniting of Europe: Political, Social, and Economic Forces 1950–1957* (Stanford, Calif: Stanford University Press, 1958) and *Beyond the Nation-State: Functionalism and International Organization* (Stanford, Calif: Stanford University Press, 1964); Inis L. Claude, Jr., "Collective Legitimization as a Political Function of the United Nations," *International Organization,* Summer 1966 (Vol. 20, No. 3), pp. 367–379, and *The Changing United Nations* (New York: Random House, 1967).
[5] Claude, *The Changing United Nations,* p. 83.

increasing legitimacy.[6] However, in one important organization, the Organization of American States (OAS), there are severe limits to the function of collective legitimization, and, if anything, this function is becoming *decreasingly* significant.

The discussion will proceed in the following manner. After a brief review of the past record of the OAS and collective legitimization a detailed analysis will be made of the action of the OAS in the Dominican crisis of 1965–1966, stressing the failure of the Organization to provide much, if any, legitimacy for United States policies. Then, recent evidence will be noted of an apparently increasingly widespread disenchantment with the Organization in Latin America largely but not solely due to its role in the Dominican affair. Finally, utilizing these findings, the author will offer a brief reevaluation of collective legitimacy in general, emphasizing its fragility, costs, and dangers.

COLLECTIVE LEGITIMIZATION AND THE OAS

To determine the capacity of an international organization to legitimize national policies by enveloping them in a multilateral framework it is first necessary to show that the organization itself is in fact widely viewed as legitimate. Viewed by whom, it might be asked? The most relevant perceivers, we would think, would be the members (defined here to refer both to governments and concerned sectors of public opinion) of the international system or subsystem that is served by the organization. In the western hemisphere North American attitudes toward the OAS are probably of less significance than Latin attitudes, for most OAS actions take place in Latin America and inter-American problems in general have a higher salience there than in the United States. By the same token, attitudes about the OAS outside the hemisphere are treated here, by omission, as even less significant.

The problem of ascertaining the legitimacy of the OAS anywhere, however, is complicated by the lack of hard data. As far as this author knows, there have been no rigorous empirical studies on Latin American attitudes toward the OAS, either of the general public or political elites. Resorting, therefore, to impressionism, it would seem that the OAS has had a not insignificant legitimizing capacity, stemming from the notion of pan-Americanism and, more importantly, from converging national interests that have allowed the Organization to perform certain widely approved tasks.[7]

In the past pan-Americanism, or what Arthur Whitaker has called "the Western Hemisphere Idea,"[8] provided

---

6 This statement is admittedly only an impression that the author is unprepared to substantiate by citation of concrete evidence, the gathering of which might require surveying an enormous range of the literature on international organization. Had the refutation of the alleged assumption been central to this article, the task would clearly be neccessary. However, our major concern here is the far more limited one of pointing to some of the costs of the "collective legitimization" function revealed by the actions of the Organization of American States (OAS) in the Dominican Republic.

7 The following analyses are mostly drawn from the author's book, *The OAS and United States Foreign Policy* (Columbus: Ohio State University Press, 1967) although some new material is included.
8 Arthur P. Whitaker, *The Western Hemisphere Idea: Its Rise and Decline* (Ithaca, N.Y.: Cornell University Press, 1954).

a certain integrative cement in the inter-American system, acting (in Easton's terminology) as a legitimating ideology. The basis of the Western Hemisphere Idea is that the peoples of the hemisphere are bound together by the common belief that they stand in a special ideological, historical, and cultural relationship to each other. This notion in turn has legitimized the inter-American tradition of the insulation, or attempted insulation, of intrahemispheric political relationships and conflict from the international system at large. How much continuing operational significance the Western Hemisphere Idea has in the formulation of national policies is difficult to say although it is at least plausible that the persistence of the idea that the Western Hemisphere is more than a geographic expression, but a political community[9] of sorts as well, becomes partially self-fulfilling and to some extent acts as an independent variable in governmental actions.[10]

Still, there is little doubt that under the impact of technology, the postwar world commitments of the United States, and growing ideological conflict within the hemisphere, pan-Americanism hardly suffices any longer as the source of whatever support the OAS continues to enjoy. Such support now depends primarily on the degree to which the Organization can consistently perform functions generally seen by system members to be necessary and useful.[11]

The main objective of the United States policies in Latin America since World War II has been the maintenance of political stability, operationally defined primarily to mean the avoidance of inter-American conflict and the exclusion of Communism from the hemisphere. The OAS has generally contributed to both of these ends, functioning quite successfully in its peace-keeping capacity, somewhat less so as an anti-Communist alliance. On the other hand, the Latin American states, all of them relatively weak, historically have been preoccupied with the maintenance of their "sovereignty." In this respect the inter-American system has been of considerable value to them, for its primary effect has been to protect their political independence and territorial integrity against external threats, whether coming from within or outside the hemisphere.

Normally, the United States' concern for stability and the Latin American concern for sovereignty have been compatible since both have usually required the maintenance of the political status quo in the hemisphere and the prevention of interstate conflict. The convergence of these objectives, then,

---

9 *The sense of political community may be described as a we-feeling among a group of people, not that they are just a group but that they are a political entity that works together and will likely share a common political fate and destiny.* (Easton, p. 332.)
10 See Michael O'Leary's essay, "The Nature of the Inter-American System," in Robert Gregg (ed.), *International Organization in the Western Hemisphere* (Syracuse, N.Y.: Syracuse University Press, 1968), pp. 157–177, for a sophisticated analysis of the Western Hemisphere Idea stressing its continued operational significance.

11 "Support" is used here in Easton's sense, i.e., approval given for expediential reasons (the production of approved outputs) as well as because of the perceived legitimacy of the organization. As Easton notes, however, if the organization persistently meets its constituents' demands, eventually it acquires generalized legitimacy as well. That is, specific support stemming from self-interest spills over into diffuse support and to attachment to the system for its own sake. (Easton, pp. 343–344.)

has allowed the OAS to perform a number of hemispheric tasks.

The most successful of these, as indicated, has been the functioning of the inter-American collective security or peacekeeping system. In this capacity the OAS has helped end numerous outbreaks of small-scale interstate conflict, especially in the Caribbean in the 1950's, and, plausibly, has deterred others. Less significant but still of some impact has been the role of the OAS as an anti-Communist alliance, which would include such activities as the mostly symbolic Latin American backing for unilateral United States actions in the Korean War and the Cuban missile crisis, the passing of various anti-Communist resolutions partially designed by their framers to legitimize United States and other subversive actions against Guatemala in 1954 and Cuba since 1959, the exclusion of Cuba from the OAS and the trade embargo against it, the pressing for cooperative counterinsurgency programs in Latin America, and the support of United States actions in the Dominican Republic after the 1965 revolution.

In recent years a new inter-American task has developed—a still relatively minor but growing OAS role in the internal politics of Latin American states stemming, too, from converging United States and Latin American interests. Since about 1960 the United States, as part of its broad anti-Communist strategy, has been pressing for domestic reform in Latin America in order that the conditions in which Communism or Castroism is thought to thrive may be eliminated. In part for the same reason and in part because of a normative commitment to greater democracy and modernization a number of Latin American governments have supported the recent United

States policies. As a result the door has been very tentatively opened for OAS action in areas previously considered outside its legitimate scope. Included here are the expanding activities of the Inter-American Commission on Human Rights, the use of inter-American commissions to observe (i.e., certify the legitimacy of) Latin American presidential elections, and, most importantly, the involvement of various OAS bodies in Dominican politics since the assassination of Rafael Trujillo Molina in the spring of 1961.[12]

In most of these tasks the main function of the OAS has been to cloak essentially unilateral United States actions in a multilateral framework, thereby providing them with a measure of legitimacy. While the United States, then, plays the key role in most OAS actions, providing leadership, logistical services, economic pressures, and, when necessary, military force, Latin American support, even when merely symbolic, helps avoid political opposition in the United States, Latin America, and the rest of the world.

The capacity of the OAS to provide collective legitimization for United States policies, however, is limited or even fragile. To put it in Easton's terms the Organization has a very limited reservoir of diffuse support—generalized legitimacy—and therefore its successful functioning depends primarily on its continuing capacity to provide widely desired outputs. In fact, though, United States and Latin American political objectives (demands) have diverged on

12 For OAS activities in the Dominican Republic in 1960–1963 see the author's article "The United States, the Organization of American States, and the Dominican Republic, 1961–1963," *International Organization,* Spring 1964 (Vol. 18, No. 2), pp. 268–291; for the post-1965 period see below.

a number of highly charged issues, thus either reducing the OAS to impotence or precipitating a sharp split in which the United States is forced to struggle so hard to get a bare two-thirds majority that the hoped-for legitimizing effect all but disappears. This has been particularly the case in the Communism issue: In the Guatemalan, Cuban, and Dominican situations the United States' concern for stability and the Latin American concern for sovereignty have clashed rather than converged, for the restoration of a non-Communist stability required that the principle of national sovereignty be ignored.

Another limiting factor is Latin American nationalism, manifested in the continuing sensitivity to "intervention," even collective intervention, in the internal affairs of Latin American states.[13] To keep the OAS from developing into a dreaded "superstate," then, the Latin Americans have kept the Organization's political capacities limited to the minimum required for keeping the peace and have generally sought to exclude it from hemispheric political and ideological conflicts not involving actual armed hostilities between states.

Perhaps most importantly, though, the legitimizing capacity of the OAS is sharply reduced to the extent that the Organization is believed to be dominated by the United States, and it is probable that this perception is growing.[14] As a result of the enormous power disparity between the United States and the other hemispheric countries there is a widespread belief in Latin America—neatly summed up in

Fidel Castro's sardonic reference to the OAS as the Department of State's "Ministry of Colonies"[15]—that the OAS merely institutionalizes and legitimates United States hegemony in the hemisphere.

In actuality the United States normally has not "dominated" the OAS, at least if that is taken to mean that its accustomed style of operation is to impose its own policies through its "majority of one." Since one of the major values of the Organization to the United States is precisely its potential to legitimize and evoke widespread consent for North American policies not only in Latin America but in the United States as well, an OAS obviously under Washington's thumb would be dysfunctional. As a result deliberate constraints usually have been placed on the employment of economic and military power in the inter-American diplomacy of the United States, and Washington's typical role in the collective decision-making process is one of bargaining, negotiating, and compromising.

Nonetheless, with the United States increasingly being forced to fight hard for bare two-thirds majorities for its anti-Communist policies—and, at that, two-thirds majorities which frequently find the largest, most populous, and most democratic states in the opposition—it admittedly becomes more difficult to argue that the asymmetries of *potential* power in the hemisphere are far greater than the asymmetries of *applied* power.[16]

[15] Cf. also the continuing popularity in Latin America of Juan José Arévalo's *The Shark and the Sardines* (New York: Lyle Stuart, 1961).
[16] For evidence see Chapter 4 of Slater, *The OAS and United States Foreign Policy,* as well as the discussion of the Dominican crisis below.

[13] Although exceptions are made, as noted above.
[14] See below for a discussion of the evidence for this assertion.

THE OAS AND THE
DOMINICAN CRISIS

Nowhere has this recent trend been starker than in the Dominican crisis where the United States did indeed dominate OAS actions. Even in that situation, however, one should be careful of overstatement, for the general impression that the OAS acted as *merely* a reluctant and perhaps partially coerced rubber stamp of the United States is a serious oversimplification. Although there was certainly widespread anger in most Latin American governments over the failure of the United States to consult with the OAS before intervening in the Dominican Republic, nonetheless thereafter there was a considerable amount of genuine support—usually more than the minimum two-thirds—for a continuing inter-American role in the Dominican crisis. This support stemmed from a variety of differing but partially converging Latin American objectives. In a number of states there was real agreement with the substance of United States policies if not always with the manner in which they were carried out. It should not be forgotten that there are many conservative regimes and military dictatorships in the hemisphere which are always ready to see a Communist menace in any revolutionary movement and which therefore were downright delighted to vote for and participate in the Dominican operation.[17] For example, the initial five-man investigating committee of the OAS, consisting of the representatives of the generally conservative regimes of Argentina, Brazil, Guatemala, Pa-

nama, and Colombia, reported that had the United States not intervened, the Dominican revolution "could rapidly have been converted into a Communist insurrection."[18] (In fact, the representative of the one fairly liberal state, Colombia, went even further, arguing that "We are in a struggle against international communism," in which the OAS states cannot "sit on the balcony to watch the end of the tragedy...as if we were at a bullfight waiting for the crew.")[19]

Nor was support for the United States actions limited exclusively to the right—the relatively progressive and democratic governments of Venezuela and Costa Rica, for example, while initially bitter at the unilateral actions of the United States[20] and suspicious of its motivations, nonetheless are extremely sensitive to the possible spread of Castroism in the Caribbean. Venezuela resolved its mixed feelings by abstaining on many of the important votes while Costa Rica usually voted

18 "First Report of the Special Committee of the Tenth Meeting of Consultation of Ministers of Foreign Affairs of the American States" (OAS Document OEA/Ser.F/II.10 [Doc.47]), May 8, 1965.

19 "Acta de la Cuarta Sesión Plenaria" (OAS Document OEA/Ser.F/II.10 [Doc. 42]), May 7–8, 1965, p. 15. (Author's translation.)

20 E.g., President Raúl Leoni of Venezuela sent the following message to President Lyndon B. Johnson:

I was deeply disturbed at the news that ...the armed forces of your country had landed on the territory of that sister Republic, in inexplicable disregard of the principles of the inter-American system....

See "Note No. OEA-00303, of April 29, 1965, Addressed to the Chairman of the Council of the Organization by the Representative of Venezuela, Presenting the Text of the Message Sent by the President of Venezuela to the President of the United States of America" (OAS Document OEA/Ser.G/V [C-d-1308]).

17 Cf. *The New York Times* of July 3, 1965, in which it was reported that El Salvador, Nicaragua, and Honduras were critical of the United States for being too *weak* in its efforts to contain the Dominican revolution.

with the majority, explaining that

It is true that we cannot accept as good that the United States decides for itself when it should send troops to prevent the triumph or defeat of a revolution. But neither can we accept as good that anarchy reigns in a brother country and...a tyrannical regime like that of Cuba [could be established].[21]

To be sure, the situation did contain elements of a fait accompli, but a number of Latin American states, anxious not to totally abdicate responsibility, supported an OAS role for precisely that reason. A very painful dilemma had been presented: Collective action might tend to legitimize the intervention, but a refusal to act on that account would leave the Latin Americans without influence either on United States policy or on the unfolding events in the Dominican Republic. While a few Latin American states, notably Chile and Mexico, chose not to depart from the nonintervention norm, others decided that the logic of the situation left them no choice but to salvage what they could. And what could be salvaged, it was hoped, was democracy in the Dominican Republic—with about 15,000 troops on the ground and under the at least nominal control of the OAS here indeed was an unprecedented opportunity to rid the Dominican Republic of the remnants of *Trujillismo*, especially in the Dominican armed forces.[22] Gonzalo Facio of Costa Rica put it like this:

It may be that the government of the United States, in its anxiety to avert worse

evils, has violated the principle of nonintervention. But that should not prevent us from acting to repair the wrong and to help our brothers.

.   .   .

In the face of an accomplished situation such as the one in which we find ourselves, the sane, the logical, the humanitarian thing is to find formulas which will permit us to correct the errors and to help a long-suffering people to find the path to liberty.[23]

Finally, the traditional Latin American desire to close ranks and solve hemispheric problems without outside interference (the Western Hemisphere Idea) eventually to some dgree reasserted itself. Even strong opponents of collective action were at times influenced by the argument that the existence of the inter-American system itself might be at stake if the Dominican crisis was not satisfactorily resolved and either abstained or voted in favor of some OAS actions.

Still, when all is said and done, there can be hardly any doubt that the role of the OAS in the Dominican crisis was at best peripheral to that of the United States. The OAS, of course, was completely bypassed in the initial decision to intervene not so much because it is slow to act and time was short (the official reasons) but because the American government was doubtful that a two-thirds majority would,

---

[21] "Acta de la Cuarta Sesión de la Comisión General" (OAS Document OEA/Ser.F/II.10 [Doc.32]), May 3, 1965, p. 12. (Author's translation.).
[22] The debates on the establishment of the

Inter-American Peace Force (IAPF) made it clear that a number of its supporters, particularly Costa Rica and Venezuela, expected it would be used positively to facilitate the return of democracy as well as negatively to prevent a Communist takeover in the Dominican Republic.
[23] "Acta de la Cuarta Sesión de la Comisión General," p. 12. (Author's translation.) Others taking roughly similar positions included the delegates of Colombia, Venezuela, and Peru.

if asked in advance, authorize intervention.[24] Moreover, it is apparent that Lyndon B. Johnson's Administration generally viewed the OAS with contempt ("the OAS couldn't pour...out of a boot if the instructions were written on the heel"[25]) if it thought of it at all. It is reported that the initial draft of President Johnson's statement announcing the landing of the Marines made no mention of the OAS; when Senator Mike Mansfield noted the omission, the President said to the Secretary of State: "Dean, that's a good idea, now you make certain it's there."[26]

After the intervention, however, the United States became quite anxious to involve the Latins, and the relatively marginal character of the OAS activities was more a function of Latin American unwillingness to assume a greater role than United States unwillingness to let them. For example, although the Inter-American Peace Force (IAPF) contained at its peak only about 2000 Latin American troops, the great majority of whom were Brazilian, the United States had actively pressed for a much more genuinely international force and had agreed that national contingents be "progressively equalized."[27] Until domestic opposition in Argentina, Colombia, and Venezuela developed, it was expected that those countries would make major contributions and that the Force would be headed by a Venezuelan general closely associated with Rómulo Betancourt.[28]

Of even greater significance was the apparent willingness of the United States, at one point at any rate, to turn over political direction of the entire Dominican operation to a multilateral commission consisting of Rómulo Betancourt, José Figueres, and Luis Muñoz Marín. The details of this affair are still not entirely clear, but it is known that immediately after the intervention the three Latin American leaders were called to Washington and asked to take over the task of finding a political solution. They apparently tentatively accepted, provided that they would be given a free hand politically and control over the IAPF, which would take the place of United States troops and be composed only of troops from the democratic countries of Latin America. These conditions were said to be generally acceptable to the United States, but the plan fell through in face of second thoughts by the Venezuelan government and strong opposition from conservative OAS states to turning over the reins to Latin American liberals.[29]

---

[24] Time could hardly have been the crucial factor, for United States officials had been intensively considering the possibility of intervention from the first day of the revolution and yet had made no move to sound out the OAS; moreover, in the 1962 Cuban missile crisis, where the Latin Americans were genuinely convinced of the need for strong action, approval of the United States blockade was forthcoming on the same day it was requested.

[25] Philip Geyelin, *Lyndon B. Johnson and the World* (New York: Frederick A. Praeger, 1966), p. 254, quoting Johnson.

[26] Rowland Evans and Robert Novak, *Lyndon B. Johnson: The Exercise of Power* (New York: New American Library, 1966), p. 517.

[27] See the resolution creating the IAPF in "Acta de la Sexta Sesión de la Comisión General" (OAS Document OEA/Ser.F/II.10 [Doc.40 Corr.]), May 5–6, 1965, pp. 2–4.

[28] Personal interviews. All interviews were on a not-for-attribution basis.

[29] José Figueres, "Revolution and Counter-Revolution in Santo Domingo," in *Dominican Republic: a study in the new inperialism* (New York: Institute for International Labor Research, 1965), pp. 43–56; personal interviews.

Subsequently, the United States in a number of ways sought to involve the OAS more deeply in the long process of negotiating a settlement of the Dominican crisis and, once that was attained, seeing that it held together under threats from the Dominican military. These attempts to further multilateralize the situation were generally resisted by the OAS majority, however. The hard-core opposition (Chile, Mexico, Peru, Ecuador, and Uruguay) consistently opposed almost all collective action in the Dominican case, standing on principle and fearing the legitimization of the United States intervention. Other Latin American states, while supporting some kinds of OAS actions, for a variety of reasons resisted greater inter-American involvement in the Dominican political process. The ideological split between the Latin American states, preventing, for example, the Betancourt-Figueres-Muñoz Marín mission, was an important factor. More generally, the non-intervention tradition still exerted enough influence to produce strong negative reactions to an overt OAS role in imposing a Dominican political settlement. Another inhibiting factor was a widespread feeling (among some delegates accompanied with annoyance but among others with relief) that the United States was really running the show in the Dominican Republic anyway and that the Latin American involvement was so much window dressing. There was considerable consternation, for example, over a rather gratuitous statement (subsequently denied) by Lieutenant General Bruce Palmer, the commander of the United States troops but supposedly acting under the overall authority of the Brazilian commander of the IAPF, that in the event of conflict between the OAS and the United States he, Palmer, would take his orders from his country. Similarly, given the United States predominance, the apparent uncertainty and shifts in Washington's objectives led to second thoughts among some states about the wisdom of participating in collective actions the ultimate purposes and effects of which were unclear. Colombia and Panama, for example, decided against contributing to the IAPF in part for this reason, not knowing against whom or on behalf of what objectives it might be used.[30] Finally, after the Provisional Government of Héctor García-Godoy took office in September 1965, the OAS rejected a plan for direct OAS assistance in the day-to-day management of the Dominican government and economy in deference to García-Godoy's strong opposition to any interference in his freedom of action.

THE IMPACT OF THE OAS ON THE DOMINICAN CRISIS

The Dominican case presents in particularly acute form a problem in analysis that is present to a greater or lesser degree in nearly all OAS actions: In what sense can it be said that the Organization was an independent variable having a genuine impact on the outcome of the Dominican crisis as distinct from a mere figleaf providing a modicum of cover for naked United States unilateralism? Or to put it a little differently (and less luridly) if the Organization had not been involved at all, in what way would the outcome have differed?

Let us begin with an analysis of the Latin American input into the day-to-day decisionmaking processes of OAS bodies involved in the Dominican crisis. The first body to be given a political

[30] Personal interviews.

mandate was the Special Committee of the Council, composed of the representatives of Argentina, Brazil, Colombia, Panama, and Guatemala.[31] The Special Committee was charged with obtaining a cease-fire and with "doing everything possible to obtain the re-establishment of peace and normal conditions," a deliberately vague mandate which could have allowed the Committee great leeway in participating in the process of arranging a peaceful settlement. The Committee chose to interpret its function as strictly catalytic, however, urging the two sides to get together and discuss a settlement, rather than using its influence to actively mediate. Moreover, there is a widespread consensus among informed United States and Dominican officials and other observers of the Special Committee's activities that it was strongly biased against the constitutionalists (rebels), lackadaisical and halfhearted in its efforts, and generally incompetent.[32]

After about two weeks in Santo Domingo and with a settlement nowhere in sight the Committee resigned in a huff, charging that the appearance on the scene of a UN observer mission (and, by strong implication, a United States mediating team led by McGeorge Bundy) had undermined its activities.[33]

Whatever the Special Committee's inadequacies, though, it is unlikely that any OAS body could have done substantially better. The real power to arrange a settlement continued to remain in the hands of the United States, a fact that was perfectly evident to the contending Dominican groups, which chose to deal with Washington's functionaries rather than those of the Pan American Union (PAU).[34] Yet a series of high-level United States representa-

---

[31] For the resolution establishing the Special Committee see OAS Document OEA/Ser.F/II.10 (Doc.11). The full title of the Committee is the Special Committee of the Tenth Meeting of Consultation of Ministers of Foreign Affairs of the American States. The markedly rightist nature of the Special Committee appeared to stem from the reluctance of more progressive states to become involved in the whole affair as well as the fact that the majority of Latin American governments in the OAS are conservative. There are some indications that the United States tried to get the neutral or even proconstitutionalist governments of Costa Rica, Mexico, Peru, and Chile to serve on this or subsequent OAS bodies, but the author has no evidence on how hard Washington pressed the issue.

[32] In the general literature on international organization peace observer and peacekeeping missions there seems to be an implicit assumption that whatever the environmental difficulties may be, such missions may be expected to be at least competent and impartial. The activities of the Special Com-

mittee would seem to demonstrate that such a presumption is not always warranted.

[33] Another reason for the Special Committee's resignation, however, may have been the traditional Latin American reluctance to become involved on the side of the United States against another Latin nation. There is evidence that the Committee feared having to take a decision which would place Latin American contingents of the IAPF on the firing line, risking a situation in which they might be forced to join with United States troops in shooting Dominicans.

[34] A nice indication of the general irrelevance of the Special Committee to the unfolding events in the Dominican Republic was provided when on May 2 the State Department told the United States embassy in Santo Domingo to ask the Special Committee, which had been charged with maintaining a cease-fire and, by implication, the military status quo, for "permission" to extend United States lines across the entire city of Santo Domingo. The Department's instructions added, however, that if the Special Committee refused, the action (which was highly significant since it had the intended effect of bottling up the constitutionalists with their backs to the sea) was to be taken anyway! The Committee, however, agreed to the United States action, despite its mandate.

tives were, at least at first, able to do little better than the Special Committee in arranging a negotiated settlement, and no one has yet accused McGeorge Bundy of laziness or incompetence. The crux of the problem, of course, was that the deep bitterness and polarization produced by the revolution made a settlement impossible until several months had gone by and both the constitutionalists and their rightist opponents had become convinced that the United States would not allow either of them to gain power.

After the resignation of the Special Committee the Council authorized the OAS Secretary General, José A. Mora, to continue working for a stable cease-fire and a return to "normality." While this was of some significance in the development of the Organization itself —it was the first time the Secretary General had ever been given explicitly political functions[35]—Mora was no more successful than the Special Committee had been. Whatever possibility Mora may have had to play an effective mediating role soon disappeared when the constitutionalists decided that he was partial to the junta of General Antonio Imbert[36] and nothing more than a front man for the United States. This was probably an unfair judgment.

It was certainly true, as the constitutionalist "foreign minister" charged, that

Dr. Mora in many ways accepts and recognizes, without heeding the origin of the ... force on which it rests, the so-called Government of National Reconstruction [Imbert junta][37]

but this was not necessarily a function of Mora's personal views so much as of the situation that had been imposed by the United States intervention. With the United States supporting Imbert at least until another provisional government could be established any attempt by Mora to throw his weight on the side of the constitutionalists would have been futile—he had no weight to throw.[38] Within this framework of established facts and minimal personal or political leverage Mora interpreted his authority broadly and worked long and hard to maintain the cease-fire, provide emergency economic relief to the citizens of Santo Domingo, and foster negotiations.[39] His ultimate failure, then, as had been the case of the Special Committee, reflected the fact that none of the major actors in the situation—the United States, the Dominican military, and the constitutionalists—were ready for a settlement.

In early June the third and last OAS

---

35 The surprisingly large vote—only Chile opposed—stemmed from the feeling in the Organization that a failure to reestablish an OAS presence in the Dominican Republic would be an utter abdication of responsibility. Moreover, the Mora mission was generally understood to be only a temporary stopgap until agreement could be reached on a new nation-state commission. See OAS Document OEA/Ser.F/II.10 (Doc.87), May 20–21, 1965.

36 A right-wing junta under the leadership of General Imbert had been set up in early May by United States officials, acting, incidentally, completely independently of the Special Committee.

37 OAS Document OEA/Ser.F/II.10 (Doc. 109), May 30, 1965, p. 6. (Author's translation.)

38 Ironically, Imbert soon joined the constitutionalists in attacking Mora, an indicator, perhaps, of the success of the Secretary General's effort to act impartially.

39 In Mora's own eyes his role was of crucial importance not merely in salvaging the prestige of the OAS as a whole but in providing an opportunity to expand and make more useful the powers of the Secretary General, as Dag Hammarskjöld had done in UN peacekeeping crises.

body, the *Ad Hoc* Committee,[40] consisting of Ellsworth Bunker of the United States and representatives of Brazil and El Salvador, took over from Mora. It was this Committee that successfully bypassed the Imbert government, negotiated a settlement based on free elections to be conducted by a provisional government, and with its control of the IAPF kept the Provisional Government from being overthrown by the Dominican military, thus assuring that the elections were held.

There is a considerable difference of opinion among participants in, and close observers of, the Dominican dram over whether the *Ad Hoc* Committee was a euphemism for "Ellsworth Bunker" or whether it was a genuinely collective body with the Latin Americans having at least some impact on United States policy. Bunker himself apparently held the latter view, at one point warning the State Department that he would have to take into account the attitudes of his colleagues in arriving at a settlement, as a result of which the United States could not expect to manage the outcome of the Dominican affair as it chose.[41] There is consider-

able evidence that the three men generally saw eye-to-eye on crucial matters and that all decisions were unanimous and reached after full discussion and give-and-take. There is also evidence that the Latin American members of the *Ad Hoc* Committee played a fairly significant complementing role to Bunker during the long and arduous negotiating process in the summer of 1965 by virtue of their diplomatic experience and familiarity with the Latin American culture, language, and general style of operation.

Still, there is no doubt that Bunker dominated the Committee, planned its general strategy, and was the source of almost all its initiatives. His status as the personal representative of the United States President would have assured his predominance in any case, but there were other factors as well. For one thing, it is probable that Brazil and El Salvador were not anxious to incur the annoyance of the United States through undue shows of independence. Moreover, Bunker's age, experience, diplomatic skill, and powerful personality won admiration and deference from all actors in the Dominican drama, even the constitutionalists. Finally, after the initial crisis had eased, the Latin Americans increasingly left matters to Bunker, apparently finding life in Santo Domingo distinctly inferior to that in Washington—on a number of occasions, in fact, Bunker was forced to fly back to Washington to consult with his colleagues or persuade them to return to their duties.

It is clear, then, that the OAS as such played only a minor direct role in the evolution of United States policy in the Dominican Republic. More importantly, though, the very fact of its official involvement probably exerted an important restraining influence on

---

[40] This body was formally known as the *Ad Hoc* Committee of the Tenth Meeting of Consultation of Ministers of Foreign Affairs of the American States.

[41] In the course of his research the author was given access to a number of private papers, documents, and memoirs which unfortunately cannot be specifically cited. With that single exception no strings whatever were attached to the use of those materials, and this article has not been submitted for prior clearance to any government official. Hereinafter, whenever an unattributed statement derived from access to these materials is made, normally introduced with the phrase "there is evidence that . . .," there will be no footnote. This procedure will not be followed unless the source is unquestionably accurate and reliable.

the United States.[42] If the inter-American body had not successfully pressed for a cease-fire in the early days after the United States intervention, for example, Washington might well have decided upon a military "solution" and ordered its troops to occupy the constitutionalist zone, even at the cost of bloody fighting.

The precise chronology of events is very important here. The first contingent of United States troops was landed on the evening of April 28. At this point their mission was only to guard the Hotel Embajador, embarcation point for Americans and other foreigners seeking to leave the country. No final decision had yet been made to employ the troops in the civil war although that possibility was definitely envisaged if the constitutionalists continued to defeat the regular military. On the following morning, April 29, the OAS met and passed a Colombian resolution asking the Papal Nuncio, dean of the diplomatic corps in Santo Domingo, to negotiate a cease-fire on behalf of the OAS pending the arrival of an OAS mission.

Meanwhile, on the same day, April 29, the State Department informed its embassy in Santo Domingo that the United States would indeed resort to direct military action if necessary to prevent a rebel victory although it still hoped to be able to avoid that. The next day, however, a few hours after the cease-fire took effect, the embassy

was instructed to cooperate and to inform the Dominican military that the United States was not now planning to take direct action against the constitutionalists.[43]

In the ensuing weeks the possibility of a military attack was not discarded in Washington, particularly as it became evident that the establishment of the United States corridor across the city had not merely bottled up the rebels but was protecting them from the regrouped and reinforced Dominican military. Gradually, though, the cease-fire came to be accepted, if only reluctantly, as a fait accompli, and the military plans were shelved.[44]

It is highly probable, then, that the quick OAS call for a cease-fire, followed shortly thereafter by the arrival of OAS mediation missions on the ground, was an important continuing factor in constraining the United States from either itself attacking or acquiescing in a Dominican military attack on the rebels. In the rapidly breaking events of April 28–30 the United States had accepted and even helped obtain a cease-fire, in part because the political implications were still unclear; it was considered possible that a temporary breathing space would help the Dominican military at least as much as the constitutionalists. Once the cease-fire was in effect, the political costs to the United States of a blatant violation would have been enormous.

Even more indirectly, the OAS played a fairly useful lightning-rod role. Both the rightists and the constitutionalists, fearing the consequences of a total break with Washington, typically

42 Other factors such as the UN presence and the skeptical reporting of the major United States newspapers undoubtedly also helped modify Washington's policies. Although it is very difficult to know what weight to assign each factor, the author's talks with United States officials have left him with the impression that the involvement of the OAS was probably the most important element over the entire duration of the crisis.

43 John Bartlow Martin, *Overtaken by Events: The Dominican Crisis from the Fall of Trujillo to the Civil War* (New York: Doubleday & Company, 1966), pp. 658–660; personal interviews.

44 *Ibid.,* pp. 661–662.

attacked "the OAS," "Mora," or "the Inter-American Peace Force" for disliked actions that were clearly primarily or exclusively controlled by the United States government, such as the seizure of the central bank, the military interposition between the two sides, and the semi-dictation of the terms of settlement. Thus, though the fiction was apparent to all, the involvement of the OAS helped keep open the lines of communication between the United States and the contending Dominican factions.

Finally, the *de facto* diplomatic recognition by OAS bodies of the constitutionalists gave them a certain status and legitimacy. Once the situation had settled down and serious political negotiations had begun, the constitutionalists were accepted as being on at least an equal plane with the Dominican military and the Imbert junta—a contending party whose demands had to be accommodated if a settlement was to be reached. Moreover, the involvement of the OAS during the long political negotiations provided the constitutionalists with a forum for public pressure against the United States, thus giving them a degree of political leverage that partially offset their military weakness and led to a settlement that was far more acceptable to them than to their rightist opponents.

LEGITIMACY, THE OAS, AND THE DOMINICAN CRISIS

Nonetheless, and this is the crucial point in this discussion, the OAS was apparently very unpopular in the Dominican Republic, and its actions were hardly seen or accepted as legitimate by either the left or the right.[45] On the

contrary, it was the focus for intense hatred and scorn, as summed up in the widesperad reference to the OEA (the Spanish abbreviation of OAS) as "Otro Engaño Americano"—Another American Fraud.[46] Particularly detested was the so-called Inter-American Peace Force, the creation of which produced no legitimization at all of the United States forces that dominated it but plenty of contempt for the few Latin American "gorillas" that joined it.

The reasons for this feeling are not difficult to discover. To begin with, not only in the Dominican Republic but all over the world the OAS was seen, whatever the oversimplification, as nothing more than a front for the United States that could not even muster up a slap on the wrist against the country that had engaged in the most flagrant violation of the nonintervention norm, proclaimed *ad nauseam* by the Latin Americans as the "cornerstone" of the inter-American system.[47] Moreover, as has been noted, the OAS refused to allow such leading Latin American progressives as Rómulo Betancourt, José Figueres, and Luis Muñoz Marín to mediate the crisis; on the contrary, at least two of the OAS

---

45 The author says "apparently" because he has no systematic data on the attitudes of the general Dominican public toward the OAS. Among the more articulate and therefore more relevant sectors, however, anti-OAS statements were widespread, frequent, and vehement.

46 By contrast, the relatively unimportant UN observation team was very popular in the constitutionalist zone, frequently being greeted with cries of "UN si, OEA no."

47 Jottin Cury, foreign minister of the constitutionalist government: "Since that moment [the creation of the IAPF] it has not been possible to distinguish between the interventionists and the OAS." (OAS Document OEA/Ser.F/II.10 [Doc.109], p. 3. Author's translation.)

bodies, the Special Committee and the IAPF, were primarily made up of conservative, strongly anti-Communist states that were openly hostile to the constitutionalists. Whatever chance the Special Committee had to play an effective role was dashed when the Committee, at a time when it was supposedly mediating between the opposing Dominican groups, publicly accused the constitutionaliists of tolerating Communist infiltration of their movement.

Other OAS actions, especially in the early months, were hardly calculated to convince the Dominicans of the Organization's impartiality and independence:

1) The fourteenth vote necessary to obtain the minimum two-thirds required was frequently provided by the Dominican delegate to the OAS, who was personally bitterly hostile to the revolution and "represented" only the overthrown government of Donald Reid; when the credentials committee of the OAS recommended that the Dominican seat be declared vacant until a recognized Dominican government was in power, the majority refused to act.

2) In the name of establishing a "neutral zone" the OAS agreed to authorize the United States to extend its lines across the entire city of Santo Domingo, thereby containing the constitutionalists in a small zone with their backs to the sea at the moment when it appeared that they were on the point of defeating the Dominican military.

3) An official constitutionalist request for an OAS investigation of charges that their movement was under Communist influence was ignored despite several attempts of OAS states sympathetic to the revolution to get the majority to respond.

4) The OAS failed to prevent or even condemn repeated violations of the cease-fire by troops loyal to the Imbert junta, including a major drive that resulted in the killing of hundreds of constitutionalists or innocent bystanders and the jailing of thousands of others.[48] Nor did the OAS do much to prevent a summer of murder and repression by Imbert's police and soldiers.

5) Nothing was done to stop the IAPF from a series of alleged overreactions to sniping from the constitutionalist zone, including a drive in June that resulted in the death of over 60 Dominicans. Not only the constitutionalists but most neutral observers believe that IAPF reactions were deliberately designed to periodically remind the constitutionalists of their helplessness and thus pressure them into concessions in the negotiations.[49]

6) Finally, several Latin American states, particularly Colombia, grew increasingly unhappy about United States domination of OAS activities in the Dominican Republic and said so publicly, thereby helping confirm the Dominican view of the relationship between the OAS and the United States government.

Even though it is irrelevant to the main point of this article—the perceived illegitimacy (in the Dominican Republic) of the OAS actions—it per-

---

[48] The chairman of the Special Committee reportedly personally favored military action against the constitutionalists, which perhaps accounts for the remarkable failure of the Special Committee to even call upon the Imbert junta to adhere to the cease-fire that the OAS itself had negotiated.

[49] The author's own research, however, indicates that IAPF reactions were probably not intended to have political side effects although it was recognized by United States officials that they did.

haps should be noted that the actuality of the OAS role, in its totality, was far more balanced than has thus far been indicated.[50] For one thing, once the United States decided to press for a compromise political solution, the IAPF did play a genuine peacekeping role, several times preventing the Dominican armed forces from launching planned "clean-up" drives against the constitutionalist zone and later, under the García-Godoy government, performing general police and internal order functions to supplement the inadequate and unreliable Dominican police. The firm refusal of the IAPF to allow the Dominican military to achieve a "definitive solution,"[51] i.e., massacre the constitutionalists, led, in fact, to bitter charges from the right of "intervention" while the left gradually though reluctantly came to realize that its safety depended on the continued presence of the Force.[52]

The work of the Inter-American Commission on Human Rights helped to supplement the IAPF's peacekeeping role and to bring about an atmosphere making an eventual settlement possible, not to mention salvaging some OAS prestige.[53] Representatives of the Commission were in the Dominican Republic from early June 1965 until the

elections a year later, investigating thousands of complaints of police harassment, political imprisonments, and outright murders of constitutionalist sympathizers throughout the country. The vigorous activities and forthright public reports of the Commission, which received widespread publicity in the Dominican Republic and the hemisphere at large, were undoubtedly instrumental in deterring worse atrocities, securing the release of political prisoners, and contributing to a significant lessening of terrorism by the end of the summer of 1965.[54]

In the economic sphere, too, the OAS (or to be precise, the United States operating in part through OAS personnel and institutions) performed a significant emergency relief and recuperation role, all but replacing Dominican government public services that were disrupted by the revolution. In the first months after the revolution OAS teams distributed large quantities of American food and medicine in the constitutionalist zone and throughout the country, and OAS funds were used to pay the salaries of the Dominican public sector—armed forces, government bureaucracy, and workers in government enterprises—constitutionalist and nonconstitutionalist alike. Later, the OAS provided millions of dollars in loans and technical assistance for emergency public works projects to relieve

---

50 In the ensuing section the United States component is included in references to the role of "the OAS," whereas earlier, in the analysis of the impact of the OAS, only the distinctly Latin American input was dealt with.

51 Imbert government note to the OAS, contained in OAS Document OEA/Ser.F/II.10 (Doc.202), June 26, 1965, p. 2.

52 On a number of occasions constitutionalist officials told the United States embassy that no matter what they said publicly, they wanted the IAPF to remain in the country for an extended period.

53 The Human Rights Commission, though an OAS body, was very popular in the

Dominican Republic, perhaps in part because the Commission took pains to distinguish itself from other OAS institutions by, for example, not flying the OAS flag.

54 See the various reports of the Commission to the Tenth Meeting of Consultation of Foreign Ministers; and Anna P. Schreiber and Philippe S. E. Schreiber, "The Inter-American Commission on Human Rights in the Dominican Crisis," *International Organization,* Spring 1968 (Vol. 22, No. 2), pp. 508–528.

unemployment and to reopen hospitals, businesses, and agricultural enterprises closed by the revolution.

Finally, and most importantly, despite its initial rightist orientation the OAS eventually came to play a decisive role in support of liberalization and democracy in the Dominican Republic. The compromise solution that ended the revolution and brought the García-Godoy government into office, was, in effect, put together by the *Ad Hoc* Committee. Ostensibly, the agreement was negotiated by the contending Dominican forces with the *Ad Hoc* Committee acting merely as mediator, but in fact the Committee went far beyond mediation, not merely because the two sides were so far apart as to preclude direct negotiations but also because the United States had ideas of its own about what constituted an acceptable solution. After a long and arduous negotiating process stretching out over several months the Committee did manage to get the reluctant support of the constitutionalists and the Dominican military for the compromise package, but the terms of the accord were mostly drawn up, and came close to being imposed, by the Committee, which had the economic and military power of the United States behind it. As time wore on, the logic of the deadlock imposed by the presence of the IAPF gradually sank in, inducing both sides to retreat from their maximum demands.

The important point, though, is that the settlement did not attempt to merely split the unbridgeable differences between the left and right but leaned much more to the left. The man chosen to head the Provisional Government, Héctor García-Godoy, was progressive, independent, and effective, and his mandate was to provide

a liberal transitional government that would make it possible to hold genuinely free elections nine months hence.

As might be expected, then, the major obstacles to the agreement came from the right, particularly from the Imbert junta that had been hastily thrown together in the early days after the intervention. While the United States saw Imbert only as a stopgap, Imbert disagreed and proceeded to do his utmost to establish himself as a Trujillo. When his intentions became evident, the main task of the *Ad Hoc* Committee became that of undercutting him, which it was able to do by mobilizing Dominican public opinion in favor of its compromise settlement and by bringing heavy diplomatic and economic pressure to bear. (With the Dominican economy shattered and collection of government revenues at almost a complete standstill Imbert was nearly completely dependent on OAS [i.e., United States] loans to keep his government afloat, even to the extent of paying the salaries of the military and the government bureaucracy. Whatever independent resources Imbert might have had access to were controlled by the Dominican central bank, but when the OAS learned of Imbert's intention to seize the bank, an IAPF contingent was sent to occupy it, and thereafter no disbursements were allowed without the authorization of an OAS official. Once agreement with the Dominican military and constitutionalists was reached, the *Ad Hoc* Committee announced that the OAS loan fund, "particularly for the payment of salaries,"[55] was about to run dry. With the handwriting thus not merely written but emblazoned on the wall Imbert

---

[55] OAS Document OEA/Ser.F/II.10 (Doc. 278), August 6, 1965.

resigned and the García-Godoy government took over.)

The installation of the Provisional Government in September 1965 did not end the crisis, for García-Godoy was able to govern successfully only with major OAS economic, political, and military support. After the return of Juan Bosch to the country in September made it clear that the *Ad Hoc* Committee and García-Godoy meant what they said about free elections, the military moved into a state of permanent revolt. Only the rapid deployment of IAPF troops prevented several coup attempts from succeeding and made it possible for the elections to be held on schedule. After the elections, won by Joaquin Balaguer,[56] the IAPF remained in the Dominican Republic for three months in order to provide the new government with the necessary support to consolidate its control of the military. There is strong evidence that the OAS was prepared to play the same role for even a longer period had a victorious Bosch so desired,[57] a remarkable comment on the evolution of United States policy in the year since its troops had intervened to prevent the victory of a revolution having as its aim the reinstallation of Juan Bosch to the presidency.

This digression should not obscure the point that whatever the complexities and changing nature of the OAS role in the Dominican Republic, what counts in legitimacy is perceptions and not reality. And it seems clear that the Arévalo/Castro image of the OAS as a mere cloak for United States hegemony not only is widely accepted in the Dominican Republic but has gained new converts throughout the hemisphere. Once again, then, as with its "success" in getting some OAS support for its Guatemalan and Cuban policies, the United States won a pyrrhic victory, adding precious little "collective legitimization" to its own policies but seriously diminishing the already shallow fund of organizational legitimacy.[58]

The evidence of the declining reputation of the OAS seems to be considerable. In a series of interviews with Pan American Union officials and the Latin American representatives on the Council the majority admitted to rising skepticism or even hostility toward the Organization in Latin America, and many did not expect the Organization to be able to play a significant role in hemispheric political affairs in the near future. Some of this feeling is even

[56] Although there was probably some military intimidation in the countryside, a great number of independent observers, most of them pro-Bosch in their sympathies, certified that the elections were remarkably free and fair and that the surprising Balaguer victory was genuine.

[57] Despite Bosch's bitterly anti-American campaign and his repeated demands for the immediate withdrawal of the IAPF he privately let it be known that if he won the elections he would want the Force to remain in the Dominican Republic for at least eighteen months.

[58] As Joseph Nye of Harvard University has suggested to this writer, United States officials may also seek multilateral endorsements to convince *themselves* or the general public of the legitimacy of their policies. The author has no systematic data on United States decisionmaker or public perceptions on the role of the OAS in the Dominican crisis, but it seems that a good many officials and much American writing took the same generally jaundiced view of the OAS as did the Dominicans and the Latin Americans. In any event, as argued earlier, the low saliency of inter-American affairs for the United States general public ensures that it is attitudes in, first of all, the host country of the operation and, secondly, Latin America as a whole, that are the main targets for collective legitimization efforts.

being expressed at recent inter-American conferences, in sharp contrast with the tradition of fulsome rhetoric that usually prevails at such gatherings. The foreign minister of Chile, for example, was quite blunt about it:

Let us state frankly a fact that is not pleasant: the inter-American system is looked upon with suspicion by the peoples of America or, at least, ignored as a thing alien to their vital interests.[59]

Indeed, so widespread is this feeling, apparently, that the new OAS Secretary General, Galo Plaza, felt obliged to tour Latin America shortly after taking office in an attempt to revitalize the Organization and, in his own publicly stated words, "dispel the image of some that the OAS is the Ministry of Colonies of the Government of the United States."[60]

An admittedly unsystematic sampling of recent Latin American writings on the OAS adds other evidence to confirm the general drift, the great majority stressing the damage done to the Organization by its recent support of United States anti-Communist policies in general and in the Dominican Republic in particular. The flat statement by Víctor Alba, a prestigious and moderate writer on inter-American affairs, that the OAS "has been destroyed" by the Dominican crisis does not seem atypical.[61]

The crisis has already had visible effects on the Organization. One manifestation was the general coolness of the Latin Americans to United States efforts to keep the UN out of the crisis.[62] Only Uruguay played an active part in the UN debates, and it took a remarkably candid pro-UN, anti-OAS position, at one point arguing that "no collective measures...can therefore be taken lawfully by that [the Tenth] meeting."[63]

But most important of all has been the halting and perhaps even reversing of a recent movement in the OAS toward increasing the political authority and capacity of the Organization to play a greater role in hemispheric political conflict. Before the Dominican crisis an apparent consensus had been

---

enthusiastically praised by most Latin Americans present. Sample:
The presence of a hegemonic power... dominated the political, social and economic lives of its weak neighbors, which are...completely integrated into the United States sphere of influence. This factor transcends into the area's regional organizations which tend to become no more than a formalization of the United States sphere of influence and...a vehicle for the endorsement and legalization of United States actions in the hemisphere.
(Unpublished paper by Pilár Calderón, presented at a conference at the University of the West Indies, Kingston, Jamaica.)
[62] Even before the Dominican crisis, however, there was a growing Latin American tendency to turn to the UN as a counterweight to the OAS. See Ronald Yalem, *Regionalism and World Order* (Washington: Public Affairs Press, 1965); Bryce Wood and Minerva Morales M., "Latin America and the United Nations," in Norman J. Padelford and Leland M. Goodrich (ed.), *The United Nations in the Balance: Accomplishments and Prospects* (New York: Frederick A. Praeger, 1965), pp. 350–363.
[63] Security Council *Official Records* (20th year), 1221st meeting, June 7, 1965, pp. 8–9.

---

[59] See OAS Document OEA/Ser.E/XIII (Doc.83), November 22, 1967, p. 7 (Second Special Inter–American Conference).
[60] Quoted in the Dominican newspaper, *Listin Diario,* July 4, 1968.
[61] Víctor Alba, *Los Sumergidos* (Mexico City: B. Costa-Amic, 1965), p. 79. Also, for whatever anecdotes are worth, at a recent conference in the Caribbean a paper emphasizing United States hegemony in Latin America and the uselessness of the OAS was

reached on the need...to strengthen the Organization's antiquated and frequently ineffective procedures, particularly those relating to peaceful settlement of interstate conflict.... At a series of three conferences between the fall of 1965 and early 1967, however, the consensus disappeared....

CONCLUSION: COLLECTIVE LEGITIMIZATION REEVALUATED

There is reason to be cautious in generalizing too much from the Dominican case, for the United States domination of OAS action and the Latin American opposition to Washington's policies were considerably greater than normally is the case in inter-American actions. In more genuinely collective operations based on a broader consensus the limits of the Organization's capacity to bestow collective legitimization are likely to be less severe. Moreover, in most other international organizations power is more evenly distributed and organizational activities more genuinely collective, so that the collective legitimization function is more likely to be a reality.

Still, the Dominican crisis involved a major operation by a major international organization and thus, with all the above qualifications, provides a significant test of the applicability of the "collective legitimization" function to international organizations other than the UN. The following conclusions, then, are suggested by the analysis. First, the capacity of an international organization to legitimate national policies is not a given and cannot be assumed but depends, obviously enough, on the degree of legitimacy the organization is perceived to have. This, in turn, may vary widely—not only from organization to organization but within every organization over time and from case to case, function to function, and institution to institution. In fact, while this analysis has focused on only the OAS, even UN action, as distinct from the vague generalities of the Charter and numerous nonoperational resolutions, is not invariably seen as legitimate: In the last few years, for example, the United Kingdom, France, Belgium, Israel, the Union of Soviet Socialist Republics, and large sectors of United States public opinion have been bitterly opposed to a variety of UN activities, with indications that specific opposition has been increasingly broadened into generalized dislike or even contempt.

Secondly, since the legitimacy of an organization depends primarily on its being perceived as the repository of the common interest or general will, the capacity of an international organization to bestow collective legitimization is inversely related to the degree to which the organization is customarily used by member states to implement their traditionally defined national interests rather than to seek consensus, resolve conflict, or build international order. Yet, as we all know, the former heavily prevails over the latter with the result that the collective legitimization function may be quite fragile.

Third, collective legitimization may even be dangerous to an international organization. As Claude has pointed out, "bad" as well as "good" policies may be endorsed, and the organization may be exploited for propaganda purposes rather than used to promote diplomatic settlement. Or, alternatively, the impact of an international organization on a national policy channeled through it may be in the "wrong" direction. "International organization," "multilateral," and "collective action" are all honorific words eliciting favorable connotations, especially among the generally liberal and internationalist elite sectors of public opinion. Thus, behind the frequent exhortations to policymakers to allow international organizations to play a greater role in national policies lies the implicit assumption that collective bodies will exert a moderating, liberalizing, or enlightening influence. But this is not invariably so: As has been shown in this article, the conservative, nondemocratic majority in the OAS sometimes made it more difficult for the United States to follow liberal policies in the Dominican Republic than if it had acted entirely unilaterally.

The final demurrer is perhaps the most serious: The very value or perceived value of collective legitimization may lend impetus to the aforementioned tendency of states to use international organizations to win short-run victories for their national policies, as the United States did in the Dominican Republic. Paradoxically, too many such victories add up to defeat—each time a state succeeds in getting multilateral support for a national policy that is strongly opposed in some quarters the organization loses a little more of its capacity to legitimize future policies. Put differently, the organization may not so much legitimize the policy as the policy delegitimize the organization.[64]

[64] Cf. Merelman, p. 554.
When policy-makers choose to attach symbols of legitimacy to policies they wish learned, accepted and implemented, they make a major investment. If the policy fails, it is likely that the legitimacy symbol will also become less useful.

Yet, it must be admitted, this line of argument cannot be carried too far, for it raises in another guise the familiar dilemma posed by international organizations with a rather shaky fund of generalized legitimacy operating in international systems with a high degree of conflict: For the organization to be effective in performing its most crucial function, the management and control of interstate conflict, it must act —but to act is to risk disaffecting key members of the system. Thus, although in the long run legitimacy certainly will depend considerably on the organization being perceived as relevant to the mainstream of international politics, in the short run legitimacy and relevancy may be often in direct opposition as major crises confront organizations with the conflicting necessities of doing something about the immediate situation but yet preserving the organization itself for the future.

In the international system of today the values of peace, order, and stability, on the one hand, are frequently in sharp conflict with the values of change and justice, on the other. Peacekeeping operations, for example, tend to work against those who seek radical internal change. Whichever set of values the organization seeks to maximize will condemn it in the eyes of a considerable segment of its constituency and, if it takes a middle course, as the UN did in the Congo, it risks failure and antagonism from all sides. But to conclude from this that an international organization should engage only in activities for which there is a solid consensus would condemn the organization to the periphery of international politics.

14

The Dominican Republic Crisis of 1965:
A Case-Study of the
Regional vs. the Global Approach
to International Peace and Security

Dona Baron

From Dona Baron, "The Dominican Republic Crisis of 1965: A Case-Study of the Regional vs. the Global Approach to International Peace and Security," in Andrew W. Cordier, ed., *Columbia Essays in International Affairs (III): The Dean's Papers, 1967* (New York: Columbia University Press, 1968), pp. 1–37.

Dona Baron is a Ph.D. candidate in the Department of Political Science at Columbia University.

Ever since the Pan American movement began in serious fashion in the late nineteenth century, Latin Americans have been torn between their desire for some sort of special relationship with the United States and a wider pattern of interaction in international politics that would to a degree insulate them from their powerful northern neighbor. "Let America be for humanity," sloganized Argentine delegate Roque Saenz Peña at the First Pan American Conference in 1889. When the League of Nations opened its doors, Latin American governments joined in part because they hoped that it might act as a counterbalance to the United States in the Western Hemisphere. In this respect, as in so many others, the League proved a disappointment: Article 21 of the Covenant proclaimed the inviolability of "regional understandings like the Monroe Doctrine," and the League treaded gently concerning matters which it regarded as within the legitimate U.S. sphere of influence. However, during the 1930s, under Washington's wary eye, the world organization did play a relatively minor role in the international negotiations surrounding the Chaco War, and it went so far as to provide a commission to administer the settlement in the Leticia conflict.

After the Good Neighbor period and World War II, regional sentiments were running higher in Latin America than ever before or since; and Latin American governments moved to consolidate the institutional framework of the inter-American system to withstand potential challenges from the

227

emerging United Nations. Then, at the San Francisco Conference, they pressured a divided U.S. delegation and other governments into writing important concessions for regional organizations into the UN Charter. Article 52 not only authorized the existence of "regional arrangements or agencies for dealing with such matters relating to the maintenance of international peace and security as are appropriate for regional action" but also provided that members of regional organizations "shall make every effort" to settle disputes at the regional level before taking them to the Security Council—without prejudice to the right of the Security Council under Article 34 to consider disputes on its own initiative or the right of member governments under Article 35 to bring disputes to the attention of either the Security Council or the General Assembly. Article 53 decreed that "no enforcement action shall be taken under regional arrangements. . .without the authorization of the Security Council"; on the other hand, Article 51 guaranteed "the inherent right of individual or collective self-defense if an armed attack occurs against a Member of the United Nations, until the Security Council has taken the measures necessary to maintain international peace and security."

The post-San Francisco era saw the development of two central issues regarding the OAS–UN relationship, defined by Claude in a pioneering monograph[1]: (1) the "try the OAS first" issue, relating to the primacy of regional organizations in peaceful settlement; and (2) the question of OAS autonomy in imposing sanctions against its members. What is perhaps the most interesting aspect of the debate over these issues is that there has been a partial reversal of United States and Latin American positions since 1945. The Cold War almost paralyzed the UN and prompted the U.S. to turn to regional alliances for the organization of security against Communism. In the process, the United States has become a staunch defender of regionalism, while Latin Americans have again expressed some reservations, especially on the "try the OAS first" issue.

As a matter of fact, most Latin American governments strongly supported U.S. defense of OAS autonomy in imposing sanctions against Trujillo and Castro. In these cases, the United States successfully argued that requiring Security Council approval would give the Soviets a "veto" over inter-American affairs and, in any event, that "enforcement action" in Article 53 referred only to the use of force. Although the OAS–UN relationship was hardly of immediate concern in the excitement of the Cuban Missile Crisis, the United States subsequently resorted to an even more circuitous argument to justify the obvious use of force involved in the OAS naval "quarantine":

---

1 Inis L. Claude, Jr., "The OAS, the UN, and the United States," *International Conciliation*, No. 547 (March 1964).

The State Department insisted that the existence of "offensive" missiles in Cuba constituted a matter "appropriate for regional action" under Article 52 and that the quarantine was not "the threat or use of force against the territorial integrity or political independence of a state" forbidden by Article 2(4), since no threat to Cuba was implied. In the U.S. reasoning, neither was the quarantine an "enforcement action," for this term referred only to Security Council military operations proceeding under international agreements which were foreseen by the founders of the UN but never negotiated after the war. The U.S. conspicuously steered away from the argument advanced by some international lawyers at the time that, in the light of technological developments in the missile age, "the inherent right of individual or collective self-defense" against an "armed attack" had to be expanded to include "pre-emptive self-defense" against the threat of an armed attack. From the U.S. point of view, the latter argument would have allowed the Soviets and other governments greater leeway in the use of force; in contrast, action under Article 52 was available only to regional organizations like the OAS!

Since the Guatemalan case in 1954, when the U.S. made skillful use of a jurisdictional conflict to delay the UN from acting before the Arbenz regime collapsed, Latin American governments have carefully stressed their legal right of access to the UN at any stage of a dispute. Nevertheless, most have stood with the United States in specific cases in maintaining that the UN should defer to the OAS, solely on the practical ground that it is better equipped to deal with regional disputes.

In the 1965 Dominican Crisis, however, Uruguay joined the Soviet Union, France, and several other Security Council members in urging the United Nations to assume a prominent role from the outset. As Baron observes in her essay that follows, the UN soon established a "presence" in the Dominican Republic and thereby moved the longstanding jurisdictional problem "from the realm of legalistic arguments based on political considerations to the realm of pragmatic contingencies in the volatile atmosphere of the scene of a political crisis." Implications for the OAS–UN relationship aside. UN entry into the dispute made it more difficult to settle.

... The Dominican experience illustrates how the coeval existence of both regional and universal organizations concerned with peace and security can tend to diminish even further the effectiveness not only of each agency respectively, but also of the sum of their efforts. Such deleterious results of the theoretically complementary relations between regional and global agencies can be seen both in the respective arenas of decision-making and in the actual attempts to implement adopted policies. ...

As the OAS proceeded to involve itself in the Dominican crisis, it punctilliously related each of its actions to its role as a regional agency subordinate to the UN. At OAS invitation, a UN observer was present at plenary sessions of the OAS Tenth Meeting of Consultation; and OAS resolutions, committee reports, and other pertinent data were forwarded to the world organization. That the OAS was choosing to assert its competence to handle the crisis did not, however, prevent the UN Security Council from considering the Dominican affair also. Despite previous United States-led efforts, notably in cases involving Guatemala and Cuba, to keep the Security Council out of disputes in the Western Hemisphere, it seemed to have been established that while Article 52, paragraph 2 of the UN Charter exhorts members of regional agencies to "make every effort to achieve pacific settlement of local dispute through... regional arrangements or by...regional agencies before referring them to the Security Council," Article 34's assertion that "the Security Council may investigate any dispute, or any situation which might lead to international friction" assured access to UN consideration to any party to a dispute.

Since May, representatives of both rival Dominican factions had been requesting that their respective delegates be accepted by the UN as certified representatives of the Dominican government. Due to the unclarified situation in the Dominican Republic, the UN Secretary General had decided that such official recognition could not yet be given to either party. It was not until May 13, however, when Dr. Jottin Cury, Minister of Foreign Affairs of the Constitutionalist Government, requested that the Security Council consider alleged movements of United States troops outside the established "security zone," that any party directly involved in the Dominican crisis specifically called for Security Council consideration of a complaint.[1] Meanwhile, under the initiative of the Soviet Union, the Security Council had begun to consider the Dominican crisis at a meeting on May 3.

Accusing the United States of having violated paragraphs 4 and 7 of Article 2 of the UN Charter, the Soviet Union proposed a draft resolution condemning "the armed intervention by the United States of America in the domestic affairs of the Dominican Republic as a gross violation of the Charter of the United Nations."[2]

As in previous cases where it had acted against a perceived Communist threat within the Western Hemisphere, the United States attempted to maintain OAS competence to handle the matter. In the face of condemnation by the Soviet Union and Cuba, which had been invited to attend the Security Council meeting on the Dominican case, and criticisms from other Security Council members including France, Jordan, Malaysia, the Ivory Coast, and Uruguay, the United States was hard-pressed to justify its initial landings of Marines and especially its rapid build-up of troops. Still, the United States hoped that by stressing OAS measures aimed at resolving the crisis, it could both further justify its own actions with the mantle of hemispheric action and, perhaps more critically, keep the issue out of the reach of Soviet influence.

Because its position in the Dominican Republic was so vulnerable to criticism and because it considered its interests there so vital to its security, the

[1] United Nations, *Security Council Official Records, Twentieth Year, Supplement for April, May and June, 1965.* S/6356. (Henceforth referred to as *SCOR.*)
[2] *SCOR,* S/6328.

United States felt compelled to exert as much pressure as possible to keep the Dominican situation under the auspices of the regional agency where it would be less visible as a target for hostile propaganda and where its prospects of exercising a decisive influence on the course of events were more favorable. Thus practical political considerations forced the United States to act as a champion of the regionalist approach to international organization. And conversely, since the Soviet Union sought the political advantages of focusing world criticism on the United States and of diluting United States influence in the resolution of the crisis, it became the advocate of the global approach to international organization. Therefore, while discussion of the Dominican crisis was related to considerations of cold war politics and, undeniably, based on considerations of the actual gravity of the situation, the debate often was couched in terms of jurisdictional conflict between the regional and the global organizations. While none, not even the United States, denied Security Council competence to discuss the crisis, the Soviet Union and Cuba were the first to press for UN direct action. At first, most other members of the Security Council were more inclined to allow the regional organization time to act.

After five meetings of the Security Council had been devoted to the Dominican Republic, the Soviet proposal had not come to a vote and no alternative resolutions had been suggested. It had become evident that despite efforts of the OAS and the United States, the Dominican situation was far from being resolved. Thus by May 11, there was increasing feeling within the Security Council that continued fruitless discussion would reflect poorly on the United

Nations as an instrument of international peace. At the 1204th meeting of the Council on May 11, Uruguay presented a draft resolution which, reaffirming the principles of paragraphs 4 and 7 of Article 2 of the UN Charter, and drawing attention to Articles 15 and 17 of the OAS Charter, expressed concern over the situation in the Dominican Republic, urged a cessation of hostilities, invited the Secretary General to "follow closely the events in the Dominican Republic and to take such measures as he may deem appropriate for the purpose of reporting to the Security Council on all aspects of the situation" and invited the OAS "to cooperate with the Secretary General of the United Nations in the implementation of this resolution."[3] As the Uruguayan delegate pointed out, although the Council had not been able thus far to reach any substantive decisions on the matter, the lack of any decision by the Council would imply its inability to fulfill its duties and hence detract from the prestige of the UN. Furthermore, a failure of the UN to exercise its authority would indicate a "serious precedent for small members of regional organizations."[4] Uruguay therefore proposed a resolution that would at least permit the Security Council to assert its authority. . . .

Although the United States objected to the Uruguayan draft on the basis that it implied that the UN did not encourage action by regional agencies and that it might inhibit a solution in the Dominican Republic, it could not stem the tide in favor of some direct assertion of UN responsibility. Thus on May 14, the following resolution, proposed by Jordan, Malaysia, and the

[3] *SCOR,* S/6346.
[4] UN, Security Council, Provisional Records, S/PV. 1204.

Ivory Coast, was adopted unanimously:

The Security Council,
Deeply concerned at the grave events in the Dominican Republic,

1. Calls for a strict cease-fire;
2. Invites the Secretary-General to send, as an urgent measure, a representative to the Dominican Republic for the purpose of reporting to the Security Council on the present situation;
3. Calls upon all concerned in the Dominican Republic to co-operate with the representative of the Secretary-General in the carrying out of this task.[5]

In accord with the resolution, an advance party headed by General I. G. Rikhye of India was dispatched immediately to the Dominican Republic and José Mayobre, the Secretary of the Economic Commission for Latin America, was selected as the Secretary General's representative. After consultations with U Thant, Mayobre arrived in Santo Domingo on May 18.

With the adoption of the three-power resolution, relations between the UN and the OAS entered a phase new to the history of the two agencies. Never before had the UN gone so far as to superimpose its direct authority upon that of the regional agency. The UN had exhorted the OAS to reach solutions before; but never had an emissary of the Secretary General entered an arena of conflict already occupied by representatives of the OAS. With both a UN mission and an OAS committee on the scene in the Dominican Republic, jurisdictional conflicts were to move, in part, from the realm of legalistic arguments based on political considerations to the realm of pragmatic contingencies in the volatile atmosphere of the scene of a political crisis.

[5] *SCOR*, S/6355.

The arrival of the UN mission in Santo Domingo immediately complicated the already incredibly confused situation. These further complications can be examnied on at least two levels. On one level, the activation of the UN made more readily available to the disputing factions another element which potentially could open avenues to political advantage. The simultaneous operation of two distinct courts of appeal and sources of political leverage increased the opportunities for parties to the dispute to attempt to play off the international agencies for their own ends. On another level, related to the first, there were the resulting frictions between the two agencies themselves. These involved not only administrative problems of coordination and division of labor but also competing corporate interests of the two agencies and differences in perspective related to the political composition of their respective constituencies.

That the Security Council's seizure of the Dominican crisis was to have political repercussions was immediately evident. The arrival of General Rikhye was greeted with great enthusiasm by the Constitutionalists who offered the UN mission all the aid and cooperation which might be required. Tad Szulc observed that crowds in the rebel area "wanted to know when the OAS would be thrown out of Santo Domingo. Obviously the rebels had spread the word in the area that the UN was their friend and the OAS their enemy."[6]

Constitutionalist antipathy towards the OAS had been increasing prior to the arrival of the UN mission. The Constitutionalists were irritated that, despite their protestations, the OAS

[6] Tad Szulc, *Dominican Diary* (New York: Delacorte Press, 1965), p. 223.

meeting in Washington was still accepting José Antonio Bonilla Atiles, who had been appointed by the Reid Cabral government, as the official delegate of the Dominican Republic. Another source of Constitutionalist hostility towards the OAS was perhaps more critical. On May 10, Colonel Caamaño had written to the OAS recommending that the [OAS five-man Committee composed of representatives of Argentina, Brazil, Colombia, Guatemala, and Panama] conduct further investigations as to the influence of Communist elements within the Constitutionalist movement. The Caamaño government regretted that the OAS Committee had not clarified this critical aspect of the dispute in their first report. Caamaño went on to recommend that the services of three of Latin America's most distinguished statesmen—Rómulo Betancourt, José Figueres, and Luis Muñoz Marín—aid the OAS Committee in this investigation.[7] Although Betancourt, Figueres, and Muñoz Marín had been willing to participate in such a venture,[8] the OAS had decided to ignore the request. In view of these sources of disillusionment with the OAS and, in addition, the role of the United States in the actions of the Imbert forces, it is understandable that the Constitutionalists would be prone to welcome the arrival of a UN representative.

Constitutionalist antipathy to the OAS had already been making the five-man Committee's tasks more difficult.

Its report pointed out that Colonel Caamaño had recently refused to meet with the Committee and representatives of the Imbert government as had been previously agreed. It is therefore not hard to see why the OAS Committee was disturbed by the entry of the UN onto the Dominican scene. Members of the OAS Committee left almost immediately for Washington and submitted their second report to the Meeting of Consultation. One conclusion of the report was that the Committee had accomplished its original objectives and considered that it had fulfilled its mandate. The report made it quite clear that the Committee believed that, in light of the UN resolution, it could no longer function effectively. The Committee stated that the appearance of the UN mission had had immediate political reverberations, as members of the Dominican diplomatic corps and parties to the dispute "looked towards the Representative of the United Nations Secretary General as a possible element of negotiation." The Committee felt that when this element was added to the efforts of "other governments seeking political solutions" its position became untenable. Thus the Committee, referring to Article 52 paragraph 2 of the UN Charter, found it:

... essential to request the United Nations Security Council to suspend all action until the regional procedures have been exhausted ... in order to avoid simultaneous action of two international organizations in a way that could delay fulfillment of the noble aims of achieving immediate peace and normality in the Dominican Republic.[9]

Within the OAS, the Committee's report evoked lengthy and heated debate. The juridical arguments which

[7] Organización de los Estados Americanos, *Décima Reunión de Consulta de Ministros de Relaciones Exteriores, Documentos Oficiales,* OEA/Ser. F/II. 10, Doc. 64. (Henceforth referred to by English initials—OAS.)

[8] Rómulo Betancourt, José Figueres, and Luis Muñoz Marín, Letter to the Editor. *Life,* LVIII (June 18, 1965), p. 23.

[9] OAS, Doc. 81, Rev.

confirmed Security Council competence to handle any dispute and concluded that thus there could be no jurisdictional conflict between the UN and the OAS were presented. On the other hand, there were those who wished to challenge the UN as recommended in the Committee report or, at least, request the world organization to coordinate *its* activities with those of the OAS. Still, the vast majority of the OAS members were most concerned with preserving the prestige of the inter-American system by demonstrating the ability of the regional organization to define its role so that it could promote the cause of a peaceful settlement. If there was disillusionment with the disruption of the hemispheric respect for the nonintervention principle, there was still concern to protect the right of the Dominican people to establish their own representative government in accord with the norms of the inter-American system. It was in this latter respect that it was felt that the OAS should play a leading role.

The members of the OAS thus turned their attention to the immediate problems of the situation at hand. The view was prevalent that the representative of the UN Secretary General would be no mere observer. As the Colombian representative noted, since Mr. Mayobre had held conversations with leaders of both factions and since the UN resolution spoke of the ceasefire, Mayobre's was "not to be a task of transmitting information but a task of conciliating two enemy bands."[10] Furthermore, it was not known to what degree the UN might choose to expand its role or to what extent extra-hemispheric elements might be empowered

to exert their influence in the situation. It was felt that in order best to promote the role of the OAS vis-à-vis the UN and to act as a positive factor in the achievement of a peaceful settlement in the Dominican Republic, the OAS should empower a representative to succeed the five-man Committee in working for a solution to the crisis. Also, it was concluded that while the authority of the regional organization should be encouraged and the role of the UN mission should not be enhanced, coordination of the two agencies should not be precluded.

On May 22, the OAS approved a resolution charging Secretary General Mora, as representative of the OAS, to work for a strict ceasefire in accord with the Act of Santo Domingo; to offer his good offices to the parties involved in order to procure the establishment of a climate of peace and conciliation which would permit the functioning of the democratic institutions of the Dominican Republic; "to coordinate in what is pertinent, action tending to the achievement of the ends determined by the resolution with that which the Representative of the Secretary General of the United Nations promotes"; and to keep the Meeting of Consultation informed of his efforts and their results.[11] The resolution was passed with no negative votes and Mexico, Chile, Uruguay, and Panama, for various reasons, abstaining on certain sections.

It is worth noting that at this juncture the United States was not compelled to goad the OAS into asserting its authority. In fact the US delegate tended to restrain Latin American delegates who wished to challenge the UN resolution. For example, United

---

[10] OAS, Doc. 87 (textually), Rev. (11th plenary session, May 20–21, 1965), p. 23.

[11] *Ibid.,* pp. 37–38.

States Ambassador Bunker stated that "since the regional organization has jurisdiction over the question...[the OAS]...ought not to read something into the resolution of the Security Council that...goes beyond what the Security Council itself was proposing to do."[12] Furthermore, while the OAS resolution of May 22 indicated an acceptance of a UN role in the Dominican crisis, on May 25, representatives of Argentina, Bolivia, Brazil, Colombia, Costa Rica, El Salvador, Guatemala, Haiti, Honduras, Nicaragua, Panama, Paraguay, and Peru addressed a letter to the UN stating that, in accord with Article 52 paragraph 3 of the UN Charter, action of the OAS as a regional organization should be encouraged.[13] It seems, therefore, that although many Latin American states have been in some respects disillusioned by the function of the OAS and have sought to preserve their right of recourse to the world organization, there remains among the Latin American states a considerable element of that regionalist sentiment which had been so manifest at the time of the framing of the UN Charter, the time when the Latin American delegates had provided the impetus for the adoption of provisions for regional organization. It could be suggested that both a corporate interest in preserving the prestige of the regional organization and a desire to protect the existence of an agency involved in activities in the economic development field from which they benefit, contributed significantly to the motivation of most Latin American states actively to defend the role of the OAS in the settlement of the Dominican crisis.

While the OAS had attempted to clarify its role, it was not possible to predict how the UN representative would interpret his mandate or how political repercussions consequent from the UN presence in the Dominican Republic and on-going events would affect the Security Council's definition of its responsibilities. After having spoken to leaders of both factions in the Dominican Republic, Mr. Mayobre reported that the situation was "extremely grave."[14] Each side had blamed the other for attacking its positions and the Constitutionalists accused the United States of giving military and logistic support to Imbert's forces. In view of continued violence in the Dominican Republic, the Security Council, on May 19, requested the Secretary General to convey to his representative the desire that he devote his urgent efforts to securing an immediate suspension of hostilities for the humanitarian purpose of permitting the Red Cross to carry out its tasks.

Through the efforts of both Dr. Mora and Mr. Mayobre, a twenty-four hour ceasefire was agreed to by both sides. The negotiations leading to this ceasefire demonstrated that when the immediate goals of the two agencies were identical and clearly defined, their actions could successfully be coordinated. The effectiveness of neither the OAS nor the UN representatives in the Dominican case can be evaluated, however, without consideration of the direction and influence of United States policy.

Although in the third week of May McGeorge Bundy was still carrying on negotiations for a Guzmán government, in Washington United States policy seemed to have taken another

12 *Ibid.*, p. 19.
13 *SCOR*, S/6409.

14 *SCOR*, S/6369.

turn. It seems to have been decided to undercut negotiations with the Constitutionalists for a Guzmán government and to allow Imbert to win the war. Thus the United States had not interfered as Imbert's forces occupied more and more of the Constitutionalist territory in the north of Santo Domingo. Once Imbert had control of the northern district of the city, the United States-manned Security Corridor became a buffer between the two Dominican forces. Thus the United States had maneuvered itself into a physical position from which it could not allow the Imbert forces to continue their advance; world opinion would be outraged by such an obvious violation of an allegedly neutral position. Now Washington seemed to hope that a military stalemate having been reached, it could ultimately force both sides to accept a coalition government. Thus the United States belatedly joined the UN and OAS mediators in their efforts to prolong the humanitarian ceasefire into a lasting truce. The latest change in United States policy was soon followed by a change in Imbert's posture. Whereas through the morning of May 22 Imbert had rejected extension of the truce, on the afternoon of May 22 he announced in a statement to the press that his government would "not initiate further warlike action. . . . It would abstain from firing, unless it were provoked, as long as conversations continued with the OAS to reach a definitive solution to the conflict."[15]

That the junta had caved in under powerful pressure from the United States was apparent. This is indicated by Dr. Mora's statements to Mr. Mayobre that the US Embassy had advised

him that the United States would not permit Imbert's forces to use "facilities that were under the control of US forces."[16]

This phase of the Dominican crisis would seem indicative of a pattern that prevailed throughout. Although representatives of international agencies, the OAS and the UN, were to perform meaningful functions which promoted the eventual settlement, fundamentally it was the position of the United States upon which all else hinged. During the third week of May, the United States had made it clear to Imbert's forces that further massive aggression would not be tolerated. Henceforth a truce was established and, although there were further incidents, there were no further large-scale military aggressions on the part of Imbert's forces. Similarly, once the United States decided to channel its efforts for a political settlement through the OAS, that body, no longer working in isolation from competing United States peace missions, became the instrument through which a political settlement was negotiated. . . .

. . . As the Security Council continued to discuss the Dominican crisis, the questions remained whether the scope of the UN mission's responsibilities would be enlarged and, if so, whether increased overlap in the spheres of action of the two agencies would increase their total effectiveness.

Once the Security Council had demonstrated its willingness to act, it was subject to increased pressure to reach substantive decisions. Through the reports of the Secretary General's representative in the Dominican Republic, personal testimony of rival claimants to represent the Dominican Republic in the UN, and communications from

---

[15] OAS, Doc. 96 (textually), Rev. (14th plenary session, June 2, 1965), p. 11.

[16] *SCOR,* S/6371/Add. 2.

the contending factions, the Security Council was now directly exposed to complaints from the parties to the dispute. In view of continued turmoil in the Dominican Republic, a French resolution calling for transformation of the humanitarian truce into a permanent ceasefire was adopted on May 22.[17] The resolution was passed 10 to 0 with the United States abstaining. The United States explained that it had abstained because the resolution did not encourage the activities of the OAS; however, it would not veto the resolution since the measure would not impede the regional agency and, as reports had indicated, all in Santo Domingo concerned with restoring the peace were working in consultation. It was pointed out, moreover, that on May 21, the OAS had passed a similar resolution exhorting the factions to convert the truce into a permanent ceasefire.

As the crisis in the Dominican Republic prolonged itself, each of the contending factions chose to exercise its right of recourse to the UN. Complaints were not confined, however, to mutual denunciations. While the Constitutionalists, understandably, were the only party to the dispute to lodge complaints against the activities of United States military forces, both parties eventually raised allegations against the OAS—particularly with regard to the activities of the Inter-American Peace Force. Each faction also denounced the other for violations of human rights. The Constitutionalists in particular complained of atrocities committed by the Imbert forces.

It should be noted that while each side protested to the UN, each continued to deal intensively with the

OAS. Complaints addressed to the Security Council were also addressed to the OAS. Some complaints were directed first to the OAS, with indications that if the OAS did not deal with the matter to the party's satisfaction, the party would then seek rectification in the world organization. In addition, in those aspects of the crisis directly relating to the working out of a political settlement, neither side appealed to the UN. Each negotiated with the regional agency which in turn informed the UN of progress being made. Examination of interactions between the UN, the OAS, and the contending parties with regard to the three key issues just mentioned—the IAPF, human rights, and the political settlement —should illuminate further the dynamics of the interrelations between the regional and world organizations on both the political-strategic and the practical-functional levels.

On May 24, the OAS transmitted to the UN the text of the constituent act of the Inter-American Peace Force, signed on May 23 in Santo Domingo. In accordance with the OAS resolution of May 6, the IAPF was placed under the command of General Hugo Panasco Alvim of Brazil and combined forces from Brazil, Costa Rica, El Salvador, Honduras, and Nicaragua with the predominant United States contingent, which still numbered over 20,000.

The establishment of such a force by a regional organization was indeed a novelty in the history of contemporary international organization. Such an innovation, realized through United States efforts to promote its political objectives, would naturally be challenged in the Security Council by the Soviet Union. As the Soviet Union and Cuba led the assault against the IAPF, the thrust of their arguments was that

[17] *SCOR*, S/6376.

such a force could not legally be justified and practically constituted a tool of foreign occupation that would aggravate the situation in the Dominican Republic. Indeed, the United States would be hard-pressed to find legal justification for the IAPF. The IAPF was attacked by the Soviet Union on the basis of Article 53 of the UN Charter which prohibits enforcement action by a regional agency without Security Council authorization. To this argument the United States replied, as it had to similar arguments raised against the IAPF in OAS meetings, that the function of the IAPF did not constitute an enforcement action within the meaning of Article 53. It was instead conceived as an instrument of restoring normal conditions in the Dominican Republic. Its proclaimed purpose was to protect the security and rights of the Dominican people and to help establish the atmosphere of peace which would permit the functioning of democratic institutions. However, if the activation of the IAPF did not constitute an enforcement action, its juridical basis was still vulnerable to arguments which had been posed by various Latin American states at the OAS Meeting of Consultation and which were subsequently brought to the floor of the UN by Uruguay. As United States political pressure and the aggravation of the Dominican crisis had overridden legal obstacles to the formation of the IAPF within the OAS, so the attitude of the Security Council to the IAPF would be molded by ongoing events in the Dominican Republic and United States-led efforts to promote the force as a necessary device for peaceful settlement of the crisis.

In further defense of the IAPF, the United States asserted that since the goals of the UN and the OAS were essentially identical and since the OAS, under Article 52 of the UN Charter, was working towards the settlement of the Dominican dispute, it would be unwise to deprecate the accomplishments of the regional organization or to give the impression that the world organization was competing with its regional agency. Although it was never suggested that a UN police force supersede the IAPF, in view of repeated violations of the ceasefire and complaints against the participation of the IAPF in these outbreaks of violence, the Security Council debated the need to enlarge the staff and facilities of the UN mission so that it could more effectively carry out its assigned tasks. While the United States continued to justify the actions of the IAPF, the Soviet Union was not without support in its condemnations of the role of the IAPF in any infractions of the ceasefire and its demands that the Security Council increase its powers to investigate the situation.

The problem of violations of human rights, especially reports of repression, assassinations, and atrocities committed by the Imbert government, provided the Soviet Union another opportunity to argue that the UN presence in the Dominican Republic should be reinforced. With regard to the alleged violations of human rights, on June 11, the Secretary General stated that he had provided his representative with sufficient staff and facilities to discharge his present mandate which involved observation and reporting. In the view of the Secretary General, this mandate did not include the investigation of actual complaints and verification of specific charges. According to the Secretary General, if his representative in the Dominican Republic were to undertake such activities, a specific clarification on the part of the Security Council and a substantial enlargement of the mission's staff and facilities would be necessary. In subsequent debate, the Soviet Union, with the firm support of France, Jordan, and Malaysia, contended that the situation in the Dominican Republic called for an intensification of the UN presence. The United States led the counterargument that the OAS was competent to handle the situation and further increases in Mr. Mayobre's staff would only lead to duplication of work already being done. The United States was able to support its position by the fact that the Inter-American Commission on Human Rights was on the scene and conducting the desired investigations.

No resolutions were proposed to alter the mandate of the UN representative. On June 18, in his summary of previous Security Council discussions, the President of the Council noted that there was agreement that Mr. Mayobre's mandate implied that he continue to investigate and report on violations of the ceasefire as he had heretofore been doing. However, there had been no discernible consensus that the UN representative should be given a broader mandate. Hence the question of staff and facilities was essentially a matter to be decided by the Secretary General and his representative.[18]

When on June 21 the UN adjourned its discussion of the Dominican crisis, it seemed that the United States had won a qualified victory in its battle to keep the settlement of the Dominican situation within the purview of the OAS. Although the IAPF had been criticized, it had not been condemned. The mandate of the UN representative had not been made more elaborate and the investigation of violations of human rights was to be continued by the Inter-American Commission on Human Rights. The competence of the OAS to conduct negotiations leading to a political settlement had not been challenged.

With the assiduous efforts of the OAS Ad Hoc Committee it seemed that progress was being made toward achievement of a political settlement. By mid-July, both factions had endorsed Héctor García-Godoy as president of a future provisional government and plans were being formulated for the establishment of such a regime and for the conduct of free elections to be held under OAS supervision. However, conditions remained both tense and unsettled. There were occasional violations of the ceasefire and continued allegations of repressions and atrocities, particularly in the areas outside Santo Domingo. While both factions continued to direct their complaints to the OAS and to work with OAS mediators, each sought to strengthen its political position in the elaboration of a political settlement by appealing or threatening to appeal to the world organization.

Thus on July 20, at the request of the Constitutionalist government, the Security Council again considered the Dominican situation. Accusing the Government of National Reconstruction of repression, illegal executions, and atrocities and, furthermore, charging "complicity on the part of the OAS in these crimes"[19] the Constitutionalist government called for the immediate withdrawal of the IAPF. The Government of National Reconstruction denied the allegations of the Constitutionalists and also requested the im-

[18] S/PV. 1227.

[19] S/PV. 1230.

mediate withdrawal of the IAPF, the presence of which it asserted was a violation of Dominican sovereignty. The Government of National Reconstruction further contended that the IAPF, by preventing the Government's regular police forces from acting in certain areas, was thus making it impossible to guarantee peace and order.

The United States felt that there was no reason for further Security Council discussion of the Dominican case and pointed out that each faction urged the withdrawal of the IAPF so that it could attempt to extend its own control. Therefore, the presence of the IAPF was necessary to prevent the outbreak of civil war. It was further indicated that the Inter-American Commission on Human Rights was making thorough investigations of all reported violations of human rights and that under the aegis of the OAS progress was being made toward a political settlement. Moreover, in compliance with Article 54 of the UN Charter, the OAS was keeping the UN fully apprised of its findings and progress in these areas.

As debate continued, the Soviet Union contended that the IAPF should be withdrawn immediately. Although there was little support for this suggestion, members of the Council expressed concern over continued breaches of the ceasefire and the perpetration of violations of human rights. France pointed out that the presence of the IAPF had not prevented atrocities. Uruguay, once more demonstrating that smaller members of regional organizations dominated by a Great Power can seek to preserve their independence by endorsing the responsibility of the world organization, urged further supervision by the Security Council.

At the final meeting of the Security Council on the Dominican situation, the President of the Council presented a report summing up the Council's discussion. The report stated that the Council members condemned violations of the ceasefire and other violations of human rights and concluded that "it has become apparent that members of the Council consider it necessary that the Council continue to watch closely the situation . . ."; therefore the Secretary General "will continue to submit reports to the Council."[20] The United States declared that it accepted the statement but wished to reaffirm the positive role which the OAS was playing in the Dominican Republic. Thus, as far as the disputants in the case were concerned, appeal to the UN had ultimately provided little political leverage; the OAS, reinforced by United States positive participation, would continue to press for establishment of a provisional government and an ultimate political settlement to be achieved through free elections. . . .

Perhaps the primary conclusion that can be drawn from the experience of the Dominican Republic crisis is that no international organization for the maintenance of peace and security, whether that organization be regional or global, can function effectively without the positive support of the world powers included in its membership. The existence of the legal framework of the OAS had been unable to prevent the United States from a unilateral act of intervention. Forced into action by a crisis exacerbated by United States action, the OAS could not function effectively to achieve a solution to the turmoil until United States policy directed that verbal advocacy of OAS compe-

[20] S/PV. 1233.

tence would be accompanied by real support for OAS actions. And this ultimate coordination was only achieved because the United States had a controlling influence in the formulation of the policies of the regional agency.

Neither had the norms of the UN Charter prevented the United States from exerting its military strength in the pursuit of national policy objectives. In the arena of the Security Council, where no action could be taken except in areas in which there could be agreement between the Soviet Union and the United States, the United States would only allow the world organziation to exercise its authority in a manner that would not substantially damage what it conceived as its national interests.

Because of the predominant motive power of national policy objectives within a context of United States-Soviet Union conflict, the Dominican Republic case does not constitute a test of the abstract principles of the relative effectiveness of problem-solving on the regional or global level. Because the United States championed the cause of a regionally derived solution and exerted its efforts to that end within the OAS and the UN, the regional agency was able to assert its competence and ultimately to fullfill its responsibilities by achieving a political settlement. Thus as a result of the Dominican crisis the powers of the OAS would seem to have been increased. However, the tensions and resentments created within the OAS by the original United States intervention would seem to negate any increases of OAS efficacy indicated by such precedents as the establishment of an Inter-American Peace Force. It is worth noting that subsequent United States proposals that study be made of the possible establishment of such a force on a permanent basis have been received with little support and much hostility within the organization. . . .[21]

21 *The New York Times,* coverage of OAS Special Conference, Rio de Janeiro, November 17–28, 1966.

15

The Situation in the Dominican Republic

J. William Fulbright

From the *Congressional Record: Proceedings and Debates of the 89th Congress, First Session*, III, Part 18 (September 14–23, 1965), pp. 23855–23861.

Senator J. William Fulbright (Democrat-Arkansas), Chairman of the Senate Committee on Foreign Relations, delivered one of the more notable post-mortems on the Dominican episode in this speech to the Senate on September 15, 1965.

In Fulbright's view: The United States, "on the basis of ambiguous evidence," assumed "almost from the beginning" that the Dominican revolution was (or would soon become) dominated by Communists, and through its military intervention stifled whatever potential existed in the situation for progressive political and social change. Indeed, according to Fulbright, the most disturbing aspect of the Dominican case was that it provided further evidence that Washington was backing away from its Alliance for Progress commitment to democratic social revolution in Latin America and aligning itself "with corrupt and reactionary oligarchies." By supporting conservative forces in the Dominican Republic, ignoring the nonintervention rule, and proceeding without advance consultation with the OAS, U.S. policy-makers "embarrassed before their own people the democratic reformers who have counseled trust and partnership with the United States" and "lent credence to the idea...that the only choice Latin Americans have is between communism and reaction." Finally, Fulbright turned to a more general analysis of the foundations "for a new and more friendly relationship between Latin America and the United States," which, he asserted, required "a loosening of existing ties and institutional bonds" and Latin American countries' "'building bridges' to the world beyond the Western Hemisphere."

At the risk of anticipating themes developed in Part II-B and II-C, we should note here that since 1965 the notion of U.S. "disengagement" from Latin America has continued to gather strength in Congress and now (for rather different motives) has found limited expression in the policies of the Nixon Administration. During the same period, Fulbright and other Congressmen of like mind have grown steadily less hopeful about the prospects both for U.S. progressive leadership in the hemisphere and for Latin

American social change under the aegis of the democratic left. Their increasing pessimism in this respect has, in fact, added steam to their advocacy of disengagement.

U.S. policy in the Dominican crisis was characterized initially by over-timidity and subsequently by overreaction. Throughout the whole affair, it has also been characterized by a lack of candor.

These are general conclusions I have reached from a painstaking review of the salient features of the extremely complex situation. These judgments are made, of course, with the benefit of hindsight and, in fairness, it must be conceded there were no easy choices available to the United States in the Dominican Republic. . . .

It cannot be said with assurance that the United States could have changed the course of events by acting differently. What can be said with assurance is that the United States did not take advantage of several opportunities in which it might have changed the course of events. The reason appears to be that, very close to the beginning of the revolution, U.S. policymakers decided that it should not be allowed to succeed. This decision seems to me to have been based on exaggerated estimates of Communist influence in the rebel movement in the initial stages and on distaste for the return to power of Juan Bosch or of a government controlled by Bosch's party, the PRD—Dominican Revolutionary Party.

The question of the degree of Communist influence is of critical importance and I shall comment on it later. The essential point, however, is that the United States, on the basis of ambiguous evidence, assumed almost from the beginning that the revolution was Communist dominated, or would certainly become so. It apparently never occurred to anyone that the United States could also attempt to influence the course which the revolution took. We misread prevailing tendencies in Latin America by overlooking or ignoring the fact that any reform movement is likely to attract Communist support. We thus failed to perceive that if we are automatically to oppose any reform movement that Communists adhere to, we are likely to end up opposing every reform movement, making ourselves the prisoners of reactionaries who wish to preserve the status quo—and the status quo in many countries is not good enough.

The principal reason for the failure of American policy in Santo Domingo was faulty advice given to the President by his representatives in the Dominican Republic at the time of acute crisis. Much of this advice was based on misjudgment of the facts of the situation; some of it appears to have been based on inadequate evidence or, in some cases, simply inaccurate information. On the basis of the information and counsel he received, the President could hardly have acted other than he did. . . .

The development of the Dominican crisis, beginning on April 24, 1965, provides a classic study of policymaking in a fast-changing situation in which each decision reduces the range of options available for future decisions so that errors are compounded and finally, indeed, there are few if any options except to follow through on an ill-conceived course of action. Beyond a certain point the Dominican story acquired some of the inevitability of a Greek tragedy.

Another theme that emerges from the Dominican crisis is the occurrence of a striking change in U.S. policy toward the Dominican Republic and the possibility—not a certainty, because the signs are ambiguous, but only the possibility—of a major change as well in the general Latin American policies of the United States. Obviously, an important change in the official outlook on Dominican affairs occurred between September 1963, when the United States was vigorously opposed to the overthrow of Juan Bosch, and April 1965, when the United States was either unenthusiastic or actually opposed to his return.

What happened in that period to change the assessment of Bosch from favorable to unfavorable? It is quite true that Bosch as President did not distinguish himself as an administrator, but that was well known in 1963. It is also true, however, and much more to the point as far as the legitimate interests of the United States are concerned, that Bosch had received 58 percent of the votes in a free and honest election and that he was presiding over a reform–minded government in tune with the Alliance for Progress. This is a great deal more than can be said for any other President of the Dominican Republic.

The question therefore remains as to how and why the attitude of the U.S. Government changed so strikingly between September 1963 and April 1965. And the question inevitably arises whether this shift in the administration's attitude toward the Dominican Republic is part of a broader shift in its attitude toward other Latin American countries, whether, to be specific, the U.S. Government now views the vigorous reform movements of Latin America—such as Christian Democracy in Chile, Peru, and Venezuela, APRA in Peru and Acción Democrática in Venezuela—as threatening to the interests of the United States. And if this is the case, what kind of Latin American political movements would now be regarded as friendly to the United States and beneficial to its interests?

I should like to make it very clear that I am raising a question, not offering an answer. I am frankly puzzled as to the current attitude of the U.S. Government toward reformist movements in Latin America. On the one hand, President Johnson's deep personal commitment to the philosophy and aims of the Alliance for Progress is clear; it was convincingly expressed, for example, in his speech to the Latin American Ambassadors on the fourth anniversary of the Alliance for Progress—a statement in which the President compared the Alliance for Progress with his own enlightened program for a Great Society at home. On the other hand, one notes a general tendency on the part of our policymakers not to look beyond a Latin American politician's anticommunism. One also notes in certain Government agencies, particularly the Department of Defense, a preoccupation with counterinsurgency, which is to say, with the prospect of revolutions and means of suppressing them. This preoccupation is manifested in dubious and costly research projects, such as the recently discredited Camelot; these studies claim to be scientific but beneath their almost unbelievably opaque language lies an unmistakable military and reactionary bias.

It is of great importance that the uncertainty as to U.S. aims in Latin America be resolved. We cannot successfully advance the cause of popular democracy and at the same time align ourselves with corrupt and reactionary oligarchies; yet that is what we seem to be trying to do. The direction of the Alliance for Progress is toward social revolution in Latin America; the direction of our Dominican intervention is toward the suppression of revolutionary movements which are supported by Communists or suspected of being influenced by Communists. . . .

We simply cannot have it both ways; we must choose between the Alliance for Progress and a foredoomed effort to sustain the status quo in Latin America. . . .

It is not surprising that we Americans are not drawn toward the uncouth revolutionaries of the non-Communist left. We are not, as we like to claim in Fourth of July speeches, the most truly revolutionary nation on earth; we are, on the contrary, much closer to being the most unrevolutionary nation on earth. We are sober and satisfied and comfortable and rich; our institutions are stable and old and even venerable; and our Revolution of 1776, for that matter, was not much of an upheaval compared to the French and Russian revolutions and to current and impending revolutions in Latin America, Asia, and Africa.

Our heritage of stability and conservatism is a great blessing, but it also has the effect of limiting our understanding of the character of social revolution and sometimes as well of the injustices which spawn them. Our understanding of revolutions and their causes is imperfect not because of any failures of mind or character but because of our good fortune since the Civil War in never having experienced sustained social injustice without hope of legal or more or less peaceful remedy. We are called upon, therefore, to give our understanding and our sympathy and support to movements which are alien to our experience and jarring to our preferences and prejudices.

We must try to understand social revolution and the injustices that give it rise because they are the heart and core of the experience of the great majority of people now living in the world. In Latin America we may prefer to associate with the well-bred, well-dressed businessmen who often hold positions of power, but Latin American reformers regard such men as aliens in their own countries who neither identify with their own people nor even sympathize with their aspirations. Such leaders are regarded by educated young Latin Americans as a "consular bourgeoisie," by which they mean business-oriented conservatives who more nearly represent the interests of foreign businessmen than the interests of their own people. Men like Donald Reid—who is one of the better of this category of leaders—may have their merits, but they are not the force of the future in Latin America. . . .

The movement of the future in Latin America is social revolution. The question is whether it is to be Communist or democratic revolution, and the choice which the Latin Americans make will depend in part on how the United States uses its great influence. It should be very clear that the choice is not between social revolution and conservative oligarchy but whether, by supporting reform, we bolster the popular non-Communist left or whether, by supporting unpopular oligarchies, we drive the rising generation of educated and patriotic young Latin Americans to an embittered and hostile form of communism like that of Fidel Castro in Cuba.

In my Senate speech of March 25, 1964, I commented as follows on the prospect of revolution:

I am not predicting violent revolutions in Latin America or elsewhere. Still less am I advocating them. I wish only to suggest that violent social revolutions are a possibility in countries where feudal oligarchies resist all meaningful change by peaceful means. We must not, in our preference for the democratic procedures envisioned by the Charter of Punta del Este, close our minds to the possibility that democratic procedures may fail in certain countries and that where democracy does fail violent social convulsions may occur.

I think that in the case of the Dominican Republic we did close our minds to the causes and to the essential legitimacy of revolution in a country in which democratic procedures had failed. That, I think, is the central fact concerning the participation of the United States in the Dominican revolution and, possibly as well, its major lesson for the future. I turn now to comment on some of the events which began last April 24 in Santo Domingo.

When the Dominican revolution began on Saturday, April 24, the United States had three options available. First, it could have supported the Reid Cabral government; second, it could have supported the revolutionary forces; and third, it could have done nothing.

The administration chose the last course. When Donald Reid Cabral asked for U.S. intervention on Sunday morning, April 25, he was given no encouragement. He then resigned, and

considerable disagreement ensued over the nature of the government to succeed him. The party of Juan Bosch, the PRD, or Dominican Revolutionary Party, asked for a "U.S. presence" at the transfer of government power but was given no encouragement. Thus, there began at that time a chaotic situation which amounted to civil war in a country without an effective government.

What happened in essence was that the Dominican military refused to support Reid and were equally opposed to Bosch or other PRD leaders as his successor. The PRD, which had the support of some military officers, announced that Rafael Molina Ureña, who had been President of the Senate during the Bosch regime, would govern as Provisional President pending Bosch's return. At this point, the military leaders delivered an ultimatum, which the rebels ignored, and at about 4:30 on the afternoon of April 25 the air force and navy began firing at the National Palace. Later in the day, PRD leaders asked the U.S. Embassy to use its influence to persuade the air force to stop the attacks. The Embassy made it clear it would not intervene on behalf of the rebels, although on the following day, Monday, April 26, the Embassy did persuade the military to stop air attacks for a limited time.

This was the first crucial point in the crisis. If the United States thought that Reid was giving the Dominican Republic the best government it had had or was likely to get, why did the United States not react more vigorously to support him? On the other hand, if the Reid government was thought to be beyond salvation, why did not the United States offer positive encouragement to the moderate forces involved in the coup, if not by providing the

"U.S. presence" requested by the PRD, then at least by letting it be known that the United States was not opposed to the prospective change of regimes or by encouraging the return of Juan Bosch to the Dominican Republic? In fact, according to available evidence, the U.S. Government made no effort to contact Bosch in the initial days of the crisis.

The United States was thus at the outset unwilling to support Reid and unwilling to support, if not positively opposed to, Bosch.

Events of the days following April 24 demonstrated that Reid had so little popular support that it can reasonably be argued that there was nothing the United States could have done, short of armed intervention, to save his regime. The more interesting question is why the United States was so reluctant to see Bosch returned to power. This is part of the larger question of why U.S. attitudes had changed so much since 1963 when Bosch, then in power, was warmly and repeatedly embraced and supported as few if any Latin American presidents have ever been supported by the United States.

The next crucial point in the Dominican story came on Tuesday, April 27, when rebel leaders, including Molina Ureña and Caamaño Deño, called at the U.S. Embassy seeking mediation and negotiations. At that time the military situation looked very bad for the rebel, or constitutionalist, forces. Ambassador Bennett, who had been instructed four times to work for a cease fire and for the formation of a military junta, felt he did not have authority to mediate; mediation, in his view, would have been "intervention." Mediation at that point might have been accomplished quietly and without massive military intervention. Twenty-four hours

later the Ambassador was pleading for the marines, and as we know some 20,000 soldiers were landed—American soldiers.

On the afternoon of April 27 General Wessin y Wessin's tanks seemed about to cross the Duarte bridge into the city of Santo Domingo and the rebel cause appeared hopeless. When the rebels felt themselves rebuffed at the American Embassy, some of their leaders, including Molina Urena, sought asylum in Latin American embassies in Santo Domingo. The administration has interpreted this as evidence that the non-Communist rebels recognized growing Communist influence in their movement and were consequently abandoning the revolution. Molina Urena has said simply that he sought asylum because he thought the revolutionary cause hopeless.

An opportunity was lost on April 27. Ambassador Bennett was in a position to bring possibly decisive mediating power to bear for a democratic solution, but he chose not to do so on the ground that the exercise of his good offices at that point would have constituted intervention. In the words of Washington Post Writer Murrey Marder—one of the press people who, to the best of my knowledge, has not been assailed as prejudiced:

It can be argued with considerable weight that late Tuesday, April 27, the United States threw away a fateful opportunity to try to prevent the sequence that produced the American intervention. It allowed the relatively leaderless revolt to pass into hands which it was to allege were Communist.[1]

The overriding reason for this mistake was the conviction of U.S. officials,

1 *Washington Post,* June 27, 1965, p. E3.

on the basis of evidence which was fragmentary at best, that the rebels were dominated by Communists. A related and perhaps equally important reason for the U.S. Embassy's refusal to mediate on April 27 was the desire for and, at that point, expectation of an antirebel victory. They therefore passed up an important opportunity to reduce or even eliminate communist influence by encouraging the moderate elements among the rebels and mediating for a democratic solution.

Owing to a degree of disorganization and timidity on the part of the antirebel forces which no one, including the U.S. Embassy and the rebels themselves, anticipated, the rebels were still fighting on the morning of Wednesday, April 28. Ambassador Bennett thereupon urgently recommended that the antirebels under Air Force General de los Santos be furnished 50 walkie-talkies from U.S. Defense Department stocks in Puerto Rico. Repeating this recommendation later in the day, Bennett said that the issue was one between Castroism and its opponents. The antirebels themselves asked for armed U.S. intervention on their side; this request was refused at that time.

During the day, however, the situation deteriorated rapidly, from the point of view of public order in general and of the antirebels in particular. In midafternoon of April 28 Colonel Pedro Bartolomé Benoit, head of a junta which had been hastily assembled, asked again, this time in writing, for U.S. troops on the ground that this was the only way to prevent a Communist takeover; no mention was made of the junta's inability to protect American lives. This request was denied in Washington, and Benoit was thereupon told that the United States would not intervene unless he said he could not protect

American citizens present in the Dominican Republic. Benoit was thus told in effect that if he said American lives were in danger the United States would intervene. And that is precisely what happened.

It was at this point, on April 28, that events acquired something of the predestiny of a Greek tragedy. Subsequent events—the failure of the missions of John Bartlow Martin and McGeorge Bundy, the conversion of the U.S. force into an inter-American force, the enforced stalemate between the rebels under Caamaño Deño and the Imbert junta, the OAS mediation and the tortuous negotiations for a provisional government—have all been widely reported and were not fully explored in the committee hearings. In any case, the general direction of events was largely determined by the fateful decision of April 28. Once the Marines landed on that day, and especially after they were heavily reinforced in the days immediately following, the die was cast and the United States found itself deeply involved in the Dominican civil conflict, with no visible way to extricate itself, and with its hemisphere relations complicated in a way that few could have foreseen and no one could have desired.

The danger to American lives was more a pretext than a reason for the massive U.S. intervention that began on the evening of April 28. In fact, no American lives were lost in Santo Domingo until the Marines began exchanging fire with the rebels after April 28; reports of widespread shooting that endangered American lives turned out to be exaggerated.

Nevertheless, there can be no question that Santo Domingo was not a particularly safe place to be in the last days of April 1965. There was fighting in the streets, aircraft were strafing parts of the city, and there was indiscriminate shooting. I think that the United States would have been justified in landing a small force for the express purpose of removing U.S. citizens and other foreigners from the island. Had such a force been landed and then promptly withdrawn when it had completed its mission, I do not think that any fair-minded observer at home or abroad would have considered the United States to have exceeded its rights and responsibilities.

The United States intervened in the Dominican Republic for the purpose of preventing the victory of a revolutionary force which was judged to be Communist dominated. On the basis of Ambassador Bennett's messages to Washington, there is no doubt that the threat of communism rather than danger to American lives was his primary reason for recommending military intervention.

The question of the degree of Communist influence is therefore crucial, but it cannot be answered with certainty. The weight of the evidence is that Communists did not participate in planning the revolution—indeed, there is some indication that it took them by surprise—but that they very rapidly began to try to take advantage of it and to seize control of it. The evidence does not establish that the Communists at any time actually had control of the revolution. There is little doubt that they had influence within the revolutionary movement, but the degree of that influence remains a matter of speculation. . . .

It is, perhaps, understandable that administration officials should have felt some sense of panic; after all, the Foreign Service officer who had the misfortune to be assigned to the Cuban desk at the time of Castro's rise to power has had his career ruined by congressional committees. Furthermore, even without this consideration, the decisions regarding the Dominican Republic had to be made under great pressure and on the basis of inconclusive information. In charity, this can be accepted as a reason why the decisions were mistaken; but it does not change the conclusion that they were mistaken. . . .

On the basis of the record, there is ample justification for concluding that, at least from the time Reid resigned, U.S. policy was directed toward construction of a military junta which hopefully would restore peace and conduct free elections. That is to say that U.S. policy was directed against the return of Bosch and against the success of the rebel movement. . . .

One is led, therefore, to the conclusion that U.S. policymakers were unduly timid and alarmist in refusing to gamble on the forces of reform and social change. The bitter irony of such timidity is that by casting its lot with the forces of the status quo, in the probably vain hope that these forces could be induced to permit at least some reform and social change, the United States almost certainly helped the Communists to acquire converts whom they otherwise could not have won.

How vain the hopes of U.S. policymakers were is amply demonstrated by events since April 28. The junta led by General Antonio Imbert, which succeeded the junta led by Colonel Benoit, proved quite intractable and indeed filled the airwaves daily with denunciations of the United States and the Organization of American States for preventing it from wiping out the Communist rebels. These are the same military forces which on April 28 were refusing to fight the rebels and begging for U.S. intervention. Our aim apparently was to use Imbert as a counterpoise to Caamaño Deño in the ill-founded hope that non-Communist liberals would be drawn away from the rebel side.

In practice, instead of Imbert becoming our tractable instrument, we to a certain extent, became his: he clung tenaciously to the power we gave him and was at least as intransigent as the rebels in the protracted negotiations for a provisional government.

The resignation of Imbert and his junta provides grounds for hope that a strong popular government may come to power in the Dominican Republic, but that hope must be tempered by the fact that the military continues to wield great power in Dominican politics—power which it probably would not now have if the United States had not intervened to save it from defeat last April 28. Even with a provisional government installed in Santo Domingo, and with the prospect of an election in 9 months, there remains the basic problem of a deep and widespread demand for social change. The prospect for such social change is circumscribed by the fact that the military has not surrendered and cannot be expected voluntarily to surrender its entrenched position of privilege and outrageous corruption. . . .

I turn now to some broader and long-term implications of the Dominican tragedy, first to some considerations relating to the Organization of American States and its charter, then to the problem of reaction and revolution in Latin America, finally to a suggestion for a free and, I believe, healthier relationship between the United States and Latin America.

Article 15 of the Charter of the Organization of American States says that:

No state or group of states has the right to intervene, directly or indirectly, for any reason whatever, in the internal or external affairs of any other state.

Article 17 states that:

The territory of a state is inviolable; it may not be the object, even temporarily, of military occupation or of other measures of force taken by another state, directly or indirectly, on any grounds whatever.

These clauses are not ambiguous. They mean that, with one exception to be noted, all forms of forcible intervention are absolutely prohibited among the American States. It may be that we should never have accepted this commitment at Bogotá in 1948; it is obvious from all the talk one hears these days about the obsoleteness of the principle of nonintervention that some U.S. officials regret our commitment to it. The fact remains that we are committed to it, not partially or temporarily or insofar as we find it compatible with our vital interests but almost absolutely. It represents our word and our bond and our willingness to honor the solemn commitments embodied in a treaty which was ratified by the Senate on August 28, 1950.

There are those who might concede the point of law but who would also argue that such considerations have to do with our ideals rather than our interests and are therefore of secondary importance. I do not believe that is true. We are currently fighting a war in Vietnam, largely, we are told, because it would be a disaster if the United States failed to honor its word and its commitment; the matter, we are told, is one of vital national interest. I do not see why it is any less a matter of vital interest to honor a clear and explicit treaty obligation in the Americas than it is to honor the much more ambiguous and less formal promises we have made to the South Vietnamese.

The sole exception to the prohibitions of articles 15 and 17 is spelled out in article 19 of the OAS Charter, which states that "measures adopted for the maintenance of peace and security in accordance with existing treaties do not constitute a violation of the principles set forth in articles 15 and 17.". . .

The United States thus had legal recourse when the Dominican crisis broke on April 24, 1965. We could have called an urgent session of the Council of the OAS for the purpose of invoking article 6 of the Rio Treaty. But we did not do so. The administration has argued that there was no time to consult the OAS, although there was time to consult—or inform—the congressional leadership. The United States thus intervened in the Dominican Republic unilaterally—and illegally.

Advising the Latin American countries of our action after the fact did not constitute compliance with the OAS Charter or the Rio Treaty; nor, indeed, would advising them before the fact have constituted compliance. One does not comply with the law by notifying interested parties in advance of one's intent to violate it. Inter-American law requires consultation for the purpose of shaping a collective decision. Only on the basis of advance consultation and agreement could we have undertaken a legal intervention in the Dominican Republic.

It is possible, had we undertaken such consultations, that our Latin American partners would have delayed a decision; it is possible that they would have refused to authorize collective intervention. My own feeling is that the situation in any case did not justify military intervention except for the limited purpose of evacuating U.S. citizens and other foreigners, but even if it seemed to us that it did, we should not have undertaken it without the advance consent of our Latin American allies. We should not have done so because the word and the honor of the United States were at stake just as much—at least as much—in the Dominican crisis as they are in Vietnam and Korea and Berlin and all the places around the globe which we have committed ourselves to defend.

There is another important reason for compliance with the law. The United States is a conservative power in the world in the sense that most of its vital interests are served by stability and order. Law is the essential foundation of stability and order both within societies and in international relations. . . .

There are those who defend U.S. unilateral intervention in the Dominican Republic on the ground that the principle of nonintervention as spelled out in the OAS Charter is obsolete. The argument is unfortunate on two grounds. First, the contention of obsoleteness justifies an effort to bring about changes in the OAS Charter by due process of law, but it does not justify violation of the Charter. Second, the view that the principle of nonintervention is obsolete is one held by certain U.S. officials; most Latin Americans would argue that, far from being obsolete, the principle of nonintervention was and remains the heart and core of the inter-American system. Insofar as it is honored, it provides them with something that many in the United States find it hard to believe they could suppose they need: protection from the United States. . . .

In the eyes of educated, energetic and patriotic young Latin Americans—which is to say, the generation that will make or break the Alliance for Progress—the United States committed a worse offense in the Dominican Republic than just intervention; it intervened against social revolution and in support, at least temporarily, of a corrupt, reactionary military oligarchy. . . .

We have embarassed before their own people the democratic reformers who have counseled trust and partnership with the United States. We have lent credence to the idea that the United States is the enemy of social revolution in Latin America and that the only choice Latin Americans have is between communism and reaction. . . .

In conclusion, I suggest that a new and healthier relationship between the United States and Latin America must be a freer relationship than that of the past.

The United States is a world power with world responsibilities and to it the inter-American system represents a sensible way of maintaining law and order in the region closest to the United States. To the extent that it functions as we want it to function, one of the inter-American system's important advantages is that it stabilizes relations within the western hemisphere and thus frees the United States to act on its world wide responsibilities.

To Latin Americans, on the other hand, the inter-American system is politically and psychologically confining. It has the effect, so to speak, of cooping them up in the Western Hemisphere, giving them the feeling that there is no way to break out of the usually well-in-

tentioned but often stifling embrace of the United States. In their hearts, I have no doubt, most Latin Americans would like to be free of us, just as a son or daughter coming of age wishes to be free of an over-protective parent. A great many of those Latin Americans for whom Castro still has some appeal—and there are now more, I would guess, than before last April 28—are attracted not, I feel, because they are infatuated with communism, but because Cuba, albeit at the price of almost complete dependency on the Soviet Union, has broken out of the orbit of the United States. . . .

Perhaps, then, the foremost immediate requirement for a new and more friendly relationship between Latin America and the United States in the long run is not closer ties and new institutional bonds but a loosening of existing ties and institutional bonds. It is an established psychological principle —or, for that matter, just commonsense —that the strongest and most viable personal bonds are those which are voluntary, a voluntary bond being, by definition, an arrangement which one is free to enter or not to enter. I do not see why the same principle should not operate in relations between nations. If it does, it would follow that the first step toward stronger ties between Latin America and the United States would be the creation of a situation in which Latin American countries would be free, and would feel free, to maintain or sever existing ties as they see fit and, perhaps more important, to establish new arrangements, both among themselves and with nations outside the hemisphere, in which the United States would not participate.

President Frei of Chile has taken an initiative to this end. He has visited European leaders and apparently indicated that his Christian Democratic Government is interested in establishing new political, economic, and cultural links with European countries. For the reasons suggested, I think this is an intelligent and constructive step.

I think further that it would be a fine thing if Latin American countries were to undertake a program of their own for "building bridges" to the world beyond the Western Hemisphere—to Europe and Asia and Africa, and to the Communist countries if they wish. Such relationships, to be sure, would involve a loosening of ties to the United States in the immediate future, but in the long run, I feel sure they would make for both happier and stronger bonds with the United States —happier because they would be free, stronger because they would be dignified and self-respecting as they never had been before.

16

The Dominican Crisis:
Correcting Some Misconceptions

Thomas C. Mann

From Thomas C. Mann, "The Dominican Crisis: Correcting Some Misconceptions," *Department of State Bulletin,* LIII, No. 1376 (November 8, 1965), pp. 730–38.

In an address to the Inter-American Press Association of October 12, 1965, Under Secretary of State Thomas A. Mann offered a concise, ex post facto defense of the Johnson Administration's intervention in the Dominican civil war. Although Mann stressed that he did not intend his speech to be "in answer to any particular commentary on our policies," the discerning reader will note that it replied almost point by point to criticisms raised by Fulbright.

In selecting a subject of current interest, I have chosen to speak about some of the issues that have arisen in the Dominican crisis principally because it seems to me that there are certain misconceptions that ought to be corrected.

I should like to make it clear that my remarks today are not in answer to any particular commentary on our policies. There has been a great deal of comment both here and abroad. My simple purpose is to clarify a number of misconceptions.

NONINTERVENTION NOT AN OBSOLETE DOCTRINE

It has been suggested that nonintervention is thought by some to be an obsolete doctrine.

I know of no Washington officials who think this way. On the contrary, I believe unilateral intervention by one American state in the internal political affairs of another is not only proscribed in the OAS [Organization of American States] Charter but that nonintervention is a keystone of the structure of the inter-American system. American states have a treaty as well as a sovereign right to choose their political, social, and economic systems free of all outside interference.

If we start from this point, it is not difficult to identify two distinct areas of confusion:

The first confusion comes from those who say, however obliquely, that it is necessary unilaterally to intervene —"support" is the word most often used—in favor of political parties of the non-Communist left.

With all respect, this thesis is justified by the same rhetoric that was used to justify our unilateral interventions in the past.

But this thesis overlooks the fact that countries want to solve their internal political problems in their own way. Latin Americans do not want a paternalistic United States deciding which particular political faction should rule their countries. They do not want the United States to launch itself again on what one scholar described as a "civilizing mission," no matter how good its intentions are.

This explains why, in the case of the Dominican Republic, we refrained during the first days of violence from "supporting" the outgoing government or "supporting" either of the factions contending for power. It explains why we and others thought it best to work for a cease-fire and to encourage the rival Dominican factions to meet together and agree on a Dominican solution to a Dominican problem. It explains why, to use a phrase of international law, we offered our good offices rather than attempting to preside over a meeting for the purpose of proposing political solutions with a "made in USA" label on them.

The second area of confusion concerns the response which an American state, or the Organization of American States as a whole, can make to intervention. When, in other words, a Communist state has intervened in the internal affairs of an American state by training, directing, financing, and organizing indigenous Communist elements to take control of the government of an American state by force and violence, should other American states be powerless to lend assistance? Are Communists free to intervene while democratic states are powerless to frustrate that intervention?

This is not so much a question of intervention as it is of whether weak and fragile states should be helped to maintain their independence when they are under attack by subversive elements responding to direction from abroad.

Surely we have learned from the October 1962 missile crisis that the establishment of Communist military bases in this hemisphere threatens the security of every American state. Surely we have learned that political control of an American state by Communists is but the prelude for use of that country as a base for further aggressions.

A number of juridical questions deserve consideration—not in an atmosphere of crisis, demanding an immediate decision, but in an atmosphere of calmness and objectivity. As illustrative of the kind of questions that ought to be considered, I pose these two:

What distinctions ought to be made, on the one hand, between subversive activities which do not constitute an immediate danger to an American state and, on the other, those which, because of their intensity and external direction, do constitute a danger to the peace and security of the country and the hemisphere?

Second, assuming that, as I have suggested, certain subversive activities do constitute a threat to the peace and security of the hemisphere, what response is permitted within the framework of the inter-American system?

I do not offer precise answers to these questions at this time. I only wish to say that the problem of Communist subversion in the hemisphere is a real one. It should not be brushed aside on a false assumption that American states are prohibited by inter-American law from dealing with it.

SERIOUSNESS OF COMMUNIST SUBVERSION

I turn now to a political question: How seriously should we regard Communist subversion in this hemisphere?

I will not take your time to remind you of the expansionist history of the Communist countries in recent years in Eastern Europe and in Asia. The history and the tactics used are well known.

Only last month the Defense Minister of Communist China, in what was described as a major doctrinal article, stated that the United States, which he considered the principal obstacle to Communist domination of the world, must be defeated "piece by piece" in "peoples' wars" in Africa, Asia, and Latin America. This doctrine is the same as Lenin's. But the Minister's candor in reminding us of Mao's dictum that "political power grows out of the barrel of a gun" is revealing. Quoting Mao, he states:

The seizure of power by armed force, the settlement of the issue by war is the central task and the highest form of revolution. This Marxist-Leninist principle of revolution holds good universally for China and for all other countries.

The so-called "peoples' wars" or "wars of national liberation" are the tactic used in cases where the direct employment of military force is not feasible. Less than a year ago Communist parties from the hemisphere met in Havana and pledged to each other an increase in their coordinated efforts to subvert free institutions in this hemisphere.

It is difficult to understand the precise reasons why some appear to be less concerned than others about attempts to expand by force and violence areas of Communist domination in this hemisphere.

One point of view I have heard expressed as late as 2 years ago is that the "Castro revolution" should be looked at sympathetically because "it has done so much for the Cuban people." "Please keep an open mind about the Castro revolution" is a phrase I have heard. I do not believe this view is held by any United States Government official, appointed or elected. But it still has a few articulate and influential proponents. If this were United States policy, only dictatorships of the right would be opposed, not Communist dictatorships of the left.

A second school of thought says in substance that the way to preserve freedom in this hemisphere is to achieve rapidly a higher level of social justice, economic progress, and political democracy. I know of no one in the Government of the United States who does not have a deep and sincere conviction that the goals of the Alliance for Progress should be achieved as rapidly as possible. We support the Alliance goals not because there are Communists in the world but because the goals are right and good and because they are consistent with our national and hemispheric traditions and ideals. As President Johnson said in August of this year:[1]

... in my nation, like yours, we are still struggling to find justice for all of our people. And because we are fortunate in abundance, we feel that morality requires that we must also try to help others who seek it for their own people, too.

The issue is not whether we should pursue the Alliance programs. The

[1] BULLETIN, of Sept. 13, 1965, p. 426.

issue is not whether faster progress under the Alliance will make it more difficult for subversive elements to achieve their purpose. The issue is whether those programs, by themselves and standing alone, can be expected to frustrate Communist subversion by force and terror.

This recalls to mind a story I read somewhere several years ago. A young man went alone into the jungle in search of a tiger. When he found a tiger he began to explain in great detail and with considerable persuasiveness why peace between tigerkind and mankind was desirable. To prove his good faith he had come without arms and—. The young man's statement of good will ended here at midsentence. At this point in the monolog the tiger ate the man.

In my experience the men who have contributed most to social, economic, and political reform in this hemisphere are men who have understood that the Communist danger is not met by good works alone.

Another theory points out that the new generations in Eastern Europe want greater freedom to express themselves and a higher standard of living. Decentralization, profit incentives, greater autonomy for light industrial plants and farms, quality rather than quantity goals—all these and other topics of debate suggest a movement away from the old Marxist practices. Historic rivalries between Russia and China are stressed. The suggestion is made that the Soviet Union will, in its own interest, inevitably draw closer to Western Europe.

I suppose everyone welcomes certain liberal trends in Eastern Europe. However limited in scope they may be—and they are limited—they represent a step in the right direction. I suppose everyone would welcome a decision by the Soviet Union to abandon the idea of world revolution by force, a decision to leave others alone, a decision to put its enormous weight on the side of those who hope for a truly pacific relationship between the Communist and the free parts of the world.

We ought to welcome liberalizing thought and action in Eastern Europe. We ought to seek ways, compatible with our own security interests and those of the free world, gradually to find a basis for a truly pacific relationship with Eastern Europe.

But it is wrong to present as a current reality that which is now only a hope for the future. All Communists still openly proclaim their belief in a world revolution achieved by force. They are still supporting subversion in the Western Hemisphere. It would be difficult indeed to convince those who have lived recently for long periods in Latin America that Communists are not working harder than ever to export the "revolution of the Sierra Maestra to the Andes."

Lastly, there is the thesis that we tend to overestimate the ability of the Communists to subvert free governments.

As near as I can discover, this particular theory comes down to this: A number of Western European and Latin American governments have been able to stand up against subversive elements; therefore it is to be assumed that all developing nations will be able to do likewise. All that is needed is more faith in democracy.

It is true that today there are a number of states in Europe and the developing areas of the world which have achieved the kind of maturity and tradition which gives them a large degree of security. But it is equally true that other states are vulnerable simply because they have not yet been able to modernize their societies and to acquire the maturity, broad popular support, the disciplines, and the traditions which are elements of national unity and strength.

It is to these weaker, more fragile societies that Communist subversive efforts will be directed in the future. One has only to look around the world today to see that great differences exist between areas and between states in terms of their vulnerability to demagoguery and to the use of force exercised by a disciplined minority. It is folly to assume that the experience of one nation or one culture is even a good indicator of what will happen in an entirely different situation.

What we can be certain of is that the greatest danger to freedom and to peace will come when the free world is confused, uncertain, divided, and weak—when expansionistic communism comes to believe that new aggressions can be committed without risk.

In addition to these generalities there are a number of misconceptions about particular United States actions in the recent Dominican crisis.[2]

MISCONCEPTION: REASON FOR U.S. ACTION

One misconception is that danger to American lives was more a pretext than a reason for United States action.

This is demonstrably incorrect.

Violence in the Dominican Republic began on April 24, 1965. By April 25–26 there had been a breakdown in the maintenance of order in the capital

[2] For background, see *ibid.*, Sept. 20, 1965, p. 477, and Sept. 27, 1965, p. 514.

city. Planes of the Dominican Air Force were strafing and bombing the National Palace and other points. Artillery fire between the rebel and antirebel forces was being exchanged in the eastern part of the city. Armed rebel bands roamed the streets looking for anyone who was suspected of being unsympathetic to their cause. The police were special targets and suffered heavy casualties; for all practical purposes the police force distintegrated and police protection broke down completely. Radio and telephone stations in Santo Domingo were in the hands of rebel groups.

The *first* important decision made in Washington was to evacuate, through the port of Jaina, all those who wished to leave.

American tourists, unable to leave the capital by commercial transportation, had requested evacuation. On April 27 a group of about 1,000 people of various nationalities, mostly women and children, gathered at and near the Hotel Embajador, which had been designated as the assembly point for evacuation. The American Embassy asked for and received promises of safe conduct from both the rebel and antirebel groups so that they could be moved from the assembly point by road to Jaina, seven miles to the west.

While the evacuees were being processed, an armed group appeared at the hotel and engaged in indiscriminate firing both in the hotel itself and on the grounds nearby, endangering the lives of many people. Only by good fortune was the first evacuation successfully carried out through Jaina on April 27 without loss of life.

On the following day, April 28, another large crowd gathered at the Hotel Embajador desiring evacuation. By this time the road to Jaina was under sniper fire; our Embassy was informed by police authorities that they could no longer be responsible for the protection of American lives.

Meanwhile the rebel government had dissolved with many of its members, including Molina Ureña, seeking asylum. There were no constituted authorities on the rebel side. There were, in fact, no constituted authorities of any kind in the city at this time and for several days thereafter. Total anarchy prevailed.

The *second* major decision was to order that some 500 Marines be landed for the purpose of protecting Americans and making possible the continuation of the evacuation process by helicopter.

This small number of Marines established a small perimeter around the Hotel Embajador area. This permitted helicopters to land and take off and gave protection to those assembled for evacuation.

The evacuation of the second group was begun as night came on the 28th. Several hundred more were evacuated then. Around 5,000 persons of many nationalities were evacuated during the crisis.

While the evacuation by helicopter was taking place, the United States Embassy and Chancery were under steady sniper fire, endangering the lives of Americans there. A small group of Marines was sent from the Hotel Embajador area to the United States Embassy in order to reinforce the Marine Guard there.

The facts which I have outlined are undisputed. Whatever may have been the requests or desires or recommendations of others, the action taken by Washington in the evening of April 28 had as its purpose the protection and evacuation of unarmed civilians.

We did not consider it necessary to wait until innocent civilians had been killed in order to prove to the most skeptical that lives were in danger. Had we done this we should have been derelict in our duty to our citizens. These facts are also obviously relevant to the assertions that we should have left those desiring evacuation on the beach until the complex machinery of the OAS was able to function.

MISCONCEPTION: USE OF MILITARY FORCE

It is charged that the administration assumed from the beginning that the revolution was Communist dominated and that it should therefore be opposed by military force.

This assertion is incorrect for the simple reason that when the second decision (to evacuate by helicopter) was taken it was still our hope that United States troops could be withdrawn as soon as the evacuation was completed. There was a sound basis for this on the 28th.

But with each passing day hope had been diminishing that the non-Communist elements on the rebel side would either reach a cease-fire agreement with the bulk of the armed forces opposing them or bring the armed civilians and paramilitary on the rebel side under effective control. By the evening of April 29 it became clear that the armed forces at San Isidro would be nothing but observers. General Wessin, for reasons best known to him, elected not to support General Montas's column, which was split up as it entered the city from the west and, after some initial success, disintegrated. As it turned out, Wessin never did move his forces into the city.

Whereas on the evening of the 28th it appeared that order might be restored by the Dominicans themselves, by the evening of the 29th the reverse appeared to be the case. Rebel bands, still without any visible cohesion except among the Communist components, were roaming at will into the city, carrying violence with them. There could be no assurance that order could even be maintained in the balance of the country.

The United States Government had, of course, long since been aware of, and concerned about, the growth of Communist influence in the Dominican Republic. This concern grew when large quantities of arms were turned over to civilians and distributed by known and identified leaders of Communist parties to their partisans in the early days of the crisis. But there is a very important distinction to be made between concern and a decision to use armed force.

Thus it was not until the evening of the 29th that a decision had to be made on whether the Communist elements in the rebel camp presented a clear and imminent peril to the freedom of the Dominican nation.

I do not know what the United States Government might have decided that evening had we not then been engaged in evacuation operations— had not the lives of innocent people been in danger. Perhaps under other circumstances we might have awaited developments for a while longer. Certainly we should have welcomed time to permit the OAS which, by this time was working on the problem, to take effective action.

But these were not the facts, and this was not the situation. We were already engaged in evacuating our citizens and civilians of many other nationalities. Thousands remained to be evacuated. We did not wish to abandon them by withdrawing our men and helicopters from the small perimeter on the western

edge of the town. We did not wish to abandon those in our Embassy under fire and other nationals without either protection or means of leaving the island.

Against this background the *third* important decision was taken in the evening of April 29th. In form it was to reinforce the small number holding the perimeter near the beach and to land troops at the San Isidro airport a few miles east of the capital.

The saving of lives continued to be an objective. But from this third decision (to land additional troops) flowed a number of actions in the following days.

First, the small perimeter around the hotel was expanded into an International Safety Zone, a safehaven for all those who wished to repair to it. This was done both for humanitarian reasons and in response to requests for protection from a number of embassies which had come under small-arms fire from snipers.

Second, a line of communication, a corridor, was established between the troops in the San Isidro area and the troops in the International Safety Zone. This corridor had the effect of interposing troops between the two contending armed factions. The interposition prevented a bloodbath that otherwise would have occurred eventually. It prevented a widening of the civil war. It helped to stabilize the countryside. It opened the way for a political settlement under the auspices of the OAS.

Much of the confusion concerning these events derives from attempts to lift official statements out of their time context. Statements made in one phase of the crisis were compared with statements made in another phase. These confusions have not been helpful to the American states in their efforts to find solutions to delicate and difficult problems.

MISCONCEPTION: DEGREE OF COMMUNIST INFLUENCE

The degree of Communist influence in the rebel movement has been especially questioned.

It will not be possible, in this short speech, to tell the complete story of the degree of Communist influence and strength in the rebel movement. The facts we already have would fill a volume. Each passing day brings additional facts to light. The danger will soon become apparent even to the most skeptical. In a very real sense the danger still exists.

All those in our Government who had full access to official information were convinced that the landing of additional troops was necessary in view of the clear and present danger of the forcible seizure of power by the Communists. The evidence we have indicates that at that stage the paramilitary forces under the control of known Communists exceeded in military strength the forces controlled by the non-Communist elements within the rebel movement. Equally important is the fact that these non-Communist elements were working hand in glove with the Communists.

The strength of the Communist component of the rebel side must be measured not only by its men and arms and its superior discipline but by the weakness, the divisions, and the lack of leadership within the rebel movement. It needs to be measured in light of the fact that the Communists were operating in a total political vacuum during the early days of the crisis. There were no moderate forces on either the rebel or antirebel side with the will and the capacity to offer effective resistance to them. Indeed, from the dissolution of the Molina Urena regime on April 27 until Colonel Caamaño formed his regime on May 3 there was no identifiable leadership on the rebel side other than that of the Communists.

MISCONCEPTION: REFORM MOVEMENTS AND COMMUNISM

Next, it is said that the United States overlooked the fact that reform movements are likely to attract Communist support; that the United States failed to perceive that, if it is automatically to oppose any reform movement that Communists adhere to, it is likely to end up opposing every reform movement and, in the process, make itself a prisoner of reactionaries.

This theory assumes that an alliance between the Communists and the non-Communist left in a popular front is an act of nature. This is really not different in essence from the Marxian theory that Communists are "in the vanguard" of all truly revolutionary movements.

In Western Europe this theory has been proved false. By and large, Communists have failed to seize power there because European reformers were their most determined and effective opponents. In contrast, non-Communist revolutionaries in Eastern Europe and elsewhere have formed popular fronts with Communists.

The need to distinguish between a reform movement allied with the Communists and a movement dedicated to reform in freedom should be emphasized over and over again. Indeed, it is precisely the failure to make this distinction—the tendency of some to lump all "reformers" together and to evaluate them solely on the basis of their rhetoric

—that causes a great deal of the confusion.

Many of you will recall De Tocqueville's conclusions about the causes of the Reign of Terror, which detracted from the real achievements of the French Revolution:

When we closely study the French Revolution we find that it was conducted in precisely the same spirit as that which gave rise to so many books expounding theories of government in the abstract. Our revolutionaries had the same fondness for broad generalizations, cut-and-dried legislative systems, and a pedantic symmetry; the same contempt for hard facts; the same taste for reshaping institutions on novel, ingenious, original lines; the same desire to reconstruct the entire constitution according to the rules of logic and a preconceived system instead of trying to rectify its faulty parts. The result was nothing short of disastrous; for what is a merit in the writer may well be a vice in the statesman and the very qualities which go to make great literature can lead to catastrophic revolutions.

Even the politicians' phraseology was borrowed largely from the books they read; it was cluttered up with abstract words, gaudy flowers of speech, sonorous cliches, and literary turns of phrase.

Popular fronts do not have as their principal objective the noble purpose of democratic reform. Their principal objective is political power. They are often formed by those who want the Communist vote in order to get elected to office. Sometimes they are formed because the help of disciplined Communists is needed to overthrow a government. They are sometimes formed by politicians already in power to "buy their peace." The rationale I have heard is a revealing one: "I know they are dangerous. But I can control them." Sometimes this estimate proves to be correct. More often it does not.

As President Kennedy said in his address at the Free University of Berlin on June 26, 1963: [3]

As I said this morning, I am not impressed by the opportunities open to popular fronts throughout the world. I do not believe that any democrat can successfully ride that tiger.

But the point I wish to make is that Communist participation is not necessary in order to carry out reforms. There are several governments I can think of which are not allied with Communists and which are doing a pretty good job of reform. I am not conscious that this great country of ours has, in cooperating with these and other countries, become a prisoner of any group.

Moreover, popular fronts serve Communist ends. Communists gain from them a respectability they do not deserve. They use this respectability to infiltrate their partisans into the educational system, organized worker and farm groups, the mass media, and, of course, the government itself. In participating in popular fronts politicians usually have in mind a short-term, personal, political, selfish gain. On the other hand, Communists are content to work today in order to prepare for tomorrow.

We do not really have to choose between reaction and leftist extremism. There is a large and growing number of people in Latin America dedicated to rapid and far-reaching reform. New political movements, organized on an institutional rather than a personalized base, give promise of organizing and leading those who so desperately want to build modern societies. The Latin American military contain in their

[3] *Ibid.,* July 22, 1963, p. 125.

ranks many able and dedicated men who do not deserve to be smeared with the brush that ought to be reserved for the few. The church is providing leadership in many areas of social progress. Many of the younger men from all sectors of society are conscious of the need for change and are helping to promote it. Organized labor is growing in strength and could be a powerful influence for progress.

AMERICA'S CONTINUING REVOLUTION

It is also said that our country is not much in sympathy with revolution and that our Revolution of 1776 was not much of an upheaval compared to the Russian and other revolutions.

Perhaps these words are to be interpreted as suggesting that in our revolution the violence was confined largely to the battlefields and that, consequently, it cannot be compared with the number of civilians killed under the guillotine or with the millions who disappeared in the familiar Communist purges. If so, I fail to see why violence itself should be considered a desirable end.

If, on the other hand, it is intended to say that the basic values of political and economic freedom, which were the principal motive force of the Revolution of 1776, are inferior to others, then there are differences in opinion which are indeed significant. Our political, economic, and social systems have produced a greater degree of individual freedom, a more even-handed, impartial administration of law, higher levels of income, a more equitable distribution of an ever-rising national product, more equality of opportunity, more religious freedom, a greater appreciation of the value of the spirit and of the dignity of man than has been heretofore achieved by any nation in history.

Our revolution did not start and end in 1776. It is a continuing phenomenon. The frontiers of opportunity, of knowledge, of health, of social justice and economic and political progress in our land are being expanded still further in President Johnson's program for the Great Society.

Certainly if one compares the achievements of our system with that of others, we have no need to be apologetic or defensive. On the contrary, we can take great pride in our accomplishments and in our determination for even greater improvement in the future.

17

Presidential Mission: 1965

John Bartlow Martin

From John Bartlow Martin, *Overtaken By Events: The Dominican Crisis—From the Fall of Trujillo to the Civil War* (Garden City, N.Y.: Doubleday & Company, Inc., 1966), pp. 672–76, 704–8. Copyright © 1966 by John Bartlow Martin. Reprinted by permission of the author and Doubleday & Company, Inc.

John Bartlow Martin was U.S. Ambassador to the Dominican Republic following the fall of Trujillo and was instrumental in engineering the free elections that brought Juan Bosch to the presidency in February, 1963. In spite of grave doubts about Bosch's ability, Martin remained a strong supporter of the new government until it was overthrown after only seven months by a rightist military coup. In early May, 1965, he returned to the Dominican Republic at President Johnson's request to assess the degree of Communist domination of the self-proclaimed pro-Bosch rebels in the ongoing civil war. Ironically, it appears that Martin's conclusion that Communists had in fact captured the rebel movement may have been pivotal in Washington's final decision to deny them power at almost any cost.

In this brief excerpt from his memoirs, Martin sets forth the evidence he relied upon for his report and attempts to answer "five main questions about our Dominican policy." It is noteworthy that he takes issue with some of the actions of U.S. Ambassador Bennett and concedes that Washington was less than candid in explaining its goals. Perhaps even more interesting is his emphasis upon the collapse of the Dominican political structure and ensuing "bloodbath." Incidentally, Tad Szulc remarks in his eye-witness account that Martin may have "let himself slide too easily into despair" at "finding chaos and bloodshed...in a country in which he had placed so many personal hopes."[1] Certainly one may detect more than a note of bitter disappointment between the lines that follow.

[Harry Shlaudeman, the State Department Dominican desk officer] had spent Saturday afternoon, and he and I spent Saturday night and Sunday, studying the massive evidence assembled by our intelligence agencies and quietly talking to Dominicans we knew personally on both sides. A frightened businessman said, "Your troops saved us from communism." And a foreign

[1] Tad Szulc, *Dominican Diary* (New York: Dell, 1966), p. 118

diplomat shouted, "You saved our lives." A rebel leader said bitterly, "Your troops killed the revolution— we had won when they arrived." One day a stranger cried happily, "Meester Martin! *¡Aquí viene la democracia!"* —that is, freely, "Here's Mr. Martin, here comes democracy!" Late one night, riding in a bucking helicopter, a man whose son was fighting alongside the rebels told me, "They have all gone crazy. All the Dominicans."

I took stock.

At the outset, the rebellion had been a long-planned military revolt led politically by Juan Bosch's PRD, aided by other politicians, in an attempt to reverse the *golpe* against Bosch of September 1963. Among the PRD leaders had been Molina Ureña and Peña Gómez, both passionately dedicated to Bosch's—and our—ideals of liberty and justice.

Among the military men, some had been well-intentioned, some adventurers. The plotting of Bosch, the plotting of the military, and Reid's own ambition had converged to overthrow him.

And the rebellion had been joined too by Castro/Communists. Among these were several the reader will recognize from my time—Juan and Félix Ducoudray, the PSP leaders; Asdrúbal Domínguez and Antonio Isa Conde of the PSP; Gustavo Federico Ricart-Ricart and Cayetano Rodríguez, both central committee members of the MPD; and Jaime Durán and Fidelio Despradel, both of the extremist wing of the 14th of June. U.S. intelligence sources listed some seventy others, including Pedro Julio Mir Valentine, PSP central committee member and friend of Fidel Castro, frequent traveler to Cuba; and Hugo Tolentino Dipp, who had received guerrilla train-

ing in Cuba and Soviet bloc countries and become the PSP chief of a Cuba-trained guerrilla unit. During the Civil War, our intelligence agents saw many of these men at rebel headquarters or strongpoints. Independently, Shlaudeman and I were told by thoroughly trustworthy sources that they were there. Both true Communist parties— PSP and MPD—were represented, and so was the extremist wing of the 14th of June. The PSP and 14th of June seem to have been the most militant, at least at the outset, although in my time the MPD had been more violent. (Later on, the PSP officially changed its name to the Dominican Communist Party, saying, in a newspaper that sprang up during the Civil War, that everyone knew it had always been Communist in ideology and its new name was adopted because it was "scientifically exact." The MPD, vying with the PSP for Dominican Communist leadership, and demonstrating pointedly its adherence to the Peking, not the Moscow, line, sent "fraternal greetings" to the "Workers Party [Communist Party] of Albania.")

And, finally, the rebellion had been joined by hundreds, perhaps thousands, of ordinary Dominicans who had emerged from Trujillo's tyranny and who had been told by me and others that the United States would help them get a better life. They had voted for Bosch, and they had seen the cost of living rising and their hopes disappearing during the Reid regime.

That, then, was how the revolt had begun. But in a flash it had changed. The military rebels had looted the arsenals of huge quantities of weapons. Quickly they and the Castro/Communists had handed out guns on street corners to anybody, as we have seen. A twelve-year-old boy, wishing to join the excitement, tried to get a weapon in his home town; unable to do so, he walked to the capital and, on the way, met a truckload of soldiers; one of them gave him a machine gun.

The killing began. Blind fury and anarchy overwhelmed the city. Dominican troops killed Dominican troops. Dominican civilians killed each other. Dominican warplanes and naval vessels attacked the Dominican capital. Nobody knows how many died, probably at least two thousand. Colonel Caamaño told me he had lost fourteen hundred men. Hospitals and makeshift hospitals filled up. Doctors operated on patients by lamplight on hospital floors without anesthetic.

On Tuesday, thinking they were losing, the rebels asked Ambassador Bennett to help them negotiate a settlement. He refused.

Thereupon, the PRD leaders went into asylum in foreign Embassies. And Caamaño and the other military men, already so deeply committed they knew they must win or die, went back to the streets to fight. The PRD leaders gone, a political vacuum existed. Quickly the Castro/Communists filled that vacuum. They took over political leadership of the rebellion.

The senseless slaughter which ensued was just that—senseless slaughter. It was, indeed, the bloodbath that should logically have followed Trujillo's assassination nearly four years ago and that many Dominicans had told me in my time was some day inevitable. For Trujillo had held the lid down tight for thirty-one years, a whole generation, and pressures built up that could not be contained forever without blood. Or so some said.

In my time, we had maintained a precarious balance. We had been very careful to distinguish among the twenty-six parties, especially among the four Castro/Communist parties—and between those parties and Juan Bosch's non-Communist PRD.

When the military-*civico* right overthrew Bosch, the delicate political mosaic into which he had tried to fit himself collapsed. Hatreds polarized, the left-right polarization we always had feared. The powerful forces that had been unleashed by Trujillo's death wracked the Republic, and the political structure failed completely, and when rebels overthrew Reid, Civil War began.

This failure of the political structure has happened time and again in Dominican history. It has happened only once in the United States—and our own Civil War resulted. When a political structure collapses, nothing can replace it but fratricidal warfare, the most terrible of all.

What happened in the Dominican Republic was the Spanish Civil War —but without content or ideas.

The bloodbath drowned the ideals and purposes which had created the rebel force. Each man had rebelled for his own reason—Boschist idealism, revenge, plunder, Communist directive, anti-Reid, anti-corruption, sheer adventure and excitement, the highest ideals of liberalism and the meanest effort to pick a winner. In those terrible hours, all ideals vanished. The old party structure, the distinctions we had been so careful to make, were swept away, as though by a flood in a mountain valley. The rebels become welded together. By the time I arrived distinctions had become meaningless. It did not matter what party each man once had belonged to, nor what his original motive had been. All had forgotten for what they fought. All had become extremists in the true sense of the word—men of violence.

Men and women like this have nowhere to go except to the Communists. All other doors are shut. And the men and women themselves become transformed by the bloodshed and hate. People I had known in the past had changed. A woman I had known as a gentle idealistic leftist, vigorously opposed to communism, went one day to rebel headquarters to obtain supplies. A teen-ager stopped her—did she have a note from Party headquarters? No. Then she must get one. Instead, she called a rebel officer and denounced the boy to him as a "counter-revolutionary deviationist." Like others, she had become, in a word, unhinged.

It is not names of Communists, or numbers, that is important. It is the process itself—the fusion process of the bloodbath.

Out of the noble French Revolution came the Terror, paving the way for the despot Napoleon. Out of the heroic risings against the Czar came the tyrant Stalin. Out of the brave opposition to Batista came the "show trials" and the *paredón*, and the Communist dictator Castro. From Trujillo's prisons emerged heroes to make a revolution—and now their revolution was about to devour its children.

In all my time in the Dominican Republic, I had met no man whom I thought might become a Dominican Castro—until I met Caamaño. He was winning a revolution from below. He had few political advisers in Santo Domingo at that time but Communists.

It makes little difference when Castro "became a Communist." It would make little difference when Caamaño became one.

In any case, after all this blood and all this hate, I saw no chance whatsoever for a political settlement at that time.

But the obvious alternative was to my mind also unacceptable—sending our own forces against the rebels. And I detected a rising determination to do it. Some Dominican military men wanted us to. Some U.S. military men considered the present U.S. military position tactically untenable (they were probably right from a purely military viewpoint, though not from a political one). I began to think our gravest danger lay in being provoked into a massacre. Indeed, now that the U.S. troops had landed and the Communists knew they could not win, perhaps the Communists' new objective was to provoke us into just that.

The only hope was to gain some time—to maintain a cease-fire and hope that people might come to their senses, that new openings might appear for reconciliation, that new leaders or new political constellations might arise. Dr. Mora and the OAS Commission, as well as the Papal Nuncio, would bring their prestige to bear to keep the peace.

I reported all this to President Johnson by telephone. At a press conference, I said the U.S. Marines had originally come here to protect U.S. lives but that in my opinion their purpose now was or should be to prevent a Castro/Communist takeover, because what began as a PRD revolt had in the last few days fallen under the domination of Castro/Communists and other violent extremists. It was the first time we had said so. The President said approximately the same thing at home in a national radio-television speech that same night, Sunday, May 2. . . .

.   .   .

Critics asked five main questions about our Dominican policy:

—Was there really danger of a Communist takeover?

—Should we have intervened militarily and unilaterally?

—Hadn't we overreacted?

—Having intervened, why didn't we espouse the rebel cause or at least maintain strict neutrality between the rebels and loyalists?

—Wasn't our policy erratic, uncertain, and contradictory? Weren't we less than candid in explaining it?...

On the first point, I have no doubt whatsoever that there was a real danger of a Communist takeover of the Dominican Republic. I have set forth the evidence in the preceding chapter. Again I wish to emphasize that this is not primarily a question of names and numbers. It is a question of the process, of the bloodbath that fuses men and women of all ideologies into a fanatic mass and erases the fine distinctions that are possible in ordinary times.

On the second point, given the circumstances that existed at the time, in my opinion President Johnson had no choice but to send the troops. There can be no question that, with the police and military demoralized and all but defeated, with thousands of armed and embittered civilians roaming the streets, U.S. lives were endangered. Had the President not sent the troops, the rebels probably would have defeated the San Isidro troops, spread the rebellion throughout the Republic, killed some Americans and many Dominicans, and in the end established a Communist-dominated government. When I speak of "the circumstances that existed at the time," however, I mean not only a breakdown in law and order, but the fact that the rebellion had fallen under the domination of Communists, not PRDistas. And, reluctant as I am to say it, in my opinion this had happened at least in part because on the first Tuesday of the rebellion Ambassador Bennett rejected the rebels' plea to help negotiate a settlement.

It is extremely disagreeable to second-guess any Ambassador. Moreover, no Ambassador can know everything; to a considerable extent he must rely on what he is told. Ambassador Bennett had returned to Santo Domingo only a few hours before he faced his crucial decision. He thought the rebels were losing; they said so themselves. But when he rejected their overtures, the PRDistas went into hiding—and the military rebels and the Communists went back to the streets to fight; and they nearly won. The only door open to them was the Communist door; Bennett had shut our door. Had he not, everything else might have turned out differently. Having said this, I must add that it might not have—Caamaño was already so deeply committed he might have fought on anyway, the Communists were gaining ascendancy anyway, Wessin had his tanks at the bridge and was in no mood to negotiate, and Bennett's move may have made no difference. Who knows? History does not reveal its alternatives. At the least, Bennett's move was important, if only because it persuaded Molina Ureña to abandon the struggle. In any case, presented with the situation as it existed after Tuesday, President Johnson had to intervene.

Intervene unilaterally? The OAS Charter specifically prohibits unilateral intervention. Therefore, our intervention was illegal, or at least contrary to the spirit of the Charter.[1] We could have asked for an emergency meeting of the OAS, but the OAS is not noted for swift, decisive action. I do not believe we could have waited; there simply wasn't time. We could, however,

---

1 Lawyers argue that any nation has a right in international law to use arms to protect its citizens' lives, hence our intervention was not illegal.

have informed the OAS before we sent the troops. This would have been no less illegal. It would have made little difference to the Dominicans. It probably would have looked better, and our reputation probably would have suffered somewhat less.

On the third point, whether we "overreacted" and sent too many troops —"more than twenty thousand troops to catch fifty Communists," as critics have put it—I would point out that in such a situation a few leaders can exert great leverage on large numbers of uninformed people. The situation in the capital was chaotic and that in the interior virtually unknown. If, as the troop buildup increased, our purpose became to prevent a Communist takeover, then prudence argued for a large force. From a purely military point of view, how many is too many? I am not competent to judge but certainly would have hesitated to send only four hundred Marines to rescue several thousand civilians in the face of several thousand armed rebels. The Marines might have been thrown out. How many did we need to patrol the International Zone and other areas? I do not know, but U.S. forces had to hold a total perimeter of more than thirty miles. At the peak, on May 17, U.S. troops in Santo Domingo totaled 22,289. Putting so many troops ashore in little Santo Domingo hurt us politically and helped the Castro/Communists throughout the Hemisphere. But the Defense Department, once called upon, takes no unnecessary risks and throws in overwhelming numbers, on the ground that doing so is the best guarantee against losing many lives on both sides. This is hard to quarrel with.

On the fourth point, we did not espouse the rebel cause because it had fallen under Communist domination.

As we have seen, we did everything possible to support President Bosch before he was overthrown in 1963. It would have been logical to support him in 1965 had he returned to lead the rebellion at its very outset. But although his men started the rebellion, and although Molina Ureña and other PRD leaders apparently expected him to return immediately, Bosch did not return. Why he did not has never been satisfactorily explained, even by Bosch himself in all his writings on the rebellion that I have seen.[2] He does say that he twice asked us for a plane. He did not ask me. So far as I know, he did not ask any American official or unofficial representative. Nor did we, so far as I know—and I inquired at the time—interpose any obstacle to his return. He could have returned in the first days without consulting us. True, San Isidro Air Base was in Wessin's hands, and Bosch could not have landed there. But had he wanted to go, he could have landed at any of several airports. He did not. Therefore, with Bosch in Puerto Rico, and Molina Ureña in asylum, and Communists dominating the rebels, we could hardly support them.

As for maintaining neutrality, we did a good deal of talking about it, and journalists criticized us severely for not doing it. My own view is that in the

[2] Bosch has written several magazine articles and given several interviews since the Civil War. He has been critical of our policy and of some of our policymakers. He has differed from me in his recollection of certain events, notably our conversations of May 2–3, 1965. Readers may find a summary of his views in *The New Leader* of June 21, 1965, and other magazines mentioned in the bibliography. He wrote his book, *Crisis de la Democracia de América en la República Dominicana,* before the Civil War. Regrettably the recent edition in English has not been brought up to date.

very beginning some of our people on the spot understood that they were there to fight communism, and this meant, to them, fighting alongside Wessin, although our policy never so dictated; that we stopped this and set up the Zone lines and the corridor and, after Imbert's offensive in the north, interposed our troops between the hostile Dominican forces and thus did in fact maintain neutrality, shooting only when shot at; and that we did our shooting mostly at rebels because with few exceptions only rebels shot at us. And my further view is that once we had decided we were in the Republic to stop communism, we should have stopped pretending neutrality. For it is incomprehensible to me how we could contain one side and at the same time stay neutral.

On the fifth point, I believe our policy seemed more erratic than it was. During the first few days, in a situation so chaotic and confused, it would be surprising if we had been able to lay out a policy neatly. (But in fact, on two fundamental points, our policy did set early and never changed: To protect United States lives, and to prevent a Castro/Communist takeover.) Most critics, however, complained that at various times we seemed to be collaborating first with San Isidro, then with Caamaño, then with Imbert, then with Guzmán. This can be called erratic; it can also be called exploring all possibilities. I myself was sent to the Republic to open a channel to the rebels, and did. Then on May 2 I said the rebellion had in the past few days fallen under the domination of Communists and other extremists because I believed it was true, because I thought it time we said so, and because I thought saying it might help split the rebels and thus save the non-Communist rebels. Then I helped set up the Imbert government, for the reasons I have stated. I see no policy inconsistency here either. Some reporters criticized us too because it seemed to them inconsistent that we labeled the rebels Communist-dominated then opened negotiations with them through Guzmán. I see no inconsistency here: A pre-condition of our proposed support for Guzmán was that his government be free of Communist influence. The reporters who criticized did not know that. They did not know because they were not told.

Reporters cannot be told everything while a negotiation is in progress, but on the whole I feel that what we did in Santo Domingo was better than what we said. Ambassador Bennett repeated to U.S. correspondents—in all good faith, I feel sure, though without checking them—atrocity stories told him by the San Isidro generals; when they turned out not to be true, the correspondents suspected him of having deliberately lied to them, and some of them never trusted him again. The President himself, again in all good faith, repeated some of the stories. Thus began the "crisis of credibility" in the Administration so much discussed for many months. A great deal of hostility toward U.S. policy and suspicion of U.S. motives that colored correspondents' stories stemmed from those early statements; journalists who think they have been lied to do not forgive. Not until Sunday, May 2, nine days after the rebellion started and five days after the first Marines landed, did we say publicly that we were there to stop communism. Previously we had maintained that we were there to protect American lives. I think we would have come out better if at the moment we sent the Marines, or certainly when we sent the Airborne, we had announced that we were sending them to protect American lives, to help restore peace, to stop the combatants from tearing their country to pieces, and to prevent a Castro/Communist takeover, calling on the OAS to help us. At the same time we should have made it clear that we had no intention of setting up or propping up a military dictatorship under Wessin or anybody else—that our purposes were to suppress anarchy and give the Dominican people a chance once more to choose their own leaders in a free and peaceful election, a chance they would never have had if the Communists had won. But, again, hindsight is easy. . . .

18

On Pentagonism

Juan Bosch

From Juan Bosch, *Pentagonism: A Substitute for Imperialism,* translated by Helen R. Lane (New York: Grove Press, Inc., 1968), pp. 20–22, 92–96, 100–102, 120–22. Reprinted by permission of the author.

With the 1965 intervention as a case in point, former Dominican President Juan Bosch charges that "pentagonism" (not Lenin's "imperialism") is the latest stage in the "overdeveloped capitalism" of the United States.

...[P]entagonism, ... has come to occupy the place that imperialism occupied until a short while ago. Imperialism has now disappeared from the globe, and the word which defined it ought to disappear with it. What is taking place at present in Latin America, in Asia, in Africa—in all the underdeveloped areas—is not the old imperialism defined by Lenin as the last stage—or the most advanced stage—of capitalism. It is pentagonism, the product of overdeveloped capitalism.

Pentagonism retains almost all the characteristics of imperialism, especially those that are most destructive and painful, but it is a more advanced form, and bears the same relation to imperialism that today's overdeveloped capitalism bears to the industrial capitalism of the nineteenth century. To state this more graphically, pentagonism resembles imperialism in the nature of its effects, not in its dimensions, just as the cannon used in the Franco–Prussian War of 1870 resembles the atomic bomb dropped on Hiroshima, in that both cause death, but not the same number of deaths.

Pentagonism nonetheless differs from imperialism in that it does not share its most characteristic feature, military conquest of colonial territories and their subsequent economic exploitation. Pentagonism does not exploit colonies: it exploits its own people. This is an absolutely new phenomenon, as new as the overdeveloped capitalism that gave birth to pentagonism.

To succeed in the exploitation of its own people, pentagonism colonizes the mother country; but since the colonization of the mother country must be achieved through the same military process as was used to conquer a colony and since it cannot wage war against its own people, the mother country sends its armies out to make war on other countries. And since sending the army of the mother country out against a foreign territory was what was done in the bygone days of imperialism, people continue to think that imperialism still holds sway. But this is not the case. The fact is that the use of military power has not changed; what has changed is the purpose for which it is used.

The military forces of a pentagonist country are not sent out to conquer colonial territories. War has another purpose; war is waged to conquer positions of power in the pentagonist country, not in some far-off land. What is being sought is not a place to invest surplus capital for profit; what is being sought is access to the generous economic resources being mobilized for industrial war production; what is being sought are profits where arms are manufactured, not where they are employed, and these profits are obtained in the pentagonist mother country, not in the country that is being attacked. A contract for bombers brings in several times more profit, in a much shorter time, than the conquest of the richest mining territory, and the contract is obtained in, and brings money in from, the place where the center of pentagonist power lies. The armies operate a long way away from the pentagonist power, but the planes are built at home, and this is where the fabulous sums produced by the contract are earned. These sums come out of the pockets of the pentagonized people, who are at the same time the mother country and the seat of pentagonist power.

The pentagonized people are exploited as colonies were since they are the ones who pay, through taxes, for the bombers that enrich their manufacturers; the mother country thus turns its own people into its best colony; it is at once a mother country and a colony, in an unforeseen symbiosis that requires a new word to define it. It is no longer a classic imperialist power

because it does not need colonial territories in order to accumulate profits. It accumulates them at the expense of its own people. A mother country that exploits and an exploited colony no longer exist. There is something else: the "impentagonal" or the "metropocolony.". . .

.   .   .

. . . The doctrine that would justify the use of pentagonist armies in any part of the world, however far it might be from the United States, would be called that of *subversive* wars. This came to be the doctrine of pentagonism.

What is the substance of this doctrine and what is the method by which it is applied?

The substance is very simple: Every effort at revolutionary change anywhere in the world is contrary to the interests of the United States; it is the equivalent of a subversive war against American order and consequently is a war of aggression against the United States which must be answered by the military power of the country, just as if it were an armed invasion coming from outside the national territory.

Until a few years ago this doctrine was simply called the right of the stronger to annihilate the weaker; it was the old law of the jungle, the law that the bloodthirsty tiger applies to the timid deer in the jungles of Asia; it had been in use since the earliest days of the human species everywhere that man remained a savage, and it seemed incredible that anyone should attempt to revive it in a civilized era. But it pleased the pentagonists so much —because it was impossible to invent any other theory—that they sought to honor it by giving it the name of one of its benefactors, and so they called it the Johnson Doctrine.

The method of applying the new law of the jungle or doctrine of subversive wars or Johnson Doctrine is as simple as its substance, and just as primitive. It is based on the idea that the government of the United States has the right to define any armed conflict, either between two countries or within the limits of one country, and has the responsibility of determining if the war is or is not subversive. The war is defined without hearing the parties concerned, by a unilateral decision made by the United States alone. Since there are already established precedents, we know that a subversive war—the equivalent to armed aggression against American territory—can be a revolution within the Dominican Republic to re-establish a democratic regime and liquidate thirty-five years of criminal habits, or it can be the war of the Viet Cong to establish a Communist regime in South Vietnam. A subversive war, when it comes down to it, is everything that the Pentagon finds good for justifying the use of armies in another country.

When Fidel Castro declared that Cuba had become a Socialist state, pentagonism was already a respectable force, but it was not yet a power coherent enough to impose itself on its own government. Even after having attained the coherence that was lacking, it needed a doctrine that would provide it with the moral force to act. President Kennedy wavered in the case of the Bay of Pigs because he did not have a doctrine to lean on, and perhaps it will some day be discovered that this hesitation placed the Kennedy Administration—that is to say, the civil power of the country—in a position of inferiority in the face of pentagonist power,

and thus was a turning point in America's destiny. There is no documentary proof of what we are about to say, but when the process of integration of pentagonism is scrutinized, one intuits that its decisive hour, the hour when it acquired its real strength, was between the Bay of Pigs and the military coup which cost Ngo Dinh Diem his power and his life.

It is easy to see that when the so-called doctrine of subversive wars came to be elaborated pentagonists were thinking of Vietnam, but perhaps they were thinking more of Cuba and the Bay of Pigs. The idea that Fidel Castro was busy organizing guerrillas in Latin America and that some day the United States would have to invade Cuba to eliminate Fidel Castro pulses in the heart of this shabby creature called the doctrine of subversive wars. The truth is that Communist Cuba made the United States lose its head; it brought the whole country to a state of panic that was inexplicable in a nation with so much power, and this panic was an important factor in the hour in which the doctrinal justification of pentagonism was created.

The acts of peoples, like the acts of men, are reflections of their attitudes. But it so happens that a country's social nature is dynamic, not static, with the result that every act provokes a response or provokes other acts to reinforce it. No act, then, can hold its own in isolation. Thus the chain of acts deriving from the principal act in the end modifies the attitude of the one who acted first and the one who carries out acts in reply. This modification can lead many places, depending on the personal, social, or national character of the one who acts and on his internal or external circumstances at the time that he acts.

The panic caused by Cuban Communism provoked important changes in the mental attitude of the United States. At first it decided to intervene secretly in Cuba so as not to violate openly its policy of non-intervention, and it resorted to the CIA in order to accomplish this. But a government based on public freedom cannot act in secret, and Castro, moreover, countered these secret activities with public executions of agents sent to Cuba, so that these secret activities were in the end known to the whole world. Caught red-handed, and rendered helpless in confronting Cuban Communism because of its irrational fear, the United States became a suspicious country, and ended up believing that every political change, anywhere in the world, was in the last analysis a change toward Communism. Since this had been what had happened in Cuba, it would happen in other places.

From its fear of Communism and its failure at the Bay of Pigs, Americans went on to fear any change anywhere, and from this fear they went on to keep the whole world under surveillance. In short, the outcome of the tangle of new attitudes and the acts derived from these new attitudes had to be—and was—that the United States ended up thinking that it had to become the police of the world.

But what sort of police? Police that establish order, through law, where the citizens are disorderly, or police that hunt down ideas and political activities considered dangerous for that society— what are called "political police" the world over?

The United States devoted itself to being the political police of the world, and this was bound to be the natural result of the so-called doctrine of subversive wars, since the word *subversive*

has a clear political implication; it describes the effort made to change a political order, the form of a state or of a government.

As the world happens to be organized today, what ideas and political activities are dangerous to society?

In a capitalist country the ideas and political activities dangerous to society are logically those of Communism, since they are aimed at changing the economic, social, and political order, the form of the state, and the system of government. But in a Communist country the dangerous ideas and political activities are those of capitalism because they are aimed at re-establishing the economic, social, and political order that was overthrown and replaced by Communism. The result is that when the pentagonist country acts as the political police of the world, it is confronted with a difficult task, because it cannot at the same time act as political police to prevent changes in both the capitalist and the Communist world; it must therefore resign itself to being the political police of the capitalist world. And the United States is, in fact, the political police of the capitalist world.

Now what agency fulfills the task of being the political police of the world?

There are those who will think that it is the CIA, but it is not. This agency sniffs out new developments, and gathers information on the places where it is possible that a revolutionary movement will break out, and that is all. Policing, properly speaking, is the responsibility of the American armed forces. . . .

.   .   .

In the political field there is, of course, a close relationship between a sense of proportion and a moral conscience, and if the former is lost the latter is effected. The opposite almost always occurs: a sense of proportion is lost because a moral conscience has been lost. Moreover, the desire for such fabulous quantities of money as are earned in pentagonist businesses necessarily leads to the loss of a sense of proportion. It therefore seems natural that pentagonism has produced these effects, and doubtless it would have been contrary to the order of nature for them not to have been produced. Every power becomes a source of transformations, or, what amounts to the same thing, every power has an effect on the medium in which it acts, and pentagonism was not to be an exception.

What does not appear logical is that these effects should go as far as they do. There are appearances that every great country must maintain. To put the President of the United States in a position in which he has to tell lies is to degrade the country in the eyes of the world, and pentagonism has done this; to put the highest officials of the nation in a position in which today they must say the opposite of what they said yesterday is to place the government in a ridiculous and distasteful position, and pentagonism does this constantly.

During the pentagonist intervention in the Dominican Republic, President Johnson was put in the most painful position that any chief of state has been in for many years. He was made to say, first of all, that on April 28, 1965, he was sending a limited number of troops in to protect the lives of American citizens, and three days later thousands of United States Marines entered the city of Santo Domingo with equipment as heavy as that which had been used to land in Normandy. He was made to say that sharpshooters had fired on the office of the American ambassador in Santo Domingo and that bullets were whizzing over the ambassador's head at the very moment he was talking to Mr. Johnson, and it turned out that, given the layout of the ambassador's office, this was physically impossible, even if someone was firing on the embassy, an event that never occurred. He was made to say that there were thousands of decapitated bodies in the streets of the Dominican capital, and that the heads of these corpses were paraded about on the ends of bayonets, and no one could produce even one photograph of a decapitated head. He was made to say that the revolution was Communist and then a list of fifty-one Dominican Communists was produced, which brought a laugh all over the world.

But in any event, and in spite of how sorry a spectacle it was to hear the President of the most powerful country in the world saying things that journalists of this same country had to deny immediately, there was something even sorrier: This was the open and shameless violation of pledges that the United States had made, in the majority of cases on its own initiative and after long struggles to convince other parties. These were pacts that the American government had proposed to governments in Latin America, that it had drawn up, discussed, and approved and that were finally made a part of American law because they had been approved by Congress.

Pentagonism did all this without denouncing these pacts beforehand, which established a new precedent. What is more, the United States is still honoring these pacts, as if nothing had happened, and the Organization of American States (OAS), which was the organ produced by these pacts, continues to function, again as if nothing had happened.

This could only come about—and did come about—after a moral conscience had been lost, and since a moral conscience is closely tied to a sense of proportion, the latter was also missing when a military power greater than that which pentagonism had in South Vietnam at that moment—the end of April, 1965—was unleashed against the defenseless little Dominican Republic.

Efforts have been made to present the story of American intervention in the Dominican Republic as a model of beneficial international action, but the story is quite a different one; it is a sad story of abuses, assassinations, and terror that has not been told because of the world control of news. A few facts will suffice to give a glimpse of the truth: From nine o'clock on the morning of June 15, 1965, until ten o'clock on the morning of the following day, without a single hour of respite day or night, the city of Santo Domingo was bombarded by the occupation forces of the United States. In these twenty-five hours of bombardment hospitals did not have enough facilities to take care of the bodies rent by pentagonist mortars.

The truth has not yet been told about events in the Dominican Republic, but eventually it will be. Pentagonism has circulated *its truth,* and it believes that this is sufficient. But it is certain that the intervention in the Dominican Republic is an episode that is not yet over. This abuse of power will have consequences in Latin America and in the Dominican Republic itself, and these consequences will oblige the United States to act in a more illogical way than it did in April, 1965. . . .

.   .   .

What pentagonism learned in Vietnam and perfected in the Dominican Republic, and what it learned in the Dominican Republic and perfected in Vietnam is going to be put into practice in other countries in Latin America, especially in those in which there are guerrilla movements.

One of the improvements of the methods used in Vietnam and refined in Santo Domingo consists of the fact that political crimes—assassinations of real or supposed Communists—are not laid at the government's doorstep, that selected groups of military leaders or police commit them, and that the President publicly protests these crimes and somehow or other lets it be known that he cannot hunt the authors down; thus terror spreads because the people feel defenseless and at the same time the government is not blamed. This was being done in Guatemala—and being repeated in the Dominican Republic—in 1967. Another strategy pentagonism resorts to is to hold "elections." The "elected" governments are then submitted—as in Vietnam, the Dominican Republic, and Guatemala—to a native pentagonism that, because it is native, is underdeveloped.

This calls for an explanation.

Pentagonism has established a governmental schizophrenia, a double power, in the United States: that of the civil government and that of pentagonism. The American armed forces obey the latter. Latin-American armed forces—with only rare exceptions—will also obey the pentagonist power rather than their national governments. The armies of the United States, however, carry on no war activities within the United States; their field of action is outside their own country, and traditionally—and because this is what brings profits to pentagonism—they will continue to act outside the country, at least until the time when a major defeat abroad obliges them to take over in their own country. The opposite is true of Latin-American armies. Their military activity is not outside the country; their men do not fight outside their own countries. Traditionally—and because their sources of profit have always been in their own countries—Latin-American soldiers are prepared only to be the military occupiers of their own countries. This is what flatters them, this is what they like to do. When they are placed in a position of obeying orders from pentagonism and not from their own national governments, their inclinations toward bringing the downfall of their own people are stimulated; as a consequence, these armies will cause a pentagonist schizophrenia, not in the international sphere but in the realm of domestic policy in each Latin-American country. As a result, of course, the powerful revolutionary current that is agitating Latin America will be both hastened and intensified.

Moreover, the native and underdeveloped pentagonism that is already beginning to function in the Latin-American countries will help to intensify the galloping discredit into which democracy has fallen in this region. In a little while the word democracy will be a synonym in Ibero-America for crimes, theft, brutality, and persecution. There are already Latin-American countries where those who spread terror call themselves democrats and call all others who repudiate their savagery Communists; this may even happen to Catholic priests.

The Dominican Republic, the first of the countries of Latin America which fell under the power of pentagonism, is one such country.

19

The Dominican Intervention
in Retrospect

Abraham F. Lowenthal

From Abraham F. Lowenthal, "The Dominican Intervention in Retrospect," *Public Policy*, XVIII, No. 1 (Fall 1969), pp. 133–48. Reprinted by permission of the author and the publisher.

Abraham F. Lowenthal is an Assistant Representative with the Ford Foundation in Lima, Peru.

Lowenthal observes that after the first wave of criticism of the Johnson Administration's marine landing in the Dominican Republic subsided, a new school of thought held that the entire operation was, on balance, a striking success for U.S. policy—one that might be repeated, with some modifications, in the future. He counters this view by highlighting weaknesses in U.S. policy which the crisis revealed, the high costs of intervention, and certain fortuitous circumstances unique to the Dominican case.

On April 28, 1965, over 500 U.S. Marines landed at Santo Domingo in the Dominican Republic. Armed and authorized to return fire, they were the first combat-ready U.S. forces to move into a Latin American country in close to 40 years. Within a week, the rapid build-up of American forces in Santo Domingo had reached almost 23,000 men, nearly half the number then fighting in Vietnam. Another 10,000 American troops stood ready just off the Dominican coast, and thousands more were on alert at bases in the United States.

The Dominican intervention of April 1965 and the various American statements and actions immediately thereafter appeared initially to mark a severe setback for U.S. diplomacy. Neutrals, adversaries, and allies condemned various aspects of American policy. Public protest welled up in almost every country of Latin America, and in many countries outside the hemisphere. Suspicions and fears were aroused or revived, and the concepts of inter-American cooperation were severely tested. Relations among the members of the Organization of American States (OAS) and between the OAS and the United Nations seemed to cloud.

Within the United States, the events

The author is grateful to the Center for International Affairs, Harvard University, for arranging the seminar on "U.S. Policy in the Dominican Republic" at which a first draft of this paper was presented, and to the members of the seminar for their criticisms and suggestions.

of these weeks produced strong adverse reactions. Although mass public opinion, as reflected in the major polls, expressed confidence in the administration's handling of the Dominican affair, significant sectors strenuously opposed the government. The five newspapers then most widely read in Washington policymaking circles—the *New York Times,* the *New York Herald Tribune,* the *Washington Post,* the *Wall Street Journal,* and the *Christian Science Monitor*—published reports and editorials so critical of the administration as to become themselves major factors in the crisis. Later, several leading public figures, most of them from the administration's own party, attacked specific aspects of American policy. Senator J. William Fulbright, Chairman of the Senate Foreign Relations Committee, delivered a particularly harsh indictment which occasioned the opening of the Senator's public breach with the Johnson Administration.

As time passed, however, what loomed at first as a major disaster came to be regarded, by many in Washington at least, as a remarkable success for American policy. Viewing the Dominican intervention in retrospect, some observers have argued that all four objectives of U.S. policy were attained: to protect American and other foreign citizens, to halt violence, to prevent a Communist take-over, and to restore constitutional processes to the Dominican people.[1] Within little more than a year of the intervention, they point out, American troops were officially withdrawn, their mission accomplished, and national elections had

brought to power a new Dominican regime with which the U.S. government could cooperate in carrying out major economic and social development programs. Except for relatively minor matters, such as admitted inadequacies in U.S. public information activities and perhaps the failure to inform members of the OAS in advance of the U.S. decision to intervene, these analysts look back on the Dominican episode as a successful exercise of American power.

At a time when many Americans are focusing on what can be learned from the failure of American power in Vietnam, some may be tempted to review the Dominican experience in search of lessons for successful intervention. A State Department publication has noted, for instance, that "When we confronted the Communists promptly and vigorously in our own hemisphere, as in the Dominican crisis, they were halted; when we failed to recognize and confront them, as in Cuba, the tumor took root and grew."[2] Such a statement may be dismissed, of course, as simplistic propaganda, but its premise —that the Dominican intervention turned out well—is very widely accepted. It may be useful, therefore, to question the complacent residue of the Dominican intervention and to warn against deriving misleading conclusions from that supposed triumph.

There are three major reasons for criticizing the tendency to regard the Dominican intervention as a success from which lessons may be learned. First, satisfaction with the perceived outcome of the intervention diverts attention from specific weaknesses of American policy during the Dominican crisis, and from the general inade-

---

[1] See, for example, Center for Strategic Studies, Georgetown University, *Dominican Action: Intervention or Cooperation?* (Special Study Report No. 2; Washington, D.C., 1966).

[2] *Foreign Policy Briefs* (June 5, 1967).

quacies of the U.S. approach to the Caribbean. Second, the judgment that U.S. policy in the Dominican crisis was ultimately successful tends to be based on an incomplete and misleading reckoning of the costs of the intervention. Finally, favorable evaluations of the Dominican intervention generally fail to focus sufficiently on unique aspects of the Dominican case which facilitated the relatively quick withdrawal of U.S. forces from the Dominican Republic.

II

A revealing measure of the widespread belief that the U.S. intervention in the Dominican Republic was successful is the notable decline since 1965 of academic, official, and public interest in the Dominican crisis. The tendency to focus concern on more current problems is inevitable, but it tends to decrease the possibilities for learning from past difficulties and even to encourage an unfounded confidence that U.S. policies in past crises have been free of major errors.[3]

Several aspects of the Dominican experience ought to be examined more carefully than they have been. Insufficient attention has been paid to the extent to which U.S. acts and omissions helped to cause the crisis by permitting the situation to deteriorate until U.S. officials could see no alternative to landing the Marines.[4] Scant analysis has been accorded to the vari-

[3] See Howard J. Wiarda, "The Dominican Revolution in Perspective: A Research Note," *Policy*, I (Fall 1968), 114–124.
[4] A more extended discussion of this and other questions will appear in Abraham F. Lowenthal, *Purpose or Process? A Study of the 1965 Dominican Intervention* (forthcoming doctoral dissertation, Department of Government, Harvard University).

ous ways in which American perceptions, policies, and actions during the first weeks following the intervention deepened the crisis, making more difficult its eventual resolution. Not enough thought has been given to the problems of intelligence which revealed themselves in the Dominican case with respect not only to data collection, analysis, and evaluation but also to the relation of intelligence to policy-making and policy justification. No published study has focused on the problems of "crisis management," of policy coordination and control, which marked the Dominican affair. Nor has any work dealt adequately with operational problems exemplified by the Dominican intervention: with the issues of civil-military relations, with the efforts to develop effective psychological and information programs, or with the problems of relief and economic rehabilitation, to cite only three of many possible examples.

Finally, the disappearance of the Dominican Republic from the morning headlines should not be allowed to obscure the deeper foreign policy issues posed by the 1965 crisis. The 1965 intervention in the Dominican Republic was not merely an isolated incident, but rather the most recent and dramatic episode in a long and disturbing history. The United States has exerted its influence openly and vigorously over the years in the Dominican Republic, yet in few places have the constraints on America's efforts to transform foreign realities been more evident. The military interventions of 1916–1924 and 1965–1966 have been the most controversial episodes in U.S.-Dominican relations, but the overall history of American participation in Dominican affairs has been a tale of repeated frustration.

The Dominican experience suggests, for instance, the need to reconsider the problems of dealing with an extensive military establishment which is not the instrument of the civil government but the very locus of political power and conflict. Ever since the U.S. occupation forces set up the Dominican army 50 years ago, American officials have talked about the need to create an honest, effective, unified, apolitical security force in the Dominican Republic, and extensive programs of military training and assistance have been devised toward that end. Yet the 1965 crisis arose initially largely because the corrupt, ineffective, thoroughly political Dominican armed forces split into warring factions. Then the crisis deepened precisely because the faction that the U.S. government chose to back proved incapable of restoring order. The eventual regrouping of the Dominican armed forces and the ultimate resolution of the Dominican crisis should not divert attention from the implications of the Dominican military's collapse in April 1965.

Similarly, attention should be focused on the problems of U.S. economic policy revealed by the Dominican case. Between 1960 and 1965 the U.S. first imposed sanctions on the Dominican economy, later provided massive amounts of aid, next cut off aid entirely, and finally renewed its aid program on a more limited scale. These steps were motivated by political objectives as U.S. aid was used in this chaotic period to pursue the immediate goal of short-range political stability.[5] It is certainly possible, however, that these

measures—which had the effect of facilitating the rapid expansion of Dominican imports in 1962–1963 and then forcing the Dominican government to impose austerity policies in 1964–1965—actually helped to heighten the pressures which produced the 1965 explosion.

More generally, the Dominican case affords an excellent opportunity for reconsidering the fundamental problem of U.S. policy in the Caribbean: how to deal with weak, chronically unstable, underdeveloped and dependent enclaves in a region considered vital to its security by the United States. First, the Dominican crisis suggests the need to reassess the nature and extent of America's strategic, economic, and political interests in the Caribbean area. It is time to ask whether the American impulse to act in the Caribbean stems from anything more than historic axiom and unquestioned habit. Unchallenged premises and preconceptions very largely determined the U.S. intervention in Santo Domingo, and constructive analysis should focus special attention on outlining and questioning these assumptions.[6]

Second, even if special U.S. interests in the Caribbean are posited, the Dominican case poses in dramatic form basic questions about the proper extent of American involvement there and about the capacity of the United States successfully to influence events even so close to its shores. Some who have participated in conducting American diplomacy in the Dominican Republic and elsewhere in the Caribbean, including Sumner Welles and John Bartlow Martin, have recom-

[5] See Lowenthal, "Foreign Aid as a Political Instrument: The Case of the Dominican Republic," *Public Policy*, Vol. XIV (Cambridge, Mass.: Harvard Graduate School of Public Administration, 1965), 141–160.

[6] See also Richard M. Alpert's related comment: "Is There an Alternative to Intervention?" *Public Policy*, XVIII, No. 1 (Fall 1969), 149–153.

mended an extraordinary degree of American involvement in Carribean affairs. They have argued that the United States simply cannot avoid participating in the affairs of the nations of the Caribbean region, and that the United States must therefore accept the need for long-term, intimate engagement in countries like the Dominican Republic. Others with extensive diplomatic experience in the Caribbean, including Laurance Duggan and Philip Bonsal, have taken a more skeptical attitude toward the propriety and the effectiveness of active American involvement in Caribbean affairs.[7] They have stressed the extreme difficulty of exerting influence and exercising power wisely in such an unpredictable environment, and have argued that the United States would be best advised to refrain as much as possible from direct interference in the domestic politics of the Caribbean nations.

What the Dominican case reveals most strikingly is that policies based on each of these historic approaches have time and again failed to achieve the stated objectives of U.S. policy. Interference of the traditional character has been counterproductive, but non-interference has been ineffective and unsatisfactory; the result has been intermittent, *ad hoc,* pre-emptive military intervention. The Dominican intervention of 1965 dramatizes the need to reflect on this troubling history and to define carefully American interests and objectives. If the United States in fact has a permanent interest in Caribbean stability, as I would argue, then it is necessary to explore new ways to approach the dynamics of political, social,

and economic development in the Caribbean area.[8]

III

The view that the U.S. intervention in the Dominican Republic was successful tends to be founded on a comparison between the chaotic Dominican situation on April 28, 1965, when American troops began landing, and the relative tranquility of September 1966, when American forces completed their withdrawal. This comparison is certainly pertinent, but a meaningful evaluation of the Dominican experience and its possible relevance in future situations depends on considering the intervention's total costs. It may as yet be too early to reach a conclusive judgment on whether the Dominican intervention provided benefits ultimately worth all its costs, but it is certainly not premature to think about its price.

Of all the costs of the U.S. intervention in the Dominican Republic, the most difficult to reckon is the most tragic entry: human agony. At least 44 American soldiers died and almost 300 were wounded in the Dominican Republic. Many, perhaps most, of the estimated 3,000 Dominican deaths are believed to have occurred after the U.S. intervened, some of them in armed clashes between Dominicans and Americans.[9] It should be noted, however, that

---

[7] See, for instance, Philip W. Bonsal, "Open Letter to an Author," *Foreign Service Journal,* XLIV (February 1967), 40, 41.

[8] Attempts to study this problem are currently being undertaken by Ben S. Stephansky at the Twentieth Century Fund and Robert D. Crassweller at the Council on Foreign Relations.

[9] The estimate of 3,000 Dominican deaths is based on calculations by the U.S. Embassy in Santo Domingo, which analyzed Red Cross reports, hospital records, and other sources. Dominicans generally accept this figure as reliable.

more Dominicans might have been killed had the U.S. refrained from intervening and allowed the civil war to continue; no conclusive statement can be made about this possibility.

The financial cost to the United States as a result of the Dominican intervention is easier to fix, and it has already been considerable. Above and beyond the cost of the military operation itself, emergency relief and assistance during 1965–1966 came to over $100 million. The events of 1965 also resulted in the assumption by the United States of the burden of an extraordinarily large aid program, which will have to be continued into the foreseeable future; the official American mission now resident in the Dominican Republic is the largest assigned in Spanish America. The cost of maintaining this massive Dominican aid program is being compounded, moreover, as general U.S. aid appropriations are reduced and funds consequently become unavailable elsewhere in the hemisphere.

The intangible costs of the Dominican intervention—in the hemisphere generally, in the United States, and particularly in the Dominican Republic —are difficult to estimate, but the impossibility of precise quantification should not preclude consideration of these consequences of the Dominican crisis. Public opinion polls and regional summit conferences, for instance, should not obscure the fact that some sectors of Latin American and world opinion found their faith shattered or their doubts confirmed by the U.S. intervention. Disagreement is possible about the extent to which the Good Neighbor policy had succeeded in erasing the legacy of interventionism or about the extent to which the Alliance for Progress had improved the U.S. image

in Latin America, but none can dispute that the U.S. actions in the Dominican case set these efforts back. Perhaps the United States achieved some positive advantages by clearly demonstrating its determination to protect its vital interests in the hemisphere even, when it deems it necessary, by armed intervention. One wonders, however, whether Latin Americans will take so seriously the rhetoric and the reality of inter-American cooperation, since the doctrine of nonintervention—which they regard as its cardinal principle— was summarily discarded by the United States. Many students of the Alliance for Progress, indeed, attribute its loss of mystique in part to the 1965 Dominican intervention, which seemed to align the United States with reactionary forces against those who favored change. Surely there are other, more profound reasons for the *Alianza*'s loss of momentum, but it cannot be denied that progressive leaders like Eduardo Frei of Chile were shocked and embarrassed by the U.S. intervention.

The Dominican experience also hurt the Organization of American States. Although the Organization may have lent some legitimacy to U.S. actions during the crisis, it undoubtedly lost standing in the hemisphere; the O.E.A. seemed, to many Latin Americans, just "Otro Engaño Americano," another American trick.[10] Some of the apparent costs of the Dominican crisis within the Organization, such as the sharp division of the members into blocs which characterized the 1965 debates, now seem not to have been permanent, but other consequences have been last-

[10] See Jerome Slater, "The Limits of Legitimization in International Organizations: The Organization of American States and the Dominican Crisis," *International Organization*, XXIII (Winter 1969), 48–72.

ing. The morale of the permanent secretariat of the OAS was undermined by the Dominican operation. The carefully cultivated efforts to build support for basic reforms of the Organization's charter and to strengthen the mechanism of the Inter-American Peace Committee lost much of their effectiveness as a result of the Dominican crisis. The idea of an Inter-American Force composed of units from democratic countries in the hemisphere also seems to have died as a result of its premature birth in the Dominican context.

The Dominican intervention may also have decreased the chances for the kind of peaceful change which the United States claims to support in Latin America. The Dominican crisis had the immediate, specific consequence in several countries of heightening frictions between opposing political groups, and between local military establishments and popular parties. Longer-term effects may arise from perceptions of the Dominican intervention as part of a pattern of U.S. policy. Some Latin American conservatives—particularly in Central America—may have drawn the conclusion from the Dominican crisis that the United States will not allow nationalist reform movements to succeed, and that therefore they need not accommodate themselves to proposed changes. On the other side, some Latin Americans committed to change may well have concluded, as has Juan Bosch himself, that the American intervention in Santo Domingo proved that the United States will oppose democratic revolution in Latin America.[11] Some defenders of U.S.

11 See Juan Bosch, *Pentagonism: A Substitute for Imperialism* (New York: Grove Press, 1968).

policy in the Dominican crisis have argued that the intervention served to warn non-Communist leftists to avoid involvement with Communists who might taint their movements, but it seems at least as plausible to suggest the contrary. Many non-Communist radical leaders may well have concluded from the Dominican case that the American preoccupation with anti-Communism makes U.S. officials incapable of distinguishing radicals from Communists; if that is true, they can retain little hope for support from the United States and have less reason to reject alliances with Communists.

The Dominican intervention may also have had serious consequences here in the United States. It is difficult, in retrospect, to separate out the Dominican crisis from the almost simultaneous escalation of the war in Vietnam, which has overshadowed all other foreign policy issues since 1965. It seems likely, however, that the Dominican episode helped to breed the deepening *malaise* about American policy which so constrained the U.S. government's foreign policy choices by 1968. The Dominican crisis, particularly the seeming twists and turns of U.S. policy during its first weeks, heightened the sense of marked distrust and even hostility between the administration and many leading journalists, scholars, and other informed opinion-shapers. The administration's obvious lack of candor in this case also contributed to increasing mutual suspicion between the Executive and some members of Congress, thus deepening domestic American unrest about this country's foreign involvements. For many Americans, the "crisis of credibility" began with the Dominican intervention.

The intangible costs of the American intervention of 1965 may well be most serious in the Dominican Republic itself. No one can state with certainty what would have happened in the Dominican Republic had its amorphous "revolution" not been interrupted by the introduction of American forces. Nor can anyone know what might have occurred had the United States been willing and able to use the opportunity afforded by its armed intervention to build closer ties with Dominican non-Communists on the left and to co-operate with them in restructuring the Dominican military establishment, then more vulnerable than at any time in recent years. It is already possible to suggest, however, that the crisis of 1965 heightened the fragmentation of Dominican politics, further decreasing the already slender chances that the Dominican Republic can soon develop effective political institutions.[12] Families, social and economic groups, political parties, the armed forces, even the Catholic Church were divided by the crisis and the U.S. intervention, and capable individuals were "burned" politically because of their participation on one side or the other or in efforts to resolve the crisis.

Although it is too early to be sure what lasting effects the U.S. intervention will have had on the Dominican polity, it is equally early to draw the comforting conclusion that a stable and progressive Dominican regime has now been established. Disturbing signs that the current Balaguer regime is less than progressive recur from time to time, and there are indications that the extreme right, now clustered around General Wessin y Wessin, may exert

increased influence in the future. As pressure mounts from both extremes of the Dominican political spectrum, and as the opposition P.R.D. continues to disintegrate into competing factions, there is reason to doubt the regime's capacity to survive. As Dr. Balaguer himself has warned, the civil war of 1965 may yet be resumed, albeit in a new form and with many new participants.

Among all the uncertain consequences of the 1965 intervention, two results are all too sure: The intervention further entangled the U.S. government in the Dominican morass and it reinforced the dependence of Dominicans on the United States. Just as the U.S. imposition of sanctions voted by the OAS against Trujilo in 1960 involved the United States deeply in the post-Trujilo Dominican political struggle, so the 1965 intervention and its aftermath have forced the U.S. government to play an even more central role in current Dominican affairs. This intense involvement may decrease in time, but the long-term prospects for the development of normal diplomatic relations between the United States and the Dominican Republic were undoubtedly diminished by the events of 1965. The political, economic, and psychological effects of renewed intervention have further undermined the possibilities for authentic national development in the Caribbean, while increasing the likelihood that, if national development does occur in the Caribbean, it will be based —as in Cuba—on virulent anti-Americanism.

12 See Wiarda, "From Fragmentation to Disintegration: The Social and Political Effects of the Dominican Revolution," *America Latina*, XI (April–June 1967), 55–71.

IV

Some will doubtless conclude, even after weighing all the costs here enumerated, that U.S. policy in the 1965 Dominican crisis was well-advised. They will stress the importance of the advantages they believe were produced by the intervention: preventing a bloodbath perhaps even worse than that which occurred, precluding the possible take-over of the Dominican Republic either by Communists or by a right-wing military dictatorship, and perhaps even discouraging radical uprisings elsewhere in Latin America. Since the Dominican intervention was limited in time and extent, they will argue, it did not entail the more permanent costs which might have arisen had hostile power been introduced into the Dominican vacuum.

To contest this judgment would require evaluating some fundamental assumptions about the nature of U.S. interests in the Caribbean, analyzing in detail the extent of Castro-Communist strength and the degree of violence and potential violence in the early days of the Dominican crisis, and examining carefully the various alternatives for U.S. policy at different stages of the crisis. Much less is required, however, to show that the Dominican intervention should not be considered a model for future U.S. actions, for *even if* the Dominican operation is assumed to have been successful from the standpoint of U.S. objectives, it should be stressed that unique aspects of the Dominican case helped account for its outcome. The Dominican Republic was a comparatively easy place for the United States to intervene and from which to withdraw. The fortuitous availability of particular individuals helped to facilitate early resolution of the crisis. Finally, official exaggerations of the dangers in the Dominican situation may obscure the perils the United States would face if it intervened elsewhere in

more difficult circumstances. The quick withdrawal of U.S. forces from the Dominican Republic does not, in short, necessarily indicate that the United States would be able to extricate itself so fast and so favorably from a future intervention.

It seems likely that military intervention in the Caribbean bears fewer costs and risks for the United States than it would in any other area. In no other region are U.S. capabilities more overwhelming than in the island nations of the Caribbean, heavily dependent on U.S. trade and susceptible to naval blockade and other exercises of U.S. power. U.S. intervention in a Caribbean island probably has far different effects on Latin American opinion and inter-American relations from those which might follow the landing of U.S. forces on the South American continent, or even on the mainland of Central America. South Americans tend to distinguish themselves from the peoples of the Caribbean on racial, cultural, and historical grounds, and many South Americans consider the Caribbean a U.S. "sphere of interest." The apparent decline in evident South American concern about the U.S. intervention after the initial outbursts and demonstrations had subsided may be due partly to the distance of the Dominican Republic—geographically and in terms of self-image—from the countries of South America.

Even within the Caribbean, the United States found it easier to extricate itself from the Dominican Republic in 1966 than it would elsewhere. Nationalist consciousness in the Dominican Republic is less fully developed than in most Latin American countries, a fact which accounts partly for the lack of effective armed opposition to the U.S. military presence. The background of U.S. participation in recent Dominican politics made Dominicans more receptive to American efforts to establish a new Dominican government during the 1965 crisis than most Latin Americans would be. Moreover, certain key U.S. officials gained, from the unusually active embassy role during this period, sufficient understanding of the personalities and dynamics of Dominican politics to perform the difficult task of helping to devise a political solution for the Dominican crisis. And when the Provisional Government formula was finally achieved, its success depended largely upon the compatible abilities of two individuals, U.S. Ambassador (to the OAS) Ellsworth Bunker and Dominican President Héctor García-Godoy. Each displayed gifts of patience and judgment which probably averted the resumption of open hostilities at several stages, and each was vindicated in several instances when their policies were questioned within the U.S. government. Should the United States ever find itself again in circumstances similar to those confronting it in the Dominican case, it might not be so fortunate as to find a statesman of Dr. García-Godoy's caliber willing to assume such a difficult post, nor could it be sure that an official of Ambassador Bunker's capacity would be available for such an assignment.

Finally, it is clear that American officials exaggerated the dangers in the Dominican crisis, and one may well consider how the U.S. government would actually fare in circumstances like those it originally perceived in the Dominican Republic. The United States government, for instance, greatly overestimated the coherence, strength, and political influence of Dominican Communist groups when the massive intervention began. Dominican Com-

munists proved to be few in number, almost totally lacking in rural support, and relatively untrained in the techniques of urban violence. Their role within the "constitutionalist" movement was not difficult to determine or to limit, as they proved relatively easy to isolate. It is likely that the United States might find elsewhere that the real strength of local Communist organizations would preclude the rapid disengagement of American forces.

United States officials also exaggerated the extent to which Dominican society had disintegrated at the end of April 1965. After U.S. troops imposed an uneasy truce in Santo Domingo, it turned out that the Dominican Republic, while shaken, had not been so thoroughly affected as some American observers had initially feared. Most of the country outside the capital city was little affected by the violent struggle in Santo Domingo, and it soon proved to be possible to maintain nearly normal economic activity throughout the countryside. As weeks passed, the U.S. learned that there were still fairly well organized forces in Santo Domingo with which to deal. The U.S. entered into aid agreements with members of the permanent Dominican national bureaucracy and also with established municipal governments and private development associations. U.S. officials negotiated with recognized political parties and encouraged existing business, labor, and professional associations to put forth their views on how to resolve the political impasse. When the time came in 1966, the feasibility of orderly and meaningful elections depended upon competition between two well-known political groupings, each headed by a former Dominican president with a substantial following in the country. The fact that the

Dominican people were familiar with the electoral process, and had reason to trust the honesty of elections held under OAS auspices because of the 1962 experience, was also helpful.[13]

In considering the problems which might some day arise in Haiti, the country probably most likely to cause the United States to consider another intervention, it is worth noting that precisely the factors which facilitated early U.S. withdrawal from the Dominican Republic would be lacking. If the United States were to send its forces into a country such as Haiti—without clearly established institutions and political groupings, without political figures of obvious stature and influence, without experience at meaningful elections, even without a functioning bureaucracy, and about which the United States has relatively little experience or knowledge—it might find it very difficult to pull them out.

Finally, it may be worth reflecting on a possibility that some administration officials mentioned at the time—that a number of leftist insurrections might occur at once. The Dominican intervention, which occurred when the U.S. had in Vietnam about one-tenth of the forces deployed there by 1968, strained the standing-force capabilities of the United States in the hemisphere. Over 35,000 troops were engaged in the Dominican operation at its height, almost 23,000 of them on shore in an area only a few square miles in extent. United States officials must examine the consequences of this overwhelming type of response to a Caribbean crisis on the capability of this country to deal simultaneously with a security threat elsewhere.

V

The various arguments set forth here suggest that no easy lessons can be drawn from the Dominican intervention. Both the vigorous criticism immediately following the U.S. landing and the satisfaction with American policy that some now express must be scrutinized. Thorough examination of American policy during the Dominican crisis may well yield valuable insights about that particular episode and about more general problems of U.S. diplomacy, but it will not provide a manual for successful intervention.

This essay is not meant to imply that the United States can or should absolutely preclude military intervention as a policy instrument in all future circumstances. The world is yet too far from a state of enforceable international law to offer such a proscription. What is emphasized, however, is the high cost of military intervention and the uncertainty of its consequences even under conditions relatively favorable for the exercise of U.S. power, and also the likelihood that a future intervention might be more costly and less effective as a way to achieve American objectives. The Dominican experience points most clearly, therefore, to the need to stress and reinforce preferable means of advancing American aims, particularly by helping to promote the political, social, and economic development of those areas, like the Caribbean, where U.S. interests are deemed important.

[13] See Henry Wells, "The OAS and the Dominican Elections," *Orbis,* VII (Spring 1963), 150–163.

B

MODERNIZATION: THE POLITICAL DIMENSION

20

Centralism and Nationalism
in Latin America

Claudio Véliz

From Claudio Véliz, "Centralism and Nationalism in Latin America," *Foreign Affairs*, XLVII, No. 1 (October 1968), pp. 68–83. © Council on Foreign Relations, Inc., New York. Reprinted by special permission of the author and *Foreign Affairs*.

Claudio Véliz is Director of the Institute of International Studies at the University of Chile, Santiago, Chile.

The division between sections II-B and II-C of this anthology is largely for the sake of convenience. It is exceedingly difficult to separate the political from the economic and social dimensions of modernization, none the least because social scientists are hard put to specify the exact relationship between them. Policies also overlap: For example, one of the arguments against bilateral economic assistance is that it tends to be political in orientation, although few would deny that multilateral aid, too, has political implications. Generally speaking, however, the editor has grouped under II-B selections dealing primarily with the domestic political environment in Latin America and the longstanding issues involved in defining unilateral United States and multilateral postures toward various kinds of Latin American governments and the Latin American military. Since security considerations have usually been foremost in the minds of U.S. policymakers, there are also unavoidable echoes of section II-A. On the other hand, II-C stresses the economic and social impact of development assistance, the mechanisms of development assistance, the foreign private enterprise question, competing strategies of development, and Latin American trade and economic integration.

In this essay, Véliz contends that Latin America is no longer as receptive as it once was to United States and European "political experiences, aspira-

tions and recommendations." This trend stems in part, he feels, from a belated recognition that foreign pluralistic models have little relevance to the "vertebral centralism of the Latin American tradition." According to Véliz, the "centralist state" serves as the focus of a "new nationalism" in Latin America today, which reflects an increasing reaction against external dependence.[1]

For the last century and a half, Latin America has been a faithful echoing chamber for every political noise uttered in the more civilized regions of the northern hemisphere. It now appears that this period may be drawing to a close, partly as a result of domestic developments, and partly because the source of models deemed worthy of imitation is drying up. This is not the end of ideology, but it certainly suggests that the era in which Latin America accepted blindly the political experiences, aspirations and recommendations issuing from the shores of the North Atlantic is coming to an end.

Practically every major political ideology which found a sympathetic echo in Latin America during the last hundred years was produced by the impact of the Industrial Revolution upon a European social structure which in turn was fundamentally modified by historical events like Feudalism and the Reformation that had no counterpart in the Luso-Hispanic tradition. Thus, under different names and guises, conservatism, liberalism, radicalism, communism and social democracy (and its Christian Democratic variant), all with deep European roots, have dominated the political life of this part of the world. Even conservatism, which could perhaps claim to be timeless and pre-industrial, never succeeded in clearing the awesome frontier of 1810; it retained a distinct republican flavor which placed it closer to modern European conservatism than to any irredentist monarchial movement with Hispanic roots.

The European origins of liberalism, radicalism and communism of course need no documentation. The aura of modernity and originality which currently adorns the Christian Democratic and Christian Socialist movements in Latin America is more than faintly similar to that which graced their European precursors, not only in recent times but also when they provided Chancellor Bismarck with some of his livelier political difficulties or when they shattered the complacency of the Bishops' Conference of 1908 at Lambeth.

The modern political arrangements of the so-called Western world—which most certainly includes the Soviet Union—are to an important degree the offspring of the transformations brought about by industry during the nineteenth century. But Latin America has been bypassed by the Industrial Revolution: industry has indeed come to these countries, but without the great changes which attended its earlier appearance on the shores of the North Atlantic. Moreover, the Latin American social structure, which has received the benefits of modern industrial technology, is different in essence from the European one which produced it.

The complex of cultural differences

[1] For a related discussion, see selection 30.

makes it hard if not impossible to establish priorities or hierarchies of significance. Nevertheless, I would like to suggest three fundamental differences which may account for the apparent inability of Latin America at present to provide a fertile soil for European ideological models and which indicate the type of development likely to dominate its domestic and international political life in the near future. The three differences are the absence in Latin America's historical experience of feudalism, of religious nonconformity and of industrial development which is individually initiated as opposed to that which is centrally encouraged. Conversely, I would suggest that it is precisely in the vertebral centralism of the Latin American tradition that an explanation of recent developments and perhaps even the key to the political future of the region will most probably be discovered.

II

The feudal experience is not part of the cultural tradition of Latin America. Of course the word has often been used pejoratively to describe the relationship between landlord and peasant in Latin America as elsewhere, but in fact feudalism as a political structure never existed in this part of the world. It is important to realize this, because the balance of power between a weak center and strong periphery, which was characteristic of feudalism, was evidently a major ingredient of European liberalism and all its social-democratic variants.

In spite of the quaint efforts by Mexican revolutionaries, the founders of APRA and others to establish direct lines of descent from the centuries before the coming of the Spaniards, the fact is that Latin America was born into the modern world during the sixteenth century, at least three hundred years after feudalism had disappeared from Western Europe; its institutional structure was fashioned wholesale in Madrid by the strongest monarchy in Christendom and on the Renaissance model of a centrally controlled polity. It hardly needs pointing out that Columbus discovered the New World precisely the year that the last Moorish stronghold of Granada was taken by the Spaniards, bringing to an end a military campaign which had lasted, with varying intensity, for seven centuries. The victorious Catholic kings ruled unchallenged and the faint attempts by regional military orders or aspiring warlords to contest their authority are of no more than anecdotal value. A full generation before Henry VIII started his quarrels with the Vatican, Ferdinand of Aragon secured from Pope Julius II the famous bull *Universalis ecclesiae regimini* which, together with earlier generosities of Rome, laid the legal basis for the absolute power, temporal and ecclesiastical, which the Spanish rulers were to exercise with considerable efficiency over their vast American territories.

The institutional structure devised for the Indies naturally reflected this unqualified centralism, and no effort was spared to ensure that distance would not facilitate the development of peripheral sites of political power; even to fill a minor post at the Viceroyalty of Peru, consultation with Spain was required, and whoever attempted to depart from the strictest reading of the colonial legislation was punished with severity. Even the most exalted colonial rulers had at the end of their mandate to make the lengthy voyage to Spain to sit at the dreaded *juicio de residencia.* Madrid's power gave muscle to the longest administrative arms in Christendom.

This system survived for three centuries and when it finally collapsed, its legalistic, centralist and authoritarian tradition passed on undiminished to the republican régimes, which had the advantage of shorter lines of communication. It must be remembered that the revolutions of 1810 were not popular uprisings but rather independence movements after the fashion of the one led by Mr. Ian Smith in Rhodesia.

The institutional habit of compromise between alternative centers of political power is not, then, part of the Latin American tradition. The feudal experience of northern Europe, where the central monarchy had to negotiate with a number of lesser centers of power, is simply not known in this part of the world. Here the center has never been decisively challenged and even its major revolutionary experience—that of 1810—was initiated in the name of legitimacy and against the French, who by then represented egalitarianism.

Political centralism remained virtually unassailed during the nineteenth century. No doubt instances can be found of uprisings by local chieftains but, apart from the fact that these were generally unsuccessful, close examination will show that even the most outspoken regional *caciques* were often feeding on the crumbs of political power which fell from the table of the central government.

The centralism of the past four centuries has survived well into our times. The three major modern revolutions in Latin America—perhaps the only real ones—have reconstructed society according to strikingly different ideas, yet they have all resulted in single-party systems: the Mexican PRI is unique in the ramifications of its centralist control; the Cuban government party, I would suggest, rules from an authoritarian center because it is Cuban rather than because it is communist; and the Bolivian MNR, although eventually unsuccessful, made a determined attempt to monopolize political power and was later replaced by another régime at least as centralist. The trend that can be perceived in other countries—without considering the outright tyrannies—is clearly toward the establishment of a dominant political party identified with the government. This is seen even in the most sophisticated and democratic states in the region.

The weight of this historical tradition has lately been reinforced by the well-nigh universal trend toward increased participation or intervention by the central government in all aspects of national life. While in, say, Britain, the United States or Sweden, this trend clashes with the prevailing pluralistic and generally liberal concept of political responsibility, in Latin America it reinforces the existing drive for greater central control.

If political centralism has worn well over the last few centuries, the same can also be said of the Catholic Church. It is a moot point whether nonconformity is, or is not, a basic ingredient of European liberalism, but it is difficult to imagine political liberalism in Britain, France or the United States, for instance, without a concomitant attitude in matters of religion. In Latin America the problem would hardly arise: there has never been anything which could reasonably be equated with nonconformity; the religious authority of the Catholic Church has never been challenged from within. No doubt priests have been shot, churches burned and anticlericalism has become an established political and social attitude, but the spiritual authority of the Catholic Establishment remains untouched. Even in a country like Mexico, where from Juarez to Zapata the major revolutionary movements have been staunchly anticlerical and where it is easier to sustain normal diplomatic relations with Cuba than with the Vatican, the Catholic Church remains the only significant national religion.

There is, of course, ample evidence of dissent within the Catholic Church in Latin America today, but this stems from anxiety over social and political issues, not over the fundamental religious tenets of official Catholicism. The inroads of Protestantism are also not to be minimized, but so far, even in Chile, where they have been most noticeable, less than 10 percent of the population is registered as belonging to the numerous Protestant sects.

In Europe and North America it was but a short step from religious dissent to political dissent; it does not take exceptional scholarship to trace the nonconformist ancestry of many of the most active reformist parties.

III

As might be expected, political and religious centralism was accompanied by economic centralism, which is not only the product of a long Hispanic tradition but also the result of the way in which industry came to this part of the world. In Europe, industrial activity arose out of a complex· cultural situation which resulted in the conscious accumulation of industrial capital over a long period of time. This process owed little or nothing to the intervention of the central government and it

led to a dispersion of power. That the central state later came to represent these industrial interests is beside the point; for it to happen, the new industrialists had to challenge the traditional ruling groups and wrest power from them.

Further, the growth of industry ran almost parallel with the growth of cities, and urbanization was a consequence of industrial activity. Industry then was labor intensive and for it to function efficiently a sizeable labor force had to be organized in urban centers. As a result the workers acquired a new political consciousness. Thus it can be said that the impact of industry on traditional European society was revolutionary at least in that it was spearheaded by a newly formed industrial bourgeoisie and it resulted in the formation of a new industrial proletariat.

None of these considerations would seem to apply to the industrialization of Latin America. Here industry has been stimulated largely by external factors such as the great crisis of 1929 (principally affecting Brazil) and the Second World War, which began the process of import substitution. It owed relatively little to domestic determinants. An urbanization in Latin America did not wait for industrialization, which was instead grafted onto a sophisticated, self-conscious, relatively urbanized society. A remarkably large proportion of the population was already living in cities for reasons other than the development of industry. More important perhaps, industrialization owed a very great deal to the direct intervention of the central state—through tariff protection, subsidies, credit policies or straightforward programs of industrial development carried out directly under the aegis of public development corporations. Lastly, the social changes generally associated with industrialization have not occurred in Latin America; there have been many changes but not the ones that scholars and politicians were prepared for.

Latin America has industrialized rapidly, but this has not been the result of the exertions of an industrial bourgeoisie; nor has it produced an industrial proletariat. In the 1870s, Britain was the first industrial power on earth and was producing her first million tons of steel. To achieve this, over 370,000 workers were employed. In Latin America today, Argentina, Brazil and Mexico are well over the million-ton mark (Brazil is moving close to four million tons per year) and a rough estimate shows that only seven or eight thousand workers are needed to produce each million tons of steel. Peru is the first fishing nation on earth, but the total labor force engaged in the fisheries and processing plants does not exceed thirty thousand men. Such examples abound and they all point to a fairly obvious development: industrial technology has changed; it is now more capital than labor intensive. The industrial labor force in Latin America is not the modern equivalent of the traditional proletariat. Working with an advanced industrial technology, it is smaller, better trained and better paid. It is in fact an aristocracy of labor with incomes which all too often rise above those of vast numbers of white collar workers in the tertiary sector.

As the capacity of industry to absorb large numbers of workers is limited, the massive transformation of peasants into industrial workers has not come to pass. With luck, the average migrant to the cities will find employment in the building industry, but more often than not he will somehow drift into the service sector, which is by far the best organized as well as the most politically active. The coming of industry resulted in a sharp decrease of self-employed artisans and craftsmen and a spectacular rise in the number of people in service occupations, but this increase was only the continuation of a process that had been going on for well over a century. These professionals, white collar employees, bureaucrats and domestic and service workers are not the Latin American equivalent of, say, the rising English middle class of 1832; for the most part they are directly or indirectly associated with, or dependent upon, either the central government or the traditional social structure. Few are involved in industry, and their political activities have been directed principally toward securing greater participation in the existing social organization rather than in seeking to demolish it and replace it with another.

The pre-industrial urbanization of Latin America is a significant phenomenon in its own right; its intensification during the last three decades has resulted in the steady depopulation of an already sparsely settled countryside. At present Latin America has a greater proportion of its urban inhabitants living in cities of 100,000 or more than does Europe; in Argentina, Cuba, Chile, Uruguay and Venezuela the proportion of the population that is urban is well over 40 percent. It is neither the "landless peasant" nor the "exploited" industrial worker who epitomizes the politically significant Latin American; it is rather the underpaid bank clerk with social aspirations.

As for the Latin American equivalent of the traditional industrial bourgeoisie—forward-looking, adventurous, willing to take risks, ready to innovate, anti-aristocratic and reformist —it simply does not exist. The force for dynamic change has been the central government. Domestic private enterprise has seldom performed with distinction except when instigated and assisted by the government. If all state subsidies and financial commitments were to be withdrawn from private industry, precious little would remain in operation. This has come about partly by default; the so-called industrial bourgeoisie and their clientele have been agile opportunists and mediocre imitators rather than adventurous challengers or originators of new ideas. With remarkably few exceptions— mostly foreign immigrants—they owe their newly achieved economic prosperity more to their social or political proximity to the government cornucopia in the years between 1940 and 1960 than to any impressive exertions on their own part.

For them, industry is just one of many ways of making money: they own industrial capital, they often have a controlling interest, but they are not industrialists in the meaningful sense of the word. More often than not they are prepared to exchange the risks inherent in effective responsibility for an agreement with a foreign company which will guarantee royalties, expert advice and a numbered bank account in Europe. Their docility has prevented them from becoming an effective pressure group except in a negative sense. This is shown, for instance, in the opposition of Ecuadorian and Venezuelan businessmen to plans for regional integration. There is in Latin America no counterpart to European industrial liberalism.

In Europe and the United States it was the dynamic industrial groups that for various reasons became the mainstay—both political and economic—of

a development policy aimed at the satisfaction of national aspirations; in Latin America, however, the owners of industry are largely responsible for increasing our external dependence. They have not been innovators, nor have they challenged the established social order or provided political alternatives. Instead they have fallen with remarkable ease into the patterns of imitation and emulation characteristic of social climbing. In fact, it would not be surprising if their major contribution to the contemporary life of Latin America turns out to be the efficient institutionalization of this process; far from weakening the traditional structure, they have become its most loyal and enthusiastic upholders.

To sum up, then, there appears to be no substantial evidence indicating that the tradition of centralism characteristic of Latin American culture is in any significant way being challenged from within. Furthermore, the pressure groups which in Europe and the United States played such an important role in forcing through the changes demanded by the incorporation of industrial technology are either not fitted or not prepared to play a comparable role in Latin America. What sector of society, then, is likely to fulfill this function in the future?

IV

Marx and Lenin have not been the only ones to accept the notion that the state is an instrument, a tool to be used by one group or another to defend its own interests. This concept of the state has figured prominently in the historical tradition of Western Europe (though perhaps more significantly in Britain and the United States). From it derives the conceptual framework which informs much of contemporary sociological and historical analysis—including the study of Latin America. Learned northern observers of the Latin American situation have thus spent much time identifying the pressure groups which are expected to be vying with each other for the control of that supposedly inert instrument, the central state. In their writings, various groups are favored as most likely to assume the leadership of the process that is vaguely described as "modernization." Some place their bets on the rising urban bourgeoisie; others hope or fear that the peasantry will march on the cities and transform everything; others are impressed by the vociferous political activity of the students; while others still stress the reformist aspirations of the "Nasserist" groups in the armed forces.

This type of analysis does not seem to me helpful, largely because it starts from the mistaken premise that the central government in Latin America is at least as "instrumental" as that typical of the European tradition and as likely to respond to the pressures, civilized or not, coming from more or less powerful groups. In Latin America the central government itself is the most powerful pressure group. It extends its power and influence t hrough a highly centralized civil service and through complex and all-embracing systems of social security and patronage which have transformed most of the vast urban service sector into an institutionalized clientele; it controls the major centers of learning and is capable of exercising almost unrestricted control over economic life. The only institutions which could perhaps be regarded as likely rivals, because of their relatively self-contained nature, are the Church and the armed forces, but in either case the rivalry would not be counterbalancing or pluralistic; rather it would tend to emphasize the central and national responsibilities of the government. Whenever pressures from these two sectors are exerted, they encourage the state to exercise still more all-embracing power from the center.

If this powerful and self-conscious pressure group did not earlier exert its potential force to the fullest, it was because the domestic and international conditions prevailing during the hundred years which preceded 1929 were such as to discourage or at least make unnecessary an activist role for the state. Conflicting interests were few. The ruling groups of the time enjoyed a more than reasonable degree of prosperity; those influential in forming political and intellectual attitudes were clearly identified with European liberalism, while the expansion of world trade and a growing demand for the primary commodities of Latin America tended to make acceptance of the tenets of laisser faire financially profitable as well as socially and intellectually agreeable.

It was not external pressures, therefore, which forced the state to accept an apparently passive role, but rather a decision made for reasons of expediency. It is worthwhile remembering that the same uncritical admiration of everything European which contributed to making Manchester liberalism so attractive to the exporters of mineral and agricultural products also eased the introduction into Latin America of English fashions, German militarism and French positivism, European tastes and methods of education. Sarmiento was not alone in thinking that for Latin America to become truly civilized, it had to become European.

The crisis of 1929 and the Second World War marked the end of the lengthy period of prosperity based on the export of commodities. It also established the conditions for the massive introduction of industrial technology, if only through the doubtful channels of indiscriminate import substitution. Yet the full political impact of the ensuing changes was postponed as a result of circumstances imposed by the Second World War and the pressures of the cold war.

Apart from other important considerations, the Second World War introduced a virtual moratorium on political development in Latin America. With the world divided into warring factions and the countries of the region more or less in the Allied camp, traditional alignments were redrawn to fit external demands. Even the communist parties and their close associates of the time postponed their struggles against capitalism and loyally collaborated in the efforts to keep the Allies well supplied with raw materials. The hope was also widely entertained that the end of the conflict would bring, as a well-earned reward, a veritable flood of assistance, which would in some undefined way bring back the plentiful days of the past.

Although the nationalistic movements in Latin America had little or nothing in common with Germany save a shared suspicion of the United States or Britain, they were often sympathetic to the Axis, and it required considerable coaxing before they declared for the Allies. It would be facile and mistaken to think that Villarroel in Bolivia, Ibañez in Chile, Vargas in Brazil, Péron in Argentina, Arnulfo Arias in Panama and so many others were simply stooges of an international Nazi conspiracy. It would be closer to the truth to say that these various nationalist movements were essentially domestic and reflected the basic aspirations or dissatisfactions of important

urban sectors. The issue of the Canal Zone was foremost in the minds of those who supported Arnulfo Arias at that time; economic imperialism and the Falkland Islands were ever present in Péron's oratory; Villarroel came to power as a result of the frustrations of the Chaco War but also on the assurance that Bolivia would not remain forever a colonial appendage of the tin industry; Vargas represented the drive toward industrialization and economic autonomy. These movements, under whatever name, represented a nationalist alternative to the traditional programs presented by the established parties of Right and Left. At their most successful, they provided the basis for what in the postwar period has generally been described as Latin American populism—perhaps the most revealing portent of the political future of the region.

The widespread feeling that rampant nationalism was the ultimate cause of World War II tended to make the domestic nationalist movements in Latin America appear like the villains of a new black legend. Internationalism became the new religion and international cooperation the accepted morality. But with the slaughter and destruction of the war still fresh in mind, a weary world plunged into yet another total struggle. Mr. Truman's doctrinal declaration dividing the world into two oddly defined camps presented Latin America with a formidable false dilemma. It was clear that Mr. Truman had not really meant each country to choose between democracy and tyranny; there were enough despotic régimes on the side of the angels to make this a doubtful proposition. On the other hand it was apparent even then—and it has since become obvious—that the communist parties in the Latin American countries had no intention of leading revolutionary movements to overthrow their respective governments. In this respect they reflected the pragmatic attitude of the Soviet Union, which accepted Latin America's being within the sphere of influence of the United States. Yet the urgencies of the international situation forced a decision, and anti-communism was raised to the status of dogma by able politicians; although these men were well aware that the local communists did not constitute a serious threat, they kept their eyes fixed on the flow of aid which was invariably directed toward those countries whose loyalty to the Western world was beyond dispute.[1]

In the anxiety of the Soviet Union and the United States to marshal their allies into supranational political and military arrangements, the Organization of American States was created. The OAS, which became the Latin American branch of the cold-war policy of the United States, can validly claim to be one of the least impressive of the many postwar pacts. For a time internationalism apparently was defined in

[1] "In other parts of the world it may be merely ridiculous to claim that the communists are not revolutionaries, but in Latin America it is a fact that the communist movement has no vigorous revolutionary tradition. There is probably no conservative or liberal party in all of Latin America that has not staged more insurrections and incited more civil wars than the communists. In a continent racked by civil strife the communists' record has been one of remarkable quiescence. Their one major attempt to seize power by force was the 1935 insurrection led by Luiz Carlos Prestes in Brazil, apart from which there have been only some instances of communist participation in risings by noncommunist groups." Ernst Halperin, "Nationalism and Communism in Chile." Cambridge: Massachusetts Institute of Technology, 1965, p. 13.

Washington and Moscow as a willingness to accept the validity of these arrangements, and the good favor of the superpowers depended on the degree of zeal with which these treaty organizations were supported. But to those Latin Americans who were not absolutely committed, the cold war was less an ideological confrontation than a struggle between two obsessively nationalistic powers intent on defending or extending their respective spheres of influence. Neither was seen as a particularly attractive model and neither received more than tepid gestures of popular support—except from the notoriously servile tyrannies.

Yet a most important consequence of the coming of the cold war to Latin America was the emphasis it placed on the dependent nature of both domestic and international political life. Political activity became largely subordinated to the vagaries of the great world confrontation; neutralism was unacceptable and nationalism severely frowned upon, while friendly internationalism was most definitely encouraged. Any reformist program, any criticism of the United States, however justified, any attempt to steer an independent policy became suspect, and more often than not was publicly tinged in deepest red. It finally required an initiative by the United States to make agrarian, fiscal and administrative reform respectable political aspirations.

V

The feeling of utter dependence has grown deep roots during the years of the cold war. But as the confrontation becomes attenuated by the challenge of France and China to the leadership of the United States and the Soviet Union, by the growth of polycentrism on both sides of the Iron Curtain, and by a measure of détente between the two great powers, a resurgence of nationalism is apparent in Latin America. "A plague on both your houses" is becoming a common attitude; as the tide of cold-war loyalties recedes, Latin Americans are becoming increasingly conscious of national aspirations submerged for too long.

The time may now be ripe for the centralist state to come into its own, fired with a new nationalism fed on an awareness that the increasing cultural and economic dependence of the region is one of its principal problems. Had circumstances even faintly similar to the present ones occurred, say, half a century ago, a fashionable European ideology would no doubt have been promptly imported by the latest batch of Latin American intellectuals returning home from their grand tour. Today this is no longer possible, partly because the mood is emphatically nationalistic and partly because the prevailing feeling is that the northern hemisphere has precious little guidance to offer: the United States and the Soviet Union are living through critical times themselves and have abandoned much of their ideological fervor in order to adopt pragmatic and short-term solutions. Even those who until recently were willing to grant the benefit of the doubt to some tried old horses—*e.g.* socialism, capitalism and their variants—are now conscious that their application to Latin America is at least questionable. Indeed, Latin America may for the first time in its history become an exporter of political symbols and ideas. This is suggested by the enthusiastic adoption of Ché Guevara by students in Europe and the United States, while here his political appeal is largely restricted to a genuine admiration for his integrity and heroism.

In the absence of a more elaborate framework within which to fit political action, men tend to fall back on elemental loyalties—tribe, family or, as in Latin America today, straightforward nationalism. Besides being undemanding intellectually, nationalism draws support from all the people, regardless of other interests.

A nationalistic ideology can perhaps get us from a confused present to a more satisfactory future, but the risks cannot be ignored. Nationalism tends to magnify the impact of external factors on domestic situations. Even if it is based on a reasonably civilized understanding of what constitutes the national interest, it courts international friction. In this kind of mood, affecting the major nations of Latin America simultaneously, rearmament, for example, assumes an importance which cannot be overlooked.

At the same time it should be emphasized that the major objective of Latin American nationalism is to reverse the present trend toward cultural and economic dependence on the United States. This, to be fair, is apparently also an objective of enlightened U.S. policy, as shown in numerous official pronouncements calling for a determined effort in Latin America to shoulder a greater part of the burden of its own development. The financial difficulties of the United States may of course make this objective mandatory. At any rate, it must be remembered that independent behavior in nations, as in human beings, cannot easily be confined to some things, excluding others. If the countries of Latin America are to act with greater independence in the planning and implementation of truly national development policies, it should not surprise anybody if they become independent in foreign policy and other fields as well. The military, for example, which until recently have been the most loyal allies of the United States, are now beginning to see the penetration and interference of the great northern power in the same light in which they formerly viewed communism—as an international threat to national sovereignty and integrity. Their indignant reaction to the efforts of the United States to stem their growing purchases of armaments is a significant example of the new attitude.

Although the numerous Latin American student movements operate from strikingly varied backgrounds, under various political auspices and with very varied purposes, they do seem to share a preoccupation with the need to encourage national research and scholarship as a means to escape the cultural penetration of the United States. These students are not necessarily militants of extreme left-wing parties; more often than is realized they are politically nonaligned or represent middle-of-the-road political movements. They themselves, of course, come predominantly from the middle and upper classes of society.

There is a widespread feeling, especially in the academic community, that Latin American integration is in difficulties partly because it is too closely associated with the United States. One of the informal conclusions of a major conference which met earlier this year in Chile to examine the problems of integration was that what was needed was a truly American process of integration instead of the present Inter-American scheme which allows the United States to play too important a role.

Until a few months ago there were three principal organizations interested in the process of integration: the Latin American Free Trade Association (LAFTA), the Inter-American Development Bank and the Inter-American Committee of the Alliance for Progress. Of these, the last two are based in Washington and depend on the financial support of the United States; LAFTA is strictly a Latin American organization but also the least successful so far. This anomalous situation has not gone unnoticed, and it may be that the move to create truly Latin American subregional organizations like the Andean Group or the Plata Basin Group is at least indirectly a consequence of this awareness.

Amidst the débris left behind by the quiet failure of the Alliance for Progress will be found a number of social-democratic movements which feel—with or without justification—that the United States did less than it could have done to assist their reformist efforts, after giving them decisive early encouragement. Their frustration is minimal, however, compared with that of the right-wing parties, which feel that after decades of giving their loyal support to every political move made by the United States and facing the domestic onslaught of the left-wing opposition to such unpopular policies as the overthrow of the Arbenz régime in Guatemala or the Bay of Pigs invasion, the Kennedy Administration stabbed them in the back by putting forward a program like the Alliance for Progress, whose principal objective was precisely to undermine the very basis of their economic and political position.

Such examples could be multiplied. The important fact is that the growing isolation of the United States in the world, whatever its causes, is now being reflected in Latin America. It is not easy to find a significant political group or sector of society willing to stand up and be counted on the side of the great northern neighbor.

Given these indicators and the concomitant resurgence of nationalism in Latin America, it is likely that relations with the United States will become difficult in the future. Moreover, the challenge to U.S. hegemony will probably come not from the extreme left wing but rather from the state itself, supported by sizeable sectors of the urban population. The United States is likely to be more vulnerable to this type of confrontation than is usually imagined. Seen from Latin America, it will resemble the fortress of Singapore on the eve of the Japanese invasion: all guns facing the sea but virtually defenseless against a land attack.

However important the negative dynamism generated by aggressive independence of the United States, I would suggest that this is not the principal feature of contemporary Latin American nationalism. Rather it is the return to a style of political behavior firmly rooted in an autochthonous centralist tradition. On this tradition is founded the structure of institutions and political habits of Latin Americans; on it, as well, are based the organizational successes of the past decades. Latin Americans are increasingly conscious that in harnessing the momentum of this tradition to the needs of national development they will acquire understanding and mastery of the problems of their nations.

Although this novel process of self-discovery is scarcely a few years old it has already offered promising first results in various fields. The original, successful and growing participation of the central government in the Mexican economy; the plans for public multinational corporations which will operate within the subregional schemes; the remarkable history of growth and consolidation of the enterprises fathered by the Chilean Development Corporation—all afford evidence of the vitality of this trend. At the same time, the writings of historians, economists and political analysts reflect both a generalized dissatisfaction with foreign imitation and an endeavor to create a new political architecture, using the materials at hand instead of importing them ready-made from elsewhere.

Latin America has been prodigal in the arts and letters—perhaps the world's best contemporary novels have been written during the past decade by Colombians, Peruvians and Argentines —but it has not distinguished itself in the field of political and social ideas. It is not unduly optimistic to think that this is due at least in part to the diligence with which its intelligentsia has in the past looked to the northern hemisphere not only for political answers but for the questions as well. It would be surprising indeed if a reversal of this trend does not prove extremely rewarding.

21

The Nixon Administration Position
Regarding Undemocratic Governments
in Latin America :
State-AID Congressional Testimony
and the Rockefeller Report

Section I from House Committee on Foreign Affairs, Subcommittee on Inter-American Affairs, Hearings (February–May 1969), *New Directions for the 1970's: Toward a Strategy of Inter-American Development*, Ninety-First Congress, First Session, Committee Print (Washington: U.S. Government Printing Office, 1969), pp. 7–8, 14–15, 28–30, 140–41. Section II from Nelson A. Rockefeller, *Quality of Life in the Americas* in *Department of State Bulletin*, LXI, No. 1589 (December 8, 1969), pp. 514–15, 504–5.

As the editor indicates later in his own article (selection 26), U.S. attitudes toward undemocratic regimes in Latin America have undergone substantial shifts throughout the years, including the 1960s. Vigorous support for political democracy, which was central to the Kennedy Administration's conception of the Alliance for Progress, was (to say the least) not high on the list of Washington's priorities during the Johnson period. The following documents offer a reasonably clear view of the Nixon position, which bears a strong resemblance to its predecessor.

The first section below is a series of excerpts from the testimony of Viron P. Vaky, Acting Assistant Secretary of State for Inter-American Affairs, and James R. Fowler, Acting U.S. Coordinator, Alliance for Progress, Agency for International Development (AID), before the House Subcommittee on Inter-American Affairs in March, 1969. These spokesmen suggest that the purpose of aid is to build the long-term socioeconomic institutional foundations for meaningful democracy, while minimizing violence and political instability in the short run. Some political instability, they argue, is inevitable and should not be allowed to interfere with aid geared to long-range development objectives. The reader should note that Vaky and Fowler were "Acting" officials during the transition from the Johnson to Nixon administrations; however, to date there has been no change in State-AID policy on the matters discussed. The Congressmen doing the questioning are: Dante B. Fascell (Florida-Chairman), John S. Monagan (Connecticut), and Donald M. Fraser (Minnesota).

The second section is an excerpt from the Rockefeller Report submitted to President Nixon in late August, 1969. Like State-AID, Governor Rockefeller holds that the United States should not permit "moral disagreement" with particular regimes to interfere with diplomatic and aid relationships which may be necessary to "help people" and "encourage" democratization. He regards the "new military" in Latin America as a possible source of "constructive social change" but warns that some of them could become "radicalized, statist, and anti-U.S." (We will examine Rockefeller's related views of Latin American military establishments as bastions against Communism in the context of the military aid issue—selection 24.)

The part of Rockefeller's Report which follows received approbation in President Nixon's major address of October 31, 1969. Nixon stated that the United States "must deal realistically with governments in the inter-American system as they are."[1]

I. STATE-AID

Mr. Fascell. . . . [W]ould it be fair to say that the Alliance, up to this point, has really been an economic development program?

Mr. Vaky. I think that this was true in the first years of the Alliance.

Mr. Fascell. Because we hadn't had time to shift gears, you mean?

Mr. Vaky. Well, largely because we were uncertain, I think, as to what really was involved in development. The further we got into it, the clearer it became to us that economic growth, while important, in itself, still had indirect effects on other aspects, such as social development, and still required additional progress in fields that one might not strictly call economic, such as education. Thus, other kinds of assistance, involving different problem-solving techniques were also needed. And, therefore, we began to move in the last 4 or 5 years, I would say, into institution-building, and into the different uses of technical assistance, and began to think not only about economic growth, but also about how to influence institutions and build capacities and influence attitudes and values that will be conducive to total development.

I think that while we have been aware of these other dimensions, they involve factors that we know very little about. Where you talk about sociocultural change and modernization, our knowledge of how these things are done, particularly how they are guided or accelerated, is simply not adequate. Our knowledge of how you can help change through external assistance in these noneconomic areas is even more limited. We are experimenting with it and I think we have become increasingly aware of the importance of this kind of activity. . . .

Mr. Fowler. I would like to comment on that question, if I may, Mr. Chairman.

1 "Action for Progress for the Americas," *Department of State Bulletin,* LXI, No. 1586 (November 17, 1969), p. 413.

I think what Mr. Vaky said is quite true, but I believe also that there were, perhaps, three or four other points worth noting.

I believe that for a long time, consciously or unconsciously, we have tended to assume that economic growth, developing and increasing per capita income, and material improvement in standards of living, somehow would automatically bring in its train political and social development. This is an unstated or perhaps unconscious premise in the thinking of people, particularly in the United States. That premise is now being very severely questioned.

As we have worked in, and studied, and participated in the development process, we are becoming more and more aware that such automaticity simply does not exist.

The second point I would make is that there is something, I believe, called the state of the art. When faced with the problems of development, it was true that in the economic sphere, we knew more—not everything, but we knew more about the problem and how to tackle it than we did in certain of these other and more subtle areas of social and political change. This led to initial responses directed toward the obvious problems that were economic in nature.

Finally, I would note that faced with all the many problems of development, one starts where one can, does what is obviously required, and this again, I think, led in the initial stages to tackling those problems which commonsense told you had to be tackled in any event at some point. . . .

Mr. MONAGAN. Mr. Fowler, one of the objectives of our participation in the Alliance for Progress might be the altruistic one of helping these countries just for the sake of helping them. A second might be that we help in the same way we try to help poor people in our own country, for the common welfare, but there are, I think, other objectives in the program, and I would like to ask you about them.

First of all, one would be, I assume, to help create political stability in that part of the world.

Would you agree with that?

Mr. FOWLER. Yes; I think political stability is obviously a desirable objective, but as Mr. Vaky said in his opening statement, we are not quite sure how political stability comes about.

I think it is very important to define that word "stability," because behind it lurks a lot of problems. If it means simply maintenance of the status quo, which is a rather stable kind of situation, that is not what many of us mean when we think of stability.

Mr. MONAGAN. Well, if we do mean that, we do have situations there, such as Brazil and Argentina, where that might be a description of the situation, do we not?

Mr. FOWLER. The maintenance of the status quo?

Mr. MONAGAN. Yes.

Mr. FOWER. I think there are evolutionary—

Mr. MONAGAN. And Panama, perhaps.

Mr. FOWLER. There are evolutionary movements going on there. The point I was going to make is that political stability, as such, should not be regarded as a static thing. In many politically stable situations, there may be very dynamic political and economic change occurring. A question is the limit to which the methods of bringing change ultimately go, and in this respect, I would think the objective is to bring about change in an orderly and evolutionary fashion which avoids the total disruptions of violence.

Mr. MONAGAN. I would agree with that, but it does seem to me that if this is one of the objectives, we should measure the success of the Alliance, in part, by what the developments have been in this field.

You have an example also, a prime example in Peru at the present time, where you had a takeover from a reasonably progressive government by the military, which certainly would be contrary to political stability.

Mr. FOWLER. I think no one can deny that the events of that type in the hemisphere are unhappy ones. Anything which interrupts constitutional government is a retrogressive step.

It is our hope that these things will be temporary, and that they will decrease as development takes place, as education takes place, as political institutions become firm and more enduring. . . .

Mr. VAKY. I was just going to say, Congressman, as I mentioned earlier in my statement, all of these nations are going through a process of change that is just going to happen because technology is what it is, and because human nature is what it is.

As this change occurs, I think it would be a mistake for us to assume too easily that it is going to occur in stable form. Change is, to a certain degree, destabilizing. We have it in our own country. Societal change brings conflict. It brings clashes of vested interests, and so forth.

But this kind of instability is, I believe, quite different from the kind of instability and violence one might expect if you had just continually stagnant backwardness, pervasive lack of progress in elemental human terms of education and so forth.

It is very difficult, when the processes start, because the state of the art, as Mr. Fowler said, involves you in certain areas of the noneconomic, of the social areas, such as education. It is very difficult to predict or control completely the process through which societies change, and about all that one can hope, and I think we have to look for this in the long term, is that the more urbanized, the more industrialized, the more rationalized the society becomes, the more decision–making power tends to be spread and pluralistic, the more this kind of progress occurs, the better the chances are that we will witness a less traumatic process and see one which is more representative in terms of a pluralistic society.

But these are very difficult to either predict or control from the beginning. . . .

Mr. FOWLER. . . . We don't have yardsticks for participatory democracies. How do you measure that? Well, I suppose one way is how many people go to the polls. Yet, the democratic process, as Mr. Vaky indicates, in much of Latin America has not yet reached the point where you can meaningfully measure it that way. Yet, if one travels through Latin America, particularly in the country, out of the cities, and in the disadvantaged areas of the cities, there is no doubt whatsoever that the Latin American people, themselves, feel a sense of participation, and involvement, a dissatisfaction, a feeling of expectation that things can be better.

Now, I would submit that that is an essential ingredient in something called the democratic process. Without it, change can't take place and certainly, without it, the objective of bringing people into some kind of role in which they feel they are controlling their own destinies can't take place.

It has not yet, perhaps, reached the sophisticated level of highly developed constitutional government that works in the sense we are aware it works in our country, but that does not mean it isn't happening. And it is for this reason that all these myriads of small things, co-ops, savings and loan associations, community development projects, all taken together, are involving people as never before. . . .

Mr. FASCELL. Well, can we in good conscience continue to support [military governments]?. . .

Mr. VAKY. Mr. Chairman, I think that what one must always keep in the forefront in dealing with any of the countries is this long-term desirability of development. Recognize that in any country, you are going to get, over a period of time, political shifts of various kinds. One can expect it. I think we have to remember to keep in mind the long term, the developmental effort, to take at any given time whatever circumstances exist, and try to determine what we can do, if indeed we can do anything, to continue those basic goals that are enshrined in the charter. Is it possible to have what one colleague once called islands of sanity? Is it possible to have development or assistance or types of help that can aid the people, that can help education for example?. . .

Mr. FRASER. . . . I think one could make the proposition that if there isn't any growth, you are not going to get anywhere. That is, that while it doesn't assure the growth of democratic institutions, without some significant economic advance, you are going to have real trouble ever getting to that point.

What I am trying to say, however— and I am saying it very poorly, because I haven't thought this through—is that I have some very real difficulty with the whole conceptual framework under which we are presently relating to Latin America. . . .

. . . I worry about the fact that the United States does not come down very hard in favor of democratic institutions in Latin America, or I should say democratic governments, as distinguished from authoritarian governments, whether of the right or the left.

I don't know what we ought to do. All I know is that if I were an active democrat—with a small "d"—in Latin America, I would have grave misgivings about many elements of U.S. policy. . . .

Mr. FOWLER. . . . [L]et there be no mistake about this—the regression in democratic institutions in specific instances here and there, not only in Latin America, but anywhere over the world, is something which we do not approve of, and obviously wish wouldn't happen.

There is, however, the time aspect. Governments change from time to time but the modernization and development process, if it is correctly measured —and I think it should be—should be measured in terms of decades and generations. Should our assistance to that development process be stopped, or turned off and on, or rise and fall simply because of these shorter term political manifestations, many of which seem to us to be retrogressive, many of which are disappointing, if measured by the democratic norms which we establish?

I think this is the way the dilemma poses itself. Can we maintain both a long-term development policy, looking toward long-term development objectives, and at the same time not appear to be condoning or supporting short-term political movements which we all find highly disturbing? I put it in a time frame rather than a politico-economic frame.

II. THE ROCKFELLER REPORT

UNITED STATES POLITICAL RELATIONS WITH THE HEMISPHERE....

Commitment to representative, responsive democratic government is deeply imbedded in the collective political consciousness of the American people. We would like to see strong representative government develop in the other nations of the hemisphere for both idealistic and practical reasons:

—Our experience convinces us that representative democratic government and free societies offer the best means of organizing man's social, political and economic life so as to maximize the prospects for improving the individual's dignity and the quality of his life.

—Practically, nations with broadly-based political systems of a democratic type are more likely to have outlooks and concepts compatible with the style of the United States and its people, and more willing to cooperate with us in establishing an effective world order.

All Americans, in fact, share a common heritage of respect for human dignity, justice and freedom of the individual. They are linked by the bonds of revolutionary ancestors who succeeded in declaring themselves separate from the nations of Europe. This heritage is evidenced in different ways in different nations, especially when they are at differing stages of development or reflect different cultural influences. Individualism in the American republics often takes a more intense form than it does in the United States which has had a successful experience with greater individual restraints for

the public benefit. It must be recognized that there is no single route to the fulfillment of human dignity.

Democracy is a very subtle and difficult problem for most of the other countries in the hemisphere. The authoritarian and hierachical tradition which has conditioned and formed the cultures of most of these societies does not lend itself to the particular kind of popular government we are used to. Few of these countries, moreover, have achieved the sufficiently advanced economic and social systems required to support a consistently democratic system. For many of these societies, therefore, the question is less one of democracy or a lack of it, than it is simply of orderly ways of getting along.

There will often be times when the United States will find itself in disagreement with the particular policies or forms of government of other American nations. However, the fundamental question for the United States is how it can cooperate to help meet the basic needs of the people of the hemisphere despite the philosophical disagreements it may have with the nature of particular regimes. It must seek pragmatic ways to help people without necessarily embracing their governments. It should recognize that diplomatic relations are merely practical conveniences and not measures of moral judgment. This can be done by maintaining formal lines of communication without embracing such regimes.

The U.S. should also recognize that political evolution takes time and that, realistically, its long-term interests will be served by maintaining at least minimal diplomatic relationships with other governments of the hemisphere, while trying to find ways to assist the people of those countries, and to encourage the governments to move toward democratic processes. Such a policy requires a very difficult balance, but is one that must be achieved pragmatically on a case by case basis. The U.S. cannot renege on its commitment to a better life for all of the peoples of the hemisphere because of moral disagreement with regimes which the people themselves did not establish and do not control. . . .

THE MILITARY

In many South and Central American countries, the military is the single most powerful political grouping in society. Military men are symbols of power, authority and sovereignty and a focus of national pride. They have traditionally been regarded in most countries as the ultimate arbiters of the nation's welfare.

The tendency of the military to intervene when it judges that the government in office has failed to carry out its responsibilities properly has generally been accepted in Central and South America. Virtually all military governments in the hemisphere have assumed power to "rescue" the country from an incompetent government, or an intolerable economic or political situation. Historically, these regimes have varied widely in their attitudes toward civil liberties, social reform and repression.

Like the Church, the military was traditionally a conservative force resistant to change. Most officers came from the landowner class. In recent years, however, the owners of land have shifted more and more to an urban industrial life. The military service has been less attractive to their sons. As a result, opportunities have opened up for young men of ambition and ability from poor families who have neither land nor professional and business connections. These ambitious sons of the working classes have entered the military to seek an education and the opportunity for advancement.

This pattern has become almost universal throughout the American republics to the south. The ablest of these young officers have gone abroad for education and are now assuming top positions of leadership in almost all of the military groups in the hemisphere. And while their loyalties are with the armed forces, their emotional ties are often with the people. Increasingly, their concern and dedication is to the eradication of poverty and the improvement of the lot of the oppressed, both in rural and urban areas.

In short, a new type of military man is coming to the fore and often becoming a major force for constructive social change in the American republics. Motivated by increasing impatience with corruption, inefficiency, and a stagnant political order, the new military man is prepared to adapt his authoritarian tradition to the goals of social and economic progress.

This new role by the military, however, is not free from perils and dilemmas. There is always the risk that the authoritarian style will result in repression. The temptation to expand measures for security or discipline or efficiency to the point of curtailing individual liberties, beyond what is required for the restoration of order and social progress, is not easy to resist.

Above all, authoritarian governments, bent on rapid change, have an intrinsic ideological unreliability and a vulnerability to extreme nationalism. They can go in almost any doctrinal direction.

The danger for the new military is that it may become isolated from the people with authoritarianism turning into a means to suppress rather than eliminate the buildup of social and political tension.

The critical test, ultimately, is whether the new military can and will move the nation, with sensitivity and conscious design, toward a transition from military control for a social purpose to a more pluralistic form of government which will enable individual talent and dignity to flourish. Or will they become radicalized, statist and anti-U.S.?

In this connection, special mention should be made of the appeal to the new military, on a theoretical level, of Marxism: (1) It justifies, through its elitist-vanguard theories, government by a relatively small group or single institution (such as the Army) and, at the same time, (2) produces a rationale for state-enforced sacrifices to further economic development.

One important influence counteracting this simplistic Marxist approach is the exposure to the fundamental achievements of the U.S. way of life that many of the military from the other American countries have received through the military training programs which the U.S. conducts in Panama and the United States.

22

Toward a New Policy
for Latin America

Frank Church

From the *Congressional Record: Proceedings and Debates of the 91st Congress, Second Session,* Vol. 116, No. 57 (April 10), S5538–S5544.

Senator Frank Church (Democrat-Idaho), Chairman of the Senate Foreign Relations Subcommittee on Western Hemisphere Affairs, has recently emerged as a leading critic of U.S. Latin American policies. He outlines his criticisms in this speech delivered in the Senate on April 10, 1970.

Church urges the United States "to lower its profile in Latin America." In his words: "We must learn to hold ourselves at arm's length; we must come to terms with the inevitable, letting changes take place without insisting upon managing or manipulating them....We should keep a decent distance away from their internal affairs, from their military apparatus and their revolving-door governments." The Senator decries Washington's preoccupation with the Communist threat and its military interventions in Latin America. Even more significantly, he argues that the AID program in both its military and economic dimensions "has proved to be—on balance —a net loss." His principal prescription: End bilateral, government-to-government aid entirely and channel virtually all aid through multilateral institutions.

[H]ope, Francis Bacon once commented, makes a good breakfast, but it is a lean supper. As Latin America enters the 1970's, her governments tremble beneath the bruising tensions that separate hope from fulfillment....

Much of Latin America entered the 20th century with a way of life inherited from 16th century Spain and Portugal. This is a way of life which in many respects is incompatible with a modern, industrialized society. Latin countries are plunging headlong into the 21st century with precious little time to make a transition that took generations in the United States and centuries in Western Europe.

Yet the imperative is clear. In countries whose per capita income presently ranges from $80 to $800 a year, only the fastest economic growth conceivable can possibly produce enough food, shelter, clothing and employment to match the spiraling requirements of the swelling population. This multitude, which now numbers 276 million souls, is growing at the rate of 3 percent a year, faster than any other population in the world; yet production, on a net per capita basis, is increasing at only half that rate. Inflation is endemic; foreign exchange is in short supply: export trade opportunities are restricted by barriers interposed by the already rich, developed nations; and overall economic growth is falling chronically short of satisfactory levels. The 1960's did not bring the much heralded "Decade of Development" to Latin America. The euphoric expectation of bountiful blessings generated by the Alliance for Progress has receded, and widespread disillusionment has set in.

Still, economists know what is required within Latin America to move it into an era of adequate, self-sustaining economic growth. There is general consensus on the necessity for far-reaching agrarian and fiscal reform, for increasing internal savings and enlarging internal markets, for regional economic integration, and for more favorable trading arrangements with the developed countries. Most of all, there is the need to bring into the national economic life the large numbers of Latin Americans, amounting in some countries to the greater part of the whole population, who are now, for all practical purposes, subsisting outside a money economy.

Obviously, if such profound internal changes can be accomplished at all, they can be brought about only by the Latin Americans themselves. The impetus must come from within. Success or failure may be marginally influenced, but it cannot be bestowed from without —neither by the United States nor any other foreign power.

It is also evident that the means adopted, the economic systems devised, the political forms chosen, will likewise have to be homegrown. Neither the leisurely evolution of modern capitalism, as it matured in northern Europe and the United States, nor the differing brands of marxism, as practiced in Russia or China, offer models for Latin America that are really relevant to its cultural inheritance or its pressing needs. Even Cuban-style communism has found a meager market in other Latin lands. Che Guevara's romantic excursion to spread Castroism to the mountains of Bolivia ended in fiasco and death. For Latin America, steeped in the Christian tradition and prizing the individual highly, communism has little appeal. Indeed, those in the forefront of the struggle for radical, even revolutionary, reform in Latin America today are more likely to be found wearing Roman collars than carrying red banners.

So, as we peer into the 1970's, we must anticipate turmoil and upheaval throughout Latin America, a decade of instability, insurrection and irreversible change. Each country will stake out and cultivate its own political and economic terrain. The spirit of nationalism will grow more fervent, and movement along the political spectrum will be generally toward the left. Inflammable sensitivities will run high.

As for the United States, we would be well advised to practice an unaccustomed deference. The more gently we press our hemispheric neighbors, the greater our influence is likely to be. This will not be easy, for self-restraint is the hardest of all lessons for a great power to learn. Too tempting and seductive is the illusion of omnipotence. Every great power would prefer to believe—and ascribe to itself—the verity of the tribute once paid by Prince Metternich to imperial France: "When Paris sneezes, Europe catches cold."

In casting our own weight about the Western Hemisphere, the United States has shown typically little self-restraint. Between 1898 and 1924, we directly intervened no less than 31 times in the internal affairs of our smaller neighbors. And we have yet to kick the habit, as our abortive Bay-of-Pigs invasion bears witness, not to speak of our military occupation of the Dominican Republic, as recently as 1965.

In addition to its direct interventions, the United States has deeply penetrated the economy of Latin America with an immense outlay of private investment. By the end of 1968, American business interests had nearly $13 billion invested in Latin countries and the Caribbean, nearly three-fourths of which was concentrated in minerals, petroleum, and manufacturing industries. The extent and growth of these holdings have inevitably—and not surprisingly—given rise to cries of "Yankee imperialism."

A recent study by the Council for Latin America, a U.S. business group, reports that in 1966, the total sales by all U.S. affiliates in Latin America amounted to 13.7 percent of the aggregate gross domestic product of all the countries of the region. If foreign-owned companies played the same proportionate role in the United States, their annual sales would exceed $130 billion.

Latin Americans have also begun to deny what was long taken as an article of faith; namely, that foreign investment promotes economic development. Hear Foreign Minister Gabriel Valdes of Chile:

We can assert that Latin America is contributing to finance the development of the United States and other affluent nations. Private investments have meant and mean today for Latin America, that

the amounts that leave our continent are many times higher than those that are invested in it. Our potential capital is diminishing while the profits of invested capital grow and multiply at an enormous rate, not in our countries but abroad.

Minister Valdes is supported by the U.N. Economic Commission for Latin America which estimates the flow of private investment to Latin America in the period 1960–66 at $2.8 billion while the repatriation of profits and income amounted to $8.3 billion. This means that over this period foreign investment caused a net loss of $785 million a year in Latin America's balance of payments.

Working with later data on a somewhat different basis, the Council for Latin America makes the very opposite claim, putting the net positive contribution of U.S. investment to Latin America's balance of payments, during the 1965–68 period, at $8.5 billion a year.

Wherever the truth may lie, it is clear that the influence of U.S. business in Latin America is enormous, and that its impact produces political as well as economic repercussions. Whether or not the Latin Americans are right in their analysis of the adverse effect of private foreign investment on their balance of payments, the important political point is that they think they are right about it.

The U.S. presence in Latin America is pervasive, culturally as well as economically. Latins listen to American music, go to see American movies, read American books and magazines, drive American cars, drink Coca-Cola, and shop at Sears. The ubiquitous American tourist is to be seen on every hand, worrying aloud about the water and food and complaining about the difficulty of making himself understood in English.

The Latin reaction to all of this is

somewhat ambivalent. Latins like the products of U.S. culture and U.S. business, but at the same time they feel a bit overwhelmed and fearful that Yankees may indeed be taking over their countries. One of the causes of internal resistance to proposals for a Latin American Common Market is the fear that U.S. companies would be able, through their sheer size, to benefit from it to the disadvantage of local entrepreneurs.

Given this situation, it has to be expected that regardless of the policies we adopt, however enlightened and beneficial they may be, the United States will long remain a national target in Latin America for criticism, misgiving, suspicion, and distrust.

The picture is not all that bleak, however. Millions of people in Latin America think well of the people of the United States. Certain of our leaders have been greatly admired—Franklin Roosevelt for his "good neighbor" policy, and John F. Kennedy for the way he bespoke the heartfelt aspirations of the dispossessed. No one can fault the sincerity of President Kennedy when he launched the Alliance for Progress in March of 1961, inviting the American Republics to join in a "vast cooperative effort, unparalleled in magnitude and nobility of purpose, to satisfy the basic needs of the people for homes, work and land, health and schools." Since then, the United States has funneled in more than $10 billion in various forms of aid.

Given the magnitude of our effort during the 1960's, we are left to wonder why it produced such disappointing results. We thought we were seeding the resurgence of democratic governments; instead, we have seen a relentless slide toward militarism. We thought we could remodel Latin societies, but the reforms we prescribed have largely eluded us. We thought our generosity would meet with gratitude; but we have seen antagonism toward us grow as our involvement in their problems has deepened. We pledged ourselves to goals which lay beyond our capacity to confer, objectives that could never be the gift of any program of external aid; by promising more than we could deliver, we have made ourselves a plausible scapegoat for pent-up furies and frustrations for which we bear little or no responsibility.

Worse still, the kind of aid we have extended has tended to aggravate, rather than mitigate, these difficulties. Bilateral in character, administered on a government-to-government basis, our foreign aid program is embroiled in the internal politics of both the donor and recipient countries. The program's very nature makes this unavoidable, but the consequences are contributing to a steady deterioration in relations.

First, let us consider what has happened to the foreign aid program, due to the pressure of domestic politics within the United States. What commenced—back in the days of the Marshall plan for Western Europe—as principally a grant-in-aid undertaking, has been transformed by the outcry against "foreign giveaways" into what is now primarily a loan program. Furthermore, in terms of accomplishing our foreign policy objectives, hindsight indicates we have gone about foreign aid backward. The Marshall plan should have been administered mainly on a loan instead of a grant basis, and the ready return of our investment would have done much to solve our balance-of-payments problems in the 1960's. In Latin America, the formula should have been reversed, with the emphasis on grants instead of loans.

Now the accumulation of these loans, and others as well, by Latin American governments, is creating serious debt problems. The Rockefeller report notes:

Heavy borrowings by some Western Hemisphere countries to support development have reached the point where annual repayments of interest and amortization absorb a large share of foreign exchange earnings. Within five years, a number of other nations in the Western Hemisphere could face the same situation. Many of the countries are, in effect, having to make new loans to get the foreign exchange to pay interest and amortization on old loans, and at higher interest rates.

This debt service problem is a major concern. If countries get into a position where interest and amortization payments on foreign loans require a disproportionately large share of available foreign exchange, then the general pace of development will be slowed by the inability to maintain imports of the capital equipment needed to support economic growth.

Of course, in fairness it should be pointed out that our foreign aid program is not the sole contributor, by any means, to this mounting debt service problem. From 1962 through 1969, the Export-Import Bank lent $1.7 billion to Latin America at commercial interest rates and generally shorter maturities than AID loans. Various European governments and banks—as well as U.S. banks—have made substantial loans, frequently at rates of 6 to 8 percent and for maturities of no more than 3 to 5 years. It is clear that both we and the Europeans are going to have to review our lending policies and explore ways for stretching out repayment schedules. Joint action between the leading nations, the international lending institutions, and debtor nations is necessary. I agree with the Peterson task force suggestions to put this strategy "into effect now to prevent an emergency—not to deal with one after it has arisen."

Not only did the pressures of domestic politics change our aid to loans, but concern over our chronically adverse balance-of-payments led the Congress to insist upon tying these loans to the purchase of goods and services in the United States. Thus our aid—so-called—became an ill-disguised subsidy for American exports. While it undeniably constitutes an addition to Latin American economic resources, it can only be used for purchases in the United States or, under the new Presidential directive, within the hemisphere, where prices are often above European or Japanese levels. Moreover, still another politically motivated restriction requires that half of the goods financed by the United States must be transported in American bottoms. It has been estimated that this provision alone reduces the effectiveness of each $100 of U.S. loan assistance by as much as $20—furnishing another irritant to developing countries.

But the worst political consequence of all has been the inability of Congress to resist temptation to use the aid program as both carrot and stick to reward or punish recipient governments, depending on how we may regard their behavior. Since 1961, the punitive sections of the Foreign Assistance Act have increased from four to 21.

Most notorious of these punitive provisions is the Hickenlooper amendment. Although it has proved useless as a deterrent to the confiscation of American-owned businesses abroad, this amendment will remain on the books. Few Congressmen would relish explaining to their constituents why they voted to repeal a provision which prohibits giving further aid to a foreign government which has expropriated an American-owned business and failed to pay adequate compensation.

Yet, the Hickenlooper amendment is only the most prominent of a whole series of penalties written into our Foreign Assistance Act. There are, for instance, the amendments designed to enforce the American view of fishing rights. On occasion, U.S. fishing boats have been seized by Ecuador or Peru for fishing in what we regard as the high seas, but what they regard as territorial waters. If a fine is imposed, our law provides that military sales and assistance must be suspended; it also provides that the amount of the fine must be subtracted from the economic aid we are furnishing the guilty government.

This provision, I must confess, was solemnly adopted as an appropriate punishment to put an end to any further meddling with American boats. But, alas, it has not worked that way. We "tie" so many strings to our "aid" that some governments have preferred to take their money in fines.

The trouble with attaching such penalties to the aid program is that, although they might give us some emotional satisfaction, they do not stop the behavior against which they are aimed. What is worse, they provide a series of diplomatic showdowns that corrode, weaken, and eventually destroy good relations.

Peru is a textbook case. The deterioration of our relations with Peru began in 1964, when the State Department, on its own initiative, started to drag its heels on extending aid to Peru as a tactic to force the government to settle the International Petroleum Co. —IPC—case. The tactic was not successful and resulted in some bitterness

on the part of the Peruvian Government, then headed by Fernando Belaúnde Terry, a man who otherwise qualified as a true Alliance for Progress president.

This bitterness was increased when we refused to sell the Peruvians F–5 aircraft. But then, when they decided to buy Mirage aircraft from France, the State Department reversed itself and offered F–5's. At this point, Congress decreed that foreign aid should be withheld from countries buying sophisticated weapons abroad. The net result is that Peru now has Mirages, a plane aptly named for the contribution it makes to Peruvian security.

Finally, a military government more radical than the reformist Belaúnde came to power and promptly expropriated IPC. The new Peruvian Government has not only failed to pay compensation, but has actually presented IPC with a bill of $694 million for its alleged past transgressions. And through all of this, there has been the continuing wrangle over fishing boats.

This sketchy review is necessarily oversimplified. The story of United States–Peruvian relations in the last 5 years contains ample mistakes on both sides. The point is that each successive stage in the deterioration has been provoked, in one way or another, by some aspect of the U.S. aid program. Indeed, more than one U.S. Ambassador to Latin America has said privately that his difficulties stemmed directly from our aid program. One can scarcely imagine a more damning indictment.

Let us now consider the political impact of a bilateral, government-to-government aid program upon the recipient countries. They are naturally interested in putting the money into places of immediate advantage, where the political payoff is greatest. Heavy emphasis falls on program, rather than project, loans, whereby lump sum transfers of dollar credits augment a given government's foreign exchange reserves. This is an indirect method of lending budgetary support. The reserves, of course, are available to be purchased with local currency by importers who desire to buy, let us say, machine tools in Cincinnati or perfume in Paris. Since it was never a part of the rationale of a program loan that its proceeds should be used to finance the purchase of French perfume, AID early limited the purposes for which program loans could be used. But money is fungible, and restrictions applied solely to the loan do not insure that the borrowing government will not use its other resources for the purchase of frivolous luxury items, while relying on the United States to finance necessities. Little if any net economic gain would be made in these circumstances.

It became necessary, therefore, to make program loans contingent on agreement by the borrowing government to regulate its imports generally in such a way as to insure that its total foreign exchange reserves were used with optimum efficiency from our point of view.

Further, the question arose as to what to do with the local currency generated by the program loan. In the absence of agreements to the contrary, this currency can be used in ways that would undermine, neutralize, or offset the intended purpose of the loan. So, to insure that these local currency proceeds are used in ways that meet with our approval, AID made agreement on this point a condition of program lending. As in the case of foreign exchange reserves, it followed, of course,

that this agreement had to encompass the Government's fiscal and monetary policies across the board.

All of this inevitably involves the United States in the most intimate areas of another country's sovereignty, its tax policies, and its monetary system. Program loans are disbursed in installments, usually quarterly and each disbursement is preceded by the most detailed review of our AID mission of the recipient country's economic performance for the prior quarter. Why has the Government's tax program not been enacted? The central bank is letting the local money supply increase too fast. Recent wage settlements have been inflationary. The currency is overvalued. A program review typically raises these and a hundred other similar questions and complaints. This is done with the best of motives, but at an exorbitant political price.

Our aid technicians must sit as advisers and overseers at the highest levels in the finance ministries of various Latin American governments. Inescapably, this places us in a patronizing position which is demeaning to our hosts. The large colony of our AID administrators, meanwhile, living in conspicuous luxury in every Latin capital, cannot help but feed popular resentment against the United States. If a militant nationalism directed against the gringos is now on the rise, it is quite possible that our own policies, largely connected with AID, have given it the spur.

One is left to wonder how so cumbersome and self-defeating an AID program has lasted so long. Again, I suggest, the answer can be found by examining the politics involved on Capitol Hill. The analysis, I assure you, is a fascinating one.

Year after year, in order to get the

needed votes in Congress, a package of contradictory arguments is assembled. The package contains something for everyone, with the result that the life of the AID program has been prolonged by a hybrid coalition of both liberal and conservative Members. Let us explore how this artful strategy has worked with respect to the two main categories of AID, military and economic assistance.

MILITARY ASSISTANCE. Conservative Members of Congress have been wooed to support this kind of aid on the ground that bolstering indigenous armies and police forces furnishes us with a shield against the spread of communism in the hemisphere. Furthermore, it is argued, strengthened military power within Latin America is to be welcomed as a force for internal stability favorably disposed toward local American interests. For the most part, these arguments are accepted as articles of faith, even though events discredit them. In Cuba, it was demonstrated that once a regime has lost minimum essential support, no army will save it. Castro did not walk over Batista's army; he walked through it. In Peru and Bolivia, on the other hand, where the Government's army seized the Governments, the new military regimes galvanized public support behind them not by favoring, but by grabbing, local American interests. Each confiscated a major American-owned business, the Gulf Oil Corp. in Bolivia, the IPC in Peru.

Liberals in Congress have been lured to support military assistance by quite different, though equally flimsy, arguments. They have been told that our subsidy brings us into close association with the military hierarchy, thus enabling us to exert a tempering influence on the politically ambitious generals, while assuring ourselves of their friendship in case they do take over. Again, argument and fact are mismated. The 1960's were marked by an unprecedented shift toward military dictatorship in Latin America. Hardly more than half a dozen popularly chosen democratic governments remain alive south of our borders. Tempering influence indeed!

Furthermore, once a military junta has installed itself behind its American-furnished tanks, guns and planes, there is no assurance that the United States will be benignly regarded. In fact, the new "Nasserist" regimes of Peru and Bolivia, among all governments of South America, are the most aggressively hostile toward us.

Meanwhile, the military missions we have installed in no less than 17 Latin capitals, add to the debilitating image of the United States as a militaristic nation. Even the Rockefeller report, which gave its blessings to military assistance, looks with disfavor upon "our permanent military missions in residence," since they "too often have constituted too large and too visible a U.S. presence."

That puts it mildly. Listen to the testimony of Ralph Dungan, our former Ambassador to Chile, given before the Senate Foreign Relations Subcommittee on Western Hemisphere Affairs:

> I believe there is no shaking the prevailing Latin conception of the United States as a society dominated to a very large measure by "the Pentagon." This perception is widely shared across the political spectrum.

Mr. Dungan went on to say that "perhaps no single action which the United States has taken in recent years including the Bay-of-Pigs fiasco was so significant in confirming the view of

Latin America of the United States as a nation willing and ready to use its vast military power unilaterally—as the unfortunate invasion of the Dominican Republic." Other friendly hemisphere observers have noted we will never know whether the Alliance was a success or failure because the program stopped the minute U.S. Marines landed in Santo Domingo in the spring of 1965.

So much, then, for our misguided military policies in Latin America, and the contrived and contradictory arguments with which they are perpetuated. Let us now turn to the other side of the American AID program, economic assistance.

ECONOMIC ASSISTANCE. Here again, congressional support has been secured on the basis of false and conflicting doctrines. Conservative votes have been solicited upon the theory that economic assistance is good for business, that it can shore up the status quo in Latin America and thus prove an effective deterrent to revolution. It is argued that our input of dollars will promote stability and thwart the anti-capitalists. Oddly enough, this proposition is widely believed, even though Cuba, the only country in the hemisphere which has gone Communist, enjoyed a relatively high per capita income along with a highly concentrated investment of American capital.

Liberals in Congress, on the other hand, have accepted the need for economic assistance on the weakness of the opposite argument; namely, that far from preserving the status quo, our financial aid is meant to promote necessary economic and social change. But as our experience with the Alliance for Progress bears out, external aid does not produce internal change. Because the money has been channeled through existing governments, it has mainly been spent for the benefit of the governing elites. It has perhaps helped, in some instances, to modernize Latin economies, but not to restructure them. In short, the liberals have also been taken in.

The conclusion I must reach is that our AID program, as administered in Latin America, has proved to be—on balance—a net loss. As our meddling has increased, resentment has grown. It lies at the root of an alarming deterioration in inter-American relations—a deterioration which has led to the assassination of one of our Ambassadors, the kidnaping of another plus a labor attaché; the riotous receptions given Governor Rockefeller as President Nixon's personal emissary, indeed, the refusal of some countries even to receive him; and most recently, the unruly student demonstrations following the arrival of our Assistant Secretary of State for Latin American Affairs on an orientation visit to Bolivia.

This does not mean that we should throw up our hands in despair, or turn our backs on the hemisphere. What is necessary is that we first get off the backs of our neighbors. We must learn to hold ourselves at arms length; we must come to terms with the inevitable, letting changes take place without insisting upon managing or manipulating them. We must begin to show some self-restraint.

Here, then, are some guidelines I would favor for a new United States policy toward Latin America in the 1970's:

First. First of all, we should begin to adopt trade regulations that give the developing countries in Latin America a better break. We should listen closely to the growing, unified Latin complaint on this score, and give the most serious consideration to their urgent appeals for preferential treatment. The political hurdles to such a course are high; the strongest Presidential leadership will be necessary; but for too long we have avoided biting this particular bullet with the palliative of the AID program.

The great independence hero of Cuba, José Martí, once warned his countrymen that "a people economically enslaved but politically free will end by losing all freedom, but a people economically free can go on to win its political freedom." To achieve the latter, which Latin Americans believe they are now fighting for, Latin products must not be squeezed from the world's markets.

Second. Next, we must start to observe, as well as praise, the principle of nonintervention. It was San Martín, one of Latin America's legendary figures, who said that we are as we act. If we are to act in accordance with the principle of nonintervention, we must not only accept Latin governments as they come, but we must also refrain from the unilateral use of our military power in any situation short of one involving a direct threat to the security of the United States. Such was the case in our showdown with the Soviet Union when the Russians tried, in the fall of 1962, to obtain a nuclear foothold in Cuba. But let there be no more military interventions, 1965 style, in the Dominican Republic or elsewhere.

Third. We should bring home our military missions, end our grant-in-aid and training programs, and sever the intimate connections we have sought to form with the Latin military establishments. After all, the recent war between El Salvador and Honduras we made possible, in large part, by our gift of arms and training eagerly extended to both sides. This is a shabby business for us to mix in.

Fourth. We should commence the liquidation of our bilateral government-to-government economic AID program, as the recent Peterson task force report recommends, effecting at the same time a corresponding shift of economic assistance to the World Bank, the Inter-American Development Bank, and other multilateral institutions. Such a transfer could be cushioned by phasing out our bilateral program in the following manner:

The United States naturally should fulfill those loan commitments already in the pipeline, but the money should be "untied" so that the recipients may put it to the most efficient use. This can be done by Presidential action, which has thus far been limited to the freeing of only those markets within the hemisphere.

The State Department should open negotiations for the reservicing of debt repayment in those instances where the burden unduly restricts necessary economic growth. This, too, lies within the authority of the President, and accords with the recommendations of both the Rockefeller report and the Peterson report. We should seek, also, to involve European creditors in this process. I would oppose stretching out debts to the United States so that debts to other creditors can be paid on time.

Financial assistance from the United States for public housing projects, schools, hospitals, family planning programs, and other social work should, in the future, be funneled through the newly established Inter-American Social Development Institute. If this institute is administered properly, it will emphasize the use of matching grants instead of loans, and it will deal not directly with Latin governments but with private groups, trade unions, rural cooperatives, and charitable foundations.

The Social Development Institute should be staffed with personnel ready to try a wide variety of new experiments, willing to refrain from sending another horde of North American directors into Latin countries, and who will share with Latin Americans the real experience of innovating and initiating new programs. In short, if the Social Development Institute is to succeed, it must be divorced entirely from the old ways of AID.

As for technical assistance, the remaining part of AID, it somehow remains as much overrated in the United States as it stands discredited in Latin America. The program's present weakness was perhaps best summed up in an excellent study by a Senate Government Operations Subcommittee on the American AID program in Chile. Speaking for the subcommittee, former Senator Gruening concluded that our technicians were "too far advanced technically—for what is required in underdeveloped countries. They are also too ignorant of local conditions and customs and serve periods too short to make a significant impact." This criticism is endemic to our technical assistance program throughout Latin America.

The limiting factor on the amount of technical assistance we have extended has never been money; it has always been people. The technician not only has to be professionally qualified; he should also know the language and the culture. He should be accomplished at human relations as well as in his technical specialty. There just are not many people like this to export abroad, and

it is better not to send technicians at all than to send the wrong kind.

Yet there remains a need to transfer technology as well as capital to Latin America. This can best be done through expanding the exchange-of-persons program to enable more Latin Americans to study in the United States, and through selective grants to a few outstanding Latin American universities. The role of shirt-sleeve diplomat, the concept which underlay the original Point 4 program, can best be played by Peace Corps volunteers.

Another promising agency has been created by last year's Foreign Assistance Act, the Overseas Private Investment Corporation, more commonly known as OPIC. Its purpose is to encourage, through a liberalized program of investment guarantees, a larger flow of American private capital into developing countries. In Latin America, OPIC could play a useful role, if it encourages the right kind of investment, directing it away from the sensitive resource areas, and pointing it toward joint ventures in which Latin Americans will share largely in both ownership and management. Here, again, everything depends on the way OPIC is administered.

The use of joint ventures deserves emphasis. I am well aware that joint ventures are distasteful to many—not all—American companies. But, in the long run, this may be the only way United States business interests can survive in Latin America.

Before concluding, let me just add one warning here. Private foreign investment is not economic cooperation and assistance: it is business, and most Latin leaders are willing to treat it in a business-like manner. What Latin Americans are telling us is, "if the

United States wants its investors to prosper in the region, then it is incumbent on the United States to make sure that investors are 'development-oriented.' "

Whether the public or private sectors are involved, it is essential for the United States to lower its profile in Latin America. Our national interests can best be served, not by helping Latin America less, but by loosening our embrace. We should keep a decent distance away from their internal affairs, from their military apparatus and their revolving-door governments. This would be best for us and best for them.

It would also disengage the United States from its unseemly courtship of governments which are living contradictions to our traditional values as a nation. When we pour our money into budgetary support for a notoriously authoritarian government, when we supply it with riot guns, tear gas, and mace, intelligent young Americans who still want to believe in our professed ideals, begin to ask elemental questions.

If we are not *against* such dictatorships, then what is it we are *for* that really matters?

In the final analysis, each country must live by the ideals it prizes most highly. That is the basis upon which governments turn to their people for loyalty and support. A crisis of spirit arises when our foreign policy comes unhinged from the historic values we hold dear as a people, and when the role of the United States in the world becomes inexplicable to its own young citizens. This is happening to us. Its occurrence is of more fundamental importance than any question of economic theory, investment policy or diplomatic tactics.

Devising the right role for the United States in its own hemisphere and the world at large, a role consistent with the admirable ideals of its origins, would go far toward restoring our country to the unique position it once held in the community of man.

23

Governor Rockefeller and
Senator Church:
Convergence on an End to
U.S. *Active* Prodemocracy Policies

From Senate Committee on Foreign Relations, Subcommittee on Western Hemisphere Affairs, Hearing (November 20, 1969), *Rockefeller Report on Latin America*, Ninety-First Congress, First Session, Committee Print (Washington: U.S. Government Printing Office, 1969), pp. 8–15, 19.

Shortly after his Report was made public in November, 1969, Governor Rockfeller discussed his conclusions with the Senate Subcommittee on Western Hemisphere Affairs. The following exchange between the Governor and Senator Church sheds additional light on both of their positions regarding a desirable U.S. posture toward undemocratic regimes. Note particularly that, despite Church's expressed concern for the decline of democracy in Latin America, he is in perfect accord with Rockefeller on the point that the United States has neither the "responsibility" nor the capability to undertake an active prodemocracy campaign. At the close, almost in paraphrase of President Nixon, he remarks: "We will have to deal with governments as we find them."

Senator CHURCH. Thank you, Governor, for your statement this morning. Again, I want to express the appreciation of the committee for your presence here.

In your statement, Governor, you say that our basic concern must be the quality of life for all in the Western Hemisphere. In determining the quality of life, would you regard as an important element the nature of the government under which a person must live?

Governor ROCKEFELLER. No question.

Senator CHURCH. Is the political form an important element in determining the quality of life?

Governor ROCKEFELLER. No question.

Senator CHURCH. I thought we might start there because this committee has been very much disturbed by the precipitous slide toward militarism in the hemisphere.

Free government, democratic government, has now become the exception to the rule. . . .

. . . [I]n reading your report, I was

disturbed to find language which all but approves the military juntas that have come to power.

For example, I read, "In short, a new type of military man is coming to the fore and often becoming a major force for constructive social change in the American Republics. Motivated by increasing impatience with corruption, inefficiency, and a stagnant political order, the new military man is prepared to adapt his authoritarian tradition to the goals of social and economic progress."

Well, language of that kind is reminiscent of the time when I was beginning to take my first interest in politics, when similar arguments were put forward in justification of the Fascist military dictatorships in Europe. I would like to start there, to give you an opportunity to clarify your own position with respect to the military governments that have come to dominate the politics of the hemisphere.

Governor ROCKEFELLER. Well, Mr. Chairman, I appreciate your going to the heart of this question because I think this is probably the most important first step we have to face and understand in facing up to the broader problems of our relations.

Now I would say as far as the quote that you read is concerned, the real question is, is that an accurate description of the situation? I would assume from what you said you feel in a sense by the analogy you gave that it is a glossing over or an apology or an explanation to try and justify something that we do not agree with.

I would like to say that in all frankness, I think that is an accurate description of the situation that exists today in this hemisphere. . . .

Now, we have to think of one other thing in discussing this. The democratic tradition of the Western Hemisphere and their belief in justice and human dignity is very real but it comes from Spain, or from Portugal, as against from England; and you have a different background there than we do. There is a much higher degree of "personalismo" of the individual so that a man may believe very strongly in democracy and dignity and justice but his concept is importantly related to himself and his family; and that gentleman and his family who are strong advocates of this under a democratic government are much less willing to accept the procedures and the regulations and the rules of the democratic structure than we are here in this country.

So there is much more instability and much less ability to achieve discipline which is essential in a free society.

Senator CHURCH. Governor, I do not take issue with the statement that there are many able and dedicated young officers in the military in Latin America, or that democracy, as we know it, is not as deeply rooted there as it is in our own country. But I am concerned about the condition of freedom, or the lack of it, in the hemisphere.

Governor ROCKEFELLER. So am I.

Senator CHURCH. You would acknowledge, would you not, that the military governments that now control Argentina, Peru, Bolivia, Brazil, Panama, and other countries in the hemisphere, were not placed in power by the vote of the people?

Governor ROCKEFELLER. That is correct.

Senator CHURCH. They took power by force of arms. Isn't that correct?

Governor ROCKEFELLER. Yes, in varying degrees.

Senator CHURCH. Yes. This strikes me as ironical, because for the past 2 days we have been sitting in executive session with Secretary Rogers and Secretary Laird, reviewing American policy in Vietnam. We have been told that the whole objective of this tremendous effort in Vietnam is to secure self-determination for the people of South Vietnam. When we press for a definition of self-determination, we are told that the purpose of the war is to obtain a free election so that the people of South Vietnam can choose their government. This is so important a principle, we are told, that it has warranted the loss of 45,000 Americans and over $100 billion in expenditures in 5 years of what has become the longest foreign war in our history.

Well, I find it hard to understand why it is so important for us to secure free elections in South Vietnam, but so unimportant that there be free elections in South America.

Governor ROCKEFELLER. I only think that the conclusion is one that I would agree with. I think it is important to achieve free elections in South America and what I am trying to say in this report is the way I think that we can best achieve the restoration of democratic institutions in this hemisphere because this is the heart of the problem, Mr. Chairman, and you and I agree on the objective. It is a question of how we get there and what the method should be.

Senator CHURCH. I think that is right.

The objective is certainly one that you and I would agree upon. I would like to turn to the methods. . . .

Do you think we should extend [military] assistance, say, to the Government of Haiti?

Governor ROCKEFELLER. Well, I would say that basically it is essential that it be extended and that we cooperate with the training and the equipment hemispherewide.

Senator CHURCH. Then you would extend it to the Government of Haiti?

Governor ROCKEFELLER. Well, I would want to be a little closer as a nation to some of these governments so that while we are cooperating in helping them meet their problems, we are also talking to them on a very realistic basis about how they can take the steps to restore the democratic process.

Senator CHURCH. Do you think you can talk Papa "Doc" into restoring democracy in Haiti? [Laughter.]

Governor ROCKEFELLER. I will give you an answer and I think the answer is "Yes."

Now, you may not believe that. I do not think he is going to last very long.

Frankly, his health is very bad and, as an American citizen, I am deeply concerned as to the future of Haiti.

There are 2 million wonderful people whom we cut off as far as aid is concerned in 1963.

The only place we have spent money in Haiti is in the American Embassy which is a Garden of Eden with a beautiful swimming pool and beautifully maintained.

Outside, throughout the nation, there is nothing but degradation and poverty and an illiteracy rate of around 90-some percent and I do not know how any of us think you are going to build democracy under those conditions.

Senator CHURCH. Governor, I am not talking about the advisability of extending economic aid that might be helpful to the people of Haiti. I am talking about extending guns, helicopters, radios, and command and control equipment to the present Government of Haiti for the purpose of helping it stay in power.

Governor ROCKEFELLER. Well, if you will excuse me, Senator, the present Government is not there through my policies and I am not here to justify that Government. I am here to talk to you about how do we prevent that in the Government and how do we encourage the evolution of those countries to democracy.

Senator CHURCH. But you are advocating a military assistance program.

Governor ROCKEFELLER. Which is essential.

Senator CHURCH. And you have indicated you would make it hemisphere-wide.

Governor ROCKEFELLER. Yes, sir.

Senator CHURCH. And the effect of this is to help such governments as the Haitian Government and other dictatorial governments stay in power.

I do not see what that has to do either with American tradition, which is based on the peoples' right to revolt against despotism, or with improving the quality of life for the people of the hemisphere.

Governor ROCKEFELLER. Senator, I have to challenge a basic assumption, that if we do not send aid and if we cut off our relations we are going to achieve the goal that you want, restoration of democracy. This, in my opinion, is the fundamental error made in this country as to how we achieve the goals of human dignity and freedom and opportunity which are our objectives. . . .

Now, let's take your argument for the sake of discussion here, that we should not give any aid to Haiti, and let's see what has happened. We followed your policies—

Senator CHURCH. I said military aid; that has been the subject of our exchange.

Governor ROCKEFELLER. But we have followed the policy of giving no aid to Haiti—

Senator CHURCH. That is another question.

Governor ROCKEFELLER (continuing). Since 1963. And if everybody in Haiti goes down the drain because of the tragic conditions, the last person to go down is going to be Papa "Doc."

Now, our policy has been an utter and tragic failure in achieving our objectives in Haiti and I think it is time that we have the courage to face up to the realities of these things, that the methods we have been using are not working.

Since the Alliance for Progress, the goals of which I share, there have been 17 military coups—more than any other period. Therefore, I think it does bring us to a point where we have to say the cliches which we have been talking about are not as effective as we thought, and maybe we have to take a more realistic examination. . . .

Senator CHURCH. I think the point, at least the point that the Chair has been trying to make, is not that we have a responsibility to set up democratic governments or attempt to establish democratic governments.

Governor ROCKEFELLER. We couldn't.

Senator CHURCH. We couldn't if we wanted to.

Governor ROCKEFELLER. That is right. That is not the way democracy grows.

Senator CHURCH. It is not our policy or objective to insist that Latin America develop in our image. I understand that. We will have to deal with governments as we find them. But the question is whether we should adopt a program of giving arms, equipment, and training to keep these governments in power in their own lands. That is the question.

24

The Departments of Defense and State and Governor Rockefeller on U.S. Military Policies and Programs in Latin America

Section I from Senate Committee on Foreign Relations, Subcommittee on Western Hemisphere Affairs, Hearings (June 24 and July 8, 1969), *United States Military Policies and Programs in Latin America,* Ninety-First Congress, First Session, Committee Print (Washington: U.S. Government Printing Office, 1969), pp. 62–64, 57–61. Section II from Nelson A. Rockefeller, *Quality of Life in the Americas* in *Department of State Bulletin,* LXI, No. 1589 (December 8, 1969), 505–6, 515–17.

In the 1960s there were several important changes in U.S. military policies and programs in the hemisphere. Washington began to deemphasize arming and training for a large–scale conventional war and to concentrate instead on increasing the Latin American military's counterinsurgency capability. Kennedy Administration policy-makers also placed greater stress on economic and social development in military training courses and tried to engage the armed forces of Latin America directly in the Alliance for Progress through civic action programs. They hoped, by making the military both more professional and more development-oriented: (1) to discourage military plotting against civilian governments; (2) to improve the domestic image of the military; and (3) to have some of the resources devoted to defense serve development purposes.[1]

Counterinsurgency succeeded in the sense that the Latin American military managed, with varying degrees of efficiency, to defeat guerrillas or to curtail their activities in a number of countries—most notably, in Venezuela, Bolivia, Peru, and Guatemala. But professionalization and civic action obviously did not put an end to coups; and because civic action contributed so marginally to development as well, there is little mention of it in U.S. government circles today.

As Church's pronouncements in the previous selections suggest, United

---

[1] See Willard F. Barber and C. Neale Ronning, *Internal Security and Military Power: Counterinsurgency and Civic Action in Latin America* (Columbus: Ohio State University Press, 1966).

States aid to the Latin American military and Latin American governments' defense spending have been the subjects of a continuous debate in recent years. In addition to complaining that money "wasted" on defense should be devoted to economic and social development, critics have frequently asserted that military assistance and spending strengthen an already overgrown military establishment, which threatens particularly those civilian governments most dedicated to the Alliance for Progress ideal of progressive democratic rule. U.S. training, the argument goes, imparts a militant anti-Communism and (along with programs like civic action) encourages the military to think of themselves as much more competent than civilians to govern the nation. Moreover, in cases where existing governments are not progressive, U.S. association with military repression of domestic discontent adds credence to the charge that this country supports the status quo.

Largely in response to criticisms like these, Congress has attached restrictions to foreign aid legislation, including the Symington and Conte-Long amendments. Conte-Long, the more stringent of the two provisions, directs the executive branch to withhold in aid to a given government in a given year the amount spent on "sophisticated" weapons the previous year. This restriction does not affect long-range commitments and thus may involve only a one-year postponement in the release of funds.

The following selection is a composite of statements made by key executive officials to the Senate Subcommittee on Western Hemisphere Affairs in July, 1969, and excerpts from the Rockefeller Report. Assistant Secretary Nutter (Defense) reviews U.S. military activities in Latin America. Both Assistant Secretary Meyer (State) and Governor Rockefeller strongly urge the abandonment of Congressional restrictions, contending that they are (in Meyer's words) "paternalistic, even patronizing" and, in any event, that they do not curb Latin American military spending. Meyer holds that military assistance is directed only against instability of "such a level as to destroy the reform process itself." However, his assessment of the limited threat posed by Communism and armed insurgency differs markedly from Rockefeller's grave predictions of urban terrorism. The former is closer to at least the initial public position of the Nixon Administration on the security issue, as indicated by President Nixon's emphasis on other matters in his speech of October 31, 1969, and his State of the World Address on February 18, 1970. (There was no mention at all of the Rockefeller proposal for a Western Hemisphere Security Council.) At this writing, what effect the new Allende government in Chile will have upon the administration's policies remains to be seen. Finally, we should point out that, in spite of Rockefeller's judgment that there should be an increase in military aid to Latin America, he does recommend closing U.S. permanent military missions. In fact, for reasons of inhospitable governments in Peru, Chile, and Bolivia, the Nixon Administration's goal of a "lower profile" for the United States in Latin

America, Congressional criticism, and simple economy, substantial cutbacks in the number and size of permanent missions are currently underway.

I. THE DEPARTMENTS OF DEFENSE AND STATE

STATEMENT OF HON. G. WARREN NUTTER, ASSISTANT SECRETARY OF DEFENSE FOR INTERNATIONAL SECURITY AFFAIRS. . . .

Categories of U.S. Military Activities in Latin America

U.S. military activities in Latin America can be divided into three general categories: military assistance and sales programs; military missions; and cooperation with Latin American military forces in combined exercises. . . .

Military Assistance Program

The military assistance program for Latin America for fiscal year 1970 is small, amounting to $21.4 million divided about equally between training assistance and materiel support. It is the product of a carefully coordinated effort by all interested agencies, including the State and Defense Departments and AID. It is based on the recommendations of country teams, headed by U.S. Ambassadors, in the assisted countries. The fiscal year 1970 program is consistent with two trends in our military assistance to Latin America. First, the level of total assistance continues to move downward, and our limited support in materiel is restricted to those countries that most need our help.

The downward trend in military assistance is illustrated by the decline in the program from about $81 million in fiscal 1966 to this year's request for $21.4 million. As a matter of fact, this year's request is lower than any

previous program since fiscal year 1956 and in real terms represents less than 60 percent of the program for fiscal year 1957. Four of the larger countries that formerly received grants of materiel now receive assistance in training only. They are Argentina, Brazil, Chile, and Peru. The materiel granted to other countries consists primarily of support for equipment already furnished; the fiscal year 1970 program includes few major items of new equipment.

Military Sales Program

With the phasedown of the grant materiel program, Latin American countries must buy, either from the U.S. or some other country, needed replacements of equipment that has become old or worn out. To help them meet their needs, while minimizing the impact on their limited economic resources, we support a limited program of foreign military sales. This program is subject to the same careful interagency policy review as the military assistance program, and it is in consonance with the statutory guidelines established by Congress. The level of cash credit sales, when added to the grant materiel program, falls well within the $75 million ceiling on grants and sales to Latin America established by the Congress.

U.S. Military Missions

The United States has military missions in 17 Latin American countries. They are there at the request of the host countries to provide technical advice and assistance to their military services. The military missions also administer the military assistance program. They date back to the late 1930's, the

1940's, and in one case the early 1920's. The formerly separate missions of the Services have been grouped in each country into a military group that is part of the country team and therefore directly responsive to the U.S. Ambassador in the host country. A military chain of command exists for support and administrative matters, but the Ambassador exercises full control over policy and operations.

The roles of the missions vary with the competence and sophistication of the armed forces in the host countries. In the smaller countries, the emphasis is on such matters as individual and small-unit training, small-unit tactics and management, and maintenance. In the larger countries, the emphasis is on organizational and administrative problems at upper levels of management.

Many benefits accrue to the United States from these military groups. They provide advice to our Ambassadors as well as to the host countries. They establish a relationship of mutual trust and confidence among armed forces, and assure that military assistance plans and programs are adequately formulated and carefully administered.

The organization and staffing of military groups is currently under review. As a result, their strength has been reduced by about one-third over the last year. As our review continues, the organization and strength of the military groups will be kept in step with the requirement for their services.

Combined Military Exercises

The third element of U.S. military activities in Latin America involves modest participation in combined military exercises. We support these exercises for two purposes: to assist in the development of regional cooperation

within the framework of existing political organizations, and, to a lesser degree, to maintain international professional relationships. I described our participation as modest. The exercises, which do not exceed three each year, are all regional in nature. Two are conducted in the Central American and Caribbean area. We participate in these by providing advice, support, surveillance on the high seas, and U.S. forces on the aggressor side. The third exercise consists in naval training off the coasts of South America, in which small naval units from the United States maneuver jointly with those from a number of Latin American countries.

Latin American Defense Efforts

Finally, I should like to offer some observations about defense expenditures and military forces in Latin American countries. The resources devoted to defense by Latin American countries are modest in volume: as a percent of GNP, defense expenditures range from 0.1 to 3.1 percent and have remained relatively constant in recent years. The percentage . . . is lower than any other region of the world except Africa south of the Sahara. The great bulk of military expenditures—from 70 to 90 percent, depending on the country—is devoted to pay and allowances. Other day-to-day costs and operations in the field of civic action consume a portion of the remainder, leaving only small sums available for new military equipment.

These financial facts do not support the charges sometimes made that there is an arms race in Latin America. The military equipment sought by Latin American countries is designed not for a major buildup of forces, but principally for replacement of aging and obsolescent equipment that has become increasingly costly to maintain. The few cases in which controversial arms purchases have been made—like the Peruvian purchase of French *Mirage* aircraft in 1967—have not brought about a scramble by neighboring countries for compensatory armaments. As a matter of fact, there has been a decrease of approximately 29 percent in the number of combat aircraft in the major Latin American countries since 1953. Inventories of other armaments have fallen as well. In short, there is no evidence of a Latin American arms race. . . .

STATEMENT OF HON.
CHARLES A. MEYER,
ASSISTANT SECRETARY OF STATE
FOR INTER-AMERICAN AFFAIRS. . . .

*Relationship Between
Modernization and Stability*

Some of the earlier witnesses who appeared before this subcommittee have correctly made the long-accepted and recognized point that the acceleration of the movement in Latin America toward the social and economic reform goals of the Alliance for Progress will naturally and inevitably be accompanied by instability. It can, moreover, be argued that social tensions and conflicts are necessary ingredients in promoting the accelerated structural changes the Alliance seeks. At the same time, there can be little doubt that the painful and dynamic process of change is exploited by elements which have no real interest in the kind of change sought under the Alliance and indeed seek to frustrate it. Consequently, there is legitimate and responsible concern that instability not attain such a level as to destroy the reform process itself. There is, then, a very close relationship between the pros-

pects for achieving social and economic reform and development goals and a necessary level of internal security and stability. This relationship, between modernization and stability, is complex even in a fully democratic, pluralistic, highly developed society such as ours. If constructive reform is to proceed, however, the acceptable forms of legitimate, healthy, necessary dissent preclude terrorism and armed insurgency.

Insurgencies of a Sporadic Nature

Inasmuch as our military assistance program was shifted in the early 1960's, in recognition of changed circumstances, toward strengthening the Latin American national capabilities to counter Communist-sponsored or supported insurgency movements, how do we assess the threat today and for the near future? We believe that there is very little likelihood of a major external threat to the area in the foreseeable future. Communist insurgencies are currently at a relatively low ebb in Latin America. At the present time, active insurgencies of a sporadic nature continue to exist only in Venezuela, Colombia and Guatemala.

The defeat of the "Che" Guevara–led guerrillas in 1967 by elements of the Bolivian Army, largely equipped and trained in counterguerrilla warfare by the United States, seems to have made the Cuban regime more cautious about initiating new areas of insurgency in the hemisphere. In view of the improved counterinsurgency capabilities of the Latin American military forces, achieved by our joint efforts and programs, and the declining appeal of the Cuban-style revolution to the Latin Americans, a significant increase in insurgency movements is not likely at this time. We must recognize, however, that despite the relatively lower emphasis Havana seems to be giving for tactical reasons to overt support of insurgencies in their various forms, we have no evidence of any fundamental change in their interest in the export of revolution.

Need to Continue Military Assistance

Inasmuch as the threat of an external attack is unlikely and the danger of formidable insurgencies is today reduced, legitimate questions arise as to the desirability or need to continue with a military assistance program to Latin America.

Although today insurgent forces are not a direct threat to the governments in any of the Latin American countries, they do continue to represent, in varying degrees, a nucleus which can be further supported from outside in the event of deteriorating economic or social conditions. This factor, coupled with the continuance of inadequate and inequitable economic and social structures which are vulnerable to subversion; necessitates the maintenance of the counterinsurgency capabilities of Latin American forces in order that an internal atmosphere conducive to social and economic progress can prevail. Our training of small, mobile, rapid-reaction forces and our grant materiel program geared to maintaining equipment for the support of such forces play fundamental roles in this respect.

Whereas formal training is provided to 17 countries, our grant material assistance has now been limited to 11 countries which remain relatively vulnerable to subversive threats and which, at the same time, are less able to cope with internal security problems solely with their own limited resources. Such materiel assistance will, of course, be phased out when these countries are able to attain and maintain on their own an effective counterinsurgency capability or the insurgent threat further declines.

Relationship Between U.S. and Latin American Military Services

Now, let us look at a different and important relationship; namely, the relationship which has existed since or before World War II between the U.S. military services and the matching services of the larger Latin American countries. In these countries we have maintained military groups which were originally designated as military service missions in concert with the request or continued invitation of the host governments (often under contractual terms). These military groups have undergone reductions of personnel . . . and are subject to current and continuous reexamination both as to functions and numbers. Because, however, this relationship is long standing, because it is a relationship with the larger nations, because three of these nations are governed by leaders from their military, and because the relative size and sophistication of these nations produce requests for up-to-date major military equipment, we, the United States, ask ourselves whether our military presence is responsible (1) for encouraging military governments, (2) for providing repressive influences against the dissent inherent in today's worldwide struggle for self-fulfillment, and (3) for encouraging and then financing the acquisition of armaments which are either an unnecessary diversion of national resources or are the beginning of an "arms race."

I am not a military man. Like many in this room, I have served in one war and have seen the post-war revulsion to things military. Today, the Nixon administration is dedicated to a just and honorable termination of a controversial military action. This action has caused or has given focus to dissent within our own country, dissent which is clearly discernible around the world. But, recognizing this as a common current does not convince me that our politicomilitary relationships in Latin America are responsible per se for its internal political struggles. Nor do I believe that our inter-American relationships will be improved by any attitude on our part which, in effect, says to the sovereign states of Latin America: "You don't need anything more advanced in military equipment than the 20-year-old items you have and, furthermore, if you elect to buy anything more advanced than what you already have from anybody, we will consider it an irresponsible act and penalize you accordingly."

Arms Expenditures by Latin America

In all fairness, it must be said that the record of arms expenditures by Latin America has to date been the lowest of any world area with the sole exception of sub-Sahara Africa. Only about 2 percent of their GNP and less than 13 percent of their total central governments' expenditures have been expended for total defense costs. Moreover, only approximately 10 percent of their annual defense expenditures has been devoted to new military equipment. Naturally, we would hope that such restraint on their part would continue. However, the time has now arrived when these nations consider that they cannot further delay their military modernization programs. They would much prefer to purchase U.S.-manufactured equipment. In this regard our policy objectives have been entirely consistent with the purposes of legislative restrictions to discourage

Latin American governments from diverting their limited economic resources to unnecessary military items at the expense of development programs. However, these legislative restrictions, intended to inhibit their purchase of "sophisticated weapons systems" are, I am afraid, sowing the seeds of political estrangement with the major countries of that area.

Latin Americans have become puzzled and even suspicious of our motives. Strong nationalist resentment has arisen over what is seen as U.S. efforts to infringe on the sovereign rights of a country to determine its own military requirements; it is especially hard to understand in those countries which cherish the sense of close alliance with us, and have showed the value they place on this association. The net result has been negative in terms of broader U.S. political interests. There has been an increasing disposition on their part to turn to European suppliers who are able to respond promptly with firm offers of much more sophisticated as well as correspondingly more expensive equipment for early delivery on attractive credit terms. Unfortunately the long-term consequence of our paternalistic, even patronizing, restrictions will be the acquisition of more expensive items, higher maintenance costs, and greater diversion of financial resources from civilian purposes. The end result could be a real arms race which fortunately, thus far, has been avoided in Latin America. . . .

II. THE ROCKEFELLER REPORT
Communist Subversion

In every country, there is a restless striving for a better life. Coming as it does at a time of uprooting change, it brings to many a vague unease that all the systems of society are out of control. In such a setting, all of the American nations are a tempting target for Communist subversion. In fact, it is plainly evident that such subversion is a reality today with alarming potential.

Castro has consistently recruited from the other American republics, and trained in Cuba, guerrillas to export the Cuban-type Communist agrarian revolution. Fortunately, the governments of the American republics have gradually improved their capabilities for dealing with Castro-type agrarian guerrillas. However, radical revolutionary elements in the hemisphere appear to be increasingly turning toward urban terrorism in their attempts to bring down the existing order. This type of subversion is more difficult to control, and governments are forced to use increasingly repressive measures to deal with it. Thus, a cycle of terrorist actions and repressive counterreactions tend to polarize and unsettle the political situation, creating more fertile ground for radical solutions among large segments of the population.

There are also Maoist Communist forces in the hemisphere. Although they are relatively small in numbers, they are fanatically dedicated to the use of violence and intimidation to achieve their ends. The mystique of Maoism has appealed most to the idealism of the young and, thus, has been the means for widespread subversion.

Now it appears in some cases that Castro and Maoist forces have joined for acts of subversion, terror and violence in the cities. These forces also concentrate on mass student demonstrations and disruptions of various institu-

tions, public and private, calling on the support of Communist labor front organizations to the degree possible.

Although Castro's propaganda casts him as a leader of the down-trodden who is opposed to United States imperialism and independent of Soviet Communism, it is clear that the Soviet Union presently has an important degree of financial, economic, and military influence over Communist Cuba. The recent visit of the Soviet fleet to Havana is one evidence of growing warmth in their relations.

This Soviet performance in Cuba and throughout the hemisphere is to be contrasted with the official Soviet government and Communist party protestations not only of peaceful coexistence but of disassociation from Castro and his program of terror in the American republics.

Clearly, the opinion in the United States that Communism is no longer a serious factor in the Western Hemisphere is thoroughly wrong. . . .

Western Hemisphere Security. . . .

. . . Forces of anarchy, terror and subversion are loose in the Americas. Moreover, this fact has too long gone unheeded in the United States.

Doubt and cynicism have grown in the other American nations as to the purposefulness of the United States in facing this serious threat to freedom, democracy and the vital interests of the entire hemisphere.

Many of our neighbors find it incomprehensible that the United States will not sell them military equipment which they feel is required to deal with internal subversion. They have been puzzled by the reduction in U.S. military assistance grants in view of the growing intensity of the subversive activities they face. . . .

In addition, the United States must face more forthrightly the fact that while the military in the other American nations are alert to the problems of internal security, they do not feel that this is their only role and responsibility. They are conscious of the more traditional role of a military establishment to defend the nation's territory, and they possess understandable professional pride which creates equally understandable desires for modern arms; in addition, they are subjected to the sales pressures and blandishments of suppliers from other nations— east and west—eager to sell. The result of all this is a natural resentment on the part of the military of other American nations when the United States refuses to sell modern items of equipment.

Thus, many military leaders in the other American republics see the United States acting to hold them back as second-class citizens, and they are becoming increasingly estranged from us at a time when their political role is on the rise. Our dilemma is how to be responsive to their legitimate desires for modern equipment without encouraging the diversion of scarce resources from development to armaments which, in some cases, may be unrelated to any real security requirement.

Military leaders throughout the hemisphere are frequently criticized here in the United States. However, we will have to give increasing recognition to the fact that many new military leaders are deeply motivated by the need for social and economic progress. They are searching for ways to bring education and better standards of living to their people while avoiding anarchy or violent revolution. In many cases, it will be more useful for the United States to try to work with them in

these efforts, rather than to abandon or insult them because we are conditioned by arbitrary ideological stereotypes.

In addition, there is not in the United States a full appreciation of the important role played by the police. There is a tendency in the United States to equate the police in the other American republics with political action and repression, rather than with security. There have, unfortunately, been many such instances of the use of police. Yet well-motivated, well-trained police, when present in local communities, enforce the laws, protect the citizenry from terror, and discourage criminal elements. At the present time, however, police forces of many countries have not been strengthened as population and great urban growth have taken place. Consequently they have become increasingly less capable of providing either the essential psychological support or the internal security that is their major function. . . .

Recommendation: National Policy Objective

The United States should cooperate with other nations of the Western Hemisphere in measures to strengthen internal security.

Recommendations for Action

1. A WESTERN HEMISPHERE SECURITY COUNCIL. a. The United States should work with the other republics to form a civilian-directed Western Hemisphere Security Council to cope with the forces of subversion that operate throughout the Western Hemisphere. The purpose of the Council would be to help the hemisphere countries work together in creating and preserving the kind of orderly environment, free from terror

and violence, in which each citizen of each country can build a better life for himself and his family. This Council would supersede the Special Consultative Committee on Security of the Organization of American States.

b. Although the United States would have membership in the Council, the Council should have its headquarters outside of our country.

2. A WESTERN HEMISPHERE SECURITY TRAINING ASSISTANCE PROGRAM. a. The United States should reverse the recent downward trend in grants for assisting the training of security forces for the other hemisphere countries. (The total amount proposed for fiscal year 1970 is $21.4 million, as against $80.7 million in fiscal year 1966.) In view of the growing subversion against hemisphere governments, the mounting terrorism and violence against citizens, and the rapidly expanding population, it is essential that the training program which brings military and police personnel from the other hemisphere nations to the United States and to training centers in Panama be continued and strengthened.

b. The name "Military Assistance Program" should be dropped because it no longer reflects the security emphasis we believe important. The program should be renamed the "Western Hemisphere Security Program."

3. INTERNAL SECURITY SUPPORT. a. The United States should respond to requests for assistance of the police and security forces of the hemisphere nations by providing them with the essential tools to do their job.

b. Accordingly, the United States should meet reasonable requests from other hemisphere governments for trucks, jeeps, helicopters and like equipment to provide mobility and logistical support for these forces; for radios, and other command control equipment for proper communications among the forces; and for small arms for security forces.

c. In furtherance of these objectives, the United States should provide, on request, military and technical training missions but should no longer maintain the permanent military missions in residence in other nations which too often have constituted too large and too visible a United States presence.

4. MILITARY SALES FOR DEFENSE. a. The Executive Branch should seek modification of the Conte and Symington amendments to permit the United States to sell aircraft, ships and other major military equipment without aid cut penalties to the more developed nations of the hemisphere when these nations believe this equipment is necessary to protect their land, patrol their seacoasts and airspace, and otherwise maintain the morale of their forces and protect their sovereignty. Realistically, if the United States doesn't sell such equipment, it will be purchased from other sources, east or west, and this would not be compatible with the United States' best interests.

b. Each country should be permitted to buy such equipment through purchase orders placed with the United States Defense Department through the Military Assistance Program, in order that each country may get full value for its military investment, more reliable delivery dates, and better maintenance.

25

U.S. Military Policies and Programs in Latin America

David Bronheim

Published for the first time in this collection, by permission of the author.

David Bronheim was formerly Deputy U.S. Coordinator of the Alliance for Progress (1965–67) and Director of the Center for Inter-American Relations in New York.

Responding to the Rockefeller Report recommendation for increased military aid, Bronheim outlines and criticizes what he believes to be the major assumptions underlying U.S. relationships with the Latin American military. Note that, except for governments "which take or hold office by force of arms," he suggests separating the question of military assistance from the issue of military hardware sales and recommends that in its allocation of nonmilitary aid the U.S. stress the adequacy of a country's budget for economic and social development rather than the appropriateness of its expenditures for weaponry.

Should the United States conduct assistance programs to train and arm the Latin American military to kill more efficiently? This is a question that goes to the heart of our relations in this hemisphere. More importantly, it is intimately connected to the issue of what we are as a nation and a people.

Our military assistance policies and programs are based on World War II, the Cold War, and the Castro scare. The experience of this three-decade period and the changes that have occurred in the world during that period are reason enough to evaluate our policies. However, there are other more pressing factors that compel the re-examination. First, more than one-half of the population of Latin America is living under military rule—a percentage greater than when the decade opened. Second, a substantial number of educated people in Latin America (and in the United States) are increasingly convinced that our military programs helped create and preserve their present difficulties with their armed forces. Third, and of most immediate importance, Governor Rockefeller's report to President Nixon on Latin American policy recommends that we increase military assistance to all governments in the hemisphere regardless of their political complexion. Communism is his fear. Security is his goal. The moral and practical problems of providing increased and improved killing power to repressive dictatorships are unanalysed. The complexities of assisting the armed forces in countries having democratic civilian institutions are ignored.

Given the potential perniciousness of the Rockefeller recommendation and its high component of nonsense, some background and analysis is in order.

Prior to the Second World War our involvement with the military in Latin America was minimal. They did their training and bought their weapons in Europe. At the start of that war, the Germans were deeply involved with many of the military establishments in Latin America. To reverse this situation, the United States began to supply arms and training. This effort was made to enable the hemisphere to resist invasion and to assist the United States in anti-submarine warfare in the Atlantic. Nelson Rockefeller was instrumental in developing and implementing these programs.

Our efforts to keep the Latins focused on combating an overt external military threat continued sporadically throughout the 1950s. Out of these Second World War and Cold War efforts there evolved such things as the joint naval exercises that are still held by the U.S. and some Latin navies, the Inter-American Defense Board, and the substantial United States military groups stationed in almost all of the Latin American countries. On the inter-American scene, all are of debatable relevance. None is in any way relevant to any war that the United States is likely to fight.

With the advent of Castro's Cuba, the Kennedys, and Vietnam, the em-

phasis of our programs changed. Latin armies were to be trained to combat covert communism, insurgency, and subversion. They were to provide the internal security and stability that was thought to be essential for the Alliance for Progress. Programs for training and equipping the police were undertaken for the same purposes.

Throughout the 1960s, thousands of Latin American officers and enlisted men were trained to combat insurgency at schools in the United States and in Panama (probably in violation of our treaty rights). Hundreds of United States military personnel were stationed around the hemisphere to advise the Latins on these tasks. Latin military colleges were encouraged to revise their curricula to encompass courses dealing with internal security, and guest lecturers from the U.S. military were available to help out. The United States encouraged the Latins to buy, and would only supply, the small, but at times sophisticated, equipment that would enable the Latin soldier to kill a countryman or a covert infiltrator rather than the equipment needed to repel an overt aggressor.

As the war in Vietnam wound on, and the number of unrepresentative, repressive, or reactionary governments in the hemisphere increased, the pressure grew in the United States to get out of the military assistance business. The executive branch, responding to strong civilian pressures within it and to more persuasive pressures from the Congress, began substantial reductions in the program. Financial assistance was reduced to a third of its $80 million 1966 high, and the number of military advisers started down from about 800 to 500. Rockefeller has recommended that the trend on assistance be reversed. It is encouraging to note that the President has not adopted this proposal.

When looking at our policy, it is helpful to keep a few basic truths in mind. Latin America had military services before the U.S. had military assistance programs. These military services would exist today, they will continue to exist in the future, and they will be significantly involved in their domestic political affairs regardless of whether the United States has a military assistance program. Also, many Latin American military men are decent people whose attitudes and characters are no worse, and often better, than those of many Latin American civilian politicans.

Our present policy is based on the rhetoric that a country with an increasingly democratic political system and a rapidly growing economy offering improved standards of living and opportunities for its people is most consistent with the U.S. national interest. The only fair way to judge our military assistance programs is to determine whether in fact they are contributing to the achievement of these objectives.

To achieve these objectives the government of the United States reached two key conclusions involving the Latin American military: first, that accelerated economic and social development required increased political stability, and, second, that a well-trained professional military would be automatically more divorced from internal political processes and more tolerant of democratic development. Both conclusions turned out to be incorrect.

The first conclusion—that concerning development and stability—is an attractive part of the conventional wis-

dom. But it may be conceptually unsound. Most of our experience tends to indicate that the development process is inherently destabilizing. Development almost by definition necessitates the redistribution of political and economic power. It raises aspirations and expectations faster than it can satisfy them. It puts serous strains on social institutions faster than it can reform those institutions. It is a very risky and nerve-racking process. We are witnessing it in our own country.

Generally the very poor and oppressed are not an explosive mass. They tend to be passive and resigned. It is only when they begin to achieve and have aspirations that they become a potentially explosive force. Development is what makes them explosive. The acceleration of the development process is naturally accompanied by increased instability. The question cannot be how to have development and suppress instability. Institutions and laws must be reformed. Property and opportunities must be more equitably distributed. Justice must be made available for all, and all must have the opportunity to participate in the political process. The army and the police cannot be used to suppress all of the accompanying ferment. We cannot try to arm the military and the police to preserve stability. Most countries must first solve the more difficult intellectual problem of how to keep instability within a range that does not threaten either economic growth or political development. The United States Government rarely addresses itself to this problem. Certainly, it has not attempted any serious discussion of these issues in its inter-American relations. Moreover, it is not at all clear that it would be morally bad or inconsistent with the national interest of the United States if some countries in this hemisphere were to have actual rebellion.

Since our military programs are designed to enable the Latin military to preserve stability and to react negatively to all manifestations of political instability, they are inherently unsound, and on occasion entirely suppress the very forces that are necessary to bring about political change. Throughout the hemisphere, U.S.-trained and -equipped military have tried to suppress vigorous political dissent, civil demonstration, riot, and rebellion. (In fairness, we should note that sometimes they are carrying out civilian orders.) Accordingly, we are now believed to be rooted to the status quo and the military and entirely opposed to real change. I cannot believe that it is in our national interest to be known as a force favoring repression against every movement for rapid change.

A more honest public examination of our policy might reveal a related but more difficult motive to isolate. Many in the U.S. government believed that instability was not merely inconsistent with development but would be exploited by the communists to the disadvantage of our vital national interests. The price that we have paid for this delightfully simplistic belief in the workings of political processes in Latin America is that many educated people in the hemisphere believe that we are the main supporters of reaction. Additionally, to add insult to injury, the military, also, are less friendly with us than they were a decade ago.

(To compound our mistakes, we have been training and equipping the police of Latin America for similar objectives. In the past five years the United States has spent almost $43 million and has stationed about eighty employees in Latin America for this purpose. Since it should be clear from our performance at home that our police departments are not all-knowing founts of wisdom in dealing with the problems that result from rapid social change, a review of our police assistance programs is probably long overdue.)

The second conclusion—that well-trained and -equipped military would be more divorced from domestic politics— was incorrect from the outset. While the first conclusion concerning instability is subject to disagreement on complicated conceptual grounds, this second conclusion was simply a gross blunder.

The Latin American military has always had a deep interest and involvement in its local political process. Our experience now shows that a significant improvement in their training and equipment does not lessen their concern, but in fact may heighten it. As a result of our "excellent" training they have become impressed with their own capacities for efficient management and increasingly impatient with the inefficiencies of civilian rule in the development of their countries. Moreover, by dunning them about internal security and the communist threat, they now have a higher tendency to see communists everyplace and to equate all opposition with subversion. This has lowered their tolerance for civilian "bungling" in dealing with all the subversion that they see around them. The coups in Argentina and Peru and the threat of one in Venezuela come in some measure from the belief by the military that they are better able to manage the affairs of their country than the less efficient civilian politicians. The last coup in Ecuador, and perhaps the next one, will be motivated by much the same reasoning. The one in Brazil in 1964, and in some part the one in Panama, was influenced by the military's view of the risk of subversion to the institutions of the country.

Additionally, a military well-trained in the U.S. and exposed to our wondrous weapons systems develops very professional tastes in expensive hardware. This creates increased budgetary pressures on civilian governments and complicates their development efforts.

In sum, there is absolutely no reason to believe that a better-trained and -equipped Latin military will meddle less in domestic politics.

From time to time other objectives of our military assistance programs come up, sometimes singly, sometimes in groups. The following seem to have been on the best-seller list longest:

(1) Strengthen collective hemispheric defense against external aggression.
(2) Fight communism from Moscow, Peking, or Havana.
(3) Improve the image of the Latin American armed forces.
(4) Reduce Latin America's economic burden.
(5) Enable the United States to be the exclusive supplier of arms and training.
(6) Enable the United States to obtain the political collaboration and friendship of the Latin American military.
(7) Expose Latin American officers to our concepts of democracy.

These objectives are not mutually exclusive, nor are they all of the same quality. They do, however, have a common characteristic. When examined carefully, they do not supply sufficient grounds to continue our programs.

1. Collective Hemispheric Defense

This point is of great rhetorical popularity but is unrelated to current military reality. There is no likely situation involving a threat to the United States that would involve hostile land or sea action against a Latin American country. This concept is a residue of the Second World War and is not credible today.

Sometimes one hears of a hemispheric threat of subversion. However, a careful analysis of this threat indicates that it is misdescribed. There may be subversion in many of the countries. Some of this subversion may be financed and equipped from outside the hemisphere, but this fact does not call for a hemispheric defense system. It certainly does not call for joint naval maneuvers in the South Atlantic. And it is equally unaffected by anything that comes out of the large collection of brass that inhabits the impressive Washington headquarters of the Inter-American Defense Board. Periodically, an inter-American intelligence collection system is proposed to deal with the problem. But our President would be well advised to ponder the moral complexities of exchanging intelligence data with a Duvalier or a Stroessner to help them deal with whatever they thought was subversive. Such a system of information exchange with many governments of this hemisphere would be morally repugnant to our principles and would not serve any identifiable U.S. national interest.

2. The Fight Against Communism

In recent years, as we have become more sophisticated in our analysis of the Cold War, the Latin military, and the political issues in Latin America, this objective has not been given as much public support as it received in the 1950s. The Rockefeller report tries to rejuvenate it.

The Rockefeller report perceives the

problem inaccurately. Equally important, even if it were to be proven right in its perception, it is unsound in its conclusions.

The report points out that political tensions are rising and that the risk and incidence of politically motivated violence is increasing; that the violence is communist inspired; that it is a threat to Western Hemisphere security; that it manifests itself in urban terrorism more than in the previously popular rural insurgency; and that it is in our national interest to help combat it wherever it appears by assisting the military and other internal security forces with helicopters, communications equipment, and small arms and ammunition.

It is true that there is a good chance that politically inspired violence will go up. It is also true that urban terror is becoming increasingly more popular than rural insurrection as a revolutionary tactic. But neither the revolutionaries nor the authorities in power have made a thorough study of the one Latin American city that has dealt with and defeated urban violence: Caracas.

In the early 1960s, the Venezuelan government was a representative government becoming increasingly democratic. It had the support of large numbers of its people. The population of Caracas was repelled by the terror. The government developed a good system of intelligence collection and rapid reaction. In large measure it was these factors—not helicopters—that ended the urban terror. Helicopters flying around New York City would not have raised the possibility of stopping the recent explosion in the Chase Manhattan Bank. Nor would they have raised the prospects of catching the perpetrators of the deed. Governor

Rockefeller's prescription is irrelevant.

In any event, it gives the Russians, Chinese, Cubans, or even the home-grown communists far too much credit to blame all the terrorism on them. By and large, the people leading the guerrilla movements in Latin America are radical nationalists and socialists. They are not under international communist discipline. They get their training, guns and money wherever they can—rebel leaders in Guatemala and the Dominican Republic were trained in the U.S. Generally they do not take their orders from abroad.

For the moment, the Russians do not have a strategy for encouraging guerrilla warfare in Latin America. The Moscow-line communists are the most reactionary parties of the left in Latin America. Moreover, since Czechoslovakia, the Russians are viewed as imperialists who are at least as unpleasant as the United States.

There is no doubt that Havana and Peking will create as much mischief as possible for the U.S. in Latin America, but it would be a mistake to credit them with causing the disturbances. The violence would exist without them. There are a lot of people in Latin America who do not like the status quo. There are many who hate the military dictatorships in Argentina and Brazil, have lost patience with the civilians in Uruguay, despise Duvalier and Stroessner, and are prepared to resort to violence to get rid of them. Whether they would run their countries better if they succeeded is arguable. The history of revolution in Latin America is mixed. But surely it cannot be vital to the national interests of the United States to have revolutionaries killed wherever and whenever they raise their heads.

Two other points related to arming the military to fight communists require comment. One involves Brazil, the other Bolivia. The Brazilian military, as much as any military in the hemisphere, has been influenced by the United States. We have preached to them about internal security, communists, and subversion. They now have a tendency to see communists everyplace and to equate all vigorous opposition with subversion. This frame of mind may heighten their tendency to create the classic political polarization by either destroying the moderate opposition or by driving it together with the violent left. Should this happen, they would have created a traditional revolutionary situation which could not possibly be in the United States national interest.

The Bolivian case is less complicated and more revealing. A white Argentine, a Frenchman, and some Cubans came to Bolivia to lead the Bolivians in a revolution. A less likely combination for success could hardly be conjured up. Guevara could not get the support of the local rural people. This fact was not connected with our military assistance program; it was in part connected to reform measures undertaken earlier by a revolutionary civilian government. The Bolivian army, with practically every advantage to be hoped for in such circumstances, almost failed. After a decade of military assistance, it could not carry out the simple tactics necessary to track and destroy the guerrillas. It had to be given emergency help. Ten years of military assistance were not of much value when a real test came.

Finally, even without our help, the military in Latin American would be anti-communist. The military generally turns out to be at best authoritarian and statist, and at worst fascist. Though this is some distance from our system, it is also sufficiently different from communism to make them natural enemies. But perhaps of greater importance is the fact that every officer in Latin America knows what Castro did to the Cuban army.

3. The Image of the Latin American Military

In the abstract, the United States could not possibly care whether a particular military force is liked or disliked. The issue can be relevant in only two areas.

First, if the military are friendly and closely associated with us, it would be nice if they were liked in their own country. However, friendship by itself is not enough to support a military assistance program. Whether we should be friendly to the military is the very thing that is under review.

Second, it is argued that, in the event of insurgency, a populace friendly to the army is of great value in combating guerrillas. Therefore, a program that endears the army to the civilian population is a vital counter-insurgency tool.

There is a glaring weakness in this argument. First, it cannot be a vital U.S. interest to have insurgency crushed whenever and wherever it appears. In Haiti and Paraguay revolution may be one of the few valid answers for changing the political system. But if that point is arguable, there is a more obvious weakness. In a progressive modernizing country the military, to get popular support, will be encouraged by domestic politics to act in ways that help develop the country. However, where a government, civilian or military, is repressive or unconcerned with development, the public relations effort of the military supporting that government will be of little value. Moreover, in that situation the United States should not be concerned with improving the image of the military.

4. Reduce the Economic Burden of the Military

This is a deceptive objective which tends to hide the real issues. Money is fungible. A dollar spent by the U.S. on one program releases a dollar for a different program. The question for the United States is not how much money should be spent by a particular government on its military. The real question is with which part of its development effort do we want to be associated.

Theoretically, a government makes difficult domestic compromises and decisions in arriving at its overall budget. If a government knows that we would be more inclined to help its agricultural effort and thinks increased military expenditures are important, they can use their own funds for military expenditures and seek our help for agriculture.

There is a curious side issue on this point. In Panama a few years back, the executive branch did not think that it could get the Congress to vote increased funds for the military. It was easier to seek funds from the U.S. than it was to burn up good will domestically on an unpopular cause. Were someone to discover the increased expenditures for the army, or if the newly expanded army did anything unpleasant, the U.S. could always be blamed.

A final point about this objective is that it tends to be self-defeating. As I mentioned earlier, there is nothing that improves taste in expensive weapons faster than our creating a professional officer corps exposed to U.S. weapons.

5. Exclusive Supplier of Arms and Training

This objective is primarily designed to reduce the influence of other nations' military forces on the forces in Latin America. Here again we have a policy left over from the Second World War. Since those likely to replace us today as suppliers would be English, French or German, no real shift of truly vital proportions is involved. No such shift affects the vital national interests of the United States in a world made up of today's configuration of military power. The Latin American military is unlikely to seek aid from Russia or China. It is not in their interest.

In any event, the political situation in Latin America is such today that the military must periodically purchase weapons from other sources to show that they are not subservient to us. Moreover, what they really want weapons for is not to protect themselves from internal subversion or European invasion, but rather to defend themselves against their immediate neighbors. We are politically unable to arm all of them for fighting each other, and we cannot stop them from doing it. When we try, they get mad at us. We might as well relax and understand that we cannot continue to be the exclusive supplier. This shouldn't trouble us. It should delight us.

During and right after the Second World War, when we were the only possible source of weapons, we developed the grandiose ideal of monopolizing the arms trade. One incentive for this was that if there was an invasion anywhere all arms and ammunition would be interchangeable and easily suppliable by the U.S. The whole concept is obsolete today.

Moreover, if some military force decided to seek arms from the Russians, this could only create a threat to our national security because of actions by the Russians. The lesson of the Cuban missile crisis is that in such a situation, we do not even bother to talk to the Latin American nation. Our conversations are with the Russians. Finally, if our relations had deteriorated sufficiently with the military of a Latin country so that they were seeking Russian arms, the issue of exclusive supplier would have been subsumed in graver matters.

6. *Political Collaboration and Friendship*

This objective has an attractive rhetorical ring—until it is examined closely. There are those who think it would be a good thing to be able to count on the friendship and collaboration of the Latin military. Even were this the case, it is not an adequate way to approach the issue.

The issue is: what is the political cost that we pay for attempting to purchase the collaboration and friendship of the Latin military, how effective is the collaboration, and how important or real is the friendship?

There are two points to political collaboration. One, dealing with Latin American domestic problems, is easiest to dispose of. Our experience to date indicates that our capacity to influence the Latin American military on important domestic questions is insignificant. Our ability to persuade the Panamanian, Peruvian and Argentine military to stay their hand and not

overthrow elected governments was nil. If we could not influence the Panamanian National Guard, we cannot influence anyone. If another example is needed, the circumstances surrounding the issuance of the repressive Institutional Acts in Brazil are relevant. Our capacity to influence our good friends in the Brazilian military to move in more truly democratic directions was not great. Finally, our ability to persuade the Hondurans and Salvadorians to forgo their recent war was nonexistent.

The second part of the collaboration issue involves international issues. It has been argued that a friendly military will support us on international issues, and when necessary, will influence an undecided civilian government.

Again, we have oversimplified the problem. It is the domestic political reality that decides a civilian government on its course. No civilian government would send troops to support us in the Dominican Republic notwithstanding military pressure. The position taken by the civilian government of Argentina was a classic example of the point. Substantial military pressure was not able to budge the Argentine civilian government.

Peru today is an example of the cooperativeness of the military when they are actually running a government. Though some of the fault results from bungled U.S. policy on the part of civilian sectors of our government, one can still learn from the present situation that the military are increasingly sensitive to their domestic political reality, and will tend to play to it in seeking support. Since they are suspected by their own people of being too close to the U.S., they are tempted to over-react and be super-patriots.

Today, the military in Peru, one of the largest recipients of United States military assistance, is by traditional tests one of the least cooperative.

The friendship point in the abstract is irrelevant. We must decide what it costs us to seek that friendship and what we get from it.

At present, the political costs of our tactics are substantial. We have alienated large elements of the civilian population who believe that we support and maintain their military against democratic forces; we are targeted with the Latin American military by all anti-military political groups; we do not have a significant influence on major issues; and even the military are unhappy with us. This is not a formula for success in the Western Hemisphere.

The final irony is that when a military government does our bidding, it is hard to find the expensively purchased benefits. When the military governments of Paraguay, Honduras and Brazil sent troops to the Dominican Republic it did little to untarnish our image.

7. *Exposure to Democracy*

Experience shows that this was one of the more naive objectives. Latins close to our military in the field did not profit at all. If anything, it made our military more sympathetic to the anti-democratic leanings of the Latins. Whether the military training in the States had beneficial political effects on the Latins is harder to estimate. There is no hard evidence that it did. Perhaps if they had been exposed to the civilian side of our society one could have more hope. But their programs and time are taken up by our military, and it is hard to see how any significant beneficial aspects of our civilian life could seep through to them.

In sum, it is easy to see the political costs incurred by our military assistance programs. Substantial benefits are harder to find. This equation by itself would be reason enough to end our military assistance program. But there are stronger reasons. They have to do with what we are to become as a nation. We must decide on our domestic purpose and clarify our ideals. It cannot be that we have a domestic purpose that is nourished by supplying guns and ammunitions to every dictator and general to be used to kill those that rise against them.

If we are deeply concerned with the unrest, violence and frustration that is growing in Latin America, we must be prepared to help them root out the basic causes. That is time-consuming, aggravating and costly. If the United States cannot afford the financial cost of helping to alleviate the causes of unrest and violence, then our consciences cannot afford the moral cost of supplying the weapons to suppress it.

RECOMMENDATIONS

1. The U.S. should terminate all assistance programs for hardware. On the other hand, we should have a clear general rule permitting most Latin American countries to buy on commercial terms most weapons in whatever amounts their domestic political process budgets. It should be made clear to the hemisphere that we neither assist in the acquisition of arms nor meddle in the domestic process of deciding how much arms are necessary.

Obviously certain things, such as atomic, biological and chemical weapons would not be for sale. There may be other weapons that we would not want to sell for psychological and moral reasons (such as napalm).

Finally, and the most difficult part of this proposal, we should rigidly embargo all sales of arms to governments which take or hold office by force of arms. It should be made clear that we are not attempting to meddle in other countries' domestic affairs. We are saying that as the leader of the Western World, and as a country deeply committed to the democratic process, we are not prepared to see U.S. arms sold to support authoritarian regimes. This requires some extremely difficult line drawing, but hard decisions are what policymaking is all about.

2. The U.S. should be prepared to continue to assist in the training of Latin American officers, but on the condition that a joint civilian-military curriculum board be set up in the U.S. to develop the training course and to assure that it has a large civil component.

3. Military missions should be terminated. If a Latin American country requests advice, it should be made available on a short-term consultant basis.

4. In determining whether a particular country should receive economic assistance, a sound development program with adequate internal financing is a prerequisite. Accordingly, were a country to be neglecting its development sectors because it was investing heavily in its military, the U.S. might refuse to provide economic assistance. My point is that we should not get involved with the military budget. Rather we should concern ourselves with the adequacy of the rest of the budget.

It should be noted that this paper deals with questions of military assistance. Other than in connection with military sales, this paper does not deal with the separate question of how the U.S. should deal with military governments. I stress this because the subjects, though related, are distinct.

26

The United States and
Political Development in Latin America:
A Retrospect and a Prescription

Yale H. Ferguson

In this essay, the editor charts a third course for the United States in Latin America between an attempt to maintain the status quo and a retreat from exposed positions of leadership: what he regards, respectively, as the Johnson-Nixon posture and the alternative urged by Congressional critics of executive policies. As background for his prescription, he (1) analyzes United States policies in periods when the "promotion of democracy" in Latin America has—and has not—been a high-priority goal, and (2) surveys the current prospects for modernization proceeding under various kinds of Latin American political regimes. He concludes with a plea for an "updated" Kennedy policy, revised in the light of the somewhat new conditions of the 1970s to favor fundamental economic and social change first and democracy second.

The author wishes to express his gratitude to the Woodrow Wilson Foundation for a Dissertation Fellowship and to the Rutgers University Research Council for a grant which helped to make this study possible. He is also grateful to Robert R. Kaufman of Douglass College, Rutgers University, for his constructive criticism. Finally, he wants to acknowledge the kind permission of the following publishers to use quotations from their publications: Doubleday and Company, Inc., for John Bartlow Martin, *Overtaken By Events: The Dominican Crisis—From the Fall of Trujillo to the Civil War,* Copyright © by John Bartlow Martin; and Houghton Mifflin Company, for Arthur M. Schlesinger, Jr., *A Thousand Days: John F. Kennedy in the White House.*

"[W]e must deal realistically with governments in the inter-American system as they are," stated President Nixon in his address of October 31, 1969, outlining major aspects of his administration's policies toward Latin America.[1] With these words, he ratified the fact that the official attitudes which prevailed during the Johnson years regarding the domestic political environment in Latin America were something more than a temporary aberration. Gone were the ringing phrases of the Kennedy period about the dawning of

---

[1] Richard M. Nixon, "Action for Progress for the Americas," *Department of State* *Bulletin,* LXI (Nov. 17, 1969), 413. (This periodical hereafter cited as *DSB.*)

a new era of democracy and development in the hemisphere. No less than seventeen military coups d'etat, the staggering gap between aspirations and accomplishments in the balance sheet of the Alliance for Progress, and the apparent decline of the guerrilla offensive that was anticipated in the wake of the Cuban Revolution—all had taken their toll.

The posture of overt pragmatism now reaffirmed by the Nixon Administration appears to reflect both grave doubts that the United States can have a substantial constructive influence upon the political dimension of the modernization process in Latin America and also—aside from any lingering threat of radical revolution—an acceptance of the status quo as generally consistent with U.S. interests.

While Congressional critics of the Nixon policies urge abandonment of anti-Communism, partly to avoid another incident like the 1965 Dominican crisis, and complain that U.S. aid bolsters unprogressive military and civilian governments, the alternatives they advance involve less (rather than more) attempted interference with indigenous patterns of Latin American political change. They would have the United States largely "disengage" from Latin America and come to terms with what they envisage as increasing diversity and nationalism in the region.

From a number of standpoints, then, there could hardly be a less auspicious time than the present (October 1970) for an essay on the subject of 'The United States and Political Development in Latin America." One senses that policy-makers with quite different goals would at least agree that there should be as little as possible to discuss under that heading!

On the other hand, the author is spurred to write precisely because he is strongly opposed both to the current "Pax Americana" and to the "new isolationism" which vies to replace it. For reasons to be advanced below, he advocates steering a third course between the Scylla of a reprehensible (and ultimately vain) attempt to maintain the status quo and the Charybdis of an equally undesirable retreat from exposed positions of leadership. This course emphasizes the *positive* contributions that the United States can yet make to Latin American political development, contributions which derive only in part from deemphasizing the negative.

The essay that follows has three basic sections. Part I analyzes past and present United States policies. Part II focuses upon key aspects of the domestic political environment in Latin America today. Part III draws upon discussions in the two previous sections to argue for a major reorientation in U.S. policies.

I. UNITED STATES POLICIES IN RETROSPECT

Looking backward over the years, perhaps the most striking thing about United States policies relating to domestic politics in Latin America has been their cyclic character: What has usually been termed the "promotion of democracy" in the area alternately has—or has not—been high on Washington's list of priorities. Although, as we shall see, there have been significant variations in comparable parts of the recurrent cycle and a concern for the best interests of the United States (read differently at different times) has undergirded them all, the cyclic pattern has been dominant. In the sense that policies on the democracy question came full circle between 1959 and 1964, this tumultuous period constituted one complete cycle. However, in the perspective of history, it is only one of several.

U.S. PRO-DEMOCRACY POLICIES

From the outset of inter-American relations in the early nineteenth century, the United States has periodically adopted unilateral policies designed to further contemporary standards of democracy in (at least) various parts of the hemisphere. The fact that most of the newly independent states of Latin America framed "republican" constitutions initially helped them to secure recognition from the United States.[2] In his famous Doctrine, Monroe spoke of a dramatic contrast between the republican governments of the Western Hemisphere and the absolute monarchies of Europe.[3] Nearly a century later, the United States underwrote the Central American (Tobar) treaties of

2 As the Latin American independence movement progressed, the conviction grew that it would lead to the establishment of "regimes whose political orientation, . . . was of the same general revolutionary and liberal type as that represented by the United States and combatted by the 'allied despots of Europe' [the Holy Alliance]." (Arthur P. Whitaker, *The Western Hemisphere Idea: Its Rise and Decline* [Ithaca, N.Y., 1954], 54.) Monroe himself explained his recognition decision as in part motivated by a desire to promote "the establishment of free republican governments." (Quoted in Arthur P. Whitaker, *The United States and the Independence of Latin America, 1800–1830* [Baltimore, 1941], 375.)

3 Dexter Perkins observes: "Against [the] Old World order, based on the doctrines of absolutism, Monroe opposed a new one, based on the right of the peoples of the world to determine their own destiny and to govern themselves." (*A History of the Monroe Doctrine* [rev. ed.; Boston, 1963], 63.)

1907 and 1923, which (among other things) denied recognition to regimes emanating from coups d'etat.[4] Wilson began an essentially separate campaign for "constitutional government" when he assumed office in 1913.[5] Hoover's

4 The 1907 treaty provided for the withholding of recognition until free elections had been held after a coup. The 1923 treaty went further, to deny recognition even to governments elected following a coup when an individual serving as president, vice-president, or chief of state was: (a) one of the leaders of the coup or a relative of same; (b) a member of the military command or secretary of state within the six months prior to the coup, during the coup, or while the election was in progress; (c) anyone disqualified by the constitution from holding these offices.

For texts of the treaties and related documents, see: U.S., Department of State, *Foreign Relations of the United States, 1907*, II, 665–727 [this series hereafter cited as *FRUS*]; and U.S., Department of State, *Conference on Central American Affairs, December 4, 1922–February 7, 1923* (Washington, 1923).

On the Tobar period, see also: Dana G. Munro, *Intervention and Dollar Diplomacy in the Caribbean, 1900–1921* (Princeton, 1964), chap. x; Theodore P. Wright, Jr., *American Support of Free Elections Abroad* (Washington, 1964), chaps. iii, vi-viii; R. L. Buell, "The United States and Central American Stability," *Foreign Policy Reports*, VII (July 8, 1931), 161–86; Buell, "The United States and Central American Revolutions," *Foreign Policy Reports*, VII (July 22, 1931), 187–204; and Thomas L. Karnes, *The Failure of Union: Central America, 1824–1960* (Chapel Hill, N.C., 1961), 198–224.

5 See his famous statement in *FRUS, 1913*, 7. On the key Mexican case, see esp. Ray Stannard Baker, *Woodrow Wilson: Life and Letters*, IV (Garden City, N.Y., 1931), chaps. v-vi; Samuel Flagg Bemis, *The Latin American Policy of the United States* (New York, 1943), chap. x; Howard F. Cline, *The United States and Mexico* (rev. ed.; New York, 1963), chaps. viii-ix; Arthur S. Link, *Woodrow Wilson and the Progressive Era* (New York, 1954), chap. v; Wright, *Free Elections*, chap. iv; Robert E. Quirk,

Secretary of State, Henry A. Stimson, tried to lay the foundations for democracy during the latter stages of the U.S. intervention in Nicaragua.[6] In 1933 Under Secretary Sumner Welles journeyed to Cuba with instructions from President Roosevelt to see to the liberalization of the Machado dictatorship or to help bring it down.[7] At the close of World War II, as U.S. Ambassador to Argentina and then Assistant Secretary for Inter-American Affairs, Spruille Braden made Perón the principal target of a short-lived democratic crusade.[8] In 1948 the Truman Administration contemplated a more modest pro-democracy effort in reaction to several coups thought possibly to be *Peronista*-inspired.[9] A decade later, the Eisenhower government went beyond mere compliance with OAS resolutions

in levying diplomatic and economic sanctions against the Trujillo regime.[10] Finally, support for democracy was again a prominent feature of U.S. policies during the Kennedy years.[11]

Policy Goals

United States attempts to foster democracy in Latin America have stemmed from the interplay of two central motives: (1) a desire to bring the blessings of liberty to benighted countries south of the border, implying the goal of democratic government; and (2) a concern for the security interests of the United States, including the objective of political stability in Latin America. Emphasis upon one or the other goal has shifted from one period to the next, but (both altruists and cynics beware) in only one instance does it appear that U.S. policy-makers proceeded on the basis of a single motive alone: This in the Tobar era when Secretary of State Hughes privately

An Affair of Honor: Woodrow Wilson and the Occupation of Veracruz (Lexington, Ky., 1962); and *FRUS* for the years 1913–1917.
6 See Bryce Wood, *The Making of the Good Neighbor Policy* (New York, 1961), chap. i.
7 See *ibid.*, chaps. ii-iii.
8 On the Braden vs. Perón episode, see esp.: Harold F. Peterson, *Argentina and the United States, 1810–1960* (New York, 1964), 443–57; O. Edmund Smith Jr., *Yankee Diplomacy: U.S. Intervention in Argentina* (Dallas, 1953), chap. vii; Arthur P. Whitaker, *The United States and Argentina* (Cambridge, Mass., 1954), 131–34, 145–50; and Robert J. Alexander, *The Perón Era* (New York, 1951), 198–217. While Braden was Assistant Secretary, U.S. Ambassador to Brazil Adolf A. Berle, Jr., pressured Vargas to honor his pledge to hold free elections by making a speech on September 29, 1945, which hailed the move as an important step in the consolidation of hemispheric democracy. See mention of this incident in: Thomas E. Skidmore, *Politics in Brazil, 1930–1964* (New York, 1967), 51; and Robert J. Alexander, *Prophets of the Revolution* (New York, 1962), 234.
9 See "U.S. Concerned at Overthrow of Governments in Certain American Republics," *DSB*, XXI (Jan. 2, 1949), 30.

10 See the following by Jerome Slater: "The United States, the Organization of American States, and the Dominican Republic, 1961–63," *International Organization*, XVII (Spring, 1964), 268–91; and *The OAS and United States Foreign Policy* (Columbus, 1967), chap. v.
11 The author's analysis of the Kennedy policies is based in part upon his interviews with leading administration decision-makers then in the White House and the Department of State.
On the Kennedy policies generally, see esp.: Arthur M. Schlesinger, Jr., *A Thousand Days: John F. Kennedy in the White House* (Boston, 1965), chaps. vii-xi, xxix-xxxi; Edwin Lieuwen, *Generals vs. Presidents: Neo-Militarism in Latin America* (New York, 1964), chap. vii; Jerome Slater, "Democracy vs. Stability: The Recent Latin American Policy of the United States," *Yale Review*, LV (Dec., 1965), 169–181; and Theodore James Maher, "The Kennedy and Johnson Responses to Latin American Coups d'Etat," *World Affairs*, CXXXI (Oct.–Dec., 1968), 184–97.

acknowledged that the Central American formula substituted no guarantee of free elections for the resort to revolution which the treaties supposedly abolished.[12]

Wilson's and Braden's policies perhaps rate highest on a scale of unabashed idealism; however, these men, too, regarded a pro-democracy posture as serving U.S. security interests. To Wilson's mind, the only way to achieve lasting stability was to allow the people to elect their own leaders and to teach them the benefits of the rule of law.[13] Braden was convinced that the hemisphere would never be completely secure as long as what he labeled "Nazi-Fascist" regimes remained in power.[14]

In other periods, the security goal has been even closer to the surface of U.S. policies. Monroe sympathized with Latin America's espousal of republicanism, but he was principally concerned about the dangers of European intervention inherent in monarchical plots.[15] The Tobar treaties were part of a U.S. design to curb civil strife in the Central American vicinity of the Panama Canal. As we have already implied, the Truman Administration bestirred itself about postwar coups primarily out of fear that *Peronismo* was beginning to spread.[16] After years of indifference, the Eisenhower government joined a vigorous assault against Trujillo not only because the U.S. needed Latin American votes to isolate Castro, but also because it had belatedly come to believe that the very presence of the Dominican tyranny encouraged radicalism in the Caribbean.[17] There is no doubt that Kennedy and several of his closest advisers were ideologically committed to democracy[18]; yet they, too—in a much wider sense than their Eisenhower counterparts—thought democracy was the only acceptable alternative to Communism in Latin America.

From the beginning, policy-makers have assumed that most of the inter-

[12] Hughes wrote: "The question whether ...the policy...is a good one is very debatable. In these...countries revolutions and *coups d'etat* are often about the only reform measures available to the people... to dislodge corruption. Elections there frequently don't mean much...[Therefore] these people are entitled to their revolutions.... But...it would have been impossible...to take the position that they must not take this step to make revolutions less likely; that we wouldn't agree to it; and that we insisted that they have revolutions [because] revolutions in Central America... are not advantageous to us. We cannot tolerate much disturbance in the Caribbean region, because of the vital importance to our self-defense of the Panama Canal.... If the disturbances are of such a character as injuring life and property that foreign governments would take control if we were supine, then it is absolutely essential that we intervene." (Quoted in Wright, *Free Elections,* 56.)

[13] Harley Notter, *The Origins of the Foreign Policy of Woodrow Wilson* (Baltimore, 1937), 268, 307–8.

[14] Braden expressed his views perhaps most clearly and concisely in a radio interview late in 1945. See "What Is Our Inter-American Policy," *DSB,* XIV (Jan. 6 and 13, 1946), 27–29.

[15] This was the implication of his warning to the Holy Alliance that the United States "should consider any attempt on their part to extend their political system to any portion of this hemisphere as dangerous to our peace and safety." (Quoted in Perkins, *Monroe Doctrine,* 28.)

[16] On this point, see Smith, *Yankee Diplomacy,* 173–74.

[17] Slater comments: "Herter's Dominican policy was based on a simple relation: 'Batista is to Castro as Trujillo is to____,' and the United States wanted to insure that it could help fill in the blank." (*The OAS,* 191.)

[18] As one adviser put it to the author: "Democracy was part of the Kennedy *zeitgeist.*"

national and domestic preconditions for the kind of democracy they envisaged in Latin America already existed. However unrealistic some policies appear in retrospect, the fact remains that many self-styled "practical" men did not consider them to be unrealistic at the time: The dictates of idealism and realism thus have often seemed to coincide. Following the American and French Revolutions and colonial victories in the wars of independence against Spain, it is understandable that Monroe might have been optimistic about the republican course of the Western Hemisphere. Wilson interpreted the increasing pressures for liberalization and self-determination experienced by various European monarchies as an indication that democracy would soon sweep the world. Braden expected that the defeat of the Axis totalitarian powers in World War II would lead to the downfall of other authoritarian regimes in Latin America, particularly those which had admired fascist models and harbored Axis agents. When Kennedy became President, long-standing dictatorships were crumbling throughout the hemisphere. Odría, Rojas Pinilla, Pérez Jiménez, and Batista had fallen; and Trujillo was obviously in trouble. After a century and a half, the age of the classical *caudillo* was clearly drawing to a close.[19]

The Kennedy Administration added a major new dimension to the policies of earlier periods. Previously, pro-democracy policies had focused solely on obeisance to essential constitutional norms and carried no specific connotations of economic and social change. Indeed, Washington had generally regarded the latter with suspicion, as possibly posing a threat to the investments of U.S. nationals. In contrast, New Frontier decision-makers posited a mutually reinforcing relationship between democracy, security (political stability), and economic and social development in Latin America.[20]

In the Kennedy view: If the "twilight of the tyrants" had come at last to Latin America, the "revolution of rising expectations" meant that it was also "one minute to midnight." Because of the rapidly escalating desires of Latin America's masses for a better life, the region was in the throes of a fundamental economic and social revolution that was as inevitable as it was explosive. The question was not whether dramatic "structural" change would soon take place, rather whether it would assume the character of peaceful "reform" ("evolution") or violent "revolution" ("chaos"), manipulated by Communists and indigenous radi-

[19] *New York Times* correspondent Tad Szulc captured the optimism of the period in his book, *The Twilight of the Tyrants* (New York, 1959).

The author recalls hearing Kennedy's campaign speech at the Alamo in September, 1960, before an enthusiastic crowd composed largely of Mexican-Americans: Kennedy commented upon the declining number of Latin American dictatorships and fervently promised that—with him as President —there would soon be no more tyrannies in the hemisphere.

[20] Another remarkable aspect of the Kennedy Administration was the sheer intensity of its concern with Latin America. Theodore C. Sorenson has written that "no continent was more constantly in the President's mind ...than Latin America." (*Kennedy* [New York, 1965], 533.) Richard N. Goodwin told the author that a day hardly passed without Kennedy's inquiring personally about current developments in the hemisphere. He took a keen interest in the minutest details: for example, in the composition—down to the last man—of U.S. delegations to inter-American conferences.

cals hostile to the United States. If other Castroite revolutions were to occur in Latin America, the traditional United States sphere of influence, it might well have a drastic impact on U.S. prestige and positions of strength the world over.

Kennedy policy-makers reasoned that they could forestall violent revolution under the aegis of Communism and native radicalism only by offering a *viable* alternative. It had to be clear to the humble citizens of Latin America that their lot could be improved some other way. Reliance upon *caudillos* or even ostensibly democratic, oligarchical regimes to suppress domestic discontent would pave the way for the very elements that the United States was striving to defeat.[21] The Alliance for Progress could provide desperately needed capital for development; however, it would not succeed unless there also existed "responsible" Latin American governments dedicated to—and capable of engineering—fundamental reforms.

Reviewing the contemporary political scene in Latin America, the groups most likely to organize such governments appeared to be the Latin American "democratic left."[22] In the judg-

ment of Kennedy and his staff, all other political groups were either too oriented towards the status quo or too radical. The Latin American military might fall into either category, depending upon whether the example selected was a typical set of *golpista* officers or a Perón.[23] Military leadership which would be more progressive than the former and less inclined to xenophobic nationalism and a demagogic ideology than the latter was initially considered an "intellectual possibility," but was ultimately dismissed as little more than that for the foreseeable future.[24]

On the other hand, prospects looked bright for the democratic left. They alone seemed to have effective party organizations, drawing support from a supposedly dynamic "middle sector" in Latin American society, and ideologies stressing evolutionary reform. Moreover, their recent political successes in Venezuela, Colombia, Costa Rica, Honduras, Peru, Bolivia, Brazil, and Argentina gave them claim to being the dominant political force in Latin America. It was presumed that they would win elections, if elections were held, and would subsequently prove willing and able to carry out the reforms they preached.

Hence New Frontier decision-makers

---

[21] Schlesinger remarks: "Kennedy fully understood—this was, indeed, the mainspring of all his thinking about Latin America—that, with all its pretensions to realism, the militant anti–revolutionary line represented the policy most likely to strenghen the communists and lose the hemisphere." (*A Thousand Days*, 201.)

[22] The administration applied this term generally to all political groups in Latin America which espoused political and socioeconomic development goals compatible with the Alliance. However, in the minds of Kennedy policy-makers, the "core" of the democratic left were the *partidos populares,* which recognized a vague ideological bond with Haya de la Torre's APRA party in Peru and whose leaders—jocularly referred

to as the "Caribbean Mafia"—shared acquaintances born of years in exile: Betancourt of Venezuela, Muñoz Marín of Puerto Rico (a personal friend of Kennedy's), Figueres of Costa Rica, Villeda Morales of Honduras, Bosch of the Dominican Republic, and so forth.

[23] According to Schlesinger, the Kennedy Administration's assessment was that when the military were not entirely unprogressive, they tended to be "revolutionaries of a sort themselves, like Nasser, and hardly more agreeable to the capital-commanding class than a Castro." (*A Thousand Days*, 198.)

[24] Interviews.

concluded that the United States should lend its enthusiastic moral and material backing to the Latin American democratic left. This support, they believed, accorded nicely with the United States' own democratic tradition *and* offered the best hope that the Latin American revolution would take a moderate course instead of embracing a radicalism inimical to U.S. security.

The Sources and Limits of U.S. Pro-Democracy Influence

The geographical scope of United States pro-democracy policies has broadened over the years. With the exception of the Monroe Doctrine (which was little more than rhetoric when it was first declared), the U.S. has applied its policies to the entire hemisphere only since the Second World War. The range of the Tobar and Wilson policies never extended beyond the Caribbean,[25] while Stimson and Welles each focused on a single Caribbean country. On the other hand, once the United States had emerged from World War II as a superpower with global operations and responsibilities, South America—even Argentina—no longer seemed so far away. Braden was as (mistakenly) confident of his ability to defeat Perón as Wilson, Huerta. Kennedy paid no less heed to coups in Argentina and Peru than to those in the Dominican Republic and Honduras.

Contributing to the pro-democracy influence of the United States has been its capacity and willingness to institute sanctions against those who dared to challenge its policies: verbal castigation, nonrecognition, severance of diplomatic relations, economic pressures, and the threat and use of force. Most Latin American governments have coveted recognition from the United States since the era of independence. The economic weapon was forged by World War II—and earlier in the Caribbean—as the United States became a leading market for Latin American commodities and supplier of arms and other industrial goods. Control over the distribution of steadily increasing amounts of economic and military assistance, culminating in the Alliance, gave Washington further leverage. The ultimate sanction, force, has continued to play an important role. Wilson precipitated the Veracruz incident in a fit of pique with Huerta. Stimson's efforts to educate Nicaraguans in the ways of democracy proceeded under U.S. military occupation. Kennedy dispatched warships to Dominican waters in November, 1961, when it appeared that the "wicked uncles" of the Trujillo family were plotting a return to power. Had the warship maneuver failed and, in another case, had Duvalier bowed to U.S. pressures to abandon the Haitian presidency upon the expiration of his constitutional term in May, 1963, it is very possible that Kennedy would have ordered the landing of marines.[26]

Nevertheless, as the Kennedy Administration at least partially realized from the outset and other administra-

---

[25] Wilson indeed believed that—in terms of political and economic progress—the ABC countries and Uruguay in South America belonged in a completely different category from the banana republics of the Caribbean area. (Bemis, *Latin American Policy,* 194.)

[26] In each case, several contingency plans were in various stages of readiness; but marine landings were definitely under serious consideration. (Interviews)

On the Haitian case, see esp.: Slater, *The OAS,* chap. vi.; and Robert D. Tomasek, "The Haitian-Dominican Republic Controversy of 1963 and the Organization of American States," *Orbis,* XII (Spring, 1968), 294–313.

tions have discovered to their dismay, the utility of sanctions is extremely limited. In the judgment of Kennedy policy-makers: The actual use of force was feasible only with respect to a few small Caribbean countries and then could prove prohibitively costly in terms of human lives and its implications for inter-American solidarity. Until 1965, Latin Americans regarded marine occupations as strictly a thing of the past. Moreover, the record of previous occupations offered no evidence that democratic practices would persist much longer than the physical presence of the United States.[27]

The practical effect of other sanctions was equally problematical. Compared with being ousted from office, U.S. nonrecognition and economic pressures presented relatively low-level threats to unconstitutional regimes. Recalcitrant governments could always tighten their belts and, up to a point, compensate by leaning more heavily upon extracontinental markets and sources of supply.[28] Finally, there was the chance that, by triggering latent anti-Americanism, coercive measures might have the counterproductive effect of strengthening target regimes. Both Huerta and Perón had skillfully manipulated nationalist resentment against *gringo* interference.[29]

With armed intervention customarily ruled out of the question, sanctions have not offered the possibility of crushing offending regimes. Their availability thus has not constituted an infallible deterrent, nor has their application guaranteed a particular outcome. However, as serious inconveniences to be avoided or removed, they have given the United States additional bargaining power before and after specific challenges have arisen.

U.S. policy-makers have envisaged their direct exercise of pro-democracy influence as merely supplementing the efforts of Latin American democrats who presumably enjoyed wide popular followings. In other words, they have relied upon the people of Latin America and democratic leaders to provide vigorous support at the domestic level for U.S. pro-democracy policies. Washington has generally been disappointed in this respect. Wilson was deeply disturbed when fighting continued after the collapse of Huerta's government and the leading contender for power, Carranza, carefully disassociated himself from the United States.[30]

---

[27] U.S. Ambassador John Bartlow Martin wrote of the situation at the time of the 1963 Dominican coup: "How could we restore a Dominican President to the Palace whose own voters did not protest his overthrow? We could do it, of course, with armed force. But ought we? ·What kind of democracy is it that can be kept in the Palace only by a foreign fleet in the harbor? By so using force to 'support democracy,' you destroy the thing you try to create. We had the force. But we could not use it. Force alone is not power. Force may be unlimited. But power is always narrowly limited. And the greater the power the narrower the limits. . . ." (*Overtaken by Events: The Dominican Crisis—from the Fall of Trujillo to the Civil War* [Garden City, N.Y., 1966], 594.)

[28] Even the allies of the U.S. did not give full support to wartime sanctions against Argentina or to those later directed against the Trujillo and Castro regimes.

[29] Cline describes the atmosphere in Mexico at the end of 1913: "After all Wilson's threats, bombast, scurryings, and alarms, a rupture of relations and war between Mexico and the United States seemed imminent. Mexicans rallied around Huerta, who now became (to his own surprise) a symbol of political independence in the face of Wilsonian pressures. Probably he was never so strong. He seemed impregnable." (*United States and Mexico,* 150.)

[30] The U.S. negotiators at the Niagara meeting reported to Washington on a con-

Braden's plans went awry when the standardbearers of a coalition of Argentine democratic parties proved no match for Perón in the 1946 election. Kennedy was distressed that few ordinary citizens appeared willing to "fight" for democracy when coups swept Latin America in 1962–63. The complete failure of the general strike called by APRA in Peru was pivotal in convincing him that the United States would have to battle the military almost alone.[31] In many Latin American countries, the middle sector was itself divided, and the rest of the populace was either unmobilized politically or so accustomed to the rapid rise and fall of governments that they despaired of any dramatic shift for the better.

Yet target military regimes themselves were unable to rally substantial popular support, and the anti-American bugaboo did not materialize. The most encouraging case was an early and exceptional one: the wicked uncles episode in the Dominican Republic. Kennedy decision-makers were pleasantly surprised when the sight of

U.S. ships on the horizon brought— not cries of "gunboat diplomacy"— but cheers from residents of the capital who celebrated in the streets.

Still another limited source of support for U.S. policies has been other hemisphere governments. Even before the nonintervention principle became the so-called cornerstone of the inter-American system in the mid-1930s, the Colossus of the North occasionally felt the need for some collective underwriting of its policies; and to this extent its pro-democracy campaigns spilled over into the multilateral sphere. Although the Tobar treaties were fostered by the United States and depended for success upon U.S. influence, they did involve formal international agreements. Wilson imperiously "consulted" with the ABC powers on two separate occasions during the Mexican crisis, once immediately following the incident at Veracruz and again when it was necessary to decide between rival claimants after Huerta's defeat.[32] In 1945 Braden unhesitatingly endorsed an abortive proposal advanced by Uruguayan Foreign Minister Rodríguez Larreta which called for inter-American sanctions against hemisphere dictatorships.[33] Three years later, Sec-

---

versation with unofficial representatives of the Constitutionalists as follows: "They insisted that they might be willing to take up the question of surrender with someone outside the mediation with which the United States had nothing to do, but that so far as mediation was concerned they would absolutely decline to receive anything from the Mediators or through the mediation; that they would not accept as a gift anything which the Mediators could give them, even though it was what they were otherwise seeking; that they would not take it 'on a silver platter.' They declined to discuss names or propose names for provisional president, saying that no one would be satisfactory that was appointed by the Mediators, even if it was Carranza himself, because anything that came from the Mediators would not be accepted by their party or by the Mexican people." (*FRUS, 1914,* 543.)
[31] Schlesinger, *A Thousand Days,* 787.

[32] Representatives from Guatemala and Uruguay also attended the second conference.
[33] See Pan American Union, *Consulta del Gobierno del Uruguay y contestaciones de los Gobiernos sobre paralelismo entre la democracia y la paz, protección internacional de los derechos del hombre, y acción colectiva en defensa de esos principios* (Washington, 1946). The timing of the proposal and the prompt approval it received in Washington gave rise to the impression (still unsubstantiated) that it had been inspired by the United States. On this point see Lawrence Duggan, *The Americas* (New York, 1949), 205–6. For Braden's denial of the charge, see "Our Inter-American Policy," 28.

retary of State Acheson received a cool response when he asked Latin American governments to consider whether the newly established OAS might take some action to discourage further *golpes*. The Eisenhower and Kennedy administrations made effective use of the multilateral "umbrella" provided by OAS sanctions in negotiations leading to the post-Trujillo democratic experiment in the Dominican Republic. Both administrations also gave strong support to the ad hoc OAS electoral assistance and observation program which grew out of the early Dominican experience. Finally, Kennedy tried to no avail to interest the OAS in planning to exercise a form of trusteeship over Haiti should the need arise.

In fact, the legitimacy of the use of nonrecognition and additional coercive measures as instruments of pro-democracy (and other) policies has long been a controversial issue in the Americas.[34] In 1930 Mexican Foreign Minister Genaro Estrada announced that his government regarded the institution of recognition as an affront to state sovereignty and would henceforth follow the practice of merely maintaining or withdrawing its diplomatic representatives as circumstances required. Many Latin American governments initially seized upon the "Estrada Doctrine" or a variant, the virtually automatic recognition of new governments, as one means of countering U.S. interventions in the days of "Dollar Diplomacy." In later years, this position has continued to attract governments who have opposed in principle external meddling in domestic politics and/or those who have had something to fear from pro-democracy offensives.

The principal challenges to the no-interference posture emerged during periods of democratic successes in Latin America (1944–48 and 1958–63) when a number of governments were charged with a spirit of democratic evangelism and an even more compelling desire for international protection. Several of these governments adopted unilateral policies denying recognition to unconstitutional regimes, explicitly or implicitly in accordance with the "Betancourt Doctrine."

Militant Latin American democratic governments also urged a similar course of action upon the OAS after World War II. Indeed, it has been they—rather than the United States—who have originated most of the pro-democracy proposals which have been considered at the international level. They maintained that the inter-American organization should support democracy not only as an ideal, but also because there existed a relationship between the promotion of democracy and the primary function of the OAS, the maintenance of hemispheric peace and security. The precise nature of the threat to security which they posited changed with the times. At the close of the war, with Axis examples fresh in mind, it was fashionable to assert that

---

[34] For full details and bibliographical information, see the author's unpublished doctoral thesis: "The Inter-American System, the United States, and the Promotion of Hemispheric Democracy: Perspectives on Intervention and Collective Responsibility in the Americas" (Columbia University, 1967). See also: C. Neale Ronning, *Law and Politics in Inter-American Diplomacy* (New York, 1963), chap. ii; Slater, *The OAS, chap. vii; M. Margaret Ball, The OAS in Transition* (Durham, N.C., 1969), 485–502; and Donald M. Dozer, "Recognition in Contemporary Inter-American Relations," *Journal of Inter-American Studies, VIII* (April, 1966), 318–35.

dictatorships were inherently expansionist.[35] More recently, pro-democracy spokesmen argued that dictatorships lead to civil strife and related international frictions (exile invasions emanating from neighboring countries) and that they are breeding grounds for Communism (oppressed masses turn to radicalism).

The inter-American controversy over

the democracy issue has produced far more debate than practical pro-democracy action. Latin American democrats failed in their effort to frame the Rio Treaty so as to place deviations from democracy on a par with other "threats to the peace" occasioning inter-American consultation and possible collective sanctions.[36] Upon their insistence,

---

[35] For an early statement of this theme, see Víctor Raúl Haya de la Torre, *La defensa continental* (Buenos Aires, 1942).

The 1942 Meeting of Ministers of Foreign Affairs at Rio created a seven-man Emergency Advisory Committee for Political Defense (EACPD). The following year the EACPD promulgated the "Guani Doctrine," recommending consultation between the American states before recognition of new governments instituted by force, to discourage the establishment of regimes inimical to hemispheric security. With the support of the EACPD, the United States proceeded to apply economic pressures against the Villarroel government in Bolivia and successive military regimes in Argentina. Several Latin American governments were uneasy about the Guani Doctrine and distressed by the coercive policies of the U.S., which— coupled with the Braden vs. Perón episode— undoubtedly made them less receptive to proposals for multilateral pro-democracy programs after the war. (For texts of the Guani resolution and the replies of governments, see EACPD, *Second Annual Report* [Montevideo, 1944]. For a discussion of the Bolivian case, see William L. Neumann, Jr., *Recognition of Governments in the Americas* [Washington, 1947], 34–38. On U.S.-Argentina relations, 1939–1945, see esp.: Peterson, *United States and Argentina*, 398–443; Smith, *Yankee Diplomacy*, chaps. iii-vi; Donald M. Dozer, *Are We Good Neighbors? Three Decades of Inter-American Relations* [Gainesville, Fla., 1959], 136–46; and Henry M. Blackmer, *United States Policy and the Inter-American Peace System, 1889–1952* [Paris, 1952], 109–30.)

At the Mexico City Conference in 1945, the Arévalo government in Guatemala presented a draft resolution calling for abstention from recognition of and diplomatic relations with "anti-democratic regimes,"

including those emanating from coups against existing democratic governments. The conference passed the proposal on for study by the Inter-American Juridical Committee (IAJC), which expressed its disapproval in an opinion that even today stands as one of the most profound analyses of the problems inherent in the promotion of democracy. (The English text of the Guatemalan proposal is reprinted in U.S., Department of State, *Report of the Delegation of the United States of America to the Inter-American Conference on Problems of War and Peace, . . .*, Conference Series No. 85 [Washington, 1946], 354–55. For the IAJC opinion, see PAU, IAJC, *Defense and Preservation of Democracy in America Against the Possible Establishment of Anti-Democratic Regimens* [sic] *in the Continent* [Washington, 1946].)

When Rodríguez Larreta made his proposal several months after the Mexico City gathering, less than half of the American states indicated interest and only a few offered their unequivocal support.

[36] See the text of the project of Uruguay in PAU, *Inter-American Conference for the Maintenance of Continental Peace and Security, Rio de Janeiro, Brazil* (Washington, 1946), 141–43. Also the project of Guatemala, reprinted in U.S., Department of State, *Inter-American Conference for the Maintenance of Continental Peace and Security, . . . : Report of the Delegation of the United States of America,* International Organization and Conference Series II, American Republics No. 1 (Washington, 1948), 96. The minutes of the debates on these proposals are in OAS, PAU, *Conferência Interamericana para a Manutencão de Paz e da Segurança no Continente, . . . : Diário,* OEA/Ser.N/2 (português) (Washington, 1965), 157–58.

It is interesting to note that while a majority of hemisphere governments gave the Bogotá Conference accepted Article 5(d) of the OAS Charter, making the maintenance of governmental systems of "representative democracy" a binding obligation of member states. However, the conference neither clarified the exact nature of the Charter democratic norm nor provided enforcement procedures.[37] Subsequently, the OAS has applied sanctions against only two dictatorships, the Trujillo and Castro regimes. Both of these cases were obviously exceptional, not the least in that Trujillo and Castro left themselves open to Rio Treaty penalties by advocating and materially as-

sisting the violent overthrow of fellow Latin American governments.[38] After Trujillo's assassination, the OAS became more deeply involved in Dominican politics than many governments had originally intended[39]; but a clear majority felt an obligation to insure a democratic outcome of the transitional situation which the organization was partially responsible for creating.

Otherwise: OAS member governments gave their approval in 1959 to a rough definition of "democracy" incorporated into the "Declaration of

---

little encouragement to pro-democracy proposals during this period, they were sufficiently irked by Somoza's unseating of the very government he had picked to succeed him in 1947 that they voted to exclude the Nicaraguan regime from participation in the Rio Conference. Nicaragua received an invitation to the Bogotá Conference in 1948 only after Somoza had legitimized his rule by holding "elections" and installing his elderly uncle in the presidency. (See the minutes of the PAU Governing Board for the meetings of July 21 and 28, 1947, and March 8, 1948.)

37 The Article 5(d) statement is: "The solidarity of the American States and the high aims which are sought through it require the political organization of those States on the basis of the effective exercise of representative democracy." The binding obligation aspect was quite clear in the debates at the conference. Indeed, Mexico offered the principal opposition to any mention of democracy in this, the "Principles" section of the Charter, precisely on the grounds that the internal organization of a state should not be the object of a "contractual obligation." (See Colombia, Ministerio de Relaciones Exteriores, *Novena Conferencia Internacional Americana, Bogotá, Colombia, ... : Actas y documentos* [Bogotá, 1953–54], III, 298ff.) This apparently minor legal victory for pro-democracy forces actually held considerable significance for the future: It made it possible for them to argue that the promotion of democracy is *not* "intervention," in spite of the fact that potential measures to this end did not

receive a specific exemption from the non-intervention principle, like that accorded to peace and security measures in Article 19. (See also references to democracy and human rights in the Preamble to the Charter, which was not of sufficient legal significance to be controversial at Bogotá.)

On the other hand, the conference rejected a definition of "democracy" proposed by Uruguay and postponed a decision on that country's suggestion that the EACPD should remain in existence for possible service as an advisory body in the democracy field. (The OAS Council abolished the EACPD in October, 1948.) A majority of governments also proved unwilling to bar undemocratic states and governments from membership and/or representation in the OAS and to establish a formal consultative procedure for the recognition of new governments.

38 The technical basis for sanctions levied against the Dominican dictator by the Sixth Meeting of Foreign Ministers in 1960 was his personal involvement in a plot to assassinate President Betancourt of Venezuela.

39 Even earlier, in January, 1961, Argentina and Brazil led the opposition to an expansion of economic sanctions voted by the OAS Council, with the Argentine representative complaining that "the proposed measures can only invoke as justification the continuance of the governmental institutions or the internal political situation of the Dominican Republic." (See OAS, PAU, Council, *Acta de la sesión ordinaria celebrada el 4 de enero de 1961*, OEA/Ser.G/II/C-a-397 [Aprobada] [Washington, 1961].) (Minutes of Council sessions hereafter cited as *Acta ordinaria* or *Acta extraordinaria* as appropriate.)

Santiago, Chile"[40] and have continued to support OAS observation and technical assistance in electoral matters, extended by the Secretariat only upon the request of the governments concerned. Urgent appeals from Latin American democratic governments menaced by the military in 1962–63 finally resulted in an OAS call for a

[40] Resolution I in the Final Act of the Fifth Meeting of Foreign Ministers. (For documents relating to this conference, see: OAS, PAU, *Reunión de Consulta de Ministros de Relaciones Exteriores, Quinta Reunión ...: Actas y documentos,* OEA/Ser.F/III.5 [español] [Washington, 1961]; and U.S., Department of State, *Inter-American Efforts to Relieve International Tensions in the Western Hemisphere, 1959–1960,* Inter-American Series No. 79 [Washington, 1962].) (The latter publication hereafter cited as *Inter-American Efforts.*)

The Fifth Meeting of Foreign Ministers also directed the OAS Council to prepare a draft convention on the "effective exercise of representative democracy"; asked the Inter-American Council of Jurists (IACJ) to study "the possible juridical relationship between respect for human rights and the effective exercise of representative democracy, and the right to set in motion the machinery of international law in force"; and entrusted the Inter-American Peace Committee (IAPC) with the task of examining the "relationship between violations of human rights or the nonexercise of representative democracy, ... and the political tensions that affect the peace of the hemisphere." Finally, the conference established the Inter-American Commission on Human Rights and resolved to have the IACJ draft a convention on human rights.

Of all the steps outlined above, only the initiatives related to human rights produced much in the way of concrete results. Through its investigation of complaints and publication of reports, the Inter-American Commission on Human Rights has made a modest contribution to the welfare of particular individuals suffering political repression under undemocratic regimes. The human rights convention has gone through several revisions to date and is still under formal consideration by the OAS.

Regarding the other measures envisaged in 1959: The OAS Council produced a

Meeting of Foreign Ministers.[41] The meeting was never convened, largely because pro-democracy ranks were by then decimated. In 1965 the Second Special Inter-American Conference reinforced what has usually been standard diplomatic practice by recommending informal consultation before the recognition of governments arising from coups.[42]

The Kennedy Administration gave

Draft Convention on the Effective Exercise of Representative Democracy; but this treaty failed to gain any appreciable support and is now, for all practical purposes, dead. (The proposed text is Appendix A in *Acta ordinaria,* Dec. 15, 1959, OEA/Ser.G/II/C-a-353 [Aprobada].) The IAJC found a "clear" relationship between human rights and democracy; however, its study strongly recommended that the American states concentrate on establishing procedures furthering human rights rather than democracy *per se.* (OAS, PAU, IAJC, *Study on the Juridical Relationship Between Respect for Human Rights and the Exercise of Democracy,* Doc. No. CIJ-52 [English] [Washington, 1960].) The IAPC asserted in its report that there existed a relationship between democracy, human rights, and peace; yet it was unable to suggest a formula for action that would not violate the nonintervention principle. (The report is Appendix E in OAS, PAU, IAPC, *Informe de la Comisión ...a la Séptima Reunión de Consulta de Ministros de Relaciones Exteriores,* Doc. No. CIP-6-60 [Washington, 1960].)

[41] Under Articles 39–40 of the OAS Charter, providing for consideration of "problems of an urgent nature and of common interest to the American States." (For the debates, see the minutes of OAS Council sessions on the following dates: July 30, 1962; Aug. 8, 1962; Aug. 10, 1962; Aug. 22, 1962; Oct. 3, 1963; Nov. 4, 1963; Nov. 12, 1963.)

[42] Resolution XXVI in the Final Act. (The text of the Final Act is in OAS, PAU, *Segunda Conferencia Interamericana Extraordinaria, ...: Actas y documentos,* Versión Preliminar, I, OEA/Ser.E/XIII.3 [español] [Washington, 1965], 489–563.) Compare this resolution with the original proposals of Costa Rica and Venezuela. (Texts in *ibid.,* IV, 545–50, 565–67.)

only cautious encouragement to proposals for multilateral action advanced by militant democratic governments.[43] Aware of the likely deadlock in the OAS on anything much beyond the voluntary election observation program, Kennedy policy-makers wanted to avoid United States identification with initiatives that were doomed to fail. Moreover, even had it been possible to agree on collective action, they were generally reluctant to trade the flexibility of unilateralism for the constraints inherent in genuine multilateralism. They far preferred meshing unilateral policies with other Latin American governments informally to channeling pro-democracy activities through the OAS, which would have institutionalized Latin American influence and committed the U.S. to specific measures embodied in an operative resolution or treaty.[44]

On the other hand, the Kennedy Administration recognized the usefulness of a multilateral umbrella in the post-Trujillo Dominican and 1963 Haitian episodes, when nothing less than a plan for national political reconstruction was involved. But a strong thread of unilateralism ran through both of these cases as well. The naval show of force that frightened the Trujillos was not cleared in advance with the OAS. Kennedy showed every intention of carrying out the marine occupation of Haiti if necessary, in spite of OAS unwillingness before the fact to authorize a possible inter-American trusteeship. Indeed, the Haitian case was not so much an instance of Washington's miscalculating on its rule to avoid advancing proposals that had slim chance of approval, as it was an attempt to lay the groundwork for the subsequent multilateralization of an operation if the U.S. had to present the OAS with a *fait accompli.*

Although the OAS was stalemated on the democracy question and only a handful of Latin American governments adhering to the Betancourt Doctrine joined the United States in unilaterally ostracizing unconstitutional regimes,[45] there was strikingly little overt hostility in Latin America to the

[43] The U.S. representative on the OAS Council supported the request for a foreign ministers meeting in 1962, but suggested that the OAS delay indefinitely setting a date for the meeting. At the same time, he forcefully maintained that the nonintervention principle did not constitute a barrier to OAS action in the democracy field. He said: "In the view of my government, aside from the grave peril of communist subversion, the great danger facing the countries of America today is *not* a threat to our *in*dependence through intervention but our possible failure to realize and act fully and jointly upon the challenging truth of our *inter*-dependence." (*Acta extraordinaria,* Aug. 22, 1962, OEA/Ser.G/II/C-a-460 [Aprobada], 2–7.) Assistant Secretary of State Edwin M. Martin made essentially the same points in his Pan American Day address of April 16, 1963. (See Edwin M. Martin, "Interdependence and the Principles of Self-Determination and Nonintervention," *DSB,* XLVIII [May 6, 1963], 710–15.)
[44] In any event, according to one Kennedy aide, the administration had a rather low regard for the OAS as an instrument of multilateral diplomacy. Theoretically, nego-

tiations in the OAS might have served as a useful substitute for the cumbersome procedure of consultations with foreign ministries situated in remote Latin American capitals. In fact, the latter procedure was unavoidable, since many Latin American governments persisted in assigning to the OAS diplomats of questionable competence or political persuasion whom they themselves distrusted. (Interview)
[45] The Chilean foreign minister cautioned the United States against the possibility of being "more royalist than the king." (Schlesinger, *A Thousand Days,* 787.)

Kennedy posture. We have already noted that the anti-American bugaboo did not materialize among domestic constituencies: The same might be said for the international reaction. Lack of public criticism—even by governments traditionally hypersensitive about "intervention" like Mexico—was evidence of the continued strength of the regional democratic ideal and of widespread support for the development objectives of the Alliance, which depended for their realization upon the Latin American democratic left. It was also silent testimony to Latin Americans' faith in the motives of the Kennedy Administration.

The Failure of Will: Self-Imposed Limits on U.S. Pro-Democracy Influence Deriving from Competing Policy Goals

The United States itself has been responsible for some of the most significant limits on its influence in pro-democracy periods. Those administering U.S. pro-democracy policies have applied them with such apparent inconsistency as to raise the question of whether a true dedication to democracy existed. They have done so largely because they were simultaneously pursuing other objectives, originally deemed consistent with democracy, which in important respects proved incompatible. We may examine these problems under the category of United States failures of will, reflecting tensions between the goals that pro-democracy policies have been designed to serve.

By far the most serious clash has been between the goals of democracy and security. Political stability has been a continuing security objective of U.S. policy-makers, and they have often supported democracy because they regarded it as the most stable form of government. Nevertheless, furthering democracy has regularly involved condoning a not-inconsiderable amount of *immediate* instability. Toppling an old dictatorship or even a new unconstitutional regime is by definition a destabilizing act—at least in the short run. The Central American Tobar treaties actually encouraged revolutions in the sense of making it more difficult for the leaders of a coup to consolidate their control. During the same period, Washington more than once found it impossible to tolerate the opposition elements (seen as scoundrels)—for example, the Liberals in Nicaragua—who might have come to power through the democratic process. Although the Grau San Martín government in Cuba clearly enjoyed wider popular support than its predecessor, Welles never forgave it for arising out of the overthrow of a provisional regime which he had hand-picked to follow Machado. Kennedy faced difficult choices when coups occurred in Guatemala and Ecuador in 1963: One of these was support democracy and accept the probable victories in upcoming elections of former presidents with demagogic proclivities (Arévalo and Velasco Ibarra respectively) or rely upon the "stabilizing" intervention of the military.

The threat of Communism has further complicated judgment. In an earlier era, immediate instability raised the prospect of another dictatorship and, at worst, the increasingly hypothetical danger of European meddling. However, by 1933 Welles's successor as U.S. Ambassador to Cuba, Jefferson Caffrey, was expressing himself as "disturbed at seemingly communistic tendencies in the [Grau] regime."[46] Of course, the later Guatemalan (Arbenz)

46 Quoted in Wood, *Good Neighbor Policy,* 99.

and Cuban experiences have placed virtually any political vacuum in a new context. Primarily because of the short-run instability problem, the Eisenhower government initially urged that the OAS press for the steady liberalization of the Trujillo regime, rather than apply sanctions which might bring about its sudden collapse.[47] Moreover, both the Eisenhower and Kennedy administrations recognized that the task of building democracy in the Dominican Republic extended far beyond the downfall of the tyrant and therefore attempted to shape a program for the political reconstruction and socioeconomic development of that country. Kennedy had a similar program in mind for Haiti.

New Frontier decision-makers saw no contradiction between support for democracy and efforts to isolate the Castro regime and to strengthen the counterinsurgency and civic action capabilities of the Latin American military. From their perspective, defense against subversion was essential if Latin American democracies were to survive and proceed with evolutionary reforms. However, administration policies may have had at least a marginal effect in encouraging Latin American coups. The United States appeared to be inviting the military to judge a given government by its attitudes toward anti-Castro measures in the OAS and toward leftists at home, as well as (or even instead of) its degree of commitment to democracy and progress. The military accepted the invitation and in case after case cited "softness on Communism" as one of the principal reasons for their intervention. In

addition, U.S. training and civic action programs helped build the military's "modern" image of itself as the prime mover in national development.[48]

The Kennedy Administration's security policies may have done a disservice to the cause of Latin American democracy in still more profound ways. The Alliance proclaimed that the democratic evolutionary road was the best route to modernization. But in the event that democratic governments could or would not move rapidly enough to meet the rising demands of their citizens, U.S.-trained-and-equipped counterinsurgency teams would insure that as little as possible (nonmilitary) violence shattered the calm of political impotence and indecision. One might argue that even more than some democratic governments needed a moratorium on violence to survive, they needed the specter of revolution to remind them constantly of the consequences of failure. Meanwhile, U.S. opposition and OAS sanctions presented Castro with an "underdog" image that was of great use to him domestically and abroad, none the least in that it served as a ready excuse for the less-than-spectacular performance of his own model for development.

To a lesser extent than democracy and security, the goals of democracy and economic and social change also proved incompatible.[49] Another impor-

---

[47] See Herter's address to the Sixth Meeting of Foreign Ministers, reprinted in *Inter-American Efforts*, 285–87.

[48] See selection 25 in this reader. (Hereafter the term "selection" refers to materials in this reader.)

[49] Curiously, Wilson started in Mexico with constitutional government as his main goal and little awareness of the socioeconomic dimension of the revolution in progress— and ended by giving priority to the latter over the former. At one point in the struggle against Huerta, Carranza's emissary succeeded in convincing Wilson that the

tant consideration affecting the Kennedy responses to coups in Guatemala and Ecuador was the fact that the deposed governments had been singularly corrupt and slow-to-action on the economic and social front.[50] For somewhat different reasons, the Kennedy Administration was disillusioned with Juan Bosch in the Dominican Republic, whose government succumbed to the military after only eight months. In Washington's judgment, only a conciliatory leader could achieve reform in a situation so threatened with assaults from both the right and the left —and Bosch, though well-intentioned, had a personal political style which polarized competing factions. Finally,

---

Constitutionalist's agrarian reform program was the precondition for political peace in Mexico. (Samuel G. Blythe, "Mexico: The Record of a Conversation with President Wilson," *The Saturday Evening Post,* CLXXXVI [May 23, 1914], 4.) Later, when the Constitutionalists were themselves divided and Carranza at last appeared to be in firm control of the capital, Wilson no longer displayed his old enthusiasm for free elections. On August 8, 1915, he wrote to Secretary of State Lansing: "The first and most essential step in settling the affairs of Mexico is not to call general elections. It seems to me necessary that a provisional government essentially revolutionary in character should take action to institute reforms by decree before the full forms of the constitution are resumed." (*FRUS, 1914–1920, The Lansing Papers,* II [Washington, 1940], 547.)

[50]The only likely reason why Arévalo would not have won the upcoming election in Guatemala was the fact that President Ydígoras was determined to impose as his successor an arch-conservative landowner whose *finca* had been a training ground for the Bay of Pigs.

Someone in the Kennedy Administration did a semi-serious calculation and concluded that President Arosemena of Ecuador was inebriated about 65 per cent of the time. (Interviews)

Kennedy decision-makers painfully realized that denying recognition and aid to an unconstitutional regime involved the dilemma of suspending the Alliance to save the Alliance. It was particularly difficult to justify this course of action when—as in Guatemala and Ecuador—the military regimes that resulted from coups were less corrupt and no more unprogressive than the governments they replaced.[51]

The Balance Sheet on the Kennedy Policies

Rhetoric and performance are equally relevant to an understanding of Kennedy pro-democracy policies.

On the one hand, unquestionably, those principally responsible for administering the Kennedy policies genuinely believed in the democratic evolution vs. violent revolution rhetoric of the Alliance and took their public commitment of the United States to a pro-democracy posture very seriously. Indeed, the Kennedy Administration's formal position on the democracy issue contrasts sharply with the unabashed espousal of pragmatism by succeeding administrations. Kennedy policies were policies of *purpose,* not an open admission of aimless drifting or perhaps (more insidious) of purposes which had to be concealed.

On the other hand, within the framework of their blanket commitment to democracy, Kennedy decision-makers adhered to the largely unarticulated guideline of flexibility. This

[51] Although the Kennedy Administration framed its response to the Peruvian coup under the assumption that the military intervention represented merely a reactionary attempt to bar APRA from power, the resulting junta subsequently proved to have some reformist tendencies which foreshadowed the later Velasco government.

approach derived mainly from the President's own political instincts, reinforced by the similar attitudes of White House Special Assistant Ralph Dungan and Assistant Secretary of State Edwin M. Martin—who had replaced the more ideologically inclined Richard N. Goodwin and Arthur M. Schlesinger, Jr., as Kennedy's key Latin American advisers by the time that the most serious threats to administration policies arose.[52] Keenly aware of the limits of U.S. influence and, to some extent, of the problem of competing goals, the President determined almost from the outset to opt for minimum democratic progress if this were necessary to limit cost to the United States. Later, the sheer number and variety of coups and the disappointing lack of active Latin American support for a hard anti-military line only increased his caution.

With the exception of pressures brought to bear for post-Trujillo democ-

ratization in the Dominican Republic and against the notorious Haitian dictatorship, the Kennedy Administration did not elect to challenge existing regimes. Whenever a military coup appeared likely to occur, the strategy was to launch a vigorous diplomatic offensive to head it off.[53] If deterrence failed, Kennedy decision-makers attempted to tailor the U.S. response to the particular requirements of each situation as it developed. Schlesinger has commented upon Kennedy's "realist's concern not to place himself in positions from which he could neither advance nor retreat."[54] Washington did *not* insist that the military return to the barracks by sundown. If there was a ready "out" for the United States, the administration seized it:[55] Against Martin's advice,[56] Kennedy decided to recognize Guido's military-

---

52 Goodwin moved from the White House to the post of Deputy Assistant Secretary of State for Inter-American Affairs in November, 1961, in a general reorganization designed to make the Department of State more responsive to presidential policies. Goodwin was only nominally subordinate to Assistant Secretary Robert F. Woodward. In March, 1962, the State Department reasserted its role in the policy-making process by replacing Woodward with Martin. Under Secretary George Ball frankly admitted that State needed "someone down there to clip Dick Goodwin's wings and keep him in channels." (Schlesinger, *A Thousand Days*, 784.) Goodwin joined the staff of the Peace Corps soon thereafter, although he continued to maintain informal contact with the President on Latin American affairs. At the White House, Dungan gradually took over from Schlesinger as the latter became preoccupied with other matters after the Bay of Pigs. Dungan and Martin had a close working relationship and were in accord on most policy questions. (Interviews)

53 The administration went so far as to have the Pentagon detach U.S. military officers from service elsewhere around the world for emergency missions in Latin America: They were asked to counsel Latin American officers whom they knew personally from previous tours of duty or training sessions against involvement in political plots. Administration sources told the author that they felt the U.S. military had performed creditably in these assignments.
54 *A Thousand Days*, 785.
55 The first coup of the Kennedy period occurred in El Salvador in January, 1961. Since it confronted the administration in Washington only a few days after the inauguration and represented merely an internal struggle among the military—the replacement of one unconstitutional government with another—it did not offer much of a test of the new pro-democracy policy. The United States soon recognized the junta, noting its pledge to hold free elections and to seek solutions to economic and social problems. (For documents relating to this case, see U.S., Department of State, Marjorie M. Whiteman, *Digest of International Law* [Washington, 1963], II, 281–83.)
56 Schlesinger, *A Thousand Days*, 785.

intimidated regime in Argentina as the "constitutional" successor to the Frondizi government.[57] Otherwise, in the cases of *golpes* in Peru, the Dominican Republic (1963), and Honduras,[58] Kennedy immediately withheld recognition and aid and searched for a way to resolve the crisis as soon as possible.[59] The eventual formula was an end to U.S. sanctions in exchange for the military's promise to hold free elections within a reasonable length of time and not to conduct any "bloodbaths" or "witchhunts" in the interim.[60] As a further measure in Peru, after recognition and a resumption of Alliance aid, Kennedy for some months left the U.S. embassy in the hands of a chargé and withheld military aid.

The Kennedy Administration's effort to eschew dogmatism in dealing with varying domestic conditions is undoubtedly praiseworthy. However, flexibility also proved to be the Achilles Heel of the Kennedy posture, because the administration too often allowed it to degenerate into simple expediency. This was the self-defeating "old politics" showing through the "pre-new politics" of the Kennedy years, the muddling through which sidetracked the "grand design" for Latin America, the shortsightedness that dimmed the administration's at least partially authentic long-range vision.

First, had Kennedy been less eager to resume normal relationships and continued U.S. sanctions until the military had actually kept their promise to return power to civilians, he might have achieved more in both symbolic and practical terms. As it was, the military soon discerned that the maximum price they would have to pay for coups was far from prohibitive and really not much more than a temporary inconvenience. With each crisis surmounted, the credibility of the deterrent presented by Washington diminished, and Kennedy pro-democracy policies thus steadily lost momentum.

Second, although there is an admittedly thin line separating the prudent decision from the gutless and/or unprincipled decision, it is a crucial

---

[57] When Frondizi was placed under arrest, Senate President Guido hurried to the Supreme Court and had himself sworn in—reportedly to the chagrin of the three military service heads, who were already forming a junta. (Lieuwin, *Generals vs. Presidents,* 17–18.)

[58] For documents on the Peruvian case, see Whiteman, *Digest,* II, 310–12. See also: Martin C. Needler, "United States Recognition Policy and the Peruvian Case," *Inter-American Economic Affairs,* XVI (Spring, 1963), 61–72. On the Dominican Republic and Honduras, see Whiteman, *Digest,* II, 73. For the background of the U.S. decision to take a firm position in these instances, see Martin, *Overtaken by Events,* 596–602.

[59] Schlesinger's report of a conversation with the President during the Peruvian episode is indicative of Kennedy's thinking: He expressed his concern, in Schlesinger's words, that "we might have staked our prestige on reversing a situation which could not be reversed—and that, when we accepted the situation, as eventually we must, we might seem to be suffering a defeat." As he saw the problem, it was "to demonstrate that our condemnation had caused the junta to make enough changes in its policy to render the resumption of relations possible." (*A Thousand Days,* 787.)

[60] Technically, it was the Johnson Administration which ultimately recognized the

military governments in the Dominican Republic and Honduras. However, Kennedy was prepared to extend recognition by the middle of October and only refrained from doing so in order not to aggravate criticism from liberal Senators. The day before he went to Texas he told one of his advisers: "Next week we'll have to sit down and find a way to recognize the Dominican junta." (Interviews) one; and the Kennedy Administration was on the wrong side of it in responding to *golpes* in Guatemala and Ecuador. What happened to democracy in Latin America was clearly more important than any immediate political considerations in either country. Nevertheless, frazzled by successive crises, Washington in each instance barely protested the overthrow, and aid programs continued unabated.[61] Following these object lessons, if not from earlier U.S. responses, the military in the Dominican Republic and Honduras can hardly be blamed for concluding that they could proceed to unseat civilian governments with little to fear from the United States.

There has been some speculation as to whether Kennedy Administration policies were substantially changing in the last discouraging months before Dallas.[62] This interpretation rests, in part, upon the obvious inconsistencies in Washington's reactions to the four coups of 1963. However, our analysis suggests that it is more accurate to view these experiences as merely the ultimate result of a tendency to carry flexibility too far.

A statement published by Assistant Secretary Martin in the *Herald Tribune* on October 6, 1963[63]—several days after coups in the Dominican Republic and Honduras—also helped generate the misleading impression that Kennedy policy-makers were reassessing their commitment to democracy.[64] Approved by the White House, this statement, in reality, represented neither a strictly personal initiative by Martin nor an administration "trial balloon" designed to prepare public opinion for a major shift in policy. Its timing and content were governed by the fact that the annual appropriations for the Alliance for Progress were scheduled for consideration in the Senate. Conservative Senators were insisting that the Alliance had failed; while liberals were clamoring for drastic measures, ranging to the landing of marines, to reverse recent military takeovers. The Kennedy Administration was anxious to avoid both a reduction in the funds available for the Alliance and amendments to aid legislation which might tie its hands in negotiating with the Latin American military.[65]

Martin's statement was a remarkably frank exposition of the fundamental formal and informal tenets of the Kennedy policies and a brief summary of the experiences of the previous two years. Among other things, it revealed that the administration by late 1963 was less confident than at the outset about the prospects for democracy in Latin America (understandably!) and, in addition, was inclined to believe

61 See: "The United States Extends Recognition to New Government of Guatemala," *DSB*, XLVIII (May 6, 1963), 703; and "U.S. Recognizes Military Junta as Government of Ecuador," *DSB*, XLIX (Aug. 19, 1963), 782–83.

Washington's lack of resistance to the coup in Ecuador looked particularly bad because the military seized power immediately following a dinner at which an obviously inebriated Arosemena had bluntly criticized the United States in front of the U.S. ambassador and the president of the Grace Line. (On the coup generally, see Martin C. Needler, *Anatomy of a Coup d'Etat: Ecuador 1963* [Washington, 1964].)

62 For example, see Slater's "Democracy vs. Stability," 176–77; and *The OAS*, 13.

63 See the reprint: Edwin M. Martin, "U.S. Policy Regarding Military Governments in Latin America," *DSB*, XLIV (Nov. 4, 1963), 698–700.

64 For this reason, as one Kennedy aide observed in retrospect to the author, the statement was perhaps "more defensible intellectually than politically."

65 Interviews.

that its initial classification of the military as either dedicated to the maintenance of the status quo or too revolutionary had been overly simplistic. But there was no indication that the Kennedy government was any less convinced that democracy remained the only possible non-Communist road to development in the hemisphere.

Martin criticized both "impatient idealists" and "defeatist cynics" for a tendency "to measure current events not against historical reality and substantive progress, but against somewhat theoretical notions of the manner in which men should and do operate in a complex world."

He conceded—indeed stressed—that current conditions in Latin America made democracy a difficult goal to achieve:

Genuine concern with an overturn of the established order, fears of left-wing extremism, frustration with incompetence in an era of great and rising expectations, and a sheer desire for power are all formidable obstacles to stable, constitutional government—especially in countries where the traditional method of transferring political power has been by revolution or coup d'etat. In most of Latin America there is so little experience with the benefits of political legitimacy that there is an insufficient body of opinion, civil or military, which has any reason to know its value and hence defend it.

The Assistant Secretary also argued that the military were not "universal supporters of those who oppose change and the programs of the Alliance." Regarding the military governments which were the products of recent coups: Those in Argentina and Peru had led to "two of the most progressive regimes either country has ever had" (the Illia and Belaúnde governments

respectively), and those still in control in Ecuador and Guatemala had announced "reform programs of substantial importance."

Nevertheless, Martin firmly maintained that it was not in the interest of the United States to allow the military full rein: "Military coups thwart the will of the people, destroy political stability and the growth of the tradition of respect for democratic constitutions, and nurture Communist opposition to their tyranny." Furthermore, "the military often show little capacity for effective government, which is a political rather than a military job."

How then should Washington respond to coups? Martin observed that "unless there is intervention from outside the hemisphere by the international Communist conspiracy, the use of military force involving the probability of U.S. soldiers killing the citizens of another country is not to be ordered lightly." Moreover, past military occupations, "even when carried out with the best of intentions," had been "politically unproductive." Neither could the United States "as a practical matter, create effective democracy by keeping a man in office through use of economic pressure or even military force when his own people are not willing to fight to defend him." In the Assistant Secretary's opinion, the U.S. really had only one choice:

We must use our leverage to keep these new regimes as liberal and considerate of the welfare of the people as possible. In addition, we must support and strengthen the civilian components against military influences and press for new elections as soon as possible so that these countries once again may experience the benefits of democratic legitimacy. Depending upon the circumstances, our leverage is sometimes great, sometimes small.

Martin closed his statement with the following remarks:

I fear there are some who will accuse me of having written an apologia for coups. I have not. They are to be fought with all the means we have available. Rather I would protest that I am urging the rejection of the thesis of the French philosophers that democracy can be legislated—established by constitutional fiat.

I am insisting on the Anglo-Saxon notion that democracy is a living thing which must have time and soil and sunlight in which to grow. We must do all we can to create these favorable conditions, and we can do and have done much.

But we cannot simply create the plant and give it to them; it must spring from seeds planted in indigenous soil.

In spite of Martin's denial that he was presenting an "apologia for coups," his statement did spark the rumor that the Kennedy Administration was abandoning resistance to the Latin American military. Kennedy himself dampened the rumor in his press conference of October 9. He said that there was no change in policy, that Martin had been "merely attempting to explain some of the problems in Latin America, why coups take place, and what problems they present us with."[66]

The President cleared the air still further with a speech in Miami Beach on November 18. This was no casual address: In the words of one of his advisers, Kennedy recognized that "there had been some slippage" in U.S. policies in the previous year, and he was concerned lest he seem to be

giving a tacit go-ahead to "all those guys down there" to seize power.[67] Delivered only four days before his death, the Miami speech was Kennedy's last testament on Latin American affairs. Among the foremost objectives of his administration, he unequivocally reaffirmed, was the promotion of democracy in the hemisphere:

Political democracy and stability . . . is at the core of our hopes for the future. There can be no progress and stability if people do not have hope for a better life tomorrow. That faith is undermined when men seek the reins of power and ignore the restraints of constitutional procedures. They may even do so out of a sincere desire to benefit their own country, but democratic governments demand that those in opposition accept the defects of today and work toward remedying them within the machinery of peaceful change. Otherwise, in return for momentary satisfaction we tear apart the fabric and the hope of lasting democracy.

The Charter of the Organization of American States calls for "the consolidation on this continent, within the framework of democratic institutions, of a system of individual liberty and social justice based on respect for the essential rights of man." The United States is committed to that proposition. Whatever may be the case in other parts of the world, this is a hemisphere of free men, capable of self-government. It is in accordance with this belief that the United States will continue to support the efforts of those seeking to establish and maintain constitutional democracy.[68]

Hence, most of the evidence indicates that Kennedy was far from ready

66 *The New York Times,* Oct. 10, 1963, 18.

67 Significantly, Goodwin wrote most of the speech. (Interviews)
68 John F. Kennedy, "Battle for Progress with Freedom in the Western Hemisphere," *DSB,* XLIX (Dec. 9, 1963), 902.

to phase out his pro-democracy campaign in the fall of 1963. Whether he would *eventually* have done so is, of course, open to speculation.

Toward the end of his presidency, Kennedy had virtually decided to create the post of Under Secretary of State for Inter-American Affairs. Even more important as a measure of his continued commitment to Latin America, he was very seriously considering giving the job to Robert Kennedy. He mentioned the RFK idea to Goodwin two days before his assassination; and RFK later told Goodwin that he thought he would have accepted the appointment, at least in the second term. He wanted to move into foreign policy and needed an independent area to avoid undercutting the Secretary of State.[69] In any event, it is difficult to conceive of the President assigning his brother—or, for that matter, any other leading administration figure[70]—to oversee an area that he was likely to leave to the tender mercies of the military.

Nevertheless, a balanced view dictates conjecturing where the flexibility guideline might have led the administration over the long haul. Given the President's high regard for U.S. Ambassador Lincoln Gordon and Goulart's erratic behavior, it is probable that Kennedy would have acquiesced in the 1964 Brazilian coup—though surely with less public rejoicing than Johnson and his Assistant Secretary, Thomas C. Mann.[71] Thereafter, if the hemisphere trend toward militarism had appeared irreversible and the guerrilla

threat had subsided to the level of recent years, who knows?

Whatever the future might have been, the record of Kennedy efforts to further democracy in Latin America is one of a few successes and numerous frustrations and failures. On the positive side: U.S. policies may have helped to avert some coups and to ameliorate the effects of others. Certainly, the Kennedy Administration was largely responsible for ushering in the Bosch government in the Dominican Republic and for the elections of 1963 in Peru. But the administration was neither able to prevent a devastating series of military coups in Latin America nor to budge Duvalier from the Haitian presidency.

Yet we should not measure the success or failure of the Kennedy policies solely on the basis of the extent to which they actually fostered democracy. They also had an important impact upon the U.S. image in the hemisphere. From the Latin American standpoint, as significant as the Kennedy Administration's support for democracy was its strong identification with the democratic left. Along with the Alliance, Kennedy's pro-democracy-policies represented a sincere attempt to place the United States in the vanguard of what then appeared to be the political forces most dedicated to constructive economic and social progress. In this respect, the policies were eminently successful, and they contributed mightily to making the Kennedy years a brief era of good feeling between the United States and Latin America.

[69] Interview.
[70] Schlesinger mentions Sargent Shriver or Averell Harriman as possible choices for the post. (*A Thousand Days,* 1002.)
[71] See "The United States Role in João Goulart's Fall"—the Appendix in Skidmore, *Politics In Brazil.*

U.S. NOT-SO-PRO-DEMOCRACY POLICIES

The other side of the cyclic pattern of U.S. policies has been relative disinterest in promoting—and, occasionally, suspicion of and outright hostility to—democracy in Latin America.[72]

Under the influence of Latin American domestic developments and the failures of U.S. pro-democracy campaigns over the years, optimism has often yielded to pessimism in Washington on the question of Latin American preparedness for democracy. Starting with the premise that, except for a very few countries, democracy is at best a long-range goal,[73] U.S. policymakers have proceeded to rationalize an emphasis on other goals as follows:

The United States must deal in a "pragmatic" fashion with civilian and military unconstitutional governments simply because they are going to be part of the Latin American political milieu for the foreseeable future. It is possible to make a case for a no-*abrazo* posture toward some regimes and even for direct opposition to a rare dictatorship that "outrage[s] the conscience of America." However, as a general rule, the U.S. can most effectively encourage democracy in Latin America by exercising subtle pressures in a "quiet, unpublicized way" on a "day to day basis" through the normal channels of diplomacy.[74] Public posturing on the

democracy issue is not only futile but counterproductive: It makes a moral question ("good guys" vs. "bad guys")[75] out of what is basically a practical problem, diminishes the prestige of the United States in the hemisphere by committing it to overly ambitious political development goals, and engenders a negative reaction from undemocratic regimes which might otherwise be responsive to friendly persuasion. Finally, overt U.S. pro-democracy action is "patronizing" and "degrading" to Latin Americans and, from a legal standpoint, violates the inter-American principle of nonintervention.[76]

---

ening democratic governments. I feel that the United States can make its influence in favor of democratic procedures felt more effectively if diplomatic relations can be maintained with all the governments of the hemisphere. The American Republics probably can work together most effectively for hemispheric solidarity if they utilize, among other means, the continuing interchange made possible through normal diplomatic channels." (Text in Whiteman, *Digest,* II, 318.)

Or Rusk's statement at a press conference after the 1964 Brazilian coup: "[I]f unhappily in a particular...country, there is ...a military takeover—this does not present us with a situation which we can simply walk away from because we and other members of this hemisphere necessarily have an interest in what happens in that situation. Therefore we have to continue to live with it, work with it, try to assist a particular country in coming back to constitutional process." ("Secretary Rusk's News Conference of April 3," *DSB,* L [Apr. 20, 1964], 610.)

Again, see Rockefeller's position in selections 21 and 23.

[75] The reference is to remarks reportedly made by John O. Bell, U.S. Ambassador to Guatemala, interpreting Mann's exposition of his policy in a closed door session at the State Department. (*The New York Times,* Mar. 19, 1964, 1, 2.)

[76] Mann, "Democratic Ideal," 998–1000. As has been the practice of other U.S. decision-

---

[72] On the Johnson policies generally, see esp.: Slater's "Democracy vs. Stability"; and *The OAS,* 14–17; and Lieuwen, *Generals vs. Presidents,* chap. ix.

[73] See, for example, Rockefeller's views as expressed in selections 21 and 23.

[74] The quotations in the preceding two sentences are from Thomas C. Mann, "The Democratic Ideal in Our Policy Toward Latin America," *DSB,* L (June 29, 1964), 999. However, we might have gleaned similar ones from other sources.

For instance, Truman's letter to deposed President Rómulo Gallegos of Venezuela, explaining why the U.S. had not imposed sanctions following the 1948 coup: "This Government,... is of the opinion that nonrecognition is seldom, if ever, effective in bringing about the broader aim of strength-

Lip service to democracy and the nonintervention norm aside, the fact remains that policy-makers in the periods under discussion have viewed the promotion of democracy as largely contrary to the security interests of the United States.

First, *caudillos* and military regimes have traditionally been strong supporters of U.S. security policies at the international level. FDR did not discriminate between various types of Latin American governments, in part so as not to interfere with the organization of security against the Axis.[77] The social calendar of the White House reflected his attitude when Somoza and Trujillo both paid state visits on the eve of World War II. Similarly, the Truman and Eisenhower administrations found conservative dictatorships among their most dependable allies in the postwar struggle against Communism. Eisenhower symbolically bestowed the Legion of Merit on dictators Manuel Odría and Marcos Pérez Jiménez. The Brazilian military publicly praised Johnson Administration policies in Vietnam and made the largest Latin American troop contribution to the 1965 Dominican operation.

Second, Washington has often regarded undemocratic regimes as bulwarks of political stability and economic orthodoxy on the domestic front. During the Truman and Eisenhower years, many Latin American democrats (José Figueres of Costa Rica, for example) were believed to subscribe to "socialistic" development ideologies which were both repugnant in themselves and unfavorable to U.S. business. But the abiding preoccupation of U.S. policy-makers—reaching almost paranoic proportions during Mann's tenure in the Department of State and in the Rockefeller Report—has been with the danger that Communists or native radicals will exploit the stresses and strains inherent in the modernization process in Latin America. With the threat of "another Cuba" looming large in their thinking,[78] they have been skeptical as to whether development can safely proceed in many cases without regi-

[78] Mann's retrospective comments on the 1964 Brazilian coup are revealing: "[W]e are not at all sorry when we see a neighbor put out a fire in his house. Fires have a way of spreading. And I am sure that all of our friends know they can continue to count on us for help if they should be threatened by communist subversion." (Thomas C. Mann, "The Western Hemisphere's Fight for Freedom," *DSB,* LI [Oct. 19, 1964], 551–52.) See also selection 16, for his discussion of the dangers of Communist subversion in the "weaker, more fragile societies" of Latin America.

J. B. Martin quotes President Johnson at the outset of the 1965 Dominican crisis: Johnson said that he did not intend "to sit here with my hands tied and let Castro take that island. What can we do in Vietnam if we can't clean up the Dominican Republic? I know what the editorials will say but it would be a hell of a lot worse if we sit here and don't do anything and the Communists take that country." (*Overtaken by Events,* 661.)

See Rockefeller's assessment of the Communist threat in selection 24.

makers, Mann coupled his homage to the nonintervention principle with mention of Resolution **XXXV** in the Final Act of the Bogotá Conference: "That the establishment or maintenance of diplomatic relations with a government does not imply any judgment upon the domestic policy of that government." See selection 16, for Mann's dig at those who insist on nonintervention and yet argue for U.S. "support" of the non-Communist left.

[77] The Roosevelt Administration also drew the conclusion from Welles's experiences in Cuba that "interference was capable of creating situations where intervention [defined as the landing of marines] might become unavoidable." (Wood, *Good Neighbor Policy,* 137.)

mentation and repression. To policy-makers so oriented, the notion of the "modernizing military" in Latin America has seemed a godsend.[79]

Nevertheless, Washington's identification with the Latin American military has not been entirely without reservations,[80] one of which applies as well to old-style dictatorships like those of Duvalier and Stroessner. Paralleling the Eisenhower Administration's final assessment of the Trujillo regime, Johnson and Nixon policy-makers have expressed some concern that excessive political repression and socioeconomic stagnation might eventually breed widespread popular opposition and violence. Yet, unlike Eisenhower (re Trujillo), they have not been sufficiently concerned to explore alternatives to support of the status quo.[81] They

have also been a little uneasy about the possibility that the military might itself develop into a radical nationalist political force. This factor helped shape U.S. unenthusiastic attitudes toward coups in Bolivia (1964),[82] Argentina (1966), Peru (1968), and Bolivia (1969 and 1970).

Mann insisted that his pragmatic stance was no real departure from the *practice* of the Kennedy Administration.[83] However, one need only cite the 1965 Dominican case and the United States' continued embrace of the Brazilian military regime long after its extreme reactionary course was established[84] to demonstrate that

---

[79] See selections 21, 23, and 24.
[80] See Rockefeller's warnings in selection 21.
[81] Nevertheless, there was one brief revival of apparently genuine pro-democracy sentiment under the Johnson Administration, beginning in 1966, after Lincoln Gordon assumed the post of Assistant Secretary and Mann left the Department of State. In that year, Gordon gave full backing to U.S. Ambassador Edwin M. Martin's vigorous efforts to head off a coup against the Illia government in Argentina. Although the decision was made not to revert to the Kennedy practice of applying sanctions, Washington subsequently expressed its distress at the Onganía takeover. (*The New York Times,* June 29, 1966, 1, 14.) Gordon indicated to the press that he did not feel that the situation in Argentina was analogous to the Brazilian case two years before: Specifically, he said he did not believe that there was any real danger of economic collapse or Communist influence. (*The New York Times,* Aug. 2, 1966, 10.) Shortly thereafter, the Assistant Secretary publicly criticized the Argentine military regime for raiding and then closing the state universities. (*The New York Times,* Aug. 5, 1966, 1, 9.)
Somewhat less openly, the United States

also opposed the coup against the new Arias government in Panama in 1968. Washington was concerned both about the threat of violence by Arias supporters and about the effect of the revolt—coming soon after the Velasco coup in Peru and launched by a military establishment so closely associated with the U.S.—in further eroding Congressional support for U.S. Alliance for Progress and military aid. (*The New York Times,* Oct. 13, 1968, 1–2.)
[82] Other considerations in the 1964 Bolivian case were the Paz government's pro-U.S. and anti-Communist orientation, as well as its related determination to resist pressures from the left (spearheaded by Juan Lechín's tin miners) while revamping the Bolivian economy along the lines urged by Washington. (*The New York Times,* Nov. 10, 1964, 2; and Nov. 11, 1964, 17.)
[83] Mann. "Democratic Ideal," 999.
[84] For example, Castelo Branco's letter of August 11, 1964, expressing approval of U.S. actions in the Gulf of Tonkin incident, elicited an effusive reply from President Johnson. Johnson wrote that "the struggle for freedom in Vietnam is closely related to the struggle for freedom everywhere" and that the Western Hemisphere had "joined in that struggle in the Alliance for Progress." He added: "We in the United States have been heartened—and I believe the whole Hemisphere looks to the future with greater optimism—because of the vigorous manner in which your government has accepted this

Mann's assertion was just another manifestation of the Johnson Administration's "credibility gap." By renouncing the blanket commitment to democracy, the administration clearly implied that it henceforth would not be answerable to criticism from the Latin American democratic left. Moreover, its analysis of Latin American political and socioeconomic "realities" betrayed an exceedingly conservative ideological bias. Indeed, Mann represented precisely that sector of governmental opinion, including the "old Latin American hands" in the State Department and the Pentagon, which Kennedy decision-makers had regularly overruled.[85]

Much the same outlook now characterizes the Nixon Administration, although Nixon officials do appear sincere in their announced goal to achieve a "lower profile" for the United States in Latin America. In this regard, they largely ignored the Rockefeller Report's dire warnings of increasing Communist terrorism[86] and late in 1970

officially adopted a "wait and see" position toward new leftist governments in Chile and Bolivia. With Latin American nationalism on the rise and many hemisphere governments under rightist control, the administration undoubtedly believes the less said about politics the better. Its philosophy seems to be that U.S.–Latin America relations may profit from what Goodwin has termed "malign neglect"—under the guise of "partnership" and a "nuts-and-bolts" approach to issues of aid and trade.

However, the emphasis on a lower profile has merely submerged, rather than irrevocably revised, the Cold War attitudes traditionally prevalent in various parts of the executive branch. In March, 1970, coinciding with the Frei government's unilateral decision to break its embargo on trade with Cuba, the Nixon Administration began a quiet diplomatic campaign throughout Latin America to muster support for continued OAS diplomatic and economic sanctions against Castro.[87] Later, shortly after Salvador Allende won a plurality in the Chilean elections, Nixon's closest foreign policy adviser, Henry A. Kissinger, ventured the prediction at an off-the-record press briefing that congressional confirmation of Allende's victory would lead to the establishment of a "Communist" government in Chile which would, in turn, threaten the neighboring countries of Argentina, Bolivia, and Peru.[88] Conditioned responses like these raise the question whether the administration will be able to resist more direct and con-

challenge." Finally, Johnson pledged his administration's "sincere support through the Alliance for Progress." ("U.S. and Brazil Reaffirm Commitment to Peace," *DSB,* LI [Sept. 28, 1964], 436.)

[85] Schlesinger recalls that Mann "had an old Latin American hand's skepticism about the grandiose schemes of the New Frontiersmen and, on occasion, even responded a little to the crotchets of Admiral Burke." (*A Thousand Days,* 202.)

In some respects, Mann's attitudes seemed to pass beyond conservatism to a personal contempt for Latin Americans. He was "famed" in the State Department as the man who said: "I know my Latinos. They understand only two things—a buck in the pocket and a kick in the ass." (Quoted in Arthur M. Schlesinger, Jr., "The Lowering Hemisphere," *The Atlantic,* CCXXV [Jan., 1970], 81.)

[86] See selection 24 for contrasts between the views of Assistant Secretary Charles A.

Meyer and Rockefeller on the issues of Communism and military aid.

[87] *The New York Times,* July 13, 1970, 13.

[88] *The New York Times,* Sept. 23, 1970, 13.

spicuous involvement in Latin American political struggles should the situation become still further polarized between the left and the right.

Meanwhile, rather ironically, United States policies currently downgrading problems of Latin American political development draw support from the Nixon Administration's leading critics in Congress. Responding to disillusionment over Vietnam and the performance of the Latin American democratic left, what began as an attack on the Johnson Administration's deemphasis of the political goals of the Alliance[89] soon developed into a call for U.S. "disengagement" from Latin America. Senators Frank Church and J. William Fulbright and other Congressmen of similar views now are hypersensitive about U.S. interventionism and paternalism and also are gloomy about the prospects for reform under almost all existing Latin American governments. In their judgment, the Kennedy policies were naive, both because they posited a Latin American commitment to fundamental reform that rarely materialized and because they assumed that an essentially nonrevolutionary country like the United States could act as the agent of change in the hemisphere. Even were the U.S. dedicated to revolutionary goals, Church-Fulbright argue, its efforts to promote radical change would inevitably deliver the "kiss of death" to progressive Latin American politicians.

This reasoning leads Church-Fulbright to the conclusion that the way for the United States to improve its image is to stop its direct support of Latin American governments. According to their prescription, Washington should limit its assistance to aid for development channeled through multilateral institutions and remove barriers to Latin American trade. Church-Fulbright concede that such policies would indirectly help bolster conservative regimes along with the few progressive ones, but they point out that the responsibility for doing so would then rest primarily with the Latin Americans themselves. Moreover, they expect that the masses will everywhere benefit to some extent from development and ultimately, through an awareness born of improved living standards, come to demand more of their governments.[90]

II. POLITICAL DEVELOPMENT IN LATIN AMERICA: A CONTEMPORARY OVERVIEW

The only sure foundation for assessing the viability of current and possible future policy options available to the United States is a clearheaded grasp of contemporary political realities in Latin America. In the 1960s U.S. policy-makers tended to overestimate the malleability of the Latin American domestic environment by democratic reformers and radical revolutionaries alike.

DEMOCRACY AND EVOLUTIONARY REFORM

Instead of the steady strengthening of democracy in Latin America anticipated by the Kennedy Administration, the years of the Alliance witnessed a

---

[89] In addition to Senator Fulbright, among Mann's principal Congressional critics were Senators Wayne Morse and (interestingly enough) Hubert H. Humphrey. See Humphrey's article precipitated by the policy shift of March, 1964: "U.S. Policy in Latin America," *Foreign Affairs*, XLII (July, 1964), 585–601. For Fulbright's critique of U.S. actions in the 1965 Dominican crisis, see selection 15.

[90] For the Church-Fulbright prescriptions, see selections 22, 23, and 28.

new series of military coups. Only Chile, Colombia, Costa Rica, Mexico, Uruguay, and Venezuela were able to maintain constitutional processes more or less intact throughout the decade. During the same period, there were some striking successes of "reformmongering"[91] (for example, the land reform bill engineered by the Frei government in Chile[92]). However, *no* Latin American democratic government managed to fulfill the Alliance mandate of sweeping economic and social reform on many different fronts simultaneously.[93]

The experience of the sixties seems to demonstrate the widespread applicability of the model of the Latin American political system which has emerged from recent political development literature[94]: a relatively "stable"

pattern of instability and violence, deriving from the competition between an ever expanding number of political elites.[95] Although Latin America's "participation crisis" has been limited by the traditional political and social

[91] For a discussion of reformmongering, see Albert O. Hirschman, *Journeys Toward Progress: Studies of Economic Policy-Making in Latin America* (New York, 1963), esp. chap. 5. As his term implies, Hirschman sees change as coming most often through a complex process of "logrolling and shifting alliances" between and among competing supporters and opponents of specific reforms —with low-level violence a common ingredient. He maintains that this is a much more accurate description of what is actually happening in Latin America than the "traditional dichotomy" of "change through violent revolution or through peaceful reform."

[92] See Robert R. Kaufman, *The Chilean Political Right and Agrarian Reform: Resistance and Moderation* (Washington, 1967).

[93] See selection 27.

[94] A partial list: Charles W. Anderson, *Politics and Economic Change in Latin America* (Princeton, 1967); Samuel P. Huntington, *Political Order in Changing Societies* (New Haven, 1968); Martin C. Needler, *Political Development in Latin America* (New York, 1968); David E. Apter, *Some Conceptual Approaches to the Study of Modernization* (Englewood Cliffs, N.J., 1968), pp. 295–350; Helio Jaguaribe, *Eco-*

nomic and Political Development (Cambridge, 1968); Irving Louis Horowitz, "Political Legitimacy and the Institutionalization of Crisis in Latin America," *Comparative Political Studies,* I, No. 1 (Apr., 1968), pp. 45–69; Douglas A. Chalmers, "Parties and Society in Latin America" in the *Proceedings* of the 1968 Annual Meeting of the American Political Science Association; Chalmers, "Crisis and Change in Latin America," *Journal of International Affairs,* XXIII, No. 1 (1969), pp. 76–88; James L. Payne, *Labor and Politics in Peru* (New Haven, 1965) and *Patterns of Conflict in Colombia* (New Haven, 1968); Carlos A. Astiz, *Pressure Groups and Power Elites in Peruvian Politics* (Ithaca, N.Y., 1969); François Bourricand, *Power and Society in Contemporary Peru* (New York, 1970); Richard R. Fagen and Wayne A. Cornelius, Jr., eds., *Political Power in Latin America: Seven Confrontations* (Englewood Cliffs, N.J., 1970); Arpad von Lazar and Robert Kaufman, eds., *Reform and Revolution: Readings in Latin American Politics* (Boston, 1969); Paul E. Sigmund, ed., *Models of Political Change in Latin America* (New York, 1970); Claudio Véliz, ed., *Obstacles to Change in Latin America* (London, 1965) and *The Politics of Conformity in Latin America* (London, 1967); Richard N. Adams, *The Second Sowing: Power and Secondary Development in Latin America* (San Francisco, 1967); Luis Mercier Vega, *Roads to Power in Latin America* (New York, 1969); Jacques Lambert, *Latin America: Social Structures and Political Institutions* (Berkeley, 1967); John Mander, *The Unrevolutionary Society* (New York, 1969); Seymour Martin Lipset and Aldo Solari, eds., *Elites in Latin America* (New York, 1967); Irving Louis Horowitz, ed., *Masses in Latin America* (New York, 1970); and Henry A. Landsberger, ed., *Latin American Peasant Movements* (Ithaca, 1969).

[95] See esp. Anderson's "power contenders– power capabilities" model in *Politics and Economic Change,* chap. iv.

hierarchy in the region,[96] it has been of sufficient magnitude to prevent governmental "legitimacy" from evolving. New social groups created by economic development have pressed their demands upon governments which have possessed few institutional mechanisms —most notably, broad-based political parties—for "managing" them.[97] The result has been a nearly continuous state of political crisis, with gradual accommodation to changing conditions often attended by coercion and the rapid rise and fall of governments.[98]

Generally speaking, the amorphous middle class has in this century captured most of the citadels of political power in Latin America and come to terms with the former "oligarchs."[99]

Reformers have been plagued with defections on both the left and right in their own parties and occasionally with an "unholy alliance" between rival middle class parties and conservatives in congress. As a consequence of political stalemate, most Latin American governments have thus far been able to meet only "just enough" of the demands of the urban working population, *lumpenproletariat*, and mobilized *campesinos* to maintain a modicum of social peace. These groups have proved far more amenable to relatively small

---

[96] See selection 20. As Véliz himself recognizes, the state appears as significant as it does in Latin America mainly because it fills a political vacuum created by the inconclusive struggle between elites in society at large ("the state itself is the most powerful pressure group"). Nevertheless, the government which *is* the state often lacks legitimacy and in this sense remains "weak" and unstable. Nationalism in this context is "thin": a device to hide inaction (in Víctor Alba's felicitous phrase, "the nationalism of the emperor's clothes") and/or a means of staving off the ever imminent threat of collapse.

[97] See esp. Huntington, *Political Order*, chaps. i, vii. Chalmer's "Parties and Society" is perhaps the best single analysis of Latin American parties.

[98] See esp.: Horowitz, "Political Legitimacy"; and Chalmers, "Crisis and Change."

[99] As John J. Johnson suggested in his pioneering study, *Political Change in Latin America* (Stanford, 1958), the term "middle sectors" may be preferable to "middle class"—to indicate that the diverse groups in question have little sense of unity. Luis Mercier Vega comments: "For the census takers, [the middle classes] represent the residue left after the working class, the agricultural labourers and the privileged classes have been accounted for. Thus one finds lumped together in this category—

though sometimes distinguished by the prefixes 'upper' or 'lower'—small businessmen, tradesmen, members of the liberal professions, civil servants, old age pensioners, *rentiers*, independent peasants, and artisans." (*Roads to Power*, 21.)

The term "oligarchy" is also difficult to define, as James L. Payne has demonstrated in his "The Oligarchy Muddle," *World Politics*, XX (Apr., 1968), 439–53.

Definitional problems aside, these points that numerous students of Latin American politics have made appear to the author to be valid: (a) it is possible to distinguish at least impressionistically between "elites" ("haves") and "masses" ("have-nots") in Latin America; and (b) middle-class political victories have added to the former without much affecting the status of the latter. (See, for example, the following by Richard N. Adams: "Political Power and Social Structures" in Véliz, ed., *Politics of Conformity*; and *The Second Sowing*.)

José Nun writes: "The expanding middle class made no attempt to change the system as a whole: it merely demanded recognition of its legitimate right to play a part in it. . . . [T]he middle class had no need of time to develop a characteristic outlook, because it merely adopted that of the oligarchy. It accepted its heroes, its symbols, its culture, and its laws." ("The Middle-Class Military Coup" in Véliz, ed., *Politics of Conformity*, 81, 85.) From this pattern, Anderson derives his "rule of Latin American political change": "new power contenders may be added to the system, but old ones may not be eliminated." (*Politics and Economic Change*, 104ff.)

favors and less receptive to radical appeals than originally was expected.[100] When the delicate balance has failed, many civilians have called upon a predominantly middle class military to restore "order," and the military has rarely abstained from intervention very long.[101]

With the election of Salvador Allende, the *Unidad Popular* coalition in Chile *may* now be engaged in testing what Frei and his Christian Democrats promised to test and, in the last analysis, did not: whether a "revolution in freedom," operating within the constraints of the democratic process, is in fact possible.[102] Whatever the desires and intentions of Allende and his supporters, there is very little likelihood of the creation of a radical revolutionary civilian dictatorship. Auguring against any such eventuality are Chile's constitutional tradition (including a strong legislature), the special guarantees that Allende made as the price of his selection by congress, the highly organized character of those who have a stake in various aspects of the status quo, and the fact that change must take place under the wary eye of the military.

As Allende takes office for a term legally limited to six years, four possible outcomes—in addition to a radical civilian dictatorship—suggest themselves. Of these, three are perhaps equally probable, and the fourth, considerably less probable.

Allende may be able to build in what might be labeled "radical-evolutionary" fashion on Frei's program and thus, with some CD support, proceed with the nationalization of copper and banks, the establishment of more state controls over the economy and foreign investment, and an expanded land reform. To accomplish these high-priority tasks, and certainly to go even further in the direction of structural change, will require nothing short of a political miracle. Allende must succeed where Frei failed: He must conquer internal divisions in his own movement. He must also arouse *and sustain* the enthusiasm of the masses for his reforms and channel this in some systematic way into the political process. If reformmongering is to be carried much beyond the CD precedent, it cannot be confined to the executive-congressional arena of politics-as-usual conflict between those who have "made it" in Chilean society.

A second real possibility is that Allende will bow to the almost overwhelming odds against him—including the acute economic crisis that began

100 See Chalmer's discussion of Latin American governments' "anticipation of demands" in selection 1. They have been particularly successful in nipping labor militancy in the bud, partly by encouraging unionization under state control. See Henry A. Landsberger, "The Labor Elite: Is It Revolutionary?" in Lipset and Solari, eds., *Elites in Latin America,* 256–300. See also Huntington, *Political Order,* chap. v.

101 See esp.: Nun, "Middle-Class Military Coup"; Huntington's analysis of "praetorianism" in *Political Order,* chap. iv; and Horowitz, "Political Legitimacy." Horowitz argues that military dictatorship in Latin America is a "conflict-model substitute for consensual politics." One of the most interesting features of his essay is its stress upon the similarities between political systems in two countries currently ruled by rightist military (Argentina and Brazil) and two other countries that have already had fundamental social revolutions (Mexico and Cuba). He concludes that the "institutionalization of crisis" and attendant reliance on violence by governmental and nongovernmental elites alike is unfortunate because it prevents the emergence of more efficient, legitimate patterns of authority. (45–46)

102 See Norman Gall, "The Chileans Have Elected a Revolution," *The New York Times Magazine* (Nov. 1, 1970).

with his election—and simply settle for a great deal less reform than he pledged in his campaign.

A third quite conceivable outcome, of course, is a rightist military takeover on the order of those in nearby Argentina and Brazil. The military may decide at some point that social strains have become so severe that Chile can no longer afford the luxury of a democratic system. Actually, the situation in Chile would appear to be tailor-made for a left-wing military coup on the model of Peru, with the military choosing to lead the drive for reform as a means of insuring that it will remain in "responsible" hands. Although this fourth outcome seems strictly hypothetical at this stage, since the Chilean military is not known to have a substantial leftist sector, the idea may gain increasing currency over time.

If Allende and the *Unidad Popular* succeed in giving evolutionary change a new lease on life in Chile, this will undoubtedly encourage both the remnants of the democratic left and other leftists throughout Latin America who advocate the peaceful road to power as opposed to the desperate gamble of guerrilla action. But generalizing on the basis of the Chilean experience will continue to be hazardous. After all, outside of Chile, there are few (if any) places in Latin America *today* where a man with a platform as radical as Allende's could run in a free election, be elected, and physically take office—let alone stand a chance of completing his term.

MILITARY RULE

Late in the Kennedy period, it became fashionable in United States academic and official circles to speak of the possible emergence of a so-called Nasserist military in Latin America: a technocratic legion of officers dedicated to nationalism and modernization, which would maintain order while instituting major domestic economic and social reforms by decree. However, prior to the 1968 Peruvian coup, the vision of a Nasserist military appeared to be hardly more than an illusion. Aside from distant examples of military leaders who did not fit into the usual mold—the generals of the 1917 Constitution and Cárdenas[103] in Mexico, the Brazilian *tenentes*, Villarroel in Bolivia, and Perón—and the recent anomalous case of El Salvador,[104] there was little evidence to point to.

On the contrary, most of the military regimes established by coups in the early and mid-1960s were not remarkable for their nationalism[105] or progressive orientation. In practice, the military remained firmly aligned with the United States on most foreign policy issues, did not attack U.S. private enterprises, and showed much more interest in order than reform. When they turned to reform, their emphasis was primarily on economics, rather than social restructuring. They gave first priority to curbing inflation, through harsh austerity measures that hurt the man on the street much more than dominant social elites. Moreover, they demonstrated a singular lack of political skill and related inability to

103 Who, in fact, was largely responsible for making the Mexican military more responsible to civilian politicians.

104 See Lieuwen, *Generals vs. Presidents,* 91–94.

105 They were nationalistic only in the sense that the military establishment—through collective leadership—often defined their role as "guardian of the state" against the "extremist" demands of the underprivileged. However, this role did offer a contrast to the personalism and corruption of traditional military *caudillos* like Trujillo.

build wide popular support. Although many civilians had initially sought military intervention, the military wore out much of its welcome fast by impolitic responses to complicated domestic political problems. As some analysts subsequently noted, most Latin American societies are considerably more complex than Egypt was when Nasser came to power—perhaps too complex to be ruled by military fiat.[106]

The outlook has changed somewhat since the coup of October, 1968, in Peru. We are as yet too close to the situation to make a firm judgment; however, it is at least tempting to view the Velasco government as a "military-revolutionary" exception to the pattern we have been discussing.[107] It is still uncertain, of course, whether the regime will implement its projected reforms with vigor and substantially redefine Peru's relationships with the United States, as well as what effect its decisions in both these respects will have on the fragile nationalist coalition generated by the I.P.C. episode.

One thing is clear: For reform to continue—short of the Velasco government's extremely unlikely conversion into a military equivalent of the Castro regime—"politics"[108] cannot be suspended for any appreciable length of time without stalemate setting in. To date, Velasco appears to have enhanced his prospects for success by avoiding serious repression and including something for practically everybody in his broad set of reforms. While adamant on the I.P.C., he has also shown that he will accept foreign investment under proper safeguards and has been cautious about any dramatic initiatives vis-à-vis Cuba. Velasco's most urgent tasks would now seem to be, first, to persuade those left-to-right of center in Peruvian politics that they stand to gain more than they will lose from supporting his entire package of reforms; and, second, to institutionalize whatever support he has.

We may be able to tell from the eventual course of the Peruvian experiment not whether a non-Castroite "spasm revolution" is possible, but whether military rule which is genuinely oriented toward fundamental change can give the reformmongering process stronger direction from the center.[109]

To what extent the military elsewhere in Latin America will emulate

106 See Huntington, *Political* Order, 228–30.

107 For background, see: Rod Bunker, "Linkages and the Foreign Policy of Peru, 1958–1966," *Western Political Quarterly,* XXII, No. 2 (June, 1969), 280–97; Astiz, *Pressure Groups;* and Bourricand, *Power and Society.* See also: selection 29; José Iglesias, "Report from Peru: The Reformers in Brass Hats," *The New York Times Magazine* (Dec. 14, 1969); and Luigi R. Einaudi, *The Peruvian Military: A Summary Political Analysis,* Rand Memorandum RM-6048-RC (May, 1969) and *Peruvian Military Relations with the United States,* Rand publication P-4389 (June, 1970); Richard Lee Clinton, "The Modernizing Military: The Case of Peru," *Inter-American Economic Affairs,* XXIV (Spring 1971), 43–66.

108 Not necessarily implying constitutional procedures.

109 Einaudi is doubtful whether the Peruvian military's decision to assume a more active policy-making role is any "guarantee of progressive development." He writes: "The thesis of 'military as salvation'—for any partisan group—fails on the fact that the normal internal political diversity of the military is heightened by the assumption of responsible political power and the encounter with the complexities of government.... Additional sources for skepticism about the military's capacity for sustained revolutionary innovation derive from the nature of Peruvian society...the unmanageability of Peru, whether it be measured in social, political or administrative terms." (*Peruvian Military Relations,* 23–24.)

the Peruvian example remains to be seen. Naturally, much depends on exactly what the Peruvian "example" turns out to be—both what the Velasco government really attempts and what it succeeds in doing. In the author's opinion, the immediate forecast for Latin America as a whole—aside from further conservative military interventions—is more coups of the Ovando variety in Bolivia: the military seizing control for familiar reasons behind a radical facade.

However, we cannot entirely discount the possibility of other military-revolutionary experiences. There are radical sectors in almost every Latin American military establishment which might come to the fore under crisis conditions. Moreover, an Ovando regime, whose radicalism is initially only for show, might have to move rapidly to the left in order to survive if conservative opposition increases and the enthusiasm of the masses declines. Indeed, it was apparently Ovando's failure to do so that led to his downfall in October, 1970, and to the formation under chaotic conditions of a new government headed by Colonel Juan José Torres. At this writing, the ideological complexion of the self-proclaimed "popular nationalist" Torres government is not entirely clear, but it bears a distinct resemblance to that of Ovando.

How long rightist military regimes like those in Brazil and Argentina can keep the lid on the pressure cooker of Latin American societies is also an open question. When the military of this persuasion occupies the center of the political stage, they suspend many of the formal and informal processes through which gradual social adjustments have traditionally been made. They do not appear to possess either the inclination or skill to make of the

central state an adequate substitute, a truly flexible administrative apparatus capable of responding imaginatively to group demands.[110] Therefore, it seems logical to maintain that the more often the rightist military intervene and the longer they remain in power, the more likely it is that social tensions will finally erupt in some sort of revolutionary explosion.[111]

NONMILITARY REVOLUTIONARY CHANGE

Many of the same factors impeding civilian and military proponents of change in Latin America—plus the almost certain resistance of an anti-Communist military (not to mention the United States)—make revolutions by "armed struggle" as propounded by Guevara and Debray seem improbable for the near future.[112]

Nevertheless, if civilian reformers and/or the radical military do not succeed in co-opting issues and leadership, there is a strong chance of additional revolutions from below over the long haul. The Kennedy analysis may yet prove to be correct, except in underestimating the length of the fuse on the powder keg of social unrest.

[110] Douglas A. Chalmers has provocatively explored some of the possibilities in this respect in his unpublished paper, "Political Groups and Authority in Brazil: Some Continuities in a Decade of Confusion and Change" (Columbia University, 1970). See also Octavio Ianni, *Crisis in Brazil* (New York, 1970).
[111] See: Huntington, *Political Order*, 237–45, 261–63; and Horowitz, "Political Legitimacy." Writing before the 1968 Velasco coup in Peru, Horowitz states bluntly: "The record of Latin American 'modernizing militarists' is dismal." (p. 64) For essentially the same argument, see also Martin C. Needler, "The Latin American Military: Predatory Reactionaries or Modernizing Patriots?" *Journal of Inter-American Studies*, XI, No. 2 (Apr., 1969), 237–44.
[112] See selection 11.

Guerrilla activity will undoubtedly continue, and population growth and political mobilization of have-nots in the urban slums and the countryside may ultimately (if not sooner) overcome governments making adjustments in the traditional ways or not at all.[113] In the interim, it is always possible that a president coming to power with broad popular support might again, like Castro, "unmask" himself on a wave of nationalist sentiment once in office. And, as Allende and the *Unidad Popular* have shown, victory at the polls is not inconceivable for well-organized groups advancing relatively radical programs in those few countries where free elections are held.

Although any future radical revolutions will probably be dissimilar from the Cuban precedent in significant respects, the past eleven years have clarified some of the benefits and costs of Castro's path to development.[114]

Most Cubans now share the same lowest common denominator of welfare, which in such fields as education and health is markedly higher than that of the lowest sectors of society under Batista. In addition, there is unquestionably among Cuban citizens a much greater sense of social equality and national purpose than existed prior to 1959, and a pride in Cuba's independence from the United States.

However, the price paid for these achievements has been considerable: Some would argue that the destruction or exile of former elites, including a

substantial part of the middle class, at the outset of the revolution was unnecessarily vindictive. Certainly it deprived the Cuban regime of valuable expertise and creative (as well as obstructionist) criticism, which, in turn, helps explain the failures of some of the most ambitious revolutionary programs despite massive Soviet aid. The revolution has also involved the establishment of an authoritarian state, centering in the personality of Fidel[115] and buttressed by an ideology stressing (in addition to positive goals) hatred of enemies abroad and constant vigilance against counterrevolutionaries at home. Apart from its incompatibility with liberal-democratic political values,[116] this form of political organiza-

[113] See Huntington, *Political Order*, 281–83, 288–300.
[114] See: Richard R. Fagen, *The Transformation of Political Culture in Cuba* (Stanford, 1969); Maurice Zeitlin, *Revolutionary Politics and the Cuban Working Class* (New York, 1970); and Edward Gonzalez, "Castro: The Limits of Charisma," *Problems of Communism*, XIX, No. 4 (July-Aug., 1970), 12–24.

[115] Fagen emphasizes the political development achievements of the Cuban Revolution. Yet he observes: "[T]his claim does not deny the continuing importance of Castro or the personalistic aspects of his style of rule. Clearly, revolutionary institutions would be deeply affected by his death and would probably move in the directions of rigidity and disunity, the polar opposites of adaptability and coherence." (*Transformation*, 161.)
[116] In this respect, the author is not reassured by Fagen's assessment: "[T]he regime —while harsh and unrelenting at times— is not even a pale approximation of Stalinism or Hitlerism. The rules of the revolutionary game are quite well understood in Cuba; there is little or no arbitrary violence directed against any sector of the population (as opposed to sporadic harrassment); and the quasi-coercive shaping of environments to channel citizen energies toward revolutionary activities is relieved by an easiness of interpersonal relationships and a widespread—though often grudging—feeling among the citizenry that all must contribute to the development of the nation." (*Ibid.*, 161–62.) One should also bear in mind that Fagen rejects the labels of "Stalinism" and "Hitlerism" to describe the *current* degree of political repression in Cuba on the ground that (unlike Stalin or Hitler) Castro is not engaged in the systematic persecution of a "selected segment of the population." (*Ibid.*) Passing quickly over the possible

tion and culture has grave implications for the future of the revolution itself. Will it be possible to maintain revolutionary commitment and to prevent the rise of a new privileged class, especially after Fidel?[117] We should remember that Guevara was not an avid admirer of the Soviet system as it had evolved since its inception. Finally, though foreigners no longer exploit Cuba to the same degree as they used to, the Soviets are still more than an occasional nuisance to the Castro regime.

III. U.S. POLICIES: A PRESCRIPTION FOR THE 1970s

The hostile reception of the Rockefeller Mission offers ample evidence of the sad deterioration in United States–Latin America relations over the last few years. Obviously, U.S. policies require a profound reorientation if they are to meet the challenges arising from the complex domestic political environment in Latin America in the 1970s.

The author has no illusions about the likelihood of a reorientation at this time when so many of the political leaders of the United States either reveal their moral bankruptcy or seem to have substituted quasi-ideological posing for constructive thought. In a period when the only doubts the executive and many Congressmen appear to have about a Southern strategy is whether it will work and when U.S. arms flow again to the Greek military, probably even adoption of the unimaginative Church-Fulbright position is beyond the capacity of the United

States Government. The author prescribes nevertheless, with the recollection that more than once in the past there have been at the helm of state policy-makers attuned to some of the major needs of the United States and Latin America.

The starting point for reorientation should be the recognition that whatever the United States does *or* does *not* do in the hemisphere has a practical impact and reflects both upon the U.S. as a society and upon the U.S. image in Latin America. It is this image, taken as a whole, that holds the key to inter-American relations: This is the background against which all our day to day contacts unfold. Whether we realize it or not, the United States is constantly being judged, classified, and categorized.

Latin Americans have a ready stereotype of the Colossus of the North. However, Latin Americans have also demonstrated a willingness to trade the stereotype for a more charitable view when this is justified. They have a remarkable ability to strip away nonessentials to perceive the extent of genuine understanding and sympathy for their affairs that prevails in Washington at any given time. Contrast the tumultuous welcome accorded President Kennedy on his several goodwill tours (incidentally, *after* the Bay of Pigs) with the experiences of Vice President Nixon and Rockefeller. The explanation for the contrast lies deeper than the charisma of a man or his Catholicism: Latin Americans knew that the Kennedy government was committed to goals which many of them shared.

Today the United States is regarded by progressive Latin Americans as reactionary or, at best, intent upon maintaining more or less the status quo. They are correct. We richly deserve our current reputation.

---

debating point that the "selected segment" involved is any and all active opponents of the regime (of which few apparently remain), the fact is that these descriptions are much more appropriate applied to the early years of the revolution.
117 See *ibid.,* 158–65.

But a shift to the Church-Fulbright disengagement alternative is not the answer. Although it stems from generally admirable motives, it is entirely too negative. It neglects our responsibility as a nation to put ourselves unequivocally behind progressive governments and forces (however few) in Latin America. There is little virtue in leaving Latin America to its fate in the name of self-determination, while easing our consciences with a small amount of multilateral aid and the vague hope that things will somehow get better, eventually, if only the United States can keep its fingers out of the pie.

The question is not whether the United States should adhere to an utterly undesirable—and, indeed, in an absolute sense, impossible—nonintervention posture. Rather it is *how* should we use our still substantial influence and, especially, *for what ends?*

What we need is an updated version of the Kennedy policies, revised for the somewhat new conditions of the 1970s: The United States position should be that we prize *both* fundamental economic and social change *and* democracy in Latin America; that—forced to choose between them—we regard change as more important; and that we intend to focus our scorn on regimes which honor *neither value.*

POLICIES TOWARD COMMUNISM, THE CUBAN REVOLUTION, AND FUTURE REVOLUTIONS ON THE FIDELISTA MODEL

Before anything worthwhile can be accomplished, the United States must abandon many aspects of its traditional anti-Communism on the scrapheap of obsolete policies.

As thoughtful Latin Americans have argued for years, Washington has grossly exaggerated the Communist/Castroite threat. Aside from Guatemala and Cuba (and Chile, via the electoral route), Communism has made no significant inroads in the hemisphere; and Castro's success in putting his unique personal stamp on the Cuban Revolution casts doubt on the meaningfulness of the "Communist" label there. It is hardly accurate anymore to speak of a worldwide "Communist conspiracy": There are now "many Communisms," and, as the example of Cuba suggests, even these involve a heady dose of old-fashioned nationalism. Moreover, nearly all of them, including Cuba, present no more of an immediate physical threat than Latin American governments should be able to handle *alone,* with modest counterinsurgency measures unassisted by the U.S. If target governments cannot, they undoubtedly *deserve* to fall, and it will ultimately take more than U.S. aid and OAS resolutions and sanctions to save them. The United States might be able to sustain a few unpopular regimes temporarily by landing marines. However, such interventions are short on morality, costly in other ways, and unlikely to make a lasting contribution to political stability.[118]

Not only has the United States magnified the Communist/Castroite threat out of all proportion, but many of the measures which we have adopted to meet it have been self-defeating. U.S. hostility and OAS sanctions may have been, on balance, more of a boon than a menace to the Castro regime. On the other hand, the campaign against subversion has seriously undermined the OAS and exacerbated U.S. relations with leading Latin American governments like Mexico, Chile, Argentina (under Frondizi), and Brazil (under Quadros and Goul-

[118] See selection 19.

art).[119] Obsession with Communist penetration has also led the United States into several ill-considered unilateral actions, in Guatemala, Cuba (the Bay of Pigs), and the Dominican Republic (1965). Finally, U.S. anti-Communist pronouncements and activities have aligned this country with a truly reactionary and status-quo-oriented civilian and military constituency in Latin America. Castro himself could not have devised a better strategy for ensuring future anti-U.S. radical revolutions.

The "threat" of Communism (*Fidelismo,* etc.) is really more in the nature of a long-range challenge to demonstrate that there are better roads to progress—which, in fact, there may be. Quite apart from any conceivable overtones of Cold War struggle, the United States has sufficient grounds to continue opposing *in principle* the Cuban Revolution as a model for Latin America as a whole. The *Fidelista* model is irreconcilable with values which we should cherish and perhaps no more likely than other less drastic approaches to change to improve the material lot of the masses.[120] Insofar as the returns are not yet complete either on the Cuban Revolution or on possible alternative paths to development, there is still time for another "act of faith" based on the hope that the latter can be found.

The point is that the United States should enter into competition with the Cuban Revolution, and any future revolutions of a similar character, stressing the positive. There is no more effective way of weakening Castro than moving to end the U.S.-OAS diplomatic and economic boycott of Cuba and placing the onus of further isolation on him. We should even express our willingness to aid Castro's regime, provided that he at least tacitly abandons physical attempts (loosely defined) to export his revolution. We can do so emphasizing that we see no merit in continuing to penalize the Cuban people for a revolution that was essentially a product of the failure of pre-Castro governments to bring about basic change.[121] Castro may well decline our assistance, but this surely should not be a matter of concern to Washington.

Infinitely more important for the United States than opposing the *Fidelista* model is indicating in an unmistakable fashion—in deeds as well as in words—what it is we support. We must rededicate all our available energies and resources to the task of strongly encouraging whatever other potential for change exists in Latin America.

POLICIES TOWARD LATIN AMERICAN MILITARY REGIMES

The first part of the task that faces the United States is to do everything

119 See selections 5 and 13.
120 Anderson's reasoning is relevant here: "It may be argued that Latin America cannot wait for...evolutionary processes to take hold, and must engage in revolution to hasten the pace of imperative change. However, there is a significant sense in which Latin America, because of its urgent needs for change, cannot wait for revolution. To create the revolutionary situation, to undergo the sacrifices that a large-scale reordering of social and economic systems entails, to endure the tumult and disorder that precede the constructive phase of revolution, may involve an extravagance of time, energy, and human and physical resources that Latin America can ill afford." (*Politics and Economic Change,* 378.)

121 The United States might use the same formula to pave the way for aid to other revolutionary regimes patterned after Cuba, but the offer of aid should be withheld until after any initial period of extreme repression is past.

within its power to "convince" the Latin American military that their place is in the barracks and not in the presidential palace—unless they are really prepared to wield their superior force in a military-revolutionary fashion.

There being little evidence to the contrary, we should publicly espouse the thesis that almost any civilian government is preferable to exercise of power by the military. At the same time, we should state that special consideration will be given to cases where a military regime undertakes significant reform measures and proceeds to implement them without undue repression. Dramatic steps like the Peruvian agrarian reform ought to be regarded as the *sine qua non* of a military-revolutionary government.

Accordingly, the United States should begin phasing out *all* aid to existing military regimes (except, at this writing, the Velasco government in Peru) and reinstitute a Kennedy-type policy of nonrecognition and non-aid to any new (nonrevolutionary) military governments which may arise in the future. Learning from the mistakes of the Kennedy Administration, we should continue diplomatic and economic sanctions until the military has actually returned power to civilians or has clearly demonstrated its military-revolutionary proclivities. Unless the president ousted by a coup is allowed to serve out his constitutional term or all major political parties agree on some alternative plan, return to civilian rule should involve at least passably free elections, with the former president participating as a candidate if he and his party so desire.

There is, of course, no assurance that U.S. nonrecognition and non-aid will always force the military to retreat. Indeed, there is a high probability that instituting such a policy will involve us in long and bitter disputes with some military regimes like those currently in power in Brazil and Argentina. However, to do otherwise is no less than to reinforce Latin Americans' worst suspicions about the United States, to waste most of our aid, and to prejudice the future political development of individual countries and possibly the greater part of Latin America.

As we mentioned earlier, one of the customary replies to assertions like the above is the argument that the United States can exercise more constructive influence upon Latin American conservative military governments through the normal channels of diplomacy. The record speaks for itself: Either we have not been trying very hard and/or subtle persuasion weighs lightly in the balance against the continued flow of U.S. aid dollars and the public *abrazo* inherent in "relations as usual." Note, for example, that Governor Rockefeller's stroll through a deserted Brazilian Congress and his meeting with student representatives[122] were feeble gestures beside the glaring fact that he was paying an official call on Costa e Silva's authoritarian and reactionary military regime.

Washington will register a gain, in the form of building a progressive image for the United States, even when its hard antimilitary line fails to wring concessions from the generals. "Prestige" is not always defined in terms of power: Latin American publics might have greater affection for the U.S. if it occasionally ventured to tilt with windmills in a good cause. But this Don Quixote metaphor may be inappropriate, insofar as the threat posed by conservative military regimes to

122 *The New York Times,* June 19, 1969, 1, 15.

Latin America's future is not imaginary but real and one of the lessons of the Kennedy years is that the generals will sometimes yield. As we have noted, they did yield at least temporarily in the Dominican Republic (after Trujillo and prior to Bosch) and in Peru (1962). And we might have had more such examples had the U.S. challenged the military more often and more tenaciously.

Taking the United States commitment to a hard-line as a given, there would appear to be three key factors determining the degree of actual U.S. influence in confrontations with Latin American conservative military governments: (1) the number of internal political divisions within the larger military establishments on the desirability of a return to civilian rule and economic and social reforms[123]; (2) the dependence of the military regime in question on U.S. aid; and (3) the availability of nationalist causes with which the military may disguise their true motives in seizing power.

Two of these factors have important implications for other U.S. policies. Factor two suggests that if the United States is intent upon actively supporting socioeconomic progress and democracy in Latin America, it would be an error to opt for greater multilateralization of development aid. On the other hand, if the U.S. is inclined to persist in its recent practice of favoring conservative regimes like that of Brazil in its assistance program or decides to dispense aid indiscriminately, it could be better done through multilateral channels. Multilateral aid is less identified with the United States, and we can be sure that the many unprogres-

sive Latin American governments will see to it that they share in any division of the spoils.[124]

Another problem relevant to both factors two and three concerns the many petty restrictions currently imposed on U.S. aid by Congress, which direct the President to suspend assistance to governments expropriating U.S. private enterprises without prompt and adequate compensation (Hickenlooper Amendment), seizing U.S. fishing vessels beyond a twelve mile limit (Pelley Amendment), and so forth. We need to remove all lesser encumbrances in order to preserve aid as a source of influence for the right kind of goals.[125]

Factor three points to the possibility that a new military regime might bolster its position through expropriations of U.S. private enterprises, thereby casting doubt upon the reasons for U.S. opposition. Hence it is necessary for the United States both to state clearly its policies towards coups *before* they occur and to disassociate itself from the properties of its nationals abroad. Regarding the latter, suffice it to say here that the United States should long ago have established the principle that U.S. corporations must be prepared to bear the risks involved in investing in Latin America alone.[126]

POLICIES TOWARD NON-FIDELISTA CIVILIAN GOVERNMENTS

Opposing the Latin American conservative military is only part of the task ahead: Washington must also bring itself to deal more critically with civilian governments.

123 See Needler, *Political Development,* 75–76.

124 See selections 22 and 28.
125 See *ibid.*
126 For other alternatives, see selections 29 and 30.

The United States should declare its firm support for the notion embodied in Latin American constitutions that periodic free elections are the best means of securing governments responsive to the popular will. As Kennedy stated it: "We should not attempt to influence voters in their choice of governments—but we should always indicate our hope that they will have an opportunity to make such a choice. . . ."[127] Elections lend legitimacy to the decision-making structures of government and contribute to the process of "political institutionalization" in other ways—most notably, by offering political parties an incentive to organize themselves more efficiently and to broaden their social base.[128]

We should recognize and at least initially extend development aid[129] to

any government which results from a free election. As a general rule, we cannot attempt to judge the honesty of an election; however, we may reserve the right to withhold recognition and aid when an election has definitely been rigged. Moreover, we should urge all Latin American governments to establish the practice of inviting OAS teams or other extranational observers to verify the conduct of elections, and we should set an example by doing so ourselves.

Nevertheless, with due regard for the goal of democratic government, the United States must indicate that its primary concern in Latin America is meaningful socioeconomic change. Although we should give elected governments every benefit of the doubt, we have to make it clear even to them that we cannot go on indefinitely buying time with aid for governments which are not disposed to undertake basic reforms. In addition, the United States should not foreclose the possibility of acquiescing in an incumbent administration's abandoning constitutionalism in whole or in part, provided this appears necessary to achieve reforms and does not lead to brutal repression of political dissidents. Our reaction in such cases ought to be that we may have to reassess our diplomatic and aid relationships with the regime in question unless the promised benefits of the new political order soon begin to materialize.

The need and potential for reform obviously varies from country to country; and in most instances the United States will certainly have to settle for something closer to reformmongering than the ambitious approach of the Alliance. Yet we must strive harder to assure that our decisions in each case stem from a realistic appraisal and not

---

[127]John F. Kennedy, *The Strategy of Peace,* ed. by Allan Nevins (New York, 1960), 137. Incidentally, the Kennedy Administration violated the first part of this maxim in openly supporting the candidacy of Haya de la Horre in the Peruvian elections of 1963. (See Goodwin's testimony in Senate Committee on Foreign Relations, Subcommittee on Western Hemisphere Affairs, Hearings [April 14, 16, and 17, 1969], *United States Relations with Peru,* Ninety-First Congress, First Session, Committee Print [Washington, 1969], 85.)

[128] See Huntington, *Political Order,* chap. vii. We may conceive of our role—in Anderson's terms—as adding (however marginally) to the "power capability" of Latin American political parties. (See *Politics and Economic Change,* 94–95.)

[129] As concerns progressive democratic governments, the author endorses Bronheim's recommendations regarding military aid (in selection 25). Although the author proposes wider sanctions with respect to conservative military regimes and believes exceptions might be made for genuine military-revolutionary governments, he also agrees with Bronheim's argument that the U.S. should embargo *sales* of weapons to governments "which take or hold office by force of arms."

simply a willingness to follow the path of least resistance.[130] In the long run, it may be better if we expect too much from Latin American governments than too little. If all but two or three governments feel that the political risks involved in reform outweigh whatever benefits accrue from the receipt of U.S. aid, so be it. In this event, we can—and should—find use for the money elsewhere.

It should almost go without saying that the United States has considerable to gain and absolutely nothing to lose by ostracizing flagrant, unprogressive dictatorships like those of Duvalier in Haiti and Stroessner in Paraguay. One finds it difficult to imagine what reasoning or utter cynicism prompted the Nixon Administration to include "Papa Doc" on the visiting list of the Rockefeller Mission. Governor Rockefeller subsequently indicated that he hoped to persuade Duvalier to begin to liberalize his regime and also hinted that the administration was worried about repercussions in the U.S. black community and around the world if a black country were to be snubbed.[131] What-

ever the excuses, they are not good enough. Rockfeller's stopover in the Haitian "nightmare republic"[132] was a national disgrace for the United States and a shocking triumph of penny-ante realpolitik over humanity.

CONCLUSION

In the pages above, the author has outlined a framework for a fundamental reorientation in U.S. policies toward Latin America. Some readers may be inclined to argue that what he is proposing is a renewed "civilizing mission" for the United States in the hemisphere.

This characterization is valid up to a point: The fact is that Latin America could stand a little more "civilization," if only in terms of more stable and representative political systems and a greater commitment to socioeconomic change. However, lest the charge be that we are insisting that Latin America develop "in the image of the United States," recall that these are the same goals which many progressive Latin Americans have themselves set for their own countries. Let us also acknowledge that the United States urgently needs to look to the kind of example it is setting at home and abroad, which at present in numerous respects is execrable.

As Latin America enters the 1970s, the United States may *either* continue

---

130 As Hirschman points out, it is important to eschew the "action-arousing gloomy vision ...that creates more gloom than action," to perceive the limited degree of change that is always taking place even in a "backward" setting, and to be alert for whatever opportunities exist for accelerating the process. "Large-scale change" of *any* variety, he cautions, is "unpredictable," "unique," and involves a "highly improbable complex of events"—yet it does on occasion happen. ("The Search for Paradigms as a Hindrance to Understanding," *World Politics,* XXII, [Apr., 1970], 329–43. See also Hirschman, "Obstacles to Development: A Classification and a Quasi-Vanishing Act," *Economic Development and Cultural Change,* XIII [July, 1965], 385–93.) In his earlier *Journeys Toward Progress,* Hirschman wrote: "The roads to reform are narrow and perilous, ... *but they exist."* (275)
131 See: selection 23; and Senate Com-

mittee on Foreign Relations, Subcommittee on Western Hemisphere Affairs, Hearing (Nov. 20, 1969), *Rockefeller Report on Latin America,* Ninety-First Congress, First Session, Committee Print (Washington, 1970), 52.
132 Graham Greene's apt description. Greene wrote to the *The Times of London* condemning Rockefeller's presentation of a letter from President Nixon to Duvalier as "an encouragement of tyranny." (Quoted in *The New York Times,* July 6, 1969, 17.)

to support the status quo *or* place whatever influence it has squarely on the side of progress. We must choose, since any attempt to avoid a choice is, by default, to opt for the status quo.

The suggested policies will not, of course, usher in an era of complete peace and harmony in the relations between the United States and Latin America. But they should vastly improve relations with those Latin Americans whose good will ought to matter the most to us. And they will definitely assure—for once—that those Latin Americans who dislike us will do so for the *wrong* reasons. Surely these would be major accomplishments which the citizens of the United States could view with justifiable pride.

C

MODERNIZATION: THE ECONOMIC
AND SOCIAL DIMENSION

27

A Review of Alliance
For Progress Economic
and Social Development Goals

AID

From "A Review of Alliance for Progress Goals: A Report by The Bureau for Latin America, Agency for International Development (February 1969)" reprinted in House, Committee on Foreign Affairs, Subcommittee on Inter-American Affairs, Hearings (February-May, 1969, *New Directions for the 1970's: Toward a Strategy of Inter-American Development,* Ninety-First Congress, First Session, Committee Print (Washington: U.S. Government Printing Office, 1969), pp. 656–753.

When the American states signed the Charter of Punta del Este in 1961, the Kennedy Administration billed the Alliance for Progress as a vast hemispheric effort to promote democratic government, self-sustained economic growth, and social justice—in short, to launch Latin America as a region into the modern world—in the brief space of a decade.[1] Eight years

[1] For background on the Alliance, see: R. H. Wagner, *United States Policy Toward Latin America: A Study in Domestic and International Politics* (Stanford: Stanford University Press, 1970); J. Levinson and Juan de Onís, *The Alliance That Lost Its Way: A Critical Report on the Alliance for Progress* (New York: Quadrangle Books, 1970); Harvey S. Perloff, *Alliance for Progress: A Social Invention in the Making* (Baltimore: The Johns Hopkins Press, 1969); William D. Rogers, *The Twilight Struggle: The Alliance for Progress and the Politics of Development in Latin America* (New York: Random House, 1967)—chap. 7 reprinted as selection 31 below; Herbert K. May, *Problems and Prospects of the Alliance for Progress: A Critical Examination* (New York: Praeger, 1968); J. Warren Nystrom and Nathan A. Haverstock, *The Alliance for Progress* (Princeton: D. Van Nostrand, 1966); Richard S. Thorn, "The Alliance for Progress: The Flickering Flame" in Cole Blasier, ed., *Constructive Change in Latin America* (Pittsburgh: University of Pittsburgh Press, 1968), pp. 117–59; Robert N. Burr, *Our Troubled Hemisphere: Perspectives on United States–Latin American Relations* (Washington: The Brookings Institution, 1967), chap. 8; Eduardo

later, the Alliance was under attack from virtually every quarter, and at the request of Congress AID undertook a study of the feasibility of attaining the Charter economic and social development goals by 1971. The resulting document, portions of which are reprinted below, is a useful review of the few accomplishments and many failures of the previous seven years, and a catalogue of some of the staggering obstacles yet facing Latin America on the road to modernization. Among other things, it demonstrates that an extremely high rate of population growth, which continues unabated, has already wiped out many significant "gains." Under these circumstances, the editor suggests that asking whether the Alliance has succeeded is perhaps less important than asking how it might have been improved and what Latin America would be like today had there been no Alliance. The report also highlights the difficulty of measuring the progress of individual countries or groups of countries either in overall terms or with respect to specific development objectives.

President Kennedy promised at least $1 billion a year in public funding from all sources for Latin American development under the Alliance, and this figure has been more than met in succeeding years for AID. Moreover, as the study mentions, President Johnson pledged in 1965 that the United States would be willing to extend its commitment beyond 1971. In spite of President Nixon's reluctance to endorse a Democratic program and his preference for the phrases "action for progress" or "a new partnership in the Americas," he and other spokesmen for his administration have said that they, too, support the Punta del Este goals. However, there remains considerable doubt as to the willingness of the United States Congress to go on financing the program, at least as it has been administered in the past. Those who decry the Alliance's lack of impact in the areas of economic and especially social reform have been joining forces with traditional opponents of foreign aid to scale down appropriations. AID's total authorizations and obligations for fiscal year 1970 were $377.7 million, in contrast to the 1966 peak of $638.3 million.

INTRODUCTION

The Committee on Government Operations requested a study to determine whether the goals of the Alliance for Progress as they apply to each country are currently realistic or attainable in light of the experience of the past seven years. . . .

Our review of experience of the past seven years indicates that total accomplishment of the ambitious Alliance goals within the decade 1961–1971, as contemplated in the Charter of Punta del Este, is not possible. . . .

This report does not attempt to treat the many, and still not fully understood, variables involved in moderniza-

---

Frei Montalva, "The Alliance that Lost Its Way," *Foreign* Affairs, XLV (April 1967), pp. 437–48; and the annual reviews by Simon G. Hanson in *Inter–American Economic Affairs.*

tion and development, but instead, is addressed to the formal goal structure of the Charter of Punta del Este. The formal objectives omit some critical elements which bear particular mention.

Major among these is the critical variable of population growth. Although omitted from Alliance goals because of its political volatility, this factor has been central to what has transpired since. In most Latin American countries, the birth rate is staggeringly high. The number of school age children not in school tends to grow at the very moment when new schools are being built at a record rate. Substantially increased food production and remarkably expanded educational facilities barely keep pace with population increase. High economic growth rates are largely cancelled out in per capita terms, as the economic pie must be shared by a rapidly increasing number of claimants. . . .

The United States has made known its willingness to assist, where requested, as the countries of Latin America come to recognize the population issue as a matter of priority concern. While there are increasing signs of this growing recognition throughout the Hemisphere, there are few countries in which the issue is yet being squarely met. Until these problems are better recognized and addressed in most of the Hemisphere's countries, the question of attaining a satisfactory level of development remains uncertain.

Another vital development priority not specifically identified as a formal Charter goal was the need for all countries to couple their firm general commitment to develop with vastly improved competence, efficiency and vigor in governmental operations. Development requires not only that the Latin American governments perform their traditional functions more efficiently and effectively, but also that they prepare themselves for a broad range of innovative, technically complex and managerially-demanding developmental undertakings. . . .

The Alliance years have left an imprint of new commitment, competence, and confidence throughout governments in the Hemisphere. Thousands of public servants have received essential training, and key governmental policy-making and executing agencies in most countries have been—or have begun to be—strengthened. At the same time, the Alliance has also been an essential factor in the new sense of commitment to development, and in the realistic perception of the means for its attainment, which appear everywhere in the Hemisphere. Whereas few governments in Latin America had even given lip service to the key issues of development prior to the Alliance, development is now everywhere the by-word of national political life. No government or political party can ignore it. This, in itself, is a momentous achievement of the Alliance. . . .

An analysis of progress towards goals raises the question of relative priorities. Viewed broadly, each of the Charter goals theoretically represents an equally high priority objective for each Alliance country. Again, theoretically, it is only through the eventual achievement of all the goals that a country can be said to have succeeded in providing access to its citizens to meaningful productive opportunity and a greater share of the benefits of progress. Yet realistically, simultaneous progress towards each of the goals cannot be expected and the priority significance of progress toward any goal or group of goals, in terms of development strategy, varies widely among countries and within the same country over time. There are great differences between one country and the next in the development bottlenecks that require early resolution as a precondition to progress on other fronts. Also, the countries of the Hemisphere differ markedly in their capacities to achieve political commitment and consensus behind various policies and goals, or to mobilize technical, financial and institutional resources behind the programs leading to the goals. While every country needs to base its development strategy on its unique development problems, priority setting for operational programs must also take account of the art of the possible within that country's political, economic, technical, and administrative constraints. . . .

Examination of progress toward the individual Alliance goals raises several cautionary points which should be underscored. First, only a few of the goals are "self-interpreting" in that they offer clear-cut quantitative benchmarks against which to measure progress. Most are susceptible to a variety of measures and interpretations. . . . *Second,* even in the few instances in which quantitative targets are specified, the significance for development of the attainment or non-attainment of any or some of the goals is not always self-evident. . . . The tangled cause and effect relationships of goals and priorities in each country, and the many essentially qualitative aspects which must be weighed in assessing development progress preclude the application of mechanistic models in evaluating Alliance achievement. Inevitably, evaluative conclusions must be based upon judgmental weighing and analysis. While the data offer basic guidance for judgment, they often mask important

inter-relationships and significance. The trends measured by the statistics need to be taken only as indicators of the direction and order of magnitude of movement. Particularly when the average annual change over the period is small compared with the annual fluctuations, any large annual change will have a relatively strong effect on the average for the period. A relatively "successful" or "unsuccessful" country may switch to another rating group as the result of an atypical year's performance which, in fact, has little or no long range significance. The reverse is also true. If annual country changes are relatively small, a country that has reversed its previous poor record may have to do well for a number of years before its average qualifies it to enter the relatively successful group.

Third, there is the question of comparability. Judging performance involves the weighing and comparing of various factors which actually may be incommensurate—an "apples-and-oranges" addition problem. How is a high level of attainment with a slow rate of improvement to be credited relative to a fast rate of improvement at a still low level of accomplishment? Thus, primary school enrollment may have increased greatly, but with one country going from 40 to 60 percent of the school age population and another from 50 to 70 percent. Or one country may have reduced mortality only of children under one year, while another only of children from one to five. Some countries performed well at the beginning of the period, and in spite of faltering, show better averages than poorer performers that recently have been progressing at an accelerating pace. Finally, there are cases especially in respect to price stabilization where we know that strong efforts have been made and deserve commendation even though accomplishment in the sense of achievement of relative price stability is as yet incomplete.

The question of whether the Alliance is attaining its goals points up the difficulty that has plagued this effort since its beginnings. There is no easy path to modernization of the traditional societies and archaic economies of Latin America. Yet the rhetoric of development has so overshadowed the reality, that reasonable men have been led to conclude that a decade of "development" could achieve progress to match that of the European nations under the Marshall Plan. The sober realities that must be faced, and the inevitable frustrations, delays and turmoil which must accompany the basic social and economic change called for in the Alliance goals, have been increasingly forced upon those concerned with this great undertaking.

We believe that precisely this problem would have made more specific quantitative and time frame benchmarks undesirable. The most unrealistic goal of all would have the attainment of all the objectives of the Alliance, however quantified, in a 10-year period. Realism required that the goals be stated generally, leaving to the individual countries the assignment of priorities in light of their own unique needs and desires, obstacles and capacities. There can be no uniform definition of the extent of these needs for all the diverse countries of Latin America, much less a uniform estimate of the nature or cost of the policies and programs which are required.

The record shows significant accomplishment by every country in some area of Alliance objectives. There is no question that the goals are being pursued and can be met. Less clear is how long the process will take. That the

original Alliance period of a decade was far too short a time span was realized long ago. It was formally recognized in President Johnson's message of November 23, 1965, to the Second Special Inter-American Conference at Rio de Janeiro:

Recognizing that fulfillment of our goals will require the continuation of the joint effort beyond 1971, I wish to inform the Conference—and through you, your respective countries—that the U.S. will be prepared to extend mutual commitment beyond the time foreseen in the Charter of Punta del Este.

President Johnson's affirmation was subsequently reaffirmed by the Presidents of the American Republics meeting at Punta del Este in April 1967.

NOTE ON STATISTICS

Throughout this study we have relied mainly on the statistical data used in the AID Congressional presentation in the spring of 1968. . . .

REVIEW OF THE GOALS

PER CAPITA GROWTH: CHARTER GOAL

To achieve in the participating Latin American countries a substantial and sustained growth of per capita income at a rate designed to attain, at the earliest possible date, levels of income capable of assuring self-sustaining development, and sufficient to make Latin American income levels constantly larger in relation to the levels of the more industrialized nations. . . . Similarly, presently existing differences in income levels among the Latin American countries will be reduced by accelerating the developmnt of the relatively less developed countries and granting them maximum priority in the distribution of resources and in international co-operation in general. . . .

It is recognized that, in order to reach these objectives within a reasonable time, the rate of economic growth in any country of Latin America should be not less than 2.5 per cent per capita per year. . . .

1. Analysis of the Goal

Among the few goals precisely quantified by the Latin American leaders in the Charter of Punta del Este was a minimum 2.5% annual increase in per capita GNP.

The slowdown in growth in many countries beginning in the latter half of the last decade and early 1960's vividly focused hemispheric attention on the need for extraordinary measures to strengthen their fragile economies. Failure to grow had many and varied root causes, with no two country situations being precisely alike. Not only were the policy and investment prescriptions different for each country, but so too, were the probable "development consequences" of attainment of this growth rate. The Charter framers recognized, of course, that the 2.5% growth target masked these very important country differences but assumed quite reasonably that meaningful and sustained development was more likely to occur in a bouyant setting of 2.5% annual growth than in one of lagging productivity. They took as their growth benchmark the rate attained by the region in the relatively prosperous early 1950's. At 2.5% per annum, per capita income would double in 28 years. At a lesser rate, for example 1½%, this would require 48 years. A slower rate would thus offer considerably less hope of relieving the massive poverty of the region. . . .

While a per capita GNP growth rate is a convenient yardstick against which to gauge development, it is a rough measure at best. It readily combines the effects of the growth of total national product and of population expansion. It also allows some limited inter-country comparisons, but masks or omits numerous other developmentally significant parameters. Also, there has been a tendency to use this short-hand index number as a measure of governmental effectiveness, such that perspicacity and vigor are uncritically attributed to governments of countries in which the rate is achieved, and incompetence or weakness to governments of countries which fail to obtain this magic number. This use of the index neglects the fact that many, if not most, of the forces which bear heavily upon GNP growth may simply not be within the immediate control of the government and that key development policies may not, on the other hand, be directly reflected in this index. Reasonable policies in such areas as investment incentives may be executed, for example, but still other factors such as adverse world prices for key export commodities may prevent the successful results sought. External factors, such as weather, and world market prices, have been very significant in affecting Latin American growth. Also, significant institutional reforms and the initiation of priority programs and investments may have little impact in the short run on per capita growth, but should make a substantial contribution to growth in the longer term. Further, as an "average," per capita growth masks the very uneven income distribution, the large gaps between rich and poor, and the disparities between urban and rural sectors, existing in many Alliance countries. . . .

Great care is also required in using

the per capita data for inter-country comparisons. Here comparisons are normally made in constant dollar terms, calculated at existing exchange rates. In reality, however, purchasing power within the many different economies in local currencies varies relative to the dollar in time, and from country to country. Thus, while perhaps a more useful index than most, levels of per capita income are not dependable indicators of relative real income among countries. Also, the short-term and artificial nature of the calendar year measuring period for national accounting often lumps together short-term fluctuations which distort or obscure important underlying trends. As a result, any single year-to-year change is apt to have little longer-run significance.

Despite these many limitations, GNP growth remains the most convenient tool to measure increases in total national production and through that the changes in the resources which each country has available over time for consumption, investment, and exports, on which both welfare and growth depend.

2. *Experience to Date*

Over the Alliance period, Latin America has averaged 4.5% growth per year of its total combined GNP. In comparison, the United States averaged 5.1% per annum over the same period, and the OECD countries, 4.3%. Among other less developed regions, South Asia (India, Pakistan, Ceylon) showed 4.2% average yearly growth and Africa showed 4.0%. On the other hand developing nations in East Asia (Taiwan, Thailand, Korea, Philippines, Malaysia) averaged 7.1% total GNP growth per year from 1961 to 1967. Such performance in part reflects the successful development efforts of Taiwan, Thailand, and Korea. Since per capita GNP is a function of both output and population, it becomes evident that Latin American nations, with populations increasing at some of the fastest rates in the world, must attain total growth rates of 5.5% and more—higher than the United States average—to attain the Alliance goals of 2.5% per capita. . . .

Turning to the specifics of the actual Alliance period and progress toward the per capita growth rate goal, the figure combining average performance of all 18 Republics over all Alliance years (1961–1967) is 1.5%. The actual significance of this figure, however, can be understood only in analyzing individual country growth rates. Seven countries surpassed the Alliance target, some by a substantial margin: Panama (4.7%), Bolivia (3.4%), Mexico (3.1%), Nicaragua (3.0%), El Salvador (2.9%), Peru and Costa Rica (both 2.6%). Those whose per capita growth rates exceeded the regional average (1.5%) but did not achieve the minimum target of 2.5% are: Chile (1.8%), Guatemala (1.7%), Ecuador (1.6%), and Venezuela (1.5%). In the low growth group fall Colombia (1.1%), Brazil (.9%), Honduras (.9%), Dominican Republic (.5%), Argentina (.4%), Paraguay (.2%), and Uruguay (−1.1%). With one exception, per capita income growth in these latter countries has fluctuated widely from year to year. Brazil's per capita growth rate, on the other hand, has been moving steadily upward from a low base since 1963 of −1.4% to 2.4% in 1967 and a projected 2.9% in 1968. Colombia's projected 1968 growth of 2.8% per capita moves it temporarily out of the low growth category too.

Although data is still preliminary,

the 1968 regional per capita growth rate will apparently come very close to the Alliance goal of 2.5%. Economic recoveries in Brazil, Argentina and Colombia as well as continued high growth in Mexico and Venezuela contribute to this achievement. A brief glance at the country groups will make evident a diversity of characteristics in respect to levels of industrialization, resource endowment, size of economy and population, relative amounts of external assistance, type of political system, level of per capita GNP, etc. Within each of the three groups, the countries combined and used the total resources available to them in varying unique ways. Bolivia's output per person in 1967 for example measured only $161, while Mexico's was $507. Yet the two countries grew at very much the same rates. . . .

INCOME DISTRIBUTION: CHARTER GOAL

To make the benefits of economic progress available to all citizens of all economic and social groups through a more equitable distribution of national income, raising more rapidly the income and standard of living of the needier sectors of the population, at the same time that a higher proportion of the national product is devoted to investment.

1. Analysis of the Goal

If the purpose of development is broadly viewed as being the attainment of a more adequate and ample income distribution this goal can be viewed as the paramount Alliance objective. In this sense the other charter objectives are means to this end.

The aim, as in the case of per capita income growth, was increased welfare for the economically disadvantaged. Greater income for the poor can come from either source. The two may be interrelated, however, in that measures to transfer income may reduce saving and investment by the higher income groups, increase the total of resources used for consumption, and reduce the rate of growth of output. The authors expressed their recognition of this problem by specifying that a higher proportion of the national product should also be devoted to investment. On the other hand, if conflict between growth and distribution policies can be avoided, it is clear that the higher the growth rate, the easier it may be, both economically and politically, to carry out policies with redistribution effects, since no groups need suffer an absolute decline in income.

Standards of living are affected not only by changes in levels of personal income in cash or kind, but by the availability, quality, and relative prices of goods available for personal consumption, and by the total environmental conditions under which people live, including the adequacy of public health and education facilities, social insurance, employment opportunities, and civil and political rights. There is no precise way to measure total economic welfare in this sense, or to compare the welfare of one group with that of another.

2. Experience to Date

While the developed countries of the world have statistical systems which turn out data relating the number of individuals or families in an economy with various levels of annual income, most Latin American countries have not collected this kind of information and none has collected it over time so as to permit measurement of change through the Alliance period. . . .

A UN Economic Commission for Latin America study issued in 1967 showed income structures of Argentina, Brazil, and Mexico that were remarkably similar with the top 10 per cent of the population receiving about 40 per cent of total income, and the bottom 40 per cent receiving 10 to 14 per cent. It seems likely that these basic proportions have changed little since the early 1960's.

Scattered data on wage rates in relation to prices (i.e., "real" wage rates) in various industries in various countries show increases, but there is no reliable way to separate any redistributive element from the positive influences of general income growth, special prosperity or union strength in specific industries, or the negative influences of anti-inflation programs, or unemployment, rural-to-urban migration and accompanying overcrowding of service trades. . . .

INDUSTRIALIZATION: CHARTER GOAL

To accelerate the process of rational industrialization so as to increase the productivity of the economy as a whole, taking full advantage of the talents and energies of both the private and public sectors, utilizing the natural resources of the country and providing productive and remunerative employment for unemployed or part-time workers. Within this process of industrialization, special attention should be given to the establishment and development of capital-goods industries.

1. Analysis of the Goal

Industrialization has long been a symbol of economic development, as well as a major instrument of produc-

tion and welfare as economies develop. The relation of industrialization to overall growth and development, however, is not a simple one. Many less developed countries have tended to promote industrial expansion while neglecting agriculture and education. In many cases, this leaves industry with an inadequate raw materials and human resource base for efficient production, while low output and income in other sectors restricts demand for industrial products.

Indicators of industrial growth, therefore, are only rough measures or outlines of what is happening in an economy. They give little indication of the desirability or efficiency of that expansion, or whether some of the capital spent on it might have been more productive if used for other purposes. Nevertheless, they remain valuable means of measuring the overall direction and rate of change of the structure of developing economies.

2. Experience to Date

INDUSTRIAL ACTIVITY. Reports on gross domestic product show that value added in manufacturing contributed a larger percentage of the gross domestic product and income in 1966 than it had in 1960 in 15 of 18 republics. For the region as a whole, manufacturing now contributes approximately one-fourth of the gross domestic product, with the second largest share, about one-fifth, coming from agriculture, forestry and fishing.

Those countries with the largest percentages of gross domestic product coming from factories are among those considered the most advanced of the region. They are, in order of the relative size of manufacturing production, Argentina, Brazil, Mexico, and Chile.

The greatest relative increases during the 1960–66 period were in Panama and El Salvador, in both of which the percentage derived from manufacturing increased by about one-fourth.

In the 12 countries for which figures are available on growth of output measured by value of end products, there was an average increase of forty percent between 1960 and 1966. Production more than doubled in Panama and El Salvador and increased by two-thirds in Peru and Mexico. The smallest increase reported was that of Uruguay, 9%, but even there the index of manufacturing had advanced to 12% above the level in 1963.

Another indication of industrial advance in Latin America is furnished by the reports on production of electric power. Output during the Alliance years in Latin America rose from 69 billion kilowatt hours in 1961 to 100 billion in 1966, with 106 billion estimated for 1967. The 45% increase from 1961 to 1966 was exceeded in 11 of the 18 countries. Output in Honduras doubled in the five years, and five other countries increased power production by 75% or more. Two-thirds of the power is produced in Brazil, Mexico and Argentina. The relative increases in these countries were: Brazil 34%, Mexico 62%, and Argentina 33%. . . .

AGRICULTURAL DEVELOPMENT: CHARTER GOAL

To raise greatly the level of agricultural productivity and output and to improve related storage, transportation, and marketing services.

1. Analysis of the Goal

This Alliance goal is not expressed in terms of the quantitative dimensions of contemplated growth or improvement, and accordingly is open to considerable flexibility of interpretation. Generality in the statement of the goal was appropriate in the face of the scope, diversity and complexity of agriculture sector problems, involving as they do so wide a variety of crops grown under so many different conditions, and encompassing not only production but a wide range of input commodities and services, supply and marketing institutions, and world market supply and demand conditions.

The indexes of agricultural production for the Latin American countries prepared by the U.S. Department of Agriculture illustrate certain of the difficulties of evaluating improvements in output. Over the 7 years from 1961 to 1968 the indexes for all but 2 countries rose markedly. It is, however, a trivial view of the goal which would deal only with gross output and not relate it to needs. Yet there is no simple way to relate production to needs, since country resource endowments are so varied, and countries can or should import and export widely differing proportions of their consumption and output. . . .

All things considered, the best general indicator of agricultural progress is the index of agricultural production per capita. A reasonable transition of the goal into a common measure would be raising the level of agricultural production at a pace greater than the growth of the population. Such a formulation would at least suggest the direction of movement of each country's ability to satisfy its needs.

2. Experience to Date

The index of agricultural production per capita over the period shows that despite the increases in total output attained, the output per head for the region as a whole did not increase appreciably over the period. However, the regional average conceals a rather wide range of individual country experiences from major increases to substantial declines. While use of single years as base and end of the period measure makes the result overly subject to the influence of especially good or bad crop years, the data for the Alliance period show 7 countries with increases of 5% or more in per capita production, 8 countries with declines of 5% or more and 3 with no significant change (i.e. less than 5%)....

AGRARIAN REFORM: CHARTER GOAL

To encourage, in accordance with the characteristics of each country, programs of comprehensive agrarian reform leading to the effective transformation, where required, of unjust structures and systems of land tenure and use, with a view to replacing latifundia and dwarf holdings by an equitable system of land tenure so that, with the help of timely and adequate credit, technical assistance and facilities for the marketing and distribution of products, the land will become for the man who works it the basis of his economic stability, the foundation of his increasing welfare, and the guarantee of his freedom and dignity.

1. Analysis of the Goal

Agriculture is the mainstay of Latin American economies, and over half of the population of the area lives in rural areas. Because of this and because of the highly uneven distribution of land, the problem of agrarian reform is one which has a direct relevance to the lives of a large percentage of the population.

Much of the best land is in the hands of a very few owners, while the great majority of the farm population is situated on plots too small to provide an adequate living. Recent studies have shown that sub-family farms (large enough to provide employment for less than 2 people) made up 43% of all farms in Argentina, 23% in Brazil, 37% in Chile, 64% in Colombia, 90% in Ecuador and 88% in Guatemala and Peru. It showed further that 60% of all farm laborers are landless in Brazil, 48% in Chile, 35% in Ecuador and 25% in Guatemala.

When non-farm employment opportunities are severely limited, control of land is also control of economic opportunity, and land ownership in Latin America is traditionally strongly related to social status and political power.

No goal of the Alliance for Progress, therefore, proposed more profound or difficult change than the one relating to land reform. The authors clearly were not proposing that land redistribution be pursued through violent revolution as in Bolivia and Mexico. That they were proposing peaceful and orderly change is reflected in their choice of words: "to encourage,... in accordance with the characteristics of each country, programs... leading to...effective transformation, where required." All the Latin American countries could be said to need improvements in land tenure, and use, and improved facilities to help the cultivator. The nature and seriousness of this need also varies widely from country to country, as does the political difficulty of agreeing on policies and programs, the technical and demographic limitations and possibilities, and the financial and administrative capacity to design and carry out programs.

These complexities also make it impossible to establish uniform benchmarks as to what each country needed to do, how much progress it should have been expected to make over a given period of time, or to measure against clear standards the value of such work as they have carried out. Also, while agrarian reform has been and will continue to be equated with expropriation and redistribution, and while such measures are necessary and possible, expropriation can generally be expected to be confined to unproductive or inadequately used properties, except under very unusual circumstances.

Expropriation and redistribution cannot by themselves solve major land tenure problems or alleviate rural misery. It is important that collateral reform measures not be neglected, particularly with regard to (1) more effective land taxation, (2) more equitable tenancy arrangements, (3) improved conditions for agricultural labor, and (4) provision of secure land titles. In particular situations, the correction of these conditions may obviate the need for expropriation, or may yield more effective results of broader significance.

The success of agrarian reform in improving the welfare of its beneficiaries is closely related to increases in productivity which require the availability of technical advice, adequate credit and improved marketing arrangements. Research, extension, credit and marketing institutions are not agrarian reform measures, but they are important complementary activities.

2. Experience to Date

Many of the countries (15) have enacted agrarian reform laws and established institutions to administer them. The laws covering agrarian reform generally provide for the expropriation of privately-owned lands (with compensation), distribution of public lands, and the provision to settlers of complementary production facilities, such as credit, seeds and technical assistance.

With the exception of Mexico, Bolivia, Chile and Venezuela, Latin American countries have been slow in expropriating privately-owned land for redistribution, and especially in the sub-division of large estates because of the basic political problems presented by such a program. Therefore, the countries have placed greater emphasis on the distribution of public lands through colonization programs, confirmation of title to squatters, and the provision of complementary production facilities to them and to other small farmers. Nevertheless, based on data received from the countries, almost a million Latin American families were settled or resettled during the period of 1960–1967. About half a million land titles were distributed, as were almost 40 million hectares of land. About half of this land was in Mexico, but other large distribution programs are found in Bolivia, Venezuela, Colombia and Chile.

Land tenure and distribution is not a very serious social problem in Paraguay, Costa Rica, or Uruguay. In these countries, the problems are those of underproductivity, with root causes in faulty market and distribution mechanisms and an administrative incapacity for effectively organizing needed, and complex investment and technical input programs which effectively reach the small farmers.

In these countries and in Brazil, Honduras, Guatemala, Nicaragua, Panama, and the Dominican Republic, relatively large amounts of land are available for new settlement, with the result that there is often less incentive to implement politically difficult land reform legislation and proposals. For example, in Guatemala less than 50% of the arable land of the country has ever been farmed and is available for settling. Likewise, with minimum inputs of capital—a simple plow, a machete and labor—10% of the land presently unused in the western 2/3 of Brazil can economically be brought under cultivation, and with more substantial inputs—seed, fertilizers, etc.— about 50% can. The substantial recent increases in agricultural productivity in Brazil, in fact, largely reflect a process of bringing new land under cultivation.

Therefore, concentration has been placed in these countries on indirect measures encouraging better land use such as cadastral surveys, studies to explore the percentage of presently unused land which can be economically brought under production, land tenure tax changes to reduce the attractiveness of holding large areas of idle land, and opening credit facilities for new settlers in areas of spontaneous colonization.

In these countries and in others of the hemisphere, the number of extension agents almost tripled during these years, thereby reducing the average amount of arable land and land in permanent crops from about 37,000 hectares per agent to about 12,000. Agricultural credit increased considerably, and almost 11 million loans were granted since 1960, with about two million farmers in Latin America receiving loans in 1967. While this growth in credit represents substantial progress—particularly insofar as the numbers themselves do not readily suggest the considerable new institutional capacity which has been created—and

which can now be built upon for fanning credit out into the sector, the remaining needs are still immense. An estimated 10 to 14 million families in Latin America remain to be settled or resettled. This figure is increasing faster than the current rate of resettlement. At an average cost of $1000 per family, close to $15 billion in agricultural credit would be needed now for agrarian reform purposes—a sum approaching total annual gross investment for the entire region.

Programs of varying magnitudes are thus underway in most countries to improve cultivator security, improve resource use, and bring improved income and welfare to the recipients. Nevertheless, actual redistribution of underutilized large estates has been slow and, particularly in the Andean region, the number of landless families added to rural society each year far out-strips the number of families benefitted. Consequently, small plots tend to be subdivided because of population pressures, inheritance, and the lack of alternative employment opportunities for rural people. Latin America is far from accomplishing comprehensive agrarian reform, and with some exceptions such as Mexico, Venezuela, and Chile, has not yet effectively tackled this major issue. . . .

EDUCATION: CHARTER GOAL

To eliminate adult illiteracy and by 1970 to assure, as a minimum, access to six years of primary education for each school-age child in Latin America; to modernize and expand vocational, technical, secondary and higher educational and training facilities, to strengthen the capacity for basic and applied research; and to provide the competent personnel required in rapidly-growing societies.

1. Analysis of the Goal

Two of the education goals of the Alliance for Progress are very closely interlinked. One is to eliminate adult illiteracy, and the other to attain, as a minimum, access to six years of primary education for each school-age child. If in fact the second goal is realized, the first will also be attained, albeit somewhat later, through the process of population aging and the addition of annual quotas of 15-year-olds who have had more recent and better educational opportunities and are more literate than their elders. This is precisely what has happened in the United States where, for some years now, it has no longer been necessary to even try to count the number of illiterates.

Primary education needs can be measured from available data by comparing enrollment of school-age children with the total numbers of school-age children in the population. This apparently straightforward index, however, must be used cautiously since enrollment per se cannot be taken to mean that all children recorded as attending school actually attend classes, or that the quality of education was adequate. Because of poor attendance and the quality of teaching, many, particularly in rural areas, enroll for many years without learning to read and write. Also, only a very small percentage of those enrolled graduate from primary school (11%) and only 7% of the population 15–24 years of age has entered secondary school.

2. Experience to Date

ILLITERACY. Statistical data on illiteracy in Latin America are in many cases inadequate, inaccurate, or not comparable from country to country. These statistics come from censuses and household sample surveys and represent responses to a question as to whether the person can read and write. To measure what progress has been made in reducing illiteracy requires at least two observations, one of which should be a recent date. The only Latin American country for which such a pair of observations is available is Venezuela, where the number of illiterates declined by 97,000 or 7 percent in a 6½ year period ending August 1967. During the same period, the adult population aged 15 years and over increased by 11 percent. The joint effect of these two factors was a reduction in the adult illiteracy rate from 34.2 percent to 26.0 percent, or about one-fourth in 6½ years.

For the other countries of Latin America, where an apt pair of observations is not available, it is still possible to perceive illiteracy trends indirectly by calculating the effects of removing from the adult population those who will die and adding back those who will each year reach the fifteenth birthday, associating with each group its attained literacy proportion at a not-too-far-in-the-past census. This requires but a single observation, and as all Latin American countries but Bolivia have had a census since 1960, it may be done readily. The process may be illustrated for Guatemala, which, according to the census of 1964 had an adult population 15 years old or older of 2,271,000, of whom 1,411,000 were illiterate. The adult illiteracy rate was 62.1 percent. If, by 1979 or 15 years after the 1964 census, there is no enlargement of primary school educational opportunities, the adult population will be augmented by successive annual waves of persons reaching their fifteenth birthday and the proportion of each wave which is illiterate will be about the same as the proportion of illiterate 13-year-old persons in 1964, namely, 51 percent. The removal from the population by death of persons 15 years old and older in 1964 will bring the total number of adult illiterates to 2,039,000, and the adult illiteracy rate should fall to about 55.8 percent. In other words, the adult population will increase by 1,384,000 or 61 percent, the number of illiterates will rise by 628,000 or 44 percent, but the rate of adult illiteracy will fall to about 55.8 percent or by about one-tenth. As more years pass the rate of adult illiteracy will continue to drift downward towards the 51 percent level.

If, however, there is an expansion of primary education sufficient to give virtually all children 6 years of schooling before the fifteenth birthday, adult illiteracy will decline far more rapidly. Should this come about by 1970, as stated in the educational goals of the Alliance for Progress, the number of adult illiterates would be about 10 percent smaller in 1979 than in 1964 despite the great growth in total adult population, and the adult illiteracy rate would be about 37 percent or about three-fifths as great as in 1964. Moreover, adult illiteracy would be concentrated among people over 30 years old, with virtually none among younger adults. The attrition of death would thereafter move the illiteracy rate inexorably toward zero.

PRIMARY EDUCATION. The enrollment of school-age children in primary schools increased by about 50% during the years 1960 through 1967 from 24 million to 36 million. Despite their limitations the data show great expansion in school facilities. During the Alliance years, school enrollment increased an average of 6 percent annually, while the population of children of primary school (5–14) increased by 3 per-

cent annually. As a result the percentage of the children not enrolled in school declined from 52 to 43 percent over this period. However, because of rapid population growth, there remained over 27 million children not registered in primary school, or 740,000 *more* than in 1960. . . .

It is expected that there will be about 69 million children of primary school-age in 1970. This is almost twice the number enrolled in school in 1967. If the present trend of 6% increase in school enrollment annually were to continue, enrollment would not reach the level of 69 million children until 1979. By that time, of course, the school-age population would be well above that level, or about 92 million, so there would still be 23 million children not enrolled in school. Not until 1986 would the entire school-age population be enrolled, if present rates of population growth and school expansion continue.

While school enrollment obviously needs to be augmented at a faster pace to meet the target in a shorter span of years, it is clear that there is no chance of getting all the children into schools by 1970. To provide schooling for 69 million children at the present rate of 31 children per teacher, would require 3.2 million primary teachers. Since Latin America now has 1.2 million teachers, it would have to train or recruit 2 million more, compared with 136,000 now graduating annually, only about two-thirds of that number actually joining the teaching force. Similarly, almost three times as many classrooms would be needed.

. . .Although the goal of primary education for all Latin Americans cannot be reached by 1970, if the rate of improvement can be increased, the objective may come within grasp during the decade of the seventies. If the current rate of increases in school enrollment were to be stepped up from 6 to 9 percent per year, the entire expected school-age population of 85 million would be enrolled in school in 1977.

SECONDARY AND HIGHER EDUCATION. ...Clearly, secondary, vocational secondary, and higher education facilities have expanded under the Alliance. In 1960 there were 2.7 million students enrolled in secondary and higher schools, constituting 7% of the population between 15 and 24 years of age. By 1967 this had more than doubled, reaching a level of 5.8 million students, or 13% of the population. Enrollment has increased in all 18 Latin American republics, and the percent of the population enrolled has doubled or more in Nicaragua, Peru, El Salvador, Bolivia, Colombia and Guatemala.

Considerable improvement, though less than in the first group, is indicated by the rise in the percent of the population attending in the following countries: Brazil, Costa Rica, Dominican Republic, Ecuador and Mexico. The remaining countries showed slight improvement. ...

GOVERNMENT EXPENDITURES. In real terms, the 18 Latin American republics increased their expenditures on education by nearly 62% between 1961 and 1967. Increases occurred in every country, ranging from 20% to over 200%. Education rose from 9.3% of total central government expenditures for the region in 1961 to 13.3% in 1967, reflecting similar increases in twelve countries. During 1967, thirteen countries devoted more than 15% of their central government expenditures to education; only five countries reported that education represented a smaller percentage of their total expenditures than it had in 1961. These expenditure data omit those by state and local governments, which, in some countries, including Brazil, provide much of the financing. ...

HEALTH: CHARTER GOAL

To increase life expectancy at birth by a minimum of five years, and to increase the ability to learn and produce, by improving individual and public health. To attain this goal it will be necessary, among other measures, to provide adequate potable water supply and sewage disposal to not less than 70 per cent of the urban and 50 per cent of the rural population; to reduce the present mortality rate of children less than five years of age by at least one-half; to control the more serious communicable diseases, according to their importance as a cause of sickness, disability, and death; to eradicate those illnesses, especially malaria, for which effective techniques are known; to improve nutrition; to train medical and health personnel to meet at least minimum requirements; to improve basic health services at national and local levels; and to intensify scientific research and apply its results more fully and effectively to the prevention and cure of illness.

1. Analysis of the Goal

...The data necessary for the measurement of life expectancy at birth are far from satisfactory. Life expectancy is calculated from age distributions of the number of deaths in the population. Death registration, however, is incomplete in many countries, and even in countries which have relatively good registration, there are large, particularly rural, areas for which registration is poor. In addition, data are often deficient for infants, many of whom are born and die without any legal registration being made of their existence. Under-registration of deaths results in the calculation of low death rates, which produce an exaggerated life expectancy. Without special and costly surveys, it is not possible to gauge the extent of under-registration. However, for our purpose of comparing death rates over a period of years from 1960, observation of statistical practices indicates that registration in Latin America has improved. Therefore, increases observed in life expectancy may safely be assumed to be conservatively stated, rather than exaggerated.

The second goal, which speaks of improving individual and public health, further lists several measures which can help to produce such improvement. Progress towards attaining these subgoals is measurable, although accurate appropriate statistics may not always be obtainable. . . .

2. Experience to Date

INCREASED LIFE EXPECTANCY. Although detailed and up-to-date information on changes in the expectation of life in Latin America since 1960 is scarce, the Pan American Health Organization has been able to estimate that the average future life span increased from 60.2 years to 62.5 years between 1960 and 1966. This represents a gain of 2.3 years in the expectation of life. Had there been a uniform annual increase in expectation of life sufficient to add 5 years to the average life span during the decade beginning in 1960, the increase by 1966 would have amounted to 3 years. Thus, the PAHO estimates indicate that during 1960 to 1966, the average life span increase was about three-quarters of the increase which would have occurred had the

progress contemplated by the Alliance goal been attained.

Specific data are available for a very few countries. In Mexico and Chile the estimated improvement in life expectation was 3.2 and 3.0 years, respectively, and if improvement continues at the same pace, these countries will each have a 5-year increase in average life span during the decade. The improvement in El Salvador is reported by PAHO as 2.1 years between 1960 and 1966, so that at the same rate through the decade, the extension of the average life span there will reach only about 3.5 years.

The increase reported by PAHO for Venezuela was only 0.2 years during the first 6 years of the decade. However, the goal of the Alliance to increase life expectancy by 5 years between 1961 and 1971 is not so urgent for countries which start from higher levels of life expectancy than for those with lower levels to begin with. Thus, an improvement of a fraction of a year in life expectancy for Venezuela, which by 1960 had already attained a level of over 62 years, would be perhaps as satisfactory an accomplishment as a gain of 3 years in Chile where life expectation was only 56 years in 1960.

Progress in increasing life expectancy depends largely on the success of another general goal of the Charter, to reduce childhood mŏrtality by 50 per cent. For Latin America as a whole, PAHO estimates that 1.0 of the 2.3 years gained, or 43%, resulted from the reduction in child mortality. Deaths of children under 5 account for 44% of all deaths in Latin America. The goal is to reduce these deaths by one-half in the decade ending in 1971; this implies reducing them by one-fourth by 1966. Infant mortality decreased by only 12 percent, or less than half this goal during the first five years. Deaths of children in the 1–4 year age group, however, have decreased rapidly, approaching the goal of the Charter. Over 90% of the decrease required for half the decade was achieved in South America, and two-thirds of the desired decrease was attained in Middle America.

POTABLE WATER SUPPLY. A leading cause of the death of children in Latin America is gastroenteritis. These deaths are preventable and to a large extent can be controlled by a sufficient supply of potable water and cleanliness.

Remarkable success has been made toward achieving the goal of supplying potable water for 70% of the urban population by 1971. Only 60% of the group had water service in 1960; this had increased to 69% by 1967. Attainment of the goal of 70% can be expected before 1971.

The goal for the rural population provides for potable water for at least 50% of the population by 1971; an intermediate goal would be 25% by 1966. However, only 19 million rural people have potable water out of an estimated 1971 rural population of 128 million. An additional 45 million must be provided to reach the 1971 goal. Present plans, limited primarily by cost factors, do not include provision for programs likely to achieve coverage of more than 10 million in that time.

SEWERAGE. There has been less progress towards reaching the goals for sewerage than for water supplies. In 1967 only 48 million persons, or 36% of the population, were provided sewerage services, leaving some 62 million to be provided for.

COMMUNICABLE DISEASES. There has been moderate success in pursuing the goals of controlling the more serious communicable diseases and eradicating those for which effective techniques are known. During the decade ending 1966, death rates from these causes declined by 48% in Middle America and 22% in South America. However, the 1966 death rates were 91.2 and 74.7 per 100,000 population in the two regions, about ten times greater than the rate in Northern America. . . .

NUTRITION. The importance of improving nutrition in Latin America is underscored by a recent study of child mortality indicating that nutritional deficiency as an underlying cause or an associated cause of death is responsible for a high proportion of the deaths of young children. Total food production in Latin America, although it has risen by 37% over the 1957–59 level, has just about kept pace with population growth during those years. According to calorie requirements estimates by FAO, only 5 of the 15 countries for which data are available have food calorie supplies above their average daily requirements. The situation is further complicated by uneven distribution of food and purchasing power within the countries.

Efforts have been made to increase the supply of protein, particularly for young children, by developing protein-rich food in the laboratory. Some success has been achieved by the production of such products as Incaparina in Guatemala and Colombia. Over 5 million pounds were produced in 1967. Other products make use of fish flour and soya. . . .

HEALTH PERSONNEL. There are marked differences in the availability of trained health personnel from one country to the next, with striking deficiencies in the rural areas in nearly every country for which data are available. . . .

In 1966 there were about 148,000 physicians in Latin America, or 6.0

for each 10,000 persons; in Northern America the ratio was 15.2 per 10,000. There was considerable variety among the countries of Latin America, from 16.4 per 10,000 in Argentina to 0.7 per 10,000 in Haiti. Only four countries had more than the average of 6.0: Argentina, Cuba, Uruguay and Venezuela.

Between 1960 and 1966, the number of physicians in Latin America increased by 30% compared with a population growth of about 19%. . . .

Growth in the number of physicians has been felt largely in the capital city or large urban areas. . . .

Low-Cost Housing: Charter Goal

To increase the construction of low-cost houses for low-income families in order to replace inadequate and deficient housing and to reduce housing shortages; and to provide necessary public services to both urban and rural centers of population.

1. Analysis of the Goal

The goal of adequate housing for all is obviously desirable, but realistically one which cannot be soon realized. The total need for housing in Latin America has been estimated as being between 15 and 20 million units. This deficit is increasing by at least one million units a year. Squatter settlements continue to mushroom. Given higher priority needs for the use of scarce internal and external resources, the countries of Latin America will not be able to meet the housing need in the foreseeable future. Economic development priorities will not in any country result in substantially larger resource allocations for housing.

The greatest need for housing is for low-income families. Unfortunately, persons in this income category can make little or no contribution to the cost of their housing, and generally require some form of public subsidy. This raises the hard economic question of the feasibility and desirability of allocating large amounts of capital to low rent housing.

2. Experience to Date

Since the inception of the Alliance, every Latin American country has created or strengthened a national housing agency charged with responsibility for providing low cost housing. All have received financial assistance from IDB or A.I.D., or both. Prior to the Alliance, those agencies already in existence produced a limited amount of housing, and this was confined almost exclusively to middle rather than lower income housing. Loans made to these agencies for low cost housing under the Alliance required matching budgetary contributions and focused some attention on low income housing needs. However, the experience with low-income housing has not been satisfactory. There remains strong resistance by national institutions to minimum standards and aided self-help, and a tendency to favor middle income housing, where demand is both strong, and unlike low-income housing, effective in terms of financial capacity.

As a matter of policy, both A.I.D. and IDB have made loans for sale of housing only, and have required that the loans be made on a self-liquidating basis. This requirement has limited the reach of externally financed efforts, since cost factors tend to make the imposition of economically required payments schedules unrealistic.

What has been accomplished to date by such external assistance has been the creation of intermediate credit institutions, such as savings and loan banks, whose experience may one day point to ways to accumulate savings to finance middle-income housing. Such financing is clearly needed, but it is not the answer to the growing slums and to the crowding of poor people into shack-towns in the cities and huts in the countryside.

Recognizing this, Brazil and Peru, whose urban slums are among the worst in the hemisphere, have begun programs for upgrading the housing in the favelas and barrios. These programs assume that tearing down large slum areas is too disruptive for the people and too expensive for the society and that some other means must be found to create acceptable living conditions for the slumdweller. But slum rehabilitation is a slow process, and far-reaching progress will no doubt turn largely upon improved economic opportunity, more than upon subsidized physical construction, community organization and planning efforts.

3. Conclusion

Latin America's housing problems will be solved only when most families are in position to demand decent housing because they can afford it. But that condition presupposes enormous economic development strides forward. At the same time, intensive efforts to reduce costs through the development of new construction techniques and material, community self-help techniques, and the elaboration of new financing approaches and methods should be intensified. Breakthrough in all or any of these areas can meaningfully advance the time frame within which the hemispheric housing need can be met.

STABILIZATION: CHARTER GOAL

To maintain stable price levels, avoiding inflation or deflation and the consequent social hardships and maldistribution of resources, always bearing in mind the necessity of maintaining an adequate rate of economic growth....

1. Analysis of the Goal

Inflation has been a prominent feature of the Latin American economic landscape.

Among economists concerned with Latin America's development, far from any clear-cut consensus, there are strongly contending schools of thought. The position taken in the Charter of Punta del Este reflects the notion that extreme price instability results not only in an unfair allocation of burdens, but inevitably retards progress through inadequate stimulus and mechanisms for savings, inefficient allocating incentives for investment, and the almost inevitable concomitant of unsettling political side effects. There is similar diversity of opinion about the causes of inflation—in somewhat capsule form:

1) The "structuralist" view, that inflation is caused by inelastic supply conditions, especially in agriculture. Attempts to expand the economy run up the prices of various kinds of commodities and services instead of calling forth additional output. The money supply then has to be increased proportionately to prevent unemployment and recession. This view is sometimes accompanied by a rather fatalistic view of politics—that public policy can't or at least doesn't respond with measures adequate to solve the underlying "structural" problems.

2) The "monetarist" view that inflation is caused by printing too much money. In its most simplified form, this view may be accompanied by the attitude that any inflation is bad and should be stopped at virtually any cost. In response to the structuralists, a

member of this school might argue that most of the "structural" obstacles to growth with price stability are the results of past, present, or expected future inflation, even though these obstacles themselves may in turn magnify inflationary forces further.

3) The "eclectic-pragmatic" view that inflation comes (a) partly from external demand pulls; (b) partly from the cost-push factors that operate everywhere (labor unions, rising land values, rising pay for services not counteracted by productivity improvements) (c) but, in Latin America, mostly from budget deficits financed by excessive money and credit creation. The budget deficits themselves result from different circumstancs in different countries, but almost all follow the pattern of political demand and legislative appropriation of funds for public services at a level which cannot be financed by non-inflationary revenues because of (i) lack of political consensus on who would pay the taxes; (ii) which in turn results in toleration of country revenue administrations' inability to collect even the taxes levied; (iii) which results in inflationary financing that is accepted as the lesser evil, or perhaps the inevitable result of the political process, depending on the vantage point of participant or observer.

The political push for expanded public expenditures both for direct welfare programs and capital investment tends to make the fiscal problem worse. As the data show, many countries feel the political pressure to lift development expenditure whether or not the "rising expectations" are generated by public awareness of Alliance goals, or underprivileged groups seeking a greater share of the national income. The availability of external financing on concessional terms for development projects may make it still harder to resist the pressure to spend before revenue is in sight. This promotes a race between the need to spend additional internal resources without inflation.

A.I.D. and multilateral agencies furnishing assistance to the hemisphere, such as the IMF and IBRD, have subscribed to various views at different times for different countries, recognizing essentially that the origin and significance of, and prescriptions for containing, inflation vary widely according to differing countries' circumstances at various points in time. The validity of the goal—containing inflation while maintaining respectable growth—is not in doubt. There inevitably is often great uncertainty about the level of inflation which can be tolerated, and the appropriate policy prescription to be applied at any time.

The economics of disinflation is not very well elaborated, either as science or the art of public policy-making. Some of the more successful stabilizations in Europe included at least temporary recession and sometimes substantial unemployment for extended periods of time. Other cases, such as Greece and Austria, suggest that all-at-once adjustments can effectively stop the inflation cycle. The recent Latin American approach of trying to cut the rate of price increase from, for example, 40% a year to 10% over three years without causing unemployment represents a compromise method seeking a practical solution.

Even if the executive authorities in the Latin American countries have full power to choose apt policies, their tools are not always up the task. Central control mechanisms for money and credit tend to be weak. However, the foremost problem is the weakness of tax systems and collection machinery.

Under these circumstances, when a government starts a stabilization program, it may find it cannot raise enough revenue or cut its expenditures enough to balance its budget. It therefore often seeks to reduce the flow of credit to the private sector. The credit reduction may succeed in depressing activity but not in halting the buildup of excess liquidity enough to prevent a continued rise of the price level.

2. Experience to Date

Nine countries in Latin America—Venezuela, Nicaragua, Panama, Paraguay, Mexico, Honduras, Guatemala, El Salvador and Costa Rica—have experienced relative price stability over the Alliance years, with less than 18% inflation, or less than 3% per year.

A second group including Bolivia, the Dominican Republic, and Ecuador experienced mild inflationary pressures over the period, up to 36% increase in prices, less than 6% a year.

A third group—Uruguay, Peru, Colombia, Chile, Brazil and Argentina were plagued by strong inflationary pressures which, in our view, weakened growth performance and ability to focus on long range development problems in each of these countries. Inflationary increases in these countries ranged from 95% in Peru to 1300% in Brazil over the period.

Because of the relative ease with which governments can increase expenditures and the corresponding difficulty of raising more revenue, one could have reasonably expected that an upswing in public expenditure in the Alliance period would have produced more inflation than actually has occurred. Yet, as a result of often very adroit programs, which in many countries have been influenced by the requirements of A.I.D. and other inter-

national lenders, the inflationary results have not been evident or have been dampened.

Most Latin American countries have managed to keep a reasonable degree of price stability. The major unsolved problems lie mostly in Brazil, Chile and Colombia, where price stabilization efforts have been made, but where stabilization is yet precarious. Even of this group of countries with hard-core problems, those which have received substantial support through A.I.D. in the form of program loans, have made basic progress in closing their budget deficits. Brazil ran a deficit equal to over 40% of its total budget through 1964, but by 1967 this figure had been reduced to 12%. Colombia and Chile, in somewhat less critical situation than Brazil (their revenues nearly always more than equalled current expenditures), both experienced declining deficits during the Alliance period. Colombia's deficit averaged over 30% of its total budget in the early Alliance years (1961–63) but dropped to around 15% on the average from 1964 on. Chile's deficit began to drop significantly after 1965, to less than 5% of total expenditures by 1967.

3. Conclusion

For the governments of the less stable countries, stabilization programs pose disconcerting dilemmas. The experience of Argentina and Brazil shows that stabilization through monetary austerity measures can produce painful business recessions, loss in real income to large segments of the population, particularly labor, and risky political consequences, without widely-felt benefits to the economy or political stability through stimulation of growth and development. On the other hand, without stabilization, inflation can clearly frustrate prospects for growth. Keeping the goal in clear focus, the question for the coming few years is whether these countries can thread their way successfully through the dilemmas by keeping inflation within tolerable bounds.

Several points give ground for optimism that countries will successfully control inflation. First, governments of the still inflationary countries show signs of genuine belief that inflation interferes with progress, and of determination to find some way to solve their problems. Secondly, partly under the stimulus of program loans and partly under their own initiative, Brazil, Chile and Colombia have started basic tax reform programs that will give them the means to close their deficits. Brazil and Chile have also made good progress at rationalizing public control of their banking systems. . . .

Government Revenues

1. Analysis of Revenue Performance

The Charter's call for tax reform aimed at improvements in (i) the countries' ability to collect levels of revenue adequate to support the various public development programs needed to reach other Alliance goals; (ii) the equity of the tax systems in order to improve income distribution; and (iii) the effectiveness of the tax systems as instruments to promote growth and development.

A major question is what to measure. Our standardized data are for central government tax and total revenues. However, many countries have state and local government revenues and also substantial social insurance collections. . . . Some countries (e.g., Chile) are highly centralized, while in others (e.g., Brazil, Argentina, Mexico), the regional and local governments have considerable taxing and revenue powers which are not reflected in central government figures.

Probably the best single yardstick that allows for some quantification of country performance in this field is the revenue or tax burden, namely that portion of total income collected by government, usually calculated as total revenue or taxes as a percent of GNP. This measure gives some idea of the government's willingness to tap domestic sources to finance public efforts in development. Another way of measuring revenue effort or tax system effectiveness is to calculate that portion of additional, or incremental, income (GNP) that goes to the government each year. Both measures are used here.

The numerical indicators by themselves, however, cannot provide an evaluation of country self-help in this field. The adequacy of revenues depends partly on the needs for public funds to finance development expenditure. Needed expenditure depends on the nature and severity of the country's problems, and the extent to which the country must rely on government activity and financing.

2. Experience to Date

Central Government Taxes as a Percent of GNP. Available data show that thirteen of the sixteen countries had increased their ratio of taxes to GNP (tax burden ratio of central government revenues) in 1967 compared with 1961 data. Chile, Colombia, Ecuador and Honduras increased their tax share of total income more than 25% between these years. On the other hand, in 1967, the Dominican Republic, El Salvador, Uruguay, and Venezuela all collected a lower portion of income in taxes than they did in 1961. In Argentina, the ratio in 1967 had just recovered to 1961 levels, after declining to a 1964 low.

By 1967, central governments were collecting 12.2% of total income in taxes, a substantial increase considering that the ratio had fluctuated between 11.1% and 11.5% through 1965. Recent efforts to improve tax administration and collection and to reform tax structure have helped achieve this increase. Venezuela and Chile collect the largest percent of GNP in taxes, 21% and 20.5% respectively. Mexico has consistently collected the smallest percentage.

TOTAL CENTRAL GOVERNMENT DOMESTIC REVENUES AS A PERCENT OF GNP. Central Governments have sources of revenues other than taxes, of course. State-run enterprises are one example. Thus, total domestic revenues, tax and non-tax, provide a clearer picture of government income than taxes alone, particularly because some Latin American countries receive as much as 20% of their revenues from non-tax sources.

In Latin America, the central governments collected 13.6% of total income in 1967, 12.2% of it in taxes. Considering the ratio of annual increases in revenues to annual increases in GNP, as another means of evaluating the trends, we find that Chile far surpasses other governments in tapping new revenue sources—with an average revenue gain equal to 44% of the GNP increase. Ecuador's ratio, 34%, is also high. The average of this "incremental" ratio for the region is 14.5%. . . .

REVENUES OF ALL LEVELS OF GOVERN-MENT. The measure of revenue that includes revenues of the central government, extrabudgetary agencies, regional and local governments, and social insurance agencies gives the best picture of all public resources. Available data show that, in 1965, five countries had revenues from all levels greater than 20% of GNP. Chile (26%) and Venezuela (23%) were again in this high group, but were topped by Brazil (30.4%) with its more federalized system of government. Mexico and Guatemala show lowest percentages (total revenues of 10.4% and 10.7% of GNP, respectively).

3. Conclusion

It is apparent that most countries have begun to make their revenue systems into effective and adequate tools for development and income distribution, and that most of Latin America must yet continue to give tax laws and other revenue-related issues specific attention. Further, reform laws that are legislated need to be effectively enforced. Almost every government has received technical assistance in tax administration and collection, and improved collections are beginning to show. But the most critical process—that of changing public attitudes toward taxation—remains a slow one. Ultimately, these attitudes turn upon both the fairness and thoroughness with which the tax laws are administered and upon public confidence in how well and wisely the government will expend revenues it has collected. Public confidence in the probity and efficiency of government is not high in most of Latin America. . . .

28

On Planning,
Existing Forms and Levels of Aid,
and the "Mix" Between
Bilateral and Multilateral Programs:
Additional Excerpts from
Congressional Hearings

Sections I and II from House, Committee on Foreign Affairs, Subcommittee on Inter-American Affairs, Hearings (February-May 1969), *New Directions for the 1970's: Toward a Strategy of Inter-American Development,* Ninety-First Congress, First Session, Committee Print (Washington: U.S. Government Printing Office, 1969), pp. 38–42, 49–54, 66, 81–82, 44–46, 78–79, 83–89. Section III from Senate, Committee on Foreign Relations, Subcommittee on Western Hemisphere Affairs, Hearings (June 24 and July 8, 1969), *United States Military Policies and Programs in Latin America,* Ninety-First Congress, First Session, Committee Print (Washington: U.S. Government Printing Office, 1969), pp. 33–35, 38, 51–53.

One of the early features of the Alliance was the Kennedy Administration's acceptance of the idea of national planning, which ECLA economists had long advocated, to the chagrin of many Eisenhower policy–makers who regarded planning as a "socialistic" device. At the outset of the Alliance, the Latin American countries were each to draft a ten-year national plan for submission to ad hoc committees composed of an equal number of OAS Panel of Nine experts (the "Nine Wise Men") and outside experts.[1] Upon approval, these plans were to serve as a basis for allocating aid from numerous public and private, national and international sources. However, only a handful of countries actually drafted acceptable long-term plans, and over the years even these have proved to be of questionable value, insofar as national performance has rarely met expectations.

In any event, when so few Latin American plans were forthcoming, the Alliance lost most of the limited inter-American character it had had initially. The Panel of Nine had virtually no control over aid, and the

---

[1] See Raúl Sáez S., "The Nine Wise Men and the Alliance for Progress," *International Organization,* XXII, No. 1 (Winter 1968), pp. 244–269.

biannual meetings of the Inter-American Economic and Social Council (IA–ECOSOC) were obviously unable to exercise meaningful supervision. In 1963 the IA-ECOSOC accepted the principal recommendation advanced in independent reports by former presidents Kubitschek of Brazil and Lleras Camargo of Colombia, to create an Inter-American Committee of the Alliance for Progress (CIAP). Ironically, CIAP as it emerged closely resembled the framework for the Alliance that had originally been proposed by the United States. Washington reasoned that Latin Americans would find pronouncements from a multilateral institution which they dominated more acceptable than those emanating from AID. But in 1961 a clear majority of Latin American governments had opted instead for the Panel of Nine approach, preferring to continue their fundamentally bilateral aid relationships with the United States to a more highly multilateralized program. Two years later, with the Alliance rapidly losing momentum, they reconsidered.

CIAP is a "political" body whose membership (increased from seven to ten in June, 1969) is selected in the same fashion as the Executive Directors of the Inter-American Development Bank (IDB). This system of weighted voting proportionate to states' capital subscriptions to the IDB assures that one member is always a North American. CIAP's formal task is to set development "priorities" in the hemisphere through an annual review of regional and national development plans and progress. The IA-ECOSOC initially envisaged that the Panel of Nine would remain in existence for the purpose of rendering "technical" advice to CIAP. In fact, the Nine Wise Men soon resigned en masse, *protesting that political rather than sound development considerations now predominated; and the Panel of Nine was officially abolished in 1966.*

CIAP has proceeded to set "guidelines" for development assistance, and its role has been enhanced by a provision which the U.S. Congress has attached to foreign assistance legislation since 1966, to the effect that U.S. aid must be consistent with CIAP's recommendations. On the other hand, CIAP is still something less than the multilateral master of the Alliance, in part because it customarily frames its recommendations in very general terms. There is a perhaps inescapable tendency in an organ of this kind to avoid as far as possible public criticism of the performance of specific Latin American governments. Moreover, CIAP suffers somewhat in comparison with AID, the World Bank (IBRD), and the IMF, both with respect to the size and professional competence of its staff and in the amount of time that it is able to devote to country reviews (a matter of days, rather than the several weeks set aside by other institutions).

Responding to recommendations made by Governor Rockefeller and a White House Task force headed by former Bank of America chairman, Rudolf A. Peterson (now chairman of the President's new Council on International Economic Policy), the Nixon Administration has announced several changes in U.S. aid programs and (as this book went to press) has proposed still others.

Rockefeller urged, among other things: continued bilateral aid emphasizing program loans; the removal of existing Congressional restrictions on U.S. aid, except for the provision making it subject to CIAP guidelines; the complete elimination of the concept of "additionality," under which Latin American governments have recently been allowed to use AID monies only for the purchase of specified U.S. goods, a list that has excluded most traditional U.S. exports to Latin America; the freeing of U.S. aid to be spent by recipients anywhere in the Western Hemisphere; and a "generous rescheduling" of Latin American debts, coupled with the creation of a special fund representing Latin American contributions in local currencies equivalent to dollar repayments postponed. The latter recommendation was directed to the growing problem of a number of Latin American countries' building up a burdensome external debt with a minimum of economic and social progress to show for the money already expended.

Mention of some of Rockefeller's proposals for reorganizing and renaming various U.S. and inter-American institutions is also in order: He suggested creating a Secretary of Western Hemisphere Affairs (with two Under Secretaries and three Assistant Secretaries) in the Department of State. More significant for our purposes here, he proposed abolishing AID and establishing a new Economic and Social Development Agency in the Executive Office of the President. In his scheme, a government corporation under the Agency, the Institute of Western Hemisphere Affairs, would administer government-to-government economic and social programs in the Western Hemisphere—with a clearance procedure involving the Secretary of Western Hemisphere Affairs and the U.S. Ambassador in the countries involved. CIAP would be renamed the Western Hemisphere Development Committee.

President Nixon has expressed his administration's general agreement with a number of Rockefeller's recommendations. He has eliminated the additionality provision entirely and has "untied" aid dollars for expenditure anywhere in the Western Hemisphere. (We should note, though, that Latin Americans still cannot use U.S. aid for the purchase of often less expensive goods in Europe and Japan.) In addition, the United States, acting in conjunction with CIAP, is asking other national and international creditors to help study the debt-servicing problem; and the President has ordered the Secretary of the Treasury to examine Rockefeller's related proposal for a local currency fund.

However, the Peterson Report[2] served as the principal basis for President Nixon's foreign aid message to Congress on April 21, 1971. The President proposed the separation of development and military aid, the latter to be renamed international security assistance and to be administered by the

---

2 *United States Foreign Assistance in the 1970s: A New Approach*, Department of State Bulletin, LXII, No. 1606 (April 6, 1970), pp. 447–67.

Pentagon, with policy guidance and supporting economic assistance from the Department of State. Under Nixon's plan, humanitarian aid (disaster relief, etc.) would be the responsibility of an Assistant Secretary of State, while AID would be replaced by two new institutions, with boards of directors made up of both government officials and private citizens. The U.S. International Development Corporation would make development loans on flexible terms and give priority to projects and programs that "promote private initiative" in "lower-income" countries and regions of "major long-term interest" to the United States. It would have authority for three years to allocate $1.5 billion in newly appropriated public funds, to borrow in the private capital market up to $1 billion, and to use repayments on past U.S. development loans. The other institution, the U.S. International Development Institute, would sponsor research on development problems and provide technical assistance through private contractors, thereby reducing the number of U.S. Government personnel needed abroad. It would have a three-year authorization of $1.275 billion. All development assistance would be coordinated by a single official, directly responsible to the President, who would serve as board chairman of these two corporations and of the Overseas Private Investment Corporation (see editor's introduction to selection 29). This official would also chair an executive committee composed of the chief executives of each of the foregoing institutions and of the Inter-American Social Development Institute (see footnote 3).

It remains to be seen how far Congress is prepared to go in reorganizing the administration of U.S. bilateral aid and what part of available funds will be directed to Latin America. There is also the question of follow-up on the Peterson Report recommendation that the U.S. channel a much larger proportion of its assistance through multilateral institutions. With specific reference to Latin America, to date, President Nixon has offered $23 million in grant funds "to strengthen the activities" of CIAP and the IDB and has also authorized a CIAP review of U.S. economic and financial programs as they affect the hemisphere.

.   .   .

In the first and second sections of the following selection, we return to the House Subcommittee on Inter-American Affairs hearings held in March, 1969.

In the first section, Acting U.S. Coordinator of the Alliance for Progress (AID) James R. Fowler, and William T. Dentzer, Jr., Deputy U.S. Ambassador to the OAS and Deputy U.S. Representative on the Inter-American Committee of the Alliance for Progress (CIAP), offer us further insights into the problems both of development planning at the country level and of coordinating AID and multilateral aid—through CIAP and other mechanisms—with country programs and policies. Mr. Dentzer also provides tables outlining U.S. gross and net, public and private investment in Latin

America, 1962–1967, and AID's role in the Alliance. As he notes and Latin Americans regularly point out, when one deducts Latin American countries' repayments on previous loans and the return to the U.S. of profits from private enterprises in the area, the net *flow of capital to Latin America has been virtually nil, even before U.S. contributions to the Alliance began to drop in recent years. The Congressmen doing the questioning are Dante B. Fascell (Chairman-Florida), Abraham Kazen, Jr. (Texas), and Lee H. Hamilton (Indiana).*

The second section focuses on the matter of bilateral vs. multilateral aid. Fowler and Dentzer argue for the maintenance of the present mix between bilateral and multilateral programs on the grounds that multilateral institutions are not equipped to shoulder a heavier administrative burden and that the United States has a continuing interest in being directly identified with Latin American development efforts. An interesting discussion ensues when Congressman Benjamin S. Rosenthal (New York) questions whether in fact the Latin American "man on the street" is aware of U.S. aid.

The third section is from the Senate Subcommittee on Western Hemisphere Affairs hearing of June 24, 1969, on U.S. military policies and programs, but the excerpt here concerns bilateral vs. multilateral aid. Senator Church (Chairman) and other participants—Senator Fulbright; George C. Lodge, Associate Professor, Harvard University Graduate School of Business Administration; David Bronheim, Director of the Center for Inter-American Relations and formerly Deputy U.S. Coordinator of the Alliance (author of selection 25); and Ralph Dungan, Chancellor of Higher Education of the State of New Jersey and formerly U.S. Ambassador to Chile (1964–67) and Special Assistant to President Kennedy (1961–63)—comment on Lodge's proposals (not reprinted) for reorganizing the Alliance for Progress. Basically, Lodge urged multilateralizing the bulk of U.S. aid under the Alliance, while reserving about 25% for an entirely new program which would involve U.S. nongovernmental groups' direct assistance to their counterparts in Latin America.[3] In spite of Church's general preference for multilateralism, he remains disturbed that this aid, too, flows to governments upholding the status quo. Bronheim asserts that a very few Latin American governments are *worthy of support and suggests that the central question is whether* either *the United States* or *multilateral institutions are capable of making the necessary distinctions. Dungan implies that he favors substantial bilateralism, with the United States exercising greater discrimination in selecting governments to assist. Incidentally, the reader should recall (selection 22) that Church has now apparently modified his earlier position— expressed here in his final "hypothesis"—on the matter of continued bilateral aid to progressive democratic governments.*

---

[3] See the following by George C. Lodge: "U.S. Aid to Latin America: Funding Radical Change," *Foreign Affairs,* XLVII, No. 4 (July 1969), pp. 735–749; and *Engines of Change: United States Interests and Revolution in Latin America* (New

I. HOUSE HEARINGS: PLANNING AND EXISTING FORMS AND LEVELS OF AID

STATEMENT OF JAMES R. FOWLER, ACTING U.S. COORDINATOR, ALLIANCE FOR PROGRESS, AGENCY FOR INTERNATIONAL DEVELOPMENT. . . .

Planning at the Country Level. . . .

Initially, in the Alliance, great emphasis was given to the preparation by the Latin American countries of comprehensive country development plans as the basis for establishing country development policies and priorities, and in order to provide a focus for international assistance.

Emphasis soon shifted, however, to the more pragmatic approach of strengthening the processes of financial resource mobilization, financial management, and investment budgeting.

While most countries have prepared comprehensive development plans and analyses of sectoral needs, the major question for each country has been how to translate development program and investment requirements into annual financial investment budgets supported by disciplined monetary and fiscal policies. . . .

Role of Multilateral Agencies: IMF, IBRD, CIAP

The major multilateral assistance agencies operating in the hemisphere are the International Bank for Reconstruction and Development (IBRD), the Inter-American Development Bank (IDB), the International Monetary Fund (IMF), and the United Nations Development Program (UNDP).

Bilaterally, there are AID and the Export-Import Bank. These agencies, in varying degrees, have an informal division of labor as to the types of assistance they offer, the sectors they emphasize, and the circumstances under which they make their inputs. . . .

Development Loans

The major AID instruments which we use in this process are deserving of some comment. The principal instrument is the development loan, a long-term, low-interest loan, repayable in U.S. dollars—which finances U.S. goods and services for particular projects or finances general imports from the United States needed for development.

Development loans are tied to specific self-help measures undertaken by the recipient country to further its own development. Development loans are the basic element of AID development aid. They are of three basic types—project loans, program loans, and sector loans. . . .

A program loan provides the foreign exchange required to finance the imports needed for a country's development program. This type of loan has been negotiated and implemented in Colombia, Brazil, and Chile over the

York: Knopf, 1970), esp. chap. 16. As Church commented in selection 22, the Inter-American Social Development Institute has the potential of evolving into a program similar to that proposed by Mr. Lodge. Created late in 1969 upon the initiative of the House Committee on Foreign Affairs (following the Subcommittee's hearings excerpted here), the ISDI is a nonprofit government corporation with an operating budget of $50 million a year. Lodge is Vice Chairman of the seven-member, public-private Board of Directors.

For additional critiques of U.S. foreign aid, see esp.: Samuel P. Huntington's two-part article "Foreign Aid for What and for Whom," *Foreign Policy,* I, No. 1 (Fall 1970), pp. 161–89—continued in No. 2 (Spring 1971), pp. 114–34; and Richard M. Bird, "What's Wrong with the United States Foreign Aid Program?" *International Journal,* XXV, No. 1 (Winter 1969–70), pp. 9–22.

last several years. It is designed to support the developmental import requirements of countries whose chronic balance-of-payments deficits limit their capacity to buy.

The second type of loan, the sector loan, is a new form of lending which is still in the experimental stage. Its focus of attention is placed upon policy actions by the government in certain key priority sectors, principally agriculture and education.

The form in which the resource transfer occurs may be the same as that in a program loan; that is, it may furnish general imports into the economy, either for that sector or generally. The local currency proceeds, in every case, however, are devoted to projects of assistance in support of government actions in that particular sector.

The emphasis on the sector approach is, I think, an important one, and reflects the progress of the Alliance to the point where countries and foreign assistance agencies can focus increasingly not only on the macroeconomic issues—monetary, fiscal, and exchange rate policy—but look beyond those to the extremely important questions of policy management in key sectors.

In agriculture, for example, price policies, marketing, distribution, storage, are all policy matters, which we believe very directly affect the growth of the agricultural sector. The sector loan is an experimental device which we are trying to work out now to see if assistance programs can be directed into sectors and to the achievement of sector objectives.

Finally, there is the project loan, with which I am sure you are all familiar. This is a loan of the type which the World Bank makes, which the Inter-American Bank makes, and which AID has been making for many years.

These projects may be of an infrastructure type, involving roads, highways, hydroelectric or thermal electric power plants, or they may involve provision of capital through intermediate credit institutions. There are a wide variety of them, but they are looked upon as discrete activities to which our resources are applied, after negotiations with the receiving entity— in some cases, the government; in some cases a nongovernmental entity. . . .

Technical Assistance

The other major element is technical assistance, which I believe all members of the committee are fully familiar with, sometimes called technical cooperation or development grants. Under this program, we send U.S. specialists abroad, and bring trainees, which we call participants, to the United States or other countries for training in priority development fields.

Technical assistance, which first began as the Point IV program, helps less developed nations acquire needed skills and know-how, develop trained manpower and build development institutions. These grants are largely carried out by American universities and by other government agencies such as the Internal Revenue Service, U.S. Department of Agriculture, Bureau of Customs, et cetera.

Food for Freedom

Public Law 480—also known as food for freedom, or food for peace, or the Agricultural Trade Development and Assistance Act of 1954—is another one of the tools that is involved in this process.

Initially, a means of disposing of large surplus agricultural stocks, Public Law 480 has increasingly come to be viewed as a part of an integrated foreign assistance package. Commodities are sold on concessional credit terms, with repayment in dollars, or are donated directly to recipient countries or indirectly through registered U.S. voluntary agencies, for disaster relief, for supplementing wages of workers employed on development projects, and for special food aid such as school lunches.

Investment Guaranties

Another tool is the program of investment guaranties. They are designed to encourage and facilitate private U.S. investments abroad which further the development of economic resources and productive capacities of less developed countries.

Guaranties are of three main kinds —the so-called specific risk guaranty program, the extended risk guaranty program, and the housing investment guaranty program. . . .

Coordination of Economic Assistance

Coordination of economic assistance to a country is effected through the interplay, on the one hand, of recipient government priority setting and programs and, on the other, through formal and informal arrangements among the major foreign assistance agencies. . . .

This process of coordination might be best illustrated, in a broad-brush fashion, by the example of program assistance to a hypothetical country. Similar practices and procedures apply as well to sector and project lending.

Assume a Latin America country is pursuing sound development policies and programs for which foreign exchange requirements are greater than projected availabilities, and that this foreign exchange gap threatens to become a major constraint on development and growth. Normally, these projected balance-of-payments assistance requirements are spelled out with care by the borrower country and made known to the international agencies and AID.

The governmental projections and the subsequent review by the lending agencies of the "gap" requirements they reflect, take into account all sources of external financing—public and private; national and international, as well as all domestic sources of financing.

A formal focus for international agency review of assistance needs and the country's policies and programs is also normally provided in the CIAP, although prior to CIAP meetings and reviews, there may be considerable informal exchange of views and analysis among the international lending agencies and with the prospective borrower government.

The CIAP review in addition provides a useful, formal forum for joint government-international agency review of the policies and programs upon which projected lending needs are premised.

Assuming that there is agreement as to the soundness and realism of the government's policies and programs, and that the foreign exchange needs are manifest, the shape of an international program package, including perhaps an IMF standby agreement, an AID program loan, as well as other international lending agency inputs will be outlined in principle at the CIAP meetings.

Within the generally agreed-upon levels and program guidelines established in the CIAP review, each agency will then negotiate its lending program with the borrowing country.

Bilateral Aid Programs—Determination of Levels

The process through which AID country assistance levels are determined spans roughly an 18-month period and, in the final analysis, turns upon the amount appropriated by Congress for our bilateral assistance program.

The first stage in this process is the preparation in the field mission of a document called the Country Analysis and Strategy Paper (CASP). This document, which is prepared under the direction of the U.S. Ambassador in each country, spells out overall U.S. objectives—including assistance objectives—in that country, and the foreseeable policy problems and choices which are open to the United States.

A projection is then made of assistance requirements in support of the U.S. strategy proposed with emphasis on the first year, but with projections extending over 5 years in all. So that, in effect, we begin with a 5-year U.S. planning document.

The second step in the process is the preparation, by the AID field mission, of the AID program memorandum. This document is based on and derives from the CASP and fleshes out in macro and microeconomic terms the priorities and strategy for U.S. bilateral assistance for the coming fiscal year and in more general terms for 4 more years in the future—thus, it is a 5-year AID planning document, also.

Projections for assistance levels and types are refined in this document from those projected in the CASP, with especial attention given to projected assistance from multilateral and other non-AID sources. As with the CASP, this document is reviewed for approval in Washington. Proposed country assistance levels are subsequently adjusted as the requirements, realism, and feasibility of specific project and program proposals become clearer in light of further detailed project feasibility and program analyses that are submitted by the field missions.

From this analysis emerge the budget recommendations for AID, which go forward to the Bureau of the Budget, to the President, and ultimately to the Congress. Overall proposed assistance levels and programs are then further adjusted after the congressional appropriation process is completed. . . .

.   .   .

Mr. FASCELL. . . . Mr. Fowler, you spoke about comprehensive country development plans. At the same time, you talked about the fact that emphasis soon shifted to a more pragmatic approach.

Now I gather from that that for all practical purposes, country plans are just nice concepts as laid down in the charter, and provide general guidelines, and nothing else.

Mr. FOWLER. I would like to comment a little further. . .on that. I don't want to detract from the importance of the country plan; it is certainly an essential factor, but I think that in the early years of the Alliance excessive attention was paid to the plan, the product, the eight volume, 10-year plan or whatever it was, and not enough attention was paid to the real objective, namely, the process of planning.

And this shift which I mentioned occurred because it became apparent that what was really important was the process of planning and the capacity to do planning, rather than the product or document that is produced as a country plan.

In recent years, therefore, all of the countries have increased their capacity to do planning. Planning institutions have been set up in almost all countries; institutions or government agencies that perform the functions of our Budget Bureau are now operating.

This approach is more pragmatic because while it sets longrun targets and goals, and defines long-term requirements, it is the annual decisionmaking process on actions, on policies, on resource allocation, and on priority determination that, in the final analysis, produces the results.

Every plan, it is commonly said, is obsolete by the time it is printed. That is an overstatement, but not much of one. By the time a plan is fully ready for publication and about to become a five-volume work, the situation usually has changed sufficiently to make some revisions and recasting of that plan essential.

The annual process by which planning is done, reexamined, and targets reset, is where the real payout comes.

This process focuses attention each year on governmental decisions on how to allocate resources, and how to establish priorities; that is the change in emphasis that I believe has occurred since the first years of the Alliance.

Today in practically every country of Latin America, you will find a planning organization of some sort. The question of its efficiency and efficacy rests on whether that planning organization is tied into the governmental decisionmaking process, or whether it exists off to the side as a somewhat abstract and academic exercise by economists and planners who plan for planning's sake. . . .

I described previously our own process for planning our programs. I think that is an example of how a good —we think, although it could be improved—planning process takes place.

We take a 5-year span, we make our projections, and look down the road 5 years, but the operational decisions that come from that process are most important for the first year; whether they are valid after that must be checked in the course of the continuing process of planning.

At the end of the first year, or during that year, we are already in the process of taking another 5-year look, and revising and recasting our projections.

It is that process of constantly pulling up the carrot to see whether it is growing that produces good planning, but you need the total framework.

I don't want to leave the impression that simply muddling through on a pragmatic, day-to-day basis, is any substitute for planning. But I do want to emphasize that the essence of planning is the process of reassessing, revising, relooking at projections, restudying data, and getting better data. . . .

Mr. FASCELL. . . . [The CASP paper], as you pointed out, is subject to many reviews and changes, both within the executive branch of the Government and in the Congress which often alters it by changing or limiting authorizations and appropriations. So that the paper with which you started out in the field, in the way of a plan, might bear very little resemblance to the program which you can put together after you finally get your money, particularly when over 18 months has gone in the budget process.

This raises a question about the development plan of the country itself. How is that plan if at all, coordinated with what AID does—both in the preparation of the CASP in the first instance, and in the final instance?

Mr. FOWLER. Mr. Chairman, that is one of the most difficult jobs that we attempt to do. Those of us who have served in the field and here in Washington are all acutely conscious of the amount of estimating, sometimes "guesstimating," involved in preparing budgetary proposals 18 months in advance when the assisted country is not necessarily working in the same time frame that we are.

This requires the best estimates,

projections, knowledge of the country, its programs and policies, personalities, that can be obtained. One person described it once, I think very accurately, as "the incredibly difficult job of trying to make two bureaucracies mesh," and I use "bureaucracies" not in a pejorative sense, but in its good sense. Our processes, by which we plan, budget, and implement our programs, have to be meshed with the process by which these other governments plan and implement their own programs, and in timespans which are basically different.

As an example, most of the Latin American countries have a fiscal year which is a calendar year. Our fiscal year, as we know, runs from July through June. We are using one fiscal year system, they are working in a different one. Projections have to be meshed, and data has to be adjusted so that these two cycles will be coordinated and actions will be complementary. This is a complicated matter.

Another problem is that one of the main characteristics of a developing country is the weakness of its own governmental institutions, structure, and the personnel in them. A great deal of the benefit from the foreign assistance efforts, not only bilateral but multilateral, is the "rub-off" effect of other country officials working jointly with the international agencies and ourselves on this process.

In the process, their agencies, their Ministers, their planning people learn at least how we do it, because they have to mesh theirs to ours. In many ways we benefit from the interchange too. We learn a tremendous amount from sitting with them and confronting their problems of planning their own resource allocation, within the limits of their laws, agencies, their personnel, and their priorities. This is an extremely valuable experience and very instructive for us....

Mr. KAZEN. Are you in constant touch with the foreign country, as you are developing your own plan?

Mr. FOWLER. Yes. Obviously we have to be in constant touch, and that is why we have missions in each of the countries. We are in constant touch, and we have to know what their plans are, as best they can articulate them to us.

They, of course, are eager to know what our plans are. But, because our plans and projections depend upon this planning process ending with congressional action, we can't make any firm commitments as to our plans. We can't give them ironclad guarantees in advance that if they do this, we will do that.

The planning, therefore, becomes very contingent. We can't really go to the country and say, "We are now ready to do X, Y, or Z", until after the congressional appropriation process is complete and the decisions are made with respect to the allocation of resources appropriated by the Congress.

By that time, in many cases, we are 1 month or 2 weeks before the beginning of their fiscal year, and at that point, some very rapid readjustment of priorities and plans has to take place, because perhaps they had been making certain assumptions about aid, not only from us, but the IDB, the World Bank and other agencies.

At that point in time, it becomes apparent that those assumptions were incorrect. They were overstated; therefore, they have to readjust and we have to work with them in readjusting, and then we are in a position to start carrying out programs.

Mr. KAZEN. Sometimes that works vice versa. They may not have reached the point where you wanted them to get. Is this correct?

Mr. FOWLER. That is correct....

Mr. HAMILTON. Mr. Fowler, I was

interested in your statement where you talk about the role of CIAP in coordination. . . .

You say there that within generally agreed upon levels and program guidelines which are established in CIAP review, each agency will then negotiate its lending program with the borrowing country. And my question pertains to the importance of the role of CIAP.

I get the impression from your statement and the conversation so far that CIAP really is the most important body in the entire assistance program, and that it really comes very close to having control over these matters. Is that a correct impression?

Mr. FOWLER. No; I think that is not a correct impression, at least at the present time. I think the importance of CIAP in this whole organization has been growing, but I would emphasize that CIAP is really a reviewing, advising, and recommending body. It does not have operational responsibilities or powers.

Mr. HAMILTON. And does establish, according to your statement, guidelines.

Mr. FOWLER. CIAP's recommendations indicate the kinds of self-help performance which it believes the country should pursue. It analyzes the problems of the country and tries to identify the bottleneck areas where action is required.

Mr. HAMILTON. Now, suppose there is a difference there between their analysis and AID's analysis on a given program?

Mr. FOWLER. Well, in the final analysis, of course, we make our own decisions. But, generally speaking, where there are differences of opinion or emphasis, and they frequently occur, these matters are discussed and negotiated.

Mr. HAMILTON. Have there been instances where you have in fact gone against CIAP's recommendation?

Mr. FOWLER. Not that I can recall. . . .

Mr. FASCELL. . . . If the charter goals and concepts are broadly defined, which we recognize, and if comprehensive country plans really exist in name only, against what does CIAP review performance? Or what does it actually review?

Mr. DENTZER. The CIAP Secretariat, through the year, compiles a document which is presented to CIAP, the country concerned and the international agencies prior to each country review. Based on direct staff investigations in the country, and international agencies' data, the CIAP document analyzes progress of the country as against its goals in the past year. What did revenue collections look like? What are the weaknesses in the planning setup? What are the weaknesses in public administration? How much growth has there been in the agricultural sector? What are the bottlenecks in education? To what extent did international assistance fill these gaps and help resolve them?

Mr. FASCELL. Let me see if you can translate that.

Let's take the year 1968, and see how does that work?

Mr. DENTZER. CIAP assesses what happened in the last year, and what the country thinks it is going to be doing in the year ahead, what its effort should be, and what international assistance should be necessary.

Mr. FASCELL. So, theoretically, at the beginning of a year, certain goals and objectives are determined by CIAP as desirable for a particular country?

Mr. DENTZER. The country says what it wants to do, but CIAP may say——

Mr. FASCELL. "Well, that's not what you should do at all."

Mr. DENTZER. In more diplomatic language than that. [Laughter].

Mr. Fascell. I know, but that is one of the purposes of CIAP: to recommend, advise, and whatnot. So a country could come up with a plan at the beginning of a year, and CIAP could review it and say, "Your goals are not realistic", or "We don't think your priorities ought to lean in this direction; they ought to be shifted", and whatnot.

Mr. Dentzer. Or that you are not ready.

Mr. Fascell. Now, at the end of the year, I am trying to decide what it is that CIAP measures against to determine whether or not any progress has been made. . . .

Mr. Dentzer. The performance is appraised in general terms. A country says, "We are going to try to stabilize our financial situation and have so much public investment going in based on public savings. We want to save *x* hundred million dollars out of public income for capital investment." Next year, CIAP asks, Have they reached that level? Has their tax action been enough? Have they made proposals to their congress, and succeeded in passing through the congress, laws providing for the level of taxation they said they wanted?

Have their gross investments in agriculture, or education, amounted to what they said they wanted? Has their public administration really been strengthened by the assignment of more qualified people to a planning office or to a budget bureau or a project office that works on the projects with the international agencies?

The categories tend to be broad, and the tendency is not to form on particular projects. Rather, the thrust is one of analysis of performance in key sectors, of fiscal policy, of balance-of-payments management, monetary policy, investment policy in agriculture, gross capital investment by the government, and of policies to encourage more private investment in the country.

Mr. Fascell. And then the experts who make up the CIAP Secretariat decide whether or not progress has been made in these broad general terms and areas?

Mr. Dentzer. In very broad terms.

Mr. Fascell. So that there is no quantitative comparison—or very little, let's put it that way. It is essentially a judgment by an expert.

Mr. Dentzer. Yes, much as you put it earlier in this hearing. A country's inability to attain a per capita growth rate in a particular year of 2.5 percent may be weighed against significant advances in organizing its public sector, in stimulating its export growth, in raising taxes, or in mobilizing its own resources.

Mr. Fascell. But from a professional point of view, there are identifiable symptoms which can spell "progress." That's the point.

Mr. Dentzer. Yes, Mr. Chairman.

Mr. Fascell. And which are not subject to quantitative analysis or measurement?

Mr. Dentzer. That is correct, too, Mr. Chairman.

. . .

Mr. Dentzer. . . . I would like to include, for the record, Mr. Chairman, an indication of what the lending records have been in AID, the Inter-American Development Bank, and the World Bank.

If you look at the figures from the outset of the Alliance, in fiscal year 1961, one sees that AID loans—then almost a new tool for the United States in the development program in Latin

U.S. Disbursements to Latin American Republics
[In millions of dollars]

	Gross						Net					
	1962	1963	1964	1965	1966	1967	1962	1963	1964	1965	1966	1967
U.S. official:												
AID	285	331	347	460	581	449	284	326	338	452	568	428
Food for freedom	128	184	241	103	112	111	125	181	236	98	107	104
Social Progress Trust Fund	23	66	67	70	69	59	23	65	64	66	63	49
Eximbank	276	147	69	139	150	188	[1] 155	[1] −1	[1] −137	[1] (1)	[1] −51	[1] −28
Total, U.S. official	712	728	724	772	912	807	587	571	501	616	687	553
U.S. private investment:												
Direct investment	−32	69	143	176	190	191						
Reinvested earnings	268	173	216	306	302	172						
Income received[2]	(−761)	(−801)	(−895)	(−869)	(−965)	(−1,022)						
Net outflows	−525	−559	−536	−387	−473	−659	−525	−559	−536	−387	−473	−659
Total, U.S. official and private	848	970	1,083	1,254	1,404	1,170	62	12	−35	229	214	−106
International:												
IBRD Group	158	272	250	187	258	256	115	217	170	131	185	183
IDB	37	75	128	112	142	183	37	74	122	99	105	149
Other bilateral official—DAC	156	205	195	231	207	189	101	130	66	67	47	(3)

1 Does not include interest payments.
2 Not included in gross total U.S. flows to Latin American Republics.
3 Not available.

Profile of the AID Program in Latin America

A. The program has averaged $545,000,000 per year since the beginning of the Alliance for Progress late in fiscal year 1961 (excluding Public Law 480 food sales and grants). It has declined in recent years.

[In millions of dollars]

	Fiscal year							
	1961	1962	1963	1964	1965	1966	1967	1968
Alliance loans......................	135.1	189.6	342.8	479.0	441.5	505.4	439.1	433.5
Alliance grants......................	35.0	83.8	112.1	93.5	88.7	88.5	95.1	88.5
Supporting assistance..............	20.4	25.2	22.7	15.3	35.7	44.8	31.8	26.1
Cont. fund and other..............	63.3	182.2	81.7	53.6	32.0	55.4	19.3	......
Total...........................	253.8	480.8	559.3	641.4	597.9	694.1	585.3	548.1
Public Law 480....................	(145.6)	(128.2)	(166.7)	(296.5)	(103.6)	(187.5)	(69.5)	(228.1)

B. The program has been heavily concentrated in Brazil, Chile, and Colombia.

	Amount of asisstance, fiscal years 1961–68 (millions)[1]	*Percent of assistance*
Brazil, Chile, and Colombia...	$2,263.8	58.7
Central America..	419.1	10.8
All other countries..	1,180.1	30.5

[1] Excluding Latin American regional programs.

C. Reflecting early experience under the Alliance and the opinions of the hemisphere presidents at their summit meeting in 1967, the program is increasingly concentrated in the critical sectors of agriculture, education, and health (including family planning).[1]

	Fiscal year							
	1961	1962	1963	1964	1965	1966	1967	1968
Agriculture...........................	18.1	34.0	18.5	11.5	9.9	26.1	16.1	25.6
Education...........................	2.3	19.4	7.5	5.2	6.3	5.1	9.6	23.4
Health...............................	4.3	13.9	7.5	4.1	.3	6.7	5.3	17.1
Total...........................	24.7	67.3	33.5	20.8	16.5	37.9	31.0	66.1

[1] Percentages exclude uses of country-owned local currencies generated by program loans.

D. Since basic institutional reform is the major requirement in these sectors, sector loans to encourage and implement these reforms are an increasingly important part of the program.

[In millions of dollars]

	Fiscal year							
	1961	1962	1963	1964	1965	1966	1967	1968
Program loans..................................		94.5	95.0	105.0	230.0	294.0	200.0	151.0
Sector loans....................................							10.0	116.7
Project loans.......................	135.1	95.1	247.8	394.0	211.5	211.4	210.3	165.8

E. *U.S. bilateral assistance* to Latin America is of critical importance. Its relationship to the U.S. Budget and the U.S. GNP is as follows:
    Annual A.I.D. Assistance (*FY 1968*) $548.1:
        As percent of U.S. Federal Budget 0.31 percent.
        As percent of U.S. GNP 0.06 percent.
F. While external assistance and financing (both public and private), including A.I.D.'s, is of critical importance in mobilizing local resources and in redirecting those resources (through encouraging reforms in the critical sectors of agriculture, education and in social and civic development), *the major task is still one for the Latin American countries themselves.*
    **Present Annual Gross Investment in Latin America (1968): $20.3 billion (est.).
    **Latin America GNP (1968): $113.1 billion (est.).
    Total External Assistance to L.A. (1968) $2,169 ($ million):
        As percent of gross investment 10.7 percent.
        As percent of Latin American GNP 1.9 percent.
    U.S. Annual Bilateral Assistance to L.A. $1,358 ($ million) (1968):
        As percent of gross investment in L.A. 6.7 percent.
        As percent of Latin American GNP 1.2 percent.
    U.S. Annual Private Investment in L.A.* $363 million (1967):
        As percent of gross investment in L.A. 1.9 percent.*
        As percent of Latin American GNP 0.4 percent.*

---

* For 1967, but amount of investment has varied from 200 to 500 million annually.
** 20 Republics.

America, since most of U.S. assistance prior to that had been technical assistance—increased from $144 million in that fiscal year—1961—to $414 million in fiscal year 1968; IDB loans went from $66 to $413 million; IBRD loans, from $158 to $385 million.

So, you can see that the amounts of resources in new commitments to Latin America have increased very substantially since the outset of the Alliance.

Now, let me add a caveat here, lest anyone get the wrong impression that this resource transfer is on a net basis.

In the first place, it is quite clear that we are still far short of meeting the total resource requirements for external assistance to Latin America. The amount of aid going to Latin America is very small in relation to the kinds of growth that can be stimulated there, and the kinds of employment creation which can be foreseen from those levels of growth.

In the second place, you have to subtract what Latin America pays back to the United States to get a clear idea of what the net flows are. AID, the World Bank, IBRD, and IDB, in fiscal year 1968 each committed about $400 million in loans annually. That adds up to about $1,200 million.

Capital assistance in terms of long-term supplier credits from the members of European countries and from Japan amount to about another $200 million annually. There is also a modest amount of capital assistance that comes from other sources.

When one starts to consider, however, what Latin America pays back to the United States and other lenders, that total amount of resource transfer diminishes very substantially. If one deducts debt payments, amortization and interest, from Latin America to the U.S. Government, the official flow of capital diminishes from something over a billion dollars a year to about $500 million a year; and if one further deducts the net flow of captial income payments to U.S. private investors in the United States, that is to say, gross remittances less new investment and reinvested earnings, that flow is about nil, in terms of bilateral U.S. capital flows. Capital income payments to U.S. investors in Latin America in the years 1964 to 1967 averaged about $514 million.

I am placing to one side, of course, the increased export earnings which come to Latin America thanks to private U.S. investment and the many other advantages of such investment— employment, tax payments, know-how, technology, and fixed facilities. I am pointing out, however, that high gross official capital flows to Latin America under the Alliance have been necessary to help Latin America deal with the problems she had accumulated previously. When you look at net capital flows and their economic effect, and after all due credit is given to the U.S. effort to step up support to Latin America, one sees that not that much money has been put into Latin America after all. . . .

II. HOUSE HEARINGS: BILATERAL VS. MULTILATERAL AID

Mr. FASCELL. . . . [One] question which seems to be rather current nowadays, and which you might want to address yourself to, regarding which is more efficacious from the standpoint of U.S. national interest, and from the standpoint of Latin American individual country interests, bilateral or multilateral aid? . . .

Mr. FOWLER. Well, with respect to this last question, multilateral or bilateral, I think the debate on that issue has become oversimplified, as debate on issues like this tend to be. I don't think the question is whether multilateral aid is better than bilateral aid. I think the question is the mix. There is room for both; there are advantages to both; there are disadvantages to both. What is the correct mix?

The development not only of Latin America but of other developing countries depends upon their own actions; to the extent that multilateralization involves the countries more closely and directly in that process, through a multilateral forum, there is a net gain.

On the other hand, I think that the participation of the developed countries in bilateral relationships, such as that between the United States and Latin America, is extremely important and should not simply be cast aside for a totally multilateral effort.

There is a very important gain, both to the United States and to the Latin American countries, I believe, from the participation of the United States bilaterally in this operation. The question is how much of which, and in what mix, and through what mechanisms.

We participate in CIAP, both through the U.S. member, whose deputy is Mr. Dentzer, and through representation of AID as one of the lending agencies. So in a sense we are represented twice, but the U.S. member on CIAP is not an instructed member. He is there in his personal capacity, asks the questions he wants to, and says what he thinks, in his personal capacity.

My agency is represented there, along with the World Bank and IDB, and as one of the international agencies providing assistance, we ask our questions, and we may come to different conclusions.

All of this occurs in the presence of Latin Americans, and with their full participation.

Now, I think there is a very strong gain in this approach because different points of view get expressed openly. I think the great value of the CIAP mechanism, as a part of the multilateral operation, is the involvement of the Latin Americans in this process of self-examination. This is what really goes on in these country reviews. The countries send a very well qualified delegation to the CIAP meeting. This delegation initially presents the country's situation as they see it, the country's successes, problems, plans, and proposals for the future.

After the delegation makes its presentation, it responds to questions in a hearing type of atmosphere. The agencies ask questions about what happened or why it didn't happen, or what the country's plans are; the members of CIAP engage in the same questioning process. All of this, in a multilateral open forum, has, I think, a very beneficial effect.

Each year's progress is measured against last year's statements of intentions. And I think the fact that the countries are now sending better and better delegations, and that more and more preparation goes into their presentation, is an indication of the seriousness with which they regard the review, because they realize that the Inter-American Bank, AID, the World Bank, and the IMF are listening and asking questions, and that our final decisions with respect to foreign assistance will be taken in light of the adequacy of their plans, programs, and presentations. . . .

Mr. DENTZER. I think we ought to realize that we have already, and have had for several years, a very high degree of multilateralism in the Alliance for Progress.

The great bulk of IDB assistance is from U.S. sources; 75 percent of the Fund for Special Operations, which is the major lending account of the IDB, comes from the United States. The level of IDB lending ought to be increasing, and I hope our share will remain at the same percentage level as it has been.

The World Bank is lending about $400 million a year as well to Latin America. It hopes to double this over the next few years, based on borrowings in capital markets in the United States and Europe.

It would be a great tragedy, it seems to me, if the United States were to reduce its bilateral effort at a time when the needs are really higher, and when AID has the capacity to transfer those resources. Theoretically, AID's funds could be transferred to the World Bank and the IDB, but, practically, it takes people and mechanisms, and structures to analyze and process those loans. AID has developed, over the last 8 years, a rather good structure in this difficult business, to analyze the requirements, and to get something useful done. It would be unwise to think that structure could somehow be transferred to another international agency, which is already stretching its own resources and structure to better meet the requirements of Latin America.

One, we are already highly multilateralized.

Two, IDB and the World Bank probably will be able to do more, and I hope the U.S. Government will support their efforts to do more.

Three, our bilateral program is extremely necessary. . . .

I think the United States still has a substantial interest in participating directly in the development of these countries. It is awfully nice, when you read in the newspapers of a country that the World Bank or the IDB have given assistance to the country but very few nationals of the country know what the IDB or the World Bank is; they certainly don't know that the United States is putting in the bulk of the funds, in fact, which the IDB uses.

And to the extent that we participate in their development, and establish a direct identification with their development, I think we stand to gain.

Mr. ROSENTHAL. Who knows in these countries? Does the man in the street know that we participate?

Mr. DENTZER. The informed man in the street knows what AID is, when it makes a loan.

Mr. ROSENTHAL. That is a lot of nonsense.

Mr. DENTZER. No. The informed man will know that.

Mr. ROSENTHAL. The informed man in the street in Washington doesn't know what AID is. [Laughter.]

Mr. DENTZER. You are saying the informed man isn't in the street?

Mr. ROSENTHAL. The informed man is not that well informed.

Mr. FASCELL. I think we can agree that they recognize that the United States is involved.

Mr. ROSENTHAL. The man in the street?

Mr. FASCELL. Well, if as somebody has indicated, they dislike us, they must dislike somebody, and they must be——

Mr. ROSENTHAL. This I can see, but I am talking about the United States Government. Everywhere I went, I had to have associates of yours as interpreters, but the man in the street didn't know we were doing anything.

Mr. DENTZER. Of course, what I am trying to say——

Mr. ROSENTHAL. The government Ministers know it.

Mr. DENTZER. An informed newspaperman, leading businessmen, leading lawyers, and so forth, know what AID is. They don't know that 75 percent of the IDB's assistance comes from the United States. I am trying to make the point of identification. . . .

Mr. ROSENTHAL. I see Mr. Fowler shaking his head. I am trying to suggest that if we continue our bilateral aid programs, are there ways to perk up the U.S. image? Some way to merchandise our good intentions, plus our concrete financial assistance? Is there a way to do that? . . .

Mr. FASCELL. . . . [A]ren't we in fact doing that now with the concept of the Alliance, and with the concept of CIAP, by taking bilateral aid and running it through this coordinating mill, which allows the Latins to participate in a more diverse and a more direct way than they ever have before, rather than be subjected to purely the head-to-head bilateral negotiation that takes place between countries.?

As a matter of fact, if you eliminated bilateral aid altogether, you would still be involved with the question of the presence of the United States, and you might not fully answer those who advocate nothing but multilateral aid as a way of working up to a better U.S. image or keeping us from getting involved?

I believe you are the man, Mr. Dentzer, who says, "We are involved anyway, regardless". So that it is really kind of naive to think that if you took all the bilateral aid and converted it to multilateral aid, we would become "uninvolved" and everything would be rosy. It is just not a fact of life, is it?

Mr. ROSENTHAL. Maybe if we can't find a viable way to earn the points for the things we are doing, maybe we should stop trying to earn points. . . .

Mr. DENTZER. I am less concerned —although I am concerned—less concerned about gaining points from our assistance. I am more concerned about whether it gets development, and whether we are seen, at least by the informed people in the private and public sector, to be taking a reasonable quantitative and qualitative interest in their development.

That doesn't mean that I kept the USIA people from putting out press releases about AID assistance; it does mean that most all of us feel that our task is to get a job done for development, and to identify ourselves with that. To the extent possible, we should also try to get the populace to understand our role, which they don't understand. The man in the street of a rural town may not know who his President is, let alone what AID is. To get this identification is a plus, but it is a difficult job getting to that man in the street. . . .

Mr. FOWLER. . . . I would just like to have the record show that I don't agree with either Ambassador Dentzer or Congressman Rosenthal's conclusion that the average man in the street. . . . [d]oesn't know about U.S. assistance in Latin America. My experience is the contrary. Now, I am not trying to say that everybody up and down all of the streets of all of the cities is aware of it, but my own experience, and I traveled in 20 of the 21 countries in the last year, is that there is widespread recognition of the role of the United States. So much so that in too many cases, the Alliance for Progress is synonymous with U.S. aid.

My experience in Colombia and in other countries I have visited is that an amazing number of people are very much aware of the fact that the assistance they are getting in co-ops, the assistance they are getting through supervised agricultural credit, the pow-

erplants that are being built, the roads that are being constructed, are being constructed with assistance from the United States.

It is in the newspapers; they hear about it on the radio; and they look at the television; our people are there; they are seen; they are on the platform when the ribbons are cut; they are out over the country.

I just don't agree with this assessment that the man in the street doesn't know anything about the U.S. assistance in Latin America. I think he does. I think a substantial number of them do. In fact, we sometimes wonder whether they are not placing too much responsibility on the United States to solve their development problems. We wish to further strengthen the Latin American sense of responsibility and self-help in their programs. This, I think, is the problem—rather than a failure to identify or recognize the role of the United States in assistance programs.

Mr. FASCELL. There must be some of that, Mr. Fowler, because I have heard some high-ranking people around this Hill insist that we get into multilateral programs so that we couldn't possibly be identified, not only not have any control over the subject, but pump the money in, and then not do anything with it, either. There must be some identification.

III. SENATE HEARINGS: BILATERAL VS. MULTILATERAL AID

Senator CHURCH. I personally agree, Mr. Lodge, with your conclusion that our policy in Latin America is mainly designed to preserve the status quo. I think that is a self-defeating policy, and no doubt contributes to the virulent anti-American feeling in many parts of the hemisphere.

But I wonder about your recommendations because, it seems to me, they would only have the effect of changing the mechanism. Presently, I agree that we undertake, through our bilateral aid, both economic and military, to preserve the status quo. There is no question that this is the effect of the aid, since we are dealing on a government-to-government basis in all of these countries.

You suggest changing the mechanism to a multilateral one. But wouldn't the result simply be that we would then be attempting to preserve the status quo through a multilateral mechanism rather than a bilateral one, since we are going to be dealing, in any case, with the governments and the agents of the governments that are in power, even though we may be channeling the aid through a multilateral mechanism?

Mr. LODGE. I think that is a very good point, Senator Church, and the reason behind my recommendation briefly, is this: I think it is essential to provide assistance for some necessary conventional development undertakings, infrastructure, education, this sort of thing.

This, however, should, I say, be done multilaterally, because we should not take unto ourselves the blame that this kind of aid has for inevitably strengthening the status quo. But I wouldn't like to see this assistance completely halted, because I think over the years it can have an evolutionary effect, particularly if it is accompanied by the sort of assistance that I contemplate being rendered through this American foundation which I see as essentially a nongovernmental device for loosing the vast pluralism of the United States to help those Latin American engines of change which are at work.

In fact, what I am trying to do in this proposal is to make the inevitable contradiction between change and stability more precise. We cannot get away from it. It is in the nature of things. But I think we can make it more precise and we can identify ourselves as a nation with the change part, leaving the stability part to the region itself.

It may sound unrealistic, and it may sound contradictory, but I think it would work.

Senator CHURCH. Well, I certainly do agree that using multilateral agencies tends to take the onus off of the United States. But it would seem to me very difficult to extend any aid—even through that channel—that would not, to a very large degree, have the effect of shoring up the status quo; and I am troubled with the underlying concept of the Alliance for Progress which was indeed a very idealistic undertaking from the standpoint of those who fashioned it early in the Kennedy years. The lack of reality, it seems to me, goes to the very point that somebody here just made, that you cannot buy fundamental change with foreign aid money, especially when you are asking the very governments to whom the money is given to alter the basis upon which their power rests. I think that may be the ultimate in naiveté. . . .

Mr. BRONHEIM. Sir, I am troubled by one aspect of your point. I think there are status quos and status quos, if you will. Where a Latin American government has a significant dedication to a redistribution of political and economic power, and a determination to accelerate the growth process, I agree rare cases, but they do exist, it would seem to me that in situations like that help to that government, and let us leave aside for the moment the question of whether it be bilateral or multilateral help, I think help to that kind of government is probably a good thing in changing the status quo.

I think the difficulty is, and I think the hard question is: Is the U.S. Government or is any multinational organization in a political position to make that kind of differentiation on a regular basis, given the way membership of organizations work, and given the way the political process in international affairs works on the United States. . . . [Y]ou look at the hemisphere and say, in terms of who we are as a democracy and our philosophy and the evolution that we would like to see and who we would like to be associated with, that there are only two governments and possibly three that we would like to stand along side of now. In terms of that decision I do not believe a multinational organization is capable of making that either. Their internal politics are very similar to the internal politics of any multimember organization and they cannot function that way.

It is extremely difficult for the U.S. Government to function that way, and such a policy will immediately lead to antagonistic statements by the other governments who are more protective of the status quo. . . .

Senator FULBRIGHT. . . . Mr. Lodge has suggested the multilateral aid approach, and I can see the danger that the chairman has mentioned, but what is the alternative? We have bilateral and we have multilateral. What is the third alternative, do nothing at all? That is a possible alternative.

Senator CHURCH. I think possibly we might give that some consideration.

Senator FULBRIGHT. I think this undoubtedly will be given consideration. But, on the other hand, and, I do think that with Latin America,

for various reasons, we have a rather special relationship and feeling. I personally think that the multilateral even with the dangers, can do some good. The dangers would arise if we dominate that multilateral organization actively. . . .

Mr. BRONHEIM. . . . I think the situation in Latin America is such that we cannot get out of the economic assistance business. We must look at our aid and trade policies as a package but we must be more, if you will, discriminating in deciding whom we become associated with and whom we do not.

Senator FULBRIGHT. What procedures do you use? Do you want to continue to use bilateral aid in the economic field, or do you prefer the multilateral?

Mr. BRONHEIM. I think were it clear that the aggregate amount of the assistance that could be made available through multilateral channels would be adequate, I suspect in terms of the political problems of the United States in general, multilateral would be better.

There is a certain kind of assistance that we might want to consider continuing on a bilateral basis because the multilateral organizations are more often limited to a certain kind of project assistance.

But I think that the much more difficult question sometimes is not the technique, although that may have political ramifications, but rather the policies that guide the technique, and I think the hard question is what type of performance does even a multilateral organization expect from a potential recipient, both on the economic side and, perhaps, with more difficulty on the political side?

Senator FULBRIGHT. I recognize the difficulties. I would not say that multilateral organizations are necessarily more efficient, wiser than bilateral, but they have great political advantages....

Senator CHURCH....[L]et me pose this hypothesis: Suppose we were radically to change our approach to Latin America in these ways: First, bring the military missions home, and rely, as we used to for so many years, upon the American military attaché in the American embassy for such relationships as should properly exist with the military establishment in each Latin American host country.

Second, put an end, forthwith, to American military assistance programs in Latin America, grants-in-aid programs, and special credit programs.

Third, extend economic aid, insofar as possible, through multilateral channels like the World Bank and its affiliate, the subsidiary agencies of the United Nations, the Inter-American Development Bank, and so forth.

Fourth, confine our bilateral aid, given directly by the United States to recipient Latin American governments, to those democratic governments that are undertaking to strengthen the rule of law and to extend the benefits of the economy to a larger number of people; in short, confine it to governments with which we identify our own national principles, in the hope of giving them such special help as they may request. But let them request it, let them come to us if they care to, and avoid stationing large cadres of American administrators in these countries which might have the effect of reducing the very governments we most want to help to the status of puppets in the eyes of their own people....

Mr. DUNGAN. Very quickly. I concur, I think in all elements that you have just outlined, Senator, with the possible exception of No. 3....

While I understand Senator Fulbright's and others' attachment to the multilateral aid concept, I think that bears more careful examination by this committee and by the full committee before one would want to fully commit to it. In a certain sense there is a tension, if not a dichotomy, between point 3, that is shifting toward a multilateral aid concept and 4, which is continuing bilateralism....

I think with respect to 3 and 4, the United States has to fully recognize that there is a political price to be paid for intervention. The question is, it seems to me, how that intervention occurs. It can occur, to draw an extreme, to use extreme terms, in an imperialistic way in which the minute details of the country's development are in a sense dictated or strongly influenced by U.S. administrators, and there is another way to do it which is with a high degree of permissiveness in which we make a political judgment based on the host country's willingness to accept certain principles of action. In other words, it is a voluntary type attachment.

If in general what that country is doing is acceptable and it is paying attention to social change, which George described so eloquently, and doing other things which are generally consistent with what I term popular democracy, then you say "Great, we will cooperate." If not, we desist from cooperation. It is not a punishment. You know, the conditions for involvement are not suitable.

But I do not think you can avoid that kind of hard political decision by shifting to the multilateral concept nor do I think it is necessarily in the U.S. interest.

29

Letter from Peru

Richard N. Goodwin

From Richard N. Goodwin, "Letter from Peru," *The New Yorker* (May 17, 1969), pp. 41–108. © 1969 The New Yorker Magazine, Inc. Reprinted by permission of the Sterling Lord Agency.

Richard N. Goodwin was formerly a speech writer for President Kennedy and one of his principal advisers on Latin American policies.

For many years the United States has contended that Latin American countries could vastly expand the amount of capital available for development by making conditions more attractive for foreign private investments. Indeed, it was not until the late fifties and early sixties that the U.S. agreed that Latin American economic and social development also required large transfers of public capital. Moreover, the United States itself has attempted to encourage its nationals to invest in Latin America (and elsewhere) by offering them various inducements, including subsidization of investment opportunity surveys, insurance for certain kinds of risks, and low-interest Exim Bank loans.

Latin Americans, for their part, have viewed foreign investment with mixed emotions.[1] On the one hand, they have recognized that their economies need whatever capital is available; on the other, they have become increasingly disturbed about the prominent place in national life occupied by foreign corporations. Of particular concern to nationalist groups have been those foreign enterprises, generally of long standing, which control key sectors of the economy (extractive industries and public utilities, for example). Many of these enterprises originally established themselves on the basis of purchases sanctioned by—and/or agreements concluded with—now

---

[1] See Roberto Campos, "The Dilemma of Private Investment," *Inter-American Economic Affairs*, XXIV, No. 3 (Winter 1970), pp. 81–84; Miguel S. Wionczek, *United States Investment and the Development of Middle America* in *Studies in Comparative International Development*, V (1969–1970), No. 1; Raymond Vernon, ed., *How Latin America Views the U.S. Investor* (New York: Praeger, 1966); Marvin D. Bernstein, ed., *Foreign Investment in Latin America: Cases and Attitudes* (New York: Knopf, 1966); and Dwight S. Brothers, "Private Foreign Investment in Latin America: Some Implications for the Alliance for Progress" in Cole Blasier, ed., *Constructive Change in Latin America* (Pittsburgh: University of Pittsburgh Press), pp. 87–116.

discredited governments. They, like other foreign corporations, aggravate the critical balance-of-payments situation by remitting a substantial part of their profits abroad; and, in the case of extractive industries, profits come from the "exploitation" of irreplaceable national resources. Critics also often charge that foreign companies have a tendency to meddle nefariously in domestic politics, as a means of protecting their investments.

For these reasons and others, Latin American governments have become steadily more sensitive about U.S. official emphasis on private capital. For instance, emanating from the 1969 Viña del Mar meeting of CECLA was a request that the United States no longer label private investment as "assistance" or compute it as part of international financing for development.

More important is the fact that some Latin American governments are exploring ways to make foreign investment more responsible to the needs of the nation. There is increasing interest in state and/or national-private-capital participation in new (and, occasionally, existing) enterprises and in a variety of measures designed to insure that profits will be reinvested where they are made. The Velasco regime in Peru has drafted an innovative set of laws affecting manufacturing, mining, banking, and general commercial activities, which will undoubtedly encourage similar experiments elsewhere in Latin America. Under the new industry code, for example, foreign-owned industries will be required to sell at least 51 per cent of their capital to the state after a specified number of years. In the interim the government will place a ceiling on profits and make provision for workers to receive a share. As an incentive to investors, the government will protect capital investments and guarantee that they will ultimately be available for repatriation, as well as extend tax advantages to industries that attain the requisite ratings under a national point system (a "report card" on an industry's "patriotism," productivity, etc.).

Expropriation of enterprises owned by U.S. citizens, of course, has long bedeviled inter-American relations. The United States has clung to the legal position that expropriation must be followed by "prompt and adequate" compensation and has defended the right of diplomatic protection when its nationals are denied "international minimum standards of justice" —although the U.S. has conceded that there must be an "exhaustion of local remedies" before a "denial of justice" can be established. Latin American governments have usually subscribed to the Calvo principle that aliens have only the same domestic channels for the redress of grievances that are available to nationals.[2]

In the event of a threatened expropriation or a stalemate in negotiations after an expropriation has occurred, the United States has had to weigh

---

2 See C. Neale Ronning, *Law and Politics in Inter–American Diplomacy* (New York: Wiley, 1963), chap. 3.

the desire to protect its citizens' investments against its own interest in maintaining amicable relations with Latin American governments. As might be expected, different administrations have resolved this dilemma in different ways. Since 1962, over the strong objections of the State Department, Congress has complicated matters by attaching the Hickenlooper Amendment to foreign assistance legislation. The key section of the amendment requires the President to suspend all aid to any government that expropriates property owned by U.S. nationals, after six months have passed without "appropriate steps" toward "speedy compensation." As the Nixon Administration has demonstrated in the IPC dispute with Peru, the amendment need not be as binding on the executive as its proponents intended: The administration to date has simply ignored the six-month deadline, citing continuing domestic litigation and international negotiations as mitigating factors.[3]

The Goodwin article which follows is a valuable contribution from several standpoints. It examines in spellbinding detail the background of the 1968 Velasco coup in Peru. It also points up the counterproductive quality of the Hickenlooper and Conte-Long Amendments, Conte-Long denying aid at a critical time to the well-intentioned Belaúnde government because of its purchase of supersonic jet fighters. But the article is more than anything else a case study of the IPC controversy: how Peruvians came to regard the IPC as a symbol of foreign "domination" and how the United States reacted to the threat of expropriation over a period of years.

In closing, the editor would like to pose a few questions relating to the private investment issue which students of inter-American relations might consider:

1. In view of the fact that private investment has never met the $1 billion-a-year Alliance for Progress target, may we conclude that U.S. business needs continued incentives from the public purse to invest in Latin America? Traditionally, higher rates of return have to a considerable extent compensated for the greater risks attending investment in Latin America. But the climate for investment in the area—including the increasing determination of Latin American governments to establish tighter controls over foreign enterprises—is no longer as inviting as it once was.

2. Will Latin Americans on their own initiative establish the conditions

---

[3] Ironically, when Washington suspended credit arms sales to Peru at the height of the IPC dispute in February, 1969, it was acting not under Hickenlooper but under a provision in the Military Sales Act that calls for a one-year suspension in such sales when a government seizes U.S. fishing boats beyond a twelve-mile limit. The Pelley Amendment to the Fisherman's Protective Act applies to the same situation, providing for a reduction in economic aid equivalent to the fines imposed on U.S. vessels. These provisions have often been waived for brief periods—as they were later in 1969—to accommodate sporadic talks on the territorial waters issue between the U.S. and Ecuador, Peru, and Chile, the three Latin American countries that have been most militant in enforcing claim to a limit of 200 miles from their coastlines. Other claimants: Argentina, Brazil, El Salvador, Nicaragua, Panama, and Uruguay.

required to lure whatever investment they want? Whitehead has raised a related question: "[G]iven the growing burden of past foreign investment and the scarcity of new investment funds on acceptable terms, will the continent now grow faster by trying to attract still more investment, or by curtailing the costs of existing investments?"[4] *He argues the latter, making a case for Latin American governments' curbing capital outflow through measures ranging from special taxes to (when necessary) outright confiscation, and he urges the developed countries to acquiesce in these steps.*

3. Congress has recently created the Overseas Private Investment Corporation (OPIC) primarily to reshape insurance programs for private investments in the developing countries. Will the OPIC be able to offer investors adequate and low–cost financial protection against expropriations? The former Investment Guaranty Program (IGP) was limited only to new investments and to those types which governments had accepted by international agreement.[5] *Should the U.S. also subscribe to Hirschman's proposal for the establishment of an Inter-American Divestment Corporation that would help governments buy out selected foreign enterprises?*[6]

4. In the absence of programs like the foregoing, how should the United States continue to defend its nationals' investments—or should it do so at all? Might the United States, as Goodwin suggests, head off some expropriations by exercising quiet diplomacy between private enterprises and national governments? In any event, should a corporation like the IPC in Peru be any more exempt from the hazards of its unique environment than, say, a motel owner in the U.S. whose establishment is bypassed by a new highway? What indeed would happen if the United States were to indicate that its protection henceforth would not be available to companies? Would the result be a series of vengeful expropriations or other drastic measures, or would those U.S. businesses in Latin America which have not already done so become acutely conscious of their own image and start to come to terms with the constituencies they purport to serve?

Early in the morning of October 3, 1968, the armed forces of Peru overthrew that country's government. Six days later, a thousand troops of the New Revolutionary Government seized the oil complex surrounding the northern city of Talara. Within a few months, the junta had taken over that complex and all other assets of the International Petroleum Company (or I.P.C.), a wholly owned subsidiary of Standard Oil of New Jersey....

[4] Lawrence Whitehead, "Aid to Latin America: Problems and Prospects," *Journal of International Affairs,* XXIV, No. 2 (1970), p. 195.
[5] See Roderick T. Groves, "Expropriation in Latin America: Some Observations," *Inter-American Economic Affairs,* XXIII, No. 3 (Winter 1969), pp. 47–66.
[6] Albert O. Hirschman, *How to Divest in Latin America and Why,* Princeton Essays in International Finance, No. 76 (November 1969). See also Guy B. Meeker, "Fadeout Joint Venture: Can It Work for Latin America?" *Inter-American Economic Affairs,* XXIV, No. 4 (Spring 1971), pp. 25–42.

It is helpful to understand how small and poor a country now awaits, with growing apprehension, the outcome of its clash with the dominant power of the Western Hemisphere. Sprawled along the western coast of South America, Peru can be roughly pictured as an upright rectangle about twelve hundred miles high and eight hundred miles at its widest point, similar in shape to California, although about three times as large.... About a third of the Peruvians are Andean Indians who live outside the national economy and society and many of whom speak only their ancient Indian languages. Peru is one of Latin America's poorer countries. The average yearly income is about two hundred and eighty dollars per person, and the total national production is worth approximately four billion dollars; that makes the nation of Peru a little more than a fourth as productive as Standard Oil of New Jersey, whose total revenues [in 1968] were more than fourteen billion dollars.

...Today, in Peru, United States interests own, *inter alia,* nearly all of the copper, probably the country's most valuable natural resource; about a quarter of the sugar and fishing industries; nearly all of the shipping; much of the oil; the telephone company; and many of the major retail establishments, including Sears, Roebuck and Coca-Cola—although the more popular Inca Cola is owned by a Peruvian family. Moreover, Peru is almost totally dependent on the American government and private banks for the refinancing of its large external debt and for the funds necessary to expand its mining. The present Peruvian government is ready to admit the self-evident—that Peru cannot develop without the continued infusion of private capital from the United States.

Still, the sheer weight of the American presence undoubtedly heightens Peruvian sensitivity to our every act and proclamation. "We want to be friends and we want American investment," the head of one of Peru's oldest and most powerful families told me. "But we cannot have *'paternalismo.'* You are big enough to be the father, but we are too old to be a son."[1]

Peru is no banana republic carved from the wilderness by Spanish conquerors. The road from Lima to the oil fields passes only a hundred miles from the plaza at Cajamarca, where, on the evening of November 16, 1532, Pizarro the Conqueror ambushed and captured the chief of the Incas and in a single stroke destroyed the power of the vast Inca civilization, whose roots reached back into still older societies that were building temples and organizing society in the eighth century B.C. After four hundred years of Westernization, of foreign aid and private in-

[1] Some cautions for the reader. Facts in Latin America, historical and otherwise, are often elusive. In some cases, the best one can do is make a reasoned judgment. In others, it is enough to show that uncertainty exists and that the evidence is not clearly and irrefutably in favor of one side or the other. It is also necessary to be aware that a sentence in an American publication can become a banner headline in Lima and an instrument of political purpose or of vengeance. Therefore, it is sometimes necessary to conceal the precise source of information and attitudes. In this exploration, I talked with the President and high officials of the present government, the President and supporters of the deposed government, the principal civilan allies of the military coup, and with the top officers of Standard Oil, its I.P.C. subsidiary, and the United States Embassy, along with many other concerned citizens of the United States and Peru. Where there is no name given, the individual has been judged well informed or a qualified representative of attitudes and convictions.

vestment, of the Good Neighbor Policy and the Alliance for Progress, Peru is far less developed in many respects than it was during the Inca rule. . . .

From this past derives another experience that helps illuminate the intensities of feeling behind the present dispute. The history of Peru is, in large measure, the history of the soil and its riches. For centuries the Indians mined and worked the gold that lured their conquerors to Peru. . . . The Peruvians' economy has nearly always rested on mineral wealth—gold and silver, copper and nitrates, pitch and oil—although in recent years they have also uncovered the riches that lie beneath the seas in the great fishing grounds of the Humboldt Current. Much of this wealth is still untouched. The copper companies plan a six-hundred-million-dollar expansion of their mining facilities. The jungle lands east of the Andes are thought to conceal enormous and diverse riches. And the oil companies know that Peru contains one of the largest unexplored sedimentary beds in the world. The sense that minerals were the foundation of the state helps explain why under the Incas, the Spanish, and under the Republic of Peru, the state alone could own the Peruvian subsoil and what it contained. Individuals and private companies could secure the right to explore and often received sweeping concessions to mine and refine, and to profit from sales and commerce. But in Peru, as in most of Latin America, no private person could own the subsoil rights. To this traditional law, for almost a century and a half, there was one exception: the La Brea y Pariñas oil field of Standard Oil of New Jersey. That exception has now been ended by the Revolutionary Government of Peru.

Now the United States must decide whether to retaliate by invoking the Hickenlooper Amendment to the Foreign Assistance Act, which directs the President to cut off all foreign aid to any country that expropriates a United States company without taking "appropriate steps" toward "speedy compensation" within six months. The amendment was enacted in 1962 over the opposition of the Kennedy Administration and has never been applied in Latin America. The original deadline was April 9th, six months after the seizure of Talara. But as that date approached without progress toward settlement, the Nixon Administration averted a clash by deciding that Peru's willingness to permit I.P.C. an administrative appeal constituted "appropriate steps" within the meaning of the Hickenlooper Amendment. Thus, the new deadline for decision is early August, when the appeal will be decided not by the courts but by Peruvian administrators, and ultimately by the President of Peru.

The Peruvian government freely admits the company's right to compensation for its seized assets, and has offered to pay a fair amount as soon as the company pays its own alleged debt to Peru. However, this claim of debt—which is the subject of the I.P.C. appeal—is based on the theory that the company had been operating the La Brea field illegally for forty-four years and therefore owes Peru the value of everything produced by that field, which amounts to a good deal more than the value of the assets. Thus, in fact, I.P.C. would get nothing. Imposition of the Hickenlooper Amendment and allied legislation would have serious and perhaps crippling consequences for the entire Peruvian economy. Formally, it would cut off aid and halt United States purchases of

Peruvian sugar, which are a major source of foreign exchange. In practice, it would dry up American financing, public and private, of badly needed industrial expansion as well as the refinancing of present debts. An Inter-American Bank expert has estimated that the amendment could cost Peru a hundred and eighty million dollars in a year—an amount roughly equivalent to all of the country's financial reserves and about two-thirds as much as the total aid Peru has received since the Alliance for Progress began, in 1961. Almost inevitably, such Draconian strokes would provoke some form of economic retaliation, perhaps against other American companies, and bright young colonels of the Presidential staff are preparing contingency plans to halt the flight of foreign currency and assets. Even more serious are the potential political consequences. The justice of the seizure is probably the only conviction that unites the historically divided and fragmented parties and classes of Peru. Peace Corps volunteers report that for the first time they hear hostile mutterings about the "gringos" as they walk through the streets of Lima slums or ride the rickety buses of the poor. Applying the Hickenlooper Amendment "would probably increase nationalistic and anti-American feeling," says the American Ambassador, John Wesley Jones. "Blood will flow in the streets," gloomily predicts President Juan Velasco Alvarado. "Peru could become another Cuba," says a high official of the exiled civilian government. Apocalyptic prophecies about Latin America are usually wrong. Still, there is little doubt that application of Hickenlooper would damage our relationships with Peru and with other countries of Latin America....

Over the years, few nations have been friendlier to American investment than Peru, and the present government proclaims its intention to continue that friendship. Why, then, did a government that is fundamentally pro-American and anti-Communist seize this company at this time? "In my six years," Ambassador Jones says, "the company has been totally generous and reasonable in trying to reach a settlement with Peru." "If you want to know what I think," another American told me, "Velasco just saw this was a good nationalistic issue and grabbed it to stay in power." On February 6, 1969, President Velasco himself declared, "The case of the International Petroleum Company is the problem of a company that has transgressed and offended our laws, usurped our rights by using all available means, and one that is determined to create conflict between two friendly governments. The case of the International Petroleum Company is unique. It is a singular case." The Foreign Minister, General Mercado, asks, "How can you apply the amendment on behalf of a company that is so bad?" And then, in the soft tones of submerged fury, he said, "The story of I.P.C. is a black chapter in the history of my country."

The story starts long before the International Petroleum Company came to Peru, and long before men knew of petroleum and the riches it would bring. Some six hundred years ago, a group of pre-Inca Indians in the remote northern reaches of Peru discovered at the foot of the Amotape Mountains, about thirteen miles from the Pacific, a cluster of small pools filled with a dark, heavy liquid that seemed to ooze mysteriously from the center of the earth. They skimmed the oil from the surface and used it to line clay jars and to mummify the dead.

After the Conquest, the Spanish dug trenches, and as the oil seeped into the excavations they combined boiling with natural evaporation to leave a thick, scummy black residue known as *brea,* or pitch. Transported down the coast, the pitch was used to caulk the hulls and tar the rigging of the Spanish fleet. During this period, the pitch mine, like all the mineral properties in Spanish America, remained the property of the crown, which granted often sweeping concessions to favored individuals and companies. In 1821, after declaring its independence of Spain, Peru reconfirmed the colonial mining ordinances, which provided that ownership of the subsoil rights to all minerals, and to other substances in the earth, belonged to the state. And in 1824 Bolívar drove the last Spanish troops from the country. Like revolutionaries before and since, Bolívar needed money to finance his struggle. One of those who helped him was Don José de Quintana. In 1826, to discharge its debt to de Quintana, the new Peruvian government deeded him the pitch mine at Amotape. The deed declares that the agents of the Peruvian government "abdicate, strip, and separate from the state which they represent all right, title, and dominion held by or appertaining to it over the said mine of 'pitch,' and they cede, renounce, and transfer the same to the purchaser." It is on the basis of this 1826 deed that successive owners have claimed a unique ownership of the subsoil rights, and for forty-five years the deed has been the legal basis of I.P.C.'s claim to title. Peru's denial of that title is the legal foundation of the claim against I.P.C., which is the principal issue of the current crisis. Peruvian experts argue that even if the deed did grant ownership to subsoil rights in the

pitch mine—which they do not admit —it could not have included ownership of petroleum, a substance whose use and value were then unknown. However one interprets the deed itself, the history of this claim is entangled with the entire history of Peru and illuminates both the tenacity of its holders and the resistance of many Peruvians to an assertion of private dominion that they have found deeply offensive to their concept of national sovereignty. As Peru became more nationalistic and more sensitive about its independent sovereignty, that resistance increased.

By 1830, Don José de Lama had merged ownership of the mine—which he had acquired in 1827—with the huge estate on which it was situated, thus creating the property known from then on as La Brea y Pariñas. Thirty-eight years later, only a decade after the world's first oil well was drilled in Pennsylvania, his daughter struck oil on the La Brea property. Shortly afterward, the Peruvian government took a new interest in this distant northern province. In the eighteen-seventies, Peru passed its first mining laws since independence. They required, *inter alia,* that all "owners of mining claims ...of coal or petroleum...present their title ... for revalidation" and registration within four months or the claims would be declared void. The laws also set up a new system of taxation. With some exceptions, all mines were to be divided into arbitrary sections of ten acres each, known as *pertenencias,* and a flat tax would be imposed on each *pertenencia.* The then owner of La Brea, Don Genaro Helguero, neither registered his title nor paid any tax, presumably on the ground that as the absolute owner of the subsoil rights he was immune from the new national mining legislation. However, in the next decade a British group became interested in buying the oil field, and we can reasonably conjecture that before making the purchase they wanted some official confirmation of Helguero's special rights and tax status other than the 1826 deed. In any event, Helguero, after a decade of indifference to the law, petitioned a local court for judicial confirmation of his title. What happened next is obscured by time and the baffling intricacy of nineteenth-century Peruvian bureaucracy. Although the judge said that Helguero was indeed the absolute owner of the subsoil, the decree of a local magistrate was clearly not enough protection. Therefore, in 1887, Helguero petitioned the Department of Mines of Peru to recognize that no tax or mining law could apply to his property, since it came to him by the "real and perpetual sale" of Bolívar's government. After the Department reported in his favor, a higher official, the Attorney General of the Supreme Court, found that "the government cannot and should not admit in the Republic rights over mines other than those stipulated by the law." There then followed a series of petitions and official decrees that registered the mining claims in Helguero's name and divided the entire property into ten *pertenencias* for purposes of taxation. None of the official acts or decrees refers to Helguero as the absolute owner of subsoil rights, and, in fact, the final decree of 1888 calls him "the concession holder." Moreover, if he was the owner there was no need for him to register his claim or pay any tax at all, since those requirements of the mining law depended on the legal proposition that the state, as owner of the subsoil, was regulating the con-

cessionaires. Later proprietors of La Brea have argued that Helguero accepted all these conditions because he was in a hurry to sell the property. However, to the outside observer this episode would seem to provide the strongest legal argument against later claims to ownership of the subsoil, although it is hardly mentioned in the lengthy Peruvian account. It could be strongly argued, at least before an American court, that even if Helguero had been the owner he had exchanged that ownership for official recognition of his rights and for a special tax status. For even though the standard *pertenencia* was ten acres, Helguero had managed to have his huge estate, of over four hundred thousand acres, divided into only ten *pertenencias,* which meant that for the next thirty-four years the annual tax on the oil field was about a hundred and fifty dollars. One could even maintain that it was then, in 1888, that the state exercised its legal right to expropriate the subsoil rights. In any event, five days after Helguero received the government's final decree he sold the property to two British citizens—a Mr. Tweddle and a Mr. Keswick—who, a year later, leased it to the London & Pacific Petroleum Co. for ninety-nine years. It may help us to guess at the atmosphere surrounding these intricate machinations to know that this was a period in Peruvian history when an American soldier of fortune named Henry Meiggs took over the construction of railroads for the entire nation, bribing politicians and importing coolie labor until his empire collapsed, leaving him to die a penniless derelict. The atmosphere of the time has been described somewhat harshly by the nineteenth-century Peruvian political leader Gonzalez Prada: "Riches served as an element of corruption, not of material progress. . . . No means of acquisition seemed illicit. The people would have thrown themselves into a sewer if at the bottom they had glimpsed a golden sol. Husbands sold their wives, fathers their daughters, brothers their sisters."

The next serious eruption of the now historic problem of La Brea began in the early nineteen-hundreds when an official mining engineer reported to the Peruvian government that somehow a serious mistake had been made in measuring the property: it appeared to be far larger than the figure of ten *pertenencias* would indicate. The government agreed, and on March 31, 1911, decreed that the owners "of the said mine do not pay the amount of taxes. . . corresponding to the number of lawful *pertenencias*" because of an "error" made in measurement. The London & Pacific Petroleum Co. protested the decree, and matters took their customary leisurely course until April of 1914, when Peru rejected the protest and ordered surveyors to remeasure the property. The argument might have dragged on for years, except that by this time London & Pacific had urgent reasons to press for a settlement. For in 1914 the International Petroleum Company had taken over the oil field, intending to buy the property. But even Mr. Herbert Hoover, then the consulting engineer and chief negotiator for the British interests, could not persuade I.P.C. to complete the purchase until there had been a final settlement of the legal and tax status of La Brea y Pariñas. By early 1915, the surveyors had remeasured the property, and in March a Peruvian decree specifically rejected British protests that the sale to de Quintana in 1826 had given absolute ownership of the subsoil and

thus exempted the oil field from mining taxes. The decree asserted that "the rights acquired by that sale could not be other than those conferred by the Mining Ordinances in force when the . . . contract was made. . . nor did it confer any greater rights. . . than those which any private individual could grant, nor was there any declaration that the absolute ownership thereof was granted." Therefore, as the remeasurement showed, the tax should be paid not on ten *pertenencias* but on 41,614. Once again the Peruvian government had denied the special and unique claim to private ownership of the subsoil rights of La Brea y Pariñas.

London & Pacific, however, had resources not available to previous Peruvian owners, and for the first time the La Brea y Pariñas problem evoked the concern and pressure of a foreign government. The British Ambassador in Lima, acting on instructions from London, delivered a note to the Peruvian Foreign Office protesting the decree. The dispute dragged on for years, with neither side willing to yield, although there is no record that the higher taxes were ever paid. Suddenly the prospects for the oil company brightened when, in 1919, dictatorial power was seized by Augusto B. Leguía y Salcedo, whose rule was to bring a large expansion of American private investment into every sector of the Peruvian economy. Two years later, the long-smoldering dispute was submitted to a three-man arbitral tribunal consisting of representatives of Peru and Great Britain and the president of the Swiss Federal Court, Dr. Fritz Ostertag. For almost half a century, this arbitration has been the subject of debate and agitation. Lawyers and politicians have built reputations and careers analyzing, attacking, and defending the award of the tribunal. It has continually antagonized the many Peruvians who have firmly believed that a specially privileged oil company was forced on them by illegal and coercive pressures from abroad. Much of the present dispute revolves around the Peruvians' contention that the award was illegal and thus I.P.C. owes them the profits of its entire operation since the time it bought the field in 1924. And the Peruvian government points out that the arbitration took place at about the time that Harding's Secretary of the Interior, Albert B. Fall, was accepting the bribes from American oil interests that later sent him to prison. Even a high official of the deposed civilian government, which was attacked for its supposed generosity to I.P.C., says that "everyone knew that the arbitration was no good." I.P.C., of course, denies this, and claims that in any event it acquired its ownership of La Brea y Pariñas not through the award but by virtue of the deed of 1826. At this point in time, no one can evaluate the charges of fraud and corruption, but the actual decisions of the arbitration are another matter. Even before the tribunal met, the representatives of Peru and Great Britain had worked out their own private agreement, which, in 1922, was dutifully incorporated by Dr. Ostertag into an international decree. One of the most important and puzzling aspects of this decree is what it failed to decide. Although the ancient issue of subsoil ownership had helped to evoke the controversy, it is left unresolved by the final document. The most probable conclusion is that the arbitrators could find no way to resolve the question. Nor did it seem necessary. For the decree recognized the British right to La Brea y Pariñas and provided that

for fifty years—until 1972—virtually the only tax the oil company had to pay (with some slight exceptions) was about fifteen dollars a year for each of the 41,614 *pertenencias* it was actually exploiting and about fifty cents for those it was not working. This special tax status, with its exemption from all other levies, inevitably was to become a source of increasing discontent. Ten years later, after the dictator Leguía had been driven from office, the new Peruvian government attacked the award and made a futile effort to bring the matter before the World Court. As late as 1959, only the appearance of the Peruvian Foreign Minister before a secret session persuaded Peru's Congress to reject a resolution annulling the arbitration. And on November 6, 1963, that Congress finally enacted a law providing that "the so-called... Award (arbitral) on La Brea y Pariñas for having violated the pertinent legal requirements [is] null *ipso jure* and [does] not obligate the Republic." But by this time Fernando Belaúnde Terry had been elected President of Peru and had begun the five-year effort to reach an accommodation with I.P.C. that ended only when the armed forces overthrew his government and seized the oil field.

No formal historical sketch can fully explain the clashing passions and interests that shaped and colored the negotiations of the Belaúnde period. For by then I.P.C. had come to occupy a special position in Peruvian life, and one seen very differently by I.P.C., the American government, and Peruvian nationalists. "We were the largest taxpayer in Peru and our labor practices were a model for the country," accurately reports an official of I.P.C., while the American Embassy asserts that over the last several years "I.P.C.

was always very generous, and honestly worked hard to reach a settlement." Yet on December 4, 1968, the Peruvian general who seized I.P.C. summed up the feelings of many Peruvians when he said, "No people can live in dignity and with respect for its sovereignty...when it tolerates the insolent arrogance of another state within its own frontiers." It is not that the truth lies somewhere in between. Rather, it is a case of parties whose assumptions, needs, and habits of action were so divergent that conflict seemed almost inevitable. Perhaps I.P.C. did not act wisely, but it acted as an oil company might be expected to act, pressing every advantage and withholding every concession within the limits of its power and the sometimes sordid possibilities of Peruvian politics and intrigue. If at the end overconfidence and shortsightedness helped undo I.P.C., it must be remembered that the company had prospered and maintained its special privileges amid growing agitation for almost half a century. And it has not lost everything yet. Peru, on the other hand, is not a business but a country and a people. The mass of Peruvians hardly knew of I.P.C.'s existence. Yet among many of those most sensitive to the dignity and independence of their country the activities of I.P.C., combined with its unique claim to a part of the Peruvian dominion, planted seeds of hatred which the years were to nourish. Only United States policy could have reconciled these diverging perceptions, for only the United States could command the respectful attention of both I.P.C. and the Peruvian government. This force was not brought to bear, and today's crisis is in large measure a result of that failure.

In the decades preceding the crucial 1963 election of Belaúnde, I.P.C. steadily expanded its operations. By the time of the seizure, the company's interests in Peru extended far beyond the La Brea y Pariñas field near Talara. It also owned a half interest in the more productive Lobitos field. It had a refinery in operation at Talara and controlled fifty-five per cent of the marketing and sale of gasoline in Peru. In addition, I.P.C. had reasonable expectations of obtaining concessions to explore for oil in the potentially rich jungle lands east of the Andes. (Mobil Oil has already invested twenty million dollars in the search.) Obviously, I.P.C.'s other assets were far more valuable than the increasingly less productive La Brea y Pariñas field (now producing at about half its former peak), yet only La Brea claimed exemption from the normal requirements of Peruvian law. Moreover, history was reshaping traditional attitudes. Throughout the nineteen-fifties, poor nations asserted with increasing intensity their right to be independent of the historical domination of the Western powers. This was the decade that brought the final disintegration of the great colonial empires, the Bandung Conference, Algeria, the retreat from Suez, and Castro. Peru, like much of Latin America, was touched by this global surge, and a mounting nationalism was combined with an anger at the United States that erupted dramatically during the Nixon trip. There was some justice to the specific grievances that fed anti-Americanism, but equally important was the fact that Latin America, alone among the underdeveloped continents, was not made up of colonies and could only assert its nationalism against the historically dominant, if noncolonial, power of the Western Hemisphere. I.P.C. was presumably aware that in such a changing environment the privileged position of La Brea y Pariñas endangered the company's whole position in Peru. In 1951, the company submitted to the regular fifty-per-cent income tax on profits, a tax it had protested, with limited success, since 1934. In 1957, for the first time, I.P.C. offered to "assign" its subsoil ownership to the state in return for an "exploitation concession" covering the same field along with expanded concessions for its other activities. The company did this, the official I.P.C. history reports, because it realized that "ownership of the petroleum property was a cause of resentment in Peru [and] inconsistent with the general pattern of petroleum legislation . . . in South America." The offer was rejected, apparently because by 1957 the Peruvian government felt it could not afford to grant further concessions for rights that many Peruvians believed to be already theirs. In this period, not only had I.P.C. made some gesture toward relinquishing its subsoil ownership but it had become an exemplary employer. Housing and working conditions at Talara were the best in the country, and the company paid excellent wages and benefits. Still, as Peru entered the nineteen-sixties the accumulated grievances of decades were steadily building. . . .

Yet despite these resentments—which were shared, one must remember, by only a small, but influential, group of Peruvians—it is probable that the government and I.P.C. could have resolved their dispute peacefully any time between the election of Belaúnde, in 1963, and the decline of his political strength, which began in late 1966. In retrospect, the failure to do so seems like some Harvard Business School version of a Greek drama, with

all parties steadfastly honoring their prescribed duties while rushing toward a foreseeable fate. Except, of course, since modern man is more given to wishful thinking, they did not foresee it. That story began in July of 1962, when elements of the Peruvian armed forces crossed the broad Plaza de Armas, in the heart of Lima, entered the Presidential Palace, and took over the country. An extremely close three-cornered Presidential election had just taken place, and although none of the candidates had received the necessary plurality, it was clear that the two candidates least acceptable to the armed forces—one a historic enemy and the other a former dictator—had agreed to combine forces in order to keep the military's favorite, Fernando Belaúnde Terry, the candidate of the Popular Action Party, from winning. Under great pressure from the United States to resume constitutional government, the military leaders scheduled a new election for June, 1963. This time, Belaúnde won a clear-cut victory, and on July 28th he took office for a six-year term.

An architect and politician, a man of the people who can trace his family back fourteen generations to the first mayor of Lima, Belaúnde had campaigned on a liberal and progressive platform of economic development and social reform. Although many later criticized his abilities as a leader, there is no doubt about his personal belief in the principles of the Alliance for Progress. A visionary, he nurtured far-flung plans to build a great highway to unite the lands on the far side of the Andes and open the rich interior to settlement. Recently, in a Lima drawing room, a guest began to criticize Belaúnde in the presence of General Velasco, the man who drove him from office. "Don't talk that way," said the General. "He was a great man. Only he was a dreamer." Dreamer or not, Belaúnde was just the sort of national leader that the United States was hoping for in Latin America, and a logical recipient of generous American assistance.

Therefore, immediately after Belaúnde's inauguration, Teodoro Moscoso, President Kennedy's Coördinator for the Alliance for Progress, flew to Peru with offers of immediate and substantial United States aid. There was only one problem. On taking office, Belaúnde had promised to resolve the La Brea y Pariñas question within ninety days. Moscoso realized that even the most reasonable settlement would create political difficulties for Belaúnde, so he decided to withhold action until the ninety days were up. Thus, the announcement of aid could be used by the Peruvian government to help blunt any opposition. No effort was made to pressure Belaúnde, and the aid was to flow whatever the outcome might be. Negotiations between Peru and I.P.C. began in early August, and by the end of October they had broken down. As a result, on November 6, 1963, the Peruvian Congress passed the law declaring that the arbitration award of 1922 was null and void and did "not obligate the Republic." Meanwhile, changes were occurring in the United States that were to have a profound impact in Peru. After President Kennedy's death, Latin-American affairs came under the direction of Assistant Secretary of State Thomas C. Mann, a former Ambassador to Mexico. Mann decided to suspend all foreign aid to Peru until Belaúnde reached an agreement with I.P.C., but to do so without delivering an ultimatum or even telling Peru that aid had been stopped.

"The idea," one U.S. aid official has explained, "was to put on a freeze, talk about red tape and bureaucracy, and they'd soon get the message. Unfortunately, they believed we were as inefficient as we said, and it took about a year for them to get the message." In fact, virtually no aid went to Peru for two full years as negotiations with I.P.C. dragged on, broke down, and began again. (A few token loans were made, in an effort to insulate the State Department from the charge that it had frozen aid to Peru; but the freeze was real and intentional.)

No provision of United States law and no principle of foreign policy required us to suspend aid in order to compel a Latin-American country to negotiate an agreement with a private American company. Nor is there any evidence that I.P.C. ever asked that any such measure be taken. Throughout this whole period, the oil-and-gas business in Peru continued as usual, and none of the company's operations were disturbed. The negotiations themselves were complicated by Peruvian claims for back taxes and alleged debts, along with a host of technical details. On the surface, the major point at issue concerned the way in which the profits should be split between the company and the government—that difference amounted, at most, to a few million dollars a year, and no other I.P.C. operations in Peru were affected. Yet during this period of discussion Peru lost up to a hundred and fifty million dollars in aid because of its failure to agree with the company. However, behind the price dispute—and probably far more important—there was the ancient question of who owned La Brea y Pariñas. The company offered to cede its ownership rights, but it insisted on retaining operating control of the field and receiving a cancellation of all alleged debts. This was obviously a sticking point with a government that had promised to "recover La Brea y Pariñas" for the nation. The manager of I.P.C. saw President Belaúnde sixty times, and each time the President said, "Just cede me your rights and assets in La Brea, and you'll see that everything will be right." Finally, in 1968, the company offered to do just that, but it was too late.

Toward the end of 1965, the United States began to reconsider its policy. It was obvious that the aid cutoff was not forcing an agreement; nor was it advancing the broader interests of the United States. Economic development was virtually at a standstill in Peru, and although there were other reasons for this, the aid cutoff was clearly a factor. In village after village, one could see children crowded into a single dim room where a teacher struggled to keep order, while, outside, a half-finished schoolhouse stood open to the dry sierra winds. In these villages, the end of aid had meant no education, or no pure water, or a half-built road. Moreover, extremist attacks were increasing against a Belaúnde administration that had proved unexpectedly conservative in office. And Communist guerrilla movements, soon to be crushed by the U.S.-trained counter-insurgency forces of the Peruvian military, had sprung up in the Andes. "We knew we had a losing aid policy," said a high U.S. official. "But we'd said we couldn't give them loans unless they settled, and so we couldn't back down."

By early 1966, however, Lincoln Gordon had become Assistant Secretary for Inter-American Affairs, and in March the State Department sent Walt Rostow to Peru. Rostow told Belaúnde that if he was not going to confiscate the company we would go ahead with aid. A surprised Belaúnde responded that he had never intended to take the company. So aid was resumed, but not for long. However, this time oil was not the reason. In 1967, the Peruvian Air Force decided that it needed supersonic jet fighters, and, after the United States turned down the request, it contracted with the French for Mirages. (At one point, United States officials told the Peruvians that if they insisted on jets they could buy some cheaper American-made F-5s.) First in order to try and prevent the purchase and later as punishment for having gone ahead anyway, the United States reversed a decision to make program loans to Peru during 1967 and 1968 (which probably cut our aid to about half of the total we expected to give). "We just didn't think the Latins were ready for supersonics," a United States official explained. The cost of the Mirages was about twenty million dollars. The loss in aid was probably about sixty million dollars. Thus, because of our oil policy and our "supersonic" policy, Belaúnde faced a complete or partial suspension of United States aid for four of his five full years in office—a fact that certainly did not lessen his economic problems and did nothing to enhance Peruvian confidence in American dedication to the goal of strengthening progressive and democratic governments.

For a while in 1966, the I.P.C. problem receded, as Belaúnde seemed to tire of the effort to reach a settlement. In August, he even concurred in an I.P.C. plan to expand its refinery at Talara, but protest from opposition political parties and newspapers compelled a cancellation. Sporadic discussions continued as the company diligently examined various proposals for tax and profit splits. In the background, however, was the unyielding issue of ownership and control. By the summer of 1967, the deterioration of the Peruvian economy had seriously weakened Belaúnde's general political position. And criticism of his delay in solving the La Brea y Pariñas problem became part of a general assault on his leadership. Once more, in meetings with the company, the President returned to his earlier demand that the field be ceded outright to Peru, and once more the company refused. And although another year of debate and negotiation lay ahead, the stage was now set for the final act. For in the pleasant suburbs of Lima a small group of military officers and their civilian friends were beginning to plan the overthrow of the Belaúnde government and the establishment of long-term military rule. And when the revolution came, the principal actors would be the same armed forces and the same newspaper, *El Commercio,* that had fought so effectively to help install Belaúnde in the Presidential Palace five years before. Oil was among the least of their motives, but oil was to give them their opportunity to strike.

No one knows exactly when specific plans for a *golpe* (the Spanish term for "coup") began to precipitate out of the vague mist of military power that necessarily enshrouds any civilian government in Peru. One of the best-qualified U.S. observers says that it was early in 1968 when a group of officers around Minister of War Doig started to prepare contingency plans for a takeover. One of the closest advisers to the new government has said the decision began to take shape in a private conversation between General Velasco and a Colonel Rodríguez, who is one of the most brilliant and influential members of the Palace staff. However the revolutionary plans began, two of the motives were the same as those that had led the military to support Belaúnde in the first place: the desire to modernize the country and hatred of the APRA Party.

For decades, the Peruvian armed forces have nourished a deep and furious hostility toward one of Peru's most distinguished leaders, Víctor Raúl Haya de la Torre, founder of the APRA Party, and Belaúnde's chief opponent in the 1962 and 1963 Presidential election.... Although APRA disavowed Communism, it called for an overthrow of feudal structures, adopted an anti-imperialist policy, and was the first party to identify itself with the desires of the miserably oppressed Indian masses. As a result, APRA was hated and feared by the governing classes of Peru, and its history was scarred by repeated and often bloody clashes with the Peruvian military.... [A]lthough his ideas are now widely accepted, even by the Peruvian armed forces, the anger and resentment bred of those earlier clashes make the thought of an APRA government— especially under Haya, who is seventy-four and vigorous—intolerable to the military. This hatred of APRA has been shared by *El Commercio,* which has warred against APRA ever since Don Luis's brother and his brother's wife were slain by a young *Aprista* assassin on a street in downtown Lima....

The other reason for military support of the liberal Belaúnde was the change in the convictions and the nature of the armed forces. Until the late nineteen-fifties, the Peruvian armed forces, in the historic pattern of most Latin American countries, represented a static or reactionary social force. They were, in the words of a young Peruvian colonel, "the strong right arm of the oligarchy." But in recent years a quiet shift has taken place in some Latin-American military establishments which may have profound consequences for the future of the hemisphere. In Peru, the unexpected focus of this potentially revolutionary change is a sprawling complex of brick buildings on the outskirts of Lima known as the Center of Higher Military Studies. There, and in other military schools, officers spend two years in advanced study. For a decade, the course material has given increasing emphasis to social and economic systems taught by civilian experts, some of whom are far to the left, and most of whom are disciples of a liberal, and highly technocratic, brand of development economics. In these schools, the importance of the military role in "social and economic progress" is constantly stressed—an approach that is fully in accord with the emphasis that the United States and its influential military missions have given to "civic action." Most officers have also received American training in doctrines of counter-insurgency. From the irrefutable thesis that guerrillas are fish that swim in the sea of the people, they have drawn the inexorable conclusion: if they are to suppress guerrillas, they must win the support of the people. Most Latin-American officers, at one time or another, attend United States military schools and often develop close relationships with officers of our overseas missions. In recent years, it has been American policy to stress the role of the Latin-American military in economic progress. This has undoubtedly been a liberalizing influence, but it has also led many officers to believe that the

job of modernization can only be accomplished under their own rule. The officers themselves are rarely oligarchs. For the most part, they are drawn from lower-middle-class families, or even from among the poor. And they believe, as one general explained, that they "are the only people who really have lived in all parts of Peru during their career, the only ones who know the country." The emerging conviction that traditional, conservative thinking has been a source of explosive inequalities is coupled with a growing contempt for the inefficiency or corruption of civilian leadership and a mounting belief that it is the mission of the armed forces to take their country in a new direction. Although the new military leadership is fundamentally nationalistic and anti-Communist, many officers are coming to share Lenin's belief that "no revolution of the masses can triumph without the help of a portion of the armed forces that sustained the old regime." It was natural, therefore, that the military had been drawn to support Belaúnde, with his liberal and reformist beliefs and his emphasis on technology and construction.

Many of these same convictions and expectations that had attracted the military and other powerful supporters to Belaúnde in 1963 were transformed by the events of 1967 and 1968 into the motive for his overthrow. Even before 1967, many of Belaúnde's efforts to bring about moderate reform, especially land reform, had been blocked by the opposition parties, which, having more than a majority in Congress, could exercise control whenever they agreed. This opposition grew in strength and determination throughout 1967, as Peru entered a period of economic crisis. By November, the weakening position of the Peruvian sol, which had been stable for a decade, compelled a drastic devaluation. From a rate of twenty-seven to the dollar, the sol tumbled to forty-eight before stabilizing at about forty-two to forty-four in the middle of 1968. The result was a sudden and drastic increase in prices affecting every sector of the economy. The poor were especially hard hit as food prices soared. Business dropped, unemployment rose, and public discontent mounted. In 1968, the hard-pressed Belaúnde was further beset by a series of scandals involving smuggling and bribery. Though the scandals did not touch him or his top officials (some members of the military were involved), they further weakened public confidence. Some of these difficulties were undoubtedly due to bad management, as the President's opponents charged, but many also flowed from circumstances beyond his control. Also, by the fall of 1968 a new austerity program had apparently set the country on the way to financial stability, and a record volume of exports, along with the anticipation of a billion dollars in foreign private investment, strengthened hopes for better times. However, many of the military and important elements of the civilian population felt Belaúnde had failed to fulfill their expectations. In their view, civilian politics had once again paralyzed the needed modernization of Peru, and, justly or unjustly, they believed that Belaúnde had lost his grip on the country and on his own government. Moreover, growing dissension and factional splits within the Belaúnde party made it likely that the unacceptable APRA would win the Presidential election scheduled for the middle of 1969. To this explosive mixture of discontent was added an incalculable amount of personal ambition and a growing sense that the time had come for the armed forces to assume their predestined mission to create a "new" Peru. By the middle of 1968, the restaurants and clubs of Lima were filled with talk of a *golpe*. It was widely known that the plans were ready and that the generals were anxious. But the moment never seemed right. The military, lacking popular support, hesitated to move arbitrarily against an elected President who still commanded a large following. They needed—depending upon your point of view—an event, a pretext, or a cause. It came when, after five years of negotiation, I.P.C. reached an agreement with Belaúnde.

In July, 1967, a restless Peruvian Congress passed a law declaring that the La Brea y Pariñas oil field belonged to the nation, and authorized the expropriation of oil-field installations and the establishment of a "regime most consistent with the national interest." (The wording left open the possibility that I.P.C. might continue to operate the installation if that arrangement seemed "most consistent with the national interest.") Belaúnde was undoubtedly reminded, as he had been before, that any expropriation would mean the application of the Hickenlooper Amendment, and the effort to reach an agreement continued throughout 1967 without any changes at La Brea. In that same year, however, the Peruvian Tax Court found that I.P.C. owed a hundred and forty-four million dollars to Peru. This figure was based on a judicial calculation of I.P.C.'s net profits for the previous fifteen years, on the theory that the company had been operating under the illegal and invalid award of an international arbitration. This money was never collected, and judicial appeals and counter-claims mounted in complexity.

Then, at the beginning of 1968, as General Doig and his staff were laying their plans for a *golpe,* President Belaúnde designated the Peruvian state oil company, Empresa Petrolera Fiscal, or E.P.F., "to represent the state in all acts related to the operation of the La Brea y Pariñas oil field, which belongs to the nation." The president of E.P.F., and from then on one of the chief Peruvian negotiators, was Carlos Loret de Mola. Technician and businessman, mild-mannered and never actively engaged in politics, Loret de Mola had been placed in charge of the state-owned company early in Belaúnde's administration. His knowledge of the oil business would strengthen the government in negotiations, while it could be expected that on any important issue he would yield to the President's wishes. Yet this routine appointment had unexpected consequences, for Loret de Mola was to prove unexpectedly stubborn, and eventually his public attack on the final agreement was to bring on the revolution. Shortly after the negotiations had been turned over to E.P.F., they broke down again. The issue was the same as that which had brought about previous failures: Peru insisted that I.P.C. turn over the oil field, while the company refused to do so unless it was allowed to operate the field as before. Thus, as I.P.C.'s official account reports, "at mid-April of 1968, there were no negotiations in progress with the Government's representatives."

Events in Peru were moving too fast to permit the impasse to continue. Belaúnde's economic and political problems were still acute, political attacks were mounting, and talk of a military *golpe* was in the air. On July 28th, Belaúnde was scheduled to make his annual address to Congress on the State of the Republic, and it was inconceivable that he should appear without announcing some solution of the La Brea y Pariñas problem. At the same time, and more ominously, a regularly scheduled change of command was being carried out in the Peruvian Army. The Minister of War, General Doig, reached retirement and lost his chance to lead a revolution. Velasco, widely thought to be a candidate for the Cabinet position, did not get it. "Belaúnde did offer it to him, but he wouldn't take it," claims a Velasco associate. "The other officers said he didn't have the ability," says a high official of the deposed government. In any event, having failed to assume a Cabinet post that would have removed him from the command of troops, Velasco was now Commander-in-Chief of the Army and the senior general on active duty. Within a couple of months, he had placed officers loyal to him in charge of the Lima Military District and the Lima Armored Division, both of which would be essential to the success of a revolution. Then Velasco waited, although, with his own retirement scheduled for early 1969, he didn't have much time.

Amid the unmistakable signs of crisis, I.P.C. suddenly changed the position it had steadfastly clung to for years. On July 25, 1968, it sent Belaúnde a memorandum offering to transfer to the state "the surface area of La Brea y Pariñas and the installations" and to renounce "any rights it could allege over the subsoil or mineralized zone of La Brea y Pariñas." This memorandum, or proposal, was, with some modifications, the basis of the final agreement between Belaúnde and I.P.C. That agreement, in turn, was to precipitate the military *golpe* and the seizure of I.P.C. Few doubt that several years earlier the same terms would have been accepted, after some grumbling, and I.P.C. would have stayed and prospered in Peru. "It was an incredibly generous offer," say officials of the United States Embassy. "In fact," says one of our chief diplomats, "when the manager of I.P.C. told me about it I was so astonished I asked him, 'But what do you get out of it?' " And I.P.C. itself claims that it "gave Belaúnde everything he was asking for." Yet within a few weeks after its proclamation the agreement was assailed as a sellout, a giveaway, and a fraud.

Undoubtedly, these assaults were greatly magnified by political passion, yet an examination of the terms of the agreement does not support a conclusion that I.P.C. was making a sacrifice. In return for La Brea y Pariñas, I.P.C. was to be allowed to expand and modernize its refinery, thus increasing the production of oil and gas. It would continue, on a regular business basis, all its other activities in Peru, including the marketing of fifty-five per cent of all gasoline sold there. (This monopolistic position seems less impressive when we know that there are only about two hundred and fifty thousand registered vehicles in Peru.) There would also be at least a "moral commitment" that I.P.C. could join Mobil Oil and Gulf in exploring for oil on the jungle slopes of the eastern Andes. And all claims for back debts would be cancelled, including the hundred and forty-four million dollars assessed by the Tax Court. In addition, I.P.C. could reasonably expect that the agreement would free it from most of the continual agitation and hostility that had often threatened, although it rarely interfered with, its activities. Certainly these terms were not onerous for I.P.C., and the refinery expansion, especially, was, in the company's words,

"a consideration of value." Of course, Peru would receive all the benefits that flow to an undeveloped country from the investment and skill of a large modern enterprise, something Peruvians may miss in the days ahead. If we compare this offer, which would almost surely have been accepted by Belaúnde in 1964, with the proposals that were in fact rejected in 1964 and 1965, the difference appears so slight that the company's stubborn, and fatal, insistence on keeping control of the La Brea field baffles analysis. In earlier negotiations, I.P.C. had offered to give up its ownership rights but had insisted on operating the field. Now I.P.C. offered to give the field to E.P.F., which would then sell the crude oil to I.P.C., which would refine it and market the product. Yet, as one plows through the elaborate maze of figures, it seems that the difference in cost for I.P.C. between operating the field itself (and paying a fifty-per-cent income tax on profits) and letting E.P.F. operate the field was about ten to fifteen cents a barrel. Since La Brea y Pariñas had been steadily running down and was producing only six or seven million barrels a year, the total increase in the cost of crude oil to I.P.C. would probably have been not much more than half a million dollars a year. Looking at this difference, which is all that separates the hopeful days of 1964, when Belaúnde was at the height of his strength, from the disaster of 1968, one can take some comfort in knowing that even at Standard Oil irrational convictions, bureaucratic inertia, or sheer delight in the exercise of power can override the logical conclusions of economic analysis

On July 28th, three days after receiving I.P.C.'s confidential and unsigned memorandum, Belaúnde went before Congress and the nation to announce triumphantly that he had solved the ancient problem of La Brea y Pariñas. The oil field would now belong to Peru. He did not elaborate on the other elements of the proposal, and, intentionally or not, he left the impression that the takeover was almost unconditional. To almost unanimous acclaim, the negotiators then sat down to hammer out the complex series of contracts necessary to transform the new proposal into an agreement. The pressure for swift action was intense, for in June the Congress had given Belaúnde extraordinary powers for sixty days that would permit him to solve the problem by executive decree. When this period expired, it would be necessary to submit any agreement to an increasingly hostile Congress. Belaúnde could not afford to wait, and he told the negotiators that he intended to fly to the oil city of Talara on the morning of August 13th and proclaim the final and definitive solution.

For two weeks, as August 13th neared, lawyers, businessmen, and politicians crowded around tables in the Presidential Palace struggling to construct a new framework for the largest oil-and-gas enterprise in Peru. Belaúnde's Prime Minister as well as his Minister of Development continually joined other government officials in the discussions. The chief negotiator for I.P.C. was the company's gentle and dignified general manager, Fernando J. Espinosa, who, after working as an economist for the New Deal, had spent twenty-three years with Standard Oil. His principal adversary was the head of E.P.F., Carlos Loret de Mola. Toward the end, the negotiations kept breaking down over one crucial point: whether I.P.C. was to guarantee a minimum price for the crude oil it was to buy from La Brea. It was during one of these breakdowns that an incident is said to have occurred that, true or not, undoubtedly contributed to the difficulties of the days ahead, since it is widely believed in Peru. Loret de Mola says that, asked by President Belaúnde to renew the talks, he went to the I.P.C. offices at about 10 P.M. Loret de Mola claims that, after offering him a drink, a company executive (not Espinosa) told him, "Standard Oil never gets out of any place without getting all its money, and the same is going to happen here." The executive then handed him a copy of the confidential memorandum, saying, "Here are our conditions. Your President shouldn't have gone before Congress the way he did, because he deceived the people." "What could I do?" asks Loret de Mola. "I had to believe the word of my President before an unsigned memorandum by a company." Even if his story is true, the substantive terms of the memorandum could not have been a surprise, since those were precisely the subjects under negotiation. However, the suspicion that all the conditions of settlement had been laid down in advance might have had a stiffening effect on Loret de Mola's attitude. In any event, the story has added to the armory of anecdotes used to justify the seizure.

Finally, at about 2 A.M. on August 13th, thinking that final agreement had been reached on the price to be paid by I.P.C. for the crude oil from La Brea, Espinosa went home to prepare for the scheduled dawn flight to Talara. Soon afterward, Espinosa received a call from the Peruvian Prime Minister, at the Palace, who told him there was still no agreement, and then, according to an Embassy official, said, in tones of mounting agitation, "If you don't come back, there'll be an expropriation," and hung up. Peruvian officials then awakened Ambassador Jones, who called Espinosa and persuaded him to return to the Palace, where discussion resumed on the price to be paid for crude oil. As dawn approached, both Espinosa and Loret de Mola, sitting in different rooms, signed the last of a series of contracts, and the entire group drove through the quiet streets to the Presidential airplane. The problem was that each man had signed a very different contract, or so they later claimed. Within a month, this difference was to erupt as "the page 11 scandal," and that storm was to tumble the last flimsy barrier to a military *golpe* and the seizure of I.P.C.

The existing copies of the contract governing I.P.C.'s purchase of the crude oil to be produced by E.P.F. at its newly acquired La Brea y Pariñas field are ten pages long. If there was an eleventh page—and that is what the dispute is about—it contained the final disposition of the one problem that had seemed insoluble until the final hours: the price to be paid for the crude oil. Under the contract as it now exists, I.P.C. agrees to pay, after discounts, $1.97 a barrel for the crude oil. However, the contract also requires I.P.C. to provide certain essential services to the oil-field operation, such as water and gas, but leaves the details, including the costs of these services, to be worked out later. "You see," explains Loret de Mola, "since we didn't know what the services would cost, we couldn't tell how much they would pay for the oil. That's why I wanted a guaranteed minimum price, one they would pay no matter what they deducted for the services." An I.P.C. representative responds that "we couldn't possibly agree to a guaranteed price

without knowing about the services." Therefore, as the hours wore on during that last night of negotiations, I.P.C. adamantly resisted Loret de Mola's demand for a guaranteed minimum of $1.0835 a barrel, although the company negotiators did agree to a clause allowing E.P.F. to cancel the contract after six months' notice in case the price fell below that amount. "What good was that?" asks Loret de Mola. "What would we do with the oil? They owned the refinery at Talara. We'd have to ship it down the coast." I.P.C.'s representatives recall that Loret de Mola bent and then yielded to the intense arguments of government officials desperate to reach an agreement as evening stretched into morning. Loret de Mola, on the other hand, says that it was I.P.C. that finally yielded. Neither Espinosa nor Loret de Mola can recall an explicit admission of defeat by the other.

Then, as the chief negotiators joined their aides in different rooms to go over the final documents, the crude-oil contract was brought to them for signature. The two men agree that the original contract was eleven pages long and that the text ended at the bottom of the tenth page. The eleventh page was bare except for a typed dateline— "Lima, August 12, 1968"—and had room for signatures. According to Loret de Mola, when the contract came to him he wrote across the top of the eleventh page, "In any event, the price for crude oil shall be no less than $1.0835," and then signed. Two Xerox copies were made, and Loret de Mola was asked to initial or sign every page of these Xerox copies "for purposes of identification." The identifying initials or signatures are in the margin of each page. He did not sign either Xerox copy at the end of the contract, as he claims to have done on the eleventh page of the original. The documents were then taken from him, and the scene shifted to the room where Espinosa was waiting to sign the agreement. He says that he was brought only the two Xerox copies, and that they were only ten pages long. The eleventh page was no longer part of the contract, and Espinosa explains that when he asked about this "the lawyer said there was too much white space above the dateline on the eleventh page and the contract could be altered later." (Of course, a few lines drawn across the page would have prevented anyone from writing above the dateline.) Espinosa signed both contracts at the bottom of the tenth page, and wrote the date and place beside his signature. Within a month, Loret de Mola's accusation that the vital eleventh page had been removed and that I.P.C. and the government had conspired to defraud the Peruvian nation was to enlarge discontent to a critical mass which swiftly exploded into a military *golpe* and the consequent seizure of all the properties of the International Petroleum Company.

Was there a page 11? The American Embassy maintains flatly that there were only ten pages, and that Loret de Mola was lying for political purposes. This is, of course, possible, and yet—at least up until the time I asked about the matter, a couple of weeks ago—the Embassy had neither studied the documents nor discussed the matter with Loret de Mola, although he is more than willing to tell his story to any who asks. If you examine the documents, one thing is clear. On both Xerox copies of the contract, the only signature that appears at the bottom of page 10 is that of Fernando Espinosa. (Loret de Mola's signature or initial is in the side

margin of every page.) It is hardly conceivable that diligent lawyers should not have made sure that both parties signed so critical a contract, as they did in the case of other, far less controversial documents on that frenzied night— unless, of course, Loret de Mola had in fact signed an eleventh page. Meanwhile, the original has mysteriously disappeared. Unless there are other facts to be disclosed, one conclusion is clear: either there was an eleven-page contract or there was no agreement at all, since few courts would enforce a contract signed by only one party. This leaves open the question whether the "page 11" controversy flows from fraud, misunderstanding, or mistake. The accounts of Loret de Mola and Espinosa are consistent with perfect good faith by each of them, and in discussing the episode each of them gives an almost overwhelming impression of sincerity and honorable intent. Nor is there the slightest evidence that President Belaúnde was aware of any of this, although it might prove interesting to interrogate some of the lawyers who were keeping watch on the evening's transactions. A number of people were anxious to reach agreement before dawn, and the most likely possibility is that in the face of Loret de Mola's stubborn insistence on a clearly defined minimum price the eleventh page was removed as the contract went from one principal to the other. Whatever the facts, Peruvians were quick to believe the accusations of fraud by I.P.C. and the Peruvian government, and the American Embassy did not make the kind of investigation that might have convinced them otherwise. When asked what happened to the original, an Embassy official first responded that "there was no original." When it was pointed out that even

Xerox's marvellous technology had not developed to this extent, he said that the original was too messy. But making a page neater while copying it is another feat that Xerox has not yet accomplished. If there were only ten pages, why didn't Loret de Mola sign at the bottom of the tenth page? "There was no room," it was explained. Yet one has only to glance at the page to see that there was plenty of room for an additional signature. None of this proves anything about "page 11," but perhaps it does illustrate some of the attitudes that have led many Peruvians to believe that the American Embassy is the faithful representative of Standard Oil.

As the dawn of August 13th approached, the weary group of negotiators rose from the table to join the President and congressional leaders for the flight to Talara. But there was, according to some of the Peruvian participants, one more ceremony to come. No formal agreement had been signed granting I.P.C. the right to explore the potentially rich jungle lands to the east. At the request of the oil company, therefore, the highest officials of the Peruvian government raised their right hands and gave a solemn oath to the representative of Standard Oil of New Jersey that a million hectares of Peru (about two and a half million acres) would be open to their exploration. Did it happen? Two Peruvian eyewitnesses swear to it. I.P.C. says only, "We did get a moral commitment, but we never thought we could count on that." In any event, Peruvians believe the story.

On its flight north to Talara, the Presidential plane passed close to the city and plains where a few hundred Spaniards strangled the Emperor and plundered the gold of the Incas. Now,

after a century-long dispute, Belaúnde was about to recover for Peru a more modern but equally legendary treasure. That morning, in the Act of Talara, he proclaimed that the oil field and its installations belonged to the nation, once again omitting any description of the rest of the agreement. However, it did not take long for the nation's applause to die out as details of the settlement began to emerge. In an effort to head off opposition, Belaúnde had previously secured the agreement of his APRA opposition to the compact with I.P.C., but unexpectedly the attack was to come instead from his former friends —the armed forces, *El Commercio,* and Loret de Mola.

Since E.P.F. could not take over the operations of La Brea y Pariñas immediately, the Act of Talara was followed by a rather vague decree permitting I.P.C. to continue operations during a transition period. Shortly thereafter, Loret de Mola wrote I.P.C. that since the oil now belonged to Peru, the total profits from its sale—about half a million dollars a month—should be turned over to E.P.F. On September 3rd, I.P.C. replied in a letter that, whatever its legal justification, could only worsen an already deteriorating situation. "We are in agreement [that La Brea y Pariñas is now] the property of the state [but until E.P.F. actually takes over, we intend to] operate the deposits...in the same way and with the same obligations which have governed our activities...up to the present time." On September 7th, the Peruvian government confirmed the resignation of Loret de Mola and the entire board of directors of E.P.F., and the next day Loret de Mola, according to an account in *El Commercio,* said that since I.P.C. "refused to pay E.P.F. the agreed-upon price of $1.0835 per barrel...the Act of Talara was an event of no consequence." That same week, the new Minister of War, Major General Roberto Dianderas Chumbianca, made the ominous announcement that "the Army was awaiting the official publication of all the annexes of the Act of Talara in order to study them and see if it should issue a statement on the matter."

Agitation grew as it became apparent that far more was involved in the Act of Talara than the recovery of La Brea y Pariñas, and that I.P.C. would continue to expand its activities in Peru freed of all claims for past debts. On September 8th, *El Commercio,* knowing of the plans for a *golpe,* began an editorial attack on the agreement, almost certainly intending to bring down the government. And a few days later Loret de Mola went on national television to make public his charges about the missing page 11. From this point on, the attacks mounted in intensity. Thirty-six generals held a secret meeting, and a pleased General Velasco called the editor of *El Commercio* to report that the vote was "twenty-nine against the agreement and seven traitors." "For a little while," reports an observer, "there didn't seem there would be a coup, but there was no way to bring the thing to rest." Then, in the last week of September, the left wing of the President's own party rebelled against the agreement and demanded the resignation of the entire Cabinet, and APRA, reluctantly yielding to mounting political pressure, withdrew its support of the Act of Talara. On October 2nd, the Cabinet resigned and a new group of ministers was appointed. They stayed in office less than twenty-four hours. Following the long-prepared scenario, at about two o'clock

on the morning of October 3rd a column of troops led by tanks of the Lima Armored Division moved across the Plaza de Armas and entered the Presidential Palace. President Belaúnde was roused and taken to the airport, where a large Peruvian jet was waiting to carry its solitary passenger to exile in Buenos Aires. General Velasco was the new President of Peru, and, except for some minor street skirmishing, the takeover was swift and peaceful. A revolutionary manifesto explained that "history will record...the loyalty and unquestioned support by the armed forces of the deposed government." However, it went on, the Belaúnde government had disappointed its followers and "these things are evidence of this: the indecision, conspiracy, immorality, surrender, bungling, improvisation, the absence of social sensitivity," culminating in "the false surrender solution given to the La Brea y Pariñas problem, which evidences that moral decomposition in the country had reached extremes so great that its consequences for Peru are unforeseeable."

The consequences for Peru are still unforeseeable, but the consequences for I.P.C. were, even then, quite predictable. A few days later, on October 9th, to the almost universal applause of press and political leaders, Peruvian troops took over the entire oil complex at Talara: the refinery, installations, and the Brea y Pariñas oil field. "The revolution is on the march," said Velasco. When I.P.C. went to court to lodge a protest, hecklers threw coins at the feet of their lawyers. Of course, since only Talara had been taken, I.P.C. was still Peru's largest supplier of petroleum products, although it was now receiving gas and oil from a refinery that had been taken over by the government. In January, when I.P.C.

protested a bill of eleven million dollars for petroleum products from Talara, the government moved to "attach" most of I.P.C.'s remaining assets as "security" for this debt. Fruitless discussions continued until February 6th, when General Alberto Maldonado Yanez, Minister of Development and Public Works of the Revolutionary Government of Peru, summoned the manager of I.P.C. to his office and handed him a bill of slightly over six hundred and ninety million dollars: the total value, as calculated by the Peruvians, of I.P.C.'s production at La Brea y Pariñas since the company bought the field in 1924. All of I.P.C.'s assets, the General said, would be held as security. Most of I.P.C.'s top officials were already out of the country, many of them pursued by criminal warrants for fraud and tax evasion. That afternoon, General Velasco announced that "Peru has taken the final step to close definitely and forever this ignominious phase in its history." The long battle between I.P.C. and the Peruvian nation was now over. The dispute was now between Peru and the government of the United States. . . .

30

National Development Policy and External Dependence in Latin America

Osvaldo Sunkel

From Osvaldo Sunkel, "National Development Policy and External Dependence in Latin America," *The Journal of Development Studies*, VI, No. 1 (October 1969), pp. 23–48. Reprinted by permission of the author and the publisher. This article was first published in Spanish under the title "Política nacional de desarrollo y dependencia externa" in *Estudios Internacionales*, revista del Instituto de Estudios Internacionales de la Universidad de Chile, Santiago, Chile, I, No. 1 (April 1967).

Osvaldo Sunkel is a Research Professor in the Institute of International Studies and a Professor of Economic Development in the Faculty of Economics at the University of Chile, Santiago, Chile.

In the postwar era, a number of leading Latin American técnicos have argued with increasing conviction that orthodox economic doctrine—reflecting the experience of now-developed countries and to some extent continuing to redound to their benefit—is largely irrelevant to the special needs of Latin America. Many of these so-called structuralist economists clustered in ECLA during the Truman and Eisenhower administrations and eventually had an impact on U.S. official positions regarding such matters as industrialization, preferential tariffs, and economic integration. Merely listing a few of ECLA's concerns suggests that some structuralist prescriptions themselves have not proved entirely workable in the Latin American setting. However, as Street has observed, structuralists have made an important "humanistic" contribution to development theory by viewing economic phenomena as "part of a larger and evolving cultural whole."[1]

This selection by Sunkel, a prominent structuralist economist formerly associated with ECLA, is an excellent example of contemporary técnico thinking about the obstacles to Latin American development and the

[1] James H. Street, "The Latin American 'Structuralists' and the Institutionalists: Convergence in Development Theory," *The Journal of Economic Issues*, I, Nos. 1–2 (June 1967), p. 62. See also: Albert O. Hirschman, ed., *Latin American Issues: Essays and Comments* (New York: The Twentieth Century Fund, 1961), pp. 3–42; and John P. Powelson, "Toward an Integrated Growth Model: The Case of Latin America" in Cole Blasier, ed., *Constructive Change in Latin America* (Pittsburgh: University of Pittsburgh Press, 1968), pp. 57–85.

strategies through which they might be surmounted. The essay also fairly abounds with "linkage" and other theoretical implications for the political scientist, which the editor will leave to the reader to explore.

According to Sunkel, Latin American countries all want to end external dependence, but they have yet to adopt the economic and social development policies necessary to this end. He notes particularly that Latin America still suffers serious balance-of-payments problems because of its continued reliance on the export of a few primary commodities. Moreover, "import substitution" industrialization has, in some respects, increased dependence because many industries are foreign-owned or must themselves import in order to produce finished consumer goods. Nevertheless, Sunkel believes that Latin American domestic conditions (social differentiation, urbanization, nationalism, the rise of the "Central State" à la Véliz, etc.) and the prevailing international environment (the willingness of the U.S. to condone almost any non–Communist road to modernization, new contacts among the Latin American states, etc.) now offer an opportunity to break dramatically from the patterns of the past. He outlines a "national development policy" with several components, designed not to make the "center-periphery" model more viable but to overcome it. His recommendations include Latin American economic integration with multinational planning and control of basic industries; efforts to boost agricultural production and to incorporate the rural and urban poor into the national economy; and government intervention to assure the expansion and diversification of exports, as well as national participation in ventures launched by foreign private investment.[2]

I. ANALYSIS OF THE PROBLEM

In an adequate historical perspective, development appears as a process of transformation of economic, social, political and cultural structures and institutions. National development policy, to be effective, must therefore stimulate and promote the institutional and structural changes essential for the achievement of desired social goals. This implies changing what is traditionally accepted, and challenging entrenched interests, both domestic and foreign. Therefore, the objectives, in-

This article is a revised version of a lecture delivered on November 17, 1966, at the University of Chile during the series of Inaugural Lectures of the Institute of International Studies.

[2] In a complementary article, Anderson has suggested that—especially in the light of the decline in aid from the developed countries and the disappointing experience to date with Latin American economic integration (see selection 32)—the most effective way for many Latin American countries to overcome dependence may be to adopt a policy of "assertive internationalism," stressing a herculean effort to compete directly with the "center" in carefully chosen types of industrial exports. Alternatively, those countries unable or unwilling to compete in these terms might (like Cuba *or* Costa Rica) "settle" for a "counter-culture of development" that accepts relative underdevelopment as a fact and gives priority to creating "workable, decent societies" with whatever resources are available. See Charles W. Anderson, "The Changing International Environment of Development and Latin America in the 1970s," *Inter-American Economic Affairs*, XXIV, No. 2 (Autumn 1970), pp. 65–87.

tensity, instrumentalization and efficiency of development policies are limited within certain margins of flexibility; their freedom of manoeuvre will depend principally on internal conditions but also on the international relations of the country concerned.

The domestic situation is affected over a period of time by the changes which the process of development itself brings about: industrialization, urbanization, occupational differentiation, changes in social structure, alterations of attitudes and values, modifications of the patterns of political participation, transformation in the social function of women, technological changes in mass media, changes in the size and functions of the State, etc.

The influence which external relations exercise on national development policy derives from the fact that the Latin American countries are enmeshed in the system of international relations of the capitalist world. This system is characterized by the presence of a dominant power, a series of intermediate powers and the underdeveloped countries ascribed to it. Like the domestic situation, this system is also essentially dynamic. Significant variations are experienced both because of changes inside the countries and as a result of the confrontation with the other principal system of international relations, that of the socialist world. Variations in this world-wide confrontation also affect the limits within which national development policy may move.

All this, of course, is not novel. Most people know perfectly well that policies in general, and development policy in particular, can range within a spectrum which at certain times is limited and at others enlarged by external conditions. Public officials, statesmen, and politicians are as conscious of

this external conditioning as they are aware of the internal political situation.

Nevertheless, if one examines the writings of economists, sociologists and political scientists in Latin America, external dependence as a subject is remarkably absent.[1] It would appear that sociology, economics, and political science in the post-war period have not been concerned with this question.

One wonders if this extraordinary phenomenon is not in itself a first manifestation of dependence. The fact is that we dare not touch this theme, either because of the political risks and connotations, or because it has not been consecrated as part of the aseptic and formalistic range of topics which today serves as academic standard of reference for specialists in the social sciences. To find serious analyses of this theme one must go back to the classical theories of imperialism, either in their Marxist[2] or non-Marxist[3] versions, but it is evident that these theo-

[1] A notable exception, which confirms the rule, is the article signed: Espartaco, 'La crisis latinoamericana y su marco externo', *Desarrollo Económico,* July-December 1966, Buenos Aires.

[2] Rosa Luxemburg, *Die Akkumulation des Kapitals, Ein Beitrag zur oekonomischn Erlarung des Imperialismus,* 1912; Rudolf Hilferding, *Das Finanzkapital,* 1910; V. L. Ulyanov (N. Lenin), *Imperialism: the Superior Phase of Capitalism* (original Russian edition in 1917); N. I. Bukharin, *World Economy and Imperialism,* 1918.

[3] J. A. Hobson, *Imperialism,* 1902; J. A. Schumpeter, 'Zur Soziologie der Imperialismen', *Archiv für Sozialwissenschaft und Sozialpolitik,* Vol. 46, 1919 (English translation in: J. A. Schumpeter, *Imperialism and Social Classes,* 1951); Jacob Viner, 'International Finance and Balance of Power Diplomacy, 1880–1914', *South Western Political Science Quarterly,* 1929; Eugene Staley, *War and the Private Investor,* 1935; William L. Langer, *The Diplomacy of Imperialism,* 1890–1902, 1935; Lionel Robbins, *The Economic Causes of War,* 1939; B. M. Winslow, *The Pattern of Imperialism,* 1948.

ries, which were elaborated almost entirely during the first three decades of this century, are largely out of date because of the profound internal changes which both developed and underdeveloped countries have experienced, and the radical transformations which have taken place in their relations with one another.[4]

Also related to the theme of dependence are the critical analyses of the classical theory of international trade by Prebish, Singer, Myrdal and others, which are represented institutionally by the work of the U.N. Economic Commission for Latin America and more recently by that of the Secretariat of U.N.C.T.A.D. Nevertheless, these touch only partially on the theme of external dependence.

In contrast with the lack of serious research on this very important topic, public discussion and partisan controversy abound. Dogmatic and anecdotical approaches to the problem of external dependence occupy much of the casual conversation of the same social scientists who refuse to be concerned with it as a topic of research. It is not surprising that if the social scientist refuses to accept responsibility for offering information, analysis and objective interpretations of a problem of serious concern to the community, the dominant attitudes in public debate are extremist, biased and superficial.

Thus for some, private foreign investment, gifts, private and official credits and other forms of transfer of resources from the developed to the underdeveloped countries are 'foreign aid', 'a disinterested sacrifice which the rich countries make to help their poor

brothers'. For others, this flow of foreign resources represents the 'new face of imperialism' through which 'the monopolies and international cartels have found new ways of sucking the blood of the backward countries in order to keep them permanently oppressed'.

Likewise, the treaties and international agreements in the economic, financial and military spheres which lead to the adoption of international and domestic policies other than those which would have been freely adopted, constitute for some 'the defence of liberty, democracy, and the traditions of Western Christian Civilization', while for others they represent the 'return to colonialism and imperialism'.

Less attention has been paid to the massive and rapidly increasing transfer of attitudes, values, patterns of consumption and styles of living, forms of artistic expression, social organization and technological development. Some see in all this the 'process of modernization and rationalization which constitutes the base and prerequisite of economic development'. Others see in it 'the most dismal process of cultural alienation in which our own values and traditions are sacrificed in the pursuit of a well-being which is mistaken with the consumption of more or less superfluous material goods'.

Like all schematic descriptions, this one is also exaggerated and something of a caricature, but it corresponds in its essentials to the actual opinions about the foreign ties of our countries. It would certainly be difficult to use this as a base for a serious discussion. I propose therefore to begin from quite a different angle. An examination of the development programmes of many Latin American countries, especially in their political versions, reveals that self-

[4] See, for example, John Strachey, *The End of Empire* (London, Gollancz).

determination, independence and a reduction in foreign dependence are among the fundamental objectives. Moreover, if one analyses the policies of development and industrialization of Latin America—and of other under-developed areas of the world as well—one observes that an essential element is precisely the desire to overcome foreign dependence. Therefore, it is possible to accept the premise that this is one of the basic objectives pursued by economic development policies.

The question arises: is every development policy conducive to the fulfilment of this objective? The answer is clearly negative. There are exceptional cases of development policies—understanding development in the sense of economic growth—which have been very successful from this point of view, but which have meant not only the emigration of an important part of the population, but also the denationalization of these countries, their absorption into other cultures and the creation of what has been aptly named 'a dependent country' ('*país sucursal*'). I believe that this is not the ideal model to which Latin Americans aspire. In fact, one of the objectives of an ideal development policy seems to be, on the contrary, the affirmation of the national personality.

It is important, therefore, to examine Latin American development policies to see if they do lead towards the fulfilment of this essential objective or if, on the contrary, they are leading towards greater foreign dependence.

The study of conventional development policies reveals the existence of contradictory tendencies, some of which reinforce the situation of dependence, while others provide a start for a policy of greater independence. The analysis of these tendencies leads me to sketch

certain alternative strategies and lines of action which, in my opinion, permit the scale to tip in the direction of reducing dependence, without conflicting with the necessary acceleration in the rhythm of economic growth.

In order not to be utopian or excessively idealistic, it is necessary to evaluate the viability of such alternative propositions starting from the situation of dependence in which we now find ourselves. All this, of course, is not more than a first attempt to explore the area of research on foreign dependence, an area which until now has been considered taboo for serious analysis, in terms which will make a fruitful discussion possible. Moreover, I must make it very clear that I shall examine the long-range tendencies which, in my opinion, influence the phenomenon of dependence, and not the particular changes derived from more or less temporary and partisan-political situations.

II. FOREIGN DEPENDENCE AND INTERNAL CHANGES

INTERNAL SOCIO-POLITICAL CHANGES AND THEIR SIGNIFICANCE

To gain a better understanding of the essence of the phenomenon of dependence in Latin America, it is useful to begin with a brief examination of the socio-economic evolution in very broad outline and starting from certain significant periods, because the present economic, social and institutional structure has characteristics whose origins date from different key formative periods.

The traditional rural structure, which was consolidated in Latin America partly before Independence and partly during the 19th century, is one which many voices from all directions have been insisting for years ought to be altered through an agrarian reform.

Between the end of the 19th century and the 1930s the characteristic structure of export and import trade and the financial links with the industrialized countries were established. It was during this time that, on the basis of foreign investment, most of Latin America developed the production of primary materials for export which still characterizes its foreign trade.

From the 1930s onwards, and especially in the major countries of the southern tip and in Mexico, a new historical phase was superimposed: this was industrialization, accompanied by rapid urbanization and the rise of social policies; systems of social security, housing, health, and education. As all of these developments imposed heavy burdens on the public sector, it was also a period during which the state expanded considerably and acquired new functions.

Each of the successive transformations experienced during these three phases influenced the pre-existing structures, but the opposite phenomenon was more striking; the stubborn resistance of the agrarian structure and that of foreign trade to the successive dynamic influences, first of the expansion of trade and later of industrialization. It is as if the development of our societies had been achieved by the addition of new structures rather than through the internal transformation and evolution of their original social forms.

The increasing diversification of Latin American societies during these periods had important effects · on the social and economic structure. In terms of social structure, they variously passed from simple dual social systems —with a dominant oligarchy and a rural mass which was not even a political body—to a much more complex system of social differentiation. This was the result of modern export activities, industrialization, the growth of cities, expansion of the state apparatus, advancement of education, etc. The greater complexity of the social structure reduced the dominant role of the traditional oligarchy. The rural and urban masses were at least marginally incorporated into the process of political participation. Between the two extremes characteristic of traditional Latin American society there appeared a varied range of social strata, groups, classes, and estates. This was particularly true of the urban sector with its industrial entrepreneurs, professionals and technicians, white-collar workers of both public and private sectors, organized labour, students, etc.[5]

In so far as these different middle groups and the rural and urban masses increasingly influence the political process, a tendency can be discerned towards greater representation of the community in the State; towards higher levels of participation by increasing numbers of the national population in public affairs. If this tendency is a fact and is associated with the process of development, then it is possible to suggest that the differentiation of the social structure and the greater participation of the national community in the political process mark the beginnings of a broadly based and decisive assertion of the national and collective interest. Therefore, efficient political

[5] See Fernado H. Cardoso and José Luis Reyna, 'Industrialización, estructura ocupacional y estratificación en América Latina', in F. H. Cardoso, *Cuestiones de sociologia del desarrollo en América Latina* (Editorial Universitaria, Santiago, 1968).

alliances of certain groups of the middle class with the great rural and urban masses become possible.

These new alliances (which ought not to be confused with the ones that have occurred in the past in Latin America) represent national collective interests and objectives in a better and different way from that which was the case in traditional, dual societies. Nationalism, development, and organized mass participation are the ideological pillars of such alliances. From this point of view it would seem, therefore, that at least potential conditions exist for a national development policy to be translated into programmes, strategies of action and concrete political movements in some of our countries.

This requires that certain middle groups be willing to assume the leadership in the organization and integration of the marginal urban and rural masses into the political process and into the economic, social and cultural life of the nation. Since a programme of this nature necessarily implies a redistribution of income and wealth, a transfer of political power and a reordering of social opportunities, as well as a considerable effort of saving and mobilization of resources, the middle groups which are now benefiting from privileged positions are naturally opposed to such a policy. But such middle groups as have not been able to take advantage of the process of development so far and which do not see in its orientation and sluggish rate prospects for future realization are likely to support it. In those countries where import substitution industrialization begins to falter, frustration is evident, especially among certain groups of professionals and technicians and technocrats of the public and private bureaucracy; amongst some of the

national entrepreneurs displaced by foreign private enterprise[6] and in institutions concerned with collective and long-term interests rather than with immediate objectives—the intellectuals, youth and the Church.

The potential 'Nasserist' and reformist role of the armed forces in Latin America has been largely frustrated to the extent that these institutions have been functionally incorporated into a Cold War situation through their acceptance of the doctrine of the ideological frontier, which lends itself marvellously to equate, either deliberately or unconsciously, a national programme of basic transformations with a subversive process with respect to the dominant domestic groups. Thus imbued with this doctrine, the armed forces become a powerful instrument placed in the hands of those ready to resist change at all costs.

Another phenomenon which can lessen the possibility of certain middle groups assuming the leadership of a truly national development policy is found in the degree of cultural alienation of these groups; the intensity of their immediate aspirations to assimilate 'modern' ways of life and consumption and the extent to which they feel that these aspirations can only be realized by associating with foreign economic or cultural entities of various kinds. On the other hand, to the extent that these middle groups are victims of mass propaganda—which has reached the point of poisoning even children's

[6] It is not possible to generalize about the attitudes of the national business communities in the light of recent development as examined, for instance, by Celso Furtado in his article: 'La concentración del poder económico en los Estados Unidos y sus proyecciones en América Latina' (*Estudios Internacionales* Año I, Nos. 3–4, Octubre 1967; Marzo 1968, Santiago, Chile).

literature, films and television—and accept the doctrine of the Cold War and the ideological frontier, they can be easily frightened and led to reject a national development policy.

The preceding analysis reveals contradictory tendencies. On the one hand, basic changes are taking place in the social structure with the incorporation of the rural and urban masses, the growth and differentiation of the middle groups, the enlargement of the process and mechanisms of political participation and the greatly enhanced importance and functions of the central State. On the other hand, there are interest groups and sectors associated with foreign activities, as well as tendencies towards cultural and ideological alienation, particularly in the middle groups, which hinder the transformations implicit in a national development programme. Therefore, if our analysis is correct, there would not seem to be inevitable historical laws or tendencies at work in one direction or another but, rather, contradictions which open possibilities of choice and of alternative action.

Given certain foreign and domestic circumstances and an adequate analytical knowledge of the process of change, the formulation and implementation of national development policy appears as a distinct possibility. In the absence of such knowledge and of a concrete programme it is unlikely that such a policy could be achieved even if a favourable opportunity were forthcoming; worse, even the perception of the opportune moment would become impossible. I believe that, at this stage, our incapacity to lessen, modify and finally overcome the situation of dependence in which we find ourselves is fundamentally the result of a lack of intellectual and scientific effort to understand our historical reality and our possibilities of autonomous action, and a lack of creative effort to find adequate solutions to our problems.

The formulation of a strategy of national development requires, therefore, a precise diagnosis of the mechanisms of dependence in all its forms: economic, political, military, and cultural. That I shall refer only to certain economic aspects does not mean that the others are not as important.

DEVELOPMENT AND THE MECHANISMS OF ECONOMIC DEPENDENCE

The historical evolution of our economies has left as vestiges certain characteristic features which must be pointed out in considering the problem of dependence and national development policy.

First, the traditional agrarian structure has largely been preserved, seriously limiting modernization and technological improvement of rural production. Agriculture has been unable to respond efficiently to the demand for farm produce which has been strongly stimulated both by the growth of population and of urban incomes and by the development of industry itself, which, at least in its initial stages, is based largely on primary agricultural materials. Among other serious consequences[7] this situation has contributed

[7] The significance of this phenomenon from the point of view of inflationary pressures and the effects on the distribution of income and industrial expansion, can be seen in my papers 'Inflation in Chile: An Unorthodox Approach', *International Economic Papers,* No. 10 (International Economic Association, London and New York, 1960); and 'El Fracaso de las políticas de estabilización en el contexto del proceso de desarrollo latinoamericano', *El Trimestre Económico,* No. 120 (October-December 1963, Mexico).

to the worsening of the balance of payments deficit, either because exports have been reduced or because agricultural imports have increased considerably.

Second, we have inherited a structure of foreign trade which, in open defiance of policy pronouncements repeated for the last 20 years, still relies principally on the export of a handful of primary commodities. Since the Second World War there has been increasing insistence on the necessity of diversifying exports and extending local processing of primary materials, but the figures show that in the majority of the Latin American countries, the degree of concentration of exports on very few products has in fact slightly increased.[8]

Third, industrialization has not produced all the expected benefits; in particular, it has not resulted in a lessening of foreign dependence which, after all, was one of its basic objectives. Even if industrialization has permitted the reduction of the proportion of the value of imports with respect to G.N.P. —the import coefficient—it has also resulted in a change of great importance in the structure of imports. If several decades ago a large proportion of available foreign exchange was devoted to purchasing non-essential consumer goods, today—at least in the most industrialized economies of the region—imports are made up almost exclusively of essential goods: tools, machinery and equipment, to maintain and expand productive capacity; primary materials and intermediate products to assure a normal level of economic activity; and basic foodstuffs

8 Instituto Latinoamericano de Planificación Económica y Social, *La Brecha comercial y la integración latinoamericana,* Siglo XXI Editores, Mexico, 1967, p. 25, Table 5.

to maintain popular consumption. That is to say, we have arrived at a situation of extreme external vulnerability because any alteration of foreign markets or any problem of foreign financing causes very grave difficulties. These difficulties may arise from the resulting scarcity and higher prices for essential consumer goods, from the restrictions on the import of primary materials and their effect on the normal development of manufacturing activity, or from the delays in imports of machinery and equipment and the resulting influence on productive capacity.

This curious result is largely the consequence of the way in which the policy of industrialization has been carried out in Latin America, the so-called process of import substitution. In situations in which foreign exchange is insufficient the importation of consumer goods has been limited. But, since the internal demand for these goods was not reduced, nor was the importation of the machinery and goods necessary to produce them limited, conditions were created which made it possible to begin to produce them within the country. Apparently protection favoured national industry, but the traditional foreign connections, by a sort of acrobatic leap, overcame the protectionist tariff and the policies of prohibition of imports. Far from disappearing, they increased. Goods which had previously been imported began to be produced domestically, but this meant not just importing equipment and machines—and even a considerable proportion of the components for the finished manufacture—but also incurring financial costs in foreign exchange which now constitute an overwhelming burden in many countries. This is due not only to the fact that a large part of this domestic industry is foreign-owned—subsidiaries of large multinational companies—and that many products are manufactured under licence or technical assistance contracts which are paid for in various ways, but also to the fact that public and private financing from abroad was necessary in order to accelerate industrialization and investment in infrastructure. Thus the process of import substitution has resulted, on the one hand, in great vulnerability of our balance of payments and, on the other, in foreign financial commitments which in some Latin American countries represent a considerable proportion of current foreign exchange receipts.

Finally, another of the characteristic features inherited from this stage of industrialization is the establishment, during the period from 1930 to the present, of a very large and active Central State, which fulfills three basic functions. Based on the appropriation of a considerable part of the financial resources of the export activity—which because of its high productivity was the only sector of the economy to generate an abundant surplus of taxable income—the State has come to fulfill three new principal functions: *as a financial intermediary,* which transfers financial resources and subsidizes the development of private industry, usually by means of development institutions; *as a mechanism for income redistribution,* allocating resources to the expansion of social security and to the extension of educational, housing and health services; *as a mechanism of public investment,* which adapts and enlarges the economic infrastructure: transportation, communications, power and also some basic industrial enterprises. As can be appreciated, the process of industrialization and development begun in the decade of the 1930s

in the now most industrialized countries of Latin America, and more recently in the others, depended on a fundamental support, the public sector. After the Great Depression the public sector began to fulfill a strategic function in development policy: the appropriation of resources in the highly productive export activities and their reassignment in order to promote industrial and social development.

In this new function the State has been confronting two contrary tendencies which are becoming more acute. On the one hand, there is an insatiable thirst for appropriating resources in order to use them in programmes of industrialization and infrastructure and especially in the area of social services. On the other hand, the goose which lays the golden eggs—the export sector —has remained relatively stagnant, due partly to heavy taxation but mainly to policies and technological developments in the world's developed industrial economies, over which the Latin American countries have little influence. Therefore, once the principal base of the taxation system stagnated and tax rates reached a certain level, revenues no longer grew at a rhythm commensurate with the rapidly increasing necessities of the public sector. The political and administrative problems of quickly and efficiently extending the taxation system to the rest of the economy, and the problems derived from the characteristics of the economic structure itself, thus determined a systematic and permanent tendency to deficit in the public sector. Moreover, given the instability of the income derived from the export sector, the deficit becomes more acute when foreign markets are depressed and lessens when the situation is prosperous, while the new functions that the State has acquired have meant new permanent financial commitments which have a dynamic of their own.

As a result of the four characteristic processes just outlined[9]—the stagnation of traditional agriculture, the structure of foreign trade, the type of industrialization and the function which the State is fulfilling—our countries are, from the point of view of the structure and functioning of the economy, entirely dependent on their foreign economic relations. An important and not always recognized fact is that this extreme dependence is rooted in several conditions: the vulnerability and structural deficit of the balance of payments; the type of industrialization and the form of exploitation of the export sector which have not permitted our countries—with a few exceptions—to acquire the ability to adapt and create their own technology; the fact that an important and probably growing part of industry and of the export activities are either foreign owned or depend on licences and foreign technical assistance, all of which weighs heavily on the availability of foreign exchange; and the fact that both the fiscal sector and the balance of payments persistently tend to deficit, which leads to the necessity of foreign financing. In certain conditions this foreign financing can mean the accumulation of such considerable debts and such a structure of maturities that the very servicing of the debt requires resort to additional foreign financing[10]—a genuine vicious circle. It is this aspect—the overbearing

and implacable necessity to obtain foreign financing—which finally sums up the situation of dependence; this is the crucial point in the mechanism of dependence.

From what has been shown it can be deduced that even if the social structure has been differentiated and the middle groups and the masses have acquired more representation and participation in the political functioning of the countries, demanding in consequence a growing attention to the general interests of the nation, it is no less certain that an extremely delicate situation of foreign financing has been created which—independent of other forms of dependence—places our countries in a particularly weak position in the face of any pressure which may be exercised on them—and not only, obviously, in regard to development policy.

III. NATIONAL DEVELOPMENT

THE NATURE OF NATIONAL DEVELOPMENT

If the preceding analysis is correct, what are the possibilities of reorienting traditional development policy? This reorientation must lead to the reduction of the forms of dependence which are rooted in the structure and functioning of the economies; such tendencies have become increasingly acute and have been concretely translated into extreme financial dependence. In other words, it must be recognized that economic independence cannot be the magical consequence of an heroic political act. Rather, it will be the medium,

[9] For a more complete analysis, see my article 'The Structural Background of Development Problems in Latin America', *Weltwirtschaftliches Archiv* (Band 97, Heft 1, 1966, Hamburg).
[10] C.E.P.A.L., *El Financiamiento externo de América Latina,* Mexico, 1964; and Inter-

national Bank for Reconstruction and Development, *Annual Report, 1965–66* (Washington, 1966).

or long-term, result—depending on the case—of the construction of a national economy which is both efficient and flexible, and also capable of generating a large and rapidly increasing surplus of resources for investment. This reality, in the technical-economic sense, is not essentially different from the reality which confronts those underdeveloped countries which are attempting to attain national development by the socialist path. Nevertheless, while in these cases the aspiration to national development is an essential part of the definition and social base of the political régime, in the underdeveloped countries of the capitalist area the very possibility of national development must be raised as a preliminary and decisive question mark. It is a crucial question mark that we want to elucidate, for the reply to it will reveal whether the construction of an independent nation is in the final analysis a viable and possible objective or if it is pure idealism. This question seems to me both basic and pertinent, since I believe that the alternatives which one or the other of the ideological camps wants to impose dogmatically on us— socialist revolution or 'dependent country' (*país sucursal*)—are not real alternatives.

One of the possibilities, a radical-socialist revolution, seems to me a very improbable historical event in the near future in Latin America, owing to a combination of external and internal circumstances of a geographic, military, political and economic nature. It is possible that there will be eruptions and even widespread guerrilla movements in some areas, but this will almost certainly tend to reinforce the *status quo* and foreign dependence, rather than the reverse. On the other hand, the 'dependent country' does not

seem viable to me in the long run for the majority of Latin American countries. Apart from the negative elements of a general kind already mentioned, the experience of the region in the last two decades seems to suggest: (*a*) that the existing model requires a volume of foreign resources which the industrialized world—particularly private enterprise—is not interested in transferring to the periphery; (*b*) that the model of industrialization by import substitution, after a period of great dynamism, tends to stagnation even in the larger countries of the region; (*c*) that in spite of the industrialization efforts and social policies, a large sector of the population remains unable to integrate itself into economic, social, cultural or political life.[11]

Therefore, while the revolutionary route is currently blocked, to persist in the 'developmentism' of the last decades—when its positive stage seems to have already been completed—is obviously leading to frustration. I am therefore convinced that these alternatives present a false dilemma: the real option lies with a truly national development policy.

In order to avoid confusion, I must at this stage reiterate what I understand by national development. The nationalism I refer to is obviously not the autarchic, xenophobic, racist, fascist, imperialistic phenomenon familiar

11 See, among others, Pablo González Casanova, 'Sociedad plural y desarrollo: el caso de Mexico', *América Latina,* Year V, No. 4, (October-December 1962, Rio de Janeiro); Andrew Frank, 'La inestabilidad urbana en América Latina', *Cuadernos Americanos* (January-February 1966); Celso Furtado, 'Desarrollo y estancamiento en América Latina', *Desarrollo Económico* (July-December, 1966, Buenos Aires); C.E.P.A.L., 'El proceso de industrialización en América Latina' (Mexico, 1966).

to Europeans and North Americans. This is 'developed nationalism'. The nationalism of the underdeveloped countries arose or was accentuated as a result, in part, of the struggle against the manifestations of developed nationalism. The underdeveloped countries not only sent their quota of forces to the allied powers during World War II, but they also resisted and confronted similar manifestations which—under a false internationalism—these same powers exhibited in their colonies and dependencies. The nationalism of development is a force of national affirmation, an aspiration to self-determination and sovereignty, a desire to participate in the benefits and creation of modern and universal culture and science, the desire to attain liberty, democracy, equality of opportunities and well-being, which the more industrialized countries enjoy to a greater or lesser extent.[12]

The advance of the process of development increases the socio-political participation of groups and social classes making it also more representative of the nation, its traditions, culture, values, institutions and history. These are the ingredients which the nation must utilize to create and achieve its own process of development and national realization. To substitute imported ingredients is to destroy the essence of the nation and to convert its inhabitants into outcasts, both from their own history but also from that of the advanced societies. What is required is a process of modernization which is imitative and creative at the same time, based on a deliberate and conscious selection of what is authentically universal in modern civilization

and culture, and based on an imagination which can construct with these elements the politics, the institutions, the ideologies and other instruments of national development.[13] But there is no doubt that all this will necessarily result in the rupture, rejection or reform of all those internal and external circumstances and situations which interfere or block not only the realization of democracy, liberty, well-being and equality of opportunity, but also the free choice of the route and the methods of a national development policy. It would be easy to confuse these healthy and positive manifestations of nationalism with xenophobia, autarchy and patriotic arrogance. It is not a question of this, but rather of recognizing in a realistic manner that dependence is structurally inherent in underdevelopment. In order to be genuine, development must tend to replace dependence with interdependence, that is, a situation in which the nation which has to confront outside pressures or limitations in its development can by itself create or choose alternative ways of responding to these situations.

THE ROLE OF LATIN AMERICAN INTEGRATION

There arises, nevertheless, a fundamental doubt: is a national development policy possible or viable in all the countries of Latin America? In even cruder terms: are the countries of the region viable nations in the economic-technical sense? There are those who maintain that they are not, and with

---

[12] Leopoldo Zea, *América Latina y el mundo* (Buenos Aires, 1965).

[13] José Medina Echavarria, *Filosofía del desarrollo,* Siglo XXI y (Editorial Universitaria, 1967) ; Celso Furtado, 'Hacia una ideología del desarrollo', *El Trimestre Económica,* No. 131 (1966).

powerful reasons. In this nuclear age, of the second industrial revolution, development seems to require vast markets, huge resources dedicated to scientific research, a labour force of highest technical qualifications, etc., conditions which few, if any, of the Latin American countries can fulfil before being incorporated as dependent areas in larger economic spaces.[14]

Faced with such a prospect, the necessity of Latin American integration acquires its real dimension and *raison d'être*. Integration, in fact, can be either a basic instrument of national realization in Latin America; or it can be the instrument of accelerated dependence (*'sucursalización'*) of the region. Present conditions and existing policies of integration would seem to favour this latter tendency, since it is the subsidiaries of non-Latin American multinational mother companies, located in various countries of the region, which are in the best position to plan their activities with a view to the optimal exploitation of a free trade zone, and at the same time to displace the national industries even in the domestic markets. This would particularly be the case with respect to the new industries of great capital intensity and technological complexity which would be attracted as soon as a free trade zone is organized.

In order that integration should fulfil the aims of national development policies, the paths to follow must obviously be different. Unfortunately, those just mentioned are the ones which naturally tend to be followed, and which are already being put into practice. However, an integration directed towards the objective of Latin American national realization and to a lessening of foreign dependence for the region as a whole and for each country in particular, requires multinational initiative in order to develop—at least in the first stage—sectors of basic production (steel, petro-chemical, electronic, mechanical, etc.) under Latin American control. It would seem to be a condition *sine qua non* for Latin America to acquire: (*a*) its own capacity of technological creation, (*b*) large-scale production in sectors with high and increasing productivity, (*c*) sectors capable of generating substantial surpluses of resources for the expansion of the productive capacity, (*d*) a structure of production which allows her to change and increase exports—diversifying them with manufactured products —and diminishing the rate of growth of its imports, substituting the import of capital goods. In other words, the immediate efforts for integration must be concentrated on the establishment of production agreements, particularly in relation to the expansion of those sectors which produce basic goods and by means of multinational Latin American enterprises or consortiums which may be either public or mixed; that is to say, on the multinational planning of existing and additional basic industrial activities.[15]

Instead of this, the present integration efforts are concentrated on the liberalization of intra-Latin American

[14] Helio Jaguaribe, *Desenvolvimento Econômico e Desenvolvimento Político* (Rio de Janeiro, 1962); also, *Political Models and National Development in Latin America*, a paper presented at the Sixth Inter-American Planning Congress (Caracas, October 1966).

[15] Inter-American Development Bank, *Factores para la integración latinoamericana* (Mexico, 1966); see especially pp. 12–70 and appendices B (Coordinación de las políticas de inversiones, by Aldo Ferrer) and F (Coordinación de las políticas nacionales, by Helio Jaguaribe).

trade. These efforts have barely managed to re-establish the relative importance which this trade had in relation to the total foreign trade of Latin America during the periods of war and the period of bilateral agreements in the middle 1950s. In fact, intra-Latin American trade managed to surpass the absolute levels of 1955 only as recently as 1964. Moreover, having reached the levels of these last years, trade concessions have become continually less significant and more difficult, and the growth of trade has slowed down.[16] In any case this increment of trade has been mainly in traditional products. It is almost entirely between countries which border on each other, and it is not significant from the point of view of contributing to the process of development through the stimulation of industrial growth, the utilization of idle capacity, the gains of large scale economies, specialization of production, overcoming foreign exchange constraints, etc.

All the above refers particularly to the process of integration in the L.A.F.T.A. area and not to the Central American Common Market, which differs precisely in its emphasis on planning related to productive capacity and additional infrastructure, and in which the traditional process of import substitution is taking place in the context of an integrated market, with a rapid expansion of trade and important changes in the structure of production. But here also the difficulties inherent in the process of import substitution which the larger and more advanced countries of the region have already faced, will sooner or later have to be

met, since the process there is also taking place on the basis of production of consumer goods and an indiscriminate participation of foreign private capital. On the other hand, the Central American Common Market is surely very limited either as a base for manufacturing activity capable of competing in the world market, or as a means of making these economies more dynamic. The above observations on the problem of integration may well be superficial and partial, but my intention is not to enter in depth into the study of this complex topic, but rather to illustrate to what extent a Latin American development policy implies the necessity of adopting completely different strategies from the ones which have been propounded until recently with so much determination and such limited success.[17]

Overcoming the 'Centre-periphery' Model

National development policy also demands substantial readjustments in domestic development strategy. As I am not in a position to make an exhaustive analysis, which in any case could not be general, since the circumstances of each country must be taken into account, I am going to refer only to certain essential aspects in relation to which I believe a reorientation is possible and would be significant.

In the preceding pages I have put

16 Miguel S. Wionczek, 'Apreciaciones sobre el desastre de Montevideo', *Comercio Exterior* (December 1966 Revista del Banco Nacional de Comercio Exterior de Mexico).

17 The Andean Group (Zona Andina) established by Bolivia, Chile, Colombia, Ecuador, Peru and Venezuela, with its emphasis on industrial co-operation and the creation of a regional development corporation, appears as an interesting alternative strategy. C. Díaz Alejandro, 'El grupo andino en el proceso de integración latino-americana', *Estudios Internacionales,* Año 2, No. 2 (Santiago, 1958).

forward an explanation of the structural nature of the problem of dependence, which in fact results in a tendency to a balance of payments and budget deficit and problems of foreign financing. For many years there has been concern in Latin America to change the pattern of foreign trade, and more recently, as a result of the period of deterioration of terms of trade from 1954 to 1962, this concern, echoed in other quarters, has led to the creation of an international body dedicated to this problem: the United Nations Conference on Trade and Development. The requests of the developing countries refer principally to: access for their manufactured products to the markets of the industrialized countries; elimination of internal taxes, tariffs, and other obstacles to the importation of primary products exported by the periphery; agreements on the stabilization of the prices of primary products, or mechanisms for financial compensation; higher levels of processing of primary products within the underdeveloped countries; less burdensome terms of foreign financing; larger private foreign investment; more financial and technical foreign aid, etc.

Notwithstanding the efforts which have been devoted to these objectives, it must be recognized that up to now they have been almost entirely fruitless. The probabilities of future success are very low.[18] The roots of this situation are to be found, in my opinion, in the fact

that all these objectives represent some concrete sacrifice for the industrial countries. I do not believe that they are going to make these sacrifices for nothing especially if one bears in mind that the resulting measures would have important economic and political repercussions domestically on certain interests, groups or regions. Even public foreign aid, in which moral motives of international solidarity are important, often reflects the economic, cultural and, above all, political interest of the donor countries. And the greater the aid, the greater the temptation and possibility of using it for ulterior ends.

Even if these measures put forth with such insistence by the underdeveloped countries should be successful, the result would only contribute to a precarious survival of the traditional 'centre-periphery' model. This is confirmed even by the most optimistic estimates of the size of the future 'trade gap', which assume various degrees of success for these policies.

The fundamental question, therefore, which a national development policy seeks to tackle is not the viability of the traditional 'centre-periphery' model, but rather the reverse, the need to overcome it. For this it seems to me that the transformation of the internal structure of production of the underdeveloped countries is as important as the nature of their foreign ties. If this is achieved, then the concessions, advantages and aid to the underdeveloped countries can yield their real fruits: a contribution to the achievement of a national development policy. But without the requisite *sine qua non* of internal transformation and changes in the nature of foreign ties, they can only result in preserving and even stimulating the 'dependent country' (*país sucursal*) model.

[18] See the excellent study by Goran Ohlin, *Foreign Aid Policies Reconsidered* (Development Centre of the Organization for Economic Co-operation and Development, Paris, 1966); also, M. Kalecki and I. Sachs, 'Formas de la ayuda exterior: un análisis económico', *Comercio Exterior* (December 1966 Revista del Banco Nacional de Comercio Exterior de Mexico).

AGRARIAN POLICIES

One of the most significant changes in the internal structure of production concerns agricultural activity. The development process typically means a highly dynamic increase in the urban demand for rural products. This arises for several reasons: the urban population frequently grows at rates of 5 or 6 per cent, the *per capita* income in urban areas rises more than the national average, a high proportion of the industrial sector—which grows faster than any other—utilizes materials of agricultural origin. Moreover, food represents a large proportion of family expenditure for the low income urban sectors which constitute a substantial proportion of the urban population. Thus, one of the essential tasks of agrarian policy must be to speed up the growth of rural production available for the cities, at constant or decreasing *relative* prices for the urban consumer. As this must be compatible with an income rise for the peasants—the rural and urban poor being the political base of this strategy of development—it will be necessary to emphasize: (*a*) a substantial increase in yields per hectare; (*b*) the maximum efficiency and reduction of costs in the process of marketing; (*c*) a lowering of the cost of agricultural inputs; and (*d*) a redistribution of income within the rural sector itself.

These are the basic aspects of the formidable task which must be carried out in agriculture for this sector to make a substantive economic and political contribution to the process of national development and—by enlarging the exportable surplus and through import substitution—to diminishing foreign dependence.

Given the present land-holding situation in most Latin American countries, and the corresponding economic, technological, social and political circumstances prevailing in agriculture, agrarian reform will usually be an indispensable part of such an agrarian policy; but at the same time this reform must fulfil the general objectives of agrarian policy and of the national development policy itself.

'EXPORT OR DIE'

One of the most important of these general objectives is an increase in exports and their diversification, not just because of the well-known instability which results from dependence on a single product, but also because the process of import substitution has led to a rigid import structure through what Prebisch has called 'the elimination of the margin of imports'.[19] That is to say, with such a limited availability of foreign exchange (after deducting the servicing of foreign financial commitments) only the importation of production goods and essential consumer goods is possible. Then, should an unfavourable situation arise in foreign markets or in export production, the only alternatives are the contraction of essential consumption and economic activity, or additional foreign indebtedness.

On the other hand, as the import of production goods has come to represent a high and ever-growing proportion of total imports, the traditional export activities have been transformed *de facto,* into our capital goods industries. The increase of exports, therefore, whether agricultural, fishing, mining,

[19] Raúl Prebisch, 'Desarrollo Económico o estabilidad monetaria: el falso dilema', C.E.P.A.L., *Boletín Económico de América Latina* (March 1961).

or manufacturing, is the essential requisite for the expansion of real national saving and investment capacity. The rapid increase of exports is thus the only possibility of basing growth progressively on national savings or on nationally-owned industry, which amounts to the same thing. Conversely, the stagnation of exports, if the rhythm of growth is to be maintained, demands more foreign savings and investment with the resulting additional indebtedness. But this implies an increasing denationalization of national wealth, either of the actual ownership of industries when the savings are brought in as foreign private capital, or as a financial claim on the wealth of the nation as a whole, when the foreign savings take the form of a loan.

In countries without a sufficiently developed national capital goods industry and with a rigid import structure, any possibility of national development depends on the expansion of exports. In fact, this is the root of the central failing of the import substitution policy: *The import of capital and intermediate goods necessary to produce consumer goods has been substituted for the import of consumer goods themselves. The structure of manufacturing production is now organized basically to produce for the consumer and the traditional export sector has been left to 'produce' the investment goods. This seems to me the fundamental reason why our economies have become more dependent, more vulnerable and more unstable.*

This is also the fundamental reason why a radical reorientation of development strategy is needed. From a strategy based unilaterally on import substitution, we must move in a decisive way to another which rests on three principal supports: (*a*) the ex-

pansion and diversification of exports, (*b*) internal structural changes in the agricultural sector and in manufacturing activity, and (*c*) basic changes in the nature of foreign financial ties.

In the case both of traditional products and of manufactured goods, the expansion and diversification of exports meets with difficulties which are well known. They cannot be overcome merely with lyrical appeals to international solidarity. Moreover, there is a very important element which is rarely referred to, which has a decisive influence on the possibility of increasing and diversifying exports. I refer to the fact that almost all the traditional export activities of our countries belong to foreign private capital, not always in the production phase, but certainly in the marketing phase. They are usually subsidiaries producing primary materials for the mother processing company located in an industrialized country; that is, vertically integrated international oligopolies. Therefore, international trade in these cases is simply the transfer of partly processed products from the 'extraction' or 'cultivation' section to the 'processing' section. In these neither a proper market nor price exists and it is impossible to determine the amount of profits realized in the primary activity. These will depend on internal decisions of the industry and will be mainly the function of the tax policies of the countries in which the mother company and the subsidiary are located.[20]

As the taxation of this type of indus-

20 Francois Perroux, *L'economie du XXeme siecle* (Paris, 1964) ; Maurice Byé, *Relations economiques internationales* (Paris, 1965). Stephen Hymer, 'Direct Foreign Investment and the National Economic Interest', in Peter Russell, ed., *Nationalism in Canada* (Toronto, 1966).

try in the underdeveloped countries is frequently higher than in the industrial countries, the export price tends to be fixed by adding a reasonable profit margin to local costs, while all the rest is profit attributed to the processing phase in the industrial country. On the other hand, given the greater external economies and economies of scale for processing in the industrialized countries, the companies always tend to leave it to be done there. Moreover to protect themselves against each other, the industrialized countries typically establish a high tariff for the finished product and a low one for the primary material. This, then, serves as an additional justification for not developing the processing phases in the primary producing countries.

Thus it is clear that a conflict of interest exists between the exporting country, which wants to maximize its export income, and the international oligopoly, which wants to maximize its own profits *as a whole*. This conflict can only be overcome by some sort of intervention in the industry—in its policy of production, processing, sales, markets and prices—either by nationalization, through its association with local private industry or the national State, by State supervision or some other form of effective intervention.

In addition it should be possible for countries which export primary materials to develop formulae of international co-operation which would allow them to increase their capacity to negotiate with big industry, to formulate co-ordinated tax policies, intervene in the markets, regulate supply, and negotiate changes in the tariff and tax structures of the developed countries, etc. These forms of co-operation could be highly significant if they were to result in an improvement in the terms of

trade which would in turn lead to a permanent transfer of additional resources to the underdeveloped world.

In other words, the incapacity to improve the terms of trade, a greater stability in world markets for basic products or a higher degree of elaboration of primary export products is largely determined by the relationship between the mother processing companies in the developed countries and their extractive subsidiaries in the underdeveloped countries. Therefore, an objective of a policy of national development should be to change this relationship in favour of the exporting country. Various means of achieving this objective are already in the hands of national governments and in fact they have abundant experience in them. But in all these cases it is a question of national intervention in traditional international practices which have been accepted since the middle of the last century. It would therefore evoke strong resistance from the interests affected. This is the logical international corollary of a national programme of basic structural transformations. In the case of Latin America, the countries which have had a national revolution—Mexico, Bolivia, Cuba— have nationalized their basic export sector. In the case of more moderate national development policies, among them the Argentinian, Venezuelan, and the Chilean, the degree of national State control over the basic export activity has been enlarged substantially by various means: marketing boards, control over the operations of the export industries, intervention in prices and sales policies, formation of mixed enterprises, development of a national export industry, both public, private or mixed, agreements among producing nations, etc.

It has already been widely recognized that development demands profound internal structural changes. But it is now time to recognize as well that this is inseparable from profound transformations in the traditional patterns which characterize external economic relations. It must also be recognized that the adoption of new policies cannot be left entirely to the good will of the industrial nations, who for a century have been the principal beneficiaries of the traditional system. Rather it must increasingly depend on the will of the affected governments and nations themselves. There is an area of great importance in the elucidation of this problem to which the social sciences in Latin America and other regions could dedicate a creative and imaginative intellectual effort: in the creation of formulae for transition to national control of the basic export sector, in the examination of possible means of reprisals and their effects, in the collection of basic information, in the analysis of related experiences, in technical advice for negotiations, in organization and administrative advice for the creation and functioning of the new institutions. In all these areas the specialized international organizations could render distinguished service if the governments of the interested countries were so to direct them.[21]

In the field of technology, too, there is a national and international task of great importance to be fulfilled which must be a fundamental part of a new policy. The traditional export activities have not had the stimulus to develop an intensive and dynamic policy of innovative technological exploitation of our countries' natural resources—except in the case of activities or natural resources which do not exist in the industrial countries—certain tropical crops for example. In other cases, the large international companies which exploit materials have an accumulated technical knowledge, derived from their experience with a particular manifestation of a natural resource, which makes them prefer it to other varieties. For example, if a certain mineral is found without the particular characteristics which the exploiting company is looking for, then that mineral does not have any interest for foreign capital, even if from the national point of view it could be an important resource if the appropriate technology were developed. In other words, to the extent that technological progress is the fundamental determining factor of dynamic comparative advantage, it is absolutely essential to stimulate it, not just to make our own natural resources more valuable, but also to assure their optimum utilization.

PRIVATE FOREIGN INVESTMENT

Diversification through the export of manufactured products has also had very serious limitations as a result of relations maintained by a large part of domestic industry with foreign business enterprises. Whether it is a question of subsidiary firms or of companies which manufacture under foreign licence and trademarks, the policy of the mother companies limits the dependent firms to the national market, thus not only preventing the export to markets in the developed countries, but also to other countries of the under-

---

[21] See, for example, the proposal of Dudley Seers, 'Big Companies and Small Countries: a practical proposal', *Kyklos,* Vol. XVI, 1963, No. 4.

developed area. In these countries either a parallel subsidiary company will exist, or one which has acquired the same licence and trademark, or else the product will be obtained by importing it from the country in which the mother company is located. There are well-known examples of this market-sharing practice in Latin America.

Therefore, even if tariff and other concessions could be obtained for the export of manufactured goods to the industrial countries—and even to the underdeveloped countries—the dependent character of a large part of manufacturing activity will seriously limit the possibilities of taking advantage of available opportunities.

Classic foreign private investment, moreover, and the national imitation of foreign products under licence and patented trademarks, have other serious drawbacks. On the one hand, it strongly inhibits the creation of technological and scientific capabilities in national manufacturing activity. Remember, for example, that a world war was necessary before the North American automobile industry produced a vehicle, the jeep, appropriate to the necessities of rural life in underdeveloped countries. On the other hand, it gives rise to an industrial structure geared very largely to the more or less superfluous consumption goods, which the policy of import substitution was supposed to eliminate.

Another potentially serious problem, which is already beginning to appear in many countries, is the high percentage that the financial commitments for remittance of profits, dividends, interest, royalties, payments for administrative services and technical assistance, etc., can come to represent in the balance of payments. Simple arithmetic

illustrates the problem. Suppose that manufacturing activity comes to represent a third of national income, that about half of industrial capital is foreign-owned or is producing under foreign licence, that normal fees are paid on royalties, profits and remittances abroad, and that foreign trade continues to expand only moderately. We can then conclude that the remittances abroad of the industrial sector could reach 20–30 per cent of the total available foreign exchange, to which the remittances of the export sector and of other activities, and the servicing of the public foreign debt would have to be added. Requiring the foreign companies to reinvest their profits in the country would seem to be an alternative, but this would lead to the denationalization of existing national industries and/or to a rapid and considerable increase of new foreign industry relative to the national industries; in any case, it would produce a considerable outflow of resources once foreign companies had reached their limit of expansion within the domestic market. It is a problem which has been raised with great heat both in an academic context and in very sharp public debate in precisely those countries in which foreign private capital has been massively invested during the last decade; this is the case of Canada, Australia, and of various European countries.

Thus, in this aspect of our economic links with foreign countries as well, we seem to have arrived at the moment for seeking mechanisms to replace or modify the traditional forms of incorporating modern technology and foreign savings.

Very interesting in this regard are the investment, trade and loan agreements which the socialist countries have been approving with capitalist countries of Europe.[22] These agreements, called co-production or industrial co-operation, are being rapidly enlarged and extended. They have developed between France and Algeria (petroleum agreement) and with Egypt (growing and marketing of fruits and vegetables) ; Japan and also the United States are seeking to realize similar agreements with Yugoslavia, Roumania and the U.S.S.R. The traditional mechanisms for orientation and decision-making with regards to trade and international investment are at present rooted principally in the big multinational, vertically integrated, oligopolies. These existing mechanisms must be replaced by direct agreements between a genuinely national entity and multinational businesses or other foreign centres of decision.

'Industrial co-operation links two centres of decision which, after negotiations tending to safeguard mutual interests, agree with the need to attain, through commonly determined conditions and defined supplies of capital, one or more determined objectives... what interests us most here are the types of industrial co-operation which create durable flows of international trade which make possible a balanced international growth.'

According to Professor Byé, industrial co-operation presents the following characteristics:

1. Institutionalized links between centres of decision.

[22] This information and the comments which follow are based on the extremely interesting article by Professor Maurice Byé, 'Cooperación en la producción y convergencia de los sistemas económicos', *Boletín de la Integración* (July 1966, I.N.T.A.L., Buenos Aires).

2. Participation by the centre of decision on the side of the receiving country, of an institution which represents the general interest (State or decentralized body of public capital).
3. Participation by the centre of decision on the side of the country of origin, of either a private firm or an institution of public capital (State or decentralized body).
4. Installation of the institutions of industrial co-operation as a result of international agreements, which either includes the possibility of the creation of such an institution and suggests its general conditions (trade agreements of 'co-operation' signed between countries of Eastern Europe); or binds them in a specific creation (agreement between States, granted by the Franco-Algerian hydrocarbon association, for an ammonia factory).
5. Definition, by means of the decree which creates the association, of a certain number of conditions, which in general would be: mode of establishing plans and programmes; financing, including eventual advances from one side; technical supplies and common research; the position to be adopted with respect to markets; distribution of the financial returns; manner of reinvestment.
6. Definition of the value attributed to the various supplies of capital as elements submitted to control; appreciation of the supplies of 'natural resources' which are not rented, but rather associated; appreciation of the supplies and the percentages of supplies in goods of different kinds (lands, building, infrastructure, transport ...); appreciation of the supply of labour. The national supplies are understood in the sense of stock and flows accounts and not as simple financial statements (a 'firm's or a State's budget').
7. Examination of the aid expected from national or international institutions. If, in particular, the state from which the capital comes understands that it must encourage the operation, it will adapt its system of foreign credit to

the necessities of the new creation. A general review of credit conditions with the object of suiting them to aid would be necessary to establish an international statute of industrial co-operation.

'We must make clear that we do not mean to present industrial cooperation as the exclusive mode of regulating the movement of capital and aid; rather we consider it as one essential strategic means for the establishment of new and more effective links in the world, but with private investment on one side, and different forms of aid on the other, each conserving its own important functions.'

The experience indicated above and this concept of industrial cooperation open the doors to new ways of association with private foreign enterprise which may overcome the disadvantages mentioned before while preserving the very positive elements which foreign private enterprise brings; financial resources, experience and capacity in technology, administration and organization. Concretely, it would be a question of ensuring that the new productive activity, created in association with foreign State or private enterprise, is transferred to the country, progressively and within a stipulated period of time, both in property and management and in technological capacity, and that the payment for foreign capital investment should be made by exporting part of the enterprise's own production or through other non-traditional exports. This latter is one of the characteristics of these agreements, and also of the loans for the installation of new productive activities, which the U.S.S.R. and other socialist countries are making to underdeveloped countries. Furthermore, this is the fundamental characteristic which made viable the 19th-century model of

foreign investment in the peripheral areas. The massive transfer of capital resources from the centre to the periphery was possible precisely because foreign private investment created an export surplus in the periphery with which this foreign investment was repaid. The industrialization process, on the contrary, has been attracting foreign capital to the development of domestic activities which do not directly contribute to create an exportable surplus. A growing imbalance between the inflow of foreign capital and the capacity adequately to service it has therefore been appearing. The new formula here described might overcome this problem.

INDUSTRIAL POLICY

Finally, it is also necessary to introduce new concepts in the field of industrial policy and to modify customs and policies which have been copied automatically from other countries and which consequently lack both sense and function in our conditions.

The insistence on the sacred principle of competition, for example, has permitted the indiscriminate proliferation of factories producing the same article, which has led to an atomization of a small and highly stratified market. Therefore, industrial production is characterized by very high costs and substantial idle capacity. Moreover, owing to its dependence on foreign technology, it is characterized by the production of articles whose size, design, capacities, maintenance, etc. are suited to the North American or European consumer, rather than by the production of manufactured goods within the means of and suited to a large potential market of a low income and largely rural population. Instead of an open-door policy and excessive stimulus to substitution industries and the absorption of foreign technology, a restrictive policy should be initiated which prohibits new activities where idle capacity already exists and fosters industrial concentration in large specialized productive units, instead of the small units turning out large numbers of different products which are common at present.

I believe that only the concentration in enterprises of economic size, with adequate scales of production and specialized in certain kinds of production or processes, can lead to the adequate utilization of existing capacity, a substantial increase in productivity, considerable reduction of costs, and the creation of productive units which can accumulate a sufficiently large volume of resources to be able to dedicate part of them to technological research and innovation and to a cumulative process of increasing productive capacity. There is no country in the world which has had success in the process of industrialization which has not entered into this phase of great industrial concentration and large enterprises. Moreover, the great productive potentialities of capitalism did not produce progressive and substantial increases in national income until they entered into the phase of big business and mass production. This, in my opinion, is a stage into which Latin American industrialization must enter if it is going to make a really significant and dynamic contribution to development. Here again we come up against the problem of the limitation of the national markets. On this point the strategy of industrial development is linked on the one hand to the agrarian policy to which we have already referred, and on the other to the role which integration can play in the consolidation and specialization of efficient national or multinational productive units.

The deliberate promotion of industrial concentration raises a considerable difficulty: the problem of the political and economic power of these large concentrations. Here is another challenge to our capacity for devising new forms of social control over big business which will function efficiently without affecting its administrative flexibility, or burdening its personnel with bureaucratic demands, or introducing anti-innovative or excessively conservative biases in its policies, as frequently occurs with traditional State companies. It is also a challenge to the organization of compensatory social forces with the power to negotiate effectively in the area of small and medium industrial and agricultural entrepreneurs, in that of consumers, in that of the urban and rural masses, etc., so that all these can have a voice in and influence on the conduct of national economic and social policy.

It has already been indicated that one phase of the policy of import substitution has been exhausted and that it becomes necessary to advance to the production of basic intermediate products and to mechanical industry. The possibility of developing these industries under efficient conditions will depend on the expansion of the markets for the national industry producing consumer goods—which in turn depends on the concentration and specialization of the latter—and the capacity to export to other countries of Latin America or to the developed countries. The latter will largely depend on the formation with other countries of Latin America of multinational companies and the achievement of industrial cooperation agreements with advanced countries.

Many other important aspects must be developed in relation to the strategies of development in the area of agrarian policy, external relations and industrial policy, to which I have briefly referred. The implications of these strategies in other key sectors must also be developed; for example, educational policy.

IV. THE EXTERNAL CONDITIONS

There remains, however, a last fundamental question: to what extent will the limitations imposed by the web of international relations within which our countries exist, permit us to adopt policies and strategies of national development such as those suggested? Or, in other words, given the repercussions which a policy of national development would necessarily have on the nature of our external relations, would the affected foreign and domestic interests be sufficiently powerful to block these policies?

I believe that, with respect to this, we are in a better position than a few years ago. From the domestic point of view it has already been suggested that conditions could be such that ideas of this nature might form part of a programme, a strategy and an ideology of development. With respect to the capitalist world, within which we are, the adoption of strategies and institutional forms such as those which have been suggested would probably have been unacceptable up to eight or ten years ago. But today it is possible to air these problems openly and new solutions seem feasible. There have been fundamental changes in the international scene [changes which were referred to by some of the participants in the inaugural series of lectures of the Institute of International Studies of the University of Chile].[23] These changes relate to the relationship between the two principal world blocs and in particular to the relationship between the two superpowers. Since the Cuban crisis made clear that the direct influence of one of the great powers in the sphere of influence of the other carried the risk of nuclear war, they have arrived at a kind of *détente*. The nuclear balance of power has eliminated the immediate danger of war between the two great powers. This threat having disappeared, the hegemonic powers have lessened their rigid control and the perfect alignment which each had demanded from the intermediate powers and the underdeveloped countries inscribed within their spheres of influence. This has permitted the rise of intermediate countries relatively free of their respective hegemonic powers, and the adoption of important innovations in the development policy of these countries designed to arrive at forms most suited to national conditions. This is the case of the transformations which have occurred in the socialist economies of Eastern Europe and of the reorientation of the policy of international cooperation which the Alliance for Progress represents for Latin America. The intermediate, relatively advanced countries were surely not comfortable within the rigid norms of complete and total alignment. Even internally, within each superpower, there has been liberalization, a decrease of rigid control. So much so that the Soviet Union is trying new forms of organization of production, tending towards a relative liberalization of the system. Moreover, control over the

23 See the articles of Richard Gott and Claudio Véliz in Vol. I, No. 1, and of Jacques Vernant and Alain Joxe in Vol. I, No. 2, of *Estudios Internacionales*.

satellite powers has been lessened so that the socialist countries of Eastern Europe have a greater degree of freedom of decision on domestic questions, and even to a certain point on matters of international policy. The same has happened within the capitalist bloc, in part because of the rise of Western Europe as a strong economic power, particularly in the case of France. Even within America the programme of the Alliance for Progress, at least in its original conception and in the vestiges which remain, approved of this desire to try new formulae. The adoption of positive attitudes towards change in the underdeveloped countries is without doubt linked to the fact that direct nuclear confrontation between the great powers is impossible. What then are the forms in which this confrontation can take place? Obviously one is the ideological struggle, particularly at the level of development policy, each side showing the world that development can best be achieved in a capitalistic or, conversely, a socialist way. Therefore it is now in the interest of the dominant powers, even though they are conscious of running certain risks, to try out formulae which might lead to rapid and satisfactory development *without rupturing the prevailing political system*. This is in fact the argument given by both the U.S. and the U.S.S.R. to justify Santo Domingo and Czechoslovakia. Situations like these are clearly possible but I believe that they are only temporary and partial setbacks in the context of a long-term process of liberalization; internal pressures for liberalization and for decreasing the world-wide commitments of superpowers continue, and nationalistic voices are mounting in the satellite nations and everywhere.

This process has had the effect not only of a thaw within each system, but has also led to the rapid proliferation of relationships between the countries of each bloc. The last five or six years show a clear evolution in this direction, both in international trade, in political relations, and also in international cultural relations. The countries of the underdeveloped world, each of which was before directly and exclusively affiliated with its own hegemonic power, have now wider possibilities of international trade, foreign aid, cultural contact, technical assistance and consultation, ideological discussion, exchange of students and professors, and of research, with the countries of the other bloc.

The thaw between the blocs was initiated primarily by and acquired most of its vigour—as would be expected—from the intermediate countries of each bloc, gradually extending to the hegemonic powers themselves and later to the dependent countries. The latter, which are the most numerous and include a large proportion of the world's population, find themselves today in a very special situation. On the one hand, since direct military intervention by one of the hegemonic powers in a country included within the sphere of influence of the other could lead to a nuclear conflagration, it can be supposed that revolutionary movements in an underdeveloped country cannot count on open and declared economic or military support from the respective great power, while the government of the country in question will be able to count on massive and declared support from its respective hegemonic power. In other words, the possibility of guerrilla movements expanding and converting themselves into victorious revolutionary movements seem remote, at least in Latin America. Would this mean the maintenance of the *status quo?* I think not.

The possibility of implementing progressive policies in Latin America will obviously depend, in the first place, on the social structure and political forces, the degree of national integration, the legitimacy of the government and other internal circumstances. But when positive circumstances are present to a greater or lesser extent, the limits of development policy can, in my opinion, expand considerably beyond the traditional boundaries.

The principal considerations which support this thesis are:

(*a*) The danger of internal revolutionary change has been practically eliminated, both because of the Great Power *détente* and because of the reorganization of national armies for 'internal defence'. The possibility of foreign war is excluded, both between the Great Powers, for the reasons already pointed out, but also between satellites of one superpower; these would not tolerate it and, given the position of economic and military dependence of the satellites, are in a position to prevent it.

(*b*) It has become evident—as even the declarations and conceptions of the Alliance for Progress indicate, although never very seriously applied—that the revolutionary dangers and tensions in Latin America have their fundamental origin in the economic and social structure of these countries. Therefore, these must be modified, but only where the political capacity exists to accomplish this transformation without risk of letting loose a revolution. Because it has also been understood that the process of change itself contains potentially revolutionary tensions similar to the pressures which arise when trying to maintain the *status quo* beyond what is reasonable.

(*c*) Contacts of all kinds between our countries and *all* the others have been expanding to the detriment of the exclusive ties with the hegemonic power; increasing contacts with the intermediate and satellite countries of one's own bloc, as well as contacts with the alternative dominant, intermediate and satellite countries of the other bloc. Concretely, this means alternative sources of trade, finance, technical assistance, human resources, consultation about certain policies, education, research and cultural vision, as well as greater contact within blocs, whether geographic (Latin American integration) or of interest (U.N.C.T.A.D.).

(*d*) The hegemonic power itself will put all its weight behind achieving the following two objectives, in decreasing order of importance: to avoid pre-revolutionary situations, and to promote development. In the first place it will be a question of stabilizing, containing and freezing potentially explosive situations, deliberately promoting military control of the situation in extreme cases, but at any rate trying to have these military groups play a 'progressive' role. Naturally, only the first part of such a programme can be accomplished—the military take-over—since the presence of the military in power necessarily means in Latin America the gathering of reactionary forces around them and the neutralization of the intellectuals, trade unions and mass parties which might support a progressive policy. In countries without a solid and effective internal progressive political constellation, external support would probably lead to the opposite situation, a strengthening of the conditions for the preservation of the *status quo*. Countries which have a political situation which is under control and which seriously attempt policies of development and structural change, have the most favourable case from the point of view of the hegemonic power, and these countries can probably depend on ample support and foreign aid, even when their methods depart from orthodoxy.

Finally, then, given the changes in the international political scene, it seems to me that the possibility of carrying out a national development policy depends fundamentally on the domestic situation, that is to say, the degree of differentiation of the social structure, the degree of political participation, and the existence or possible formation of new political movements which would constitute a functional response to the concrete socio-political problems in terms of a programme, a strategy and an ideology of national development.

To summarize what I have wanted to suggest in these reflections—the only aim of which is to stimulate a more positive debate on these matters than that which we have had up to now— what I have tried to do is the following: to accept that *national* development is the fundamental objective of the policy of development; second, to indicate that the fulfilment of the objective of reducing external dependence requires very important re-orientations in traditional development strategy, particularly relating to agrarian policy, integration, foreign relations, and industrial policy; third, to indicate that in some countries of Latin America economic, social and political changes and transformations have been occurring which seem to indicate the possibility that such new policies could be formulated and applied; fourth, to suggest that in these particular cases, the changes in the international situation would seem to have created conditions which are sufficiently tolerant and flexible to permit the application of policies of national development.

[This paper owes much to the ideas which Anibal Pinto has elaborated on this topic, and to his specific comments on an earlier version. Nevertheless, the opinions expressed here are my responsibility.]

31

Latin American
Trade and Integration

William D. Rogers

From William D. Rogers, *The Twilight Struggle: The Alliance for Progress and the Politics of Development in Latin America* (New York: Random House, Inc.), pp. 147–176. Copyright © 1967 by William D. Rogers. Condensed version reprinted by permission of the author and Random House, Inc.

William D. Rogers was formerly Special Counsel to the U.S. Coordinator for the Alliance for Progress (1962) and Deputy U.S. Coordinator for the Alliance for Progress (1963) and is now a partner in the Washington law firm of Arnold and Porter.

In this chapter from his book on the Alliance for Progress, former Deputy U.S. Coordinator of the Alliance William D. Rogers analyzes the "trade gap" that has produced a chronic shortage of foreign exchange in Latin America and the "solutions" which have been advanced to meet it.

Commodity stabilization has thus far been only partially successful with respect to coffee, and the prospects for similar agreements affecting other Latin American products do not appear bright. Aside from the difficulty of negotiating them, the principal problem with stabilization programs is that they tend to encourage continued production of uneconomic commodities through the maintenance of artificially high prices.

Through a careful system of quotas, tariffs, and other devices, powerful U.S. domestic interests have managed to limit competition from cheaper Latin American imports both of several key primary commodities (like sugar and oil) and of manufactured and semimanufactured goods. Latin Americans have responded with a call not only for an end to discrimination in the U.S. market but also for preferential tariffs. Although Rogers would like to see nondiscriminatory entry of Latin American products, he doubts whether Congress is ready to drop restrictions; and he notes that, in any event, the impact on the balance-of-payments problem would be minimal for some time to come. Moreover, he warns that U.S. preferential tariffs might have the effect of freezing EEC preferences in favor of former European colonies.

Writing just after the 1967 Punta del Este Summit Meeting had produced a new wave of optimism about the future of Latin American economic integration, Rogers (like Sunkel) is hopeful that expanding hemisphere and domestic markets will ultimately enable Latin America to overcome its balance-of-payments difficulties through increased exports of manufactures and semimanufactures. But he cautions against too much "trade restraint" and points out the melancholy fact that further industrialization will probably aggravate the lack of foreign exchange in the short run.

It is interesting to compare Roger's views with current developments in the field of trade policies. Rockefeller proposed—and the Nixon Administration agreed—to move ahead with a plan for granting tariff preferences to Latin American imports if Europe continued to resist extending generalized preferences to all developing countries. This strategy accorded with Latin American reasoning that Europe's recalcitrance was no reason for them not to be enjoying some preferences and indeed that the only hope of opening the European market to their goods was to threaten reprisals against products receiving special privileges from the EEC. In October 1970, UNCTAD announced that all parties concerned had successfully concluded an arrangement for a system of generalized preferences, hopefully to be approved by the legislatures of the so-called market economy (industrialized) states in 1971 for a ten-year period. The arrangement suspended the GATT most-favored-nation principle, that a trade concession made by one trade partner to another must be extended to all, and the industrialized states have also agreed not to ask for reciprocal concessions from the developing countries. However, Washington is insisting that the developing states pledge to eliminate special trade concessions for some industrialized countries—a condition aimed at the "reverse preferences" the EEC presently enjoys from former European colonies. In March 1971, the EEC implemented the UNCTAD agreement by granting duty-free entry to manufactured and semimanufactured products from the developing countries (several countries excepted, including Cuba, in Latin America).

Another encouraging step from the vantage point of Latin America was the establishment in February, 1970, of a standing subcommittee of the Inter-American Economic and Social Council to hold regular meetings primarily for the purpose of considering issues of trade. Shortly after the UNCTAD agreement was made public, a U.S. spokesman informed the subcommittee that the Nixon Administration would ask Congress early in 1971 to raise the duty-free amount of Latin American products entering the U.S. from 50 to 60 per cent. He said the administration would seek duty-free entry for all manufactured and semimanufactured goods (except textiles, shoes, and petroleum), as well as additional concessions for specific agricultural and fisheries products and raw materials. Will Congress now be prepared, during a period of rising protectionist sentiment, to join the EEC in removing a number of traditional barriers to expanded trade with Latin America?[1]

---

[1] For the brightest possible view of patterns in U.S. trade and balance-of-payments relationships as of 1970, see the following by Assistant Secretary of the Treasury

Undoubtedly anticipating a struggle, President Nixon remarked in his 1970 State of the World message: "We shall have to face frankly the contradictions we will find between our broader foreign policy interests and our more particular domestic interests. . . . A liberal trade policy that can support development is necessary to sustain a harmonious hemispheric system."

World trade has expanded rapidly since World War II, but most of the expansion has gone to the industrial countries. Modern industry in Europe and North America has developed synthetic substitutes for some raw materials; their factories are more efficient and have reduced the commodities needed for a given level of output. Consumers, as their incomes go up, tend to use a relatively larger share of that income for the products of industry, rather than for coffee or bananas. The poor nations—the miners of metals and the growers of sugar, particularly in Latin America—have not shared much of the new international prosperity.

Latin American trade has stagnated. By virtue of its heavy dependence on primary products throughout the 1940s and 1950s, the region enjoyed only a 10 percent increase in sales to the United States, the world's major importing market, at the same time as total U.S. imports rose some 80 percent. Total export volume increased but prices sagged. Exports by Latin America to the rest of the world for the period from 1950 to 1962 went up from $6.1 billion to $8.6 billion—25 percent. This was small compared to the trade growth elsewhere in the world and microscopic when compared with the spurt in exports by the industrialized nations of the world. Latin America's share of total world trade was almost cut in half between

1950 and 1962, falling from 11 percent to 6 percent. By the end of the period, in fact, even its share of the exports of underdeveloped regions had dropped from 38 percent to 29 percent.

Throughout the period, of course, Latin America's population was increasing rapidly—so rapidly, in fact, as to cancel out even the small rise in export earnings. Latin America's per capita purchasing power abroad was stagnant throughout the 1950s.

The raw-material exports which made up the bulk of Latin America's earnings were subject to wild price fluctuations. Coffee dropped by something like a third between 1953 and 1962. Sugar, selling on the world market for upward of twelve cents in 1963, fell to less than two cents per pound in late 1966—below the cost of production. Cocoa doubled in price in the two years between 1965 and 1967.

The weakness of export earnings during the fifties and early sixties slowed Latin America's economic growth. Imports were depressed. Latin America was forced to borrow. Largely because of the impact of European exporter credits, loaned at extremely short terms, the hemisphere's annual debt obligations soared. Public external debt doubled between the birth of the Alliance and 1967. The annual cost of servicing this debt also rose substantially, at the same time as payments of interest and dividends by Latin

John R. Petty: "The U.S.-Latin American Trade and Payments Relationships," *Inter-American Economic Affairs*, XXIV, No. 2 (Autumn 1970), pp. 88–95.

America exceeded the $2-billion-a-year mark. This mortgaged each year's export earnings during the Alliance period to pay for previous imports. Debt service, for several countries, had reached the astonishing level of 25 percent of yearly export earnings by the time the Alliance began.

International trade, once the exclusive domain of the economist, has therefore become a matter of public debate. Commentators and politicians in Latin America make a great deal of the export stagnation and tend to lay the blame for Latin America's underdevelopment at the doorstep of world commerce; they argue that Latin America's balance of payments difficulties are exclusively attributable to the deterioration in foreign exchange earnings in the last decade and a half. From this, there has grown up throughout Latin America an impression that the developed countries not only are advantaged by the decline in the terms of trade for raw material exports, but that there is some form of subtle international conspiracy to maintain the present system of "spoliation" of the underdeveloped world, and that this conspiracy is led by the United States. The implication is clear: the United States profits by Latin America's poverty and knows it.

The intervention of the United States in the Dominican Republic excepted, nothing has poisoned relations between the United States and Latin America through the Alliance period more than trade problems. The conspiracy theorists come close to suggesting that everything the United States had done in support of the Alliance is pretense. Latin America's political and social structure is geared to the production of raw materials. If, they argue, the United States is advantaged by buying raw materials cheaply, its basic interest is to maintain Latin America as the subservient supplier. Hence, they contend, the United States in fact hopes to maintain the hacienda farm systems, the poverty of the miners in Bolivia and the lowest price for Chile's copper, and that anything which may upset the traditional way of doing business is a threat to its real interest, despite what the United States may say about the Alliance for Progress.

Whatever the data may show with respect to price relationships during the past fifteen years, they do not reflect anything inherent in the system of international trade which works to the perpetual disadvantage of the developing nations. If the analysis is pushed far enough back, one can as easily argue that commodity prices have tended to fluctuate around a fairly constant norm and that primary commodity producers are about as well off as they were forty or fifty years ago. As Victor Urquidi has pointed out, those who calculate what Latin America might have earned had the high 1950 prices continued through the past decade and a half make no allowance for the even greater competition which would have grown up from the mines and farms of Africa and South Asia to take advantage of higher prices. Logic, however, has little power against entrenched belief, and many in Latin America believe in the conspiracy theory of international trading.

Latin America, however, is also convinced that the success of the Alliance depends ultimately on breaking out of the present trade relationships, and in that it is correct. The problem, of course, is not conspiracy. The fact remains that the present system of international trade and finance has left Latin America, by and large, with a shortage of foreign exchange of woeful proportions. This dollar gap has been both a cause and an effect of the economic and political difficulties now facing the hemisphere.

Some comparisons illustrate the point. Mexico has shown outstanding progress in growth during the last decade. Its income per head has moved up something like 3 percent per year; the statistics are weak but the trend is clearly hopeful. Mexicans like to see this as the fruit of the revolution. Unquestionably, Mexico's revolutionary élan, its willingness to try new ways after 1910, and the social values and semipopulist ideology which the revolution inspired opened the way for the process of change and political peace. But one element which permitted these forces to move ahead was foreign exchange. Mexico has enjoyed an extraordinarily favored position as a tourist haven within an easy striking distance of Texas and California; tourism in the past two decades has produced a shower of foreign exchange for Mexico. In addition, Mexico has increased its export earnings. As a consequence it has avoided inflation with the aid of sound domestic fiscal policies, enjoyed a high level of imports, attracted new investments, built roads and dams and laid the foundations for an economy which is now at the breakthrough point. Mexico's fortunate foreign exchange position equipped it to take advantage of the energies and idealism released by its revolution. In all likelihood, had Mexico been plagued with the same foreign exchange bottleneck as the other nations of the hemisphere, it would have had difficulty avoiding the inflations, political tensions and stagnation which have been so pernicious elsewhere. The Mexican case illustrates the importance of foreign exchange.

Venezuela also supports the point, though its experience is more recent. It

has been inflation-free and has astonished the hemisphere with its political resilience under the very guns of Fidelista terrorists. It too has begun reforms in the countryside and is attracting a stream of investments to new factories. Again, Venezuela has enjoyed a remarkable foreign exchange position as a result of its exports. The inspiring progress of the Betancourt and Leoni administrations might well have been blunted without this.

The contrast between Mexico and Venezuela, on the one hand, and the other major countries of the hemisphere—Argentina, Uruguay, Chile, Brazil and Colombia, in rough order of per capita incomes—is striking. Each of this latter group has suffered bouts of inflation. Each has been starved, at one critical point or another, for imports essential to industrialization. Each has had to impose one or another device to husband its scarce foreign exchange. Each has devalued its currency on more than one occasion between 1961 and 1967.

Shortage of foreign exchange is particularly dangerous when a nation has moved a few rungs up the ladder of industrialization, as each country of this second group is discovering. Each one set out on a policy of import substitution during the fifties, selectively raising tariffs against outside goods in order to stimulate domestic production. The policy succeeded. Each nation has now created a local industry, inefficient in world terms, monopolistic, it is true, but industry nevertheless. The difficulty arises from the fact that these new industries contribute nothing to export earnings. In a sense, they actually create new vulnerabilities to exchange shortages; when export prices fall there is little fat to be trimmed from the stream of imports in the way of nonessential consumer goods. To restrict imports when they consist largely of machinery, replacements and intermediate goods is serious medicine.

The correlation between steady availability of foreign exchange on the one hand and financial calm, political stability and successful social change is disturbingly high. Although technicians may dispute the theoretical precision of the relationship, experience suggests that dollar shortages can go far to frustrate the Alliance. Of course, a favorable foreign exchange position is not enough by itself. Experience also demonstrates that Latin America's policymakers are quite capable of fumbling opportunities presented by high export earnings. Uruguay's export tax is a case in point; this measure more than anything else depressed sales and caused Uruguay's exchange crisis at the time when world meat prices were favorable. Nonetheless, the evidence seems fairly clear that unless the rest of the hemisphere can somehow achieve the more comfortable foreign exchange position of Mexico and Venezuela—and put those resources to productive use—continuing trouble is inevitable. If the Alliance hope for forced draft development is to be realized, it is essential to solve in a major and dramatic way the pernicious foreign exchange crisis.

There is no single, easy solution. Exchange rate reforms are critical. Mexico and Venezuela not only earned foreign exchange through tourism, diversified exports and oil, but also were able to avoid dissipating those earnings by maintaining sensible exchange rate practices. Mexico's tourist earnings would quickly dry up if its exchange rate made tourism unreasonably expensive. On the other hand, those nations whose currencies decline in international value as a result of domestic inflation, but which refuse to allow their official exchange rates to follow, pay a heavy price. Exports suffer, and so there is little temptation to invest in industries designed to produce the exports of the future. Imports receive an artificial subsidy and so increase the drain on dollar reserves. Foreign investors are reluctant to bring in new funds for plant and machinery when the exchange rate is out of line. Capital flight becomes too attractive for even the most patriotic to resist. No permanent solution to Latin America's foreign exchange crises—and, indeed, its total development effort—is possible without exchange rate reform.

Most Latin Americans who search for foreign exchange solutions tend instead to focus on the problem of raw-material prices. The fact that Latin America depends for something like 90 percent of its foreign exchange earnings on these traditional exports has led many to urge that commodity prices be strengthened artificially. The easy way would be a system of international commodity cartels, to protect producers against further competition and maintain prices at a high plane. Unfortunately, such agreements for the most part are unworkable and dangerous—unworkable in the sense that it is practically impossible to maintain world markets against price warfare; dangerous in that they tend to lull producer countries down the dead-end street of increased investment in products for which international demand is stagnant.

Less ambitious programs designed not to raise prices artificially but to smooth out price fluctuations are more promising. The International Coffee Agreement is an example. It is the most important commodity measure since the Alliance for Progress began, since coffee accounts for half or more of the export receipts of six countries, including such key nations as Brazil and Colombia. The new agreement seeks to link their interests with those of the consumer nations. The members hope to achieve the production-consumption balance essential to some sort of price stability by a coordinated series of restraints on new coffee by each of the grower nations. To put teeth into the system of self-imposed restraint, the consumers and producing nations agreed to a system for balancing supply of coffee with demand through three major instruments: quotas on all member exporters; reporting on imports by importing countries; and further policing powers against producing countries which exceed their quotas. All were designed to insure against leaks into the market of coffee produced and exported outside the agreement.

The system has its difficulties. The United States almost destroyed the program by delaying for over a year the final approval of the implementing legislation. Producers have found it easier to agree to the principle of production control than to translate that principle into specific quota figures for individual nations. Nonetheless, the agreement's early, if partial, success is encouraging evidence that the industrialized and the developing countries can cooperate in this subtle area.

The possibility of expanding the principle of the Coffee Agreement to other basic commodities, however, is fairly dim. Negotiations over a similar pact for cacao broke down over the issue of price—and cacao quickly fell from twenty-four cents to twelve cents per pound. The United States and Germany have both abstained from the International Tin Agreement.

Sugar is a special case. Attempts to smooth out prices have failed. The International Sugar Agreement was signed in 1954 and renewed in 1959, while sugar prices have moved up and down in dizzy fashion. The basic difficulty is that the agreement covers marketings of only 40 percent of the sugar sold across international borders. The United States, as well as the United Kingdom and the Common Market, are not members. Instead, the United States maintains a high and artificially steady domestic price for sugar, whatever the ups and downs of international prices, and determines by legislation, rather than free price competition, the amount of Latin American cane sugar which will be permitted into its protected market.

U.S. sugar policy is vulnerable on a number of counts. Latin American cane sugar, by and large, is less costly to produce than domestic beet. To increase the share of the U.S. market allocated to domestic beet is not only uneconomical—the cost to the U.S. consumer runs into millions of dollars —but, to many Latin Americans, seems wholly inconsistent with the assurances of the Charter of Punta del Este. Furthermore, the legislative technique of allocating the relative shares of the U.S. market among foreign suppliers, which Latin America eyes nervously each time the Sugar Act comes before the House of Representatives, is not calculated to inspire faith in the democratic process. Tarnished by an army of special-interest lobbyists and by a House Committee which makes no secret of the arbitrary way it determines national quotas, the system is more domestic politics than international statesmanship.

Unfortunately, sugar is not the only commodity of which the United States limits imports. The oil import program is a transparent exercise in national myth-making. Designed to limit shipments of crude oil as well as refined products and heavy grades of fuel oil —the latter scarcely produced in this country—this exception to liberal trade is justified on paper by the need for greater exploitation of the high-cost oil of Texas and Oklahoma in order to maintain national defense. The fact is that the restraints on fuel oil imports are of no consequence to domestic oil interests, but have a substantial economic effect on U.S. coal production. It is coal, and particularly the miners' union, which are most seriously interested in maintaining these import restrictions. The national defense justification is a rationalization for a domestic political compromise.

It might be that Latin America would not fare particularly well if all restrictions on commodity imports were dismantled. Other raw-material producers as well as Latin America would be in a position to bid if, for example, the U.S. market were thrown open to the cheapest sugars available, and Middle Eastern and African oil might present stiff competition to Venezuela. Furthermore, there is no real possibility of eliminating these import controls; the domestic political investment is too high. There is, however, a strong national interest in expanding opportunities for Latin American producers by reducing the subsidies and preferential treatment accorded domestic interests within the existing systems. Venezuela and other potential oil producers such as Colombia ought to have a greater share of the future U.S. market for fuel oil as well as for crude oil. Domestic beet sugar production ought not to rise above current levels and the future growth of the U.S. market [ought to be] allocated among producing countries, not by legislative fiat, but by those responsible for overall foreign policy—of which trade opportunities are such an integral part. Latin America ought to be permitted to export part of its sugar production in a refined form.

Europe's record on Latin American trade is little better and in many respects is worse. For most Latin American commodities—bananas, tin, copper, coffee, cacao—the United States maintains a policy of free or virtually free entry. Europe, on the other hand, has pinched its own markets for Latin American exports of these products. Germany maintains high internal taxes on coffee; the European Economic Community gives preferential treatment to banana imports from former overseas territories.

Though the Soviet Union and East Europe may eventually take more food from Latin America, there is little possibility of finding any major solution through expanded Bloc trade. Present trade between Latin America and Soviet East Europe is now only a small fraction of Latin America's total exports. These nations maintain state trading systems and traditionally prefer to clear their trade accounts bilaterally. Because they have relatively little need for Latin American products, efforts to find profitable outlets have usually been unsuccessful.

A growing sense of frustration with traditional solutions to commodity problems has forced a search for more radical measures. It seemed to many that the answer might lie in a more intimate trade link between Latin America and the United States. After all, they reasoned, the United States had pledged in the Alliance Charter to make special efforts with respect to Latin America's development. As the

Inter-American Committee for the Alliance for Progress said in 1965 in its year-end report to the OAS:

It is inequitable for the products of some of the developing countries to enjoy preferences outside the Hemisphere plus nondiscriminatory access to the United States market.

The United States is the world's largest and richest consuming area. Europe has created its trading bloc. If the Alliance was to become a really meaningful cooperative effort, many asked, why not create a preferential trading system in the hemisphere in which Latin America could export its goods to the United States free of tariffs?

The proposal began to receive serious attention. Some Latin Americans had reservations, feeling that a trade bloc device would increase the area's dependence on the United States and divide the world into spheres of influence. Nonetheless, in 1965 the Peruvian Congress passed a resolution favoring a trade bloc. The press reported that high officials in the Johnson Administration, including Assistant Secretary Thomas C. Mann, were attracted to the idea. Senator Javits asked that the Congressional Joint Economic Commission look into the proposal.

The difficulties are serious indeed. For the United States to create a tariff preference for tropical agricultural products such as bananas, coffee and cacao would mean imposing duties where none now exist on African and Asian exports. Such a step would hardly improve relations with India and Nigeria. With respect to other Latin American exports, such as sugar and oil, U.S. import legislation involves well-entrenched quota limitations which, because of the interests of domestic producers, are not very susceptible to tampering.

For manufactured goods, on the other hand, tariffs present no overwhelming problem. Precious little of Latin America's overseas sales are manufactured goods. Yet it is obvious that if Latin America is to solve its trade gap it must become competitive in this field. U.S. tariffs on most manufactures which might come from Latin America are already down to an average of 15 percent; it is not U.S. tariffs which have kept Latin American manufactures at a depressed level. At present tariff rates, there is a vast range of products which Latin America could produce at current wage and productivity rates and sell at competitive prices in U.S. markets. The inhibition has been the inhibition of habit and custom: inefficiencies, high costs, low volume, and a traditional reluctance to search out new markets, either at home or abroad. Temperament, and something of the technology of modern marketing, would by all odds be more significant than a preferential dismantling of tariff barriers for an increase in Latin American manufactured exports to the United States.

Furthermore, U.S. policy is already aiming toward a substantial, albeit general, tariff reduction through the Kennedy Round of tariff negotiations. The Kennedy-Round reductions will be open to all producing countries, developed and underdeveloped, Latin American and African alike. Hence, the success of the Kennedy Round of tariff negotiations means even less relative advantage to Latin America in a hemisphere with a discriminatory preference system. Now even if tariffs on Latin American exports were reduced to zero, the benefit would be marginal at best.

This is just as well. The larger interests of the free world, Latin America included, are tied to the creation of a more dynamic trading system. Preferential blocs could tend to separate the world. To give another impulse to Europe's already too special relation to Africa, by establishing an inward-looking Latin American–United States trade grouping, could burn whatever thin bridges exist between Europe and Latin America. Latin America needs Europe. Hemispheric preferences would be a step backward, and though they would not create much new investment in Latin America or expand exports, they would reinforce the bipolar Western Hemisphere relationship with which neither the rich nor the poor of the inter-American community are quite content. Assistant Secretary of State Anthony Solomon suggested to the Joint Congressional Economic Committee in 1965 that the "course we should follow seems to me reasonably clear. We should seek ways by which existing discriminatory arrangements can be phased out or their injurious effects neutralized; and we should continue to counsel others against the institution of new preferential arrangements."

The issue came to a head at the Summit Meeting of presidents in Punta del Este in April of 1967. The Latin delegates pressed, some discreetly, some vigorously, for trade concessions by the United States, and a number renewed the demand for hemisphere preferences to match Europe's. The United States countered with a new proposal for non-discriminatory preferences by all the developed countries for the manufactures and semimanufactures of the developing countries. Such a system would mean a substantial shift in European trade policy, but there was hope

that once the associated African states recognized the advantages of preferential access to the U.S. market, they would accept the removal of discriminatory barriers against Latin American products in Europe. By 1967, at least, the hemisphere was searching for solutions to the pressing preference issue in the right places.

Latin American economic integration, on the other hand, which received a major new impulse at the meeting of Alliance presidents at Punta del Este in April of 1967, stands a fair chance of making over the long pull a contribution to the solution of Latin America's critical exchange shortage. This will occur in part by substituting domestic production for dollar imports, but more importantly by giving Latin American businessmen a proving ground in which they can learn the lessons of international competition. The notion of a unified Latin America is at least as old as Bolivar. During the 1950s, ECLA, inspired by Raúl Prebisch, accelerated its efforts to broadcast the message of economic integration and free trade. ECLA divined that import substitution through tariff restraints had run full course. Brazil, Argentina, Mexico and Venezuela had exhausted the list of bicycle, cosmetic and sulphuric acid industries they could create by keeping out foreign competition, as long as those new industries were limited to narrow markets of 8, 40 or even 80 million people with average per capita incomes of $200 or $500. On the other hand, the European Economic Community had demonstrated to Latin America some of the possibilities which economic integration opens up. Finally, ECLA's preachings had a certain ring of exclusivity which appealed to those who were hostile to or uncomfortable with the United States. A drawing together could, at the same time, be taken as a kind of declaration of independence. Hence integration received thumping approval in the Charter of Punta del Este, and became a key part of the Alliance ideology beginning in 1961.

Curiously enough, most Latin American theorists claimed too little for integration. Its customary justification has been in terms of distributive analysis. Integration, it was thought, would yield a more rational allocation of limited savings, taking import substitution to the next logical stage. Little weight was given to the effect of integration on loosening up archaic markets. The European Economic Community has shown, however, that further import substitution is less important than the impulse which integration can provide to the total growth of the economy. EEC has generated new levels of investment which otherwise would not come forward, a strong impulse toward entrepreneurial innovation and a larger scale to plant operations. Regional integration not only rationalizes, it also spurs, growth. . . .

The final results of the Punta del Este Summit Meeting of March 12–14, 1967, were a triumph for the forces of progress. President Johnson had been disappointed only the week before by the defeat in the Senate of his resolution proposing an advance U.S. commitment of $1.5 billion over a five-year period for integration, education and agriculture. Nonetheless, the President promised the strong support of the United States for the common market effort, and spoke glowingly of additional assistance to ease the pain of industrial adjustment, as well as for the multinational roads, power systems and communications necessary to the new unified market. But the momentous

decision, like all self-help, was not purchased by promises of aid. The critical fact was that by 1967 Latin America had come to understand that common effort was essential to success in the development task. Having exhausted other devices, the hemisphere was prepared to try unity. At this, the third meeting at Punta del Este since the Alliance began, and the first foregathering of heads of state since 1956, the member states agreed to lower their customs barriers in automatic stages so that by 1985 there would be free trade throughout Latin America. Or at least so the language of the joint Declaration of Presidents seemed to say. Whether the words could later be translated into a new, binding treaty remained to be seen.

Punta del Este III thus opened a new chapter and new opportunities for the Alliance. Economic integration, however, poses a risk of monopoly. There is a strong thread of trade restraint to integration theory in Latin America. The Central American Treaty originally would have guaranteed certain "integrated industries" against competition, while within LAFTA there has been support for restricting regional shipping to Latin American vessels. Happily, neither notion has moved too far. None of the Latin American nations has had any real experience in effective public regulation of trade restraints. Europe foresaw the possibility that dismantled trade barriers might constitute an open invitation to transnational cartels, and instituted an antimonopoly regulatory system. There is nothing now in the way of a positive program of antimonopoly regulation in the Latin American integration programs.

The expansion of markets across national borders should be accompanied by an effort to broaden markets within each Latin American nation. Traditional Latin American thinking about trade has tended to ignore the fact that the consumption of manufactured products is limited to a thin edge of the population. In Brazil only a small fraction of its 80 million people buy the products of the new factories. The bulk may purchase salt, matches, tobacco and some staples, but little else. Ways must be found to bring these people into the market for bicycles, inexpensive shoes, tools and farm implements. The demand is there, indeed, that demand is the real meaning of the "revolution of rising expectations." What is lacking is simple credit, stores and outlets stocking a variety of inexpensive goods, a modern equivalent of the itinerant peddler. Most important, a revolution in the attitudes of Latin American businessmen is necessary, so that they come to see the great mass of the poor of the hemisphere, not as objects of social welfare, but as consumers.

Economic integration and the widening of each nation's own international markets should constitute the next phase of Latin America's industrialization. By pushing sales more deeply at home and across national markets, factories can begin to achieve real economies of scale and competitive experience. Common external tariffs against the industrial nations will insure that these industries will not be drowned by more powerful technology and capital. Experience with the problems of plant expansion and new marketing techniques could be a kind of finishing school to equip Latin American industry to meet the far greater challenge of large-scale marketing of manufacturing products in the industrial markets of the United States and Japan.

For the ultimate solution to Latin America's foreign exchange pinch is to be found in the export of manufactures and semimanufactures. Latin America has not yet begun to exploit its opportunities. No nation had emerged by the end of the 1950s as a substantial exporter of manufactured goods. Not only had Latin America failed to emulate Japan, which, with a per capita income roughly equal to Argentina's and Venezuela's, had succeeded during the twentieth century in becoming one of the real international traders; in fact, there was not even an enclave such as Hong Kong or Taiwan capable by mid-century of competing effectively for major world markets. Of India's exports, for example, 40 percent were manufactured goods; no nation in Latin America could claim much better than 10 percent. Mexico has a spectacular geographic advantage on the very rim of the world's largest market. Other nations such as Brazil, Argentina, Chile and Venezuela could find innumerable outlets for factory goods outside the hemisphere. Yet no nation has established a really effective export promotion program, or a development agency equipped to turn up trade opportunities and help local businessmen to exploit them with capital, worker training and modern factory technology, as Puerto Rico has done so successfully.

Such efforts could be significant five or ten years hence. But under the best of circumstances they cannot raise trade in manufactured goods fast enough to fill today's staggering foreign exchange gap. It is equally unlikely that new foreign private investment from the United States, Europe, Japan and Canada will rise fast enough to solve the problem. Though private foreign investment has an important role to play in Latin America's future economic development, it has yet to meet even the relatively modest target—$300 million of net new flows per year—which Secretary Dillon set for it at Punta del Este. . . .

Thus, there is no easy answer to the foreign exchange shortage. In the current stage of development raw materials will continue to represent the great bulk of Latin America's sales in international commerce. The best that can be hoped for is a major expansion in Latin America's sales of industrial products to itself, through deeper penetration of local markets and a quickened pace for intraregional trade. Such a development will not only fail to solve the hemisphere's foreign exchange shortage caused by sluggish raw-material sales; it may actually intensify that shortage. A major jump in industrial activity to meet large internal market opportunities will probably call for a quantum increase in imports. Thus the vicious circle: to break out of the iron grip of raw-material exports, Latin America must industrialize and integrate. To industrialize for an integrated market may, for the near term, only exacerbate the foreign exchange shortage.

Latin America is already down to the bare bones of imports. Any breakthrough in sugar or oil exports to the United States or a change in cotton export subsidy policy would call for an act of international statesmanship probably beyond the United States Congress. Some exports of sophisticated products may be in the offing, but not enough to fill the gap. Latin America cannot pay for its needs through reserves; Mexico, Venezuela and Peru[1] aside, the cupboard of reserves is fairly bare. Plainly the only real hope is in major public resource transfers. Aid must be increased.

[1] The IPC dispute had an immediate draining effect on Peru's reserves, and the military government faced a major task in rebuilding them (Ed.).

32

The Rise and Decline of
Latin American
Economic Integration

Miguel S. Wionczek

From Miguel S. Wionczek, "Integration and Development," *International Journal,* XXIV, No. 3 (Summer 1969), pp. 449–62. Reprinted by permission of the author and the publisher. The author has revised his article for this collection.

Miguel S. Wionczek is an Adviser with the Center for Latin American Monetary Studies in Mexico City. The views expressed in this essay are solely those of the author.

In this selection, Miguel S. Wionczek, one of the foremost authorities on Latin American economic integration, explains why "no Latin American common market along the lines of the 1967 Punta del Este agreement is in the cards for 1985." In fact, he demonstrates, there is considerable doubt about the future of LAFTA and the CACM.

The reader may recall that Sunkel urged the Latin American states to recognize that a "national development policy" to overcome foreign dependence involved an acceptance of interdependence *in the form of further regional integration. However, as Wionczek indicates, many governments have been reluctant to opt for new cooperative arrangements which promise a distant payoff but an unequal sharing of benefits in the interim—especially when the traditional pattern of commodity marketing and import substitution has not yet brought them to the brink of total economic collapse. Other factors discouraging integration have been continuing bilateralism in aid and Latin Americans' fears of increased dependence on foreign–owned multinational corporations. And in Central America: the disastrous Soccer War.*[1]

[1] Additional studies on Latin American economic integration include: Miguel S. Wionczek, ed., *Latin American Economic Integration: Experience and Prospects* (New York: Praeger, 1965); Ronald Hilton, ed., *Movement Toward Latin American Unity* (New York: Praeger, 1969); Sidney Dell, *A Latin American Common Market* (London: Oxford University Press, 1966); David Felix, *The Political Economy of Regional Integration in Latin America* in *Studies in Comparative International Development,* V (1969–1970), No. 5; Joseph S. Nye, Jr., *Central American Regional Integration* in *International Conciliation,* No. 562 (March 1967); James D. Cochrane, *The*

There is no good faith in America,
nor among the nations of America.
—Simon Bolívar (1829).

I

Bolívar's words quoted above, about the state of Latin American political cooperation two decades after the beginning of the insurgency against the Spanish Empire, describe fairly well the present stage of the Latin American economic integration process that started in the atmosphere of big expectations and official enthusiasm in the late nineteen fifties. The Latin American Free Trade Association (LAFTA), established in 1960 with the active assistance of the UN Economic Commission for Latin America (ECLA) and leading technocrats in most of the region, has just publicly acknowledged its failure. The Central American Common Market (CACM), that originated in a treaty signed in Tegucigalpa, Honduras in 1958 and looked for a long while like the most successful common market in the whole underdeveloped world, lies in shambles as the result of the ludicrous armed conflict between two of its five members—Honduras and El Salvador. While on the Pacific coast a new subregional integration scheme is emerging under the name of the Andean Common Market (with the participation of Colombia, Ecuador, Peru, Bolivia and Chile, all of them LAFTA mem-

bers), and the former British West Indies have signed a treaty establishing a Caribbean Free Trade Area (CARIFTA), practically no one in Latin America is willing to recall that less than three years ago all the heads of Western Hemisphere states (with the exception of non-participating Canada and abstaining Ecuador) solemnly committed themselves to setting up, by 1985, the Latin American Common Market. Mentioning the 1967 Punta del Este conference of American presidents, hailed at its time as a major breakthrough toward accelerated regional economic cooperation, is considered these days in Latin America of almost such poor taste as a revival of the memory of the Kennedy Alliance for Progress would be in the Washington of President Nixon.

In spite of overwhelming evidence that not only has the regional common market never taken off, but also LAFTA and CACM crash-landed after the early and apparently successful take-offs, few voices are heard in the region admitting the utmost seriousness of the situation. The major reason is that it is completely contrary to Latin American political customs to blame oneself for a failure. Since in the case of the regional economic integration movement, the blame for its misfortunes can hardly be put either under the door of the "imperialist Colossus of the North" or that of the "international communist conspiracy," the public discussions of this subject

Politics of Regional Integration: The Central American Case (New Orleans: Tulane University Press, 1969); Roger D. Hansen, *Central America: Regional Integration and Economic Development* (Washington: National Planning Association, 1967); Carlos M. Castillo, *Growth and Integration in Central America* (New York: Praeger, 1966); and Gary W. Wynia, "Central American Integration: The Paradox of Success," *International Organization,* XXIV, No. 2 (Spring 1970), pp. 319–34. (Wynia reviews Nye, Cochrane, Hansen, and Castillo.) See also bibliographical footnote in the editor's introduction to selection 8.

are much less than frank, oscillating between two major schools of thought. The first, composed of many long-time supporters of regional co-operation, proclaims that both LAFTA and CACM are passing through a series of serious crises which might endanger their futures. The second, led by spokesmen for the LAFTA and CACM secretariats and other Latin American institutions, like the Inter-American Development Bank, which are deeply involved in integration efforts, suggests that the present difficulties of the two schemes are only "crises of growth" that will eventually be overcome if only because integration is vital to the economic development of the region. To complicate the picture even further for the unsophisticated public, high officials in some Latin American republics continue to express their confidence in the future of integration, while qualifying their support with statements to the effect that domestic interests and objectives must have clear priority over regional growth and co-operative goals. Others give to understand that the subject of the integration difficulties should be treated with the utmost care, because sharp criticisms may kill the little that was achieved.

These conflicting opinions lead one to wonder where in fact Latin America is going a decade after the first experiments with regional integration were launched in the midst of general applause. The available factual evidence suggests that in respect to integration, as in respect to all major economic policy matters unfortunately, Latin America is drifting without any clear direction in response to the mounting pressures of unsolved internal and external problems. Consequently, it is extremely difficult to predict where the region will find itself not just by 1985,

when according to the 1967 Punta del Este agreement a Latin American common market was to be established, but even by 1980, the new date set for the LAFTA's becoming a full-fledged free trade zone. This uncertainty in respect to the short and middle-range future has its roots in the fact that both Latin America as a region and most Latin American republics individually found it impossible to undertake or were enjoined from implementing long overdue economic, social and political reforms in the years since World War II. Unable to resolve the problems inherited from the past, Latin America is thus poorly equipped to deal with those which are emerging in a world characterized by technological revolution, rising consumer expectations, and demographic explosion.

It is not that Latin America did not witness economic growth in the past two decades. The region's gross national product has increased about three times in real terms since 1945 and an impressive degree of industrialization was achieved by the large and middle-sized republics. But the area's population doubled in the same period and in most places growth did not translate itself into development. In socio-political terms, Latin America of the late 1960s is probably the most tradition-minded and conservative part of the world. As a leading Chilean political scientist put it recently:

In spite of its reputation for frequent and violent upheaval perhaps the principal contemporary problem of Latin America is excessive stability. There exists in the region a resilient traditional structure of institutions, hierarchical arrangements and attitudes which conditions every aspect of political behaviour and which has survived centuries of colonial government, movements for independence, foreign wars and invasions, domestic revolutions, and a confusingly large number of lesser palace revolts. More recently it has not only successfully resisted the impact of technological innovation and industrialization, but appears to have been strengthened by it."[1]

This social and political stagnation breeds an apparent inability to approach external and domestic economic difficulties in a modern and rational way. It is also largely responsible for the present deep crises in the ambitious attempts at regional integration that seemed to have such a bright future less than ten years ago.

II

The idea of economic co-operation was born during the 1950s in the minds of a particular coalition of Latin American technocrats and reformist politicians. Experts recruited from the region by ECLA, led by Raúl Prebisch, then the commission's executive secretary, looked upon economic integration as a potentially powerful development factor in two senses. They postulated that, first, it would stimulate the abandonment of a traditionalist export trade and, second, help modernize the Latin American economies by forcing them to specialize within the framework of an expanded and protected regional market. The general ECLA proposition was phrased in the convincing way:

Latin America's basic long-run development problems can be solved only if the following fundamental fact is recognized: Latin America, however great the assistance

it receives, however high the rate at which its exports expand—and they cannot do so very rapidly—will be unable to carry out its development plans, will be unable even to regain the rate of growth achieved in the ten post-war years, unless it makes a sustained effort to establish within its own territory the capital goods industries of which it is in such urgent need today, and which it will require on a large scale during the next quarter of century.... In order to produce these capital goods and develop all the intermediate goods industries required to launch these highly complex dynamic industries.... Latin America needs a common market.[2]

While accepting ECLA's general development theses, some individual political figures saw in economic integration also an important political vehicle that would permit them to redress somewhat the lack of balance in hemispheric relations. By the mid-fifties economic growth in most of Latin America, induced largely by World War II and sustained by the international commodity boom during the Korean conflict, petered out; at the same time the chief member of the inter-American system, the United States, continued to pay little attention to the development problems of the region. Thus, it was thought, closing the ranks and fostering intra-regional economic cooperation would force the U.S. to change its policy to the area.

Beset by foreign trade problems, lacking external capital assistance and moved by the idea of spiritual and cultural unity, Latin Americans found the proposals for regional co-operation attractive. Between 1958 and 1960 the Central Americans established their common market. At the same time, in

1 Claudio Véliz in his introduction to *Obstacles to Change in Latin America* (London-New York-Toronto, 1965), p. 1.

2 *The Latin American Common Market,* U. N. Publication No. 59.II.G.4, New York, 1969, p. 1.

a parallel but geographically broader movement, six South American republics (Argentina, Brazil, Chile, Paraguay, Peru and Uruguay) and Mexico opted for a free trade zone scheme that during the seventies—it was hoped—would evolve into a common market covering the whole subcontinent. Drawing upon the example of Western Europe, both schemes put an accent upon trade liberalization as a vehicle for regional division of labour. The Central American arrangement provided for the creation of a common market by 1966 for all but a few commodities. The Latin American free trade zone was to be set up by 1972, through annual product-by-product tariff negotiations.

The Central American regional co-operation scheme provided not only for commercial but also for financial, monetary, fiscal and industrial co-operation. In the early 1960s, an impressive array of institutions supporting the common market emerged in the area, among them a regional development agency (the Central American Integration Bank), a monetary council, a clearing house, and an industrial research institute. While these agencies worked with relative efficiency, co-ordination of major economic policies, particularly in respect to the siting of new industries and the common treatment of foreign investment, has proved very difficult. The inability to reach agreements in the key field of industrialization, partly because of an absence of national economic planning mechanisms in Central America and partly because of the opposition of powerful external political and economic interests, proved in the late 1960s to be the major source of CACM's difficulties.

The LAFTA agreement (known as the Montevideo Treaty) was less spe-cific in respect to non-commercial co-operation mechanisms. However, it did commit the participating countries— whose initial number of seven increased to eleven by 1968—"to facilitate increasing economic integration and complementary economies" by making "every effort to reconcile their import and export régimes, as well as the treatment they accord to capital, goods, and services from outside the Area." Furthermore, the Montevideo Treaty envisaged "progressively closer coordination of the corresponding industrialization policies" through agreements "among representatives of the economic sectors concerned." Very little, however, has been achieved in these fields during the first eight years of LAFTA. No regional agreement about the coordination of foreign trade and industrialization policies has been reached, and none is in sight. Neither was it found possible to agree upon a common treatment for private foreign capital. Only a few agreements designed to make industrial developments complementary, by specialization of production in individual industrial branches with concomitant freeing of trade for their output, have been signed. Only one of them (covering chemicals and signed in 1968) deals with an important industry. While some degree of co-operation was achieved in respect to the multilateral clearing of regional trade balances and maritime transport, these agreements had very little impact upon the expansion of intra-LAFTA trade and no effect whatsoever upon the acceleration of regional economic growth.

The achievements of CACM and LAFTA have been measured to date mainly by the growth of trade within their respective areas. Consequently, by 1968 it appeared that the Central

American Common Market was an unqualified success whereas the Latin American free trade zone was making only slow and hesitant progress. In fact, trade within Central America responded to the establishment of a common market with amazing dynamism. Regional trade flows, measured in terms of imports, increased from US$37 million to $259 million between 1961 and 1968, or by about 35 per cent a year. About two-thirds of intra-Central America trade consists of manufactures, mainly consumer goods, pointing to a significant diversification of zonal commerce and the progressive although limited impact of the common market upon the region's production structure.

LAFTA trade achievements are much less impressive. The signing of the Montevideo Treaty was followed by five years of a relatively rapid intra-regional trade expansion, partly in response to early progress in tariff negotiations. By 1966 intra-LAFTA export trade (excluding Bolivia and Venezuela who joined the scheme in 1967) exceeded US$700 million (10 per cent of the member countries' total export trade) as compared with $300 million (6 per cent) in 1960. The regional trade of some newcomers—Mexico, Peru and Ecuador—grew very rapidly from the low levels registered at the end of the 1950s. The bulk of commercial exchange continued to be concentrated in the three southern republics—Argentina, Brazil and Chile—which had a long tradition of reciprocal trade and still account today for close to three-fourths of intra-LAFTA trade. In spite of the impressive number of tariff reductions (exceeding 11,000 by the end of 1969), very little was achieved in respect to regional trade diversification in products. In 1967 the foodstuffs and other primary products traditionally exchanged by South American republics still represented something like 70 per cent of intra-LAFTA trade. But the biggest setback to LAFTA was that regional trade almost ceased to expand in 1967 and grew only slightly (by 10 per cent) in 1968. It has stood at slightly over $700 million in 1967 and at some $780 million in 1968, although LAFTA trade with the rest of the world has continued to register healthy growth rates.

From the statistics it might seem that while the rapid setting up of a common market in Central America proved an efficient way of accelerating trade and growth within that small area, the trade liberalization measures of the Montevideo Treaty were too weak to produce a similar effect within LAFTA. But it is not only LAFTA which became progressively paralyzed at the close of the sixties; the CACM faces even more serious difficulties as the result of the Honduras-El Salvador war, directly related to the growing social crisis in the area. One is led to suspect that although regional trade liberalization programs may be necessary to stimulate economic growth, they do not by themselves guarantee much to the underdeveloped participants in such schemes.

III

A close analysis of the CACM's experience before the outbreak of the war in the area suggests that the positive impact of common market arrangements of a traditional type upon the economies of its underdeveloped member countries has been over-publicized. In the absence of joint or even national long-term development policies, particularly of an industrial and fiscal type, the establishment of a common market brought relatively little real growth to Central America, all the impressive figures on intra-area trade notwithstanding. Some independent sources estimate that only 1 per cent of the annual 7 per cent average growth rate in the GNP between 1961 and 1966 came through common-market-induced activities. The setting up of a regional trade barrier considerably higher than the previous tariffs of the individual countries did not lead to serious industrialization but rather to the rapid expansion of all types of "final-touch" industries in the integrated area. Many consumer goods imported in finished form before 1960 are now imported in parts or at intermediate stages in production. After undergoing final processing (bottling or packing only in a few extreme cases) they circulate in the region as "Central American" manufactures.

The high regional protection offered to finished goods, the low tariffs extended to raw materials and intermediate products, the race of CACM member countries for "new industries," together with the oligopolistic structure of the market, led to an impressive expansion of intra-regional trade in "manufactures" at a considerable economic and social cost to the area. Among the economic costs of this particular type of regional integration are a rapidly growing bill for imports from third countries, a decline in fiscal revenues, the high prices of new regional "manufactures," and the exorbitant profits accruing mainly to foreign-owned manufacturing enterprises which moved massively into CACM, once aware of the profitability of the new ventures. To make matters worse, the haphazard industrialization that followed the emergence of CACM led to political complications by accentuating

differences in intra-regional development levels. Most of the new "final-touch" industries settled in the more advanced countries—Guatemala and El Salvador—which—followed by Costa Rica—became the principal exporters of manufactures to the area. Since the liberalization of agricultural trade proved an intractable issue, the least developed members—Honduras and Nicaragua—found themselves in an uncomfortable situation. They became markets for expensive manufactures from the rest of the region while being unable to increase much their intra-regional exports of traditional non-competitive agricultural commodities.

As long as the over-all balance-of-payments position of Central America was satisfactory, relatively few complaints about the growing imbalance in regional development and trade were heard. But in 1967 the area found itself facing a major payments problem *vis-à-vis* the outside world. The rapidly growing import bill was due both to CACM industrialization and to the high level of luxury imports resulting from the extremely unequal income distribution in the area, reflecting its social backwardness. Subsequently, the CACM ran into heavy criticism from its less developed members. The unequal distribution of benefits accruing from integration became the key issue, and Honduras and Nicaragua began to press the rest for special concessions. The conflict became exacerbated when the attempts to deal with the regional balance-of-payments difficulties through tariff surcharges on most imports from third countries and an equalized consumption tax on a large list of luxury commodities of regional origin met with opposition from Costa Rica, dictated by purely domestic political considerations. In early 1969 Nicaragua, which had accumulated a sizable commercial deficit within the region and was unable to export agricultural goods to neighboring countries, introduced—without warning and in clear contravention of the CACM treaty—levies on regional imports. It lifted them only after the other members ratified the pending regional protocols. The most important of these was a protocol for the equalization of fiscal incentives, its absence in the original treaty having permitted the practically unlimited race to attract foreign industrial investment.

Within a few months after the Nicaragua-induced crisis had been solved, a war broke out between El Salvador and Honduras that put the whole future of the CACM into question. Since most probably little attention is given in Europe to that armed conflict between the two small "banana republics," a few words about its origin are in order. CACM has brought about the freeing of almost all regional trade, and capital movements have enjoyed considerable freedom in Central America for a considerable period of time—in spite of monetary restrictions in some CACM member countries. However, the issue of free movement of labor, considered a political and security problem, has never been allowed to be discussed and solved by the economic integration institutions, although a considerable free movement of labor—largely illegal—has been taking place in Central America since the thirties. It consisted mainly of the outflow of unemployed rural and urban labor from the overpopulated tiny El Salvador to Honduras, Nicaragua and Guatemala. The majority of Salvadoran rural squatters have been settling for several decades in the empty but fertile hinterland valleys of Honduras. The ensuing frictions were kept under control until 1969 when the economic growth of Central America, helped by CACM but unaccompanied by social reforms, brought about the appearance of strong social tensions both in the overpopulated but relatively rich—in terms of *per capita* income—El Salvador and in the undersettled and extremely poor Honduras. According to the best Central American tradition, from which only Costa Rica stands out as an exception, both countries happened to be run by military regimes on behalf of large landowners. In the face of the growing domestic unrest, the Honduran military opted in favor of a land reform to attenuate tensions among landless peasants. Since the politically most viable land reform was obviously that which would not affect local landed interests, parts of the country inhabited by Salvadoran squatters proved to be a most logical choice for the reform's implementation. The preparatory stages of that land reform in Honduras lasted long enough to give the military counterparts in El Salvador time to prepare countermeasures.

In July 1969, the Salvadoran army launched a *blitzkrieg* against Honduras that was expected to repeat the Israeli feats during the Six-Day War in the Middle East. But Salvadorans proved not Israelis and quite unexpectedly Hondurans—not Arabs. While El Salvador's army got stuck across the border, the conflict became particularly bloody on both sides with the Salvadoran illegal population in Honduras taking the heavy toll. The outbreak of hostilities took practically everybody by surprise, although it is understood—from very well informed Washington sources—that the United States was well aware of the coming armed clash. Since no communist or Castroist threat was perceived emerging on either side, the U.S. is reported to have opted for a hands-off attitude. The armistice imposed finally on both sides by the OAS—and broken again in January 1970—came too late to prevent the most serious undermining of CACM. Not only did the trade between belligerents become completely suspended but Honduras put an embargo upon transit trade flows between El Salvador and Nicaragua and Costa Rica. Moreover, the working of most of CACM agencies became immediately paralyzed. More than six months after the outbreak of the war Honduras's economic blockade of El Salvador continues largely successful, while integration mechanisms are at a standstill. While it seemed in late 1969 that the arbitration attempts of Guatemala, Nicaragua and Costa Rica aimed at restoring the economic and trade situation prevailing in the area before the war were making progress, the new outbreak of hostilities in early 1970 increased the long-run dangers to CACM considerably. Moreover, as should have been expected, the war did not solve anything and the price paid by both parties for diverting public opinion from real local social issues looks quite heavy. Most of the Salvadoran economy is reported to be paralyzed, since that country's industries depend to a considerable extent upon access to CACM members' markets. Presently, El Salvador's regional export trade is limited to exports to Guatemala and shipping of some goods by sea to Nicaragua. Honduras, on the other hand, paid for its victory by the most serious financial dislocations.

The fact that the economic future looks quite bleak to all CACM members, permits some observers to hope for the early solution of the conflict. But even if peace is brought back to the region, the Central American Common Market will for a very long time work under extreme handicaps. The war, together with the fact that the long-simmering conflict of economic interests between the more developed CACM members (Guatemala, El Salvador and Costa Rica) and the poorer ones (Honduras and Nicaragua) has never been successfully resolved, will continue to feed nationalist attitudes in individual countries, and tremendous negotiating skill will be needed to keep CACM alive. Moreover, while the issues of equal benefits for all member countries may somehow be resolved, another one continues to overshadow the area. Both the Central American left and many local conservatives insist with growing vehemence that whatever gains from CACM may accrue to the region, foreign industrial investors are the principal beneficiaries of the common market arrangement. Given the force of nationalism in the underdeveloped countries, such a frame of mind can hardly be considered conducive to the future orderly progress of the Central American economic integration scheme, especially considering that ten years after the setting up of the common market the area is socially and politically as backward as before. The message seems to be clear. Economic integration is a poor substitute for socio-political reforms.

IV

LAFTA's story is not a success story either. Within LAFTA, the disenchantment began even before intra-regional trade stopped growing in 1967. A number of attempts to accelerate the implementation of the non-trade commitments of the Montevideo Treaty were made, starting in 1964, by the main proponents of regional integration, including President Eduardo Frei of Chile, Raúl Prebisch, and the president of the Inter-American Development Bank, Felipe Herrera. These initiatives led to the establishment of LAFTA's Council of Ministers and indirectly to the conference of American presidents at Punta del Este. But after two meetings in 1966 and 1967, the Council of Ministers ran out of ideas, while the Punta del Este declaration calling for the establishment of a Latin American common market was quietly shelved. External and regional political difficulties proved stronger than the superficial idea of Latin American solidarity.

LAFTA's inability to proceed on schedule with the original Montevideo Treaty commitments has been finally admitted openly in mid-December 1969 through the signature of the so-called Caracas Protocol at the Ninth Annual Conference of LAFTA's Contracting Parties. The Protocol postpones the establishment of a free trade zone among eleven Latin American republics from 1973 to 1980; slows down the pace of tariff negotiations by committing each LAFTA member country to make annual tariff cuts equivalent to only 2.9 per cent (formerly 8 per cent) of its weighted average of duties applicable to all imports; and suspends the implementation of the so-called common list of products freely traded at least until 1974, the date by which negotiations toward a "new stage" of LAFTA are to begin. It is no secret in Latin America that the Caracas Protocol represents a victory of the three major countries(Argentina, Brazil and Mexico) that have lost interest in anything but the purely commercial aspects of regional economic integration and that assume—perhaps correctly—that

the point reached in tariff cuts assures them enough room for export expansion in the area for some time to come without forcing them to undertake any non-commercial commitments toward the less developed LAFTA members. Significantly, the Caracas Protocol makes only a token reference to a common market by resurrecting two rather nebulous Articles of the Montevideo Treaty which call for "creating conditions favorable to the establishment of a Latin American Common Market," and for "adapting [LAFTA] to a new stage of economic integration." The Protocol sets no deadline for creation of a common market.

While there are many reasons for LAFTA's disappointing performance and the clear lack of enthusiasm for a common market, some of them are particularly important. One is the ambitious geographical scope of LAFTA. In the name of a Latin American community of interests, economies of all sizes and at all levels of development were put under one roof. The highly publicized declarations of regional solidarity notwithstanding, the events of the last few years proved that each of the three groups within LAFTA (the industrial "giants"—Argentina, Brazil and Mexico; the middle group led by Chile, Colombia and Venezuela; and the most backward republics— Bolivia, Ecuador and Paraguay) faces specific problems which hardly lend themselves to joint action. All the major conflicts that arose in LAFTA involved the economic relations among these three groups. The poor members and the middle group insist quite correctly that they are getting little if anything from the regional free trade scheme and in fact are running the risk of becoming markets for the industrial surplus of the "big three". And while Argentina, Brazil and Mexico are obviously interested in markets in neighboring countries, their dependence on exports to the rest of LAFTA is not great enough to force them to grant the unilateral commercial and other concessions for which the less fortunate republics have persistently asked. Recently Argentina made it clear that its interest in LAFTA and any future regional common market is limited strictly by considerations of domestic economic development. While Brazil and Mexico abstain from making public statements, their position is basically similar.

While the differences in economic development levels within the LAFTA family may be the main reason for its disappointing performance, a second obstacle has its roots in the flaws in the ECLA doctrine that served as the rationale for the establishment of a Latin American free trade zone in 1960. ECLA claimed, though the reality of the 1960s has disproved it, that the Latin American countries must integrate because the import-substitution process on a national level had run its course by the mid-fifties. But the post-LAFTA experiences of the "big three" and of some of the middle countries have shown that the national industrialization programs can continue in Latin America for a considerable time without an increase in the level of protection. In response to the differentiation of domestic demand for industrial inputs and final goods, new manufacturing establishments continue to appear in Argentina, Brazil and Mexico ten years after ECLA's declaration that this type of industrial growth was running into a blind alley. Eventually, perhaps within a decade, these large republics may run into the diffi-

culties predicted by ECLA, but as long as they are not too severe and the nationalist ideology remains strong, none of the three countries sees a manifest necessity to support LAFTA fully.

The possibilities of continuing such inward-directed industrialization in the middle group of countries are somewhat more limited. This may explain in part their interest in an Andean subregional common market, a project under negotiation since 1966 and subject to a formal treaty, signed at Cartagena, Colombia in July 1969 by Bolivia, Colombia, Chile, Ecuador and Peru. At the last moment Venezuela opted out of the Andean scheme, proving that the private sector in that republic believes that national industrialization programs are still feasible in most places regardless of market size, natural resources endowment, and the availability of modern technology. Industrial entrepreneurs in Venezuela have been very vocal in this respect, predicting a major national disaster in the case of the opening of Venezuelan borders to the "cheap labour" products of neighboring countries. There is little reason why industrial interests in Venezuela should think otherwise. After all, they are reaping very handsome profits behind high protective barriers. And in traditional and conservative Latin America, profits and national interest are easily equated. Moreover, Venezuela represents a particularly interesting case of close cooperation between local industrial interests and U.S. exporters to that country. In exchange for special treatment offered Venezuelan oil in the United States, Venezuela grants special tariff concessions to U.S. goods. At the same time, the actual participation of U.S. capital in Venezuelan manufacturing activities is high and growing. Under such conditions Venezuela's entry into the Andean arrangement makes little sense both to local and U.S. economic interests. It would only open the country to the competition of the third countries at a possible loss either to U.S. exporters, to Venezuela, or to U.S. manufacturers in that country or their Venezuelan partners, or to all of them.

Paradoxically, the third major obstacle to regional co-operation arises from the improvement in the international commodity trade picture, registered in recent years under the impact of the economic boom conditions in the advanced countries. Contrary to the pessimistic ECLA predictions, the external demand for Latin America's traditional commodities improved considerably in the 1960s. Although the rate of expansion of the region's exports stayed behind that of trade among industrial countries, the results were better than expected. Between 1963 and 1968 Latin America's merchandise sales increased by 25 per cent from US$9,200 million to $11,400 million. If Venezuela's oil exports which behaved sluggishly over the period are excluded, the five-year increase in export revenue of the region amounted to 30 per cent. The improvement of the export picture made internal industrialization efforts much more attractive politically than the alternative, a negotiation of regional industrial co-operation schemes which might have affected certain interest groups in individual countries. As at other times and in other places, once the atmosphere of impending crisis began to dissipate, long-term problems were conveniently forgotten.

The preference shown in the capital exporting countries for the practices of tied public loans and of private suppliers-credits in lieu of untied foreign aid only strengthened the propensity of Latin American countries to think in terms of national inward-directed development and industrialization. Whatever their external payments situation might have been, in the 1960s Latin American republics were swamped with offers of external credit for individual industrial projects involving the import of capital goods. These offers were readily taken up. As a consequence, the duplication and overlapping previously characteristic of primary activities in the region was extended to the industrial sectors. With new high-cost foreign-financed self-contained industrial plants springing up even in the most backward countries, economic integration became more rather than less difficult of attainment during the present decade.

The absence of co-ordinated aid policies toward Latin America among the donor countries and the United States' lack of interest in supporting LAFTA politically and financially brought another important obstacle to integration.[3] Through its aid agencies the United States gave financial support to the Central American Common Market from the very start. The CACM members agreed in turn to accept the "proper" rules of the game by abstaining from any interference with free market forces and foreign investment. Moreover, the possibility of a political challenge to the United States from the Central American integration scheme was virtually nil while

[3] For details, see Miguel S. Wionczek, "Latin American Integration and United States Policies," in Robert W. Gregg, ed., *International Organization in the Western Hemisphere* (Syracuse, N. Y., 1968).

the acceleration of that area's growth was attractive to the United States as a possible means to lessen the socio-political tensions in a strategically important part of Latin America.

The United States' attitude toward LAFTA was considerably more ambivalent, however. In the 1950s the United States gave no support to Latin American integration efforts if only because the initiatives came from an ideologically suspect ECLA. With the emergence of the Alliance for Progress in 1960, the United States position began to fluctuate between a "hands-off policy" and "neutral benevolence." Only in 1965 did the United States begin to express qualified support for Latin American integration. In the winter of 1966–67 prior to the conference of American heads of state, President Johnson offered aid for the readjustment of the economies that might be affected in the process of the gradual establishment of a regional common market. But the United States Congress refused to support the executive's offer, and in any case the amount of aid offered was considered by most Latin Americans to be ridiculously low.

This aid, informally promised, has never materialized. The United States claims that Latin American lack of interest in the implementation of the Punta del Este agreement made any external financial help superfluous. The Latin American countries, in turn, put forth the view that they would perhaps be ready to take the Punta del Este common market proposals more seriously if only the United States had not backed out on its promises. Obviously, this is merely verbal shadow-boxing. Both the United States and Latin America put other matters far ahead of broad and serious regional economic integration, and both are fairly satisfied with traditional bilateral methods of hemispheric aid distribution. Given the attitudes prevalent in the United States Congress, the Executive Branch can hardly ask for additional funds for integration. Moreover, in a period of declining aid, the maintenance of bilateralism is not unattractive to the countries receiving aid. Each hopes that it will somehow get more than others because of its "special" relation with the powerful donor. Besides, since the earmarking of certain funds for integration might affect the amount of bilateral aid available, no Latin American country is willing to press for financial assistance for integration. Thus, traditional aid distribution patterns continue, while both Latin America and the United States find themselves in the comfortable position of being able to blame the other side for the failure of the agreements arrived at by the heads of state in 1967.

The final major obstacle to LAFTA's efficient functioning and to its evolution toward a regional common market arises from the latent conflict between Latin American societies and foreign private investment, particularly the giant multinational corporations.[4] In many Latin American quarters fears are expressed that because of their managerial and technological power these corporations would reap the major benefits from integration and in the process destroy many weak domestic industries.[5] In principle, these prob-

4 For details see Miguel S. Wionczek, *Lateinamerika und das Ausländisch Kapital,* Institut für Iberoamerika-Kunde, Hamburg, 1969.
5 The most recent Latin American official attitude on this subject is presented in the so-called Latin American Concensus of Viña del Mar, adopted at a special meeting of the Committee for Latin American Coordination (CECLA) held in Viña del Mar, Chile in May 1969.

lems might be taken care of by regional harmonization of policies toward foreign private capital and by special financial and technical assistance on a regional scale to the domestic industries. In practice, the harmonization of such policies seems a forbidding task. Less developed LAFTA members claim that the introduction of equal regional treatment for foreign investment would result in its concentration in the few large countries. The latter, in turn, insist that offering the poorer republics the right of more liberal treatment for foreign capital on the top of unilateral regional trade concessions would result in the swamping of Latin America with manufactures assembled by foreign firms in the less developed republics. Unable to resolve this particular regional dilemma, LAFTA members continue to maintain highly varied national foreign investment policies geared mainly to individual industrialization needs. Thus, on the regional level a curious argument emerges. While each country talks about the dangers of foreign domination of the free trade zone or a future common market, only foreign investment located outside one's own national territory is considered a threat. And since local foreign-owned enterprises become somehow the extension of national economic power, negotiating battles are fought to give them access to the neighboring markets. Under such conditions the elaboration of a regional foreign investment policy is more than a forbidding task. It appears an impossible exercise.

V

It has been argued earlier in this paper that many of CACM's difficulties prior to the Honduras-El Salvador war were arising largely from an overemphasis on regional trade liberalization,

on the one hand, and, on the other, a neglect of joint industrial policies that would have avoided the economic inconveniences of the spurious "final touch" industries and assured political satisfaction by "equal" participation in the industrial process for all member countries. An attempt was also made to identify the major obstacles to the progress of the LAFTA scheme: large differences in development levels in the area; the existence of a sizable margin for national import-substitution policies in the large and middle-sized republics; the defence of the status quo by domestic industrial groups thriving behind national tariff walls; the improvement of the traditional export sector thus relaxing the pressure for structural modernization; the aid and credit practices of the capital exporting countries; and, finally, the fear of the predominance of foreign private capital in an expanded regional market. What is the future of Latin American economic integration under these circumstances?

To prophesy that it may take Latin America thirty years to integrate economically because it was disintegrating for a century and a half, as OAS Secretary General Galo Plaza said recently, dodges the issue.[6] Speculating about the shape of the world in the year 2,000 à la Herman Kahn may be a fascinating intellectual exercise, but those speculations look somewhat idle from the vantage point of the underdeveloped world. By the year 2,000 Latin America's population will reach 700 million people as compared with

[6] Galo Plaza is credited with a statement made in early 1969 to the effect that "The process of economic integration in Latin America will perhaps take three decades; it is, however, a relatively short period when compared with one and one-half centuries of economic distintegration..."

150 million in 1945 and almost 300 million today. What kind of adjustment in social organization will be needed in the region in the face of these demographic developments is anybody's guess. Will a traditionally conceived regional economic integration scheme run by traditionalist national élites still be relevant to Latin America's social adjustment needs in the year 2,000? Will these élites still exist, if only because they have happened to be around in different disguises since the early nineteenth century? These Toynbee-esque questions seem impossible to answer.

But if one shortens the time horizon and talks about the next ten to fifteen years, the shape of things to come is somewhat clearer. No Latin American common market along the lines of the 1967 Punta del Este agreement is in the cards for 1985. It is also extremely difficult to envisage the substantial strengthening of LAFTA. That scheme has progressively degenerated into a weak preferential arrangement whose main virtue consists in stimulating marginally intra-regional trade that would have been taking place anyway.

Under the LAFTA umbrella two developments are probable: first, the economic *rapprochement* between neighboring countries like the Rio Plata riparian states (Argentina, Brazil, Paraguay and Uruguay) aimed at a joint exploitation of energy and water resources through binational or multinational projects stimulated by the Inter-American Development Bank; secondly, the setting up of sub-regional common markets among the middle-sized and small underdeveloped countries. The scheme providing for the establishment by 1980 of an Andean common market points in that direction. Since there are reasons to hope that despite periodic crises the Central

American Common Market will somehow survive, if only because most of its members are not viable economic units individually, then the best that can be expected is a proliferation of similar groupings in other parts of Latin America. If such groupings prove relatively successful, one might envisage various kinds of arrangements between them and Argentina, Brazil and Mexico. This type of loose economic cooperation is already developing between the CACM and Mexico.

All this falls very much short of ECLA's proposals of the late 1950s and the American heads of state commitments of 1967. While the responsibility for the present decline of economic integration schemes lies mainly with Latin Americans themselves, the actual policies of the advanced countries are of little help too. Moreover, few changes in these policies can be expected judging by the contents of the two recent policy reports, prepared respectively for the U.S. Government by the Rockefeller Mission that visited most of Latin America in 1969, and for the World Bank—by the Pearson Commission.[7] The Rockefeller Report, widely criticized both in the U.S. and Latin America for a particularly low level of political and economic imagination and for obvious inability to look at Latin America as a region, dedicates exactly three lines to the economic integration issue by stating tersely that "the United States should lend its support to regional

---

7 See *Quality of Life in the Americas* (Report of a U.S. Presidential Mission for the Western Hemisphere), Agency for International Development (Washington, 1969); and *Partners in Development* (Report of the Commission on International Development under the chairmanship of Lester B. Pearson) (New York: Praeger Publishers, 1969).

markets as they develop in the area, including participation in regional development banks." The Pearson Report, a much more impressive effort aimed at analyzing the whole structure of the relations between the advanced and the underdeveloped countries, is more specific than the Rockefeller exercise, but still looks upon integration attempts in Latin America and elsewhere as of marginal importance though useful. Reflecting the UNCTAD philosophy, the Pearson Commission expresses a belief that the expansion of trade among developing countries on a global level is badly needed and "where appropriate, should be supplemented by regional trading blocs." Consequently, it recommends that bilateral donors and international agencies provide financial assistance to institutions such as development banks and clearing and payments unions which are designed to promote trade among developing countries on a regional scale. It also urges aid-giving countries to give special attention in their aid allocation to projects which have the effect of strengthening old, or forging new, economic links among groups of developing countries. But these are just two out of some 150 recommendations of the Pearson Commission. Moreover, since they are supported with little if any factual analysis of economic integration problems and difficulties of the sort encountered by LAFTA and CACM, the impression is left that not only the Rockefeller, but the Pearson Report group as well, continue living in a world of nation-states and not in that of potential economic groupings.

It may well be that this represents a realistic appraisal of the strength of nationalism in the developing regions. But such attitudes do not bode well for the future of economic integration schemes in Latin America. Without a clear external assistance and without social and political modernization of the region, Latin American economic integration will most probably remain an empty dream for some time to come.

33

Economic Integration and
the Political Process:
Linkage Politics in Venezuela

Robert P. Clark, Jr.

Professor Clark originally prepared this article for presentation at a conference on Venezuelan politics held in Washington, D.C., in November, 1969. Professor Philip B. Taylor, Jr., Director of the Latin American Studies Program at the University of Houston, organized the conference, and it was jointly sponsored by the School of Advanced International Studies of Johns Hopkins University and Standard Oil of New Jersey. Professor Clark's article will be appearing in a volume of conference documents edited by Professor Taylor, and the editor of the present collection wishes to express his personal thanks to Professor Taylor, as well as to the author, for making it available to him.

Robert B. Clark, Jr., is an Associate Professor of Political Science at the University of Tennessee at Chattanooga.

As Wionczek noted, Venezuela's oil wealth, industrial development, and ties to foreign economic interests have placed it in an anomalous position both with respect to LAFTA and the more promising new subregional Andean Common Market. Professor Clark's case studies of Venezuela's decisions to enter LAFTA and to remain aloof from ANCOM shed further light on that country's unique situation. More important: Clark's essay is a distinct contribution to linkage analyses of foreign policy decision-making and to our knowledge of the domestic political dimension of Latin American economic integration.

I

During the decade of the 1960's, one of the most important, recurring questions of economic policy-making in Venezuela concerned the ties which that country would establish with the other nations of Latin America. Although in terms of drama and visibility the issue of economic integration has not always occupied center stage in the Venezuelan political arena, it cannot be denied that in the long run the future development of that nation's economy will certainly be affected significantly by its relations with other Latin American states.

This study will be concerned with the question of the economic relations of Venezuela with its Latin American neighbors, and how that issue has been handled through the political process of Venezuela. We shall discuss, specifically, two case studies of economic integration decision-making: the first will deal with Venezuela's approach to membership in the Latin American Free Trade Association; and the second will be concerned with the failure of Venezuela to adhere to the treaty providing for trade liberalization of various countries in the Andean region of South America. Following that, we shall examine the various linkages between the Venezuelan political system and its external environment where the issue of economic integration is concerned. We shall examine, for instance, the ways in which linkage actors perceived Venezuela's role in the international economy, as well as their own role in Venezuelan politics. We shall look at the ways in which certain attitudes and processes affected the debate over economic integration; and finally we shall offer some tentative conclusions on the future of the economic integration issue in Venezuela.

We are indebted to Professor James N. Rosenau for the formulation of the concept of linkage politics as a method of tracing a polity's interaction with its external environment.[1] For Rosenau, any effort to analyze the relationships between a national system and its international environment should utilize as its basic unit of analysis the linkage,

which is defined as "any recurrent sequence of behavior that originates in one system and is reacted to in another."[2] Rosenau has proposed a linkage framework, which is essentially a list of points at which a national political system is linked with, comes into contact with, or overlaps with its external environment. The framework consists of a matrix containing certain national polity components on one axis and the polity's external environments on the other.

The present study has required a slight modification of the basic Rosenau framework. Specifically, we shall be concentrating on the internal polity in the areas of executive officials, civilian bureaucrats, interest groups, political culture, and interest aggregation. Inasmuch as the issue in question concerns only resource allocation, all of the external environments—contiguous, regional, and "center-periphery" (our version of Rosenau's Cold War)—will be considered as a part of the resource environment.

At this point, then, we present some of the core hypotheses which will guide the empirical inquiries below.

1. From 1958 to the time of writing (fall, 1969), the issue of economic integration has been one of the most important areas of debate in Venezuelan economic policy-making circles.

2. Venezuelan leaders throughout the period have consistently chosen not to become involved in multi-national economic integration schemes; or, if they did become involved, they did so under conditions which minimized the impact of participation on the nation's economic system.

3. The configuration of linkage components—actors, attitudes, institutions

---

[1] For a complete exposition on linkage politics, see James N. Rosenau, "Toward the Study of National-International Linkages," Rosenau (ed.), *Linkage Politics: Essays on the Convergence of National and International Systems* (New York: The Free Press, 1969), pp. 44–63. The remaining essays in the book are all attempts by various authors to employ the linkage framework in empirical studies.

[2] *Ibid.,* p. 45.

and processes—in this particular issue has virtually guaranteed that Venezuela would not participate in multi-national integration or would do so only under conditions of minimal participation.

a. The only linkage group actively favoring economic integration consisted of a small cadre of government economists and one or two leaders of political parties. In general, these men were not successful in manipulating the issue and leading Venezuela toward economic integration, either because they were poorly placed, because they were poorly disposed by personal characteristics to be reformers, or their political culture diluted their personal influence.

b. The only linkage group actively opposing economic integration was a small handful of industrialists, cattlemen, farmers and merchants. These men were able to wield so much influence within the private business sector's interest group, FEDECAMARAS, that they were successful in either swinging the association over to their way of thinking, or blocking it from taking any institutional stand at all.

c. In the absence of any strong leadership on behalf of integration from Venezuela's executive branch, either to create new pro-integration linkage groups, to sway old anti-integration linkage groups to take a new position, or to offset anti-integration strength through compensation efforts, any future Venezuelan participation in multi-national economic integration in Latin America will be either blocked completely or diluted so as to be meaningless. Indeed, the very nature of the economic integration issue seems to make inevitable the development of linkage components which will be opposed to any pro-integration policy.

II

Venezuela's most important encounter with multi-national economic integration has been through its relationships with the Latin American Free Trade Association (LAFTA). As we shall attempt to show below, Venezuela joined LAFTA relatively late, and its participation in the Association has been sharply circumscribed, because of a basic lack of pro-integration consensus among the various linkage groups in the country.

Although the economic integration movement in Latin America can be traced back as far as 1948, with the creation of the United Nations Economic Commission for Latin America (ECLA),[3] we will begin our story about 1959, when Venezuelan policy makers began to show some interest in the movement. In May of that year, ECLA held a series of meetings in Panama to sum up the findings of several exploratory investigations on the feasibility of the economic integration idea for Latin America, and to set the goals for future efforts. Although there had been a small amount of discussion of a region-wide economic integration plan prior to that time, Venezuela had taken little note for two reasons: the issue was still very ambiguous and poorly defined; and the government of Venezuela had undergone drastic change during the period. In little more than a year, Venezuela had seen the fall of General Marcos Pérez Jiménez in January, 1958, the creation of an

---

[3] Placido Garcia Reynoso, "Prologo," in José Antonio Mayobre, *et. al., Hacia la Integración Acelerada de América Latina* (Mexico City: Fondo de Cultura Económica, 1965), p. xi.

interim government, free elections in December, and the installation of democratically elected President Rómulo Betancourt in March, 1959.

It is appropriate to note, then, that Venezuela's first overt response to the idea of economic integration was a very negative one, both from the officials of the public sector as well as from the representative associations of the private sector.[4] Finance Minister José Antonio Mayobre carried to Panama the message that, while Venezuela might be in favor of such a proposal in theory, in practice the country would not be able to take part unless the "peculiar conditions of the economy [were] taken into account in a satisfactory way."[5] Responses from business associations were similarly phrased. The Federation of Chambers and Associations of Trade and Production (FEDECAMARAS), Venezuela's "peak association" for business interests, passed a resolution shortly before the Panama meeting which included the comment that "...in the present circumstances of our country, the customs measures inherent in the creation of a common market...would produce ...results contrary to the stability and progressive development of our economy..."[6] And, shortly after the Panama sessions, the President of the Caracas Chamber of Industrialists (CIC) commented to the press that "The Chamber of Industrialists has always been opposed to the Latin American common market. All the conquests which have been achieved by protection

of our industry would be annulled and Venezuelan industry would disappear..."[7]

After this first, negative reaction from Venezuela toward region-wide economic integration, the issue slipped somewhat into the background of public sector discussion. Three reasons can be adduced for this hiatus. First, the response from other Latin American nations at Panama had convinced Venezuela that it would not receive special, preferential treatment in any region-wide market. Second, for a period of about two years, Venezuela pursued the possibility of a three-nation integration scheme involving Colombia and Ecuador. And third, for several years following the overthrow of Pérez Jiménez, the Venezuelan government and the economy went through a period of severe lack of confidence and economic depression, which served to produce heavy strain on the value of the national currency, the *bolívar,* and on the country's foreign currency reserves.[8] This crisis, which reached its most severe level in November, 1960, was not finally resolved until January, 1965, when the last of a series of decrees completed a gradual devaluation of the *bolívar* to bring it more in line with economic realities.[9] Throughout the country, it was generally assumed that the government would undertake no radical change in foreign economic policy as long as the status of the *bolívar* was so much in doubt.

While Venezuelan attention was

4 In Venezuela, the business, commercial, industrial and agricultural sectors are referred to collectively as the "private sector." We shall conform to this usage in this paper.
5 *El Universal* (Caracas), May 23, 1959.
6 *El Universal* (Caracas), March 20, 1959.
7 *El Universal* (Caracas), May 14, 1959.
8 A good description of this subject can be found in W. John R. Woodley, "Exchange Measures in Venezuela," *International Monetary Fund Staff Papers,* XI, 3 (November, 1964), pp. 337–66.
9 *El Nacional* (Caracas) and *El Universal* (Caracas), January 5–6, 1965.

directed elsewhere, however, the economic integration movement continued to gather momentum. After six months of preparatory work, the LAFTA treaty was drafted in Montevideo, Uruguay, in September, 1959; the final version was signed in Montevideo in February, 1960, by seven countries (Argentina, Brazil, Chile, Uruguay, Paraguay, Mexico and Peru); and the Treaty of Montevideo formally entered into effect in June, 1961.[10] Colombia and Ecuador joined in October and November, 1961, respectively, thus rendering invalid the Venezuelan hope of a separate three-nation grouping of the Andean countries.

For these reasons, President Betancourt was persuaded by pro-integration members of his administration to begin to re-evaluate Venezuela's position with regard to LAFTA. The first concrete steps in this regard came in July, 1961, with the naming of the first LAFTA study commission, to be headed by Venezuelan Alejandro Power, who was recruited from the ECLA office in Santiago, Chile. The final report,[11] issued in December, 1961, concluded that Venezuela's entry into the Free Trade Association was "an advisable step."[12] Power's conclusions were based on the argument that Venezuela's industrialization effort would soon encounter the obstacle of insufficient markets, which would prevent large-scale production. Only by having access to all the markets of Latin America would Venezuelan industrialization be able to continue apace once import substitution had failed to provide sufficient stimulus.

Following the publication of the Power Report, the issue of economic integration underwent another period of suspended discussions until August, 1962, when the Venezuelan government moved to open some tentative channels with LAFTA. It was announced that Venezuela would send an observer with the rank of ambassador to the LAFTA Conference meeting in Mexico City, August–October, 1962; and a representative of the Ministry of Foreign Affairs revealed that "Venezuela is considering very seriously its possible entrance into the [Latin] American common market organization. . ."[13] The private sector, stimulated by these proposed changes, moved into the arena at this time. The leadership of FEDECAMARAS announced that they were going to create their own study commission to analyze the LAFTA issue, because, as they said (significantly) ". . .sooner or later [Venezuela] will have to enter the Latin American Common Market, since it is inconceivable that any country ought to remain isolated from a trade treaty [of this nature]."[14] The Venezuelan Exporters Association and the Caracas Chamber of Industrialists sent an observer to the Mexico City meeting; upon his return he announced that entry into LAFTA should be delayed until LAFTA members were willing to grant Venezuelan exports special treatment, or allow Venezuela more time in which to reduce tariffs.[15]

Early in 1963, it became apparent

---

10 Víctor L. Urquidi, *Free Trade and Economic Integration in Latin America,* trans. by Marjorie Urquidi (Berkeley, Calif.: University of California Press, 1962), pp. 134–35.
11 Alejandro Power, *Consideraciones En Torno Al Eventual Ingreso De Venezuela A La Asociación Latinoamericana De Libre Comercio (Tratado de Montevideo).* Versión preliminar. (Caracas: Cordiplan, December, 1961), pp. 159.
12 *Ibid.,* p. 36.

13 *El Universal* (Caracas), July 29, 1962.
14 *El Universal* (Caracas), August 15, 1962.
15 *El Universal* (Caracas) and *El Nacional* (Caracas), September 27, 1962.

that President Betancourt was eager to make the decision to join LAFTA, as his presidential term in office was due to expire the following year, and he could not succeed himself by law. He was especially desirous, however, of making the decision supported by a pro-integration consensus within the private sector (namely, FEDECAMARAS), and for this reason, he placed great emphasis on the work of the Federation's LAFTA study commission. When this commission was created in November, 1962, its terms of reference were to present a report to the next FEDECAMARAS annual Assembly, scheduled for the city of Barcelona in the spring of 1963. Equipped with this report, then, the Assembly could adopt an institutional position (supposedly pro-LAFTA) which could then be transmitted to the government.[16] The government, for its part, was eagerly awaiting this position, since it wanted to be able to include FEDECAMARAS in its pro-LAFTA coalition. As the Director of Cordiplan, Hector Hurtado, pointed out: "[The results of the Barcelona meeting], as well as [the study] which the government is making on its own through official specialized agencies, will be the base for the final decision."[17]

As the Barcelona convention neared, however, it became obvious that FEDECAMARAS was so badly split on the integration issue that they could not agree on a basic position. Therefore, the FEDECAMARAS leadership decided that the organization could not take a stand at Barcelona, and that it would have to be postponed until the 1964 convention.[18] With this deci-

sion, President Betancourt's dream of leading the country into LAFTA was destroyed, inasmuch as he did not want to make such a decision in the face of determined private sector opposition.

Although President Betancourt saw that he would not be able to make the decision to join LAFTA, he nonetheless was able to set in motion a thorough study of the economic integration issue, which eventually led to a major government attempt to win converts among the private sector. In May, 1963, Betancourt announced the decision to create a mixed public-private study commission to conduct a fundamental review of the LAFTA question.[19] The work of this commission, conducted over a space of six months, produced two basic conclusions: (1) that Venezuela stood to gain most from LAFTA membership in the area of sectoral integration in heavy industry (specifically, chemicals, petrochemicals, steel, aluminum and automobiles); and (2) the government should hold a special seminar to inform businessmen about the advantages of LAFTA membership.[20]

The decision to move ahead on the special seminar had to wait until after the December, 1963, elections, which resulted in the victory of Raúl Leoni, candidate of Acción Democrática and in fundamental agreement with Betancourt as far as Venezuela's membership in LAFTA was concerned. Evidence indicates that Leoni was determined to make the decision to join as soon as possible; but he, like Betancourt, wanted the private sector

---

16 *El Universal* (Caracas), November 16, 1962.
17 *El Universal* (Caracas), April 23, 1963.
18 *El Universal* (Caracas), March 21, 1963, and *El Nacional* (Caracas), May 9, 1963.

19 *El Universal* (Caracas), May 24, 1963.
20 Based on minutes of meetings of the study commission and its subcommissions, on file in the office of the Technical Secretariat, National Commission on the Latin American Free Trade Association (CONALALC), Caracas.

to make a public statement supporting integration. Thus, the seminar was held in April, 1964, in an attempt to swing enough members of FEDECAMARAS over to the integration position to push a pro-LAFTA resolution through the next Federation Assembly scheduled for the city of Maracay in June, 1964.

Even though the Macuto Seminar (so-called because of the hotel where it was held) was supposed to consolidate the government's position on LAFTA within the business community, the actual effect of this confrontation between the two sectors was to highlight the deep divisions within FEDECAMARAS regarding integration.[21] In debates during the course of the seminar, no fewer than four separate positions on integration were evident among business circles; and several prominent members of the business elite advanced definitely pro-LAFTA arguments. For these reasons, the FEDECAMARAS leadership decided to postpone the decision again, and not act on any LAFTA resolutions at their upcoming Maracay convention.[22]

With this, President Leoni decided that enough time had passed, and that he would have to move positively if Venezuela were to enter LAFTA during his administration. Therefore, at the final ceremonial session of the Assembly, Leoni, in making the traditional closing speech, astounded the delegates with the following statement:

I want to take advantage of the magnificent opportunity which this FEDECAMARAS Convention gives me to announce the decision of the National Government to join, within the next few months, the Latin American Free Trade Association. . .[23]

As one of the President's top advisors remarked later, the President decided to "light a fire under the private sector" in order to force them to come to grips with the issue of economic integration, and to participate in the government's decision-making process.[24]

Far from acquiescing in the government's decision, however, FEDECAMARAS fought back through their own publications[25] and through press releases and public statements. Within months of the Maracay announcement, the President of the Caracas Chamber of Industrialists was telling reporters that LAFTA had proven itself to be a "failure" because of defects in the Treaty of Montevideo;[26] and the Caracas Chamber of Commerce announced that it had "serious reservations" about joining an organization like LAFTA which had become stagnated and whose future was very dubious.[27] This drumfire of public criticism has continued virtually up to the time of writing (fall, 1969),[28] thus providing ample evidence that, instead of moving into a pro-integration con-

21 See "Venezuela y la Integración Económica Latinamericana," *Política* (Caracas), III, 33 (April, 1964), pp. 109–33. Also José Gerbasi, "Venezuela y la Integración Económica Latinoamericana," *Comercio Exterior* (Mexico City), XIV, 5 (May, 1964), pp. 312–14. Also, *El Nacional* (Caracas), March 17, April 12, April 16–20, 1964.
22 *El Universal* (Caracas), April 29, 1964.
23 For the complete text of President Leoni's speech, see *Política* (Caracas), III, 35 (June-August, 1964), pp. 105–15.
24 Interview with Hector Hurtado, Director, Cordiplan.
25 *FEDECAMARAS Ante la ALALC* (Caracas: FEDECAMARAS, October 15, 1965), p. 13.
26 *El Nacional* (Caracas), September 9, 1964.
27 *El Nacional* (Caracas), July 21, 1965.
28 See "La ALALC en Crisis," *El Nacional* (Caracas), February 15, 1968, for an example.

sensus, the Venezuelan private sector has hardened its nationalist attitude.

In light of this, President Leoni had to move very carefully and slowly to enter LAFTA, even after his announcement of June, 1964. Enabling legislation to authorize Leoni to ratify the Treaty was not submitted to the Venezuelan Congress until the last day of the 1965 legislative session, November 30. Since Leoni did not control a majority of either house of Congress, he was forced to utilize all of his consensus-building skills to obtain congressional approval of the ratification. According to one source, the President, in order to move the issue through Congress, was forced to make two key commitments: (1) that Venezuela would not participate in any arrangements which would expose its monetary policy (among the most stable and inflation-free in Latin America) to inflationary impulses from other countries, or which would drain its hard currency reserves (usually the highest in Latin America) to pay for trade deficits; and (2) that the Venezuelan government would continue to grant a certain amount of protection to already-established national industries.[29] Whatever the case, ratification was finally approved by both houses of Congress on June 30, 1966; Leoni formally promulgated the decree on July 11, 1966; and the document of adherence to the Treaty of Montevideo was deposited with the Foreign Ministry of Uruguay on August 31, 1966.[30]

Thus, Venezuela joined LAFTA not only in the absence of a pro-LAFTA consensus, but in the face of anti-

LAFTA sentiment on the part of the private sector. There remains the question of how this absence of consensus has affected Venezuela's participation in the Free Trade Association. It has been observed that the LAFTA debate was so bitter that the government would be forced to move slowly during the actual tariff reduction negotiations in the Association. As Aaron Segal put it, "The struggle to enter LAFTA virtually forces the Venezuelan government to adopt a cautious policy in the acceleration of tariff liberalization, for fear of provoking a new struggle."[31]

In evaluating Venezuela's participation in LAFTA, we should take into account the fact that it has been a member such a short time that reliable, long-term data is not available. However, understanding that caveat, we will look at several indicators of participation, to estimate the degree to which Venezuelan leaders have moved with caution within LAFTA.

On the question of the negotiation of annual tariff reductions (what LAFTA calls the National List), evidence indicates a very cautious attitude. Following the deposit of ratification of the Treaty in August, 1966, Venezuela waited for a year before it attempted to negotiate its first tariff reductions with other LAFTA members. At the Fourth Special Meeting of the LAFTA Conference (the tariff reducing body), Venezuela negotiated 275 tariff concessions, which was increased to 434 by the Seventh Regular Meeting of the Conference, held later in 1967.[32] Venezuelan concessions for the first full year in LAFTA amounted, then, to 4.2% of the total concessions granted by all countries. Of the Venezuelan conces-

---

29 Aaron Segal, "Venezuela y la ALALC," *Comercio Exterior* (Mexico City), XVII, 1 (January, 1967), p. 58.
30 *Comercio Exterior* (Mexico City), XVI, 9 (September, 1966), pp. 643–44.

31 Segal, *op. cit.,* p. 62.
32 *Comercio Exterior* (Mexico City), XVIII, 11 (November, 1968), pp. 953–58.

sions, however, thirty-seven were still controlled by prior licensing arrangements which serve to nullify the actual tariff concession, no matter how great it may be. In addition, these concessions went into effect immediately only for six countries (Colombia, Chile, Mexico, Paraguay, Peru, Uruguay); Argentina and Brazil were granted the concessions late in 1968; and Ecuador still had not been granted the concessions as of this writing.[33] Thus, if negotiation of the National List is any indicator, Venezuela is still not a full member of LAFTA, since their National List does not extend to Ecuador. Unfortunately, at this writing, detailed data on concessions granted in 1968 are not available; however, reports from Caracas indicate that the new administration of President Rafael Caldera, elected in December, 1968, has begun to revise Venezuela's planned concession list for the 1969 negotiating conference, and has asked FEDE-CAMARAS to participate in the revision. The effect can only be to lessen the liberalizing impact of the concessions on the Venezuelan economy.[34]

As far as composition of the first concessions is concerned, we can see that here, too, Venezuela has been playing it safe. Venezuela's negotiating strategy has been to grant concessions on items which are not likely to be exported by other Latin American countries (chemicals, machinery, etc.), and to save the really hard concessions (food, for example) for later.[35] On the first National Lists, over 60% of Venezuelan concessions consisted of chemicals and related products, machinery, and metals and semi-processed metal products.[36] In addition, if these concessions *do* result in any increased imports, the new items will probably be competing with state-owned industries (petro-chemicals, for example), and the private business sector will continue to be protected.

LAFTA's other type of tariff reduction, called the Common List, is the product of a negotiating conference held every three years, and is supposed to include those reductions which are irrevocable (National List reductions can be withdrawn under certain conditions). Further, at the end of LAFTA's twelfth year (1973), the Common List is to contain substantially all (interpreted as 80%) of intra-Latin American trade.

Venezuela participated in the negotiation of LAFTA's second Common List late in 1968; but that country attached so many reservations to the list that they admitted only the following items to the list without restrictions: mica, tin (in various forms), chromium, tungsten, titanium, antimony, silver, liquified amonium, urea, postage stamps and portraits of Latin American authors painted entirely by hand.[37] Such politically sensitive items as wheat, chocolate, tuna, powdered cacao and straw hats were subjected to provisions which serve to protect Venezuela entirely from these concessions.[38]

Another indicator of Venezuela's participation in LAFTA can be found in the negotiation of the Treaty's com-

[33] *Comercio Exterior* (Mexico city), XIX, 1 (January, 1969), p. 8.
[34] *El Nacional* (Caracas), July 6, 1969.
[35] Segal, *op. cit.,* p. 62.

[36] *Comercio Exterior* (Mexico City), XVIII, 11 (November, 1968), pp. 953–58.
[37] *La séptima conferencia extraordinaria y la marcha del comercio intrazonal.* Supplement to *Comercio Exterior* (Mexico City), XIX, 2 (February, 1969), pp. 8–12.
[38] *Ibid.* See also *Comercio Exterior* (Mexico City), XVIII, 1 (January, 1968), pp. 8–9.

plementarity agreements, those accords contracted among several LAFTA members which are designed to stimulate the integration of certain sectors of production. It will be recalled that Venezuelan leaders had concluded that these sectoral integration agreements would be the key to successful participation in LAFTA. Of the seven complementarity agreements negotiated by LAFTA members prior to December 31, 1968, Venezuela had agreed to participate in one—that pertaining to chemicals (in which Venezuela will obviously have significant comparative advantage). The other signatories were Argentina, Brazil, Colombia, Chile, Mexico and Peru. However, the accord was reached on December 17, 1967; and to date, the Venezuelan government has not deposited the ratification placing this agreement into effect. It remains a dead letter.[39]

A more detailed account of Venezuela's participation in LAFTA cannot be undertaken here because of lack of space and because of lack of trade statistics for 1968. In all likelihood, inasmuch as the first tariff reductions did not go into effect until September of 1967, trade patterns between Venezuela and LAFTA countries have not changed much in 1968. Venezuela continues to send about 5% of its total exports to LAFTA, while imports from LAFTA constitute about 2–3% of the total. Judging from the very conservative nature of Venezuela's participation in LAFTA to date, these figures are not likely to change; and the integration of the Venezuelan economy with those of other Latin American states is not a great deal closer to realization in 1969 than it was in 1959.

[39] *Comercio Exterior* (Mexico City), XVIII, 11 (November, 1968), pp. 953–58.

III

Interwoven with the debate on region-wide economic integration, we find another, quieter debate being conducted with regard to Venezuela's opportunities to achieve economic advantages through a union of more limited jurisdiction. At a very minimum, this smaller integration scheme would include Venezuela, Colombia and Ecuador—the countries of Simón Bolívar's creation, Gran Colombia. At the most, such a union would consist of these three countries plus Peru, Bolivia and Chile. This latter six-nation proposal, called the Andean Group, is the scheme which will attract most of our attention, although our story must begin with a resume of the antecedents of the Andean Pact.

From 1958 to 1961, it was clear that Venezuela's hopes for inclusion in a broader economic setting lay with the much more restricted idea of cooperation with Colombia and Ecuador, with integration being permitted to take place on a very modest scale. Beginning with the three-nation Declaration of Bogotá, signed August 10, which foresaw "... the negotiation of basic agreements for a future common market...,"[40] and continuing through numerous meetings of the three countries, Venezuela sought to offset the ill effects of their failure to participate in the broader LAFTA framework.[41] However, after Colombia and Ecuador opted to join LAFTA in 1961, Venezuelan leaders in the pro-integration community decided to abandon the

[40] *El Universal* (Caracas), August 12, 1958.
[41] United Nations, Department of Economic and Social Affairs, *Multilateral Economic Cooperation in Latin America: Volume I, Text and Documents* (New York: United Nations, 1962), pp. 137–65.

smaller union idea for the time being, and to redirect their efforts to bringing Venezuela into LAFTA.

Within a few years, however, the sub-regional idea of economic cooperation began to gain ground again, this time within the LAFTA framework. After having experienced several years of competition with the "Big Three" of LAFTA (Argentina, Brazil and Mexico), several of the more industrious smaller members—especially Chile and Colombia—decided that they needed some machinery developed within LAFTA which would protect their interests. The first step toward creating this machinery was the meeting of the heads of state or their representatives of five nations in Bogotá, Colombia, in August, 1966, to declare their desire to move toward an Andean grouping of states on economic matters.[42] Venezuela's participation in this enterprise was to bring to the surface again many of the salient points of linkage politics on the issue of economic integration.

Even though the Andean Group had pledged itself to more vigorous economic cooperation, some time was to pass before specific steps were taken to make these pledges concrete. To be precise, the Andean Group had to await the blessings of a special meeting of Latin American Presidents, held in Punta del Este, Uruguay, April, 1967, before they could move forward on their plan to form a bloc within a bloc.[43] With this obstacle out of the way, several initial planning meetings were held in June and July, climaxed

with a meeting of the Andean Group Mixed Commission in Caracas in August, 1967.

The Caracas meeting produced two instruments of economic integration. The first was a plan to create an Andean Development Corporation, a multinational public development enterprise whose purpose would be to stimulate trans-national development projects, both in the private and public sectors. Called by some observers the key to Andean development, the Corporation would be capitalized initially at an amount between $50 and $100 million, to be divided as follows: Venezuela, 40%; Colombia and Chile, 20% each; Peru, 16%, Ecuador, 4%.[44]

The second instrument drafted at Caracas was the basic document of the Andean Pact, called "Bases for a Sub-regional Agreement among Colombia, Chile, Ecuador, Peru and Venezuela."[45] As subsequently modified slightly by meetings in Lima, Peru (December, 1967), and Bogotá, Colombia (February, 1968), the document foresaw significant differences between the Andean grouping and LAFTA. Specifically, it was proposed that the Andean Group adopt a much faster and more nearly automatic method of reducing tariffs among members, that they move quickly toward adopting a common external tariff, and that more emphasis be placed on joint planning and on the "harmonization" of the foreign trade policies of the members.

---

[42] The original countries in attendance at Bogotá were Venezuela, Colombia, Chile, Peru and Ecuador. Bolivia indicated its interest in joining and began to participate in planning sessions in 1967.

[43] *Comercio Exterior* (Mexico City), XVII, 11 (November, 1967), pp. 871–73.

[44] *Comercio Exterior* (Mexico City), XVII, 9 (September, 1967), pp. 688–89. Bolivia had not yet begun to participate in meetings.

[45] For the text of this document, see *II Reunión del Consejo de Ministros; IV y V Reuniones Extraordinarias de la Conferencia.* Supplement to *Comercio Exterior* (Mexico City), XVII, 9 (September, 1967), pp. 13–17.

It was fairly clear, therefore, following the Caracas meetings in August, that the Andean Group leadership had in mind an economic integration scheme that went considerably beyond that envisaged in the LAFTA treaty, both in scope and in speed of change. It should not have come as a surprise to anyone, then, that Venezuela's private sector launched a vigorous program against entry into the proposed Andean grouping.

In October, 1967, FEDECAMARAS took the first step toward preventing Venezuela's participation in the Andean project with the publication of its own analysis of the document described above.[46] In their analysis, the Federation clearly argued against Venezuelan participation in the Andean group. Two points stand out as forming the basis for their opposition: (1) the rapid reduction of tariffs would not give national industries sufficient time to adjust to "the new conditions of competition," especially in the fields of textiles, beverages and shoes; and (2) the establishment of a common external tariff would force Venezuela away from their traditionally strong trade ties with the United States.[47]

The Fifth Meeting of the Andean Group Mixed Commission, held in Bogotá in February, 1968, provoked especially loud cries from FEDE-CAMARAS, inasmuch as the delegates to the meeting proposed to push ahead toward agreement on a final draft of the integration treaty as fast as possible. In this desire, President Raúl Leoni surely was in agreement, since he must have seen that unless he brought Venezuela into the Andean Group before

the spring of 1968, he would be caught in the final days of his term unable to move positively on the issue. Nevertheless, FEDECAMARAS unleashed such a strong campaign against Venezuelan entry that even Leoni was forced to concede ground.[48] Thus, on April 5, 1968, Leoni anounced that Venezuela had asked for postponement of the Sixth Meeting, which had been planned as the final drafting session of the Group's treaty.[49]

When the Sixth Meeting was finally held, in Cartagena, Colombia, July–August, 1968, Venezuela did take part; but on the most important issues, their delegates took positions of frank opposition. Venezuela pronounced itself to be against the proposed 2/3 majority voting rule (and in favor of the veto for each nation); they argued in favor of the continued right of each government to grant protection to industries already in existence; and they fought for a lengthening of the proposed period for complete elimination of customs duties. Obviously, finding themselves at odds with the other members on such crucial issues, the Venezuelans withdrew, announcing that they had made no decision on participation in the Andean integration effort. This, in effect, marked the end of President Leoni's attempt to bring his country into this grouping.

The issue of economic integration underwent another suspension in Venezuela until after the 1968 presidential elections in December, which resulted in the election of Rafael Caldera, candidate of the Christian Democrats

---

[46] FEDECAMARAS, *FEDECAMARAS y las Bases del Acuerdo Subregional* (Caracas: author, October, 1967), p. 37.
[47] *Ibid.,* pp. 14–15.

[48] See *El Nacional* (Caracas), February 22, 1968, and *El Universal* (Caracas), February 25, 1968, for examples of FEDECAMARAS' blistering attacks on the Andean Group.
[49] *Comercio Exterior* (Mexico City), XVIII, 5 (May, 1968), pp. 382–83.

(COPEI). Some observers predicted that Caldera would move more strongly in favor of integration, because Latin American Christian Democrats (under the leadership of Chilean President Eduardo Frei) have generally favored multi-national cooperation of this sort.[50] However, Caldera's insistence on pursuing a minority government has forced him to rely even more on private sector support than did his two predecessors; and this reliance has caused Caldera to move with great caution on the integration issue.

Accordingly, the first act of President-elect Caldera in the area of economic integration was a request of the Andean Group countries to postpone consideration of the final treaty until his government had had time to get settled and to study the issue. In a speech to more than 1,000 businessmen shortly before taking office, Caldera assured them that their interests and opinions would be taken into account before any government action, especially on the issue of Andean integration.[51]

True to his word, after less than a month in office, Caldera's foreign ministry moved to establish close contact with FEDECAMARAS on the integration question; and plans were made for subsequent working sessions to discuss any outstanding questions the businessmen might have. The new Minister of Development, a former economist with one of the country's largest industrial combines, announced her complete confidence that the government and the private sector would reach satisfactory agreement on the Andean question.[52]

At last, however, the moment of truth had come; the definitive meeting of the Andean Group could be postponed no more; and, with Colombia threatening to sign the treaty with or without Venezuelan participation,[53] the final drafting session opened in the Colombian city of Cartagena, May 5, 1969. It was apparent from the beginning of negotiations in Cartagena that inclusion of Venezuela in the treaty would be extremely difficult. The Venezuelan Foreign Minister made clear that the government and FEDECAMARAS had come to complete agreement on the requirements for Venezuelan entry,[54] and the concessions that the private sector was asking for would have all but emasculated the treaty. Among other items, the Venezuelan delegation asked to have the Andean treaty modified to do the following things: (1) establish a special category of products for which customs duties would be reduced within an "indefinite" time limit; (2) preserve the right of national veto; (3) eliminate the automatic provisions for tariff reduction; (4) establish guarantees to ensure balanced trade among all members; (5) not set up any barriers to Venezuela's traditional markets and sources of investment in the United States.[55] Without these concessions, the Venezuelan delegation argued, the treaty would never get through their country's senate.[56]

Nevertheless, the other countries refused to give way; and, after much drama and hard bargaining, the Venezuelan delegation was brought home, and the Andean Pact was signed May 24, 1969, by Bolivia, Colombia, Chile, Ecuador and Peru. Venezuela re-

---

[50] *Comercio Exterior* (Mexico City), XIX, 1 (January, 1969), p. 46.
[51] *El Nacional* (Caracas), March 2, 1969.
[52] *El Nacional* (Caracas), March 23, 1969.

[53] *El Universal* (Caracas), May 5, 1969.
[54] *El National* (Caracas), May, 4, 1969.
[55] *El Nacional* (Caracas), May 7 and May 18, 1969.
[56] *El Nacional* (Caracas), May 8, 1969.

mained with the option to sign until December 31, 1970.[57]

The failure of Venezuela to join the Andean grouping, and its growing dissatisfaction with LAFTA operations coincided with a sense of great concern about the future of its foreign trade policies. Unwilling to open its economy to its neighbors in Latin America, unable to compete with industrialized countries in manufactured items, and facing almost certain stagnation of its industrialization effort because of the narrowness of its national market, Venezuela in the summer of 1969 was seen grasping for a solution to its potential economic difficulties. Although Venezuela is unique among the developing countries in having such great natural resources, it has still encountered the classic dilemma of nations in the developing world: the conflict between economic nationalism and industrialization on the one hand, and the growing sensation on the other that the individual nation-state is becoming an inadequate political unit to solve many of the problems of economic development.

IV

By way of summary, then, we may point out some of the more significant features of the economic integration issue in Venezuela, and of the way in which that issue has been processed by the Venezuelan political system.

First, in looking at the ten-year span included in this study, we have a good opportunity to examine the actions of

three different Presidents, representing the two major democratic forces in Venezuela. We conclude that the three Presidents—Betancourt, Leoni and Caldera—were remarkably similar on most facets of the issue of economic integration.

In the area of perceptions, the objectives of all three with regard to the issue were similar. All three accepted the premise that a truly independent nation-state in today's world cannot continue to be overly dependent on the great industrial complexes of the "center" countries. Further, they all saw the need for Venezuela to begin to expand exports in the relatively near future if its hard-won gains in industrialization and manufacturing were not to be lost because of its small national market. These economic reasons would probably have been enough to prompt the three Presidents to be in favor of integration; but, in addition, each of the three had a political reason: a desire to strengthen ties among political parties of similar beliefs in other Latin American countries. For the two Presidents of Acción Democrática, the precedent was already well-established that leaders of all the democratic left reform parties in Latin America—Haya de la Torre in Peru, Figueres in Costa Rica, Muñoz Marín in Puerto Rico, etc.—cooperated closely with one another. Caldera also shared this objective; it was certainly an aim of the Christian Democrats throughout Latin America to stimulate and help the growth of brother parties in other Latin countries.[58]

In contrast to this intellectual advocacy of integration, however, the

[57] *El Nacional* (Caracas), May 25, 1969. One interesting by-product of the Cartagena negotiations was the rough treatment the Venezuelan delegation received from the Chilean Christian Democrats, their ideological counterparts. Venezuelan observers predicted cool relations between the only two Christian Democrat regimes in Latin America as a result of this conflict.

[58] This aim has probably been diminished in the case of Caldera after the difficult time his representatives had in negotiating with the leaders of Chile's Christian Democrats at the Cartagena Conference.

three Chief Executives were seen to move very slowly on all matters related to economic integration. Betancourt was barely able to initiate studies on the question; Leoni did enter LAFTA, after a delay of two years, but he failed to effect entrance into the Andean grouping; and, of course, Caldera's response was so restrictive as to guarantee virtually that Venezuela would not be able to join the Andean enterprise. We can attribute this hesitancy to two factors in their perception of the issue. First, in all likelihood, the Presidents did not perceive the issue as one of crucial and immediate importance, as one for which they should risk the viability of their regime. Second, they all probably sensed that vigorous opposition from the nation's business sectors would rob them of valuable support which they would need for other undertakings. For Caldera, there was little doubt of this need, since the private sector had supported him in the 1968 electoral campaign. However, Betancourt and (to a lesser extent) Leoni, although enjoying a base of support which did not include the business sector, also had cause to try to mollify this group. Without at least the tacit support of the economic and political conservatives of the country, the Venezuelan government in the early 1960's would have been highly susceptible to conspiracy and *coup d'etat* from the right wing of the country's armed forces. On issues which were not of the highest importance, Betancourt and Leoni could have been expected to yield to the private business community for the sake of the more important question of survival of their regime. Thus, Venezuela's presidents have apparently adopted a decision rule which requires private sector consensus on any pro-integration policy.

Second, we found that the foremost advocates of integration consisted of a small group of reform-minded economists located in various places within the Venezuelan bureaucracy—Cordiplan (the government planning agency), the Ministry of Foreign Relations, the Ministry of Finance, and eventually in the technical secretariat to the National Commission for LAFTA (CONALALC).

The strong advocacy of this group for Venezuelan entry into any integration scheme comes from their training as economists, and (for most of them) their early exposure to the ideas of Raúl Prebisch. Many of them worked in ECLA in the mid-1950's, while in exile. They are all convinced that a developing state's first economic priority lies in severing the bonds of excessive dependence on the industrial West (especially the United States), and that usually implies the strengthening of ties among the developing countries themselves.

It was precisely because of their early training, however, that the pro-integration *técnicos* in Venezuela were personally not well suited to the task of "selling" the idea of integration to the business community. Their idea of an economist was one who prepared a technically "clean" document for the use of the "political level" decision-makers; they were temperamentally unsuited to become deeply involved in the "dirty" business of politics, especially as it is practiced in Venezuela. As a case in point, the technical secretariat to CONALALC, the group which eventually formulated LAFTA policy for Venezuela, was reluctant to install a press office in their organization, even though the anti-integration Caracas press often carried false stories and rumors about LAFTA and about government intentions.[59] This attitude about political negotiation and bargaining can only have hampered the pro-integration forces in Venezuela; the only actors in the system who were advocates of Venezuelan participation were psychologically ill-prepared to fight to achieve their goal.

Third, indicative of the restricted nature of the integration debate in Venezuela, when we refer to linkage interest groups, we have in mind only one: FEDECAMARAS. Other potential interest groups which could have performed a linkage function on this issue, such as organized labor peasant associations, were either never interested in the question, or performed along the margin of the debate.[60] However, as we shall see, opinion was so divided within FEDECAMARAS that, in fact, we have an opportunity to examine several different points of view within the private sector.

By far, those sectors most opposed to integration were the rural interests, small manufacturing and bankers. The rural sectors, the farmers and livestock raisers, have usually formed a minority within FEDECAMARAS decision-making bodies; as of 1969, of the 146 constituent associations, only fifteen represent farmers, only nine represent livestock raisers, and five represent some mixture of which agricultural interests form a part.[61] In the early days of the Federation, the rural associations definitely had to accept a

lesser position of power. However, in the last several years, the vigorous defense of their interests, coupled with shrewd coalition politics within FEDECAMARAS, has provided for an increase of the power of the rural sectors. Farmers and ranchers in Venezuela have opposed entry into any integration scheme primarily because of their perception of Venezuela's contiguous environment: the competition to which they would be subjected by their counterparts in Colombia. Any association which permits the import of Colombian meat and agricultural products is anathema to FEDECAMARAS' rural interests. There is ample evidence to indicate that FEDECAMARAS' hard line on the Andean Pact was a result of such strong opposition from the farmer-rancher coalition within the Federation.[62]

If the rural interests have opposed the Andean Pact because of fear of competition from Colombia, the small manufacturer has fought integration with the larger industrial states of LAFTA—Argentina, Brazil and Mexico. Although FEDECAMARAS was founded in 1944 by trade associations for the most part,[63] the expansion of the industrial sector in the country since the 1940's has brought about a consequent increase in the power of the industrial and manufacturing interests in the Federation. Of the 146 associations in the Federation, fifty represent industrialists, and twenty-nine more represent manufacturing in some combination with other sectors.[64] Until the resurgence of the agrarian associations about 1964 or 1965, the manufacturing groups could usually achieve their objectives easily within

59 Interviews.
60 Aaron Segal, writing sometime in mid-1966, in *op. cit.*, p. 57, professes to see "great interest in integration" among the Venezuelan labor movement. The author, in his investigation in 1964–65, was able to find no evidence of labor interest; and subsequent developments have done nothing to alter this conclusion.
61 *El Universal* (Caracas), May 5, 1969.
62 *El Nacional* (Caracas), June 15, 1969.
63 *El Nacional* (Caracas), July 17, 1964.
64 *El Universal* (Caracas), May 5, 1969.

FEDECAMARAS. Even when forced to share their strength with farmers and ranchers, they still constitute a powerful bloc in the Federation. The manufacturers who most oppose LAFTA integration are those in the small, traditional industries such as food processing, cigarettes, beverages, shoes, cotton textiles, and so on. These men are profoundly afraid that they will be destroyed by foreign competition because Venezuela is a high wage country when compared with other LAFTA members. These manufacturing interests, then, have argued that any Venezuelan participation in integration proposals must provide for two things: (1) continued protection for any presently existing industry; and (2) enough time and government assistance to adjust to competition.

A third important group which has opposed integration is found in banking circles. While these men do not constitute any great numerical strength within FEDECAMARAS, their key role in the maintenance of Venezuela's laudable monetary stability made them a force which merited attention. In addition, for most of the debate on integration, these men could count on an ally within the government—the Central Bank.[65] Opposition from bankers centered on the fear that Venezuela would open up its monetary strength to drainage because of the inflationary policies practiced in most of the LAFTA countries—Brazil and Chile, especially. In order to appease these critics, Leoni had to promise that Venezuela would not join any kind of customs union which might allow other countries to unload useless, soft currencies on Venezuela in exchange for that country's relatively hard *bolívar*,

or for Venezuela's valuable supply of United States dollars. As Segal put it, "the government had to cede an important part of its future negotiating strength in LAFTA in order to achieve an attitude of indifference on the part of the [Central] Bank."[66]

We would be hard pressed to find significant sectors within FEDECAMARAS favoring integration; but this author has no doubt that they do exist. They are found in various large-scale industrial combines which have the power not only to absorb foreign competition, but actually to export items to newly-opened LAFTA markets. As an example, in 1965, the Mendoza Group, one of Venezuela's largest private corporations, was already studying ways in which it could take advantage of new LAFTA markets. And leaders of Mito Juan, the first private all-Venezuelan Petroleum company, fought within FEDECAMARAS to obtain a pro-LAFTA resolution in 1964.[67] But, for the most part, these men did not try to affect the position of the representative association of the private sector. At the most, they were active from 1963 to about 1965; but there is little evidence that they continue to be concerned about the matter as of this writing.

Fourth, the political culture of Venezuela, the attitudes that a political actor holds about the system in which he acts, was a salient feature of the integration debate in that it affected the way in which businessmen and government officials perceived their relations with one another. Essentially, we found that communication between the two sectors—private businessmen on one side and bureaucrats and mem-

---

65 Aaron Segal, *op. cit.,* p. 56.

66 *Ibid.*
67 Interviews.

bers of Acción Democrática on the other—was badly strained by the hostility with which each group viewed the other. The process of rapid political change in Venezuela between 1936 and 1958 had left the chief participants in the integration debate so embittered toward each other that there were few men whose passions would let them cast aside old prejudices and take part in the debate in an objective manner.

The private sector, for its part, could never forgive the leaders of AD for helping to overthrow the government of Isaías Medina Angarita in 1945. The business class had been one of Medina's closest supporting groups; and they had rallied to his side when he showed promise of leading the country into democracy while maintaining that feature of political life so dear to the heart of the entrepreneur—stability. The leaders of AD, on the other hand, were tainted with Marxist leanings; and it was often said that Rómulo Betancourt, who had flirted with the Third International while in exile in Costa Rica, had not really left his Communist ties behind upon returning to Venezuela. For many observers, the animosity between the business class and AD was symbolized by the bitter presidential campaign of 1963 which business-supported candidate Arturo Uslar Pietri (Minister of Interior under Medina) waged against Raul Leoni.[68]

The leaders of Acción Democrática, on the other hand, have considered many members of the economic elite their sworn enemies. The AD reformers came to power in opposition to the vested interests of the old oligarchy of Venezuela; and, although the busi-

[68] John Martz, *The Venezuelan Elections of December 1, 1963: Part I* (Washington, D. C.: Institute for the Comparative Study of Political Systems, 1964), p. 29.

ness groups of the country have undergone great transformations in thought and style over the past twenty-five years, the *adecos* have maintained an anti-business attitude. They were particularly incensed over the willingness of private businessmen to cooperate with the dictatorship of Pérez Jiménez. In addition, they generally believe that businessmen, who are conscious only of their own profit and loss statements and their own business problems, should not be consulted on questions of national, macro-economic policy. On matters of complex economics, they have neither the time nor the training, say the bureaucrats, to understand fully the implications of specific proposals.

It should be clear that the conflict in attitudes which we have described was quite important in the economic integration debate. In the various encounters between government and private sector representatives prior to 1969, the observer often had the feeling that what he was seeing was not a dialogue (a favorite word among consensus-conscious Venezuelan political leaders), but two simultaneous monologues, neither of which was being appreciated by its respective target audience. In the end, of course, Presidents Betancourt and Leoni demonstrated considerable understanding of the *power* of the business class; but, over the period of the integration debates, one is struck by the fact that there seems to have been very little, if any, mutual re-education on the issue of economic integration.

Finally, as our closing point of analysis, we shall discuss briefly the problems encountered by FEDECAMARAS in reaching an institutional agreement on the issue of economic integration in both their 1963 and 1964 meetings.

Interest aggregation, the adoption of

a common policy on issues, was a relatively simple affair in FEDECAMARAS when the Federation was founded in 1944. The lack of diversification in the Venezuelan economy was translated into a unity of viewpoint in that organization which permitted the rapid achievement of a common statement of purpose.

As the economy has become more and more diversified, however, FEDECAMARAS has become a more complex organization. The Federation has insisted, nonetheless, on maintaining its over-arching structure, attempting to retain the role as representative for the entire private economy. As a result, of the 146 member chambers or associations in 1969, twenty-eight represented trade and commerce, fifty represented industry and manufacturing; twenty-four, industry and trade combined; fifteen, farmers; nine, ranchers; and fifteen, service chambers (banks, insurance, etc.).[69]

The result of this proliferation of interests has been a decline in FEDECAMARAS' decision-making ability. The leadership has continued to place great emphasis on presenting a common front to the public and to the government; but, differences of opinion within the organization make each serious policy discussion the arena for bargaining, negotiation, consensus-formation and compromise. One of the foremost organs for this activity is the *ad hoc* study commission, formed periodically by the Federation to examine potentially disruptive questions. These study commissions are invaluable aids to the discovery of consensus, since they offer an opportunity for opposing viewpoints to be heard, and they move the entire acrimonious debate away from the formal FEDECAMARAS organization-al structure, and into a relatively quiet environment.

All of these features can be seen clearly in the debate over Venezuela's entry into LAFTA. Prior to 1962, the Federation had little trouble coming to a common position since there was little overt sympathy for a pro-integration resolution. However, when the LAFTA study commission was formed in early 1963, signs of disunity immediately began to appear. The pro-LAFTA forces, now given a forum for their views, began to press for a modification of FEDECAMARAS' previously anti-integration stance; and the hopes of the Federation leaders to bring the issue to a vote in 1963 were dissolved (much to the dismay of President Betancourt).

The same debate continued into 1964, and gave evidence of disrupting the 1964 convention, whereupon the Federation's leaders attempted the same delaying tactics. This time, however, they had not reckoned with a new President who would not be put off. Following Leoni's announcement at the Maracay convention, FEDECAMARAS struggled mightily to reach a compromise position; but, the two extreme positions would not yield and in the end the issue was brought onto the floor of the convention in a precedent-breaking move. The result was a resolution which registered FEDECAMARAS' disapproval of the decision to enter LAFTA, and recommended to the president that he create a special National Commission on LAFTA to consider future policy on economic integration.[70] In so doing, FEDECAMARAS was seeking to move

---

[69] *El Universal* (Caracas), May 5, 1969.

[70] For the full text of the final resolution, see Federación Venezolana de Camaras y Asociaciones de Comercio y Producción, *Acuerdos y Resoluciones de la XX Asamblea Anual* (Caracas: author, 1964), pp. 112–16.

the debate away from their own institutions, and into a more neutral environment where it could not spill over and contaminate the Federation itself.

Since 1964, the LAFTA issue has presented FEDECAMARAS with little problem in internal decision-making, inasmuch as the pro-LAFTA members have abandoned the fight for more productive endeavors. The question of the Andean Pact was handled a great deal more easily, because of the threatened predominance of Colombia in the new union (which drove the farmer-rancher combination to new heights of opposition) and the depth and speed of tariff reduction (which likewise motivated the small manufacturers). Nevertheless, the basic problem of consensus-formation in a highly differentiated organization continues in FEDECAMARAS; and it will continue to plague that organization in its future attempts to participate in the national decision-making process.

V

As we look back over the preceding analysis, we see little cause for optimism regarding the future of the economic integration issue in Venezuela. As we postulated at the beginning, the configuration of the linkage components on this issue is such that whatever Venezuela does with regard to integration with the neighboring countries of Latin America will almost surely be diluted and robbed of most of its significance.

We can foresee three separate conditions which might occur in the future which would alter Venezuela's current approach to economic integration: (1) the achievement of self-sustained industrialization as well as solid growth in agriculture; (2) a radical change by the United States in its petroleum import policy; or (3) the advent of

a vigorously pro-LAFTA government which could restructure the present linkages and, thereby, build a solid consensus in favor of integration.

The first two conditions are somewhat outside our analysis, lying more in the area of the economists. We would simply mention that the first condition, while it might make integration less unacceptable to various groups in the private sector, is a long-run development which cannot be counted on in the near future. In addition, to presume that Venezuela could afford to pursue an active pro-integration policy only *after* the main goals of development had been achieved would refute the basic premise of LAFTA. The second condition, involving a fundamental shift of policy by the United States, would obviously force the Venezuelans to reassess their entire foreign trade policy; but, such a change is highly speculative, and, as such, does not merit further discussion in this paper.

Which leaves us with the prospects for a more vigorous, consensus-building, pro-LAFTA government. With what chance of success may a particular pro-integration leader undertake to reform the integration linkages of Venezuela to create an atmosphere more conducive to his beliefs? And what strategy should he use to accomplish this reformation?

Harvey S. Perloff and Rómulo Almeida have written on this problem in a general sense; and their arguments appear to this author to be particularly relevant here.[71] These writers see the main task as essentially one of convincing groups in society that they have

[71] Harvey S. Perloff and Rómulo Almeida, "Regional Economic Integration in the Development of Latin America," *Economia Latinoamericana*, I, 2 (November, 1963), pp. 150–79.

benefits awaiting them in certain "pro-integration" decisions of the government. Government leaders can cope with opposition groups in two ways: (1) they can be "re-educated" to see that their "true" interests lie in supporting integration; or (2) countervailing groups, previously uninterested in the issue, can be sought out and enticed to take a supporting stand. The desire to seek protection from competition, say Perloff and Almeida, is a natural one, and can be combatted only if the government makes clear how each group stands to gain from pro-integration decisions. As these authors put it:

... free trade area negotiations, lacking demonstrative, positive attractions—*gains apparent to the key groups in each country*—tend to be carried out in a cautious and protective atmosphere, rather than in an atmosphere dominated by expansionism and the possibilities for the future.
... It is not unexpected that caution should rule when the gains to be had are still rather vague and in the distant future, while the threatened losses through new competition seem both real and immediate. *The problem, then, is to make the potential gains understandably concrete,* so that countries can countenance some small immediate losses.[72]

The situation of Great Britain and its relations with the European Economic Community, while obviously far different from that of Venezuela in many important respects, appears to us to offer at least one area of analogy—that of internal consensus building. A recent case study on Britain's decision to enter the EEC[73] makes clear

that Prime Minister Harold Macmillan, in the space of eighteen months, and in the face not only of apathy but also of strong opposition, was able to formulate a fairly respectable pro-EEC consensus. Certainly, it is suggested, had France not vetoed Britain's entry, the consensus would have been sufficient to support a positive policy once Britain had entered. Such a challenge awaits the leaders of Venezuela; whether they meet it or not will determine the place of Venezuela in the international economy, as well as the continued dynamism of Venezuela's economic growth for decades to come.

We are not especially sanguine, however, about the prospects for this latter development. As mentioned at the beginning of this study, economic integration seems, by its very nature, to produce a configuration of linkage components which will oppose or block every pro-integration step proposed by the political leadership. Stated briefly, the costs of economic integration are immediate, visible and (in the short-run) rather high, while the gains are difficult to demonstrate and likely to be enjoyed only in the long run. Further, economic integration is more likely to produce adverse effects for existing groups and beneficial effects for potentially interested groups, than *vice versa*. These inherent difficulties surrounding economic integration as a political issue mean that only the most secure, stable and firmly established governments can afford to undertake the structural reforms necessary to pursue an activist pro-integration policy. As we have attempted to demonstrate, during the decade of the 1960's,

72 *Ibid.,* pp. 153, 163. Emphasis added.
73 Eric A. Nordlinger, "Britain and the Common Market: The Decision to Negotiate," in Roy C. Macridis, ed., *Modern European Governments: Cases in Comparative*

Policy Making (Englewood Cliffs, N.J.: Prentice-Hall, Inc., 1968), pp. 47–67.

Venezuela was not led by a government which felt it could sacrifice the small amount of political capital it possessed for the sake of an active pro-integration stand. We must conclude, then, that in Venezuela (as in most of Latin America) a flourishing economic integration movement must await the development of institutions and processes strong enough and durable enough to cope with the strains inherent in such a movement.